Economic Nationalism and Globalization

Studies in Critical Social Sciences Book Series

Haymarket Books is proud to be working with Brill Academic Publishers (www.brill.nl) to republish the *Studies in Critical Social Sciences* book series in paperback editions. This peer-reviewed book series offers insights into our current reality by exploring the content and consequences of power relationships under capitalism, and by considering the spaces of opposition and resistance to these changes that have been defining our new age. Our full catalog of *SCSS* volumes can be viewed at www.haymarketbooks.org/category/scss-series.

Series Editor
David Fasenfest, Wayne State University

Editorial Board
Chris Chase-Dunn, University of California–Riverside
G. William Domhoff, University of California–Santa Cruz
Colette Fagan, Manchester University
Martha Gimenez, University of Colorado, Boulder
Heidi Gottfried, Wayne State University
Karin Gottschall, University of Bremen
Bob Jessop, Lancaster University
Rhonda Levine, Colgate University
Jacqueline O'Reilly, University of Brighton
Mary Romero, Arizona State University
Chizuko Ueno, University of Tokyo

Economic Nationalism and Globalization

Lessons from Latin America and Central Europe

By
Henryk Szlajfer

Translated from Polish by
Maria Chmielewska-Szlajfer

Haymarket Books
Chicago, IL

First published in 2013 by Brill Academic Publishers, The Netherlands.
© 2013 Koninklijke Brill NV, Leiden, The Netherlands

Published in paperback in 2014 by
Haymarket Books
P.O. Box 180165
Chicago, IL 60618
773-583-7884
www.haymarketbooks.org

ISBN: 978-1-60846-344-2

Trade distribution:
In the U.S. through Consortium Book Sales, www.cbsd.com
In the UK, Turnaround Publisher Services, www.turnaround-psl.com
In Australia, Palgrave Macmillan, www.palgravemacmillan.com.au
In all other countries by Publishers Group Worldwide, www.pgw.com

Cover design by Ragina Johnson.

This book was published with the generous support of Lannan Foundation and the Wallace Global Fund.

Printed in Canada by union labor.

10 9 8 7 6 5 4 3 2 1

Library of Congress Cataloging-in-Publication Data is available.

For Marysia and Helenka

CONTENTS

Note on Terminology ix
Introduction 1

PART ONE

RETHINKING ECONOMIC NATIONALISM

1 Setting the Agenda 11

2 Precursors 37
    Mercantilist Antecedents: 'The Improvement of
    Our Lands' 37
    Friedrich List and His *System*: 'An English State Secret' 49
    John Maynard Keynes: 'If We Happen to Want It' 63

3 Categories 77
    National Economy: Elusive Concept? 77
    Holistic and Particularistic Nationalisms 91
    Digression: The State 99

4 Against 'Wishes and Dreams': Foreign Capital and Economic
    Nationalism 109
    Foreign Capital as the Enemy? 109
    Commodities, Capital, Migrations 121
    Protectionism and Foreign Capital 132

5 Beyond Liberalism: Transformations of Political
    Nationalism 147
    Toward Integral Nationalism 147
    Anti-Liberal Temptation: Autocracy and Integral
    Nationalism 155
    Latin American Liberal-Conservative Consensus 161
    Populist Response 175

PART TWO
ECONOMIC NATIONALISM AT WORK

6 A Proto-Nationalist Interlude 183
   The Kingdom of Poland and Latin America:
   Similarities and Dissimilarities 183
   After *Discontinuité Structurelle* 191
   Variants of Industrialization 198
   Selected Problems 209
   Failure and Some Long-Term Consequences 220

7 Issues in Primary-Sector Nationalism: Latin America 223
   The Heritage: A Note 223
   An Internationalist Protectionist State 228
   Varieties of the Export Sector and Economic Nationalism ... 244
   The Regional Dimension 255
   Transformational Potential of Primary-Sector Nationalism ... 262

8 Pieces of a Puzzle: Toward Holistic Nationalism 269
   The Restrained Nationalism of Industrialists 269
   Holistic Nationalism as an Enforced Process 284
   Against Foreign Domination: Yes, but 295
   'Those Who Don't Obey the Rules Win': Beyond Orthodoxy ... 313
   Economic Independence as State Business: *Étatisme* 328

Conclusions 347

References 357
Index 395

NOTE ON TERMINOLOGY

The notion of nationalism is understood—if not stated otherwise—as a value-free generic category referring to national cultures, ideologies, programs, movements and policies (Szacki 2002: 170f). I extend it to patriotism which has a positive connotation in the Central European tradition, including economic patriotism, the category proposed by Jan Kofman (1997: 193f), denoting a variant of defensive nationalism.[1] Yet, the notion of patriotism, subjected to a critical analysis, poses interpretative problems as complicated as in the case of nationalism. Anthony D. Smith (1998: 212) is right when he observes that civic nationalism-cum-patriotism, usually treated as open and referring to Western Europe, in practice did not rule out forced assimilation of minority groups or cultural ethno-cide.[2] This is by no means surprising. Both nationalism as well as patriotism, construed as value categories, are defined by their particular contents and context. This in turn can demolish the boundaries one can find in any over-ambitious typology of nationalism, of this "scrappy, uncertain, ill-disciplined subject" (Robinson 1964: 117). On the other hand, the value-free approach mentioned is no panacea shielding against mistakes and/or misinterpretations. The terminology used in this book is thus objectivist in the Weberian sense and at the same time eclectic; yet, in view of the subject at hand of *economic* nationalism—concerning a certain segment of the wider problems of nationalistic practices and ideas—it is difficult to avoid. My only hope is that my attitude to the particular variants of the nationalistic policy and ideology will result clearly from the context of my deliberations.

The concept of the globalization (or global economy), from the second half of the 19th century until the 1930s, is understood as a result of the simultaneous occurrence and interplay of two kinds of processes. The first was the process of closing the national space, expressed in the consolidation of the Westphalian order in the economic dimension (replacing

---

[1] In Polish political debate over the last century, traditionally patriotism has been firmly opposed to nationalism. See, for example, Czarnowski (2002: 103–107), Waldenberg (1992: 18–24).

[2] From the 'A-B-C paradox' Hans J. Morgenthau formulated nearly five decades ago it results that the notion of oppressed and oppressing nations is equally vague. According to this paradox, "yesterday's oppressed cannot help becoming the oppressors of today because they are afraid lest they be again oppressed tomorrow" (quoted in Snyder 1990: 1f).

hitherto supra- and/or non-state regional ties with national economies). The other one was the process of opening of the emerging national economies by trade, movements of capital and migrations, accompanied however in major industrial countries by the 'Sombart paradox', i.e. by the relative decline of export trade measured against total output (*die fallende Exportquote*) (Sombart 1954: 369ff).[3] The result of both those processes was commodity price convergence and relative factor price convergence on the world market as the measure of the achieved level of international integration (and specialization), coupled with world-wide interstate polarization and the appearance of separate "income (convergence) clubs" (Bairoch and Kozul-Wright 1996, O'Rourke and Williamson 2000, Dowrick and DeLong 2003, Williamson 2006). An important aspect of the birth and consolidation of the first modern global economy was also either the forced (colonialism) or spontaneous (Latin America and Central Europe) economic re-organization and selective modernization of backward areas.

Unlike presentations that confine the first globalization to the year 1914 in my deliberations I extend the timeframe by including the interwar period as well. This results from my treatment of the first globalization as a special cycle. It can be perceived as the hegemonic stability of the international system (in its economic dimension) going through the phases of birth, consolidation and crisis.[4] Thus the interwar period contains first the abortive attempt to return to the *belle époque* of the prewar stability—without any fundamental changes in its institutional arrangement which would respond to the rapidly emerging hegemonic vacuum—and next, the ultimate collapse of "the first major phase of economic globalization" in the 1930s (James 2001: 5). Delayed and inconclusive attempts at creating national economies, this time in the peripheral areas of Central Europe and Latin America, were a fragment of that process.

I use interchangeably terms such as periphery, underdeveloped or backward countries and, correspondingly, developed countries, the center or core countries. Every one of them has its own history and is attributed to certain theoretical schools. This eclectic attitude toward the terminology

---

[3] See also Deutsch and Eckstein (1961: 267f). For a different view see Cunningham (1891: 649ff): "for England and Englishmen [the nationalist policy] is dead." An attempt at empirical verification of the 'Sombart paradox' for the interwar period and the few years after the WWII was made by Helander (1955). A more nuanced and critical analysis concerning the United States was presented by Lipsey (1963).

[4] The concept of economic hegemonic stability, modeled after its political variant popular in IR studies, was proposed by Rogowski (1989: 169f).

used in the book results from my desire to avoid such secondary (from the point of view of the problem discussed) identification.

Interchangeably also used are terms such as agrarian-raw-materials nationalism and primary-sector nationalism when reference is made to ideas and actions concerning and/or referring to agrarian and mining interests. The term primary sector follows Colin Clark's classical three-sector model.

INTRODUCTION

The excellent historian Carlo Cipolla once observed sarcastically,

> The story of the East India silks and calicoes that were imported into England and caused difficulty for the English textile industry ... does not need to be told here. It was fortunate for England that no Indian Ricardo arose to convince the English people that, according to the law of comparative costs, it would be advantageous for them to turn into shepherds and to import from India all the textiles that were needed (quoted in Magdoff 1978: 159).

This is how one could start a history of economic nationalism, which I am not going to do here.

My interests focus on the economic nationalism of the peripheries as on the research topic, and on a discussion about the set of analytical categories that will allow—and which I shall be trying to prove—a better understanding of the logic and sources of a certain kind of answers given in the period studied to the phenomenon of modern backwardness. I mean at the same time categories historically specific, and thus reflecting what Barrington Moore, Jr. (1966: xiv) described in his *opus magnum* as "a strong tension between the demands of doing justice to the explanation of a particular case and the search for generalizations." Therefore, if an attempt at grasping the theoretically specific nature of economic nationalism is not to lead to trivial deductions and generalizations, it requires a reference to a special control mechanism. This mechanism involves the historical context, a multidisciplinary perspective and a comparative approach.

As a research topic economic nationalism is a fragment of the political science agenda, particularly of political economy and international political economy to the extent that they describe, most generally speaking, relations established at the intersection between the state and the economy and society, and the interdependence of internal and international factors (Gilpin 2001).[1] In other words, economic nationalism concerns the

---

[1] Economic nationalism falls also into the research agenda outlined by the school of the European world-economy (or World-Systems Analysis), which, although it refers to a different conceptual framework of comparative studies, is a part of international political economy. See Wallerstein (1974, 2004).

problems of the tangle of interests and economic motivations in the international context furthered through the mediation and with the participation of the state. Contrary to certain recent interpretations of economic nationalism (Abdelal 2001), the role of the state is of key importance. This means that the category of economic nationalism is also a fragment of a wider problem of political choices the state as a collection of institutions faces, and, therefore, is a part of a research agenda of political conflict and coalition-building as well. At the same time, I lay emphasis on the problem, not on the research method, because in my deliberations I do not refer to just one specific set of assumptions characteristic of the current theoretical interpretations. Particularly, I wish to avoid in my analyses the age-old dispute between the schools of political rationality and of economic rationality (Staniland 1985). However, a preference for Weber and Marx-inspired historical sociology, the neo-institutionalist approach of the Douglass North variety–with its emphasis on state, power games and inefficient institutions–and the path-dependency argument will be clearly visible in the book.

Economic nationalism, interpreted as a set of analytical categories, refers to social phenomena that cannot be reduced to the sphere of economic choices as understood by modern economics (compare Pickel 2005) or to the unitary-actor approach of the realists and neo-realists. Economic nationalism is at the same time an idea motivating political actions, an expression of inter-group conflicts, a cultural context (national and ethnic context included) and economic policy. And this, in turn, means that the conceptualization of economic nationalism requires a reference to the research proposals and findings of a number of disciplines, particularly of economic history and, to some necessary extent, of the history of ideas. The works quoted reveal the extent to which I take their arguments into consideration. Extensive use of the achievements of economic historians does not require an elaborate justification as the epoch of the first globalization, i.e. the century preceding the outbreak of WWII, constitutes the timeframe of my deliberations.[2]

---

[2] One should, however, take note of the growing gap in the sophistication of research on economic history of 19th and 20th century Latin America, and East and Central Europe. In the case of Latin America one can also speak about a paradigm shift and the boom connected with the new economic history approach and deepened research specificity; yet at the price of losing the great historical 'narrative' and interest in the Big Questions (Gootenberg 2004, Coatsworth 2005). In the case of Polish historiography the stagnation started already at the end of the 1970s and this notwithstanding the appearance of a handful of excellent contributions made by a small group of scholars (Jezierski and Wyczański 2006: 8). There remains a lack of wider interest in economic history today.

Finally, diverse histories of economic nationalism, resulting largely from the multitude of national/cultural communities to give 'answers' to impetuses coming from outside, and also the different effects produced by nationalist moves indicate the expediency as well as the need to use the comparative perspective. It allows one to read the tendencies typical of the economic nationalism of a given historical time (Skocpol 1984: 378f). In my deliberations I refer to the respective historical experience of Latin America and Central Europe, with special emphasis on Brazil and Poland. In this regard, concentrating on the peripheries, I shall treat economic nationalism as a specific example of Reinhard Bendix's "concept of limited applicability" (see Bonnell 1980: 161). However, I do not rule out a priori the possibility of considering economic nationalism as a macro-category. The works by Kofman (1997) and Liah Greenfeld (2003), skillfully using comparative perspective in their research, indicate—if analyzed together—such a possibility (see Chapter 1).

Most generally, I would posit the argument raised in the book in the following way: In the period examined, the economic nationalism of the peripheries was not just an economic policy and—in some instances—an attempt at theorizing. It was also, like political nationalism, a kind of a *Weltanschauung* or, in the Weberian meaning, "a specific kind of pathos which is linked to the idea of a powerful political community" (Weber 1978: 398), able to ensure prosperity. It was an emotional answer to backwardness, to the question monotonously asked for at least two–three centuries about the causes of the division between rich and poor nations (Landes 1998, Olson 1996). Like the 17th- and 18th-century disputes about capitalism prior to capitalism itself, economic nationalism was a blend of rationally pleaded material interests and violent passion—an aspiration for power, glory and prestige (Hirschman 1977b), which however all too often only led to misery.

As "a specific kind of pathos" but also a set of convictions about bad and good policies, economic nationalism did not confine itself, in the historical perspective, to the states and peoples which are underdeveloped now. It was part and parcel and an essential aspect of the process of modernity forming, and particularly of the innovative, motivating dimension, focused–as stressed by Greenfeld–on competitively organized economic activity, and on transforming–to follow Albert O. Hirschman terminology–passions into interests. Without investigating here whether these theses well render the birth of the acquisitive mentality and the spirit of capitalism, I find it significant that the economic nationalism of the peripheries appears as a response to the existing external conditions.

From the economic history perspective two of them were of paramount significance in the epoch of the first globalization: the transport revolution (railroads, cable communication, telegraph and steamships) and the rise of modern industry (Williamson 2006). The peripheries must stand up to these conditions through catching up, without participating actively in their creation. Economic nationalism thus appears as a special case of reform: an active and in fact rebellious "attempt at adapting the structure of the [national] system to its environment" (Kamiński 1994: 29).

Unable (and unwilling) to change the basic goals imposed by modernity, the economic nationalism of the peripheries is formed around two kinds of demands. The first demand recalls the experience of nationalism of the pioneers of modernity and emphasizes the need for growth and participation. The second, being a response to the existing (internal and external) conditions, raises—using John Rawls' terminology (2002: 116ff)—what one might describe as a demand for distributive justice. To the ideology of the economic nationalism of the peripheries, the second demand acquires a special importance, leading to, among other things, concepts combining into one a hypothesis about a functional usefulness of underdevelopment from the point of view of the world system as a whole with a hypothesis about its dysfunctionality from the point of view of backward areas. Incidentally, it is worth noting that the first hypothesis has been undergoing a fundamental transformation in the nationalist discourse in recent years: from the point of view of the center, the functional usefulness of backwardness (including colonialism) has been replaced by a hypothesis about the irrelevance and lack of interest–at least in the peripheries of the peripheries (save raw materials and supply-oriented FDI). Statistics comparing distribution of international capital flows between core and periphery in 1913 and 2001 show clearly that in this period international investors followed wealth, not cheap labor: "only mutual investments between rich countries have increased dramatically, rich–poor capital flows remain far below historical levels" (Schularick 2006: 351). The result was a relative marginalization of the underdeveloped part of the world.

Certain economic historians argue that even at the height of the British industrial drive, say from the mid-18th century until mid-19th century, the forced and voluntary contribution of the peripheries to the growth of the core countries was rather limited (O'Brien 1982, Bairoch 1993). The contributions made before the 18th century and next from the end of the 19th century are a different story. However, one would probably agree with the careful wording proposed by Ralph Davis (1973: 137), concerning the economic role of slavery: "It is far from true to say that the Industrial Revolution in Europe was built on the necks of millions of African slaves; but their contribution to its preconditions was not a negligible one" (for a different view see Pomeranz 2002). Paul Bairoch (1993: 172), projecting the tendencies of economic history of the developed world from the early 19th century until 1938 onto the future, arrived precisely at the kernel of this change, arguing that, "The fact that the West did not need the Third World is good news for the Third World." However, only to a certain extent: the lack of interest was (and is) selective. The dynamic third-tier NICs with their growing share of world industrial production and FDIs, and their surplus labor effectively keeping in check worldwide wage levels, seem to be a functionally well integrated part of the global system today.

The historical circumstances in which this catching up was taking place and also the kind of coalitions formed by "societal actors"–a unique combination of interests, organization and function (Gourevich 1986: 59, 245)– led to a significant evolution of nationalist responses. I try to render its essence ("Part One: Rethinking Economic Nationalism") with the use of the categories of *holistic nationalism* and *particularistic nationalism* (in close relation to the notions of national economy and the state), which are of key importance to my deliberations. In a nutshell, the basic difference between the two types of nationalism can be presented as follows: inasmuch as in the case of particularistic nationalism we have to deal with a tendency to colonize or conquer in some way the state and the economy by special interests (particular industries, branches and even individual big firms), in the case of holistic nationalism one observes a different tendency—the increasingly autonomous state and its institutions which etatize nationalism and try to colonize these special interests in the name of 'national interest' and the creation of a well-internally-integrated national economy. Unlike particularistic nationalism, holistic nationalism was a relatively new phenomenon, although not without an interesting record preceding its definite appearance in the interwar period (see Chapter 6). On the other hand, particularistic nationalism, closely related to the rent-seeking approach of particular societal actors occurred almost at the beginning of the history of underdeveloped areas in their contacts with the world economy. I discuss the formation of the two types of nationalism, and especially their complex interactions, in the second part of the book.

At this point, one should add that the transformation of particularistic nationalism into holistic nationalism—whose transformation was not completed in the period examined—was accompanied by changes in the package of instruments of the nationalist economic policy: from mainly tariff protection to complicated systems combining tariffs with quantitative import restrictions (QR), to direct and indirect subsidies, to suppressing the market operations of foreigners and, finally, to an expansion of state-run enterprises. In particular countries that general trend was observed in diverse forms, though, as separate packages in every state (Chang 2005: 59–66).[3] Obvious however was the switch to increasingly complex and sophisticated instruments, widening the scope and intensity of the activities of the state institutions.

In the period examined, nationalist measures did not produce any conclusive long-term results, especially in Central Europe. After WWII, development of that region was switched to another line, this time to that of the communist economic nationalism. On the other hand, in Latin America the kind of nationalism opted for, and particularly the kind of political and social coalitions to support economic nationalism–led to sub-optimal results (perhaps with the exception of Brazil and Mexico). It became very clear against the background of economic nationalism as practiced in East Asia (Kohli 2004, 2009). However, the outcome was difficult to predict in the 1920s or 1930s. It is the history of the later, post-WWII, period that implies such conclusions. In the 1930s the growth of GDP per capita in Japan was only marginally higher than in Brazil (Maddison 2003: 143, 182). The same concerns intra-Latin American divergences in the last century. It was difficult to predict in 1914 that Brazil would in the decades to come overtake in performance the enormously successful export economies of Argentina and Uruguay (Bértola and Porcile 2006). Strongly accentuated after 1929, Brazil's *dirigisme* and state-led industrialization were thought to be a prescription for failure not a chance for relative success.

There is no doubt however that the historical laboratory for all these experiments was the first globalization, begun in the second half of the 19th century—both at the stage of growth and expansion of the world economy as well as at the time of a prolonged economic and political crisis. But the interwar period, particularly the 1930s when the first globalization collapsed completely, revealed the significance of economic nationalism to the periphery. It also revealed the inherent potential for national growth —made use of in successive decades by some, as well

---

[3] I deal to a limited extent only with economic nationalism defined as a set of specific instruments. For a comprehensive discussion on this topic see Kofman (1997) and the literature he quotes. Reading Bhagwati (1988) and Irwin (1996) has helped me better understand certain basic issues related with nationalism-as-protectionism.

as the potential for destruction. However, its symbiosis—with a few exceptions—with the authoritarian variants of the new, integral political nationalism, has for years underpinned its largely negative assessment.

So, when all is said and done, what was the economic nationalism of European and Latin American peripheries which emerged in the epoch when modern industry "has established the world-market" and the bourgeoisie "has been the first to show what man's activity can bring about" (Marx and Engels 1998: 36, 38)? It was, to reiterate, after Jerzy Jedlicki, a dream of a part of the political and economic elites in underdeveloped countries. A desperate dream about the possibility of finding—if necessary, at the expense of political freedom—a shortcut to narrow the distance to those on top.

*

* *

For many years the subject raised in this book had been reappearing in the discussions I have had the privilege to engage in with my friend Jan Kofman, the author of the path-breaking theoretical and historical analysis of economic nationalism in East and Central Europe in the interwar period (1997). As a result, at the end of the 1980s, the two of us attempted to outline a comparative perspective also including Latin America. Ryszard Stemplowski joined us in this research endeavor. Thanks to the support of the late Paul Bairoch, director of the Centre for International Economic History at the University of Geneva, and Dr. Jean Batou our essays have appeared as the Centre's publication (Szlajfer 1990).

However, in times of neoliberal reforms worldwide, and at the start of the market-oriented transformations in East and Central Europe the topic of economic nationalism appeared to many as outdated and even exotic. Sir Robert Skidelsky (2001) would probably say: "an old curiosity shop." Beautifully said but the message seems a bit biased and detached from reality. Thus, I prefer to follow the lesson of an eminent German historian, "[i]f anything should give occasion not to overestimate the significance of the majority view of economists, it is the history of protectionism" (Borchardt 1991: 2). I believe it also applies to the state.

It was my intuition that the history of economic nationalism is not over. The past can, in a way different and difficult to predict, reappear as the present. Today, with the bitter (and inconclusive) experience of the world financial crisis of the years 2008–2010, and the reshaping of the world economy going at full speed, economic nationalism (narrowly described as protectionism) appears once more as a menacing possibility to some, and a promise of success to others. Market-state interaction, expressed in regulated competition, may lead to increased competition but not to freer markets (Levi-Faur 1998: 674f). Add the long-forgotten concept of state capitalism which suddenly reemerged as an important issue in the mainstream globalization debate. In short, contrary to liberal internationalists and/or enthusiastic globalizers, the coupling of growth and nationalism (and the state) is an aspect, not a distortion, of the second globalization. Bearing in mind that peculiar nexus, one can claim that the history of the first globalization is still with us. It matters.

The Polish edition of this book (Szlajfer 2005) appeared as a publication of the Institute of Political Studies, Polish Academy of Sciences. However, while working on the English-language edition I decided to make a number of substantial revisions and additions to the original Polish text. Extensive comments I got from Antoni Z. Kamiński, Jacek Kochanowicz, Jan Kofman, Ryszard Stemplowski and Jerzy Tomaszewski were of great help in preparing this in fact new book. While acknowledging with gratitude their friendly criticism and support, I should immediately add that any mistakes and shortcomings one will find in this book are mine. Also, I am most grateful to Professor David Fasenfest, the editor of Brill's series Studies in Critical Social Sciences, for encouragement and indispensable judgement.

And finally, I want also to acknowledge the financial support I got from the Centre of Latin American Studies of the Warsaw University for the translation of one of the chapters.

PART ONE

RETHINKING ECONOMIC NATIONALISM

CHAPTER ONE

SETTING THE AGENDA

A fully shaped national self-identification and political nationalism are unthinkable without a key component, which includes economic motivations and interests. One can defend this hypothesis no matter whether we are in favor of the model of nation-building resulting from the joint action of the state and political nationalism or of the linguistic-cultural model of the emergence of nationalism(s) and the nation(s).[1] "The history of economic nationalism," notes Louis L. Snyder (1990: 84), "runs closely parallel to the story of political and cultural nationalism." However, years ago Hans Kohn (1967: 17f) opposed this hypothesis by taking a different approach which treated economic nationalism as a phenomenon much younger than political or cultural nationalism. According to him, the idea of securing the well-being of the individual by the the economic power of the nation did not emerge until the closing decades of the 19th century. Such a radical shortening of the history of economic nationalism does not sound convincing.

However, from the statement that economic nationalism is an essential part of mature political nationalism there results no specific hypothesis regarding a causal relation between the two. Such a statement merely suggests that there exists a certain interrelationship between the two categories of nationalism, which needs to be examined, referring to an analysis of specific historical cases and circumstances. For example, with reference to Welsh nationalism, which has been reviving in recent decades, Gwyn Williams (1981: 308) points to the need "to understand nationalism in terms of the manner in which economic changes serve to generate group formations which have contradictory positions and interest in the economic order."[2] Earlier, Max Weber discussed the possibility of linking

---

[1] Out of the vast literature concerning the theories and theoretical-historical analyses of political nationalism, particularly useful were the following (quoted in alphabetical order): Anderson (1983), Breuilly (1985), Chatterjee (1986), Chlebowczyk (1983), Gellner (1983), Greenfeld (1993), Hobsbawm (1990), Hroch (2000), Kohn (1967), Kula (1991), Moore, Jr. (1966), Smith (1998), Szporluk (2003), Tamir (1993), Waldenberg (1992), Wehler (2001).

[2] See also Nairn (1977: 47, 59). For a critical review consult Smith (1998: 49–55, 57–60). Also Gellner (1981: 767f) discusses this kind of relationship to some degree.

trade to political unification; he considered the case when "purely economically determined market relations have a politically unifying effect." At the same time he warned however that the "causal nexus by no means always points in a single direction" (1978: 913). Nevertheless, the history of political nationalism that developed at the turn of the 19th and 20th centuries, in connection with rapid economic changes, for example in Australia and other Western offshoots, and also in the Caucasus and in colonial India (Lloyd 2003, Gatrell and Anan'ich 2003, Chandra 1979) supports the hypothesis. It seems also that the growing sense of economic deprivation among some of the nations of the Yugoslav federation, accelerated by the external financial shocks and IMF conditionalities in the 1980s, played an important role in the final formulation–in an auspicious international situation–of political demands for national sovereignty as a precondition for their further national development (Štiblar 1997, Borak 2000, Hechter 2000).

At this point, however, I have to stress my reservations about monocausal interpretations. In any case, Hans-Ulrich Wehler (2001: 207) wrote emphatically when referring to the great interest the building of a national economy and other economic questions aroused in the German national liberal movement of the first half of the 19th century: "The array of the movement's goals never came mono-maniacally down to economic demands alone" (see also Mayall 1990: 70). Earlier, Ernest Renan (1996), in his famous essay, wrote that the nation was "[m]ore valuable by far than common customs posts and frontiers," and that a *"Zollverein* is not a *patrie."* One can hardly question this. Yet, it would be equally hard to pass over the role trade marks and the sense of rapidly growing economic power played in the legitimization of Bismarck's (and his successors') German Reich and of German political nationalism. Between the economy-centered reductionism and the instrumentalization of the state by vested interests on the one hand, and the absolutization of the influence wielded by the world of national ideas (including culture) and the state on the other, there extends a vast area that covers diverse national experience and experiments.

As far as the regions under study are concerned, of much greater significance seems to be another hypothesis, namely that in certain historical situations it is precisely political nationalism, and put more precisely the state and its political project, enunciated by a political elite and/or political movement, that favor the sharpening of the sense of national identity *and* of territorially based economic interests. "Germany," argued Weber

(1978: 913), "has been made into a unified economic territory only through custom frontiers at her borders, which, in their course, were determined in a purely political manner." Political unification of the country took place "against the economic determinants as such." The building of the United States' economy as a unified area, too, was a political project, launched by 'the English better than the English themselves', the most dramatic moment of which was, apart from the revolution itself, the civil war. It seems the same may be said with reference to Latin America and with regard to Central Europe however, only with reservations. In view of situations like these one can paraphrase Ernest Gellner's well known statement that political nationalism "invents [economic nationalisms] where they do not exist–but it does need some pre-existing differentiating marks to work on, even if ... these are purely negative" (quoted in Smith 1972: 117).

A radical version of this hypothesis, referring to the birth of political nationalism, appears in a work by Liah Greenfeld (1993). She presents nationalism as a historical process–not confined to the 18th or 19th century–of the formation and evolution of a certain kind of idea and of collective consciousness (the Weberian "specific sentiment of solidarity"), referred to a sovereign community consisting of equal members. A crucial aspect of that evolution, initiated in England at the beginning of the 16th century and continuing over the next two centuries, was the fundamental transformation of the meaning of the amorphous sovereign community (already understood as a nation). More strictly defined concepts of sovereignty, of belonging and of a 'unique' community of values, led to strong identification of the nation with the 'people'. From the perspective of the history of ideas, István Hont forcefully argues that the previously separate trajectories, followed by the concept of state and the concept of nation, finally merged at some point: the 'nation-state' as oxymoron was transformed into tautology. As a result, he writes, the nation-state emerged as "an 'absolutist' state that is legitimate, whose subjects or citizens identify themselves with it and regard it as a collective expression of themselves, conceiving the collectivity as a 'nation'" (Hont 2005: 462, 463, 489). Bearing in mind that Gellner (but other researchers as well) dated the phenomenon of nationalism to the birth of the modern state and industrial economy, Greenfeld (1993: 23, 21, 18) introduces a basically different point of view. "Historically," she writes, "the emergence of nationalism predated the development of every significant component of modernization." And in a direct polemic with Gellner and Benedict Anderson, she challenges both of them: "Rather than define nationalism by its modernity,

I see modernity as defined by nationalism."[3] Greenfeld further developed this interesting hypothesis in her analysis of economic nationalism. However, at this point one should mention serious problems encountered in applying it to Latin America's historical experience of nation-building.

To clarify the relationship between political and economic nationalisms requires, first and foremost, defining the area of study, i.e. the set of relations and phenomena to which the notion of economic nationalism refers. Should we accept Harry Johnson's (1967: 126) approach of seeing in economic nationalism no more than "the implications of nationalism for the ideology of economic policy"? Or rather, in contrast to Johnson, is it more fruitful to speak about such economic phenomena, policies included, which, subjected to the impact of political nationalism, cannot be reduced to ideologies and/or political measures expressed in economic categories?

The first approach, the prevailing one in the literature, is, to a certain extent, an aspect of a broader hypothesis according to which nationalist ideology and policy play and important role in the formation of modern states and nations. To some extent Greenfeld leans toward such an approach in her Weber-inspired deliberations on the birth of economic nationalism as "the competitive and forward-oriented collective spirit of capitalism," and, to be more precise, presenting economic nationalism as an "economic expression of the collective competitiveness inherent in [political] nationalism." Thus it is not Protestantism (or Sombart's Judaism) but economic nationalism that plays the role of the key factor that leads to the birth of capitalism and modernity. Economic nationalism was a phenomenon belonging to the category of motivations which were important if they encompassed not "one powerful minister," as Greenfeld says quoting the example of Russia's Sergei Witte, but strategically located social groups. At the same time she makes a reservation that "the orientation to economic growth is not a necessary product of [political] nationalism;" and that we deal with it only in the situation "where the economy is included among the area of international competition in which the nation in question wishes to participate" (Greenfeld 2003: 107, 114, 473f).

---

[3] However, such a perennialist position, in contrast to Hobsbawm (1990: 14) and other modernists, cannot be reduced to nationalist primordialism, and does not imply support for the thesis that national identifications "precede history." The empirical and historical perennialist position, Smith (1998: chapter 7) argues, would stress both continuities and discontinuities in the process transforming pre-modern ethnic communities (*ethnie*) into modern nations.

Indeed, Greenfeld concentrates on economic ideas created in the countries which in different but usually effective ways have generated the motivations she described, and only indirectly does she touch upon the question of the economic nationalism of backward areas that interests me.

When referring to my earlier presentation of the notion of national economy and its relationship with economic nationalism, the outstanding historian of Latin America, Marcello Carmagnani (1990: 257), went much further, actually denying economic nationalism's 'substantialist' dimension. He argued instead that "the concept of the national economy ... is merely a pretext for the rationalization of the inadequacy of resources to needs." As with every nationalism, he underlined, economic nationalism also continually refers to the concept of national economy; in point of fact it acts as a front for the state of the populace's collective mind in the face of real or imagined economic failure.

This is a debatable proposal. At the same time the question posed by Hobsbawm (1990: 28), "How indeed could the economic functions and even benefits of the nation-state be denied?" seems to be a good introduction to this subject.

The answer to this question was probably not difficult for mercantilist writers as producers of ideas and, for some of them, people involved in commercial endeavors. But when mentioning mercantilists I do not mean the world of ideas alone. The rejection by many historians of the causal relation between the theories of mercantilist policy and the state on the one hand, and the real processes on the other, for obvious reasons does not imply the negation of *mercantilist practice*. The emergence of territorial states in place of city-states and the emergence of the European world market—for a certain time along with the Asian world market—were a fact. It was a fact that in the 16th–17th centuries the final shape of a specific trade policy was arrived at and that in particular European countries (England, the Netherlands and France) interesting answers were given to signals coming from the international market. Those signals did not yet result from an advanced convergence of prices, but were connected with flourishing international trade (O'Rourke and Williamson 2000). Finally, it was a fact that the *introductory stage* of the consolidation of national economies was accelerated. However, one could speak about the advancement of that process only two centuries later, in the railroads era: "Before the coming of the railways France was not really a national market" (Braudel 1990: 467).

However, the initial stage of the consolidation process already made possible synchronization of the elements of the triad essential to the definition of the modern state, i.e. sovereignty (including national purpose), territorial unity and state-and-territorial legitimism. In the long perspective that triad did question the primacy of the hitherto regional ties, which developed above and beyond what were quite illusory borders. It is another question whether that was to the benefit of all the populace concerned. At the same time, processes of political, cultural and economic consolidation—but also those of their collapse or even reversal—had been from the very beginning located within the framework of wider and complex mechanisms of the emerging world economy and also in the framework of *inter*-national relations, which in a way forced competitive behavior. All in all, if we recap the perspectives defined by the deliberations by mercantilist theorists and deliberations on the extent of such theorists' effects on the policy of a state, mercantilism was for other legitimate reasons a distinctive feature of European policy for at least two centuries. The limited impact of the theory was accompanied by the active mercantilist practice of new state-owned and private business entities.

In such a context the economic role of the state and national economy can no longer be interpreted solely as an aspect of ideology. They become a web of institutions, interests and motivations of a relatively lasting nature. The feedback between political nationalism and the rising economic nationalism becomes increasingly complicated, and the two concepts difficult to disentangle. The transition from mercantilism to modernity may thus be interpreted not so much as a reversal of the causal relation but as a creation of a kind of modern nationalistic syndrome. Kofman (1997: 9) defines this process in regard to Central Europe between the two world wars as a transformation of economic nationalism into the "crowning" of political nationalism. Greenfeld for her part, as mentioned above, discerns the 'spirit of capitalism' in economic nationalism.

I will now return for a moment to Carmagnani's thesis quoted above. Although I do not accept it, I cannot pass over an element connected with a particular challenge involved in the process of constituting a modern nationalist idea, which is important for understanding economic nationalism: the growing awareness of backwardness and inequality. And "injustice perceived," as David Landes (1998: 309) observes, "is injustice felt. Men are not moved by bread alone." Gellner, too, noted that element, saying that "nationalism is a phenomenon connected not so much with industrialisation or modernisation as such, but with its *uneven diffusion*" (quoted in Szporluk 2003: 260; see also Wallerstein 2000: 303). Isaiah Berlin (2004: 215ff) also sees nationalism as a consequence of underdevelopment and 'wounds sustained'. Such an awareness makes–and at this point one should agree with Carmagnani, and also with Greenfeld (1993: 6–17) when the latter writes about the key role of resentment in the formation of nationalistic ideas–an indispensable element not only of political nationalism, but also of a concept of national economy as a political and economic project. There are, however, interesting exceptions to this rule. Economic motivations are associated with resentment not only in a very intricate manner, but in certain cases the sources of that resentment should be perceived also in the problems posed by *effective* and *successful* economic modernization, and not just by its delay or collapse. At this point the case of Scotland in the last forty years comes to mind (Breuilly 1985: 280–290, Findlay 1995: 151f). So do the examples of Catalonia and Wales. In any case, years ago Alexander Gerschenkron, in his pathbreaking essay, presented an excellent description of the non-economic prerequisites for effective economic nationalism to be able to confront the problem of backwardness:

> To break through the barriers of stagnation in a backward country, to ignite the imagination of men, and to place their energies in the service of economic development, a stronger medicine is needed than the promise of better allocation of resources or even of the lower price of bread. Under such conditions even the businessman ... needs a more powerful stimulus than the prospect of high profits. What is needed to remove the mountains of routine and prejudice is faith (Gerschenkron 1965: 24).

Many in the economics profession would probably disagree. Their belief in the reality-transforming power of a growth equation, which by adding human capital to capital and labor can produce economic miracles, seems to be unshakable. However, the late Ernst Gellner and Mancur Olson would probably ask: what kind of capital and labor? under which conditions? with the help of what kinds of institutions and ideas? In principle, to recognize that ideas and ideologies matter does not mean they have already found a proper place in economic history literature. On the contrary: "There is a danger ... that the role of ideology in modernization will be ignored not because it is irrelevant but because it is intractable" (Sylla and Toniolo 1991: 21).

Arcadius Kahan deals with the questions mentioned here and also with other issues connected with the subject in an interesting essay devoted to 19th century economic nationalism in Western Europe. He opens his argument with the following statement:

CHAPTER ONE

> When analyzing and describing manifestations of economic nationalism, one ought not to consider the whole set of economic measures designated directly to strengthen the nation's political and economic power (Kahan 1967: 17).

In his opinion, the notion of economic nationalism should be related only to the cases of intentional association of the demands of political nationalism with rational economic activities, aimed at the promotion of economic growth or at the satisfaction of particularistic interests. At the same time such differentiation induces him to propose two sequential, historically different, variants of economic nationalism. Inasmuch as in the 19th century the prevailing type of nationalism stressed that "American Motors is better for the United States than British Motors and therefore deserves support," in modern times (i.e. roughly since 1945) there has prevailed an economic nationalism that refers to the principle according to which "what is good for the United States is good for American Motors." Furthermore, Kahan argues that in the 19th and the beginning of the 20th centuries the activity of states inspired by nationalist ideology exerted a negative impact on economic growth (1967: 17f, 20).

I think, however, that these interesting theses formulated by this outstanding historian are one-sided generalizations, and they hardly do justice of the historical reality not just of the United States and Western Europe, but European and Latin American peripheries as well. The dispute between advocates of 'Republican (economic) nationalism' and 'Democratic nationalism' (symbolically: John Quincy Adams and Henry Clay versus Andrew Jackson) in the first three decades of the 19th century was a dispute about the directions and intensity of state intervention and about forms of state support and control. Except for the South, the principle of protecting national economy was not questioned as a general rule (Dangerfield 1965: 289). That internal dispute between the advocates of nearly total tariff protectionism on the one hand, and moderate protectionists on the other (focused on 'improvements' first and foremost in infrastructure), reflected a reality which was in fact a symbiosis—not a sequence—of both types of economic nationalism indicated by Kahan. I shall return to this in Chapter 4.

However, it is worth mentioning that seeing protectionism, the key element of economic nationalism, as by definition a barrier to economic growth in the period discussed is one of many economic myths put into doubt by Paul Bairoch (1993) already in the 1970s. Recently is has been intensively debated and questioned by other economic historians (Williamson 2002, 2006, Bértola and Williamson 2006). As with the myth of economic liberalism, it was generally believed to be characteristic of the period beginning with the Cobden–Chevalier Treaty in 1860, which ended in 1914. The concurrence of free trade and unlimited mobility of capital and labor–the very essence of economic liberalism–lasted only a short time. The tariff-growth paradox was in fact a part and parcel, not the distortion of the developmental dynamic in the majority of core countries during the first globalization (Clemens and Williamson 2001). The gold standard, the crowning of the liberal credo, had an even shorter reign in the world economy, and particularly in Latin America. Thus the researchers mentioned have in a more refined and methodical way proved the earlier hypothesis of Barry Supple (1973: 340) that "[e]conomic liberalism was only a brief episode in the history of industrial capitalism." But judging from the comparison of British, French, Dutch and 'German' (*Zollverein*) tariffs, even in this short period, say from the mid-1850s to the mid-1870s, the United States, the new emerging economic power, drastically deviated from the free-trade principles.

However, irrespective of the decades' long disputes–carried on with equal vigor among economists and economic historians–the thesis of Kahan (who is not alone in his opinion) is disproved first and foremost by the fact of the thorough reorganization of global economic potential toward the end of the 19th century. That fact corroborated the success of *some* of the protectionist late-comers—of the "second graduate class," as W. W. Rostow (1990: 445f) describes them (the "first class" was of course Great Britain)—who in the years 1830–1850 passed the maturity exam in the take-off into accelerated growth (the USA, Germany and France). The "third graduate class" was composed of Japan, Russia and Italy, but also Australia and Canada (Argentina is a debatable proposition).[4] What is more, instances of "graduates" who would not, with various intensity, practice protectionism and/or strong non-tariff support to national producers, are extremely rare at best (Gould 1973: 287). For all intents and purposes the appearance of the "graduate class" causes serious difficulties for a counterfactual analysis aimed at proving the basic divergence between the actual trend and the potential, more promising, trend based on the assumption eliminating protectionism and other externalities resulting from the activities of the state. On the other hand, however, since we can speak of the successes of only a few states practicing a protectionist policy

---

[4] O'Brien's (1986) insightful critique of the concept of take-off (and of Gerschenkron's "spurts") concerns the problem of the models of industrialization, not the question of reorganization of the world system, which arose because of the emergence of "graduates."

it is obvious that such a policy does not suffice on its own to ensure economic success.

Still, Kahan's theses provide a good starting point for further discussion. The relationship between political and economic nationalisms, between the latter and industrialization and the identification of different variants of economic nationalism are the main aspects of the problems addressed by this book. In the deliberations below I will follow the already mentioned, more forceful, approach to the category of national economy. I perceive in it not only a major point of reference for policies of economic nationalism, but also its historically-shaped dimension (Chapter 3).

I would imply that the category of national economy constitutes an irreducible part of the historical process of state- and nation-building, and in this sense it is also a non-contextual notion. Social, economic and political relations, defining the content of this category, are also a sort of investment which not only brings in—under favorable circumstances—increasing returns that sustain its permanence and, indirectly, strengthen its resistance to changes, but also an investment that is hard to reverse. The set of these relationships is a key element of the path-dependent development–as interpreted by Kenneth J. Arrow (2004).[5]

As a result, economic nationalism can be conceived of as–conditioned and legitimized by the ideology of political nationalism–a set of actions undertaken by social groups (and mediating representatives of their interests) within the framework of formal and informal institutions, implying a change in the direction of the country's economic development, and questioning the so far prevailing general and partial equilibriums. Such actions also assume–as a fragment of structural transformations called for or as an

---

[5] In economics the path-dependent development hypothesis is connected first and foremost with works by David (1985) and Arthur (1989), who emphasized the key role of random events and of increasing returns. Arrow implies something different: that at the source of path dependence we find mainly the irreversibility of investments, not increasing returns. In such a case, diminishing returns would not necessarily lead to optimizing solution. Thus if in the light of Arrow's interpretation, the randomness of changes and increasing returns are not unique preconditions for path dependency, results linked, in turn, with diminishing returns, such as enforced efficiency and flexibility, can no longer be treated as obviously given. Path dependence hypothesis was interestingly applied in an analysis of the state by, for example, Krasner (1989: 86–88), and with reference to a wider agenda of political science–by Pierson (2000). Pierson examined, among other things, the possibility of a lack of automatism in the return to institutions optimizing the use of resources, and thus the question earlier discussed by North (1990: chapter 11). For applications of path-dependency hypothesis to Latin America see, for example, Cárdenas, Ocampo and Thorp 2000, Mahoney 2001.

independent goal–changes in the distribution of economic gains. The distributional conflict, built into the logic of political and economic nationalisms, takes place both at the international as well as the domestic level. Its outcome is conditioned by political nationalism's discourse and by conditions of participation in the international system. Depending on the variant of nationalism, it is concentrated either on the maximization of particular gains (*particularistic nationalism*) or on the achievements–in the complex interaction between the state and societal actors–of certain collective goods operationalized by the state (*holistic nationalism*). These goods are usually defined as 'national interest', including the demand for economic growth and the consolidation and strengthening of the national economy. As a specific domestic and international distributional conflict (including one along the nationals-foreigners axis), economic nationalism brings in the state and is unthinkable beyond its framework. However, depending on the variant of economic nationalism, the state is perceived in various ways (as an autonomous actor, strategic relation, arena, epiphenomenon of pluralistic structures and institutions).

This above outlined approach to economic nationalism stands in contrast with the prevailing interpretations, usually proposed by economic liberals. Having at my disposal Kofman's thorough analysis of their ideas (1997: chapter 1), I shall limit myself here to indicating that the approach I propose does go beyond the horizons outlined, under the influence of the experience of the 1930s, by Michael Heilperin, the liberal economist and author of a major critical analysis of economic nationalism. According to him, the essence of economic nationalism, understood as a set of national policies, can be summed up as first and foremost the aspiration for "the loosening of the organic links between economic processes taking place within the boundaries of a country and those taking place beyond these boundaries" (Heilperin 1960: 17, 27). At the source of this kind of policy, he adds, we find "collectivism," which, even if for practical reasons, does rule out autarchy, but without doubt strives after strengthening economic self-sufficiency. Elsewhere Heilperin also mentions the aspiration to achieve "a greater degree of diversification of production and a better-balanced national economy" (1960: 20). This, however, concerns primarily the 1930s. But it is exactly this short remark which to me seems crucial to understanding the longer-term consequences of the 1930s in Latin America and Central Europe.

Incidentally, with European powers and also the USA and Japan in mind, such an approach by liberal economists to economic nationalism has spurned an attractive, in view of its simplicity, thesis combining the aspirations of the big powers to control raw materials and sales markets (the condition of 'self-sufficiency') with aggressive international behaviors ('imperialism'). This way, generalizing these countries' experience and, at the same time, ignoring the histories of Latin America and a part of Central Europe, for example Robert Skidelsky (1995: 48f) implies one-sidedly a strong connection between the economic nationalism 'doctrine' and militarism. However, if militarism implied a growing share of defense expenditures in the state budget and/or in GDP, such a tendency appeared in Central Europe relatively late, in the 2–3 years preceding the outbreak of WWII. In strictly economic terms the economic nationalism-as-militarism hypothesis seems to be not corroborated by available statistics (Hauner 1986: passim).

The problem of collectivism is definitely more important. The use by Heilperin of an extremely broad concept of collectivism does in point of fact hinder the understanding of the multitude of forms in which the 'collectivist impulse' appeared at a certain moment of the evolution not only of economic nationalism but also of broadly defined economic development. Of course, one cannot deny its relation to certain historical forms of economic nationalism. But at the same time one cannot reduce this 'impulse' to such nationalism. Collectivism is also a structural characteristic of the 20th century democratic systems and developed market economies. In this connection Skidelsky (1995: chapter 2) rightly suggests that it would be more interesting to approach collectivism as an ideologically neutral method of non-market coordination of economic life, irrespective of the political aims its advocates wanted to set themselves. This problem arose also as the linking of economic nationalism and collectivism with a definite kind of state and political regime. In particular authoritarian-corporative or populist regimes, but also fascist and communist ones, were lumped together and perceived as a functionally indispensable element of economic policy, particularly in backward countries. This is not only an oversimplification, but one that, in effect, eliminates the issue of the kind of state and political regime as a complex *political* answer to both path-dependent development as well as to the situations of political and economic crisis.

On the other hand, in the approaches to economic nationalism followed by liberal economists—under the strong influence of the post-WWII decolonization process—the emphasis was laid first of all on changes in the distribution of gains between foreigners and nationals. Thus the consequence of a focus on the distributive conflict is a pushing to the foreground of the problem of national control over resources and at the same time the demystification of "national gains" related to the nationalization of these resources. This finds its expression first of all in the concept of Anton Breton (1964, Breton and Breton 1995).

When extending the list of problems one should also raise the question of different dimensions of economic nationalism's rationality, which cannot be reduced to the narrowly understood sphere of economic activities. (This problem has been indicated by Carmagnani and Gellner, already quoted here, and earlier by Breton and Eliezer B. Ayal.) Ayal (1966: 237) indicated for instance that "not only are the contents of the nationalistic ideology important for economic development but also the ancillary social effects resulting from its adoption." This is an interesting observation, subsequently developed by Ayal and other authors in a path-breaking work on one of the important dimensions of economic nationalism, namely the indigenization of resources, in the post-colonial South East Asia as a part of nation-building. They point out at the same time that the inclusion in the descriptive definitions of economic nationalism of such criterion as "the share of members of the national society in the ownership, management and control of productive assets, and their share in the allocation of prestigious and materially rewarding economic functions" is, in principle, a "recent years" phenomenon (Golay, Anspach, Pfanner and Ayal 1969: 6f). The history of economic nationalism in the regions under study implies that this is in fact a much older phenomenon. Indigenization, in Central Europe called nostrification (and linked with 'ethnicization' campaigns) and/or inward-oriented economic nationalism, accompanied the maturation of interwar economic nationalism in the region (Kofman 1997: 73–85).

However, as is usually the case, *c'est le ton qui fait la chanson*. And so Dudley Seers (1983: 10), the founder of the Institute of Development Studies at the University of Sussex, recollects that "like many of those educated in the Anglo-Saxon cultural tradition, I saw nationalism as fundamentally irrational." The characteristic way economic nationalism is being rehabilitated in modern mainstream economics seems to be an endeavor not too distant in tone from the cultural tradition mentioned by Seers.

Inasmuch as mainstream economists raise the issues of nationalism, they propose a kind of second-best argument: while in its economic dimension economic nationalism was (and is) a total failure, this does not mean that in other dimensions (the psychological and/or political) it has not produced some benefits. So, if it was earlier argued that economic nationalism was a zero-sum game in all dimensions of social and economic life, now they make their assessment more flexible, grudgingly accepting the peculiar substitution of nationalism's economic and non-economic goals. This is manifestly stressed in the models of economic nationalism proposed by Albert Breton and, above all, by Harry G. Johnson. The former emphasizes that "investments in nationality are not so much income-creating as income-redistributing;" hence Breton classifies the consequences of this process as harmful and in keeping with the model of the rent-seeking approach (1964: 376). Johnson thinks likewise. He concludes his deliberations by stating that "nationalism will tend to direct economic policy toward the production of psychic income in the form of nationalistic satisfaction at the expense of material income" (Johnson 1967: 14). Also Golay, Anspach, Pfanner and Ayal (1969: 11, 462) write about indigenism's negative impact on income per capita.

This kind of approach–first and foremost the one-sided assessment of the long-term effects of economic nationalism in European peripheries—was questioned by Kofman (1997: 204ff). A decade later Greenfeld offered a similar assessment, although she concentrated her attention not on the Central European peripheries, but on Great Britain, Germany, France, the USA and Japan. Thus, inasmuch as Greenfeld shows the ideological context and conditions connected with the formation and consolidation of effective nationalist policies, Kofman analyzes the complicated processes, crowned with a qualified success, of the economic nationalism of the peripheries at the time of the collapse of the first globalization. Ugo Pagano, too, is critical of the Breton-Johnson approach, of the thesis opposing distributive conflict to growth in particular. In his opinion,

> the contrast between rent-seeking and wealth-creating approaches should not be overstated. In many cases, both explanations may apply; in some other historical situations, only one explanation is appropriate (Pagano 1995: 189).

While supporting this view, I must emphasize at the same time that while the interpretation stressing the rent-seeking approach eliminates from the discussion the concept of collective goods, the approach I adopt does not rule out its usefulness, especially with regard to holistic nationalism. Probably the best short description of the role economic nationalism could play–following the 'spirit' of Gerschenkron's approach–was presented not by an economist but an anthropologist. In the same volume in which Johnson presented his second-best argument for economic nationalism, one can find the following evaluation by a social and economic anthropologist:

> Economic nationalism may be a necessary input for economic development, and what superficially by the rules of immediate optimal allocation appears counter-productive may be the best investment that a developing nation can make (Nash 1967: 84).

Let me return, however, to Kahan's theses. First of all, I want to express my doubt whether, if we refer to specific historical processes, it is possible at all to draw a sharp dividing line between political goals (including military ones) reflected in economic action and economic goals conditioned by both political and economic nationalism. Is a divorce from the "total historical experience" (Mitchell 1967: 87) possible? And seeking copybook, analytically attractive and pure solutions to the catching-up by backward countries in particular seems to be an artificial endeavor (see Burnell 1986: 21ff). How could one separate these two goals in the case of the industrializing spurt initiated by Sergei Witte in Russia in the 1890s or the case of transition to modernity in the Meiji period (1868–1912), or the construction of the Central Industrial Region (COP) in Poland at the end of 1930s and the steel industry in Volta Redonda in Brazil in the early 1940s? How should one interpret the Hungarian Győr Program, which "was born not in any economic department of the state but in the Ministry of War" (Ránki and Tomaszewski 1986: 41) and its long-term results? It was in a memo written to President Getúlio Vargas by an important coffee planter and industrialist Alexander Siciliano Jr., where ambiguities concerning the interplay between political and economic goals–in the case of the Brazilian steel industry–are in the forefront:

> For me the steel problem is primarily a simple technical problem, secondarily an important economic problem, and finally a very delicate political-military problem. But there are those who, perhaps rightly, would invert the order (quoted in Wirth 1970: 72).

Kuznets, when discussing the role of armed conflicts (a "pathological" variable) and other conflict-related factors in shaping modern economic growth in the long run, gave a clear answer: "the process of growth should be defined to include its pathological deviates–which may be quite important for the understanding of the natural [peaceful] process" (Kuznets 1951: 34). A century ago it was Werner Sombart (1913b)–as a brilliant economic historian not yet the ideologue of *Deutscher Sozialismus*–who forcefully raised the problem of the "duality of war" (*das doppelte Gesicht des Krieges*) against the example of the development of modern shipbuilding and the navy up to the end of 18th century. On the other hand, do geopolitical and military factors fully explain the pace, directions, forms and (gruesome) costs of the Soviet industrialization of the 1930s, and also definitely lower costs in Poland and in other communist countries at the turn of the 1940s and 1950s? How should one describe, according to the communist model of economic nationalism, the place not so much of political and military priorities, but of the ideology (in its many mutations) and the related styles of action?[6] The widening of the scope of analysis through the introduction of problems of the international system, which was increasingly competitive in the period examined, and characterized by high and growing risk related to the gradual disintegration of the Pax Britannica, only deepens the doubts about Kahan's proposals.

The questions mentioned thus oblige us to give some thought, *first*, to the conclusions that follow from the discussion over mercantilism as the most glaring historical example of the conflict (but also an interplay) between "defense" and "opulence" (to use Adam Smith's (2005: 371) famous phrase), and over Friedrich List's *System*. In this context, it will be useful to point out some nationalistic implications of John M. Keynes' employment theory (Chapter 2). An analysis of precursors' ideas, of the intellectual tradition leading from mercantilism to "nationalist capitalism" and finally to "technocratic capitalism" (Calleo 2001: chapter 1), makes it possible to clarify two variants of economic nationalism: *holistic nationalism* and *particularistic nationalism* (Chapter 3).[7]

Second, discussion concerning economic nationalism requires that we give some thought to the theoretical status of the category of national economy (Chapter 3). Coming back to the question already mentioned: What are the reasons for singling out the problems of national economy (the main subject of economic nationalists' interest) from general economic theory which revolves around such abstract concepts as capital, interest, profit and wages? Perhaps the concept of national economy, and economic nationalism along with it, is a mere ideological artifact of the state as a political structure? This is by no means an unfounded doubt,

---

[6] Concerning the latter question, extremely interesting were discussions with Mancur Olson on the draft of his book *Power and Prosperity: Outgrowing Communist and Capitalist Dictatorships*, organized in the years 1996–1997 (see Olson 1999). Olson sustained his thesis that in the Stalinist autocracy the role of ideology had been of secondary importance. Earlier, Gerschenkron (1968: 69, 475f), too, laid an emphasis first and foremost on the circumstances not on the ideology.

[7] Their introductory version (Szlajfer 1990) was embraced by Batou and David (1996), and by David (2009). The presented by Evans (1995, 1992) concepts of the developmental state as the provider of definite public goods, and of the "predatory state" subordinated to interest groups do not seem contrary to the two variants of nationalism proposed.

especially that in a standard university textbook we read the following statement: "The essential difference between external and internal trade is *political* only: one involves a foreigner, the other does not" (Root 1978: 148). Period. There immediately comes to mind a note kept in Jacob Viner's papers, recounting a story about a certain German professor who used to explain the fall of the Roman empire by the fact that the empire had kept growing until it spread throughout the entire known world at the time, and as a result its foreign trade had been reduced to zero (see Machlup 1986: 244). In such a context, the state and national economy emerge as the second-best solution, compared with the ideal of supranational integration (and the unlimited mobility of commodities, capital and labor), i.e. as an extension of methodological individualism.

Third, should we treat the nexus linking economic nationalism with industrialization as a general rule, restricting the use of economic nationalism only to specific historical processes taking place in industrial and industrializing societies? The answer one finds in the literature is usually positive (Gellner 1991, Smith 1972, 1998). And yet, I cannot see any *prima facie* arguments in favor of such a restrictive assumption, especially in relation to the areas examined in this book (Chapter 7). What is more, the tendency for deindustrialization and ossification of primary, underdeveloped economies have been until recently bound up with the development of modern industry in metropolises. Such peculiar symbiosis reflected the division of labor based on "simple, vulgar complementarity," as Henryk Tennenbaum (1942: 126) put it with reference to relations between Germany and East and Central Europe in the interwar period.

It would be downright incomprehensible if peripheral economies did not create occasions for consolidation and articulation of different variants of nationalistic ideologies, both those that focused on the defense of the agrarian-raw material status quo, as well as such that questioned the hitherto specialization and dominant position of the related interest groups. Economic protectionism and political nationalism are not unique characteristics of those social groups who represent industrial interests and coalitions formed around them. Coalitions formed around agrarian and merchant groups can be protectionist and nationalistic just as well. It is difficult to give a better example than the violent reaction of agrarian societal actors in Germany and France to the competition from cheap grain from Russia, the USA and other countries toward the end of the 19th century (Gourevich 1986, Gerschenkron 1989). In the interwar period this kind of protectionism/nationalism became endemic in East and Central Europe (Kofman 1997, Köll 2006). What is more, that was not a nationalism founded on a basic opposition to free-market principles. In the economic dimension—but not necessarily in the political or ideological one—the agrarian interests in countries exporting agricultural products belonged, so to say by definition, to the free-market bloc. The Stolper–Samuelson theory of foreign trade gave a proper explanation of such behavior (see Williamson 2006). However, only in certain conditions. Nationalism, narrowly understood as an international bargain, was (and still is) a natural part of market behavior. And if we go beyond the perspective of economic nationalism, reduced to the notion of protectionism and industrial society, it is necessary to give attention to the interesting concept of "liberal economic nationalism" (David 2009, Helleiner 2002). It relates support for free-trade policy, especially in peripheral countries, to the more general processes of state- and nation-building.

Fourth, the problem of foreign firms and investments, and of the foreigner in general, takes a special place in the nationalistic discourse. I would argue that in this particular case we are often dealing here with glaring cases of historical anachronism. The experience of and reflections on post-WW II economic nationalism, shaped under the strong influence of communist ideology (and practice) and of the process of the second decolonization, are mechanically read into an analysis concerning earlier periods.

Without a doubt the crisis of the first globalization that reared its head in the 1930s, in many countries initiated (or intensified) processes which led to non-market practices, including nationalization of foreign assets, discrimination against national minorities and a considerable extension of the scope of state activity. One should bear in mind, however, that the post-WWII experience was in many respects a peculiar repudiation and not mere radicalization of the concepts and policies of the 1930s. That is why I attach such importance to clarifying the role of foreign capital. I set this issue against the background of an equally important transformation of political nationalism: from its liberal variant to integral nationalism (Chapters 4 and 5). During that transformation a change of attitudes toward foreign investors and foreigners in general was stressed. Yet, in the majority of cases, the threshold separating dislike for or attempts to instrumentalize foreign capital from its total elimination was not crossed.

Still, the question remains unanswered as to whether the evolution regarding 'internal foreigners' (here: national minorities) in Central Europe in the 1930s inevitably led to their radical political and economic marginalization. For sure, the intensity of disputes but also of the discriminatory measures was growing. To what end? Anything one can say here would be pure speculation. Allow me only to mention that the opinion of a Jewish historian on that matter was rather pessimistic. He was not alone when stressing that the developments in the 1930s indicated a possibility of disaster: "the demise of democracy and liberalism and the triumph of right-wing integral nationalism ... served to destroy whatever hopes had existed for peaceful coexistence between Jew and gentile" (Mendelsohn 1983: 256). And that concerned not Jews alone.

Fifth, like political nationalism, economic nationalism, too, has its history. It is not confined to mercantilist precursors and/or the traumatic experience of the interwar period. Therefore in Chapter 6 I make an attempt at a comparative analysis of *economic proto-nationalism* in the areas under study in the first half of the 19th century. The concept of economic proto-nationalism, patterned after Hobsbawm's concept of political proto-nationalism, was propounded by Thomas David (2009) and David and Elisabeth Spilman (2006), who at the same time rightly questioned discussing this kind of attempts as examples of past-oriented 'neo-mercantilism'. I should add that neither of them had anything in common with the concept of proto-industrialization, widely discussed in the literature. In a nutshell, the concept of economic proto-nationalism refers to phenomena related to attempts at top-down industrialization in the first half of the 19th century in some countries of Central Europe and Latin America. I would argue that, like political proto-nationalism, its economic equivalent could be seen as a fragment of the process of adopting ideas and practices aimed at establishing a new point of reference in economic life, which would be contrary to the model of 'natural' development. In contrast with the popular proto-nationalism, the relation of which with modern state-centered political nationalism Hobsbawm (1990: 47, 73–76) rejects, the other variant of proto-nationalism he singles out, which refers to the nationalism of the nobility and the elitist political nation, already implies a concept of a state-territorial 'whole' and/or memory of state tradition.[8] The second variant of Hobsbawm's proto-nationalism constitutes a sufficient basis permitting the use of the concept of economic proto-nationalism. The latter was downright unthinkable outside the processes of state building and—bearing first of all Central Europe in mind of re-defining the concept of the nation.

---

[8] Smith (1998: 122, 127f) does not agree with the thesis stressing the lack of continuity between the popular proto-nationalism–in fact ethnic ties–and modern political nationalism.

The last of the issues mentioned ultimately leads us to the question about the heuristic value of comparative studies which take into account the historical development (and the specificity of underdevelopment) of Latin America and Central Europe in the period examined. However, I want to underscore at this point that in this book I am not concerned with this issue as a methodological problem. Today, the usefulness of the comparative perspective, stressed particularly strongly in international political economy, the political sciences and historical sociology, is no longer questioned, although specific approaches are hotly debated.

Why then Central Europe and Latin America?

"The first developing capitalist countries," wrote Polish economic historian Witold Kula (1983b: 165), "founded sugar or cotton plantations across the ocean, and found cereal 'plantations' in Eastern Europe." When approaching the problem of the historical roots of Poland's underdevelopment, Marian Małowist emphasized not only the interplay of the international market and of the social structure of the country in 15th–16th centuries but also the paradox, which was later repeated in the Latin American booming export economies:

> The earlier dependence of Polish agriculture on the western market led to the sui generis colonization of the Polish economy; at the same time, it ensured a considerable income to the Poles, thanks to the foreign trade surplus and the inflow of money from the West (Małowist 2010: 242; see also 1973).

It is worth also mentioning here Franciszek Bujak's observation made at the beginning of the 20th century that the development paths of Poland and Central Europe as a whole and those of Latin America diverged from the stages-centered scheme of the German Historical School, focused on the Western European experience. This concerned above all the transition from the national economy (*Volkswirtschaft*)–preceded by the territorial state and economy (*Territorialstaatenwirtschaft*)–to world economy (*Weltwirtschaft*). According to Bujak, from the 16th century until the end of the 19th century the two regions were characterized by underdeveloped domestic markets, lack of economic differentiation, absence of an economic center, and the predominance of primary export orientation. As a result, already in the 16th century the two regions had "jumped over the stage of national economy and moved directly to the highest stage, i.e. to the world economy" (Bujak 1976: 456ff, 528ff). The stages-centered approach was not in a position to take such an 'anomaly' into account.

However, despite the fact that both Central Europe and Latin America made first large-scale laboratories of underdevelopment which came into existence as an element of the emergence of the modern European world economy, and despite the striking similarity of certain basic economic structures in the two regions, comparative studies on them still are at the initial stage (Łepkowski 1988, Szlajfer 1990).[9] It is particularly noticeable with regard to the problems of economic nationalism. Therefore in Chapter 8, continuing reflections on economic proto-nationalism but with regard to the first three decades of the 20th century, I show, aside from clear differences, also similar tendencies occurring in both areas. Their common denominator is the response to backwardness, the appearance of important elements of holistic economic nationalism, especially in the period of the Great Depression, as the response of underdeveloped economies and societies to crisis and to the fact of their underdevelopment (Szlajfer 1990: 9). The key category suggested by this response was the state committed to industrialization. The name of such a state–the developmental state–will appear later.

The theoretical concept of such a state, like the term itself, developed under the overwhelming influence of the postwar debates. Paul Baran (1976: 366), in his classical Marxist analysis of underdevelopment, used a different name: with India and Indonesia in the 1950s in mind, he proposed calling these states "New-Deal type régimes." Today Atul Kohli (2004) suggests calling them "cohesive-capitalist states." However, in Latin America the concept of the developmental state grew first and foremost from the experience gathered at the time of the Great Depression and in the years 1939–1945. It was in the 1930s that in Brazil "economic nationalism became an ideology of development" (Wirth 1970: 13). Thus it should come as no surprise that it was precisely in Latin America a few years after WWII that Raúl Prebisch proposed a program linking center-periphery relations, worsening terms of trade of underdeveloped countries and the call for industrialization. After all, the same can be said about the earlier concepts of the industrialization-as-the-big push and about the active role of the state in overcoming backwardness, discussed during the war under the influence of the interwar experience of East and Central Europe.

---

[9] Kochanowicz (1983) saw the possibility for a comparative analysis in connection with Witold Kula's model of Polish feudalism (second serfdom). For more on this subject see Sosnowska (2004). However, Braudel's and Wallerstein's *les grandes histoires* of the world economy exerted a rather limited impact on Polish historiography. In recent years, published has been a monograph by Love (1996), a tour de force in comparative analysis of conceptualizations of backwardness in Romania and Brazil.

I mean here above all the works of Paul Rosenstein-Rodan and Kurt Mandelbaum.

Thus the analysis presented in Chapter 8 is, to some extent, also an attempt at recovering pieces of the history of the developmental state. Such states had existed before economists, political scientists and historians discovered them and named them as such (Bagchi 2000: 398). From this point of view, the two areas studied in the book are extremely attractive. For in Latin America and Central Europe which exemplify the phenomenon of modern backwardness, the historical experiment of transition toward the developmental state appeared as a consequence of processes that for several centuries had been closely related with the building of developed economies and societies. It was the flip side of modernity.

An important fragment of this process was also the break that took place in 1917 in Russia and then after 1945 in East and Central Europe and in some Asian countries. In this connection it is worth recalling here that already in the 1930s the communist economic experiment was, sporadically and with obvious simplifications, defined as economic nationalism not just by critical observers from the West. In 1929, during a discussion organized by the New York-based Foreign Policy Association, the Soviet trade representative to the USA said:

> Can the system which exists in my country be called 'Economic Nationalism'? I would accept this term if one would understand by it a striving for a relative independence, but the essence of the system as practiced in my country can be defined best as an endeavor to advance as far as possible from the position of a colony. I would define the object of Soviet trade as 'decolonization' (quoted in Hodgson 1933: 48).

In this way the Stalinist model of enforced industrialization–a combination of imported technology with ruthless transfer of resources from agriculture and with Gulag camps labor employed in infrastructural projects, mines and forestry–was introduced into the debate concerning backwardness and competing models of modernity. I interpret this model as communist economic nationalism (Szlajfer 1997). With regard to many key variables (property rights, market coordination and rationality), the experiment initiated in 1917 questioned the institutional foundations of the developmental state of the interwar period. In terms of its economic logic and rationality it was an economic system sui generis (compare Małecki-Tepicht 2003). Therefore it seems that an attempt to see communist economic nationalism as simply an incarnation of the Breton–Johnson model writ large (see Ferrero 1995) was both an understatement and misinterpretation.

Obviously, studies on the economic nationalism of backward countries may not ignore the context of such nationalism. This applies both to the ways political nationalism was conceptualized in those countries and to economic nationalism as a general category. At this point, I refer briefly only to the second issue.

Economic nationalism as a *general category*, encompassing the experience of escape from various forms of backwardness of both the countries presently developed and of the peripheral ones, does not exist. This presumably, however for reasons other than those which cause the continuous absence of a general theory ('core doctrine') of nationalism (political nationalism included) (Smith 1998: 221–228). Still, in the case of political nationalism we have, despite the absence of a general conception, more or less convincingly argued typologies, including proposals to single out 'western' and 'eastern' variants of nationalism.[10] With regard to economic nationalism we have at hand here primarily an unusually one-sided, dismissive and hostile approaches.

Writing in 1945, Edward H. Carr (1983: 192) treated as obvious that "[i]n the nineteenth century, Germany and the United States had both learned and profited by [List's] lessons. It was now taken up by new and smaller nations all over the world." In actual fact, the 'Western' variant of economic nationalism which accompanied the birth of economic modernity, and which was next re-read from the angle of interpretations related to the political liberalism and laissez-faireism of the period of Pax Britannica, has been forgotten. Similarly forgotten was the role of non-economic factors. A British historian writes cuttingly: "By that time men of the pen, especially of pens of political economy, had forgotten and did not wish to be reminded of what the first industrial nation owed to men of the sword" (O'Brien 2003: 32). And to the men who drafted tariffs. Economic nationalism, rapidly developing in the forty years preceding the WWI at that time called protectionism was treated as an anomaly related first and foremost with 'export monopolism' and the activities of cartels and/or as an unfortunate incident, caused by the behaviors of the states and their civil-military bureaucracies competing with one another in backward areas.

---

[10] Such an approach was implied by the debatable dichotomous typology ("voluntarist" and "organic" variants of nationalism) proposed by Kohn (1967: 574) on which modeled is the misleading in many respects (viz. Latin America) division of nationalism into the "eastern" (ethnic and closed) and "western" (civic and open) ones, presented by Plamenatz (1976: 34). The influence of Kohn's typology can be also sensed in Gellner's (1994) discussion concerning "the time zones of Europe."

The same concerned imperialism (see Schumpeter 1974: 76–96). J. A. Hobson's and Marxists' (Rudolf Hilferding's and Rosa Luxemburg's) interpretations of these phenomena as economic imperative were until 1914 rarely (if at all) debated among the mainstream economists.

As a result, the growing protectionism of the end of the 19th and the beginning of the 20th centuries was defined as a sui generis phenomenon, bearing no relation to the economic nationalism of the interwar period (Heilperin 1960: 25f). A kind of epistemological *rupture* or amnesia. However, forgotten as a general category, economic nationalism reappeared and was defined as a regional phenomenon, restricted to some backward countries (including British dominions). In point of fact, in the developed world, it was rediscovered and generally noticed only during the Great Depression, and this in the interpretations which raised mainly–not without reason–its politically and economically destructive impact (see, for example, van Zeeland 1933, Simons and Emeny 1935).

Such an approach combined with the absence of historical memory had, as it were out of necessity, to find reflections on the ways in which economic nationalism that had been on the rise in backward regions from the end of the 19th century was perceived and evaluated. As a rule those evaluations were crushingly unfavorable (see, for example, Pollard 1981: passim). What is important, conflicting assessments of the effects of such nationalism in the interwar period are noticeable also in studies by economic historians of Central Europe and Latin America published in recent years: historians of Latin America assess the same period much better than historians dealing with Central Europe.[11] Consequently, before the Great Depression such nationalism, as a regional phenomenon, was in the 1920s closely related with the 'Eastern' variant of political nationalism, and evaluated negatively. It is characteristic that the first scholarly work devoted to economic nationalism, published in 1928 by Leo Pasvolsky, concerned the Danubian (succession) states which, except for Austria and the Czech part of Czechoslovakia, were model examples of economic backwardness.

On the other hand, the experience of Latin America, particularly of the circumstance-enforced adjustments in the production profile at the time of WWI, remained for the most part unregistered by Europeans.

---

[11] As far as East Central Europe is concerned, one can juxtapose the pessimistic assessment by Berend (1998) and the majority of the contributors to Schultz and Kubů (2006) to a more nuanced approach by Kofman (1997). On Latin America see Bulmer-Thomas (2003), Thorp (1998), and contributions to Bulmer-Thomas, Coatsworth and Cortés Conde (2006).

Political and economic elites in the United States, however, were well aware of it. They observed with apprehension and hostility the attempts at selective imitating of Mexican-style economic nationalism in other countries of the Western hemisphere. Stability, business-friendly states, docile labor, favorable market conditions and access to oil, copper and other raw materials were of primary concern. Yet, the United States forgot its own experience of radical economic nationalism. Hence, from the passing in February 1917 of the constitution nationalizing the country's natural resources, Mexican nationalism was in the years to come ideologized and demonized as being very close to Soviet experiments (mistakenly) and as an anomaly suggesting a possibility of development of 'artificial' industries in the country that had hitherto been primary goods producer (correctly) (Krenn 1990: chapter 4). Chile with its unique experiment of economic nationalism-cum-state socialism under the short-lived 1932 Socialist Republic was another troublesome case (Stemplowski 1996).

In this respect, one can maintain that economic nationalism as a *general category*, not limited to the ideological formula of the 'Eastern' variant, bound instead with the historical examples of escape from backwardness and also with a complex mix of reactions to the first globalization, remains an undeveloped field, tackled by only a few researchers.[12]

---

[12] See nevertheless contributions by Kofman (1997), Levi-Faure (1997), Greenfeld (2003), Helleiner (2002, 2005), Kohli (2004), Pickel (2005), Chang (2005) but also by Abelal (2001) and Maynall (1990).

CHAPTER TWO

PRECURSORS

MERCANTILIST ANTECEDENTS: 'THE IMPROVEMENT OF OUR LANDS'

The intellectual roots of economic nationalism should be sought first and foremost in mercantilism–"a word invented after the event" (Braudel 1992b: 53)–and in mercantilists' conceptions.[1] Friedrich List, a nineteenth-century theorist of modern industrial protectionism, in his *opus magnum* frequently referred to their ideas (1922: 93ff). What is more, the system he proposed may be considered as a *dynamic* variant of *some* important threads of mercantilist thought–adapted to new conditions–that were created by the industrial revolution. Thus, his approach to wealth creation and his approving attitude toward free trade–provided some conditions are met–are reason enough not to see in List simply a follower of 16th–17th century thinkers (Nicholson 1922: xxv, Harlen 1999). Contemporarily, the notions of mercantilism and mercantilist policy appear in different clothes–and out of their historical context. 'Mercantilism' is thus seen as an analytical category and option in trade policy equated with state activity supporting particular industries, and even selected companies (Gourevich 1986: 43–48, 50–53) or it is understood as a policy applied in situations where government utility functions and tax equations are introduced into economic analysis; they result in an asymmetric distribution of benefits from trade and in deepening differences in development levels on an international scale (Hymer and Resnick 1971: 474, 476).

What distinguished mature mercantilist conceptions was a holistic approach framed around the national economy. This kind of holism, building on the foundations of a dynamic balance between private interests and the state, made it necessary to adopt a specific conception of both the world economy and the relation between the state and the economy, and–in response to international competition–required taking into account the changes in internal resource allocation. Let me briefly explore these questions, recalling at all times that although mercantilism

---

[1] Cameron (1996: 145) treats mercantilism as a misnomer and consistently employs the term "economic nationalism."

preceded the birth of the modern market economy, the ultimate form of the latter was nevertheless shaped only under the industrial revolution (Polanyi 1957: 67). The chief actors of mercantilism's glorious (and brutal) history disappeared before the mid-18th century in the clash between "irrational and rational capitalism ... that is, capitalism in the field of fiscal and colonial privileges and public monopolies, and capitalism oriented in relation to market opportunities" (Weber 1966: 258).

Surprising as it may sound, no definition, let alone a fully developed concept of national economy, can be found in mercantilists' writings. It appears as an implicit, undisputed premise. This premise, made more specific by references to certain key discriminants, such as 'the Treasury' or 'Crown revenue', and finally 'national income', were so to speak obvious especially for England, a country which "internally was exceptionally unified and from a relatively early period" (Wallerstein 1974: 231; see also Cunningham 1891: 649). The process of national economic unification was in principle completed by the time of the Restoration (1688–1689). It was also at that time that the first consolidated Crown budget and its projection were drafted by the mercantilist Charles Davenant, and in a more sophisticated form by his contemporary Gregory King (Maddison 2003: 15f). (Modern national accounting appeared as late as the 20th century and was connected with the names of Colin Clark and Simon Kuznets.) In France, however, things were more complicated although the unification activities of Louis XI in the 15th century followed ruthlessly by Louis XIV and Colbert in 17th century should not escape our notice. I do not mention Germany, where the goal of merging about 1,900 territorial units (including 335 states and statelets that existed in the pre-Napoleonic era) into one state was achieved only in the second half of the 19th century.

Hence, when specifying the main goals of mercantilism, Eli F. Heckscher (1969: 20) stressed–not without the influence of Gustav von Schmoller, one of the most outstanding representatives of the younger Historical School–that beside the use of "the resources of their countries in the interest of the political power of the state" there was an obvious tendency toward "unification of the territory of the state economically." Schmoller (1897: 50, 51) himself put forward this premise in the following way:

> [mercantilism] is nothing but state making–not state making in a narrow sense, but state making and national-economy making at the same time; state making ... which creates out of the political community an economic community.

However, in further discussions Schmoller's insistence on the dual character of mercantilism (Wilson 1957: 184) was, to a large extent, pushed aside under the overwhelming criticism of modern 'mercantilist' malpractices and in connection with the inner-German switch toward a fascination with national power. Even today one can read that "the traditional business of the mercantilist state" was that "states [were] concerned principally with state building and the extraction of revenue from domestic society" (Abdelal 2001: 40). Nevertheless it was not forgotten completely. The 'dualistic' interpretation and reading of mercantilism reappeared among nationally-oriented authors from Central Europe. For example, the leading representative of the Polish 'national school' of the beginning of the 20th century argued that the "epochal significance of mercantilism" was expressed in the fact that its point of departure was "the development of the national whole" (Rybarski 2002: 362).

The concept of national economy is, in the first place, the basis for the theory of the balance of trade, which found its full expression in Sir Thomas Mun's *England's Treasure by Forraign Trade*, and then in a critical treatise by Sir Josiah Child. The former, however, when writing about "the true form and worth of forraign trade," meant not only *"The means of our Treasure"* and *"The honour of our Kingdom"* but also *"The Noble profession of the Merchant, The School of our Arts, The supply of our wants, The employment of our poor, The improvement of our Lands"* (Mun 1895: 119). Child, on the other hand, when presenting the difficulties in calculating the trade balance based on information on exports and imports, emphasized another dimension of the national economy, which touched upon national control over trade and financial transfers. He worried that

> in case the trade of England should be carried on by absentees, then the supposition ... that when the exports over-ballance the imports, the surplusage is returned into England, will prove a mistake, and in bullion the contrary will be true, viz. that the surplusage shall be conveyed into foreign parts, to the places of the residence of such absentees (Child 1751: 119).

Child, anticipated in this respect by Antonio Serra, pointed also to another extremely important aspect related to the premise of national economy. He wrote namely that it was in England's interest to "encourage those trade most, that vend most of our manufactures, or supply us with materials to be further manufactured in England." Obvious practical conclusions were: "Prevention of the exportation of our wool" and at the same time support to "our woollen manufactures" (1751: 128, 129). Antonio Serra (1958: 105–112) expressed this postulate earlier in his seminal– going beyond a fascination with bullion– analysis of the sources of wealth. He contrasted "particular factors" (*accidenti propri*), among which he counted gold and silver mines or soil fertility, with "common factors" (*accidenti communi*), occurring in every country, although to varying extents (crafts and manufactures, education and culture of the population as well as the policy of the state). In Serra's schema,

> monetary phenomena are consequence rather than cause, and symptomatic rather than important in themselves. And the author .... brushes against ... the proposition that a prosperous country ... can have all the gold and silver money it may require (Schumpeter 1986: 354f).

Serra's and Child's treatises were not, however, a mere appeal for 'industrialization' and, by the development of new branches of manufacture, for the longer-term enhancement of the competitive position of the country. Equally important were the consequences of the postulates that their authors only touched upon. What I mean here is the offloading onto the competitors of what is currently referred to as disjunctive exchange effects; these, in turn, result from concentrating production potential of a competing country in 'bad' trade (i.e. in goods manufactured in sectors characterized by low productivity) (see Andersson 1976: 24f). In parallel, England's process of economic structural diversification led to the acceleration of changes–prompted by civil wars and Tudor policy–in the composition of the dominant social groups (new aristocracy) and to the rise of the germ of new ones (gentry).

The involvement of English merchants and state in the Atlantic competition strengthened those tendencies immensely. Direct benefits (profits) and, for the most part, indirect ones (acceleration of institutional changes), resulting from that involvement played an important role in the process leading to the 18th-century economic breakthrough. The Revolution of 1640—1660 was the decisive factor in the fundamental change of relations between already strengthened private interests and the institutions of the state. The consequences of that "revolution in the system of authority," paving the way for autonomous elites and innovative institutions, in fact created the English exceptional case. What happened was first and foremost the fundamental reversal of thus-far traditional relations between the political authority and the aspirations and interests of the new aristocracy and gentry, followed by amorphous, but increasingly strong, groups of local merchants and manufacturers. Property rights and freedom to pursue economic activities, protected by law and the power of the state, were accompanied by the institutionalization of "checks on the executive" (which was the other side of the coin in the process of the consolidation of property rights). English mercantilism was increasingly becoming the policy of the new state and of the emerging first "modern nation"

(Hill 1969, Munck : chapters 5 and 12, Greenfeld 1993: chapter 1, Acemoglu, Johnson and Robinson 2005).

These long-term consequences of the process of diversification of the economic structure were perceived by mercantilists above all as being in a close relation with the aspirations to increase the share of the international market and to secure a level of income for the dominant social groups. Only in a few cases were the pushed-for changes in the production structure raised in the context of growth factors (to put it in present-day terminology). When considering other important motivations conducive to the differentiation process one cannot pass over another weighty issue. Namely, the desire to establish new and complementary branches of manufacturing. This was an extremely important aspect of searching for a solution to the problem of poverty and of uncertainty related to the rapidly growing 'poor class' (one of the major consequences of demographic growth in that era), dramatically felt at the turn of the 18th century. Classical mercantilism, originally focused on bullion and trade relations, thus evolved toward not only a new structure of domestic production, but also toward a peculiar "social mercantilism" (Wilson 1969: 136). To relieve the potentially dangerous social tensions moves were necessary whereby cheap labor ("sturdy and valiant beggars" in Sir Thomas More's words) would be sent, most often compulsorily, to new branches of manufacturing (or to colonies). This was supposed to create, apart from jobs, also additional and attractive opportunities for wealth creation. However, the economic viability of such a kind of enterprise was low, not only in England, but also on the continent. One should probably assess their political and social stabilization role differently, however (Garraty 1978: chapter 3).

Still, the reaction to the emergence of this social mercantilism and, at the same time, to a threat of England's deindustrialization as a consequence of increased imports of cheap textiles from India and elsewhere in Asia, was remarkable. All these issues exploded during the dispute on the activities of the East India Company, responsible for a significant part of such cheap imports. In the works by Charles Davenant and, above all, Henry Martyn, of the 17th and early 18th centuries, an attempt to respond to that threat, one can find already sophisticated argumentation showing how growing international competition, remaining outside the control of the state, should induce in conditions of inflexible wages, concentration upon the problem of improved efficiency/productivity (mainly through new work organization methods). Both Davenant and Martyn argued also that a fragmentary deindustrialization, albeit painful, when seen as a challenge, might in the end deliver positive results. What counted was the response to cheap Asian calicos (and labor), whereas the development of peculiar 'social employment' certainly was not one. According to a succinct phrase by Martyn, even "if the Riches of the Kingdom are not greater, they are not less for being procur'd by fewer Hands" (quoted in Hont 2005: 248). István Hont, in a path-breaking analysis devoted to these authors, demonstrated how in the disputes of that time there emerged issues of free trade, protectionism, restrictions imposed on the policy of the state by the international market, deindustrialization and internal adjustments, international wage competition, etc., which proved crucial for economic theories of the later period (see also Irwin 1996: 56–59).

The concept of national economy—as the premise of tackling economic problems, employment levels and the most efficient methods of wealth creation—was connected in mercantilist thought with a debatable approach to the problem of statics and dynamics:

> It is true that mercantilists believed in their almost unlimited ability to develop the economic resources of their own country ... but they only hoped to do so at the expense of their neighbours. That the wealth of the world as a whole could increase was an idea wholly alien to them, and in this they were 'static' to a degree (Heckscher 1969: 25f).

Thus, in the entry *'Patrie'* in *The Philosophical Dictionary*, Voltaire complained against the conventional patriotic-statist tradition (and mercantilist truth) that "to wish for the greatness of one's country is to wish evil to one's neighbours" (quoted in Hont 2005: 502).

In the case of England, one important factor making this approach more attractive was also the chance of seizing (through an aggressive trade policy) the advantages of economies of scale, bearing in mind the limited size of the home market at that time (that limitation eased off considerably in the 18th century). Going into the details of the decades-long disputes on the role of foreign trade in creating the conditions for and then the start of the industrial revolution seems to be unnecessary here. Suffice to note, I believe, the calculations of Ph. Deane and W. A. Cole, who found that the-then leading wool industry (and since the mid-18th century also the linen and iron industries) was at the same time an export industry which grew at a rate probably higher than that of the growth of national income or of other, non-export industries. This finding—if referring to the ratio of total exports to national income in the 18th century—has been questioned until recently. Domestic consumption, it was argued, was rising fast, making it possible to form a solid base for general growth and appropriate diversification of the economy (see Minchinton 1969: 36–52; O'Brien 1982: passim; Bairoch 1993: 82). However, recent studies have tried to some extent to rehabilitate the 'colonial model' of Great Britain's growth, though with mixed results.[2] Pondering the causes for France's lagging behind in international competition, Braudel (1990: 458) wrote somewhat exaggeratedly, "I have often thought that among its other advantages over [France], Britain was favoured by its comparatively small physical size: big enough to be a nation, small enough to have a unified economy."[3] Presumably the British merchants engaged in colonial trade reasoned in a similar way. For that group (and also for financiers), which represented the "summit" of market operations. i.e. "capitalism" in Braudel's terminology (1992a: 395, 417), Great Britain was too small, yet indispensable.

In the dynamic approach, the concept of limited resources of the world economy is, of course, untenable. However, things look differently in the short term or during stagnation or crisis. In such moments competition between national economies is based on the either-or rule, following the logic of the deadly zero-sum game. 'Jealousy of trade', discussed by Hont against the example of classical mercantilists, reappears in such situations with full force. After nearly three hundred years, this important thread of the mercantilist thought appeared as a threatening *and* rationally argued possibility in Keynes' *General Theory*. Mercantilists, he wrote, "were under no illusion as to the nationalistic character of their policies and their tendency to promote war. It was *national* advantage and *relative* strength at which they were admittedly aiming" (Keynes 1964: 348). The problem of foreign trade surplus and effective demand found its dramatic confirmation in the trade practices of the time of the Great Depression.

Mercantilists' holistic approach bound "defense" and "opulence"—the key notions in the theory of the state and economic development—into a tangled web of interdependencies. Nonetheless, Heckscher's thesis that the rising power of the state was, apart from territorial unification, mercantilists' second main, and maybe primary, goal aroused serious

---

[2] According to the calculations by N. F. R. Crafts (quoted in Findlay and O'Rourke 2001: 16), the share of exports in Great Britain's national income was rising in the crucial years 1700–1760–1801 as follows: 8.4, 14.6 and 15.7 percent. See also Hobson (2004: 270–273). How and to what extent this upswing was translated into the domestic investments is unclear. O'Brien's arguments (and doubts) are still valid.

[3] From a somewhat different perspective, a similar hypothesis was propounded by V. Kiernan, who argued that the states that had appeared in Europe since the time of mercantilism were large enough to survive and, at the same time, small enough to enable the authorities to exercise effective central control and coordination (see Badie and Birnbaum 1983: 71).

reservations among historians. In a balanced reconstruction of the main threads of mercantilist thought, Jacob Viner (1969: 67) argued that "Heckscher fails to cite a single passage in which it is asserted that power is or should be the *sole* end of national policy, or that wealth matters *only* as it serves power." However, even if we leave out here all historical forms in which such interdependence was expressed (the Navigation Act, trade wars, export ban on weaving machines, etc., and also a steep rise in corruption and in waste of public money), the problem of the relationship between the economy and politics still remains unsolved.

One can nevertheless suggest that mercantilists did not perceive that relationship as a problem. Most of them were clear-headed advisors to the throne (like Colbert) and practitioners in international trade (like Mun and Child, directors of the East India Company). All the more so, they did not perceive it as a serious check on the process of national wealth creation. On the contrary, the state and its power were the factors which created—in a situation of exacerbating competition for scarce resources and markets—simply indispensable preconditions for individual and national success. And so Child (1751: 132) regarded as natural that "it is our interest by example, and other means (not distasteful) ... to prevent, as much as may be, the importation of foreign manufactures." The same way as David Hume, other theorists and practitioners of mercantilism, too, took it for granted that international trade had become an affair of state, a *raison d'état* (Hont 2005: 186f). That, however, had its consequences and price.

Bearing in mind the era preceding mercantilism, and the financial problems of the territorial monarchies of the time (prior to their transformation into 'commercial states'), one can marvel at an essentially mild domestic response to the unparalleled increase in the revenues of the English (since 1707, British) Crown. In the 18th century Great Britain "became one of the most heavily taxed nations in Europe. The British state extracted more in taxes from its subjects than did absolutist France" (Hellmuth 2002: 21). During one hundred years between 1680 and 1780, in times of peace, tax revenue increased, in absolute numbers, nearly fourfold, and in times of war—sixfold (the share of Crown expenditures in the national income rose as much)—without upsetting, for a time, the precarious balance between fiscality and enterprise (O'Brien 2003: 12). The British parliamentary monarchy proved to be extremely effective in producing state revenue, without resorting to meticulous, bureaucratic control over entrepreneurs' activities (except for support given to monopolies and selected sectors of manufacturing). At the same time, however, it created an almost twelve thousand-strong state machinery to deal mostly with taxes. The financial revolution, underpinned by a kind of 'nationalization' of the system of collecting dues and distributing state revenue, and by the crucial Dutch-style innovation, that of consolidated debt, and all that based on trust and respect for one's own obligations, made Great Britain unique at that time (Braudel 1992a: 525–528). While praising these achievements, we should not forget however to leave a margin of tolerance for the flaws and weaknesses of human nature, including the temptation of corruption. The descriptions in the *Diary* of Samuel Pepys, the Chief Secretary to the Admiralty, one of the founders of Great Britain's greatness, remains unparalleled in this respect.

The effectiveness of the British system contrasted with, for instance, France at the time of Colbert and his successors. Fiscality and growing debt, but also the growing incomes of subjects—sometimes as a result of none-too-commendable methods—were in Great Britain the subject of tirades and cautions by, for example, Adam Smith. With regard to the same matter, continentals witnessed besides dwindling tax sources also pamphlets and treatises, and, in 1789, barricades being put up. Thus Heckscher is right to question William Cunningham's description of British mercantilism as "parliamentary Colbertism." In none of the important threads of domestic politics analyzed was it Colbertism, either literally or by analogy. Certainly, at that time Great Britain, like France and Prussia, was an example of the fiscal-military state (with more than 80 per cent of tax revenue allocated, directly or indirectly, to army and navy). Nonetheless, its developing political institutions, above all Parliament and decentralized authorities, supported by the autonomy and the increasingly prominent role of the parish and voluntary associations, withstood absolutist temptations (Hellmuth 2002: 21, 23–26). Writes Hont (2005: 461):

> Recent British historiography, finally, has demonstrated what generations of German historians and politicians had always suspected, namely that Britain was extremely successful in 'state-building', and that the country had not only modern armed forces and a superior navy, along with a very advanced financial system ... but also a very effective centralized 'state-building' administration.

Outward-oriented mercantilism, using an increasingly extensive set of sophisticated instruments of rationing and control, did not ultimately determine the form of internal centralization, that is the process of unifying the British economy and national state. The process of creating institutions that were essential for the later industrialization spurt was not reversed. It is astonishing indeed that Great Britain's 18th century aggressive (and increasingly costly) foreign policy did not lead to major distortions of the country's political institutions and to the deterioration of its economic condition. Furthermore, after the economically enfeebling twenty-year series of Napoleonic wars ended, it was in Great Britain where the gradual involution of the fiscal-military state was started. In the 19th century, the interventionist and at the same time bureaucratized state of the era of industrial transformations became continental Europe's specialty.

One should also bear in mind the fact that mercantilism, which as a set of theoretical concepts emerged, as emphasized by Heckscher (1969: 21), in response to the common practices of the time, was in fact a "practice leading unintentionally to theory." Even if mercantilist theories never directly influenced the economic policy of the state (Coleman 1969: 117, Cameron 1996: 146) the phenomenon of practical mercantilism, the original source of the ideas of the time, remains an important subject of reflection. In this regard, a historian's opinion on the actual consequences of the "political economy of diplomacy and political strategy" is unequivocal:

> Defence formed an integral part of opulence. Expenditures upon armed forces (and the strategic concentration on the navy) provided 'preconditions' for a significant part of the economic growth achieved between 1688 and 1815. Links between power and profit connect the navy through the defence of the realm and foreign trade to the ongoing industrialization of the economy (O'Brien 2003: 22f; see also 1986: 296f).

When one reads these words, there immediately comes to mind Schmoller saying (1884: 72):

> For it was precisely those governments which understood how to put the might of their fleets and admiralties, the apparatus of customs laws and navigation laws ... at the service of the economic interests of the nation and state, which obtained thereby the lead in the struggle and in riches and industrial prosperity.

And at the beginning of the 20th century, precisely such a connection between defence, development of the navy and the birth of the modern economy was the subject of Werner Sombart's analysis (1913b), now forgotten but pioneering at the time. National economy (still a project rather than a well-integrated economic space), the state and international market form, within this political economy, an increasingly integrated whole.

Before concluding this brief recapitulation of certain threads of mercantilist thought, a short digression on the ideological sources of nationalist concepts in economic thought seems to be necessary here. It is important inasmuch as such notions as national economy or the state (in the economic dimension) are still, quite arbitrarily, associated exclusively, or almost exclusively, with German, 19th-century Romanticism (in its various forms) and then, with the ideologies of 'power', developed by the German historical school. According to George Grantham (2003), this "nationalization of economic history," whose original source was the deliberations of Adam Müller, List and Schmoller, has survived until this day, distorting in fact the debate on the problems of economic development.

This is a rather selective reading of the history of ideas, the process of their reception and emulation.

By no means did either Adam Smith in the 18th century or John Stuart Mill in the 19th century—but not their popularizers or political supporters of free trade—give up emphasizing the national (and more precisely: state-centered and nationalist) point of view. It did not come down merely to the famous statement that "defense is of much more importance than opulence." An outstanding historian of economic thought found this statement to be a "careless" comment by the author of *The Wealth of Nations* (Blaug 1996: 14). Smith's analysis of Great Britain's dependence on trade with its colonies and the advice to diversify the sources of supply and markets certainly were an expression of a skillful combination of economic nationalism of the emerging leader of the world economy and the policy of free trade (Hirschman 1980: 5f, 73f, Greenfeld 1995: 577f, Greenfeld 2003: 31, Weiss 1967, Hobson 2004). His disquisitions on the activities of the state in the sphere of taxes or debt referred to one particular nation-state. Then, half a century later, economic nationalists on the continent argued (usually in the convention of a 'conspiracy') that Smith, who had been reluctantly supporting the idea of the independence of the British colony in North America, had not done so for the mere sake of defense of the principle of free trade. As a matter of fact, Smith (2005: 500f) did not conceal that the loss of the American colonies (and trade privileges) could cause serious perturbations in Great Britain and be "mortifying to the pride of every nation." However, he did not dramatize the long-term consequences to trade of the possible cutting of colonial ties. His concern was fully justified, and his prediction—a bold one, considering that during the fifty years between 1722/1724—1772/1774 preceding the American Revolution the value of British industrial exports to the Western

Hemisphere grew almost sixfold, while the two Americas' share in total industrial exports rose from 19 percent to 47 percent (calculated on the basis of the data provided by Davis 1969: 119f). Jean-Baptiste Say (1960: 346) writing after the proclamation and effective defense of US independence, was pleased to note that the loss of its colonies in North America were essentially of great benefit to England. This way the advantage of free trade and British economic leadership were confirmed.

In a word, the frequency and intensity with which the adjective 'national' appeared in German but also American, French and Italian 19th-century writings should not be read wrongly; in particular, it seems misleading to arbitrarily reduce them to the unique German experience. The history of the notion of national economy and its presentation (or arrogant passing over) in theory is certainly longer and much more complicated than implied by Grantham.[4] Hobsbawm (1990: 25f) writes that for 19th-century liberal economists or liberals in general, who accepted the neutral language of classical political economy, the problem was that "they could only recognize the economic significance of nations in practice, but not in theory." The case of Moliere's character discovering that he had "been speaking prose" was not strange to the leaders of the world system. They discovered that skill at a time of elemental struggle for leadership and of crisis. To paraphrase Braudel (1992b: 53), one may say that Great Britain was nationalist "at certain very rare moments–precisely those at which she was aware of an external threat. As a rule unchallenged, she was able to practice free trade with impunity since it could only benefit her." That such 'discoveries' were ever made resulted from the fact that at any moment of its history England (or later Great Britain) would be unthinkable outside the context of practical work carried out within the framework of the nation-state, and also in a clash with it, in attempts to use and/or redefine it.

Getting back to mercantilists: the interpretation proposed by Jacob Viner of the interdependence between "defense" and "opulence" in their concepts sounds convincing. He writes:

---

[4] See the studies published in the collection edited by Albertone and Masoro (1994), and particularly those concerning France, Portugal, Italy and the USA. For an earlier view see Moffat (1928). One should also mention the concept of *kokueki*, i.e. the prosperity of the country, which became one of the main symbols of the capitalist modernization of Japan after 1868. It had been originally developed by merchants from the Tosa province in the 17th century, in response to the crisis of revenues and in opposition to the power of shogun. See Roberts (1998), Greenfeld (2003: 307ff).

wealth is an absolutely essential means of power ... power is essential or valuable as a means to the acquisition or retention of wealth ... wealth and power are each proper ultimate ends of national policy ... there is long-run harmony between these ends (Viner 1969: 71).

Certainly, such interpretation is a compromise, considering the divergent attitudes of participants in the discussion (which, after all, has never been finished). This is however the kind of compromise that allows the discernment of the multitude and importance of the topics raised.

Friedrich List and his *System*: 'An English State Secret'

With regard to the 19th century, has the holism of the mercantilists turned out to be of no use at defining economic nationalism? Was the nationalism characteristic of that period nothing but a policy of "promoting particular or group interests," as Kahan (1967: 23) seems to suggest? This is a questionable hypothesis.

Nineteenth-century economic nationalism undoubtedly did not concentrate on just one sector of the economy. What at first glance seems to have been a one-sided fascination with industry was in fact subordinated to a larger vision of the national economy and of national political and economic interest. Also, the then emerging economic nationalism (the very term was invented much later) was a fragment of a wider response to already unquestionable British hegemony and–if Greenfeld (1993) is correct in her assessment–to the only non-imitative modern nationalism, i.e. the English one. Hence the nationalism of the then protectionists could be justifiably described as a holistic, and not a particularistic, one. With one reservation, though: It would be reckless not to discern its involvement in the promotion of private ventures, often far from the 'nationalist ideal'. The blending of ideals of national development with the pursuit of special profits by individuals as well as particular pressure groups was nothing out of the ordinary. The critics of mercantilism and protectionist practices gave ample examples of such motivations and behaviors.

Economic nationalism, its holistic variant included, had its natural roots in the ideas formed by certain major strands of mercantilism. Small wonder, then, that post-mercantilist practice, referring to those strands selectively, was often criticized as a step back, as a return to long obsolete concepts and theories. However, the period of 19th-century nationalism was definitely different. The Industrial Revolution and railroads created a new context. The dispute over protection and regulations, over support from the state and over tariffs was embedded in that new context. Words could sound the same, yet the circumstances and consequences were quite different.

Therefore one should recall here that Alexander Hamilton, secretary of the treasury in the years 1789–1795, in a style known already from the mercantilists' time, forced through the need to industrialize the United States. He did this in his reports on public debt, the central bank and, above all, manufactures, using the argument of defense and opulence. Although a conservative and elitist, in his public activities and economic projects he was a real radical, and a precursor of American economic nationalism (Mitchell 1967: 90–102). That nationalism, in opposition to Jefferson's, was ready to subordinate certain fundamental national principles—as they were defined at the time—to the needs of national defense, the rising class of industrialists and financiers, and of greater prosperity. Hamilton's moves regarding debt consolidation and the principles of the redemption of the public debt aroused resistance from the point of view of 'justice' (and, above all, of relations between states and the federal government), while the creation of the central bank required, as we read in his famous letter to Washington (Hamilton 1958: 164–169), an extremely subtle reinterpretation of the constitution.

The assessment of Hamilton's achievements, made by Vernon L. Parrington (1987: 307), although harsh, was not groundless: "one to whom our industrialism owes a very great debt, but from whom our democratic liberalism has received nothing." Oh, all right. Jefferson in his notes left an exciting description of a political duel between Hamilton, a high Tory, "rather English than American," and Adams. During a discussion on the British constitution, wrote Jefferson,

> Mr. Adams observed, 'Purge that constitution of its corruption, and gave to its popular branch equality of representation, and it would be the most perfect constitution ever devised by the wit of man'. Hamilton paused and said, 'Purge it of its corruption, and give to its popular branch equality of representation, and it would become an *impracticable* government'(Jefferson 1968: 159).

Certainly, Hamilton was not an idealist democrat. Probably, he was not a democrat at all. However, one could not say about him that the concept of public good appeared in his ideas (and activities) as a pretext or staffage. He was the first water holistic economic nationalist and 'practitioner of economic policy' and his concepts and activities oblige us to recognize him as an embodiment of the ideal of the national economic strategist

(Schumpeter 1986: 199; McCraw 1994: 48). By the way, such a combination of conservatism and economic radicalism appeared in other countries as well, although with various intensity and effectiveness (see Chapter 6).

It is important however that the Hamilton-proposed policy outlived its originator. Following the painful economic experience of the war of 1812, President Thomas Jefferson, personifying American democratic liberalism and attachment to the principles of free trade, toned down his earlier enthusiasm for agriculture (and bucolic self-sufficiency). Inasmuch as in 1784 he wrote that "[t]hose who labor in the earth are the chosen people of God," and as regards manufacturing, with the exception of a few cases, "let our workshops remain in Europe" (Jefferson 1958: 270) then, after 1812, he hesitantly accepted Hamilton's arguments supported by other followers of the so-called American System (the phrase introduced by Henry Clay during the 1824 debate on customs tariff): "Experience has taught me that manufactures are now as necessary to our independence as to our comfort" (quoted in Arieli 1966: 160; see also Rostow 1971: 193–196). All in all, disputes between supporters of 'Republican (economic) nationalism' and 'Democratic nationalism', although essential from the point of view of developing the sense of American national identity, did not lead to the fundamental questioning of the policy of protectionism. According to a none-too-refined definition by a certain Congressman from Pennsylvania from the early 19th century, man is "an animal that makes tariff speeches" (quoted in Bairoch 1993: 33). This was certainly the case before the adoption in 1828 of a compromise customs tariff, which was still a prohibitive one with regard to many goods. However, the debates preceding the Congress decision clearly indicated that presidential candidates Adams and Jackson would not achieve their goal if they stood openly against the principle of protectionism (Dangerfield 1965: 277).

Meanwhile, an acute conflict was growing in the shadow of these disputes. In ideological controversies and unstable political compromises, the clash of protectionism and the modern industry of the North with free trade and the agricultural export interests of the slave South had been ripening for decades. Friedrich List, an émigré from Wuttenberg and the author of *Outlines of American Political Economy in Twelve Letters to Charles J. Ingersoll,* played quite an important role in the debates held in the 1820s. His book–a result of his involvement with the activities of the Philadelphia Society for the Promotion of National Industry–was an indirect polemic with the arguments of a Southerner by affinity and British by birth Thomas Cooper, expressed in his *Lectures on the Elements of Political Economy.*

Lists's treatise *Das nationale System der politischen Ökonomie*, a "delightfully eloquent work" published in 1841 (Gide and Rist 1916: 268), was the clearest example of the holism of protectionist thought in the industrial era. The author's theoretical skills stood without a doubt no comparison to those shown, for example, by David Ricardo in his *Principles*. Not a theoretical innovator, List however "used pieces of the existing analytic apparatus judiciously and correctly. And this ... spells *scientific* merit" (Schumpeter 1986: 517). But the main message of List's *System*, falling into the broadly-defined area of economic policy and development, was powerful and has had an enormous and lasting effect. Thanks to List's *System*, Clay's arguments for the development of the domestic market and protectionism have not remained a limited, solely American experience.[5]

As with mercantilists, in List's approach also the relationship between the demands for national power and economic development had the character of complex interdependence. It was only in later interpretations of the *System* that this type of relationship was distorted, and the emphasis was laid on power (*Machtpolitik*). When analyzing List's approach, one should not therefore limit oneself to the sentence most often quoted, "On the nature of *nationality*, as the intermediate interest between those of *individualism* and of *entire humanity*, my whole structure is based" (1922: xliii). This sentence, "nationalist ontology" of a kind (Helleiner 2005: 222), is a mere introduction, the first signal of a problem. Read outside the context, by and large, it does not stray from apologies for the nation, then common (since the Napoleonic wars) in German political publications. The context was interesting, however. List argued that when dealing with the question of the economic future of Germany and other countries on the threshold of industrialization, one had first to consider the obvious fact: *Hic et nunc* there are nations (including the divided German nation) and states. Next—and at this point we touch upon the fundamental question—the concept of the nation organized into a state, is closely connected with the concept of national economy (an actual or an emerging one) as a mediator between the individual and world trade, and as a point of reference of industry-oriented economic policy. Historians of economic thought saw this in the following way: List "rightly treats nations not

---

[5] Stressing the benefits from the development of the domestic market, Clay (1958: 273f) argued that such a development would ensure the "creation of reciprocal interests," "more [transactional] security," "growth of consumption" and, as a result, "comfort resulting from increasing volume [of goods] and reduced prices."

merely as moral and political associations created by history, but also as economic associations" (Gide and Rist 1916: 288). Gellner's reading of List's *System* followed a similar logic. He argued that "[t]he national road to either capitalism or socialism was not only viable, but mandatory. It was the *national* path to industrialism that was essential" (Gellner 1994a: 13).

In the *System*, nation is expressed in two ways: as a direct reference to the already shaped Herderian *Kulturnation,* and as a concept of a state, even though in case of Germany, in List's lifetime, a united national state was merely a political project. Therefore Szporluk (1991: 12) is not persuasive when he emphasizes that "List based his program not on the state but on a 'cultural nation' ... for this was what the Germany of his time was." It is, as it seems, a misconstruction, subsequently replicated by other researchers (Abdelal 2001: 19f). List's *System* is outright inconceivable, and his arguments and polemics inexplicable without the concept of the state as an indispensable element ensuring the practical implementation of the project of national economy. The *Kulturnation* and the *Staatsnation*, separated by the political and economic fragmentation of the German space, must merge—if the *System* is to prove its usefulness and open the road to German industrialization. From the point of view of the *Kulturnation* concept, Germans already constituted a nation—at least in the opinion of a considerable part of bourgeois and bureaucratic elites—from then on, they had to become a state.

Thus we are dealing here with a process that is to a degree classic with regard to nations shaped by culture and nationalistic ideology, and, on the basis of these two pillars, demanding the realization of the ideal of the nation-state. Gellner suggests that Italy presumably was another clear example (1994b: 115; see also Wehler 2002: 325). I would also add Poland and Hungary. Yet, this was not an entirely 'classic' example if we recognize England as such. It was where the state and the nation emerged as two autonomous aspects of the same process (Acton 1907). Nevertheless the stress Szporluk lays on the role of the nation and national ideology in the *System*, and thus on its dimension that goes beyond narrowly defined economic analysis, is no doubt justified and correct (see also Abdelal 2001). For as a rule when the *System* is talked about, it is reduced to a set of certain practical moves (a protective tariff connected with the infant-industry argument), often misinterpreted, while the state is treated as an unspecified agent of change (the state-centered approach). But even in this case, Henderson (1983: 148f) and Shafaedin (2000) note, the reading of the technical aspects of the *System* concerning, for example, the intensity, selectivity and stages of industrial protection, is not very careful.

In List's era, the symbiosis between economy and nation that *System* called for was not a novelty, particularly on the edge of industrializing Europe. Such symbiosis appeared, for example, in Poland where List's message was strengthened by the fact of the loss of independence. But, for obvious reasons, the same fact blunted the sharpness and dimmed the clarity of analyses regarding both the role of the state and the necessity to have "the *kind* of nation" which industrialization would inevitably engender (Gellner 1994a: 11). It is worth mentioning, however, that the symbiosis between the economy and the nation, discerned on the threshold of independence by one of the founders of the Polish 'national school' of economics, implied a nearly total concentration on the national premise of List's *System*, and not on its consequences with regard to the policy of industrial protectionism. The message of Henryk Radziszewski provides a perfect example. It is also a testimony to an unshakeable patriotic belief that the concept of national economy without a doubt first appeared in the oppressed and divided Poland:

> The cradle of the national economic school [is to be found] nowhere else but exactly in Poland. ... Staszic and Surowiecki may be included in the national school, and, in any case, they should be considered the harbingers of this school. But unquestionably, it is not List in Germany but our Fryderyk Skarbek who may be regarded as the founder of the national school, considering that Skarbek's works preceded List's work by as many as two decades, and it was Skarbek who stood firmly on national grounds (Radziszewski 1918:103).

Let me however return to List. In 1845, Marx, a faithful reader of Smith and Ricardo, and also an increasingly disappointed participant in the German liberal movement, challenged the basic premises of the 'national system' and the concept of modernization anchored in protectionist industrial policy. Marx passionately charged the author of *System* that by pointing to the premise of national economy and to protectionism he represented the "German Philistine" who wished for the impossible. To List (1922: 313), who underscored that "internal competition and the security from destructive competition by the foreigner has wrought ... this miracle," Marx (1975) responded:

> Competition, which gives [the German bourgeois] his power inside the country, cannot prevent him from becoming powerless outside the country ... the state, which he subordinates to bourgeois society inside the country, cannot protect him from the action of bourgeois society outside the country.

The prospect of 'necessity', connected with the rampant and brutal process of capital formation on the supranational scale, did not offer any chance of a national answer. As a matter of fact, in his attack on List, the future co-author of the *Communist Manifesto* seemed to imply that not only the proletarian, but the bourgeois as well, especially from a less developed country (such as Germany), had no—although for different reasons—*Vaterland*. To resist the transition toward the free market was to check the progress of the modern economy and delay the liberation of the proletariat and humankind (see also Szporluk 1991: 31, 35).

So much for Marx's polemics with List, the economist of German unity. Such unity had almost from the beginning seemed suspicious to Marx in view of the increasingly obvious compromise between the landed aristocracy and bureaucracy (whom he hated with all his heart). Yet, several years later Marx treated the same ideas, but proposed by Henry Carey in the USA, with greater tolerance and calm. They were no longer the voice of the "Philistine," but just a view that was utterly wrong, although not devoid of the hallmarks of greatness. For, uninvolved in the problems of Europe, Carey represented a "contemporary historical principle of North America"—a society built on completely new economic foundations, untouched by European-style compromises (Marx 1973: 885ff).[6]

The premise of national economy implied, as in the case of mercantilists, a significant limitation on the freedom of choice regarding the means to establish power of the national state. List emphasized that the state protection of long-term private interests required bringing two curves closer to each other: the curve of political power and the curve of economic growth (1922: 341, 27). Growth depended directly on the development of industry, new institutions and, above all, on something he called "productive powers" (*Produktionskräfte*). List specified that general idea both at the macro- and micro-economic levels, although in his deliberations the macro approach prevails.

---

[6] Having hurled a number of epithets at List on this account, Marx wound up his 1848 speech *On the Question of Free Trade*, assessing favorably the protective tariffs in Germany, treating them as "weapons against feudalism" and a means "for the realization of free trade within the same country." However, at the end of his speech he stuck to his opinion that, in general, tariffs were of a conservative nature. According to Greenfeld (2003: 6), it was exactly the reading of List that gave Marx a direct stimulus to studying the theory of economy. The hypothesis is not well-founded. Neither Szporluk (1991) nor Mandel (1971) sustain it. However, as far as the impact of List's ideas is concerned, it was Engels who "was much more impressed by the teachings of Friedrich List and his theory of infant industries" (Gerschenkron 1989: 33).

As a holistic system, List's theory highlights not so much the arguments in support of particular interests of infant industries as the industries of the infant country as a whole. Arguments typical of particularistic nationalism are raised within *System* as historical specification of the problem of a broader vision of economic development and the shaping of a new division of labor on both a national and European scale. The benefits the industrializing Germany, unifying under the *Zollverein*, could obtain from such change were obvious to him. By building industry, he argued, that missing "other arm" of the national organism,[7] and a transportation network to unify the economic space, Germany was creating a division of labor, typical of the modern economy (on the pattern of the division discussed by Smith with reference to a single manufacture and also, in a wider context, to agriculture and towns). At the same time, having an economy that was diversified and internally complementary, Germany would take up an advantageous position on the international market (List 1922: 122, 130; see also Senghaas 1977).

Nonetheless, List's nationalism is not an example of a radical holistic nationalism as it was described in the liberal literature of the 20th century. For instance, unlike Fichte and Müller before him, and Schmoller in the already different context of the rapidly developing German industry after him, List did not call for autarchy. With one reservation, though. His concept of international trade, which was based on the vent for surplus model outlined by Smith (2005: 477ff), and not the Ricardian concept of comparative costs, did not rule out a relative self-sufficiency within large political and economic areas.

This imperial dimension of List's deliberations was, however, once again, a result of his specific interpretation of the British colonial experience. His treatment of Central Europe and the Balkans as surrogates for overseas colonies raises some doubts. However, he was not alone in this. At the turn of the 19th and 20th centuries Otto Hinze argued that "from the trade point of view Poland was ... for Prussia what the colonies were for England" (quoted in Pollard 1981: 174). Polish historian's, among others, presentation of the concept of economic autarchy showed the impact of such thinking on discussions on imperialism and the European powers' practice of delineating "vast areas:"

---

[7] Lajos Kossuth, the Hungarian national hero, who under the influence of List's book converted to protectionism, used List's metaphor when declaring: "Without industry, a nation is a one-armed giant" (quoted in Berend 2003: 140).

> In practice, the tendency for autarchy (self-sufficiency) must lead to territorial unification, *crossing the strictly national borders* ... and thus to the recognizing as the national territory parts of foreign territories if they contain natural resources another nation's economy needs" (Handelsman 1973: 35).[8]

Also, List's *System* lacks a more elaborate discussion on state property and etatism. Nevertheless, one can safely say that List's protectionism and, more generally, economic nationalism did not imply the omnipotent state-as-producer. In accordance with liberal views, he saw the state as first and foremost an instrument to support the economic activity of the middle class which served the creation of indispensable institutions and other general conditions for increasing national wealth.

The stress he laid in his deliberations on the problem of the broadly understood institutional conditions of development was clear. Its traces could be found in works by Thorstein Veblen and in the socio-economic institutional approaches which appeared several decades later. In practice, although the intrusive 'industrial policy' did until the 1860s speed up development within the *Zollverein* area, still, with the passage of time it complicated decision making immensely. Creating institutions in conditions of state fragmentation frequently led to their duplication and to economic absurdities. The unification of Germany under the aegis of Prussia and the liberalization of domestic economic relations, the transition to industrial freedom (*Gewerbefreiheit*), provided new development impetus in the second half of the 19th century (Kindleberger 1996: 153f). With minor modifications, mild protectionist tariffs were still an integral part of it–until the 1870s.

At this point, however, one can reflect that had it not been for the essentially different approach to the question of protectionism and the civilizing role of industry, List's deliberations on the role of the state would not have differed much from Smith's three-part "system of natural liberty." It can be suggested that they were their continuation, not refutation. One should remember that, according to the author of *The Wealth of Nations*, the state has three duties:

> [firstly,] of protecting the society from the violence and invasion of other independent societies; secondly, the duty ... of establishing an exact administration of justice; and, thirdly, the duty of erecting and maintaining certain

---

[8] That view, widespread at the time, and, in practice, equating economic nationalism with imperialism, found its sinister resonance in the Nazi plans, which from 1938 were put into practice. See, for example, Schacht (1937) and Hossbach Memorandum (1949). On the other hand, Hodgson (1933: 46f) pointed rightly to the need to differentiate these notions.

> public works and certain public institutions, which it can never be for the interest of any individual, or small number of individuals, to erect and maintain; because the profit could never repay the expense to any individual or small number of individuals, though it may frequently do much more than repay it to a great society (Smith 2005: 56of).

The third of the duties mentioned encompasses such a wide spectrum of problems and possibilities for the activities of the state that precisely for this reason Milton Friedman was ready to reject Smith's approach. Rostow (1990: 49f), for his part, found it close to the 20th century development economics ("push" theories). Indeed, the conception of the third duty of the state is not only at odds with the popular interpretation of Smith ('the invisible hand of the market'), but also with the neoclassical approach. "Certain public works and certain public institutions" mentioned by Smith involved transaction costs, the existence of which prevented–even with well-defined property rights–the reaching of an optimizing solution. List however posed this problem in his own way as in the author of *The Wealth of Nations* he saw not an ally, but an opponent.

All in all, List's *System* constituted the first comprehensive and well-argued attempt at theoretical questioning of the universalism of free trade, and of the theory of comparative costs. More than a hundred years later, it was Joan Robinson (1964: 117) who in the true spirit of List wrote that

> [the] hard-headed Classicals ... were arguing against the narrow nationalism of Mercantilists in favour of a more far-sighted policy, but they were in favour of Free Trade because it was good for Great Britain, not because it was good for the world.

However, List's *System* was also a passionate criticism of the conception of the long-term benefits of a narrow primary-products specialization in the already new conditions created by England's industrial revolution. It would be difficult to exaggerate List's fascination with that fundamental change of context. Hence the frequent references to the negative example of Poland as the country which was not able to give a proper answer to the new challenges. What counts in the long term, he argued, is the creativity of the economic structure, its "manufacturing power," epitomized by a combination of industry and human knowledge. Development is not just an increase in aggregate output, but first and foremost a modern output mix. What counts is the increase in efficiency and productive potential, unattainable without universal education, development of industry and the application of its products in other branches of production (1922: 108).

And unlike Marx and other critics of capitalism less radical than the author of *Das Kapital* List did not assume the permanence of the dialectic symbiosis between modern industry and unskilled, cheap labor.

Therefore one may ponder whether List's violent attack on Smith and the whole "cosmopolitical" or "popular," as he wrote, theory of free trade did not result from the fact that the author of *The Wealth of Nations* had actually not tackled the problem of the industrial revolution, which had started in his lifetime: "Indeed, there is nothing in the book to suggest that Adam Smith was aware that he was living in times of extremely unusual economic change" (Blaug 1996: 34). In turn, List could not fail to refer to that question, at the same time placing the demands for free trade in the new context, defined by Great Britain's overwhelming industrial superiority. Still, a careful reading of *The Wealth of Nations* once again affords many surprises. For example, in the chapter on physiocrats we find not paeans to free trade alone. Even if halfheartedly, nevertheless with a sharpness of view that commands respect, Smith admitted the possibility of an (although limited) rationality of measures to support 'industry':

> Those systems ... which preferring agriculture ... impose restraints upon manufactures and foreign trade, act contrary to the very end which they propose, and indirectly discourage that very species of industry which they mean to promote. They are so far, perhaps, more inconsistent than even the mercantile system. That system, by encouraging manufactures and foreign trade more than agriculture, turns a certain portion of the capital of the society, from supporting a more advantageous, to support a less advantageous species of industry. But still it really, and in the end, encourages that species of industry which it means to promote (Smith 2005: 560).

List believed that a temporary, educational, protectionism was also a policy enabling through the development of the domestic market–more effective control over national economic processes as well as lesser dependence on the global situation and on the demand of 'others'. According to List, such protectionism also was a response to the breach of the doctrinal rules of free trade by the hegemonic leader of the time (through, among other things, the maintenance of the Corn Laws until 1846, and of other instruments for the protection of manufacturing) (1922: 129f, 150). In the present-day economic parlance, it would read as follows: if market distortions caused by British operations disturbed free-market equilibrium, the adjustment process became undetermined. That in turn was a good reason for state intervention and protectionism. And finally, dramatizing the last argument, List pointed to the experience of the Continental Blockade ("an event which marked an era in the history of both German and French industry") and, more generally, of wars which, he observed sarcastically, acted "like a prohibitive tariff system" (1922: 69, 136, 147). The economic results achieved by some German states during the Continental Blockade were of no minor significance here.

As a result, one may reconstruct List's fundamental thesis in the following way: industrial and civilizational development of agricultural nations cannot be deduced from the principle of free trade and market-automatism. The causal relationship operates in a different manner: from industrialization protected and backed by the state to free trade. Such a sequence, with the final goal being a return to free trade, however on already new terms, suggested also that the economic nationalism of List did not assume the concept of the zero-sum game with regard to international relations. Competition, even if fierce, did not inevitably imply aggression and monopoly through annihilation. Thus it was an "example of benevolent version of economic nationalism," capable of a working compromise and of considering (their own and other actors') interests related to the international system as a whole (Levi-Faure 1997: 367; see also Hont 2005: 154).

In the Western European context, where the British economy set the standard and the challenge, List's economic nationalism was also a defensive nationalism, while politically it demonstrated a strong affinity with the liberalism of the time. List's American experience mattered quite a lot here. Although his mind of the economist suggested he should side with the radical protectionists in the bitter arguments of the 1820s, his political heart and the interests of the German-speaking community in the US inclined him to the 'democratic nationalism' of Andrew Jackson. That was not, however, a question of mere political sentiments. The economic nationalism of the first half of the 19th century, just like political nationalism, was not a clearly defined antithesis of the liberalism of the time, but constituted an important complement to it, which was nevertheless difficult and not quite acceptable.

Still, there were certain limits to that defensive nationalism, even if they were not typically German, but rather (Western) European. The question of adjective is important here. It indicates that aspect of List's system which found its expression in five stages of national and economic development–from "original barbarism" and the next "pastoral" stage to the stage of "agricultural-manufacturing-commercial condition" (List 1922: 143). In List's opinion, only some of the Western European countries and the United States were able to reach Great Britain's level of development with the help of protectionist policy. South America, Eastern Europe and Asia were the areas which were only in the period of transformation from "original barbarism" to the "agricultural condition." That could be realized only thanks to a state-imposed policy of free trade and free competition between industrial countries in those areas, including of course the inflow of manufactures (List 1922: 93, 143, 152f).

The concept of stages was not an original idea of List's, it was taken from Smith (Gide and Rist 1916: 271), although economic historians treat it as first and foremost a part of the paradigm of the German Historical School (Kula 1963: 20–26, 180–183, Gould 1973: 421). It has to be remembered that approval of forced commercialization as a way of preparing underdeveloped areas for 'civilization' within the system of free trade appeared at that time quite regularly. All these questions were the subject of animated debates also in the Kingdom of Poland in the first half of the 19th century, concerning, among other things, 'natural', evolutionary paths leading to new forms of national wealth-creation (Jedlicki 1999, Kizwalter 1991).

Nevertheless, even in this case List did not argue that free trade would be beneficial to those countries merely aspiring at an "agricultural" economy in the sense given to that notion by comparative costs theorists. At that point he understood benefits in the longer-term perspective, as the 'effect of civilization'–a process facilitating the emergence of new behaviors, attitudes and institutions, and the creation of new needs and skills. He did not maintain, however, that the primary specialization of the agricultural countries secured their equal share in the gains from international trade (1922: 152f, 176f).[9] In the policy-oriented part of *System* he wrote, without hiding his emotions, about William Pitt's encouragement to France as to an agricultural and wine producing country:

> Not a word here of the old maxim of England, that a nation can only attain to the highest degree of wealth and power in her foreign trade by the exchange of manufactured products against agricultural products and raw materials. This maxim was then, and has remained since, an English State secret (List 1922: 296).

Still, there was nothing to prevent an interpretation of List's theory (despite its ethnocentrism) as a theory of economic nationalism of areas

---

[9] See those fragments of *System* where he discusses the example of the pre-partition Poland and the adverse effects of persistent agricultural specialization. Equally significant are those fragments where List makes a comparative analysis of the long-term industrial and agricultural growth potentials. Senghaas (1970: 86) takes the opposite view.

that were although underdeveloped still capable of initiating industrialization. After all, this is how the theory was actually interpreted. The Nobel Prize winner W. A. Lewis (1978: 221f) wrote that List's *System* had become "the bible of all industrializing countries in the nineteenth century, except Great Britain." Theodor von Laue (1969: 57), a historian of Russia's accelerated industrialization in Witte's time, added that List himself had become "a prophet of the ambitions of all underdeveloped countries," and Seers (1983: 52) recollected that Raúl Prebisch told him once that he was influenced by List. To all those descriptions Szporluk (2003: 270) threw in his own, calling List "the Marx of nationalism." Yet, this new Bible, or *Das Kapital*, was interpreted in various ways and to various effects, more often than not, especially in the 20th century, to pitiful effect–both politically and economically. But it was able to raise enthusiasm. The future co-founder of a free-trade order in Europe, Richard Cobden, reflecting on his stay in Vienna in the mid-1840s, mentioned that "Dr. List ... gained such an influence on public opinion that professors of political economy cannot expound free trade in their lectures for the youth" (quoted in Berend 2003: 14).

All the same, it is a paradox that the Eurocentric, stage-centered aspect of the Smith/List theory was not only in the 19th century, but also in the early decades of the 20th century a peculiar credo of primary sector nationalism in underdeveloped countries. Likewise, Smith's popularity, for example in Latin America, resulted not from those fragments of his theory where he emphasized the role of the internal division of labor, but from statements defending free trade and the role of foreign trade ensuring cheaper manufactures, which was complementary to agricultural systems. Regarding the same issue, Th. Cooper, a theorist of the slave-agricultural South, referred to Ricardo's *Principles* (Dangefield 1965: 278f). Even though criticized by Smith, the views of French physiocrats enhanced that selective and eclectic process of the reception of 'the latest trends' from Europe.

It therefore comes as no surprise that for instance at the turn of the 18th and 19th centuries Bishop José Joaquim da Cuhna de Azeredo Coutinho, one of the intellectual fathers of Brazilian independence, following the physiocracts, unshakably believed that "[s]ugar, wood, coffee, cocoa, and a myriad of other natural products ... were the true source of wealth," both in the Portuguese empire and in Brazil (Burns 1964: 149; see also Jacobsen 2005). He was not alone in thinking that way, either in Brazil or outside of it. The world of the Brazilian plantation or the Polish manor at the close of the 18th and the beginning of the 19th centuries was not prepared to accept the rationality (and mentality) of the new rapidly emerging market economy. In the preceding centuries that world learnt to coexist with capitalism (in the Braudelian sense) in its refined worldish or cosmopolitan form, with a capitalism that only indirectly interfered in the delicate social matrix of the slave- and serfdom-based systems. Any change caused a shock to and a sense of disgust in many people. When at the end of the 18th century, when ideas arose that directly affected the traditional customs of the *szlachta* [Polish gentry], for instance free trade in grain, it was as if someone had attacked "something so far as sacred to the whole of the Polish *szlachta* as the elective throne" (Jedlicki 1976: 232). The rural economy-based "laissez-faire of the *szlachta*," conservative and hostile to change, was in strong opposition to the dynamic and expansive laissez-faire of modernizers (Janowski 1998: 261). Then, several decades later, an opponent of Drucki-Lubecki's state-led industrialization in the 1820s, wrote about his policy that

> in place of the ability to do away with poverty and to vaunt this ability, Prince Lubecki built in Poland an altar of Mammon ... It is true that buildings and factories arose in towns, but on the other hand, plenty of swindlers, dishonest profiteers and unreliable Jews became moguls (quoted in Górski 1963: 228; see also Jedlicki 1999, Kizwalter 1991: chapter 2).

JOHN MAYNARD KEYNES: 'IF WE HAPPEN TO WANT IT'

If we pass over here the German younger Historical School from the end of the 19th and the beginning of the 20th century, which continued certain threads of List's *System*, then an explicit reference to the national economy as the subject of theoretical reflection re-appeared with full force in J. M. Keynes' economics from 1923 onwards. According to Schumpeter (1986: 504),

> List had one of the elements of greatness, namely, the grand vision of a national situation, which ... is a prerequisite for a certain type of scientific achievement–that type of which, in our own day, Keynes is an outstanding example.

Keynes's theory of employment and the concept of self-sufficiency matured in the years of the Great Depression. Against the background of both we find the category of effective demand or, more precisely, wrote Keynes, "a theory of the demand and supply of output *as a whole*" (Keynes 1947a: 190). That it was a revolutionary idea, running against the dominant methodological individualism, clearly follows from the remark made years later by Paul Samuelson (1986: 280):

> What made Keynes different ... was the fact that [his theory] did not take a narrow look at one or two isolated parts of the economy. He ... provided the economists with new ways of looking at how the entire gross national product is determined.

But such an understanding of the importance of Keynes' economic ideas came with some delay. The hotly debated question of tariffs and protectionism testifies to that. Paul van Zeeland, the former vice-governor of the National Bank of Belgium (and in 1936–1937 Belgian prime minister), wrote at the height of the Great Depression about protectionism:

> All the international conferences which have dealt with [protectionism], and all the meetings of experts which have examined it, have always come to the same conclusion that the accentuation of protectionism is injurious for all nations and for each one of them.

He added resignedly:

> meanwhile, with the same unanimity in practice as in theory, but in direct contradiction thereto, the states have not ceased to emphasize unilateral measures designed for the protection of their domestic markets (Zeeland 1933: 19f).

Next, there was a rather common understanding that Keynes' theory is applicable first and foremost to developed industrial economies. However, from the point of view of underdeveloped areas important is that part of his approach which, even if it does not make Keynes an ideological economic nationalist, at least explains the rationality of the concept of national economy and of the interdependence of national investment policy and the international market in the 20th century economy. And of protectionism in case of urgency.

It should not come as a surprise that as a theorist *and* economic policy expert, at the time of the Great Depression Keynes tried to rehabilitate, among other things, the mercantilist fascination with the problem of trade balance. Thus, in the *General Theory* we find an excursion into the history of economic ideas—with the clear intention of reemphasizing the importance of his innovative concept of aggregate demand and supply. In his presentation of mercantilists he followed Heckscher, even though, as he remarked, Heckscher was "much less sympathetic to the mercantilist theories than I am" (Keynes 1964: 341). Incidentally, the first reaction of Alvin H. Hansen, the future Keynesian, to the *General Theory* was negative: he saw in it a "reversion to the economic doctrines of mercantilism" (Skidelsky 1992: 576).

Anyhow, Keynes argued that in conditions of laissez-faire and the gold standard, the striving for export surplus was actually the only instrument to ensure full employment in a given country. He also pointed out that at the time of the world crisis and a general decline in effective demand, the struggle for the balance of trade, in some measure, rehabilitated protectionism—in its tariff form and/or through devaluation of the local currency. In the short run, protectionism and devaluation, which favored the creation of export surplus and protection of one's own production, could contribute to a rise in employment in individual countries, although not in the world economy as a whole. Hence the possibility of exporting unemployment and of the beggar-thy-neighbor trade policy and devaluations (Keynes 1964: 339, 382f, Robinson 1939, Eichengreen 2008: 87). Therefore the logic of such an essentially aggressive approach was simple: since the world economy was sinking, a politician who would not try to save his own country from disaster would be irresponsible. Calls for a balanced approach, even if addressed to the greatest economic powers, are of little avail in situations like this.

In the interwar period such a balanced approach and responsibility were really missing. The United States showed that with the introduction of the prohibitive Smoot–Hawley tariff in 1931 and then, in 1933, when during the preparations for the World Economic Conference in London, on which great hopes were pinned, it devalued the dollar and abandoned the gold standard. Already during the proceedings of the conference US delegation rejected the plan for currency stabilization. Keynes' reaction was enthusiastic: "President Roosevelt is Magnificently Right" (quoted in Skidelsky 1992: 481). At that moment the conference became pointless (Kindleberger 1987: 201–229, Röpke 1942: 202, James 2002). Great Britain had abandoned the gold standard two years earlier. Following the banking crisis in Austria and Germany, and a strong attack on sterling, on September 21, 1931 Britain suspended convertibility, and this fact "more than any other event, symbolized the interwar gold standard's disintegration" (Eichengreen 2008: 82). Suspension of convertibility was accompanied by sterling depreciation. Thus, trying to save itself, Britain at the same time made the international chaos worse. But its economic position relatively improved. With delay, the US followed suit. The passionate arguments of the advocates of protectionism and of the "First things [i.e. US] first" policy prevailed (see, e.g., Donham 1933). The new president of the United States decided to concentrate his and the country's attention on domestic priorities and national answers to the crisis. In a word, willy-nilly the US joined the club of countries using "methods of extremism," which combined high tariffs, quotas, embargoes, exchange restrictions, and depreciated currencies. This (negative) description of the behavior of 'others' appeared in the address of Secretary of State Cordell Hull at the London conference (1933: 169f). President Roosevelt's negative decision concerning currency stabilization came later. Not without compelling *in given circumstances* reasons. The situation in the USA was really desperate. From 1929 to 1933,

> money income fell 53 percent and real income 36 percent … Per capita real income in 1933 was almost the same as in the depression year of 1908 … At the trough of the depression one person was unemployed for every three employed (Friedman 1997: 18).

Keynes, when communicating his views to the US Department of Agriculture in 1936, found the delinking of the US currency from the gold standard and other interventionist measures taken by the American administration sensible. What troubled him was rather the prospect for the eventual relaxation of the un-orthodox economic policy. This happened, with rather disastrous effects, in 1937. Earlier, however, at the end of 1933, in his "Open Letter to President Roosevelt," he expressed some doubts concerning the proper timing of measures aimed at short-term "Recovery" and those initiating the structural long-term "Reform." Taking a critical stance toward the National Industrial Recovery Act just adopted by Congress, he underscored the following: N.I.R.A. "which is essentially Reform and probably impedes Recovery, has been put across too hastily, in the false guise of being part of the technique of Recovery." His own preference was different: "I put in the forefront … a large volume of Loan-expenditures under Government auspices." In his critical assessment of the improper timing of "Recovery" and "Reform" he made an additional point: a premature Reform "will upset the confidence of the business world … before you have had time to put other motives in their place" (Keynes 1933b). Let us mention here that the distinction between "Reform" and "Recovery" was not new to Keynes' thinking. In another place he spoke about a distinction between "importance" and "urgency."

In the 1936 conversation the question of "Reform" did not appear, and for rather obvious reasons. Amid setbacks, misallocations and bureaucratic mismanagement, the structural and institutional reforms initiated by the Roosevelt Administration were implemented at full speed. Instead, Keynes raised points of a different nature. He argued that in view of the general slump in world trade on the one hand, and of the size of the American home market on the other, the question of striving for export surplus was of secondary importance. If domestic demand grew, the foreign trade volume would grow and simultaneously its relative importance would decline. At the same time, following the ideas from the *General Theory*, Keynes promoted a policy oriented toward an increase in domestic demand through stimulating private investments, not consumption. Such a move, he argued in a way resembling arguments from the "Open Letter," would ensure the necessary cooperation of industrialists. And two years later, in 1938, in another letter to President Roosevelt, he wrote vividly that to ensure effective control over businessmen's behavior it would be wise to treat them "not like wolves and tigers, but as domesticated beasts" (quoted in Garraty 1979: 228). He also stressed the need to lay greater emphasis on maintaining the appropriate level of social welfare expenditures (a topic he mentioned also in the 1933 "Open Letter"). Without them, he argued, politically capitalism would not survive another possible shock similar to the 1929 crisis.

However, Keynes associated any nationalistic conclusions following from his conception with the fundamental proposition of his *General Theory*, which stressed that the world economy as the system could be rescued only through *parallel* and *coordinated* measures taken by individual countries:

> It is the policy ... of a national investment program devoted to an optimum level of domestic employment which is twice blessed in the sense that it helps ourselves and our neighbours at the same time. And it is the simultaneous pursuit of these policies by all countries together which is capable of restoring economic health and strength internationally (Keynes 1964: 349).

Three years earlier a similar approach was pressed by well-known historian of the AFL and labor union advisor Lewis L. Lorwin; for him the alternative of either self-sufficiency or world cooperation was patently false. A proper solution should be sought in a policy

> which would reconcile the economic and social needs of individual nations and ... build a world society which would recognize and incorporate the legitimate demands of rational nationalism (Lorwin 1933: 362).

Keynes' optimistic vision, put forward in 1936, was not realized. All the more so that by the "parallel and coordinated measures" he advocated, liberal economists of the time understood something different: a return to the gold standard and the fight against protectionism and "dumping in all its forms" (Zeeland 1933: 137). However, the 'new protectionism' reigned supreme in the world economy until the outbreak of World War II. According to a League of Nations report (1942: 147), this meant the transformation of emergency defensive measures into permanent instruments of offensive economic policy, the emergence of autarky as a principal objective of policy, and the extension and consolidation of state control over trade.

Beside the structural disequilibrium characteristic of the world economy of the time, no doubt the absence of world leadership, particularly economic leadership, was a major factor explaining this adverse course of events. Five years before the Great Depression blew up, Keynes declared "the end of laissez-faire" and stated an urgent need for "a new set of convictions." "Material Prosperity," he argued in his 1924 lecture, published only in 1926 (2003: 595), "removes the incentive just when it might be safe to take a chance. Europe lacks the means, America the will, to make a move." Economic hegemonic stability at the time of the Pax Britannica was already history. In Kindleberger's (1987: 289) interpretation, presented several decades later,

> the 1929 depression was so wide, so deep, and so long, because the international economic system was rendered unstable by British inability and US unwillingness to assume responsibility for stabilizing it.

But one should also take into account that the US continuation of the gold standard until 1933 made taking on the role as a world economic leader rather impossible (Eichengreen 1992). As a result the absence of a lender of last resort precluded any coordinated action.[10] However, the lesson learnt from the absence of firm leadership was well remembered. This question reappeared during the preparations, started still during the war, for the post-war world system of economic and financial institutions and the return to international trade. The joint overcoming of the crisis, about which Keynes wrote in the *General Theory*, lay at the foundation of the post-war Bretton-Woods system. And this lesson was not forgotten when the world financial crisis unleashed in 2008. Better *inter*-national and *inter*-institutional cooperation coupled with greater willingness to expand money supplies and to run larger budget deficits made it possible to prevent—at least for a time—a repetition of the 1929 scenario.

---

[10] James (2002: 95, 208) in his interpretation of the Great Depression emphasizes the lack of coordination and inflexibility of the financial system of the time, based on stiff treaty obligations (the 'Genoa–Geneva consensus') which increased its susceptibility to shocks and disequilibria. At the end of the day, this consensus "had to survive on goodwill or hot air." From Autumn 1929 on goodwill was a scarce commodity.

In 1933, three years before the above-mentioned conversation in the Department of Agriculture and the publication of the *General Theory*, Keynes went beyond the horizon of short-term analyses, just as he did in *The End of laissez-faire* and his later publications. In the essay on "National Self-Sufficiency" he lent critical support to autarchic conceptions, broadening and actually radicalizing his earlier criticism of the ideology of free trade, enterprise and the benefits of international specialization presented in *The End of laissez-faire* (see Irwin 1996: chapter 13). However, his vision of "an experimental society" developed in the essay was not a short-term solution but a long-term perspective: "What I have been discussing is not a sudden revolution, but the direction of a secular trend." This was an important point, usually neglected by critics of "self-sufficiency," and also omitted by Skidelsky (1992) in his monumental biography of Keynes. It made it possible to understand Keynes' clearly spelled out declaration included in the essay: "I must not be supposed to be endorsing all those things which are being done in the political world today in the name of economic nationalism. Far from it" (Keynes 1933a).

Explaining the idea of self-sufficiency he wrote:

> I sympathise ... with those who would minimise, rather than with those who would maximise, economic entanglement between nations. Ideas, knowledge, art, hospitality, travel–all these are the things which should of their nature be international. But let goods be homespun whenever it is reasonably and conveniently possible.

Having in mind, among other things, the processes of diffusion of technical changes, he added:

> Experience accumulates to prove that most modern mass-production processes can be performed in most countries and climates with almost equal efficiency. ... National self-sufficiency ... though it costs something, may be becoming a luxury which we can afford if we happen to want it.

Technical changes going hand in hand with national control over finance and a policy increasing the weight of the domestic market in relation to exports, all those measures seemed to Keynes possible and, if need be, necessary.

This was yet another break with the prevailing economics, this time in the area of the international division of labor, defined since Ricardo's time by natural factor endowments. At the same time, Keynes' stand undoubtedly strengthened the position of the then advocates of the autarchic variant of economic nationalism, and, after all is said and done, this is how it was rather one-sidedly interpreted by critics. Despite the passage of several decades, such a view of Keynes is manifest, for example, in remarks by Heilperin. Without denying that Keynes' views on autarky had evolved, he nevertheless treated the author of *General Theory* as an out-and-out intellectual accomplice of illiberal and undemocratic systems: "If [Keynes] was a liberal, then he was that extraordinary kind of liberal whose practical recommendations consistently promote collectivism" (Heilperin 1960: 125). Also Skidelsky (1992: 478) commenting on the essay, and discarding the part devoted to criticism of Hitler, Mussolini and Stalin, wrote: "It was the nearest he ever came to endorsing communist, or fascist, economics."

However, the principal *political* charge against Keynes rests mainly on one sentence from his introduction to the German edition of the *General Theory*, published in Nazi Germany in 1936. In a rather out of control condemnation of Keynes, one of his critics wrote that it was precisely that introduction that was "the most convincing evidence of Keynes' strong fascist bent" (Rothbard 2010: 51). Let us then quote the passage in question. He argued there, not without a certain measure of pessimism, that

> the theory of output as a whole ... is much more easily adapted to the conditions of a totalitarian state (*eines totalen Staates*) than ... under conditions of free competition and a large measure of laissez-faire. Although I have .... worked it out with a view to the conditions prevailing in the Anglo-Saxon countries where a large degree of laissez-faire still prevails, nevertheless it remains applicable to situations in which state management is more pronounced.

In this regard he was wrong and over-pessimistic. The American New Deal was, increased 'collectivism' notwithstanding, a democratic, Keynesian in spirit, answer to unemployment and falling output (Bairoch 1993: 9–14). At the same time, if we treat this remark as an appeal for better coordinated actions—with the participation of the state, not above it—we can agree with the (slightly wicked) description of Keynes' ideas by Milton Friedman (1997: 20, 21). The author of the *General Theory*, he note, presented to the public a combination of two basic concepts: "first, the public interest concept of government; second, the benevolent dictatorship concept that all will be well if only good men are in power." Skidelsky (1992: xxviii) used different words: what Keynes proposed was "the 'managerial' response to the breakdown of values." Friedman, however, added resignedly: "We must act within the system as it is. We may regret that government has the powers it does ... but so long as they exist, it is ... better that they be exercised efficiently than inefficiently."

The charge leveled by Heilperin against Keynes *the economist* was obviously one-sided. If truth be told, not Keynes alone should be in the dock. Keynesian ideas appeared not just in the *General Theory*. Of course, Keynes' attitude to the theoretical contributions to economics appearing outside his circle in Cambridge is well known. In the words of the historian, the *General Theory* "was written in an intellectual vacuum. ... Essentially, Keynes fed on Keynes" (Garvy 1975: 393). However, a groundbreaking, in many respects, theoretical approach to the business cycle, types of markets ('degree of monopoly'), effective demand and income distribution, and government spending had been proposed by the Polish economist Michał Kalecki (1984). According to Robinson (1971: 4; see also 1980: 186–189), "Kalecki's version [of the *General Theory*] was in some ways more truly *general* theory than Keynes".[11] One should also recollect the contributions made by German economists in the last years of the Weimar Republic, in the midst of the Great Depression. The proposals by Wilhelm Lautenbach of the Ministry of Economics made in September 1931, the programs prepared, among the others, by W. S. Woytinsky, Ernst Wagemann and others concerning deficit spending, countercyclical monetary and fiscal policies and their (futile) attempts at questioning the deflationary psychosis reigning in Germany testified to the rather general disappointment with economic liberalism. The same can be said, especially after Great Britain's coup de grâce to the gold standard, about the policy proposal prepared by economists in the United States (Garvy 1975: 397ff, Garraty 1979: 203f, 223, Blaug 1996: 663). In a word, the bits from the Keynesian tool box were proposed and applied independently of Keynes' ideas. The delayed acceptance of Keynes' *theory* was, however, a different story.

Keynes' basic intuition was clear: after several decades of profound changes that affected both the institutional structure of markets as well as the ways the market operated, a defense of liberal values could not be based on a simple continuation of the hitherto symbiosis between political and economic liberalisms–usually understood in an oversimplified manner. In his 1926 essay and other publications which preceded the Great Depression Keynes laid an emphasis on structural transformations of market economies–changing among the other things, economies of

---

[11] The attitude of Skidelsky (1992: 594n) toward this question–important from the point of view of the history of economic thought–cannot be described in any other way than as an example of Anglo-Saxon-centrism. "At the time," he wrote, "no one who mattered in economics or public life in Britain or the United States had heard of Kalecki, but everyone had heard of Keynes." Granted. But he simply missed the point raised by Joan Robinson: when mentioning Kalecki, she was speaking not about the practical impact of his innovative ideas in Great Britain and the USA but about the "claim to priority." For a balanced and detailed discussion about this issue see Chapple (1993, 1995).

scale, imperfect competition, absentee ownership—and on the question of the state, and thus of a limited though necessary collectivism. His critical stand on the gold standard was clear. The author of *The Economic Consequences of the Peace* (1919)—a book which Veblen (1920) criticized as an example of a liberal defense of the "Democracy of Property Rights" and others as a devastating criticism of the economic aspects of the Versailles Treaty (Mommsen 1996: 97)—did undergo a fundamental evolution, and he admitted that openly. "I regarded," he wrote in an essay on self-sufficiency, referring to his earlier views, "departures from [free trade doctrine] as being at the same time imbecility and an outrage." Three decades earlier, in a private letter written in 1903, he did not mince his words: "I hate all priests and protectionists ... Free trade and free thought! Down with pontiffs and tariffs!" (quoted in Turnell 2002: 32). The experience of the Great Depression was the decisive factor in the change of his position.

Keynes treated the dramatic events of 1929 and the years that followed as a clear signal of the end of the old epoch of private competitive capitalism and of the entry into a period of uncertainty and transition that ruled out the reconstitution of the world economy on the 19th-century pattern. With a clearly perceptible resignation he wrote that "to-day one country after another abandons [classical] presumptions. Russia is still alone in her particular experiment, but no longer alone in her abandonment of the old presumptions." Therefore in that period it was inevitable to abandon old dogmas concerning free trade and protectionism, which would make it possible "to make our own favorite experiments towards the ideal social republic of the future." At that experimental stage, he added, "we wish ... to be our own masters." Additionally, considering that the hitherto system of treaties had gone bankrupt, a greater degree of national control over finance would favor restricting irresponsible speculative international transfers caused by "the divorce between ownership and the real responsibility of management" (Keynes 1933a). And finally, Keynes argued—actually not very convincingly—as if quoting Fichte, that "a greater measure of national self-sufficiency and economic isolation among countries that existed in 1914 may tend to serve the cause of peace." Lorwin (1933a: 366) was more realistic on this point: national self-sufficiency would inevitably lead to the creation of regional, aggressive and imperialistic blocks "gravitating around the major industrial countries." Friedrich Pollock (1933), co-founder of the Frankfurt Institute for Social Research, reasoned in a similar way. For him not national but "imperialist autarchy" was "the logical conclusion" of Keynes' idea of self-sufficiency.

In the years that followed, such pessimism of the theory as well as the sense of crisis, contributed to the development of conceptions of economic stagnation and the disappearance of investment opportunities, put forward by authors of decidedly different political affiliations (from Alvin H. Hansen, President of the American Economic Association, to Paul M. Sweezy, a brilliant young Marxist economist) (see Joelsohn 1952). Meanwhile, Soviet Russia and also Italy, Germany and Japan went their own way, practicing economic nationalism and collectivism based on quite different principles. It needs to be stressed, though, that Keynes did not have any political illusions about Nazi Germany or Stalin (the text was written in 1933, at the time of the industrialization spurt and forced collectivization of agriculture in the Soviet Union). Supporting the need for experiment he emphasized nevertheless thinking primarily of political freedoms: "Let Stalin be a terrifying example to all who seek to make experiments" (1933: 769). In the *General Theory,* after declaring wittily that "[i]t is better that a man should tyrannise over his bank balance than over his fellow-citizens,"he wrote a passage which can be read as a kind of a short manifesto:

> The authoritarian state systems of today seem to solve the problem of unemployment at the expense of efficiency and of freedom. ... But it may be possible by a right analysis of the problem to cure the disease whilst preserving efficiency and freedom (Keynes 1964: 374, 381).

Keynes' comments on self-sufficiency, although not voiced in the subsequent years, seemed to open a new theoretical perspective for underdeveloped countries which had already reached a certain minimum potential for industrial transformation. One may suggest that the 1933 essay did not contradict the basic assumptions of the *General Theory.* Once you make national economy ("aggregate demand and supply") a reference point in the discussion concerning growth and employment there is nothing to prevent accepting the rationality of moves aimed at structural changes and defining anew the forms and the intensity of a given country's participation in the world economy (see Kalecki 1938). Keynes referred to that question once again, although in a more indirect and watered-down manner, saying during the above-mentioned visit to the Department of Agriculture that if the hypothesis of the stagnating level of the world production and consumption were rejected, the opposition between economic nationalism and international trade was no longer inevitable. A relative increase in self-sufficiency, understood as a weakening of dependence on foreign trade, could go hand in hand with the growing participation in world exchanges, expressed in the absolute volume of trade. He was consistent in his views: in the 1933 essay he already presented the idea, implying that the income elasticity for domestic, non-tradable goods is higher than the income elasticity for imports. This was an interesting point, originally raised by Sombart in 1902 in his grand, and rather poorly argued, scheme of *die fallende Exportquote*, and after Keynes taken in a more methodical way by, among others, Deutsch and Eckstein (1961), and Lipsey (1963).[12]

List *redivivus?* Perhaps. Certainly, however, Keynes' "reconversion" to the principles of classical economy, about which Heilperin (1960: 118f) wrote, referring to the war years that if it really had taken place (which I doubt), it did so without his resigning from the basic postulates of *The End of laissez-faire* and the *General Theory*, including "possible improvements in the technique of modern capitalism by the agency of collective action" (Keynes 2003: 594; see also Hansen 1947: 203–207). Collectivism and control, if not limited to the experience of totalitarian systems, made up an important part of the answer to the crisis of the liberal order (and its ideological justifications). They also made up the most important characteristics of the transformation of market economies (Heilperin 1960: 28f, Skidelski 1998: chapter 2, Garraty 1979: 225–232). In a word, Keynes was enough of an optimist to believe that capitalism would survive the blow taken in 1929. At the same time he was enough of a pessimist to notice that exactly at that time capitalism's survival begged for fundamental reform of theory and economic policy. What really distinguished him from his neoclassical predecessors was "his bold ascription to government of a central role in the determination of the momentum of the system itself" (Heilbroner and Milberg 1995: 17).

The rediscovery by Keynes in the Bretton Woods discussions of the value of international trade did not restore his faith in the 19th-century idyll of free trade and automatic adjustment mechanisms. For the Bretton Woods system, the germs of which were clearly noticeable in Keynes' conception of the International Clearing Union, included also a number of ideas and instruments of action which were far from the principles of

---

[12] The arguments presented by Lipsey (1963: 77) concerning the United States and underscoring the differences between the quantity- and value-measured trends sounded convincing. He wrote: "A comparison of the value of exports and imports with the value of domestic output confirmed the view that there has been a decline in the ratio of trade to output. ... The volume of trade, however, shows no such long-run decline in importance. ... The contrasting behavior of current- and constant-dollar trade rations [was] caused by the substantial decline in the ratio of export and import prices to domestic prices."

laissez-faire; instead, they took into consideration certain lasting consequences of the Great Depression. In his speech before the House of Lords in December 1945, Keynes (1947b: 393) left no doubt that American-British agreements

> represent the first elaborate and comprehensive attempt to combine the advantages of a freedom of commerce with safeguards against the disastrous consequences of a laissez faire system which pays no direct regard to the preservation of equilibrium and merely relies on the eventual working out of blind forces.

In such circumstances, a spontaneous harmonization of policies naturally had to be complemented with (and sometimes outright replaced by) the mechanisms of both political and economic negotiations. This was somehow inevitable. Together with "the broadening of the horizons of economic policy" there appeared new goals of such a policy such as "a maximum rate of employment and growth, the stabilization of prices, the improvement of working conditions, assistance to weaker economic sectors" (Triffin 1963: 251).

This tendency was additionally and increasingly intensified by the (arising in the subsequent decades) awareness of the problem of backwardness. During the crisis of the first globalization, in the interwar period, that issue was merely signaled–although forcefully–by Central Europe and Latin America.

CHAPTER THREE

CATEGORIES

NATIONAL ECONOMY: ELUSIVE CONCEPT?

A strong association between the concept of national economy and economic nationalism, above all the holistic one, influenced the way national economy was perceived and evaluated. Bearing in mind the experience of Nazi commercial policy in the 1930s, toward the end of the war Hirschman (1980: 79) wanted to launch a "frontal attack" on this concept and this way to uproot economic nationalism. W. Arthur Lewis (1949: 200), who was otherwise far from criticizing attempts at industrialization in underdeveloped countries, like Hirschman, was allergic to the abuse of the concept of economic sovereignty by the Axis countries. The conclusion he drew from his review of the situation in the interwar period was unequivocal: "National sovereignty in economic relations spells chaos." In successive decades these two outstanding economists were in the group of the foremost representatives of development economics. The point of reference of this economics was the notion of national economy and sovereign economic policy.

All the same, these understandable in 1945 or 1949 reactions do not waive the question whether the concept of national economy (and economic sovereignty) finds any equivalent in real economic processes. Was Felipe Pazos (quoted in Adler 1967: 205) right when he claimed years ago that "a workable capitalist system is one which is made up of local capitalists, not foreign capitalists and local workers"? Incidentally, at this point he, unknowingly in a way, echoed Józef Supiński, who, disappointed in the 1870s at the activities of foreign entrepreneurs in the Russian partition sector of Poland and at the same time being realistic about the country's limited capital resources, propagated the phrase: "Foreign [loan] capital, not foreign capitalists" (quoted in Kowalik 1992; 22).[1] In the already

---

[1] When toward the end of the 1920s the Soviet government nationalized the few foreign investments made under the NEP, the then Premier Alexey I. Rykov repeated Supiński almost word for word: "We need foreign capital but we do not need foreign capitalists" (quoted in Lewis 1948: 167). Also in colonial India toward the end of the 19th century Indian authors maintained that "if foreign capital was required ... India should import only the

different conditions of the second globalization, in connection with the 2008–2010 crisis, former Polish Prime Minister discovered that "capital does have nationality. In the EU as well as in the USA" (Bielecki 2011: 18). A similar discovery was made by a top financial expert: among the 20 biggest banks operating in Poland, 15 were foreign-owned controlling 80 percent of total assets. "Such a situation," he concluded, "is unhealthy and worrying" (Kawalec 2011: 22).

Such questions can be multiplied. Positions taken in literature are equally many (and divergent). Root (1978: 148), the author of the textbook already quoted here, in the notion of national economy saw mere political interference in the sphere of economic activity, while according to Nicholas Kaldor (1970), from the economic viewpoint, the *modus operandi* of the domestic regional economy was not identical to the *modus operandi* of the national economy. For List, and next for Schmoller, Bücher and the entire German Historical School, national economy was the 'real existence' and not a mere heuristic approach. *Nationalökonomie*, entangled in then popular debates on 'society as organism', was not just a negation of Menger's methodological individualism and antihistoricism. According to Hodgson (2001: 64), adherents of *Nationalökonomie* "hinted at a conceptual and empirical method of treating economic systems: by focusing on behavior at the aggregate level." In German debates national economy appeared as an important subject of theoretical and historical reflection "long before the emergence of macroeconomics proper in the Anglo-American world." Paul Samuelson, writing about Keynes, would probably agree. Roman Rybarski and Stanisław Głąbiński, eminent economists of the Polish 'national school', adopted the German economists' approach. Let me also mention here deliberations by Joan Robinson (1964: 117f), the most outstanding of Keynes's collaborators. When writing on the basic 'rules of the game' of economic analysis, she put nationalism first. No matter whether we speak of mercantilism or free trade doctrines and economic growth, all categories of economic analysis refer, according to Robinson, to the national context. Put in a nutshell: "The very nature of economics is rooted in nationalism." Without quoting Robinson, a similar approach has been recently proposed by Takeshi Nakano (2007). Questioning the "conventional wisdom," he presents both Adam Smith and Alfred Marshall as "economic nationalists" *par excellence*.

---

capital and not the capitalists. They favored loan capital as against entrepreneurial capital" (Chandra 1979: 113). For similar attitudes in Brazil in the 1930s, see Dean (1969: 147).

Conventional presentations treat national economy as political and economic givens. Reservations concern first and foremost the economic rationality of the very existence of many politically delimited areas. The main argument used in conventional presentations is the lack of congruity between the size of particular nations and "the optimum economic area," although some authors would add that "[i]t is not obvious ... that there is any one optimum size for the nation or the firm" (Kindleberger 1962: 29f, 1974: 342). In a presentation like this, although it refers to the Smith-Ricardo-Mill tradition, we do not find any reference to Smith's thesis (2005: 559, 307) that "[t]he greatest and most important branch of the commerce of every nation ... is that which is carried on between the inhabitants of the town and those of the country."

A number of international trade theories have reservations about Smith's thesis, though. The division between foreign and domestic trade is treated as first of all a reflection of the differences in mobility of the factors of production. Thus limitations of mobility can occur within a nation just as well as in the international economy (Blaug 1996: 202f). Other scholars, as for instance Ingvar Svennilson (1963: 1, 6, 339), do not question the opinion that "a nation can be regarded as a *unit of action* in economic analysis." Nevertheless, in their conclusions they lean toward the conventional approach. Although Svennilson points out that discontinuities in mobility of factors of production and commodities at national borders imply that such concepts as the "national" wage level, the "national" standard of living, and the "national" income distribution are "relevant to economic analysis," yet they do not have to be of an absolute nature. Discontinuities are the result of policy and circumstances, although of long-term consequence. Therefore a change of policy and circumstances can bring about relativization of the concept of nation as a unit of economic analysis.

However, for the economists and/or economic historians engaged in the comparative study of economic growth a conventional approach was definitely not satisfying. This was the case with Simon Kuznets (1951, 1966). Compared to Svennilson's presentation of the problem of nation, Kuznets's approach regarding the choice of the sovereign state as the proper unit of analysis was clearly less ambiguous, more positive and sophisticated–and more convincing. In the opinion of Gerschenkron (1965: 42), it was "indubitably correct." I will return to this question at the end of this section.

While passing over for a moment the limitations of Svennilson's presentation, it should be pointed out nevertheless that indirectly it signals an important problem of changes with regard to the degree of unification and integration of particular markets, the international market included. Braudel's deliberations on the economic "identity of France" seem to be the most lucid presentation of the difficulties the emergence of an integrated national economy encountered. The never accomplished task of linking vertical international interests and ties with largely immobile local markets, the complicated and protracted integration of the latter into a cohesive nation-wide circulation of goods, elimination, at great expense, of peculiar internal colonies, all these processes made up a syndrome that put economic and political motivations and interests into the same basket. Hervé le Bras's studies show, for instance, that the relative slowdown in French industrial growth in the years 1860–1914 was caused, among other things, by massive investments in administration, education and transport infrastructure in the rural and culturally distinct south. According to le Bras, "the industrial imperative was eclipsed by the political imperative of unity" (quoted in Braudel 1990: 542).[2]

Returning to conventional presentations, what is most striking is their lack of historical perspective. Braudel's descriptive presentation took note of the complicated, spread-over-time process of building national economies. In fact conventional presentations ignore the question asked by Gellner (1994a: 18), "[D]oes a viable economic-political unit, capable of surviving [under conditions of industrialism], also need to be a national one?" Gellner's answer was positive: industrialization required a nation, but of a definite kind, formed and/or remodeled in the very process of industrialization (see also Pagano 1995). And the fundamental question which arose at a certain stage of development of capitalism and affected the concept of economic nationalism is that of the drastic limitations to the previously unlimited labor mobility. I write more extensively about it in Chapter 4, but I think that worth mentioning here is the following remark by James Mayall (1990: 87): "The fact that even in the most liberal societies, immigration is regarded as a privilege not a right, suggests that there are compelling practical arguments in favour of the national state." If so, national economy becomes a public good appreciated all the more as international differences in income levels grow. The same applies to a time of crisis.

---

[2] According to Pollard (1981: 253), until the second half of the 19th century difficulties in building well-integrated national economies implied that it was not the territorial state but regions that should become the point of reference for studies on the economic history of Europe. Only in the 1870s did "frontiers [begin to] gel ... into economically meaningful barriers."

Mancur Olson made an interesting attempt to point out the importance of the issues discussed here from the institutional and public-goods perspective. Already in his earlier work (1982) he considered this a pessimistic prospect due to the "institutional sclerosis" manifested in the petrification of "coalitional structures and processes." He treated that "sclerosis" as a hint at the broader problem of changing hierarchies and development potentials of national economies. In part, differences in the potential of particular countries were accounted for by such factors as lack of flexibility manifested, for instance, in inter-group relations and/or in the appearance of non-dynamic institutions which hampered growth. Elsewhere, Olson (1990: 98) wrote vividly that the distributional coalitions of interest groups had transformed the mobile British "nation of shopkeepers" into an institutionally paralyzed "country of clubs and pubs." Thus taking the democratic constitutional structure as given, Olson's cure for the malaise and slow growth caused by distributional coalitions is, Rose-Ackerman pinpointed (2003), "disorganization and uncertainty ... because they limit the entrenched power." The next step in Olson's theorizing led to the model of a conflict-ridden relationship between the "roving bandit" (narrow interests collusions) and the "secure stationary bandit" (encompassing interest of self-interested autocrat) applied to the communist system and the interpretation of its collapse (Olson 2000).

Still, the question about the causes of the growing basic differences among nations remained unanswered.

As in *The Rise and Decline of Nations*, in the answer Olson gives national economies are again placed at the forefront. In addition, he challenges the fundamental assumption of the economic theory that "any gains that can be obtained are in fact picked up" (1996: 3).

Having considered the impact factors such as knowledge, capital and natural resources can exert on income differences between nations, Olson makes (critical) use of Landes's hypothesis (1998: 516ff), according to which: "[i]f we learn anything from the history of economic development, it is that culture makes all the difference." Olson (1996: 16), in his own way, makes Landes's hypothesis more specific: he singles out "personal culture" as individual marketable human capital, and "civic culture" as public good capital, which manifests itself in convictions about good policy and/or good institutions. The latter can increase individual income only indirectly, "by influencing public policies and institutions."

According to Olson, the experience of international migrations clearly implies that personal cultures cannot explain the basic differences in the income the migrant earns before and after leaving his/her home country.

Therefore, as the variables cited here do not seem satisfactory, another explanation is necessary. Olson looks for such an explanation in the factors that influence civic culture. The "structure of incentives" (1996: 22) is the crucial variable, he argues. It is worth adding here that the significance of this variable is connected with a strong argument following the theory of public goods: with regard to a certain category of goods, individual rationality does not guarantee social rationality. Olson argues that to bring the two types of rationality closer to each other thus requires acting at the level of public goods (of the state and national economy). Such a hypothesis seems, however, at variance with the neoclassical theorem which assumes that as long as property rights are precisely defined and we do not encounter basic difficulties in the realization of the contract, individual rationality is capable of including externalities and the related transaction costs just as well. Finally, Olson concludes that as long as "borders ... mark the boundaries of different structures of incentives," differences in wealth among nations arise from "differences in the quality of economic policies and institutions" (1996: 22, 19).

A similar conclusion can be found in publications by the whole group of researchers who refer to the role played by institutions and institutional change (see Acemoglu, Johnson and Robinson 2004). I particularly mean here both the theoretical analyses as well as historical exemplifications presented by Douglass C. North (1990). It is always worth bearing in mind the North and Thomas dictum (1973: 2, 157): innovations, economies of scale, education, capital accumulation "are not causes of growth; they *are* growth. ... Growth will simply not occur unless the existing economic organization is efficient." Such a conclusion, they add, would certainly meet the approval of both Adam Smith and Karl Marx. In economics, this type of assumption found its place in the new theory of growth which included technical progress and knowledge as endogenous variables in the growth equation.[3]

The difference of opinion in Marxist literature is equally great. Supporters of post-Marxism emphasize, above all, the conflict inherent in

---

[3] According to Gilpin (2001: 116), "the new growth theory suggests that national economic structures, institutions, and public policies are major determinants of technological development and economic growth," and also that "an initial advantage of one country over another in human capital will result in a permanent difference in income level between the countries." See also Evans (2005). Therefore one can imply that institutional determinants of the endogenous growth theory increase and not eliminate the importance of, among other things, political and/or economic nationalism. Skidelsky (2001), juxtaposing Greenfeld's theses and new growth equation, does not take that into consideration.

the dynamic of capital, which incessantly challenges national borders, without doing away with them, though. They refer indirectly to (young) Marx's thesis that civil society (*bürgerliche Gesellschaft*) "transcends the State and the nation, though ... it must assert itself in its foreign relations as nationality, and inwardly must organise itself as State" (Marx and Engels 2004: 57). Incidentally, Gellner (1994b: 107), writing about nationalism, presented this dualism in a similar way: "The rhetoric of nationalism is inversely related to its social reality; it speaks of *Gemeinschaft*, and is rooted in a semantically and often phonetically standardized *Gesellschaft*."

The tension and conflict, but also interdependence between the unifying and globalizing dynamic of capital on the one hand and the state and the nation on the other had their consequences clearly visible toward the end of the 19th century. The approach taken by the authors of the *Communist Manifesto* (1998: 39), which emphasized the rapid disappearance of the "national ground on which [industry] stood," was no longer satisfactory (or was ahead of its time). Indeed, toward the end of the century the first globalization was a fact; all the same it was unthinkable without the rising role of the state and national market. In practice, even before Marx's death, the concepts of state and nation found their place in the policy of European socialist parties. The concepts of internationalism and solidarity, too, underwent a fundamental transformation. They did not disappear, but became 'nationalized' (Lademacher 1988; Van Tijn 1988).[4]

The pressure of reality? No doubt it was an important factor. Bismarck and the newly united German state were staunch opponents of German social democrats. As regards French socialists it was hard for them to swallow the national defeat of 1871. Prospects for revolution were receding, whereas the nation-state and the national market were becoming not so much an opponent as an increasingly important point of reference for socialist practice. Moreover, imperialism related with the nation-state and its territorial dimension, just like attempts to challenge it, became a fact

---

[4] The Gotha Program of 1875 thus declared, to Marx's indignation (1922: 36): "The working class strives for its emancipation first of all within the confines of the present-day national state." Greenfeld (1993: 390–395, 1995: 558–564) ignores this issue in her, actually borrowed from J. Toynbee, interpretation of the hidden sense of Marx's ideas as a kind of "resentment." In her opinion, nation and romantic nationalism were always present in Marx's thought. Marx–as a Jew and a German–construed the concepts of 'proletariat' and 'capital' as actually reflecting the struggle of Germany with the power of the West (Great Britain and France). In this fragment of Greenfeld's deliberations there is certainly more homespun psychology than facts. It is worthwhile reading the firm rebuttal of Toynbee by Karl Popper in *The Open Society and Its Enemies*.

difficult to ignore. Therefore there were no principal objections to Rudolf Hilferding's observation (1958: 661) that it was a matter of course that the main goal of anti-colonial movements was "to create a ... national state as a means to attain economic and cultural freedom." Nikolai Bukharin (1973: 135), in turn, while critical of Hilferding's concept of "ultra-imperialism," argued that

> the development of world capitalism leads on the one hand to the internationalization of economic life ... and on the other, and to a *much bigger* extent, this very process generates an extreme intensification of the tendencies to 'nationalize' capitalist interests.

In the successive period of crisis, following the deep slump that started in 1929, and which indicated the ultimate end of the first globalization, the Left and economic liberals together got back to emphasizing that contradiction. This time, however, they gave more emphasis to the elements of political folly in measures taken by populist demagogues (liberals and conservatives) and to immanent, doom-laden 'contradictions of capitalism' (the Left).[5]

Last but not least is Immanuel Wallerstein and the school of European world-economy (or World-System Analysis) connected with his name. According to Wallerstein (2000: 87, 1974: chapter 7, 2004: 54ff), capitalism and its birth, like state and nations, "[were] from the beginning an affair of the world economy and not of nation-states." Nation-states (or multination states) are only a part of the triad characteristic of the world-economy: a single division of labor, multiple state structures and multiple cultures. In such a perspective, the national community Gellner describes as *Gemeinschaft* refers not to the national *Gesellschaft*, but to the world *Gesellschaft*. Nation and state, and along with them the concept of national economy, appear in Wallerstein's conceptualization as elements of the functionally integrated and at the same time vertically stratified greater whole: the world-economy. Thus we are dealing here with core-states (which by definition are strong), peripheral and semi-peripheral areas (which by definition are represented by states that are weak or not so strong). Although within the world *Gesellschaft* autonomy of the national

---

[5] In the next decades, despite euphoria about the rapid acceleration of the second globalization, Sweezy and Magdoff (1972; 96) repeated that "the very idea of a unit of capital divorced from any nationality ... is a contradiction in terms." See also Stephen Hymer's pioneering contribution (1971) to the theory of MNE and FDI and "uneven development." Today the view that "capital does have nationality" is shared not only by Gilpin (2001: 297–304), but also by the theoreticians of "strategic trade" and of the "competitive advantage of nations" (see Irwin 1966: chapter 14).

economy, just like that of the state, does not disappear, nevertheless one can no longer speak of its *theoretical* autonomy. Therefore Wallerstein (2000: 120, 122f, 306) discards "the dominant historical myth" and "the liberal-Marxist consensus" as exemplifications of the stage- and state-centered approach of Karl Bücher. For this leading representative of the Historical School, Wallerstein argues, development means the "widening economic circles, in which the major jump was to go from a 'local' economy to a 'national' economy ... located ... in a national state." In such an approach, Wallerstein concludes, the "world" appears "essentially as an epiphenomenon."

Wallerstein's approach concurred to some extent with Braudel's concept of capitalism as the opposite of the nationally or locally limited market economy and all-encompassing "material life" (or "daily life"):

> Whether favourable or unfavourable, the modern state was one of the realities among which capitalism had to navigate, by turns helped or hindered, but often enough progressing through neutral territory. How could things have been otherwise? If the interests of the state and those of the national economy as a whole frequently coincided ... capitalism was by contrast always to be found in that section of the economy which sought to participate in the most vigorous and profitable currents of international trade. It was thus engaged in a game played on an infinitely wider plane than that of the ordinary market economy ... or than that of the state and its particular preoccupations. Capitalist interests ... naturally extend beyond the narrow boundaries of the nation (Braudel 1992a: 554).

According to some neo-Marxist researchers, a conception of an empire of a new type as a political structure best suiting the conditions of the current globalization "when the state and capital effectively coincide" becomes a solution to this constant tension between the state and capitalism. In such a situation "[t]he decline of nation-states is in a profound sense the full realization of the relationship between the state and capital" (Hardt and Negri 2001: xiii–xv, 236).

Let me also briefly mention that in studies of the communist system, the concept of the national economy was treated as the main point of reference, and the structure of industrial economies of the interwar period as a model to be copied. The policy of quasi-autarchic development demonstrated the costs and benefits of the economic system with a high degree of internal complementarity, although, let me add, with an institutionally limited degree of technological innovation. Hence, for instance, Polish authors dealing with the problems of the world economy took the following point of departure: "We accept national economies to be the fundamental elements of the world economy." In the descriptions of such economies they stressed the high level of inter-industry integration, the existence of common economic goals and the creation of the so-called minimum industrial complex. Then, taking into consideration the effect of the world economy on the national economy, they singled out in the latter zones of indifference, compatibility and mutual convergence (Kudliński and Siwiński 1985: 11, 12–15, Kleer 1975: 407–425). This highly descriptive and selective approach of mainstream economists exemplified the prevailing *ideology* of the Soviet-type economy. The analytically more promising concepts of 'shortage economy' and 'closed system' appeared relatively late: during the already evident decay of the Soviet-type economies or only after their collapse.

The conclusions suggested by this brief review of opinions indicate that national economy as a *category of practice* has not been questioned in at least two hundred years. At the same time, the theoretical positions discussed, particularly the conventional approaches and those referring to the communist economy, reflect different variants of *methodological nationalism* (Wimmer and Glick Schiller 2002: 303–308): from the theorizing "banal nationalism" (states, nations and national economies treated as "obvious") to those treating problems of the nation-state and national economy in only a loose relationship with the global context ("territorialization"). It seems that in this area one should not expect too much from mainstream economics. Economic historians and/or researchers practicing comparative historical sociology and international political economy have much more to say here.

As an addition to the analyses presented so far, two detailed questions should be considered.

Under the first globalization, the concept of national economy was inextricably linked with the project of independent industrialization. There can be no serious doubt about that. Of course, there is no way to express what this independent industrialization meant in the past and what it means at present in a definition that lays emphasis only on quantitative information. For instance, the decades-long and on-going dispute about the concepts of growth and development testifies to that.[6]

---

[6] For a concise summary of this debate, preceding the turnabout at the beginning of the 1980s toward the neoliberal growth models (and policies), see Gould (1973: 1–11). The debate was resumed in the 1990s, among other things, under the influence of the work by Sen, and especially the hypothesis stressing, in place of income per capita, the concept of capabilities. For a concise analysis of this approach see Evans (2005).

Anyway, for the sake of further analysis, it would suffice to refer to the approaches pursued by such different scholars as Deepak Lal and Robert B. Sutcliffe.

In Lal's presentation (1998: 19–21) we find two models of growth: the "Smithian" and the "Promethean" (Schumpeterian) ones. The first model was based almost exclusively on an increasing division of labor, expansion of foreign trade and markets included. Stagnant technology, organic energy and land frontier were the main constraints on it. In the "Promethean" model of growth, the division of labor is combined with new, mineral energy sources, with knowledge and with technical progress. Only the second model of growth ensures that Malthusian constraints are overcome and that the economy enters a path of a sustained increase in per capita incomes.[7] Lal discusses the transition from one model of growth to the other against the wider context concerning the formation of ideas and world views ("cosmology") favoring (or blocking) changes.

Sutcliffe's approach (1972: 174–176), in turn, is concentrated on the enumeration of general conditions for the second Industrial Revolution of the turn of the 19th and 20th centuries, and so he refers precisely to the period that overlaps with the subject of my interest. He points out that an independent industrialization calls for a correlation between the processes of shaping a) the domestic market, b) a wide range of industries (including capital goods industries), c) local capital resources, and d) the ability to copy, develop and adopt (or at least to choose) a technology.

A marked change in structure (and rise in the cost) of industrial growth was an important, although sometimes passed over, element that marked the second Industrial Revolution. That was a consequence of the transition from growth based on railroads, steam power and the textile industry to growth stimulated by electricity, steel, engineering and chemical industries. The fact that growth became more expensive, first referred to in Walther Hoffman's typology, and next considered by Kuznets, Chenery and other scholars, inevitably found its reflection in development strategies, that is in the change in the conditions that allow the attainment of the ideal of independent industrialization. Thus, the development of separate capital goods industries–in the case of the United States, in the years 1840–1880–was not an expression of nationalist rent, but an indispensable condition for technical progress and a rise in productivity in the economy

---

[7] These variants sound similar, to a degree, to the Ricardian and Kaldorian models of growth and foreign trade, which refer to the natural factor endowments and to growth based on investments and technical progress, respectively. See Schwarz (1994: 61–63).

as a whole. The picture associated with the first Industrial Revolution, when "[m]achines were, by and large, produced by their ultimate users on an *ad hoc* basis," belongs to the past. The emergence of a specialized sector of machine production was "a major episode ... in the process of industrialization" (Rosenberg 1976: 12; see also Wright 2003: 400, Landes 1998: 302ff).[8] Economic nationalism, which appeared in backward areas on a larger scale at the turn of the 19th and 20th centuries and crystallized in the interwar period, thereby faced a new challenge. To some extent, its prefiguration was the history of the Russian industrialization spurt initiated in Sergei Witte's days.

The question of changes in the character of industrialization involves the problem of the degree to which the first globalization was not so much limited as tightly connected with the consolidation of national economies. This problem can be viewed through the lens of the extent and effects of the internationalization of economic relations. As concerns the internationalization of capital, particularly industrial capital, until 1914 the process had been—taking into account the volume of financial operations—only in its initial stage. At the same time, a relative decline in foreign investments, compared with growth of particular national economies, was characteristic of the post-1918 period, although first and foremost of the 1930s. In major Latin American countries the ratio between the flow of foreign investments and GDP was on the rise between 1900 and 1914 (except in Argentina and Urugway), and declined substantially in 1914–1929 (except in Venezuela and Mexico). Similar trends were observed in foreign trade (Kuznets 1967: chapter 6, Bairoch 1975: 93, 97, Kindleberger 1962: 179–183, Lewis 1949: 147). That, by definition, reduced the mediating role of international competition and the immediate effect of incentives connected with price convergence. It is also against this background that one should interpret the interest in the 'Sombart paradox' also in such peripheral countries as Poland (Rybarski 1932: 86–88).

However, of late, in the discussion focused on the interplay among industrial growth, foreign trade and protectionism, Bairoch and Kozul-Wright

---

[8] The evolution of technical progress that had taken place since the first industrial revolution, brought about fundamental changes in the ratio of consumer goods industries to capital goods industries. In Great Britain in 1851 that ratio was 4.7 to 1, in 1907 only 1.7 to 1, whereas in the USA already in 1880 it was 1.8 to 1. In the successive decades the ratio was 0.7–0.5 to 1. Thus, thinking about the present time, Gould (1973: 385) points out that "capital requirements in most industries for a production unit of optimum size are now enormously larger than a century or two ago." See also Pollard (1981: 221).

have proposed quite a new, revisionist approach. According to them, the tendencies to 'nationalize' economic growth, industrial growth in particular, that were observed in the interwar period, had also appeared during the forty years before 1913, at the height of the first globalization. The authors imply that it is

> economic growth [that] leads to international trade not vice versa. ... during the 20 years following the reintroduction [in the 1870s] of protectionist policies the annual growth of output increased by more than 100 percent and the volume of exports grew by more than 35 percent (Bairoch and Kozul-Wright 1996: 14, 20).

A comparison of the rates of growth of domestic output, exports and productivity suggests a similar conclusion. In the long period of 1890–1938 the growth of GDP and productivity in the major Western European countries and the USA was faster than that of exports. Rapidly industrializing Japan was the reverse example: here the growth of exports was well ahead of the rate of growth of GDP. Also in the period 1913–1938, i.e. of a clearly accentuated decline in the importance of foreign trade, the rate of growth of productivity was on the rise (Saxonhouse 1993: 154 table 6.2).

In the course of the first globalization, conditions of supply and reactions to changes in international demand were thus in great measure formed at the national level, in response to the signals coming from the world market, but not at its exclusive diktat. The globalization was in fact a result of the growth of and ever more intensive competition among developed or just emerging national economies. The role of trade as an 'engine of growth' in the core countries was important but not overwhelming. This was not, however, the case for peripheral economies. Developments taking place in core countries were accompanied by the reopening of Latin America and Central Europe via trade and foreign investments. The "derailed" development of those regions, a unique combination of growth and "increasing backwardness" (Berend 2003, Kula 1979), was also a structural characteristic of the first globalization.

These considerations lead to several conclusions.

National economy without doubt is a non-reducible element of the nationalist conceptions related to the state and an indispensable condition for the fulfillment of the fundamental ideas of political nationalism; it enables the strengthening of political nationalism in the set of long-established material interests, irreducible to ideological epiphenomenon. Even where economic nationalism appears as the ideology of a national group encapsulated within a multinational state, economic nationalism, together with political nationalism, will legitimize attempts to create a peculiar national quasi-economy. Measures taken at the turn of the 19th and 20th centuries by Czechs and Poles were telling in this regard (Albrecht 2001, Chlebowczyk 1983: 326–334, Łuczak 1988: 69–74, 85–94). Bearing the Polish experience of the partitions in mind, Rybarski (2002: 370) wrote: "Nations deprived of sovereignty attempt, nonetheless, to organize their own economic life, to free themselves from the bonds of a foreign state." Nevertheless, he was quick to add, "a nation that has no state of its own shall neither have a national economy in the proper meaning of this word."

National economy is thus a product of historical process, even though it is only in the conditions of industrial revolution and the related first globalization which followed that one can speak of the final shaping of the national economy in the world-system centers. Braudel (1977: 99) emphasized:

> A national economy is a political space, transformed by the state as a result of the necessities and innovations of economic life, into a coherent, unified economic space whose combined activities may tend in the same direction.

Kuzntes (1951: 28. 29, 35), when choosing the sovereign state as "a natural unit in the study of economic growth" in an epoch marked by the dominance of the industrial system, would probably agree. His choice of the unit was based on a history-sensitive approach enabling the satisfaction of three basic criteria: specificity (i.e. the possibility of applying quantitative measures), independence in decision-making and in setting the conditions for economic growth (not, however, eliminating the influence of a "suprastate" and/or "supranational factors") and internal interdependence (i.e. the unit chosen "should not be reducible to subdivisions"). And it is in the complicated interplay between that "natural unit" and its international economic environment that the process of emerging national "inequalities in the rate of growth and differences in its structure" can be tackled.

In a nutshell, like the state, so the national economy too is a key element of a path-dependent development (see also Krasner 1989: 92–94, Kamiński and Kamiński 2004: chapters 2, 5). The fact that national economy is an irreversible (or difficult to reverse) 'investment' defines its role and importance.

Holistic and Particularistic Nationalisms

At this point let me make more specific the relationship between the two variants of economic nationalism and national economy.

In keeping with the approach proposed (Chapter 1), economic nationalism can be defined as, conditioned and legitimized by the ideology of political nationalism, a set of actions undertaken by social groups (and mediating representatives of their interests) within the framework of formal and informal institutions, implying a change in the direction of the country's economic development, and questioning the general equilibriums achieved. Such actions also assume–as a fragment of structural transformations called for or as an independent goal–changes in the distribution of economic gains. As a specific internal and international distributional conflict (including one along the nationals-foreigners axis), economic nationalism brings in the state and is unthinkable beyond its frame. Moreover, it has been pointed out that, depending on the nationalism variant, it focuses either on the maximization of particular gains (*particularistic nationalism*) or on the achievement–in complex interactions between the state and societal actors–of certain collective goods, defined as national interest, including the demand for economic growth and the consolidation and strengthening of the national economy (*holistic nationalism*).

Of course, the authors who referred, even if selectively, to the theoretical proposals of the German Historical School and of nationalism were accustomed to think in terms of 'national interest'. This was the case of Max Weber. He pointed out in 1893 that "[c]olossal illusions were necessary to create the German Reich." Watching, however, with resignation and anger the disintegration of the German political scene following Bismarck's death, he added that "illusions ... fled with the honeymoon of German [political] unity." Weber's favorite case was Prussia. In his view, the short-sighted egoism of the politically and economically declining Junkers was preventing a defense of German interests and *Deutschtum* in the east and was opening the way to the growing presence of the *Polentum* (see Mommsen 1984: 31, Abraham 1991: 43ff). This way, cheap labor of the Polish migrant workers and slow but continuous expansion of land-hungry Polish peasants effectively competed with the task of consolidation of the German economic space. Two years later, in his famous Freiburg inaugural address, "The National State and Economic Policy," after the declaration: "We economic nationalists," he observed, with brutally shocking frankness, that "[f]rom the standpoint of the nation, [Junkers's] large-scale enterprises which can only be preserved at the expense of the German race deserve to go down to destruction" (Weber 1994: 20, 12). However, this was a mere introduction to the main subject of his address.

With equal frankness Weber told the audience that in practical analyses and action, the "political criterion of value" and "nationalist value judgments" were crucial. And he explained: "The economic policy of a German state and, equally, the criterion of value used by a German economic theorist, can ... only be a German policy or criterion." He argued that from the point of view of this criterion, an assessment of the "political maturity" of the classes leading the country (or aspiring to leadership) required answering the question as to their ability to understand that "the ultimate and decisive interests which economic policy must serve are interests of national *power*." The bearer of these long-term economic and political-power interests, the German nation-state, "should have the final and decisive say in all questions of German economic policy." He indicated also that "economic power and the vocation for political leadership of the nation do not always coincide." And finally, his assessment of the German bourgeoisie and its leadership was scornful: "if I ask myself whether the German bourgeoisie has the maturity today to be the leading political class of the nation, I cannot answer this question in the affirmative *today*." After Bismarck's resignation the bourgeois leadership manifested itself in "the petty maneuvering of political epigones." The assessment of the leaders of the workers' movement was equally scornful: "They are wretched minor political talents, lacking the great *power* instincts of a class with a vocation for political leadership" (Weber 1994: 15–17, 20, 23f, 26).

Representatives of the Polish 'national school' also argued in a similar fashion when they were outlining the tasks facing the political and economic elites after 1918, i.e. after the recovery of independence, and in the crisis-ridden 1930s. It is crucial to understand, claimed Rybarski (2002: 362) a year after Poland regained independence, that "national economy is not a side effect of national and social consolidation, but a conscious goal of economic policy." And at the end of the 1930s he emphasized that "particular efforts should be subordinated to the goals of the powerful national economy ... even if it temporarily involved heavy cost" (Rybarski 1997: 253f). In Latin America, in post-revolutionary Mexico, on the other hand, thinking in such categories was expressed in the left-wing semantics. The achievements of the so-called 'national school of economy', shaped in the 1930s and 1940s and associated with the National Autonomous

University of Mexico (UNAM), testify to this.[9] Taking as an example Brazil in the 1930s, Wirth (1970: 13) asserted that "a new kind of economic nationalism had been prepared by the depression."

Incidentally, thinking in terms of 'state' as representing 'the whole', borrowed in many countries from the German academic tradition of the end of the 19th century (*Staatswissenschaft*), exerted also a strong impact on the formation of the political science in the United States at that time. It was understandable that in the Progressive era attention was focused on the state:

> [it] symbolized unity above factional politics; common purpose in place of the seemingly random purposes generated by the constitution; patriotic endeavor over crass, liberal self-interest. ... Consequently the pluralists' attenuated conception of the state and their challenge to the monistic account of sovereignty simply did not ring true to an American political science discipline enamored of a scientific conception of the state and the *Staatslehre* conception of unitary public good (Grady 2002: 2, 3f).

"The interests of the whole people" and "effective State" were also the main threads of the New Nationalism campaign President Theodore Roosevelt launched in 1910. Reference to national interest was meant, among other things, to exorcise the devil of corruption and special interests' selfishness.

The Weberian approach which referred to the nation *and* the state exemplified holistic nationalism in a pure, one can say ideal-typical, form. But at this point I pass over the relationship between this type of nationalism and the 'great power' destiny of Germany, a question on Weber's mind not only in 1890s. Mommsen (1984: chapter 4) in his path-breaking volume analyzed thoroughly this aspect of Weber's political thought. As a result, he devastated to a large extent Parsons' stylized picture of the author of *Economy and Society* as the incarnation of a liberal value-free sociological theorist. That giant of modern sociology was also an ideal representative of German liberal imperialism.

On the other hand, although like the holistic variant, particularistic nationalism, too, refers to the state, nevertheless it aims clearly at eliminating the premise of national economy. Particularistic nationalism

---

[9] Nonetheless, one should not make the following mistake: semantics "was not 'revolutionary socialism' in Marx's sense of the term but rather 'the socialism of the Mexican revolution'," a way of organizing political potential and the "belief" enabling to "pull... Mexico out of economic backwardness" (Babb 2001: 49, 60–67). Put in a nutshell, it was revolutionary nationalism.

fundamentally reinterprets 'national interest': it gets reduced to the level of sectoral interests. Perhaps the history of the US South up until the 1930s reveals most clearly this type of nationalism, a kind of particularistic nationalism of free trade. Peter Molyneaux, a Southerner and a well-known journalist, leveled passionate criticism at the federal government's protectionist policy in the years of the Great Depression, which hit the export interests of the Southern states. He pointed out that, from the historical perspective, the US domestic market had been developed at the diktat of the industrializing states "north of Potomac," behind the shield of high tariffs. At that time the South

> was occupied in providing raw materials for rapidly developing industry in Europe [and] was not primarily concerned with [the domestic] market. It probably had little choice in the matter, but it turned its back on this market (Molyneaux 1933: 32f).

But at the time of crisis the South needed assistance, i.e. a rejection of protectionism. The results of the American Civil War, continued Molyneaux, ruled out other solutions to that matter. Thus the South could no longer repeat the threatening words of Thomas Cooper who after the imposition of tariff in 1824 said that time had come to "calculate the value of the Union" to the cotton states.

Therefore when I write about particularistic nationalism, I point to demands for protection of sectoral interests as part of every form of the domestic market. Developing under the influence of industry, the well-integrated national market is not the only point of reference. Industrial interests do not necessarily represent the idea of holistic nationalism, either. They are the indispensable but not a sufficient condition for the emergence of such nationalism. Bearing the above in mind, there arises a need to introduce a supplementary criterion for the classification of various types of particularistic nationalism. Its point of reference is the structure of national product, its product-mix. Thus, on the basis of this criterion it is possible to distinguish the particularistic nationalism of primary sectors and particularistic nationalism of industrial groups. As a result, we deal with differentiated attitudes of different types of particularistic nationalism toward the domestic market. They all, however, substitute the premise of the national economy with other points of reference.

The situation is different, let me repeat it, in the case of holistic nationalism. It is inconceivable outside the concept of national economy (and 'national interest'). At the same time, this concept implies the point of reference in the form of a diversified structure of the national product (the historically changeable combination of industry and agriculture). Holistic nationalism, defined as both a set of goals and an instrument of economic policy, was to make that ideal real. When summarizing the experience of the interwar period from the perspective of Poland, Tennenbaum (1942: 116) stressed,

> You cannot understand the modern world if you fail to realize that industrialization of unindustrialized countries is not merely a matter of offering jobs, a matter of raising the standard of living, but a matter of national importance.

The German liberal economist grasped well the changes in progress when he wrote in his reflections on the new forms of economic nationalism emerging in 1930s:

> Under the influence of the ideal of national economic stabilization, dominating all other goals of economic policy, economic nationalism has ceased to be limited in aim and character, and now it tends to become 'total' ... with a view to supporting or to making possible a policy of regulating the national economic process as a whole (Röpke 1942: 2002).

A few years earlier, Walter Lippmann (1933: 158, 156) pointed to a new phenomenon when he wrote about "nationally organized economies" and "a new social philosophy." He indicated that the process of building up the former "received its first great impetus from the tariff policy of the United States on the one hand, and from the planned economies of Russia and Italy on the other." The "social philosophy," clearly outlined already at the beginning of the 1930s was expressed in "the fusion of nationalism with collectivism." Lippmann related it first and foremost to the communist economy.

In turn, Sir Arthur Salter, the chief economist of the League of Nations and one of the foremost opponents of the protectionist experiments of the interwar period, was unambiguously more critical, especially after the failed 1933 World Economic Conference. In 1929 he described economic nationalism as "all those tendencies of thought or politics in practice which tend to make the economic unit in the competition of the world not the individual but the nation" (quoted in Hodgson 1933: 48). In 1933 Salter (1933: 181f, 176f) became more radical. He outright rejected the possibility of treating protectionism as a result of the idea and policy going beyond particularistic interests–with a view to public interest. In that rejection Salter was not particularly revealing. Gide and Rist (1916: 282), historians of economic thought, wrote before World War I that "tariff duties are never of the nature of an application of economic doctrines." Decades later

Samuelson (1985: 489) argued likewise that selective protectionism was very seldom based "on the niceties of demand and supply elasticities." In real life it was "a mishmash of political compromises." Therefore Salter's thesis could be read as follows: regardless of the slogans spread, protectionism always subordinated macroeconomic efficiency to the logic of rent-seeking, and this inevitably led to misallocations and inefficient, suboptimal solutions. In a nutshell, Salter ruled out the possibility of the emergence of holistic nationalism. Hence, he defined economic nationalism as "[a] policy composed ... of the sum of sectional demands." Elsewhere he implied that a tariff "is not an expression of national policy, wise or foolish, but a sum of competitive–or corruptly concerted–pressures." Its opposite was a "collective and deliberate," international cooperation-oriented policy that responded to world market incentives. Thus, when writing about the state which "can really make the *res publica* effective over sectional interests," Salter really meant the state capable of standing up to economic nationalism *in toto*–and of restoring the pre-crisis conditions (with certain modifications taking account of the aspirations to diversify the economic structure in particular countries).

Still, the implications of Salter's criticism, seen against the concept of holistic nationalism, are much more complex than his conclusions would indicate. It is so because holistic nationalism was in fact both the negation of the simple "sum of sectional demands" and the "corruptly concerted pressures" and a policy that furthered certain selected group interests. In 1929 Salter was aware of such an interplay between public and private goods (and interests) when he wrote that

> [s]ometimes ... policies [of economic nationalism] use the machinery of government to reinforce the private individual in his competition, sometimes they try so to direct the efforts of the private individual as to make the country nationally stronger in war.

Few years later such interplay disappeared. In 1933, when concentrating attention exclusively on the predominance of the "sum of sectional demands," Salter could have quoted Smith's famous remark (2005: 364): "I have never known much good done by those who affected to trade for public good." In the 20th century it was not that obvious any more. At the time of the Great Depression van Zeeland (1933: 108) noted:

> When ... private business reaches a high degree of extension ... their own interests are so ramified, and cover so vast a field, that they virtually mingle with the general interests of the country itself; and so some of the leaders in such affairs come readily enough to think and to plan in terms of the public

interest, even while they pursue the eventual advantage of their individual enterprise.

One cannot ignore such opinion of the former vice-governor of the National Bank of Belgium. Years earlier, Walther Rathenau, an important representative of modern, vertically integrated branches of German industry, was arguing along similar lines (Pogge von Strandmann 2001: 12–21).

But even if we unreservedly agree with Adam Smith, it will still be impossible to avoid the dilemma and uncertainty related to the preferences of the state (its production function) and the selectivity of its decisions. Like economics, the state "is concerned with allocations and choices" (Heilbroner and Milberg 1995: 107). In holistic nationalism the problem manifests itself directly, which is due to the concept of state understood as a public good and at the same time, if we follow Bob Jessop (1990: 341f, 303), as an institutionalized and relational process of (co)molding the "common interest" and the "common will." In the situation where the state is a "strategically selective terrain," such a process will always be asymmetric, pushing certain interests to the sidelines while privileging others.

Yet, from such a general outline of the role of the state one can deduce directly neither the directions of the choices made nor the quality of the decision-making process. An analysis of the state as a specific "strategically selective terrain" and of the effectiveness of a specific policy of holistic nationalism requires that at least taken into consideration be the following factors: the influence exerted by political nationalism and culture, the way of defining priorities, the results of a particular confrontation between distributive coalitions representing group interests and the "rational ignorance" of the majority of citizens (Olson 1990), perception of external and internal threats, and also the character of the political regime. This seems to be the proper way to understand the varieties of nationalistic practices and the appeal of economic nationalism even if at the end of the day it leads not only to success, but also to suboptimal and even catastrophic results. Polanyi (1957: 154) was fully aware of that when he was analyzing protectionism as a social and cultural phenomenon:

> Once we are rid of the obsession that only sectional, never general, interests can become effective, as well as of the twin prejudice of restricting the interests of human groups to their monetary income, the breadth and comprehensiveness of the protectionist movement lose their mystery.

Moreover, it should be mentioned that both holistic as well as particularistic nationalism is to some extent connected with imperfect competition, an important factor favoring protectionism. However, from a historical perspective, such a relation was neither necessary nor direct. Schumpeter (1975: 100n, 54f) touched upon this problem, writing that "protection of agriculture and a monopoly of agrarian products are entirely different things." From a different angle, Ludwig von Mises (2004) argued similarly: "There can be protectionism in a country with domestic free trade, but where there is no domestic free trade, protectionism is indispensable."

That was an important observation, although one should not forget the adage made popular in the US by the president of the Sugar Trust: "The mother of all trusts is the customs tariff bill." To this we should add: size breeds power, power breeds selectivity and selectivity favors non-market collusions. Schumpeter was far from denying this. His criticism concerned monocausal explanations, i.e. attempts at treating "the monopolistic element ... as the sole *causa causans*" of protectionism (1975: 55). Nevertheless, regarding the period studied we should try to find the main sources of economic nationalism in the underdeveloped countries not so much in the processes that intensified imperfect competition (although this phenomenon must not be ignored), as in the general situation of these countries exposed to strong international competition in a hierarchically structured world economy. That is why Hilferding (1958: 622) and Oskar Lange (1973: 52) after him, in conformity with List but without referring to his deliberations, stressed the differences between the educational protectionism of industrially backward countries and the "high tariff wall meant to stay" of the cartels in developed countries.

On the other hand, however, imperfect competition undoubtedly favored and strengthened demands for protection. And with tariffs and other protectionist measures in place a vicious circle appeared to be unavoidable. This was perfectly clear (see Frieden 2006, Baran 1976). Why it was so was quite a different matter. And the explanation provided by Schumpeter (1974: 78f), which emphasized both the "popular sentiment" and the survival of an "antiquated method of doing business" or the mélange of "small entrepreneur groups" with "non-capitalist element," did not sound persuasive. Anyhow, it was much easier to expound particularistic interests and press for protectionism in the case of 'trustified' sectors than in the case of competitive branches of production. In specific situations, big companies, but large rural estates as well, thus also were among the leading initiators, not just supporters and beneficiaries, of particularistic nationalism. In the interwar period, in backward countries where budding modern, large-scale business was as a rule connected with the state, nationalistic appeals almost automatically became more attractive and operationally more effective. To a certain extent the appeals coming from these sectors complemented the traditional nationalistic invocations made by agrarian elites, particularly at the time of crisis.

Digression: The State

Except in the cases of colonies and/or nations encapsulated in imperial structures, economic nationalism (just as political nationalism) without the state or the "milieux in which the existence of the state is ... very much taken for granted" (Gellner 2006: 4) is an empty set. Nonetheless, even in the cases of nations deprived of their own statehood the state-centered nationalism frequently appears as a policy goal and/or an important point of reference in their aspiration to change an existing political and economic order. When analyzing the concepts of Zygmunt Balicki, one of the founders of modern Polish nationalism at the turn of the 19th and 20th centuries, Joanna Kurczewska (1979: 276) pointed out that that nationalism had acted as a major substitute: it served as a "clandestine Polish state" or a "country in a state of emergency [at the time of the partitions]."

However, in a historical perspective the relationship between capital (and capitalism) and the state cannot be reduced to competition/cooperation within the already established national and international institutional frameworks (encompassing also the hierarchic structure of the world economy). The transition leading to the establishment of the state-capital nexus, the processes which each time bring about new political and economic structures and new equilibrium are as important as the equilibrium itself. In a word, it is impossible to understand the history of the market economy without the simultaneous understanding of not only the history of the world economy, but also the history of the state and other important elements of modernity, like war or the role of luxury (see Sombart 1913a, 1913b). As Niels Steensgaard (1981: 272) observed, "the coincidence of two unique historical phenomena: the rise of the modern state and the rise of capitalism" is a basic problem and, let me add, a continually unraveling mystery of the history of modernity.[10]

---

[10] From the perspective of historical sociology, the issue was discussed by Weber (1966: 249): "Out of ... [the] alliance of the state with capital ... arose the national citizen class, the bourgeoisie in the modern sense of the word. Hence, it is the closed national state which afforded to capitalism its chance for development." See also O'Brien (2003: 32), Hobson (2004), Chang (2005). Needless to say, the bibliography of works dealing with state-formation and its relationship with the rise of capitalism is voluminous.

First, let a historian speak.

Fernand Braudel paid attention to the significant aspect of that process, connected with the natural limitations of the concept of the state when confronted with the concept of power. Thinking about the state, we usually refer to Weber's (1978: 54) succinct remark that "[a] compulsory political organization with continuous operations will be called a 'state' insofar as its administrative staff successfully upholds the claim to the *monopoly* of the *legitimate* use of physical force in the enforcement of its order." For Braudel (1992a: 555), in turn, the crucial concept of power cannot be reduced to the concept of the state. For one should bear in mind that

> the *power apparatus*, the might that pervades and permeates every structure, is something more than the state. It is the sum of the political, social, economic and cultural hierarchies, a collection of means of coercion where the state's presence is always felt, where it is often the keystone of the whole, but where it is seldom if ever *solely* in control.

Thus, Braudel's approach both embraces and at the same time goes beyond Weber's laconic definition. We know, however, that Weber linked the concept of the modern state with the appearance of rational bureaucracy. The phenomenon of the dispersion and the multidimensionality of authority, stressed by Braudel, can be traced in Weber's comments on incomplete separation between rational bureaucracy and property and economic interests (see Badie and Birnbaum 1983: 20–23). Incidentally, it is worth noting at this point that the question of rational bureaucracy acquires key significance also in the context of the escape from backwardness, in the conceptualization of the developmental state (Evans 1995: 29f).

Braudel's comments point out, though, an important phenomenon, namely an unceasing interaction between the state as the basic element of the hierarchy of power and its other dimensions. Such an interaction involves–which is of special interest to me–also direct participants to economic conflict/cooperation and representations of their interests. Taking a wider perspective, one can notice also basic similarities between Braudel's observations and Polanyi's (1957: 46, 67) concept of the state and other economic categories as 'embedded' in social relations. Thus we have to deal not only with the question of the role of the state, but first and foremost with the problem connected of building a state of *effective* economic nationalism.

In the two basic variants of economic nationalism singled out, the state and its machinery occupy important, although different, places. Let me briefly consider this problem, referring to approaches which take as their basic premise the competitive nature of the international system together with the concepts of the state as an "actor" and an "arena."

Within the international competitive system the state tries first and foremost to influence the conditions of the presence of actors participating in the economic race and of their bargaining power. It is one of its most basic functions in both types of economic nationalism. This is a natural consequence of international competition among states, as Theda Skocpol asserts (1979: 23), following Otto Hinze. Wallerstein (2000: passim), in turn, emphasizes the conflict between functionally structured European world-economy on the one hand, and the multitude of competing political structures and cultures on the other. In both cases the state appears, as in realist and neorealist theories, as a unitary actor who has at his disposal organizational and financial potential that allows it to take part in international bargaining (Waltz 1979, Gilpin 2001: 15ff). In the case of holistic nationalism such bargaining concerns the place of a specific national economy (and the state) in the hierarchical structure of the world economy and determines "the amount of elbow-room in the world" (Weber 1994: 16). In the case of particularistic nationalism, the state takes part, first of all, in the conflicts over the distribution of benefits among nationally different private competitors.

Tariff policies, export subsidies, exchange rates, government expenditures, regulations concerning foreign capital, etc., all these instruments of state policy define the framework within which contact with the 'foreigner' (states, firms) takes place; at the same time such a framework makes favoring the 'ours' (or 'our' state) possible. Yet, from the structure of these instruments, their technical perfection or deficiencies, one cannot deduce their effect.

In the case of particularistic nationalism, this type of activity of the state is the outcome of the game played and the impact exerted by private interests. "The state-as-political arena" (Skocpol 1979: 25) seems best to define precisely the relationship between the state and societal actors under particularistic nationalism. Still, Skocpol contests such a model of the state too hastily. The oligarchic state in Latin America–a case reflecting the concept of the state-as-political-arena–related *grosso modo* to the century preceding the 1930s was a reality. In certain countries it implied a pattern of functional relations (often also personal ones) between the dominant interest groups and the state, which considerably limited the state apparatus's possibility of autonomization. Meanwhile, the frequently dictatorial regimes of the 20th century caudillos unquestionably were autonomous in the political sphere, and in extreme cases one can speak about their transformation into "sultanistic regimes" (Chehabi and Linz 1998). As a rule that did not mean autonomy vis-à-vis the dominant economic groups, although it increased immensely the opportunity to pillage and/or distort resource and wealth allocation. In the case of small countries it also meant a small or zero margin of freedom in international relations. Also in Brazil, despite the *economic* autonomy of the state, increasing in the period of the Old Republic (1889–1930), the concept of the oligarchic state made sense. The leading theoretician of Brazilian developmental nationalism described it ironically as *Estado Cartorial* (literally the notarial state or sinecure state), which

> includes the middle class in an ever-expanding military and civilian bureaucracy ... actually providing more or less useless jobs for political clientele. This system preserves the status quo and maintains ... the oligarchical rule of the establishment (Jaguaribe 1969: 395).

Also, the concept of the patrimonial state was an attempt to grasp the precarious equilibrium between the autonomy of the state and its intimate relation with the then economically dominant elites, a process that had been growing as early as during the Old Republic. The famous coffee valorization scheme from 1906–about which more later in the book–was an example of both strengthened state autonomy and of the victory of the coffee *fazendeiros*. The key trait of the patrimonial state was "the absence of mobilization in the political system and the consensus among the elites on limiting popular participation" (Roett 1978: 28). Luiz Carlos Bresser Pereira (2009a: 143ff) is more specific when defining the Brazilian state until 1930 as the oligarchic patrimonial state: a mélange of a patrimonial status group of déclassé aristocratic *senhores da terra* and of the rising middle-class politicians, the military and bureaucrats, relatively autonomous vis-à-vis dominant coffee and other rural-based interests, and supported during the Old Republic by local oligarchic bosses–*os coronéis*.

One can also imply that the model of the state as a "civil association," corresponding to the tradition of Smith and Hume,[11] is a particular variant of the state-as-political arena, although referring to conditions other than in Latin America and Central Europe. Such a variant, it should be stressed,

---

[11] A concept of such a state as well as of its opposite, i.e. the state as an "enterprise association," was propounded by Michael Oakeshott. See Lal (2001: 111ff). This applies also to functionalist and pluralist theories of the state (a variant of the Marxist theory of the state included). See Badie and Birnbaum (1983: 3–11), Jessop (2001).

is not identical to the concept of a weak state. Far from it. It involves, however, a particular kind of relationship between its political and decision-making potential and the mediating representations of societal actors. Hence, with regard to Great Britain, this relationship is described in the following way: although the central authority "is more powerful than that of any other democracy ... the relative power of the British state vis-à-vis British society is sharply limited" (Rockman 1989: 183; see also Friedman 1997: 21).

In the case of holistic nationalism, the above-mentioned instruments of state intervention and mediation are applied with greater intensity, and their economic and political sense is changed. This is due to a different political and social context in which they are put into action. I mean here first and foremost the change of the point of reference (national economy) and the appearance of new actors taking part in the game. The most important of them is the state itself, which is "more than a simple vector of given [social and economic] forces" (Wallerstein 1974: 355). Let me once again refer here to Skocpol's terminology (1979: 29). She insists that we should "take the state seriously as a macro-structure. The state properly conceived is no mere arena in which socioeconomic struggles are fought out." State bureaucracy asserts its independence, creates its particular interests and area of activity, its own clients and social environment. Meanwhile, inter-state competition forces moves that in certain situations can lead to a temporary questioning of the dominant private interests or to a strong intervention in market mechanisms. Autonomy of this kind can be expressed in various ways, which Jagdish Bhagwati (1989: 98–100) describes as issuing "prescriptions" or "proscriptions." The advantage of the former over the latter does not lie in being immune to mistakes, but in leaving a vast area to individual enterprise not subjected to meticulous state regulations. That is why inasmuch as proscriptive governments "are more likely to be adversarial to private entrepreneurship," prescriptive governments show a greater inclination toward "a symbiotic relationship with private entrepreneurs." This is not always the case as far as "proscriptions" are concerned (*viz*. different forms of limiting imperfect competition), but this question can be omitted for now.

Nonetheless the neorealist paradigm focused on the growing autonomy of the state does not suffice not just from the point of view of the general theory of the modern state or historical sociology of international relations (see Jessop 1990: 278–288; Hobson 2002: passim). Without pondering here the question that has been intensely discussed for many years, suffice to point to Bresser Pereira's interesting hypothesis (1993: 1338f) that "state intervention expands and contracts cyclically, and ... in each new cycle the mode of state intervention changes." Consequently, accepted can be neither those static theories "which assume a given level of state intervention as ideal" nor those assuming the "long-term tendency toward the statization of the economy."

Presumably such a cycle can be reconstructed with regard to the first globalization, although the relationship between such a cycle and economic fluctuations is not clear. One can imply, however, a relationship between such cyclical fluctuations and the approach Kalecki proposed in an article on the political business cycle as early as 1943. The intensity of state intervention, its level and structure were closely related to the intensity of the economic and political shock caused by the Great Depression. In that context, he wrote, the taboo of deficit spending and full employment was broken. However, there was no guarantee that the lesson would be remembered in the long run. The state-financed bailout of the market economy was also a lesson about how the strength of the state could be manipulated by powerful coalitions resenting full employment mainly on political grounds (Kalecki 1972). In a word, cyclical fluctuations in state intervention, mentioned by Bresser Pereira, in fact, reflected the changing impact of political and economic conflicts on the acceptable level of employment/unemployment. Reaching long-term equilibrium that would meet the conditions of the first-best solution was not pre-determined. As Acemoglu (2003: 648) accurately observed, "efficiency considerations cannot be separated from distributional conflict." The way this dilemma was settled largely determines the direction of the cyclical fluctuations in state intervention.

The neorealist paradigm is unsatisfactory also with regard to an economic nationalism-state. Certainly, in many underdeveloped countries, in view of the weakness of the social groups able to become a point of reference for holistic nationalism, the autonomous state emerges as the organizer, coordinator and frequently a unique agency able to take measures to realize such nationalism. In a word, it acts as an "enterprise association." This means easing the restrictions imposed on the state's decision-making potential, widening its production function and reformulating its intermediary functions with regard to societal actors (Rockman 1989: 195f). However, autonomy of this kind, as long as it is expressed in a zero-sum game between the state and 'the rest', may easily lead to the emergence of an anti-developmental "predatory state" (Evans 1995: 45ff).

That was not, however, the case in the areas examined, especially in respect of bigger states. When referring to them, one should rather underline, in a context wider than the one outlined by Bhagwati, the question of "symbiotic relationship," the process setting "the limits and identities" to both the state and society, and also the selectivity of the decision process (Jessop 1990: passim). Barkey and Parikh (1991: 545f) presented the question in a similar way when they indicated that the borderline between the state-centered and society-centered approaches was in point of fact fluid: "variables such as autonomy, capacity, and state strength are usually defined in relation to society." This was however a generous interpretation. Hobson (2002: 70) is less generous when criticizing the approach taken by Skocpol, a co-founder of the "first-wave Weberian historical sociology." According to him, Skockpol's theorizing about the state "merely reproduces a pure neo-realist logic."

If effective holistic nationalism is expressed in the developmental state, such a state must combine autonomy with rational bureaucracy and embeddedness, where the latter "implies a concrete set of connections that link the state intimately and aggressively to particular social groups with whom the state shares a joint project of transformation" (Evans 1995: 12, 59, 72). Such a state is thus feasible only as long as it combines "internal cohesiveness" and the loyalty of bureaucracy with "dense external ties." In crisis situations cooperation and/or competition between the state and societal actors and representatives of their interests acquire special importance (Gourevich 1986).[12] The existence of such ties does not imply a mere passive adjustment. Autonomy, meaning the ability to impose selective choice, assumes that "institutions may alter their own environment," and thus influence the "distribution of power among social groups in civil society" (Krasner 1989: 88).

Last but not least, in the period under study the political form of the regimes pursuing a policy of holistic nationalism was not predetermined. Examples of democratic governments in the Western offshoots, in Czechoslovakia and in Chile, which practiced economic nationalism intensively, justify such an opinion. On the other hand, however, with

---

[12] At this point I pass over the problem of the 'technical' aspects of autonomy and rational bureaucracy. Referring to contemporary Latin America, Portes and Smith (2008: 108) name three conditions indispensable for effective bureaucracy of the developmental state: meritocratic recruitment and promotion, resistance to bribe taking and to "captivation" by special interests, absence of entrenched "islands of power" capable of subverting institutional rules to their own ends. In the interwar period the creation of such bureaucracy in Latin America and Central Europe was only at its beginning. Perisinotto (2003) depicts this process interestingly against the example of conflicting interests of the state and the coffee elite in Brazil until 1930.

regard to the majority of countries in both regions, one can speak of at least concurrence between the anti-liberal state, attempts at top-down corporatism, economic nationalism and an industrialization drive. Thus, in his interesting analysis of fascist Italy, A. James Gregor (1979: 312, 328) suggests distinguishing, within the category of developmental state, the sub-category of developmental dictatorship, i.e. an attempt at grasping "a functional connection between development and totalitarianism."[13]

In fact it was not a novel approach. In Latin America of the 1970s, the affinity between industrial development and the authoritarian regimes was an intensely debated issue. Although the debate focused on post-WWII developments, particularly in Brazil and Argentina from the mid-1960 onward, nevertheless the basic question about the functional connection related not just to that particular period of Latin American history.

The debate concentrated on the concept of the bureaucratic-authoritarian political systems, which was an attempt at interpreting the political-military response to economic, social and political problems mounting at the beginning of the transition to the new capital-intensive stage of import substitution industrialization (O'Donnell 1979a, 1979b). One can thus speak of a strong affinity between the type of political regime and the achieved level of economic and social modernization. At a more general level, a similar theoretical conceptualization of Latin America's historical development was propounded by Florestan Fernandes (1975: 292) who pointed out "a strong pragmatic divergence between capitalist development and democracy." A similar suggestion one can find in Kohli's (2004) explanation of the concept of the nationalistic "cohesive-capitalist state."

Without going into details of that important debate, I wish to make two brief comments here: first, touching upon the relation between the bureaucratic-authoritarian state and the choice of the policy package; second, concerning the political autonomy of authoritarianism.

Regarding the first point, in the case of Latin America one can with certainty say today that in the 1930s authoritarianism was not a sine qua non of an effective anti-crisis macroeconomic policy. Fernando Henrique Cardoso's (1979: 51f) observation that "[i]t is not correct to deduce from

---

[13] However, the excessive use of the concept of 'totalitarianism' raises doubts. From the moment Juan Linz (1975) proposed a precise distinction between totalitarian and authoritarian regimes, confusing the two should be avoided. Therefore in my own approach, I treat fascism and communism as categories sui generis, separate from the developmental authoritarian system.

the formal character of authoritarian regimes what type of economic growth policies they will pursue" and that "it seems impossible to identify a one-to-one correspondence between forms of authoritarian regimes and a set of homogenous economic interests" is fully applicable to the period under study. The authoritarianism of the 'developmental' Estado Nôvo differed markedly from the authoritarian and economically conservative rule of general Oscar R. Benavides in Peru. What is more, in the 1930s industrialization could be carried out by an authoritarian-populist regime–as in Brazil, by a conservative regime–as in Argentina, or a democratic regime–as in Chile (Díaz-Alejandro 1984: 47, Kaufman 1990: 119). However, as regards East and Central Europe, historians have not reached a consensus on the matter yet. Although certain countries under authoritarian rule (Poland, Hungary, Bulgaria) attained in the interwar period slightly better results than democratic Czechoslovakia, still, the same could not be said about Romania or Yugoslavia. The correlation between the level of development and transition to the modern economy on the one hand and authoritarianism on the other seems to have been weak (Good 2003: 148, 149f; see also Berend 1998, Hofbauer and Komlosy 2000). Despite such inconclusive findings regarding the 1930s, Kofman (1997: 204f) does not rule out the possibility that changes initiated at that time in Poland, Latvia and Estonia were the beginning of the long-term structural transformation.

But what did make authoritarian-populist developmental systems different from conservative regimes were the answers given to growing distributional conflicts. In the period under study, it was of considerable significance to Brazil, but also, although later, to Argentina. Unlike the Brazilian authoritarian Estado Nôvo, which in a tightly controlled fashion was co-opting workers and other urban classes, in the 1930s the divided Argentine conservative elite paid scant attention to mounting demands for the social and economic inclusion of the 'lower classes'. Some progress notwithstanding, "it was still true that only a minority of workers belonged to unions were covered by accident insurance or pension schemes, or were able to participate more than marginally in the benefits of economic growth" (Lewis 1990: 126). This can be a partial explanation of the delayed and forceful emergence of Peronism in the 1940s (Kaufman 1990: 119).

As concerns the second point, it should be stressed that the authoritarian form of the state and its policy only in part resulted from the economic conditions and the related challenges. Authoritarianism was not solely or even primarily an instrument to enforce (and safeguard) economic change and developmental ideology. Fernandes' above quoted hypothesis delinking democracy and capitalist development in Brazil should not be interpreted as historically predetermined. What is more, in many Latin American and East and Central European countries the emergence of authoritarian systems bore no relation whatsoever to developmental goals. Authoritarianism was first and foremost an autonomous political institution, a response to political and social conflicts, and only indirectly a reaction to economic crisis and the related economic challenges. To explain the phenomenon of authoritarianism (its developmental variant included) requires a reference, first of all, to the autonomy of the political sphere and the theoretical perspectives focused on political conflict and collective action. To put it differently: one should not attribute the sources of the interwar 'Czechoslovak (democratic) anomaly' to the weakness of economic nationalism and lack of developmental ideology. Quite the opposite, economic nationalism was relatively strong and institutionally well entrenched in Czechoslovakia. The sources of this 'anomaly' should rather be attributed to the social and political environment which made the combination of economic nationalism (particularly agrarian nationalism), developmental ideology and the democratic agenda possible.

And at the end, let me add that in East and Central Europe the emergence of authoritarian regimes was connected with a certain additional factor, which was largely absent in Latin America: "objectively, in the 1930s [authoritarianism] acted as a neutralizing agent in the face of a danger from radical movements, chiefly fascism but also communism" (Kofman 1997:192). In Brazil, aborted revolts of communist-backed Aliança Nacional Libertadora and fascist Ação Integralista Brasileira were a pretext rather than a major reason to impose and subsequently to strengthen an authoritarian regime. The factor mentioned by Kofman heightens the autonomous nature of authoritarianism even more. It also points to the complex process of adopting fascist models, although until the outbreak of WWII a fully-fledged fascist regime had emerged in none of the regions under study, while strong fascist tendencies had been observed in a few countries only.[14]

---

[14] In the majority of cases authoritarian regimes in East and Central Europe did not oppose selective imports of fascist or Nazi models. However, the way they were adopted in point of fact, at least until the outbreak of WWII, had blocked the fascist parties' road to victory (Borejsza 1981, Rothschild 1974).

CHAPTER FOUR

AGAINST 'WISHES AND DREAMS': FOREIGN CAPITAL AND ECONOMIC NATIONALISM

FOREIGN CAPITAL AS THE ENEMY?

Many 20th-century attempts at theorizing about economic nationalism approach the question of foreign capital, and more broadly speaking, of 'foreigners' as its invariable, constitutive, element. They treat the interventionist state likewise. I do not question this. But my approval goes only thus far. The way both these questions are tackled seems to constitute one of the most controversial fragments of the conceptualization of economic nationalism. It is worth remembering here that, according to Breton (1995: 98f; see also 1964), "economic nationalism revealed itself in the allocation of resources to alter the distribution of tangible (measured) assets or wealth between the 'foreigners' and the 'nationals' of a jurisdiction."

From the historical perspective, the place of foreign capital and state in the nationalist discourse, emphasized by Breton and other scholars, was not predetermined. One can imply, however, that the relevant changes were to some extent correlated with the evolution of nationalist ideas (Chapter 5). But in this case also, there was nothing automatic, especially regarding the relationship between the evolution of nationalist ideas and the perception of benefits and threats related to foreign capital. During the transformation of liberal nationalism into integral nationalism, this important element of the nationalist syndrome in practical policy appeared as an example of moderation and caution of a kind. Except for the elites and ideological trends hostile to change or being in favor of a radically different order, never in the period under study was the often sharp criticism, aimed at foreign economic domination, an expression of a theoretical dogma. More often than not it was a matter of circumstances. After all is said and done, the notion of 'foreigner', too, had many dimensions. Not only foreign companies but also national minorities were perceived as a 'foreign' internal threat.

Therefore, while raising the matter of circumstances, I suggest at the same time that the rhythm of development of political ideas, and the rhythm of 'economy' demonstrated a considerable degree of autonomy.

In addition, internal diversity of economic nationalism complicated a possible synchronization.

Incomplete synchronization created and maintained tensions first of all between the idea and practice of *political nationalism*. As the idea political nationalism ever more insistently multiplied exclusive rights, trying to duplicate the ideal of culturally closed community and/or ethnic 'uniqueness'. Real or imagined external threats worked toward the same goal. However, as practice such nationalism inevitably was a compromise between the doctrine and unpredictability. As a result, faced with threats, the formation of in-group identity and cohesion appeared as a never ending process resembling moving along the asymptote. All the more so that the source of such threats usually was–at least in the eyes of ideologues–the external environment, and also its internal 'agents'. Nationalist policy could only partially control these. Lack of precision and fluidity were thus inbuilt into the evolution of political nationalism.

Tensions built into political nationalism were bound to affect the perception of *economic nationalism*. From the historical perspective, lack of synchronization was, although with a few exceptions, just as striking. Transformation of liberal political nationalism into integral nationalism only partly accounted for the way the elements of economic nationalism and their importance were perceived. Even in the holistic variant, continuously rising hostility toward foreign capital was not inevitable. In this case incoherence appeared as a dilemma: a clash between political nationalism in its new, integral and illiberal form versus the requirements of the implementation of the nationalistic idea as an economic project. In the 19th century the dilemma looked as follows:

> Poland did not have sufficient capital, credit, technological know-how or machines, nor the industrialists and mechanics, or even an adequately qualified labor force, to create and manage industry independently. ... Nevertheless, the wish for industry and commerce to be strong without foreigners managing them and drawing profits from them was to be one of the *leitmotifs* of Polish economic nationalism throughout the nineteenth century. ... This is the dream of the middle class and the intelligentsia of every developing country (Jedlicki 1999: 44).

'The wishes' and 'dreams' Jedlicki quoted reflected emphatically the tension and lack of synchronization between the ideal and the practice of economic nationalism.

It is not a paradox that conceptually coherent theories of economic nationalism appeared in the regions under study, except for the ideas borrowed first of all from List, relatively late. The nationalist economic practice of the end of the 19th century, strengthened in the 1930s, was atheoretical, particularly in Latin America. According to Victor Bulmer-Thomas (2003: 398), in Latin America the crucial turn toward theories emphasizing internal development "began too slowly ... and went on for too long. In the 1930s and even the 1940s the export-led growth model was still seen as providing the only coherent long-run option in many republics." Joseph L. Love (1996b: 209) drew attention to the fact that in practice, it looked somewhat differently. "Industrialization in Latin America," he observed, "was fact before it was policy, and policy before it was theory." A similar assessment can be found in Stephen Haber's (2006: 538) concise analysis of Latin American industrialization: "economists in the 1950s gave intellectual legitimacy to developments already taking place." Incidentally, the fascinating discussion on the role of foreign capital in the Russian economy up until 1917 and on the type of capitalism that emerged in the empire, 'denationalists' and 'nationalists' held in the USSR in the 1920s, has remained a forgotten episode in the intellectual and political history of the Soviet Union.[1] Last but not least, in the countries which, like Japan, had never experienced a long-lasting exposure to the European world economy in the period preceding the Meiji Restoration, the formation of economic nationalism was nothing but a manifestation of the birth of capitalism and modernity. Exaggerating a bit, nevertheless rendering the essence of that basic relationship, Greenfeld (2001: 326) writes that "Japanese nationalism from the outset was focused on the economy and developed as economic nationalism in the first place" (see also Boulanger 2002).

That was only at the height of Latin American import substitution industrialization (ISI), i.e. in the 1950s and at the beginning of the 1960s, that there appeared a politically expansive conception of developmental nationalism ('national capitalism'), in its theoretical aspect dominated by structural approaches and 'inward-oriented growth'. One of its variants, the best known, were theses presented from the end of the 1940s by ECLA/CEPAL and in works by Raúl Prebisch. The division of the world into the

---

[1] In the Polish literature the discussion has been presented by Knothe (1985). 'Denationalists', in their approach close to the critics of Witte, saw in foreign capital a real threat and a factor transforming Russia into a colony. On the other hand, 'nationalists', who, in fact, shared Witte's optimistic vision, emphasized Russia's ability to assimilate foreign capital (especially the industrial one) without losing control over the country's economy as a whole. If we disregard the political instrumentalization of 'denationalists' by Stalin (from backing them to accusing them of 'Trotskyism'), their arguments will appear independently several decades later in different variants of the dependency theory.

center and periphery, secular worsening of terms of trade, development of industry and the role of the state, these and other questions were the visiting card of the new ideology and economic policy (Love 1996a, 1996b, Rostow 1990: 403–407, Cardoso 1979b). Less known was the Brazilian variant of developmental nationalism, developed in the 1950s by first and foremost the Instituto Superior de Estudos Brasileiros (ISEB), and especially by Hélio Jaguaribe and Werneck Sodré (Toledo 1998, Oliveira Filho 2007).

A response to ISEB's developmental nationalism was the São Paulo school of sociology (Florestan Fernandes, Fernando Henrique Cardoso, Octavio Ianni and others), skeptical of the 'national capitalism' thesis. In the preface to the English edition of their already classical statement of 'situations of dependency' analysis, Cardoso and Faletto (1979: xxiv) made it clear that their expectations concerning the capitalist development of the peripheral countries were very limited. What is more,

> It is not realistic to imagine that capitalist development will solve basic problems for the majority of the population. ... what has to be discussed as an alternative is not the consolidation of the state and the fulfillment of 'autonomous capitalism,' but how to supercede them.[2]

The appearance in the mid-1960s of a critical dependency theory(ies), next developed into an already less popular theory of 'autocentric development' (see Senghaas 1985) coincided with the crisis of 'national capitalism' and the ISI in the ECLA/CEPAL variant. In this respect Latin America undoubtedly was the pioneer in the Third World. The countries of the second decolonization went through these stages with a marked delay.

The crisis of the Latin American way of theorizing on 'national capitalism' and the crisis of the specific nationalist practice, however, did not spell the ultimate end of economic nationalism as a global phenomenon. The non-conclusive example of Latin America, until the mid-1960s followed with certain modifications by South East Asia countries (Golay, Anspach, Pfanner and Ayal 1969), made a contrasting background for the efficient East Asian variant of economic nationalism. The latter countries, after the not excessively prolonged ISI stage, at the time of the Latin American crisis were just starting on their march to modernity, coupling strong state intervention (*dirigisme*) with earlier land reforms, outward orientation and an export push strategy (Bradford, Jr. 1990: 33). That strategy made use of nearly all the instruments of economic nationalism,

---

[2] Thus, Kohli's (2009: 387) stylized interpretation of Cardoso from the 1960s and 1970s as a supporter of the "national capitalist model of development" seems misleading.

but also of such parameters as "culture" or "cosmology" (according to Lal's terminology). In a nutshell, "states and economies in Asia have been more nationalist and autonomous than in Latin America" (Kohli 2009: 387). At the same time the successful strategy of rapid industrialization and outward orientation was devoid of superfluous attacks and generalized accusations aimed at foreign capital. In a brief and accurate statement Barbara Stallings (1990: 55–58) described those different experiences as a confrontation of two paradigmatic conceptualizations: Latin American *modernization-dependency debate*, focused on the negative influence on and the contribution of foreign capital to the development, versus East Asian *statist-dependency debate* which, while looking more favorably at the role of specific kinds of foreign capital, at the same time portrayed the state "as capable of using foreign capital, rather than the other way around." The East Asian experience with foreign capital demystified its role: "The question of whether foreign investment helps or hurts economic growth is probably a wrong question. ... much depends on the terms on which FDI comes into a developing country" (Kohli 2009: 397, 391). Incidentally, the viability of national capitalist development, confirmed by the example of Asian countries, contributed several years later to the reemergence of the substantially revised concept of national capitalism and 'national-dependent development' in Brazil grounded in national strategy aiming "to defend national labor, knowledge and capital" (Bresser Pereira 2009b: 24).

Nevertheless, until the end of the 1930s, the lack of coherence and conceptual lagging behind the circumstances-led practice of industrialization and economic nationalism were striking. One of the few exceptions was the theory of protectionism (and industrialization) of Mihail Manoilescu, the Romanian economist (with fascist leanings) and theoretician of corporatism. Despite the criticism of mainstream economists (Jacob Viner and Bert Ohlin), relatively quickly his arguments found supporters both in certain Central European countries as well as among Brazilian economists and politicians (Kofman 1997: 14ff, Love 1996a: passim, Irwin 1966: chapter 10). In the 1930s, Werner Sombart gained some popularity too.[3] His gloomy analyses of the changes, which were at that

---

[3] By the way, it was in the second edition of Sombart's monumental work (1928: XIV) where the division into the "center" (Great Britain and Western Europe, and the east coast of the United States) and "peripheral countries" appeared. The former *"sind die führenden, aktiven Nationen,"* while the latter are *"die dienenden, passive Länder."* Love (1996a: 222) and FitzGerald (1994: 94f) suggest that Prebisch could adopt that dichotomy precisely from Sombart.

time in-progress, and the future of capitalism were known, among others, in Poland, but also in Chile (Stemplowski 1996: 401). They included ominous predictions for the developed countries of *Spätkapitalismus*: First, "'[e]mancipation of the colored' [will] proceed... at full speed;" second, contrary to expectations, industrialization of the peripheries is by no means tantamount to growth of industrial exports from Europe or the USA (Sombart 1932: 35–39). The second prediction, hotly debated among economists at the time (Kenwood and Lougheed 1971: 233ff), proved wrong, from both the medium- and long-term perspectives.

Let me once more go back for a moment to List and his *System*. Forestalling critics so to speak List admitted that initially protected industrial products would be more expensive and technically backward than the British ones. That was a truism. As the stern opponent of development planning observed ironically years ago, if you subsidize any production, by definition it is unprofitable (Bauer 1972: 143). The author of the *System* maintained optimistically, however, that behind that temporary waste lay not so much a nationalist rent, causing distortions in resource allocation (as in the Breton-Johnson model), as the rent expressed in an expected increase in production potential (List 1922: 117). In a word, there was a chance to shape new, more favorable factor endowments. Schumpeter (1974: 90), although far from supporting protectionist policies, also pointed out that "[a]ll tariffs, rights, and the like became the seed bed for economic growth that could have neither sprung up nor maintained itself without them." One of the basic methods of limiting the negative effects of the use of educational tariffs that List proposed (1922: 183), was, on the one hand, selective protectionism and support for domestic market competition, and transfer of foreign capital on the other. At this point, List gave up 'macroeconomics' for the 'microeconomics' of protectionism.[4]

In the light of the post-WWII experience of economic nationalism, List's favorable attitude toward foreign capital was surprising. In the second half of the 20th century, in many Latin American countries it would probably be construed as representing the opinion of "nation-selling" elites (*vendepatrias*). In passing, this was the term used in special circumstances in 1896 by Argentinian socialist Juan B. Justo, otherwise an enthusiastic supporter of free trade. The dramatic collapse of the powerful

---

[4] Therefore Greenfeld (2003: 203) does not sound convincing when she maintains that the author of the *System*, being fascinated by the nation's economic power alone, attached little importance to individual welfare. Earlier, such an opinion on economic nationalism after WWI was forced through by Gregory (1933: 56).

British Baring Brothers Bank provoked a violent nationalist campaign in Argentina, aimed at both the Argentine government and British capital. So much, and only so much.

However, it is worth recalling that until WWII the attitude toward foreign capital of many programs of economic nationalism, unlike that toward imports of goods, was not unambiguously negative. Certainly, in economic practice attacks on foreign companies were not generalized. Needless to say, so to speak by definition, critical of foreign companies and generally of foreign influence were the eulogists of the rustic past and, for other reasons, after 1917 the communist movement. Nor will we find slogans of economic nationalism, understood as an attack on foreign capital *in toto*, among the main program demands of the Mexican revolution.[5] It is worthwhile paying some attention to this issue.

In an interesting study on the pre-revolutionary northern state of Chihuahua where the presence of foreign investors was very much accentuated, Mark Wassermann (1973: 309f) points out that "the anti-north-American sentiments were not dominant ones either before or at the beginning of the revolution." It was the powerful, oligarchic Luis Terrazas–Enrique Creel family which was the main enemy of the revolting middle class in that state (see also Knight 2000: 134). In the successive years of the revolution the situation changed, but not dramatically: American companies became easy prey (through heavy taxation and forced contributions) for both the government of President Carranza as well as Pancho Villa, who was ruling in the north. After the adoption in 1917 of the constitution that nationalized natural resources, US oil firms behaved as if nothing happened: they ran at full steam. Devastations and investment restrictions applied primarily to foreign-owned mines and to landed property (Wilkins 1974: 36ff).

It is only at the beginning of the 1920s that an essential change in the investment strategy of oil companies took place. Venezuela, firmly in the hands of the dictator Gómez, became their main partner. But also under the Presidents Calles and Cárdenas, despite the nationalization of banks and railroads, Mexican economic nationalism was not a headstrong,

---

[5] However, the history of the 1906 bloody crackdown by the Mexican army and Arizona Rangers on the strike in the Cananea copper mine, controlled by an American investor, was a major instance quoted in the revolutionary propaganda since 1910. See Knight (1985, 1990: 145–148). The Rangers' intervention added a political argument to the 1907 nationalization of some of the railroads and to taking already less energetic measures aiming at adopting new mining regulations. See Gonzales (1994: 679).

dogmatic enemy of foreign capital. The Mexican government nationalized big properties (particularly agricultural properties) of both Mexicans as well as foreigners. That is why Thorp (1998: 68) wrote, not without irony:

> How far the revolution was anti-foreign is a matter of controversy. US investments certainly flowed into the export sectors and to industry in the 1920s. Ford, Dupont and Colgate-Palmolive were to be found among the new arrivals.

These new arrivals reflected quite an interesting tendency: that in 1929 and 1938 despite many years of revolutionary and post-revolutionary upheavals the ratio between the stock of foreign investments and GDP was in Mexico the second highest among the big Latin American countries (Haber 2006: 573). In the years 1910–1930 the degree of foreign control of capital invested in all the major non-agricultural sectors of the Mexican economy remained for all practical purposes untouched. It is only in the 1930s that foreign control in those sectors (except commerce) started to decline. As in other Latin American countries (Twomey 1998: 188, 194). The 1938 nationalization of the oil industry as an example of "outright discrimination against foreigners" (Lewis 1948: 151) was an exception. But in this case, too, acceptable is an interpretation indicating that the policy toward oil companies was by no means an issue of major contention between Mexico and the United States.[6] The dispute over oil was a sign of a much wider problem. The foremost issue was the US politicians' and businessmen's negative perception of the entirety of economic policy of successive revolutionary governments (Krenn 1990: 47f). And those stubbornly stuck to the hard-won right to an autonomous formulation of their development goals. Such an approach violated the established order of things and the division of labor in its hitherto known forms between the developed North and its underdeveloped neighbor from the South. However, from the point of view of oil companies, the lesson of Mexican nationalization was quite important (although was taken on board with some difficulty, as post-WWII developments document):

---

[6] The climax of the dispute over oil concessions occurred during Calles' Presidency. In 1927 US Secretary of State F. B. Kellog submitted to the Senate a memorandum on "Bolshevik Aims and Policies in Mexico and Latin America." Rumors were also spread of a possible armed intervention. See Krenn (1990: 55ff), Dobrzycki (1986: 198f). The conflict was staved off at the price of concessions from Mexico. Nationalization carried out in the late 1930s by L. Cárdenas coincided with the very different policy of the F. D. Roosevelt Administration toward Latin America. However, the boycott of Mexican oil followed the nationalization and the creation of the state oil monopoly (PEMEX).

> More than any other event in history–much more than the Russian revolution–the Mexican expropriation taught executives of the principal U.S. oil companies that foreign governments *did* have the power to confiscate, that talk *could* be translated into action, and that they *must* shape the policies of their enterprises in a fashion to mitigate the threat of nationalization (Wilkins 1874: 239).

Besides, if we go back a couple of decades, in many countries generalized attacks against foreign capital would be perceived with surprise, particularly among supporters of modern development. That was an extremely interesting aspect of economic nationalism which we find, among other things, in the Polish publications of the period. Józef Supiński had no doubts in this respect when in 1862 he wrote in *Szkoła polska gospodarstwa społecznego* [The Polish School of Social Economics] that foreign capital meant "knowledge and work accumulated not by us but for us;" hence export of industrial capital, he argued, meant

> a service offered by powerful peoples to weak peoples, and which weaker peoples sometimes reject because of deeply rooted prejudices, misguided patriotism, and ignorance of the laws which govern society" (quoted in Jedlicki 1999: 96; see also Kowalik 1992: 31ff).

Earlier, similar arguments were put forward by both Fryderyk Skarbek, a supporter of a 'natural' economic development of Poland, and Wawrzyniec Surowiecki, the author of the idea of the state-induced industrialization (Górski 1963: 166, 196). We find a similar thought in the assessments of government policy formulated by the parliament (*Sejm*) of the Kingdom of Poland in 1830 (Sejm Królestwa Polskiego 1995: 412). Disappointment with the activities of foreign investors, but also a sense of helplessness, came only later, vide the case of Supiński. That disappointment was not, however, strong enough to question the need and usefulness of foreign capital in general. The negatively assessed direct investments, argued Supiński, should be replaced with loan capital.

The national composition of the emerging group of industrial entrepreneurs and financiers in underdeveloped countries was somehow a separate matter. As a rule, the presence of variously defined foreigners (including the 'internal' ones) was a factor dynamizing both political as well as economic nationalism. In Latin America, until the 1930s, the bargaining position of migrants engaged in the development of industry and other sectors of the urban economy was not very strong. As it was the migrants who made up a significant number of the urban entrepreneurs–and in Argentina in 1913 even their clear majority (Lewis 1990: 16)–industrial interests were clearly underrepresented. They were, however, an easy target for critics. But this can mean that the escalation of criticism and attacks was, to some extent, an attempt at combining sin with virtue: intensifying criticism of certain types of capital without attacking foreign capital *in toto*. In Brazil, until 1930, nationalism

> had a liberal content as it was rarely directed against foreign capital. ... Most assaults were reserved for Portuguese, German, and Japanese immigrants who allegedly either engaged in monopolistic and speculative commercial practices or failed to Brazilianize and thus constituted a perceived security threat (Topik 1980: 614).

In interwar Poland such a nationalism found its expression first of all in hostile attitudes toward German companies and business activities of the Jewish minority.

Therefore one can assume that in the countries entering the path of industrialization, despite numerous reservations and ideological quandaries, the inclusion in the policy of economic nationalism of the demand for a more or less free inflow of foreign capital was not an artificial move forced by circumstances. To assume otherwise would have been at odds with the practice common since the 19th century. In the countries at different levels of economic development and industrialization, protected by high tariff walls, this demand was raised only too often. It was pointed out that, for instance,

> the McKinley bill of 1890 and the Dingley bill of 1897 in the United States, the Russian tariff laws of 1891 and 1903, the French tariff of 1892, and the Austro-Hungarian one of 1906 were extremely favorable to the establishment of foreign branches in the tariff-levying country (U.S. Tariff Commission 1934: 96).

In Paraguay from the mid-19th century until the war of the Triple Alliance (1865–1870) a high tariff barrier, which played a major role in the creation of investment surplus, went hand in hand with the efforts to attract British technology and experts (see Chapter 6). Even the politicians and economists who in the 19th century countered British political imperialism in Brazil, made favorable comments about "the aid which British capital had rendered Brazil in opening roads and developing national industries" (Manchester 1933: 285ff; see also Rippy 1959: 208–211). It was the same in the Kingdom of Poland at the end of the 19th century, where industry developed due, among other things, to the empire's protective tariff (until a certain moment) and the inflow of foreign capital (and transfer of knowledge and skills).

Bearing these in mind, one should not, however, lose sight of those cases where foreign firms were nevertheless seen as a real economic threat. That concerned the situations where their operations on the domestic market either encroached upon local commercial interests or openly restricted local producers' development capabilities. The emotions stirred up by such clashes could not be ignored, although only in rare cases did they result in immediate policy changes. The clash at the end of the 19th century between Moscow and Łódź, over the Łódź textile industry's expansion into the Russian market was such a case. Tariffs on raw materials imported from Russia by the Łódź industry were raised. So were freight charges (Jezierski 1984: 138–141). In Chile heated arguments in the mid-19th century about the British competition endangering the interests of local coal and copper mines resulted in 1860s in basic policy changes, too. Until the mid-1870s the nationally controlled mines–the backbone of the export-oriented economy and modernization–were booming. It is another matter that the oligopolistic control over these sectors the local producers gained led to a drastic decline in production and exports of copper in the subsequent decades. That opened the doors, this time effectively, to the financial, technological and managerial dominance of foreign companies (Fox Przeworski 1978: 172f, Zeitlin 1984: 62ff, Pike 1963). The second stage of the Chilean drama, in hindsight even more important, took place in 1891 under president José Manuel Balmaceda, in the 'nitrate epoch'. In this case the clash between the government's goal of autonomy in policy making and the alliance of Chilean and foreign nitrate interests resulted in blocking alternative, industry-centered development (Zeitlin 1984: chapter 3). However, one should not underestimate the long-term impact also of such nationalistic outbursts centered on particularistic demands: they "helped to call attention to foreign domination of the nation's economy and to heighten ... nationalism" (Ridings 1994: 123). And in case of Argentina in the aftermath of the financial crisis triggered by Baring bank's collapse, one can note among the long-term results of the debt-settlement the growing control of foreign capital over the profitable railroads and port facilities, and the limitation of the role of the state in the economy, both, as Carlos Marichal (1989: 168f) suggests, "the bitter and final legacy of financial dependency." In historical perspective such a solution to the crisis contributed to the growth of nationalism and, at the end of the day, to the emergence after the 1930s of the victorious populist alternative.

Yet, in the 19th century and the first two decades of the 20th century, in many underdeveloped countries the attitude toward foreign capital was not a criterion according to which one could distinguish between supporters of economic nationalism and supporters of free trade. What is more, even a sometimes negative attitude toward individual foreign companies did not automatically entail a nationalist position at the government policy level. Moreover, from the end of the 19th century, owing to the appearance of British financial and industrial competitors particular Latin American governments' bargaining power was strengthened. "The increasingly cosmopolitan character of the Latin American loan activity," writes Marichal (1989: 172), "reflected the intense economic rivalry that characterized this age of 'high imperialism'." This was confirmed, among other things, by "a great burst of speculation in Latin American bonds and stocks, which continued unabated until 1914." Beside the British and French flags, the flag representing German commercial interests, too, as dreamed of by List (but also Weber), was flying high in Latin America (not to mention East and Central Europe) at the turn of the centuries. Between the 1870s and 1914 German commerce, shipping and to a lesser extent investments were growing in Brazil and Argentina by leaps and bounds. The Theodor Wille company became the largest coffee export house in Brazil. In Argentina electrical installations were firmly in the hands of German investors. The 'made in Germany' scare developed in Great Britain in 1896 (Forbes 1978: 389, 391, 394). North Americans began to appear in Brazil in the 1870s, and not in connection with coffee alone. And in Porfirio Diaz's Mexico a subtle game was played by government to counterbalance the predominant US influence by encouraging European banks and investors (Riguzzi 2009).

In a word, negotiations, even if tough, neither meant the negation of the economic internationalism nor did they a priori rule out a foreign capital presence within the framework of nationalist economic policy. Even in the 1930s, growing suspicions and hostility toward foreign banks and firms notwithstanding, the total elimination of foreign capital was not on the agenda of peripheral states. Major changes took place only after WWII. The already quoted Breton-Johnson theory refers first of all to these new, post-WWII conditions.

Therefore List's proposals (and the practical experience mentioned) should be interpreted, first, in the proper historical context, second, in connection with other elements of his holistic economic nationalism. This applies to the state and foreign capital in particular.

As concerns the first question, it is enough, I believe, to refer to the consequences of the British economic leadership up to more or less the 1870s-1880s. Until then "both developed and underdeveloped sectors of the world had an equal interest in working with and not against the British economy, or when they had no choice in the matter" (Hobsbawm 1969: 138). In practice, one and the other came into play. That concerned especially the areas British companies recognized as important to their interests, and thus Latin America and dominions to a greater degree than Europe. Things stood differently with regard to the location of French, Belgian and German companies. In 1914, more than 54 percent of French foreign investments were located in Europe, including 28 percent which went to Eastern Europe. In the case of German investments the situation was similar (Kenwood and Lougheed 1971: 45ff). Interpreting the beginning of the rapid expansion of US capital in the Andean republics in the years 1897–1914, Pike (1977: 159) writes in a similar way: "Facilitating the southward thrust of U.S. capitalism at the turn of the century was an approximation in hearts and minds between the influential classes of North America and Andean America." Hobsbawm (1969: 140), too, shows that among the three flows of international transfers: of goods, population and capital, the latter maintained until 1931 a relatively unconstrained character, not blocked by economic nationalism.

This is an important observation directly linked with the problem of factors conducive to the emergence during the first globalization of modern economic nationalism.

Commodities, Capital, Migrations

In the 19th century and in the first decades of the 20th century growth and consolidation of economic nationalism took place primarily as a reaction centered around commodities, i.e. internationally traded primary products and next locally produced industrial goods supplying domestic markets. However, until WWI this commodity-centered nationalism was accompanied by a rapid expansion of foreign trade. The transport revolution, which from the latter half of the 19th century forced dramatic reductions in freight rates, contributed to the accelerated convergence of prices for internationally traded commodities. Cuts in price gaps between countries amounted in 1820–1914 to 81 percent (Lindert and Williamson 2001: table 1). The world tonnage of sea-going vessels increased from 49 million tons in 1860 to over 125 million tons in 1880 (Mulhall 1884: 171). In this sense, with regard to the last quarter of the 19th century and the beginning of the 20th century one can speak of the first globalization which also affected directly income distribution, resource allocation and international specialization (O'Rourke and Williamson 2000, Williamson 2006). Apart from certain detailed questions, this thesis does not arouse any major controversies today.

But on the other hand, one should bear in mind that almost two thirds of world trade at the time concerned agricultural products and raw materials. Compared to the 18th century, growth of complementary and vertical trade in the 19th century and at the beginning of the 20th century (Gould 1973: 235ff) was indeed revolutionary. That applied to Asia in particular. The transformation of colonial India into an importer of industrial goods, mostly textiles, and a source of liquid capital meant a U-turn in Europe-Asia relations shaped in the previous centuries. To a much lesser degree did new vertical trade stray from the pattern characteristic of the Atlantic economy from its origins in the 16th-century. But the change of scale was dramatic.

Yet, vertical trade which permitted the inclusion (or reinclusion) of peripheral areas into the world system was a phenomenon frequently oversimplified in interpretations. First of all, that trade was not bound up exclusively or primarily with exchanges on the North-South axis. Integration or re-integration of the South into the world economy was in a way a side effect of trade expansion within the broadly defined North, which also included the beginnings of intra-industry trade (Bairoch and Kozul-Wright 1996: 13, Saxonhouse 1993). According to data provided by Mulhall (1884: 106), the share of the four industrially most developed European countries in British foreign trade increased from 24 percent in 1860 to 28 percent in 1880. The share of Latin America in those years declined from 5.3 percent to 4.9 percent. In 1913,

> close to forty percent of total world trade was taking place between European economies, and broadening the perspective to all industrial economies the figure was around 60 percent. Much of this intra-North trade was, of course, trade in primary products (Bairoch and Kozul-Wright 1996: 9).

This is an important observation. As it turned out, on account of the overall rise in the volume of world trade, a 40 percent share of vertical trade on the North–South axis was enough to integrate peripheral areas of Latin America, Asia and Africa into the world market.

Nevertheless, this new and at the same time old structure of international specialization was not *ex definitione* contrary to the logic of the growing nationalism of the center and the periphery, at least for a time. Although the economic nationalism of the peripheries, primarily the particularistic one and rising usually at the time of business slump, was a protest against the distribution of gains from international trade, at the same time it required increased supplies coming from criticized vertical trade. Emerging nationalism, the dramatic rise in primary production, free trade mentality and expanding volume of trade went hand in hand. Even in those countries where evolution to holistic nationalism was advanced, as in the USA and Australia, for understandable reasons one could hardly expect a sudden and immediate change in fresh "graduates" export trade structure. An interesting exception was Germany, which quite soon joined the exclusive group of exporters of industrial products, capital goods included.

Thus, vertical trade was both a threat and a promise. As regards the majority of Latin American states, it would be difficult to interpret their embracing of free trade after the 1850s as an effect of direct, external intervention (Central America and the Caribbean Basin were a different case). Of course, attempts at coercion were made, however mainly in connection with specific trade and/or payment of debt disputes. The most glaring cases of such debt coercion were the military intervention of France (Great Britain and Spain abstained) in Benito Juárez Mexico, and the Venezuelan crisis of 1902–1903 involving Great Britain, Germany and Italy. Also in 1898, when negotiating the Funding Loan as part of debt restructuring, Brazil was allegedly threatened by the Rothschilds banking house–until the early 20th century *the* bankers of Brazil–with foreign intervention (Topik 1980: 611). This was probably an exaggeration, although already in 1892 Rothschilds house was under strong criticism for its suspected opposition to government intervention in support of the cotton industry (Stein 1957: 93). However, the terms imposed in 1898 by the Rothschilds on the Brazilian government (then on the verge of financial collapse) were severe: "[t]he resulting financial triumph (for Rothschilds) reflected Brazil's limited bargaining power" (Flandreau and Flores 2010: 19). In the 1920s military coercion (or the threat of such coercion) was replaced by different, mainly political and economic, instruments of pressure. In a nutshell, the choice of the development option, theoretically, lay in the hands of the elites of primary-economies countries. One can, however, agree with Desmond C. M. Platt (1977: 9) that "[t]he question is not so much the sovereign political power of Latin American governments ... as the practical limits to the use which governments could make of it in their relations with foreign business." However, with the exception of Japan, North America, Australia and the countries of Northern Europe, more often than not that undeniably was only a theoretical choice. The fast growing trade in primary products and inflow of foreign capital were defined as *the* modernity. Within the framework of the so defined modernity and in the context of the continuing process of (financially intensive) state-building in Latin America, there appeared limited and particularistic "liberal economic nationalism" (Helleiner 2002) as an extension of predominantly competitive mentality and booming exports. On the other hand, colonial areas and dominions, apart from Australia, New Zealand and Canada, were left with no choice at all.

Commodity-centered nationalism came together with a rapid increase in capital exports. According to Kuznets (1966: 326f), in the years 1874–1913 the rate of growth of the cumulative total of foreign investments was "significantly higher than the rate of growth of national output and foreign trade, whether of the creditor countries or of all debtor countries taken as a whole." However, contrary to monocausal interpretations, in the period discussed the appearance on the periphery of economic nationalism that protected local markets and local industries and/or treasury income was not the sole or even the main factor which determined decisions taken by capital exporters. The relationship between the growth of supply-oriented FDIs and protection of domestic markets in Latin America and Central Europe was weak, to say the least. But certainly commodity-centered nationalism offered many attractive opportunities for capital placements by those investors who were not entangled in the operations (and rationality) of export enclaves. Differences in return rates on overseas investments also played a role: "British-owned foreign railroads earned about twice as much as those in the United Kingdom" (Frieden 2006: 50). However, in this as in other cases of returns on capital invested and trade one should take into account diverse national experiences. In Brazil and Mexico early in the 20th century freight rates on foreign-owned railroads started to be *at some moment* a subject of intense state regulation favoring domestic market-oriented producers (Haber 1997a: 26). Likewise, changes in terms of trade were a factor affecting capital movements, although they, like tariffs, were not the sole or fundamental factor. Nevertheless, changes in terms of trade, to which I will return later, undoubtedly affected tariff policies and the intensity of economic nationalist demands.

Also, despite the rapid rise before 1914, capital exports did not become an effective substitute for trade. Let me refer to Kuznets once more. If we take into account the three major creditor countries (the United Kingdom, France and Germany), it will follow that "the average outflow of foreign capital investment [amounted] to less than a tenth of the foreign trade volume, and in most periods much less" (Kuznets 1966: 326). On the other hand, capital flows influenced consolidation of markets and interregional specialization within vertical trade, and, at the same time, they "were mainly an anti-convergence force" as far as productivity levels, wages and incomes on a global scale were concerned (Lindert and Williamson 2001: 19). The positive convergence on the North-North axis (extended to Western offshoots) was accompanied by the negative convergence on the North-South axis, expressed in growing income and wage gaps. Trade was pushing in the same direction. In the second half of the 19th century, the already strong tendency to form separate 'income (convergence) clubs', correlated with different economic structures, gained momentum. The relative gap between different 'clubs' was wider in 1914 than it had been in 1870. Intermediate cases, particularly in Latin America, were an element of such polarization. For a time the model primary-export economies of Argentina and Uruguay were taking part in the income convergence among Northern countries (Dowrick and DeLong 2003: 192, 198, Bairoch and Kozul-Wright 1996, Findlay and O'Rourke 2001, Lindert and Williamson 2001).

The main recipients of capital exports were the regions increasingly involved in industrialization and some of them strongly protected by tariffs, i.e. Europe (27.2 percent of foreign investments in 1913), North America (25.2 percent), and Latin America (20.3 percent) (Schularick 2006: 344, Thomas 1967: 10). Such geographic distribution of capital transfers demonstrated that capital followed industrialization and migrations, and growing economic nationalism. Such coordinated movement was not inevitable, though. It occurred on certain conditions. And before WWI only a few countries met them. I will deal with this question in a moment.

As concerns nationalism linked, particularly in the USA, with international migrations, this question went beyond List's deliberations (and time). It was, however, one of the most essential psychological and economic reasons for both the transformation of political nationalism and consolidation of economic nationalism which began in the last quarter of the 19th century and continued in the next few decades. Its grassroots version was a part of the process, represented, among other things, by labor unions, but also, in an already different historical epoch, by mass-scale indigenization of resources and jobs in Asia and Africa. In the political dimension, Carr recognized this issue as maybe the most important characteristic of the fully-shaped integral nationalism and changes leading to the interwar clash of nationalisms:

> The link between 'economic nationalism' and the socialization of the nation emerged clearly in the decisive and fateful step taken by all the great industrial countries after 1919–the closing of national frontiers to large-scale immigration (Carr 1985: 190).

The international migrations in the 19th century and at the beginning of the 20th century included *grosso modo* two or three essentially distinct flows. Until the 1870s, the USA, the single most important destination country for the dramatically rising migration of the 19th and at the beginning of the 20th century, accepted almost exclusively migrants from Western Europe. At the end of the 19th century migrants from East and Central and Southern Europe began to predominate. Emigration from Asia to the USA was abruptly stopped by the 1882 Chinese Exclusion Act and the 1907 Gentlemen's Agreement concerning the Japanese. The 1924 Immigration Act sealed off large-scale immigration to the United States. Australia's immigration policy developed in a similar way. Already in the 1840s this country ceased to be mainly a penal colony and began granting privileges to first and foremost white immigration, primarily from Great Britain and Ireland. 'Yellow' people were strongly discouraged, although between 1863 and 1904 about 65,000 indentured laborers from the Pacific Islands were brought in (Lloyd 2003: 422). A part of European migrants landed in Latin America, mostly in Brazil and Argentina. Last but not least, there was Asian immigration quantitatively equal to (if not exceeding) that from Europe. There were over 50 million seasonal and permanent Asian immigrants, mainly from China and India (Hatton 2010, Timmer and Williamson 1998). Apart from the relatively few who settled in the USA, Latin America, the Caribbean, East and South Africa, Asian immigrants looked for settlement chiefly in Asia itself. So they settled there–together with their wage levels (Lewis 1978b: 188).

Such distribution of migrations played an important role in the determination of the main trends concerning respective factor endowments in developed and peripheral countries, and as a result in the determination of the per capita income levels. In Lewis's approach (1978a, 1978b), by now classical, this is of fundamental importance.

The conclusions following from Lewis's theory were not optimistic about the periphery. As in the case of temperate zone products, price levels for tropical products (including raw materials) depended on the level and direction of change in labor productivity, on the availability of labor and wage level, on access to land and other productive assets, and on price and income elasticities of world demand. The effect of these factors was such that the tendency to drive down the prices for these products to the level of Asian wages persisted for a long time. The main factors were the dramatically growing gap between the rates of productivity growth in food production in the center and the periphery and the unlimited supply of labor in Asia. Compared to the wave of migrants, the presumably insufficient increase in global demand for tropical products deepened the destructive influence of that supply (Dowrick and DeLong 2003: 199).[7] Hence, says Lewis, the divergent evolution of factoral terms of trade, labor in particular, in underdeveloped and developed countries formed the basis for unequal distribution of income on the international scale. Hla Myint arrived at a similar conclusion in his classical path-breaking article. He made the following observation:

> in the latter half of the nineteenth century immigration labour, particularly from India, may really be regarded as an international commodity having a uniform price rather than as a factor of production. Wherever it was imported, it decisively pulled down wages and incomes ... to the very low level appropriate to the over-populated countries (Myint 1954–1955: 135).

The persistence of such a "conventional level of low wages," Myint argued, cannot however be assumed to be a result of optimizing economic mechanisms. Hence the distribution of gains from international trade between the 'national' and the 'foreign' factors of production involved in underdeveloped economy reflected the strong impact of both non-economic and monopolistic elements and practices.

Although the later analysis by Lindert and Williamson (2001: 11f figure 4, table 2) and Williamson (2006), centered on a single variable, namely the evolution of the rent/wage relation, does not imply so dramatic a conclusion, it nevertheless suggests a relative worsening of this relation in land-abundant immigrant countries like Argentina and Uruguay. Also in the USA, Brazil and Australia the impact of migration on real wages was negative. Let me add here that the way out of this trap, as developed, for example, in the United States and Australia, was not repeated in Latin America. Of course, one can wonder why in Latin America, that is in a region characterized by (potential) land abundance and labor scarcity, the mechanism described by Lewis worked too (although at a level definitely higher than the Asian wage level). It seems that in this case a powerful combination of economic, social and political factors was at work, which in the primary-export economies favored 'rent' over 'wage', prevented the efficient protection to the scarce factor (labor) and created artificial land

---

[7] Taking into consideration the income and price elasticities for tropical products at the time, to discuss this issue may be interesting only as an experiment in counterfactual analysis. Substantial changes could occur only in the case of industrialization of a greater number of countries, including those in the tropical zone.

scarcity and artificial labor abundance. With serious consequences in terms of class and urban-rural cleavages.

Conclusions from Lewis's and Lindert and Williamson's analyses also show the problem of terms of trade in a different light. If exchange of primary products for industrial goods takes place on neutral or favorable terms of trade, it can lead to the ossification of underdevelopment (Bairoch 1975: chapter 6; recently Williamson 2002, 2006: 18f). And vice versa: following Hans Singer's remarks, a worsening of terms of trade could create strong incentives for questioning the hitherto path of development and for initiating structural changes. However,

> the underdeveloped countries are in danger of falling between two stools: failing to industrialize in a boom because things are as good as they are, and failing to industrialize in a slump because things are as bad as they are (Singer 1950: 482).

The paradox of the historical economic development of the periphery was precisely that the perverse short-term benefits were bound up with long-term negative consequences in the social and economic structure and in the distribution of political power and influence. In a word, a perfectly dysfunctional outcome of short-term perfectly rational responses to market signals. The consequence was a vicious circle: a disjunctive exchange[8] and its related economic interests resulted in the absence of an integrated national economy.

At the same time there occurred ossification of the mechanism which limited the possibilities of industrial development through staple growth. One should keep in mind the contrasting cases of Canada, Australia and New Zealand on the one hand, and of Argentina and Uruguay on the other. One can hardly disagree with Carlos Manuel Pelaez's observation (1976: 281) that "the coffee trade constituted a golden opportunity for modernization in nineteenth-century Brazil." However, bearing in mind the cases

---

[8] The concept of disjunctive exchange introduced by Andersson (1976) refers to the production and exchange of goods exerting different effects on a given economy. The goods exchanged and the related production processes and productivity levels can be of such a kind that their effect on the parties taking part in this exchange can be nonequivalent. See also Hirschman (1977: 91–94), Kindleberger (1962: 199–204). The Díaz-Alejandro-proposed concept of "commodity lottery," which describes differentiation of backward and forward linkages relating to a given product (see Bulmer-Thomas 2003: 14f, 43), sounds similar to the concept of disjunctive exchange. In the interwar period Zimmermann (1931) made an interesting attempt at describing the "hierarchy of resources or commodities" and its effect on development and on the distribution of gains from trade.

of Canada and Australia, the conclusion this eminent economic historian draws is already less convincing:

> the coffee trade permitted Brazil to effect its first transition to modernization and industrialization. The mechanism was similar to the 'engine of growth' trade processes of the areas of recent settlement (Pelaez 1976: 287).

Indeed, the mechanism was similar, however, in view of the divergent directions of the evolution of factoral terms of trade and the divergent socio-political alliances involved in modernization (and industrialization), the long-term effects were different. Elaborating on Singer's remarks, Williamson (2006: 101) captured well the impact of trade and favorable terms of trade shocks on the periphery:

> To the extent that the periphery specializes in primary products, and to the extent that industry is a carrier of development, then positive price shocks reinforce specialization in the periphery and cause deindustrialization there, offsetting the short-run gains from the terms-of-trade improvement.

Thus, there is no sense in preaching to the converted and proving that until the end of the first globalization, industrialization in Australia and in Argentina–in both countries supported by primary exports–created two very different worlds. In 1929 the share of industry in combined total production of agriculture, mining and industry in Australia reached 42 percent and in Argentina 28 percent, while industrial production per capita in Australia was 2.45 times bigger than in Argentina (Landau 1939: 128f, 122).

In a word, the problem of gains or losses from trade associated with the movement of commodity terms of trade, although important from the point of view of cyclical fluctuations, loses its autonomy. It can no longer be treated as an explanation of underdevelopment in a long-term perspective.

Lewis's hypotheses concerning the origins of cheap labor do, however, raise some doubts. This concerns particularly, if we are to stick to the example of Asia, the very scant treatment of the impact of colonial structures on the rapid changes in factor endowments. I mean here, among other things, the frequent, colonial administration-forced blocking of non-agricultural (mainly industrial) activities or disregard for and underdevelopment of non-export sectors. Thus there was very little 'naturalness' in the colonial economy, except for the sun, abundant labor and raw materials. What happened was an active modeling of factor endowments and of comparative advantages. Asians were not destined for plantations, especially that as Lewis (1978b: 187) points out, "[a]t the beginning of the nineteenth century the plantation system hardly existed in Asia." Similarly, Myint (1958: 324) argued convincingly that export expansion in backward countries "cannot really be explained in terms of comparative-cost theory based on the assumption of given resources and given techniques." However, his attempt at reducing the colonial powers' negative impact to skewed distribution of gains from international trade only does not seem persuasive. Neither should one forget about the negative impact of colonial rule on the formation of autonomous political and economic elites. And finally it would be a mistake to pass over in the deliberations on the origins of cheap labor the effect of such factors as space and location. Taking as an example Latin America, Engerman and Sokoloff (1997: 276, 294) emphasize the relation between the initial factor endowment at the beginning of European expansion and "the directions in which institutions evolve" and that "government policies and other institutions tended generally to reproduce the sorts of factor endowments that gave rise to them." The role played in such a reproduction both under Spanish colonial rule and under independence by "politically powerful classes" was crucial, they conclude. The strong links between initial factor endowments and wealth concentration suggested by both historians met with a rebuttal from Coatsworth (2005: 139f), who in fact was echoing Lewis's above-quoted argument. However, his further contention delinking colonial institutions and the misfortunes of 19th century modernization does not sound plausible. Thus, I would suggest that as in the case of divergent responses to terms of trade shocks, also in the persistence of unfavorable 'man-made' factor endowments, one can trace a full background to the political, social and institutional history of the periphery.

Nevertheless, none of these reservations challenge Lewis's main hypothesis pointing to the structural conditioning of nationalism connected with migrations. Such a nationalism did not appear as a mere irrational defensive reaction motivated in case of Asian migrants by racism alone. Xenophobia, although it appeared in a wider cultural context, can be treated as a defensive, perverse strategy resulting from the inability "to sustain what Schumpeter called 'the gail competition'" (Breton and Breton 1994: 112). Thus "[t]he factoral terms available to the tropics ... offered the opportunity to stay poor–at any rate until such time as the labour reservoirs of India and China might be exhausted" (Lewis 1978b: 192). Let me add that that was not inevitable as proved by Japan, which did not wait until its reservoir of cheap labor was exhausted. Simultaneously with the migration of over a million Japanese people, Japan initiated fundamental restructuring of its economy. A similar emigration safety valve had worked earlier in Germany, Ireland, Norway and Italy. The impact of migration on real wages was positive in Germany (a 2.4 percent rise), Ireland (31.9 percent), Italy (28.6 percent) and in Norway (9.7 percent) (Lindert and Williamson 2001: 11f figure 4). In the rhetoric of Italian nationalism, emigration, defined as the search for land, was described, for instance by Robert Michels in 1914, as "the imperialism of poor people" or "proletarian imperialism" (De Rosa 2002: 177). However, neither China nor India had such political and economic space for manoeuvre. In their cases migration meant drainage of superfluous labor only, with no attempts—or chances—at internal economic restructuring.

Thus immigration bred defensive reactions and nationalism. "Nobody understood this better," remarks Lewis bitterly, "than the working classes in the temperate settlements themselves (and in the USA)." Workers realized that if immigration were not stopped, "it [would] drive wages down close to Indian and Chinese levels. In the same way white American labour did all it could to restrict the jobs available to blacks" (Lewis 1978b: 192). Labor market segmentation, also along race and ethnic lines (but also the employed versus unemployed), is a fragment of the same answer to the same problem. Subsequent waves of new migrants were confronted by those

> who had immediately preceded them and who now occupied the lowest rung on the local social ladder. In the United States the Irish turned on the Italians, who turned on the Jews, and all of them turned on the black internal migrants from the American South (Frieden 2006: 53).

In this sense, economic nationalism unavoidably referred to and exploited the 'migration argument'. "Welfare chauvinism," about which Jürgen Habermas (1993: 27) writes with reference to modern Europe, has its rich and tumultuous history. At the same time it was presumably used more often by workers (particularly from the endangered sectors) and politicians than by entrepreneurs. Republicans justified the McKinley Tariff of 1890 by "the need to safeguard the wage levels of American workers" and "to give the agricultural sector more protection" (Bairoch 1993: 36). As far as prejudice and xenophobia are concerned, the red-necks phenomenon was not limited to the poor South. *Some* labor unions and other organizations representing unskilled workers also contributed to the hostility toward immigrants in general: "the impetus to resist immigration was far more sensitive to labor market conditions than to immigration level" (Timmer and Williamson 1998: 744).

On the other hand, entrepreneurs had nothing against cutting labor costs, regardless of their attitude toward racism and/or protection of national and civilization values (Frieden 2006: 53). It was obvious yesterday, and it is obvious also today, although now the focus of their attention has shifted to low-wage industrializing, catching-up countries. Anyhow, this was the case in California and Hawaii. In 1909 the outgoing President Theodore Roosevelt fulminated against such an attitude "due to the short-sighted greed of the sugar planters and of the great employers generally." In a letter to the future Secretary of State Knox, concerning the Japanese immigration to Hawaii and the minority presence of white settlers there, he presented one of the first interpretations of the "clash of civilizations:"

> So far as possible our aim should be to diminish the number of Japanese in the islands without any regard to the fortunes of the sugar planters, and to bring in Europeans ... in order that the islands may be filled with a white population of our general civilization and culture (Roosevelt 1909).

He argued that the prospect "of turning Hawaii into an island of coolie-tilled plantations" was unacceptable.

Indeed, for decades the United States shut itself off to Asian people (and others as well). After all, in the long period from the 1860s until the end of the 1920s the United States demonstrated striking consistency in its immigration policy: "while the United States exhibited a steady drift away from free immigration [except in 1888–1916], the others closed their doors in fits and starts" (Timmer and Williamson 1998: 742). After WWI the United States and 'the others' closed ranks behind anti-immigration policies.

Protectionism and Foreign Capital

Interpretation of certain instances of government intervention in the economy in the 19th and the beginning of the 20th centuries constitutes an equally intricate problem. I mean here above all certain aspects of the complicated tangle of tariff protectionism and other forms of government activity on the one hand and foreign entrepreneurs' operations on the other. The thesis that economic nationalism is unthinkable without active state involvement does not necessarily imply state property and/or direct interference in private sector operations. Treating them as one would be a historical anachronism. Dissociating himself from such ideas, List emphasized that regulations he proposed organized the market, but did not interfere in the decisions of entrepreneurs. What is more, even in dealing with state property one should approach an interpretation of its role with caution.

To equate every form of government intervention with nationalism—a view increasingly popular since the end of WWI—would lead to the distortion of, for instance, the history of the first railroads in Chile in the mid-19th century. After all, such a kind of government involvement was observed not only in this country. Years ago Supple (1973: 326ff) pointed out, thinking of continental Europe, that inasmuch as the Industrial Revolution in Great Britain started without railroads, all followers built their railroads with the help of the state or the state took over this task (as well as risk and ownership). Needless to say, in some cases the construction of the railroad initially had other aims than economic development (e.g. in Russia) or led to the waste of resources (e.g. in Ireland) (Pollard 1981: 207ff). Weber (1978: 915) wrote about the "means of communication (railroads today) ... determined politically." In any event to catch up with the economic leader required new *modi operandi.*

The government's involvement in railroad investments in primary economies were also a fragment of the catching-up, but applying different logic. In the case of Chile, the government's and export sector's investments and, next, the nationalization of the railroads were not aimed against foreign capital (which co-financed railroads). Concentration of resources in primary export production was not disputed either. Just the opposite. The state and state-owned companies widened the bases of Chile's export-oriented policy and at the same time took on the burden of financing externalities (Oppenheimer 1982). The development of railroads in other Latin American countries could be interpreted in a similar way: they "tended to reinforce the pattern of export specialization rather than to encourage diversification" (Bulmer-Thomas 2003: 105; see also Summerhill 2006: 318). However, one should not push this argument too far. The construction of the Ferrocarril Central de Lima (a technical miracle) and the Ferrocarril del Sur aimed both at the economic integration of the country and facilitation of access to a traditional silver-mining region (Marichal 1989: 88ff).[9] Both goals were (and should be) seen as legitimate. Debating the case of Brazil, Paulo Singer (2009: 62) thus argues that

---

[9] It was symbolic that the first railroad line in Latin America was built in 1838 in Cuba, which was vigorously driving Brazil and other countries out of the world sugar business (Bulmer-Thomas 2003: 35). In Chile the railroads nationalized toward the end of the 19th century contributed substantially to the state budget, which was rather unique on the continent (Ortega 1985: 158, 166).

"the same infrastructure that made possible the growth in production for the global market also served to unite physically the domestic market." The assertion that "[t]he railroad was not merely a highway to external dependency" (Salvucci 2006: 292) is perfectly valid. However, serious doubts remain as to the extent to which the development of the railroad network in specific countries prevented and/or limited Dutch disease (for Peru see Bonilla 1974: 59–63).

Let me return again here to the issue of foreign portfolio and direct investments.

Unlike foreign capital contributing to the North–North convergence, which already at the beginning of the 20th century included elements of inter-industry specialization (Bairoch and Kozul-Wright 1996: 9f), on the North-South axis this capital was first and foremost an important supplement to and enhancement of vertical trade. The structure of British investments in Latin America in the years 1865–1913 shows this clearly. Almost 70 percent of British capital flows were loans and investments in infrastructure, which

> increased the capacity of primary producing nations to export marketable surpluses to Europe. ... it is abundantly clear that British funds did not directly foster the development of extensive overseas industrialization as less than 4 percent of the total capital called was invested in manufacturing (Simon 1967: 42 and statistical annex; see also Rippy 1959: 75–78, Taylor 2006: 69).

US investors, too, strengthened the logic of vertical trade: their main goal was control over the supply of raw materials and tropical exportable foodstuffs, that is supply-oriented investments (Wilkins 1974: 55–59). Foreign capital inflow was backed up by Latin American governments and, with some misgivings, economic elites as a part of the project for outward-oriented modernization. The nationalist implications of the opening up to foreign capital were connected primarily with accelerated state-building, and not with the building of an industrial society. However, the economic activity of the state and the role of foreign loans, for example in Mexico and the Kingdom of Poland in the first half of the 19th century, should be interpreted in a different way (see Chapter 6).

It seems therefore that the issues of foreign capital and state interventionism cannot be pondered and their role specified precisely outside the historical context of the period of the first globalization. This context should take into account, among other things, not only the accessibility of definite instruments of nationalist economic policy, but also the real regulating potential of the state at that time (Babb 2001: 37, Gourevich

1986: 52f). This seems to be the proper way to interpret the possible nationalist consequences of particular practical steps taken by governments. In a nutshell, List's favorable attitude to foreign capital should be treated as an integral part of a certain historical form of economic nationalism.

According to the holistic point of view, foreign investments contributed to a rise in the production potential of the national economy. Indeed, they had their price (royalties and an outflow of profits); in return they created new production resources in the country. At the same time it was obvious to List that those investments were made where they should be made, i.e. in the industrial sector and in infrastructure (the concept of *Produktionskräfte*). With regard to the industrializing European countries he rejected the so-called colonial (primary sector-oriented) and/or enclave model of foreign investments. This one he reserved for the countries at the "original barbarism" stage.

It has been already implied that such demanding requirements were difficult to meet in the 19th century, though not impossible. The experience of List's own country and of other "graduates" bears testimony to that. We know that until 1914 foreign capital played an extremely important role in the development of Canada, Australia and Norway, and to a lesser extent of the USA. Between 1870 and 1910 its share in investments in Canada fluctuated from 30 percent to 50 percent. Likewise in Australia and Norway. In Argentina, in the years 1900–1919 that share amounted to 37–43 percent (Kuznets 1966: 332f). Of course, in the period until 1913 investments in railroads weighted heavily in total foreign placements. But if we limit the analysis only to FDI outside of railroads, the balance seems still impressive: in Mexico the relation between the stock of non-railroad FDI and GDP reached in 1913–1914 97 percent, in Canada 26 percent, in Argentina 47 percent and in Brazil 81 percent (after the inclusion of railroad investments the proportion rises in Brazil to 296 percent) (Twomey 1998: 173). However, unlike in Argentina and Uruguay, in Australia and the USA foreign companies found their place in the industrialization project even if their initial preference for non-industrial, export-supportive infrastructural investments seemed to repeat Latin American examples.

During the first globalization Japan constituted a highly selective, government-controlled variant of the foreign capital inflow. From the end of the 1890s, after joining the gold standard and the establishment of the Industrial Bank of Japan, which controlled both the supply of and demand for foreign capital, the inflow of foreign funds rose dramatically. Acceleration took place after the victorious war with Russia. Japanese policy distinguished itself not merely by the centralized control exercised by government-sponsored institutions. All the more so that after WWI, the financial autonomy of enterprises, especially those belonging to the Zaibatsu groups, increased. The most interesting feature of that policy, continued also after WWI, was a focus on technological development, in capital goods industries and industrial infrastructure in particular. Japanese authors underline that the country's main goal was, especially after 1905, to raise the productivity of the economy as a whole:

> the Japanese industry needed more advanced foreign technology rather than foreign capital. Thus, in most cases direct foreign investments took the form of joint ventures, which were often supported by technical licensing agreements.

And they add: "It was fortunate for Japan to be able to obtain foreign capital from individual investors. This helped Japan to prevent powerful foreign capital from dominating Japanese industries (Okita and Miki 1967: 149, 155). Accelerated economic development continued in the interwar period, too, although with already a more limited contribution of foreign capital. The role of the state was gradually changing as well. The private sector, primarily conglomerates from the Zaibatsu groups, strongly connected with the government, gradually replaced state firms in capital goods industries. Instruments of the state policy and intervention were adjusted to the new situation accordingly (Allen 1972: passim).

So, where established were institutions and political alliances that forced the creation of a new balance between the agrarian and the emerging urban-industrial interests, and where such a balance was backed up *also* by the state, foreign capital ultimately adapted to the new political and business environment. The effectiveness of the anti-industrialization bias of foreign capital in the period of the first globalization had its limits.

Thus the mentioned earlier concept of chronologically different types of economic nationalism proposed by Kahan passes over the coexistence and overlap of particular nationalism and holistic nationalism in various historical periods. An interesting article by Mary A. Yeager (1980: 34, 37) concerning the US steel industry is of salience here. Treating protectionism as a special kind of commodity, Yeager makes a distinction between the "public protection market" and "private protection market." The former comes into being as a result of measures taken by the government in the interest of the economy as a whole or its important branches. The latter, for example dumping and cartel agreements, employed by large firms does not need state intervention. Yeager identifies the public protection market substituting for the private protection market in two historically different periods of the economic development of the United States: protectionism after the end of the civil war and the Smoot–Hawley tariff of 1931. In both cases protectionism was "unilateral, nationalist, and home-oriented." The relevant changes introduced in the 1930s (Reciprocal Trade Agreements Act of 1934) introduced a new element into the protectionist policy: protectionism became an internationally traded commodity, involving nation-to-nation bargaining. Other researchers pointed also to the positive correlation between tariff protectionism and the development of the steel industry (Baack and Kay 1973/1974). If we consider products other than steel, the history of the two types of protectionist markets turns out to be much longer. The US textile industry, until a certain time the leading sector of the non-agricultural economy, was saved in the difficult period after 1812 and in the decades that followed thanks to a combination of both types of protectionism (Bils 1984, Rosenbloom 2002). Incidentally, even critics of protectionism admit that without those tariffs, by the 1830s the British competition would have crushed the US industry. For the later period, they maintain, tariffs were neutral in view of a non-competitive division of the American market between the British high-quality textile exports and local low-grade production (Irwin and Temin 2001). This is not a fully convincing argument, but to consider it here is not necessary.

The disregard for the coexistence of various forms of nationalism results in turn from a playing down or ignoring the importance of economic processes described as holistic nationalism and the relationship between this type of nationalism and definite instruments enabling increased microeconomic efficiency. For these processes and instruments were perceived only as examples of the harmful and arbitrary interference of political nationalism that ignored economic realities and as a source of costly experiments. This is how one can explain Kahan's (1968: 19) approval of Schmoller's remark that the 1891 Russian tariff blocked the country's economic development. Sergei Witte (1921: 63–68) had a decidedly different view on the matter. Nonetheless there is no doubt that the tariff itself–an important but not the only instrument of state intervention–was not drawn up very fortunately. After all, the same can be said about German and Italian tariffs from that period. For example, Gerschenkron wrote about the Italian tariff that "at least in principle, Italy's industrialization could have been aided by a rationally conceived and executed tariff," whereas the tariff introduced reflected the state's "concentration on the least deserving branches of industrial activity" (1965: 80f).[10]

However the crux of the matter is that Kahan uses the one-sidedly interpreted example of the Russian tariff to formulate a general thesis meant to prove a fundamental contradiction between nationalism and economic development. Likewise, Frank B. Tipton Jr. (1981) argues in his revisionist picture of the economic policies of Germany and Japan in the period of industrialization in both countries that a politically-motivated government intervention slowed down the pace of industrial growth–for it was guided first and foremost by "the gradual emergence of a commercial culture" and "world factors exogenous to government policy." Obviously there is no reason for contesting that such an exogenous factor as WWI saved Japan's balance-of-payments and created favorable conditions for continuation of industrialization in the 1920s (Allen 1972: chapter 6). The way this factor was made the most of, also by the interventionist state, sped up rather than slowed down the pace of structural changes. At some cost however. The overoptimistic expectations concerning the post-war continuation of the war boom created a phenomenon of crowding in, an overinvestment frenzy and at the end of the day the bubble burst. Let us notice that a hundred years later the Republic of Korea and Taiwan (second-tier NICs) ignored these kinds of arguments, too. Their economic policies went far beyond the self-adjusting market theory and the "neoclassical principles of good economic management" (Wade 1990: 260). As in Japan earlier, the role of the government in both countries was not limited to a mere creation of mechanisms facilitating adjustment to market signals, a kind of economic environment fine-tuning. The move to skill- and capital-intensive export-oriented development in the second-tier NICs economies "required considerable government intervention in the context of a long-term industrial strategy" (UNCTAD 1996: 143). (For a different opinion see Lal (1998: 138), although he also points out that the problem of agency arose in these countries at the capital-intensive stage of industrialization.)

---

[10] The discussion between Gerschenkron and Rosario Romero concerning Italy at the turn of the 19th and 20th centuries highlighted problems with the assessment of the long-term effects of a given structure of a protectionist tariff (Gerschenkron 1968: chapter 5). In the case of Japan, until the end of the 19th century tariffs were of minor importance in view of the 1866 treaty-imposed drastic lowering of import tariffs (to 5 percent). Thus, Japanese economic nationalism made a more intensive use of non-tariff instruments of protectionism. See Allen (1972).

Both of these positions are debatable and somehow abstract in view of the historical conditions in which Germany and Japan opened themselves up to modern development. If we pass over the extreme case of a war economy, where the criteria of economic efficiency are pushed into the background, then, apart from this special case, we are dealing with different, historically specific variants of the combination of a yearning for political power and striving for economic development. Their analytic distinction can be of heuristic value, but it cannot be treated as a decisive criterion to assess a practical policy.

The role of political motivations, and in the case of Russia also of fear about the future ability to maintain power status, apparent after the defeat in the Crimean War, was obvious. Those motivations were an integral part of the process that led to a gradual change in attitudes, to the elimination of serfdom and finally to the initiation of modern growth. A few decades later, Sergei Witte–who in the years 1892–1903, as finance minister, initiated accelerated industrialization–while defending his policy, in a 1900 memo addressed to the tsar warned him: "Our economic backwardness may lead to political and cultural backwardness as well" (quoted in Laue 1969: 3). Of course firmness in decision-making and a proper assessment of the situation are factors difficult to quantify. They are, however, a kind of "X factor" which plays a crucial role in the *political* process and which opens the way to an economic breakthrough and emergence of new economic mentality and behaviors.

Unlike Russia, Japan–also thanks to its economic history prior to the Meiji Restoration–found such a factor in its own culture and political tradition. I have here in mind, among other things, the tradition described as the 'directed society': the country's economic and ideological leadership was expressed in a simultaneous rejection of direct administrative management and pluralist concepts, which got support from formalized interest groups (Rozman 1990: 177). But not only that. Years ago Barrington Moore, Jr. (1969: chapter 5) paid attention to the fact that those factors were supported, first and foremost, by the way the problem of commercialization of agriculture had been solved. In the long run the solution adopted by conservative modernizers consolidated the agrarian-commercial alliance and industrial interests and at the same time allowed a significant margin of flexibility for the state and its institutions as the guarantors of enforced peace in the countryside. This in turn, combined with expansive political nationalism, in the subsequent decades opened the doors to the Japanese variant of fascism. It seems simply impossible to understand Japanese industrialization and authoritarian modernity without referring to the fundamental idea of *kokutai* (linking into one organic whole the state and nation treated as an extension of the family writ large). The same applies to the perception of threats posed by the increasingly competitive international system. After all, the same concerns also the turbulent history of radical social thought in that country, which, willing to be both radical and Japanese, in the 1920s and 1930s inevitably evolved toward the Japanese variant of national socialism (Hoston 1994: 93 and passim; compare Lal 1998: 146).

It was also obvious that the increasingly strong incentives coming from the world system were largely beyond the state's control. One possible reaction to the problem of effective and active adaptation was to increase the tendency to take measures aimed at regulation and control of these areas which could be effectively controlled with the help of nationally defined means (Rosenau 1989: 35). Finding oneself in the "graduate class" depended on the response to those incentives, on the way they were 'domesticated', for, as Witte argued, "[i]nternational competition does not wait." Their effect could be accelerated industrialization just as well as a sudden deindustrialization or simply a persistent passive involution. Like today, so also in the period discussed the observation made by a contemporary liberal economist should be taken into account:

> The key question is not whether there is governmental action in the Far East economies, but rather how these successful economies have managed their intervention and their strategic decision-making better than the unsuccessful economies (Bhagwati 1989: 98).

Not only conservative critics of industrialization, but also Narodnik populist economists, above all W. Woroncow (1965), when analyzing peculiarities and effects of industrialization preceding the spurt initiated in the 1890s, pointed first and foremost to the barriers preventing capitalist transformation of Russia (see also Walicki 1965). However, contrary to their intentions, their criticism can also be read in another way: as a challenge and agenda for action. Witte transformed *the barriers* (primarily limited access to foreign markets and a very narrow domestic market), *new circumstances* (accelerated technological change, an increase in the scale of production and the introduction of labor-saving technologies) and *new instruments* (the state) into a program of an enforced industrial spurt. That was a program that not only opposed plans for non-capitalist development, but also ignored the Narodniks' moral indignation at the social costs of industrialization. "Legal Marxists" (Peter Struve, Tugan-Baranovsky and others) treated the question the same way as Witte did.

They derived the inevitability of capitalist development not from liberal, but from "materialistic" premises. In connection with this, Walicki (1983: 96) mentions that "Witte himself, when justifying the government program, spoke sometimes about its conformity with Marxism." Thus if List anchored the plan for industrialization of Germany in nationalism, then in Russia, Marxism advocating the inevitability of capitalist development became an important ideological justification of the industrial spurt (Gerschenkron 1965: 25).

Therefore one should expect of critics convincing arguments that Germany, Japan or Russia could break out of backwardness in a fundamentally different way, without protectionism and other forms of strong government intervention. Such intervention manifested itself, among other things, in the strongly accentuated role of banks (in the case of Germany), in state-regulated (with the help of the Industrial Bank of Japan) selective access of foreign capital and in non-tariff protectionism, and also in the clearly stressed authoritarian nature of their political systems.

I believe that to present such a counterfactual analysis is rather impossible. It does not suffice to merely criticize different national tariffs and the resulting misallocation of resources. In a word, although Gerschenkron's theoretical approach has been repeatedly pronounced as falsified, it is still relevant today. This concerns both the specificity of backwardness as well as the concept of "substitutes." Put in a nutshell, it concerns the questions David Landes (1990: 48) has defined as *Problemstellung*: "Is late development different? (Answer; yes.) How? (Answer: it requires special effort and institutional arrangements to mobilize factors and catch up.)" Witte wrote the following in his memoirs, with Germany and the USA also in mind:

> It is said that I took artificial measures to develop our industry. What a silly phrase! How else can one develop an industry? ... The measures taken by me were much less artificial and drastic than those practised by many foreign countries (Witte 1921: 76).

Let me stick, however, to the example of Russian tariffs. It seems that interpretations isolating the introduction of these tariffs from general political and economic conditions of the industrialization spurt would in point of fact lead to a distortion of the logic of Russian economic nationalism up until 1914. The 1891 tariff (I do not assess its structure and effectiveness here) and the 1894 Russo-German treaty undoubtedly were designed to protect Russian industrialists from competitive imports and to ensure the German market for Russia's grain exports. Both those instruments fitted perfectly the logic of particularistic nationalism. The claim that "state tariff policy was dictated by revenue needs rather than by a coherent industrial policy" (Gregory 1991: 74) seems to support such an opinion. It is however obvious that the role of revenue-maximizing tariffs was not limited to improvements in the state budget alone. An analogous problem was posed by the high tariffs in Latin America at the same time, about which I will come to later in the book. Nonetheless, the rapid inflow of foreign capital after Russia joined the gold standard in 1897 subjected Russian industrialists to sharp competition pressures on the domestic market. The FDIs were strongly supported by the minister of finance and part of the state bureaucracy with the aim to increase the economic potential of Russia as a whole (the logic of holistic nationalism), not the monopolistic position of Russian firms. This question seems to have been of decisive importance, although doubts arise as to the extent to which the inflow of foreign capital was a result of the state's drafted policy:

> the Russian state's contribution to attracting foreign capital is unclear. It is clear that fiscal and monetary conservatism created a stable currency. The evidence, however, is persuasive that foreign capital was principally attracted by higher rates of return in private markets (Gregory 1991: 75).

However, the FDI coming into Russia also brought with it a more varied investment focus. Unlike British and US capital in Latin America, foreign capital invested in Russia (mainly French, Belgian and German) did not concentrate solely on raw materials and on infrastructure to support primary exports. The bulk of foreign investments went into a rapidly developing industry (including machine-building and engineering, iron and steel, and chemicals) and also into the mining, oil and banking (Woroniecki 1990: 218 table 1, Pollard 1981: 238–243). Witte's famous 1899 memorandum to the tsar should be read in such context. This is how he explained in it the reasons to introduce the 1891 tariff:

> Without the help of foreign capital ... a tariff is merely preventive and not creative; such a tariff can destroy a country. The tariff of 1891 was a beneficial measure only because of the subsequent trade treaties and of the influx of foreign capital (Witte 1954: 73).[11]

This general statement holds an already more complicated picture. The play for industrialization resembled simultaneous chess game. Only an

---

[11] Giffen (1904: 148ff) underlined only this disruptive aspect of the tariff when in 1898 he criticized the advocates of protectionism in the British agricultural dominions.

identical, winning result of the play on all chessboards ensured a prize. Hence Witte's desperate appeal to the tsar for help in better coordination of the government activities with regard to economic policies. This issue was of key importance to Witte (1954: 65). The Russian state during that time, although functionally weak, was nevertheless strong vis-à-vis poorly coordinated private interests and capable of providing the first impetus toward accelerated industrialization. At that stage the state appeared to be the unique agency exercising direct control over economic processes as a whole as there were no other candidates for this role. However, this should not be interpreted as the lack of a favorable economic environment and earlier incremental changes that would have facilitated acceleration in the 1890s: "government successes of the late 1890s were possible because they were built upon prior achievements" (Crisp 1991: 263). To continue industrialization was already more complicated–not least because of the growing opposition from nearly all social groups. Contrary to Badie and Birnbaum (1983: 75), it was precisely at this stage of industrialization, not at its initial push, that the significance of such factors as "limited capacities of coordination, and fragmentation of legal and political systems" grew. Witte's appeals and his concept of transition to a new, more efficient autocratic state indicated difficulties involved in the continuation of top-down industrialization in a more complex situation. Writing about the second stage of Russian industrialization in the years 1906–1914, with a more accentuated role of banks and the relative retreat of the state, Gerschenkron (1965: 137) underlined that in that period alone the factors mentioned played a key role, supporting, among other things, the excessive 'bigness' of Russia's industrial structure: "Interest in small enterprise would have strained the organizational and supervisory powers of the banks, just as it had proved unmanageable for the bureaucracy."

While demanding that the policy of tariff protection be continued, at the same time Witte attacked opponents representing particularistic nationalism from the position that can be described as 'microeconomics' of holistic economic nationalism:

> the influx of foreign capital is disadvantageous primarily to entrepreneurs who are harmed by any kind of competition. Not only our own, but also foreign, capitalists who have already obtained an advantageous place in Russian industry join in these heart-rending complaints (Witte 1954: 69).[12]

---

[12] The behavior of foreign subsidiaries mentioned by Witte had many interesting aspects. On the one hand, those subsidiaries supported demands of Russian entrepreneurs (as well as their own interests); on the other they tried to block the inflow of non-German

Spurring both sides into action was, in essence, like playing simultaneous chess game.

All this was taking place with rampant corruption in the background. Also, attacks from Slavophile nationalists opposed to industrialization were growing. On the other hand, liberal circles–still attached to bucolic Russia (Gatrell and Anan'ich 2003: 223f)–were increasingly strongly raising the demands for freedom and political representation. Witte (1921: 74) recollected that the former, backed by the tsar, had "argued that Russian natural resources should be exploited by 'true' Russians." Witte, who was a harsh critic of many aristocratic members of the court camarilla begging for concessions (calling them "scoundrels and hypocrites"), added that, for instance, the concessions for a railroad granted to 'true' Russians had been quickly changing their holders, ending up in the hands of foreigners, while the 'true' Russians had "pocketed a round sum of totally unearned money." And finally, like List, Witte (1954: 73) too understood inflow of foreign capital as, above all, industrial investments: "[a]ny obstructions to the influx of foreign capital will only delay the establishment of a mature and all-powerful industry." In spite of opponents' violent attacks, in principle this condition was fulfilled. What is more, "Russia was the first major country to launch a 'take-off' on the basis of know-how imported alongside foreign capital" (Gould 1973: 355). This thesis of Gould seems to be exaggerated, given Japan's experience of imports of foreign technologies and expertise from the end of the 1890s until 1914. Russia was not the only one to act this way. It seems moreover that Japan's policy toward foreign capital was much better thought out and more effectively executed. Preference for joint ventures was in harmony with the controlled opening up of the country.

In the 1900 memo already mentioned, Witte raised once again the issue of threats to the transformation initiated several years earlier. Also, he placed greater emphasis on the connection between tariffs and inflow of foreign capital on the one hand, and the development of local Russian entrepreneurship on the other:

> If we do not take energetic and decisive measures, so that in the course of the next decades our industry will be able to satisfy the needs of Russia and

---

foreign investments, and that was conducive to Russian imports of supplies from the headquarters in Germany. See Kirchner (1981). Regarding exports of German capital, the Reich government expected German foreign investments to be "the means for attaining national ends" and serve "national labour" at the same time (Thomas 1967: 12). The results of the German investment drive fell short of these expectations.

of the Asiatic countries which are–or should be–under our influence, then the rapidly growing foreign industries will break through our tariff barriers ... This may gradually clear the way also for the triumphant political penetration [of Russia] by foreign powers (quoted in Laue 1969: 3).

The degree of foreign control over Russia's industry, raw materials and banks could indeed arouse anxiety, but presumably no more than that. Russia was not transformed into a colony or semi-colony (Witte 1954: 66, 72). Development from 1905 up until the outbreak of WWI was not a move away from industrialization. Just the opposite. Most of all, groups of local entrepreneurs active in modern sectors became considerably stronger. The production of textiles and other non-durable consumer goods was already firmly in the hands of the Russians. A gradual change of "substitutes" was also clearly visible: the prominent position held in Witte's day by the state bureaucracy were gradually taken over by banks and other financial institutions. Coordination, however, remained the weak point. In a word, "Russia on the eve of the war was well on the way toward a westernization, or, perhaps more precisely, a Germanization of its industrial growth" (Gerschenkron 1965: 142).

These classic arguments were put forward, however, in definitely new economic conditions, different from those in Germany or the United States, and in a new political context. In Russia and Japan industrialization was undertaken in a political environment only touched by the ideals of liberalism. On the one hand Russian autocracy as a model for itself, and on the other hand Japanese nationalist modernization, which skillfully used native tradition, imported British technology as well as Prussian institutional patterns (including the constitution), were a symbolic signal of that change. At the same time Russia and Japan were polar opposites as concerned the effect of political nationalism on the shape of collective mentality, of economic elites in particular, and, as a final result, on the effectiveness of the policy of economic nationalism. The Russo-Japanese War was a painful test of the quality of the Russian variant of nationalism. The social and political 'prehistory' of the two countries, which preceded their late entry into the industrial era, explain a lot in this respect. I refer here first of all to hypotheses proposed by Moore, Jr. (1969), and also by Pipes (1990), Landes (1998), Lal (1998), Hoston (1994), Greenfeld (2003) and Lewin (1985, 1995). One may also suppose that the different extent and nature of the two countries' involvement in the world economy and politics also played a considerable role. Ultimately the correlation between these two factors determined the result of long-term consequences of the responses given to signals coming from the external environment.

Conclusions one can draw from these discussions are as follows: in the period of classical liberalism, and next of liberal nationalism, the presence of foreign capital was seen as an obvious element of liberal *Weltaschauung*, policy and economy. Then, the emergence of integral nationalism led not to elimination, but to instrumentalization of that capital within the framework of a different political and economic project. Transition from liberal nationalism to integral nationalism was accompanied by a usually favorable, sometimes ambivalent and *Hassliebe*-like attitude of economic modernizers toward foreign firms. Therefore, in the next chapter attention shall be paid to certain distinctive features of the transformation of political nationalism. They are important from the point of view of further considerations on the logic of holistic nationalism that was shaped in the era of the first globalization, and, next, at the time of its crisis in the 1930s.

CHAPTER FIVE

BEYOND LIBERALISM: TRANSFORMATIONS OF POLITICAL NATIONALISM

Toward Integral Nationalism

The period separating List and Witte, the two great figures of economic nationalism, was also one of a fundamental transformation of political nationalism and liberalism. Changes were continent-wide, although the half century before 1914 is still believed to have been the zenith of the liberal order, which is perhaps something of an exaggeration. The political and economic consequences the Long Depression of 1873–1896 brought about, for example, in Germany and the Austro-Hungarian monarchy were profound indeed (Rosenberg 1943). Also, liberal ideas constituted an important argument in the battles for modernization of societies, economies and the newly established sovereign states fought for by the elites of Central Europe and Latin America. For obvious reasons, in Central Europe the second task took a definitely different form.

According to the Italian philosopher and historian, and witness to the crisis of liberal nationalism, transformation symbolically manifested itself as a clash of the "Cavourian ideal with the Bismarckian:" "If the Italian Risorgimiento had been the masterpiece of the European liberal spirit, [the] rebirth of Germany was the masterpiece of political art in union with the military virtues" (Croce 1933: 265, 253). In a less literary style Kohn (1955: 50) pointed to the transformation of "liberal humanitarianism" into an "aggressive exclusivism" and "exaltation" of government, whereas Mommsen (1990: 217) wrote about nations assuming "distinctive authoritarian features."

This basic change was however neither the only nor the first one. The "Cavourian ideal" had already exemplified an earlier transformation: the adjustment of the ideas of individualistic liberalism to collectivist identities and policies strengthened by the French revolution and the Napoleonic wars. Social changes accompanying the economic revolution, too, were conducive to such transformation. In List's time classical liberalism was entering a new era. Individual freedoms were increasingly often associated, not without opposition, with first and foremost nationalism, but also increasingly with democracy and 'communism'; in short, with the problem of the ties accentuating group identities. Together with Mazzini, Kossuth, Polish Romantics, but also with the workers' 'coalitions' that were just taking their first steps, the ideas of the author of *The Social Contract* were coming back with redoubled intensity. He made people realize that "[h]e who dares to undertake the making of a people's institutions [speaks in fact] of transforming each individual ... into part of a greater whole from which he in a manner receives his life and being" (Rousseau 1923: 35).

What would that "greater whole" be? The answers that were given to this question diverged far from the ideal of the individualistic and civic nation expressed in the British and American experience. The political and social consequences of industrialization had delivered a "devastating blow" to liberal principles: "The need for community feeling, rootedness and security turned out to be stronger ... than the sumptuous need for freedom of thought, conscience and action" (Jedlicki 1993: 38).

Classical liberalism was facing an already visibly different form of nationalism. The latter pushed to the fore a symbiotic relationship between ethnic criteria and the state, even where the concept of an open civic community seemed to prevail (Smith 1998: 127). Habermas's thesis (1992: 4) that "only briefly did the democratic national state forge a close link between 'ethnos' and 'demos'. Citizenship was never conceptually tied to national identity" should be treated solely as a mere expression of hope. In the period of the first globalization real tendencies were different. Acton was well aware of this. When confronted with the theories of "equality, communism, and nationality," although he did not accept any of them, he was definitely more disdainful of the last one. He treated it as usurpation which eliminated the natural autonomy of the state and of the nation, the autonomy perfectly embodied in the British experience. Mill's approach to national aspirations was as a matter of fact similar: because they could not be checked they therefore required assimilation in the wider context of liberal values.

It still was an argument, not a mortal duel, even though the chance of preventing a divorce looked bleak. Individual freedom and the parliamentary system, openness in public life and the free press, that is the foundations of classical liberalism, were confronted with values and loyalties of another order, which assumed a new form of unity. Already bringing liberalism and mass-based democracy to a compromise was a difficult and time consuming process, while conflict between them "never disappeared" (Bobbio 1998: 54).

In such a situation it seemed outright impossible to link together liberalism and the nationalist idea on the grounds of political theory and philosophy. One should take note however of Yael Tamir's (1993: 80, 79) interesting attempt to give "an interpretation of nationalism that cherishes reason and open society, [resting] on ... a coherent set of universally applicable values." From such a perspective, in multinational/multiethnic states liberal nationalism becomes a project connecting "the particularity of culture ... with the universality of human rights." Such an approach contains however a heroic assumption: to bring liberalism and nationalism together will become possible if we assume that nationalism is defined as culture, not as the state: "it is the cultural rather than the political version of nationalism that best accords with a liberal viewpoint" (Tamir 1993: 58). Yet, this premise is basically different from the approaches that treat nationalism as, above all, a movement striving to gain control over the state and as a doctrine justifying these kinds of aspirations (Breuilly 1985: 2, 9).

As a result I am more inclined to accept Szacki's opinion (1994: 68f) that in the long run liberalism and nationalism could coexist in practice only as a political compromise. But they could not create an ideological and/or theoretically meaningful synthesis (for a different view see Janowski 1998: 265). Evolving classical liberalism, while actually recognizing the role and political importance of the nation, did not have to treat national feelings and loyalties as an endogenous variable. Certainly in discursive terms at least, *practical* liberalism was culturally specific and at the same time conflict-ridden as the realization of liberal goals in a multicultural environment could always encounter strong resistance. For example, it is difficult to resolve a conflict between liberal values and illiberal national minorities by referring to shared principles. Therefore the only option available is "to rely on some other basis of accommodation, such as *modus vivendi*" (Kymlicka 1996: 168).

In sum, a replication of the fundamental conflict between nationalism and the idea of civil society took place. In this case, too, political praxis could be treated as a reference point:

> Unquestionably, the realities of the modern world include ... nationalism and nation-states, therefore every sensible theory of civil society must take them into account (Szacki 1997: 45).

Here one may also refer to Gellner's remark that a multitude of languages and nationalisms does not imply any sensible theory concerning the desirable number of national states. Moreover, realism tells us that as a rule this problem was solved with the help of instruments far from liberal procedures. Last but not least, Rawls (2002: 59–70), writing about the law of peoples, lays emphasis not on a symbiosis between liberal and nonliberal values, but on toleration. He relates the latter only to the variant of a possible agreement between "liberal people" and "decent nonliberal peoples" who accept the law of nations.

Small wonder that liberal thinkers gave decidedly different answers to the question about the desired form of relationship between the state and the people. The dispute between Lord Acton (a multinational state "is a test, as well as the best security of its freedom") and Mill ("the boundaries of governments should coincide in the main with those of nationalities") was the most significant. In a word, almost from the moment it appeared in the European polity, liberal nationalism constituted a shock-sensitive compromise.

The national revolutions of 1848 provided abundant evidence that such fear was well-founded. Regarding the period preceding 1848, in Jedlicki's opinion (1999: 17), in Poland the axioms of national community were "inscribed in liberal ideology and were by no means at odds with the idea of the community of European civilization." Brian Porter (2000: 39), for his part, emphasizes that "[t]he idea of the transcendent Polish nation had pushed ethnicity so far into the background" (see also Janowski 1998: 73). After 1848 the world was different. In the latter half of the 19th century, compared with the national idea, the weakness of liberalism was apparent: "It was a peculiarity of the Polish intelligentsia's liberalism that it did not go through the phase of individualistic philosophy which was so characteristic of more middle-class societies" (Jedlicki 1999: 230). The nation and liberty ceased to be a tautology.

Such an opinion applies also to Hungary and pre-Bismarck Germany. It is indicative of the style of practicing liberalism in the entire region. The dramatic Hungarian experience of 1848 proved its limitations: the fragile balance between nationalism and liberalism was violently upset to the advantage of the former. During the national revolution the balance was replaced by peculiar integral proto-nationalism, an abrupt end of the transformation of the aristocratic, non-ethnic *natio hungarica*, into a collectivistic and ethnic *Magyar* nation (Islamov 1992). The liberal reforms of the revolutionary government became a part of a wider process that included the confirmation of the *Magyar* hegemony and patriotism. That aroused resistance. František Palacký, a Czech patriot, expressed it drastically in his letter to the Frankfurt Parliament of 1848:

> [T]here can be no question of the Danube Slavs and the Wallachians [Romanians], nay the Poles, voluntarily joining the state which proclaims

the principle that one has first to be a Magyar and only then a human being (quoted in Wereszycki 1975: 116).[1]

In the "small and young nations," coming to life as nations, conflict substituted for compromise. The defense strategies they adopted increasingly stressed the collectivist-ethnic criteria (Chlebowczyk 1983, Hroch 2000).

The appearance of the successive transformation of nationalism, of the German integral variant connected not with the reactionary *ancien régime*, but with the modern state and economy, entailed that "even liberals were distressed by doubts of their own faith." Expansive nationalistic "activism" led to the rejection of the ideal of liberty, thus deepening the liberals' dilemma (Croce 1933: 254, 341ff). On the other hand, liberalism was ill-served by new ideological currents represented by Comte and then by Spencer, but also by theoreticians of racism and ideologues of anti-Semitism. Such changes "gradually replaced the Victorians' celebration of discussion" (Maier 1992: 137).

Let me put assessments aside, however. Although Croce (1933: 318) bridled that "a hollow positivism and evolutionism stultified men's minds," there is no doubt that exactly these theories largely justified *practical* liberalism during the selective modernization in Central Europe and Latin America in the latter half of the 19th century. Polish positivism combined Spencer's and Mill's concepts into one, and was defined as liberalism (Jaszczuk 1986: 150ff). But that was not all. Polish, Czech and Hungarian liberals of the latter half of the 19th century

> saw positive sides of state centralization, propagated national ideas ... in their theory combined individual and collectivist elements, and considered ... modernization to be more important than individual freedoms. And after all there was no doubt that they were true liberals! (Janowski 1998: 272).

---

[1] Critical historians' opinions do not differ much from Palacký's argument. According to Berend (2003: 113), "[t]he Hungarian liberal nationalists offered a broad range of human and personal liberties, but exhibited a biased assimilationist, state-nationalistic view and denied the existence of any nation in Hungary but the Hungarians." See also Chlebowczyk (1983: 337, 340), Deák (1990). In Poland, however, a shock similar to the one in Hungary did not occur. The trauma caused by the defeat of the 1830 November Insurrection did not wear off, while Russia's war machine was confronting an already disarmed people. Such shock occurred only during the post-1918 reconstitution of the state, within integral nationalism already fully-shaped in Europe. That perhaps made Janowski (1998: 112ff) interpret the events of 1848 as, first and foremost, a will to compromise, not a harbinger of sinister consequences. Kohn (1995: 52) sees it in a different way when he writes: "The new spirit of violence, of glorification of heroic deeds ... phenomena which came to darken the horizon of the twentieth century–was first noticeable in 1848."

What is more, liberalism's evolution toward positivism and the "liberals' centralist etatism" provided a bridge leading to already different ideological proposals:

> Liberalism was, so to say, drained out from the inside, and at a certain moment general liberal categories were rejected as useless, because the ideology of national egoism was more fitting to justify new concepts (Janowski 1998: 280).

And in Latin America the phenomenon of "liberals' centralist etatism" occurred as one of the most important features of the liberal credo. However, it is not clear whether on that continent, too, prepositivist liberalism was as strongly associated with the issue of backwardness as in Central Europe (Janowski 1996/1997: 75f, Gootenberg 1993).

Another change which occurred in Mill's and Acton's days is also worthy of a mention. The social aspect of the 1848 explosion, which Tocqueville described penetratingly as transition from traditionally understood political struggle to "a struggle of class against class" (quoted in Maier 1992: 128), opened the doors not only to the emancipation of lower classes. In the subsequent decades it also favored the appearance of new antithetic political tendencies among the middle classes. The liberalism-conservatism dualism was no longer the most important point of reference for political discourse. Democracy and social rights entered as further formidable challenges to individualistic theory. In Carr's opinion (1985: 185, 190f, 193), the place of the middle-class nationalism of the first half of the 19th century, related first and foremost to demands for political democracy ("democratic nationalism"), was ever more obviously taken as a "nationalism of the masses." It was the other side of the process of the socialization of the nation when the economic demands of the masses became "a concern of national policy." This was characterized by extraordinarily fluid political affiliations. "Nationalism of the masses," Carr added, formed a new basis for economic nationalism, which at a certain moment found its expression in both a negative attitude toward immigrants as well as in "nationalization of economic policy." Growing trade protectionism was coupled with Bismarck-decreed domestic "solidarity protectionism" (Rosenberg 1943: 71).

Croce (1933: 313ff) interpreted this problem as an inevitable breakup of the syndrome that combined into one the political ideals of liberalism (freedom and individualism) and economic demands (free trade and unrestricted competition). In answer to the rising importance of the social question, and also the appearance of trusts and cartels and growing inter-state competition, the economy, he argued, became subjected to the illiberal activities of the state. In the case of economically underdeveloped Italy such activities were fully justified. But this new tendency was in point of fact the most serious challenge to trivial liberalism. Croce (1933: 320) showed that "since the concept of free trade had been hazily associated with that of liberalism ... mistrust in the free-trade formula generated mistrust in the very truth of political liberty." Earlier, Mill (1992: 91), too, had declared that "the principle of individual liberty is not involved in the doctrine of Free Trade." In our times, such a view is shared, among the others, by Szacki (1994: 47):

> Examining economic liberalism against the background of a general history of liberalism, one is inclined to treat it as one of the possible aspects of the liberal option and one of its possible realizations, not as an integral and essential part.

As a result, it is possible to reconcile the political credo of liberalism with different variants of collectivism. At the same time it goes without saying that the scope and intensity of the intrusiveness of regulations must not infringe the essence of property rights (Skidelski 1995: chapter 2).

The tendency cited by Croce can be considered from another perspective, the one Polanyi (1957: 57, 132) proposed years ago, presenting the concepts of "embeddedness" and "double movement." The former emphasized the utopian nature of the category of *homo oeconomicus* and of the idea of the self-regulating market with regard to the crucial categories of labor, land and money. All of them were something more than the economist's "crude fictions;" they also meant social relations which the concept of the self-regulating market tried to transform into "an adjunct to the market." "Instead of economy being embedded in social relations," Polanyi wrote, "social relations are embedded in the economic system." It is in this tendency that one should search for the sources of the "mistaken doctrine of the essentially economic nature of class interests." Actually, in their activities, both individuals as well as social classes relate to the issue of "social recognition," and their interests "are primarily not economic but social."

On the other hand, the concept of the "double movement" juxtaposed the utopia of the self-regulating market–the result of a deliberate action of the state–to the self-protection of society. It was in point of fact a spontaneous response implying lower classes' and the others' demand that the state counteract the consequences of the utopia. In a nutshell, "*Laissez-faire* was planned; planning was not" (Polanyi 1957: 153, 141). In such a theoretical-historical interpretation economic liberalism as a utopia of the self-regulating market was an important ideological component justifying the breaking with the non-market order. However, the actual relations that ensured the duration of the modern economy strayed far from the liberal ideal. The self-protection of society, expressed in the demand for "social and national protectionism," led to ideological concepts and practical solutions that were often antithetic:

> The great variety of forms in which the 'collectivist' countermovement appeared was not due to any preference for socialism or nationalism ... but exclusively to the broader range of the vital social interests affected by the expanding market mechanism. ... Fascism, like socialism, was rooted in a market society that refused to function (Polanyi 1957: 145, 161f, 239).

The political and economic history of handicraft and small-scale industry and their organizations in Germany before Hitler seized power had shown in a copybook fashion the Janus face of the demand for self-protection (see Winkler 1976).

In the international arena that turnabout, sped up during the Long Depression of 1873–1896, was accompanied by the ultimate rejection of the balance of power based since 1815 on the Concert of Powers. The Crimean War, the unification of Italy and the rise of Bismarck's Reich ended the period of more or less formalized control over the European polity. The Concert, which left behind *also* the tradition of "an international system of political equilibrium based on benign shared hegemony" (Schroeder 1994: 580), was replaced with a less formalized and less stable system of relations among European powers. It was disturbed by the growing symbiosis between politics and economy, which was enhancing the bargaining power of states and, as a result, of imperialism (Clark 1991: chapter 7). The relationship between the latter and nationalism, although strong, was not inevitable. In certain countries the change occurred as the explosive mix of nationalism, growing competition between industrial powers, rising instability of the international system and, as a consequence, the loss of geopolitical certainty. From the 1880s onwards the empire building "came to be considered an essential element of national politics quite independently of considerations of economic or material advantage of any kind" (Mommsen 1990: 220; see also Hall 2003: 4, 7, 9–12).

Economic nationalism, at that time still described as protectionism, was becoming an ever more strongly emphasized and debated phenomenon. It could no longer be ignored or treated as an accidental disruption of market relations.

Anti-Liberal Temptation: Autocracy and Integral Nationalism

List belonged to the period of the first transformation of liberalism, symbolized by Mazzini, Cavour and Central European Romantic patriots. Although his understanding of the "theory of liberty" went already beyond the frame set by the classics, his concepts still fell within the scope of the basically liberal political discourse. For List, combining nationalist demands with the liberal *Weltanschauung* was a matter of course (Heilperin 1960: 60).[2] Against such a background, Sergei Witte's ideological choice looked different and more dramatic.

Without a doubt Witte was a proponent of List's economic theory, his arguments stressing the need for industrialization and temporary protectionism. The theory-implied promise of Russia's growing might and extrication from the circle of backwardness sounded appealing. However, the fulfillment of this promise came at the price of questioning of, first, hitherto increasingly outdated political equilibrium, and, second, the socio-economic equilibrium that was ossifying Russia's backwardness. Witte was not going to upset the former, but he wanted to change the latter. In actual fact, contrary to his deepest convictions, his top-down forced industrialization policy incited Russia to rebellion (Gerschenkron 1968: 211).

The political and social shock was proportional to the pace of economic changes. The strongly emphasized spatial and technical concentration of the nascent modern industry, migration of millions of peasants to the cities and the rapidly rising fiscal burden of rural Russia, all these factors strengthened polarization. Foreign capital played a triple role in the process: as a model of modern civilization, as a carrier of technological progress and as a multiplier speeding up the domestic resource mobilization and the pace of change.

While alienating peasants and the landed gentry, Witte could not at the same time appeal to the possible alliance of the emerging class of industrial entrepreneurs and urban workers. For protectionism as, theoretically, the element cementing such an alliance appeared as not only the condition necessary for forced industrialization, but also as a blow to the urban consumer, without adequate protection of the lower classes. The "police

---

[2] According to Snyder (1990: 195), "List, in reality, rejected the very idea of liberalism." This does not sound convincing. Greenfeld (1995: 569f), in turn, draws a line linking List with fascism. Gellner (1994a: 16) forestalled this kind of accusation, writing: "Not national socialism, but national capitalism was his aim."

socialism" offered to the leaders of the rebelling workers by the secret police (*Okharana*) (Bazylow 1966: chapter 7, Hingley 1970: 86–90) did not become, and was never intended as, an effective element to cement the crucial, but never formed, alliance of the urban classes. It was a question of an alliance capable of defying the autocratic state and well-entrenched agrarian interests, and of forcing political reform without at the same time questioning industrialization. *Okhrana*, an instrument of political repression–not socio-economic reform–staked on the division of the urban classes. Their unity was outside of *Okhrana's* interests. After all is said and done, in that particular case Witte turned out to be both a poor sociologist and an equally poor politician. His understanding of "collateral changes" accompanying industrialization was very general and sometimes desperately wrong (Harcave 2004: 73f). As far as the working class was concerned, he claimed in 1895 that "in Russia there exists no working class in the same sense as in Western Europe, and hence no labor question" (quoted in Harcave 2004: 74). The adverb "hence" says it all. Peasants-turned-workers were different, indeed more rebellious.

As a result, with the help of the state and its bureaucracy Witte triggered accelerated growth and enforced selective social modernization, mobilizing everyone against himself at the same time. In place of, say, the Prussian model of conservative modernization, founded on an alliance between agrarian elites, industrialists and the bureaucracy, in 1904–1905 there appeared an anti-systemic and anti-liberal volatile alliance between the "Reds" and the "Greens" (Rogowski 1989: 49ff, Gerschenkron 1965).[3] This was a kind of prefiguration of the later fateful symbiosis between the Bolshevik urban-based revolution and the anarchic peasant revolt. The top-down industrialization was stopped at a critical moment, as a result of the outburst of protests and defeat in the war with Japan. Industrialization was resumed after 1905, although at a slower pace.

Attacked by revolutionaries, landowners and rebelling peasants, workers and liberals, and also new entrepreneurs, Witte pinned his hopes on autocracy. He was a co-author of the October Manifesto of 1905 which pledged modest political reforms, and at the same time he was

---

[3] On the one hand, peasants enhanced their economic strength (in the years 1861–1911 "the amount of land owned by nobles ... fell by almost 45 percent"); on the other, "until 1904 courts could sentence peasants to whipping." Meanwhile, Russia's emerging middle class was for the most part politically and mentally tightly connected with the bureaucratic state and the *dvorianstvo*. Russian liberals did not play a significant role in the difficult, conflict-ridden process of transformation of the peasantry from an "order (*soslovie*)" to a "class" (Blum 1978: 425f, 430, 432, 435).

a politician who actively resisted a transition to a constitutional monarchy. At the end of the day, rejected by the court camarilla and at the same time hated for his role in the repressive measures of 1905, he resigned convinced of the need to preserve–within the limited system of representation–the basic attributes of tsarist autocracy. For Witte the marriage of the industrial class and the throne according to the formula of the "constitutional *samoderzhave*" seemed the proper solution. As a matter of fact he was copying the "enlightened despotism" of the 18th century (Krieger 1975: chapter 3); he believed that constitutional *samoderzhave* would solve the contradictions between the need to continue industrialization and the destabilizing demands for political representation (Jaśkiewicz 1982, Pipes 1994: 34).

It was not mere tactics, either in 1905 when he was fighting with both radicalized liberals and arch-conservatives in the tsarist court, or earlier, when he triggered off accelerated industrialization. It was first and foremost a matter of time and beliefs: a matter of time as the process was planned for decades and required consistent action, centralization and coordination; above all it required political stability retained at any price. In foreign policy as well. Hence his opposition to the adventurous policy leading to the war in the Far East. It was, in a word, the classic dilemma of the authoritarian modernizer. "Imperial nationalism" in the court diehards' version, an ideological supplement to the autarchic concepts of "Slavophile nationalism" (Laue 1969: 284ff), probably was an alternative model of stability. However, from the point of view of the program of top-down industrialization and modernization, the ideologues of the "Russian idea" were Witte's implacable enemies.

The *ancien régime* thus had to accomplish a risky act: to initiate self-reform while remaining hostile to the concept of change. If change is inevitable, its political scope should be restricted, at least in the short run. Suppressing peasant revolts and workers' strikes along the way. Still, what seemed to be tactics was actually a poor substitute for strategic perspective. As a matter of fact, no strategy was adopted until the fall of tsarism. The solution to this dilemma, proposed (without much conviction) by Witte still in 1899 in his reflections on "Autocracy and the Zemstvo," was based, in a utopian manner, on an attempt at combining Russian autocracy with the Bismarckian *Rechtsstaat*. Such a synthesis was also meant to play a significant part in the initiation of structural changes in the countryside. A long-term project to extend modernization to rural areas anticipated breaking with the tradition of *obshchina* and of relationships based on community ownership and patrimonial ties. The activities of another authoritarian reformer, Pyotr Stolypin, reflected similar views. At the time of the brutal post-1905 repressions, he adopted Witte's ideas (Laue 1969: 160f, Gerschenkron 1968: 236ff), although both men shared a deep dislike for each other. However, the way he carried them out met with resistance from Witte, as reflected in his memoirs:

> Like myself, Stolypin intended to develop a class of small private landowners from among the peasants [but] the reform [was] being carried out ... as if it were a mere police measure and not an act of overwhelming national importance (Witte 1921: 388).

Stolypin's agrarian reform, which took off in 1906 and was continued also after his assassination in 1911, was a qualified success: "By 1914, only about 20 percent of the peasants had obtained ownership of their land, while 14 percent of the land had been withdrawn from communal tenure" (Ascher 2001: 164). The consequences of the autocratic reformers' failure were far-reaching. The slow pace of the structural transformation of the countryside contributed in 1917 to the agrarian revolution which preceded the Bolshevik seizure of power, and subsequently to the formation of a tactical alliance between the "Reds" and "Greens," which cleared the way for the communist experiment (see Lewin 1995: 8–13).

In Witte's case seeing liberalism as a threat was also a matter of belief. Although he authored a pamphlet on List's economic theories, he was not an enthusiast of the List-proposed political reforms which could be damaging to autocracy. In that pamphlet "one will not find a word of List's liberalism nor of the larger social and political implications to Russia of his advice" (Laue 1969: 62). The primary challenge was "the formation of an educated middle class" and of institutions to meet "the requirements of industry," which the author of the *System* stressed. The conclusion was obvious: the wealth of individuals and *Produktionskräfte* grow "in proportion to the liberties enjoyed, to the degree of perfection of political and social institutions." History, List stressed with Russia in mind, "contains no record of a rich, commercial, and industrial community that was not at the same time in the enjoyment of freedom" (1922: 75, 89).

However to the powerful finance minister, freedom, if it were to be expressed through a parliamentary system and pluralist polity, was a mortal threat:

> to Witte, Westernization meant forced industrialization, to the Russian liberals a Russian parliament. But constitutional government ... precluded rapid industrialization; Russian liberalism was largely agrarian in orientation and opposed to foisting economic sacrifices upon the population (Laue 1969: 305f).

Next, Laue supplemented this accurate observation with an already less obvious forecast, writing that "under Russian conditions the Western model could not be adopted in its entirety, with both its industrial and constitutional components. Russians had to choose between freedom and power." In Witte's day that was probably correct, although even in this case one should show caution. It was not obvious–as already observed by Gerschenkron (1968: 452f)–that a resumption at the end of the first decade of the 20th century of industrial growth would, in the long run, inevitably lead to a catastrophic dilemma. Contrary to von Laue, Stalins' dictatorship was not inevitable.

Unlike in Russia, in Central Europe the fragile and unstable liberal-nationalist compromise, although in the last two-three decades of the 19th century giving ground to integral nationalism, nevertheless remained an important experience. This despite all weaknesses and limited political influence. Szacki (1994: 61, 73) gave a much harsher interpretation of the issue. Writing about the phenomenon of "dispersed liberalism," he indicated that "in Eastern Europe there *occurred* liberals there ... but there was no liberalism as a permanently present orientation one could not ignore while describing ... the political scene in the 19th and 20th centuries."

Nonetheless, in a comparative perspective such an unambiguously negative assessment seems difficult to accept, although it cannot be totally rejected. The deformation of political culture of Central Europe (Bibó 1991: 35–48) reflected the social limitations of liberalism and democracy as practiced in the region. The tsarist autocracy and the Austrian-Hungarian K&K 'institutional sclerosis' cast a shadow over all that. All these factors warped policy in the region. But they did not create unsurmountable barriers to certain–even if more often than not partial–liberal-democratic measures. After 1918 they were either connected with the activity of the state or undertaken within the framework of other forms of political mobilization and national integration related par excellence with national-democratic and socialist projects or with peasant movements, strong in some countries (Stokes 1989). No doubt, however, that in circumstances prevailing in the region liberal-democratic parties could play only a marginal role. In pre-1939 Poland, the problem was exemplified by the ideological hegemony of National Democracy (*endecja*), a party representing an anti-liberal concept of the state as well as integral nationalism (Wapiński 1980, 1988, Porter 2000).[4]

---

[4] Up until the end of the 1930s *endecja* played a crucial role in the ideological reform of the nation, creating, in fact, modern integral nationalism. It encountered however strong

On the other hand, the case of Witte and Russia, like that of Japan, dramatizes the historical split between political nationalism and holistic economic nationalism, and liberalism. That split did not result from a long-term reorientation of political society in the two countries. The symbiosis between political authoritarianism, growing illiberal 'state nationalism' and state-led industrialization was not a means to solve the dilemma that arose from liberalism's own dynamics. That symbiosis was however the way in which the autocracy–which was falling behind economically and militarily–tried to adapt to the new international realities and internal challenges, outside the liberal experience and against it. Japan, forced to open itself up to the Western world, exemplified a similar developmental model in the Far East. That however was based on different political and social coalitions, cultural heritage and economic transformation.[5]

In a nutshell, liberal nationalism gradually and selectively lost ground to integral nationalism. At the same time in the economy there appeared 'organized capitalism' and growing protectionism. Early auguries of such twin processes appeared for the most part in Germany during the Long Depression. That was however a long-drawn-out process, and the victory of the integral variant was obvious or likely not everywhere. The German case did not become a pan-European norm.

Still, effective economic nationalism did not inevitably have to result in the transformation of political nationalism into an authoritarian collectivistic-ethnic variant. The case of Australia, whose nationalism and economic success were built on the historical compromise between labor and capital and under the political umbrella of Great Britain, but also the experience of the USA, Canada and many Western European countries, justify such a suggestion. Irrespective of anti-Asian xenophobia. Interpretations that link in a direct and simplified manner late industrialization with the character of nationalist ideology and the authoritarian state do not make the explanation of such divergent results any easier. One can equally well argue that it is the form of the state and political regime, including the degree of its openness, that actually determines the contents of nationalist demands (Hall 2003: 4).

---

competition not only in rural Poland, but also in the town: from the socialist party and, first and foremost, from the authoritarian movement centered around former socialist Marshal Józef Piłsudski.

[5] Still, some researchers doubt the significance of Japan's forced opening up to the Western world as a breakthrough in that country's economic evolution. See Hobson (2004: 88–96), Frank (1998: 104–107).

At any rate, it was a fact that anti-liberal integral nationalism and the ever stronger symbiosis between its "civic" and "ethnic" components became from the end of the 19th century an important fragment of the political landscape. In relatively homogenous Western European societies such nationalism appeared in its direct form particularly in Germany, but also in France, at the turn of the century. On the other hand, in the USA and Great Britain there was a peculiar exteriorization of integral nationalism. In the former country, it concerned the issue of assimilation of foreign (for some time) immigrants and the "negro problem;" in the latter, it was transferred onto the territory of the empire in the form of both political and economic, but also cultural domination and racism, which was directed also at the Irish. Small wonder that Rabindranath Tagore, when lecturing in Japan and the USA during WWI had quite a clear picture of nationalism of the time as an ideology that taught that "a country is greater than the ideals of humanity." And thus in both countries the conclusion of his disquisition, "I am not against one nation in particular, but against the general idea of all nations" (2002: 116, 120), was received with undisguised hostility.

In Central Europe (with the exception of Czechoslovakia), in the interwar period the victory of the variant based on a symbiosis between integral nationalism and authoritarianism was absolutely crushing. At varying paces, the majority of countries in the region amalgamated– although in changing proportions–integral nationalism based on opposition to 'foreigners' at home and beyond, authoritarianism and economic nationalism. Meanwhile, Japan, like Germany, was a model example of both authoritarian integral nationalism as well as its transformation into effective economic nationalism (Greenfeld 2001: chapter 5). Central Europe and Latin America stopped, so to speak, in the middle of that process. In their case, economic success was not so obvious.

Latin American Liberal-Conservative Consensus

In Latin America the combination of nationalism and liberalism was almost from the beginning of a unique character. Initially, anti-Spanish revolutions were an exercise in state- not nation-building. In Latin American countries the origin of integral nationalism and its character were unique, too. The composite category of nation-state (Hont 2005: 125, 463) appeared relatively late; European categories of 'aristocratic nations', 'proto-nationalism' and of the nation as a specific 'ethnic corporation' had no clear equivalents in the region. As a result, "the nations of Spanish America fit uneasily, if at all, into existing typologies of nationalism" (Miller 1999: 12; see also Berger 2000). One can defend the hypothesis that it was precisely integral nationalism, usually occurring as populism, which was the first coherent conception to give meaning to the notion of Latin American nations, permanently binding them with the state and 'the people'. With regard to Latin America, it would be difficult to defend Greenfeld's and other perennialists' thesis about nationalism and national communities preceding modernity. When Collier and Sater (1996: 25) argue that "[c]onsciously or unconsciously, a Chilean nationality *was* being born in colonial times," one wonders to what extent this counterfactual case–when looked at from the perspective of the emerging independent Latin America as a whole–can be transformed into a generalized rule.

It does not seem necessary to explain here that that uniqueness resulted from the fact that Latin American states came into being as a consequence of revolutions aimed primarily at political emancipation of Creole elites. It would be difficult to recognize their cultural affiliations as "national" ones. The centuries-old conflict between Spaniards born in Spain (*peninsulares*) and Spaniards born in the colonies (*creoles*)–documented by Thomas Gage's *A New Survey of the West Indies* of 1625–1637 and Humboldt's accounts in the early 19th century–did not create such affiliations. And this notwithstanding the fact that the intensity of that conflict presumably was higher as in the British colonies in North America: "the definition of the creole as a distinct social category remained in British America overall less intricately articulated than it was in Spanish America" (Bauer and Mazzotti 2009: 41). The British and Spanish colonies had moreover one feature in common: they both referred to the 'universal principles' the metropolises were violating. *Libertadores'* continental ideology, too, reflected the lack of national arguments. Put in a nutshell, at that time to speak of cultural and/or ethnic differences–crucial elements of political nationalism (Breuilly 1985: 6f, Kohn 1967: 291–294)–would be an anachronism. The conflict between *peninsulares* and *criolles* (*Americanos*) was merely a harbinger of such differences. The inclusion of the concept of 'the nation' as the founding principle in the first constitutions of new independent Latin American states should not be read wrongly: "The Spanish American fathers of the constitutions knew only too well that the national concept ... did not correspond to the reality for many reasons, yet in all the instances it described a futuristic project" (Pietschmann 2009: 71).

The factor that made a real difference was the very administrative structure of the Spanish colonies, which strengthened the strong regional loyalties and the sense of different interests–and geography. The Bourbon reforms of the 18th century, which resulted in the adding of two new viceroyalties, Rio de la Plata and New Granada, to New Spain and Lima, aggravated the already smoldering conflicts inside colonial Spanish America; they strengthened resentments in the peripheral regions of Venezuela, Chile and Paraguay against the dominant regional centers. Historians have rightly paid attention to these developments (Pietschmann 2009: 64, Anderson 1983: 63f), as Victor Andrés Belaunde (1965: 287ff) had done earlier when he wrote about "local nationalism," and Jorge Basadre (1965: 295. 299f) when he emphasized the role of the emerging *conciencia de sí*. The importance of this factor was increased by the legitimacy crisis which developed in relations between the Spanish American colonies and French-occupied Spain in the year preceding the *primer grito libertario de América* in Upper Peru (present-day Bolivia) of 1809. When analyzing the case of Chile, Collier and Sater (1996: 25–29) added the differences in cuisine and spoken Spanish.

What is more, in certain cases, such as the Viceroyalty of Peru, the independence was actually imposed from outside by Bolivar and Sucre. Taking into consideration the impact of the Indian rebellions, which broke out during the emancipation process (above all in Mexico) or which preceded that process (Túpac Amaru II's uprising in Peru in 1780–1781, but also revolts engaging primarily *la plebe*) only strengthen this characterization (Perez 1977). The related experience of creole elites decidedly curbed their enthusiasm for the emancipation that could demolish *all* stratification structures, and also widen cultural and racial distances on the eve of independence. Cultural and racial dualism, strongly stressed in Mexico, Peru and Bolivia, suppressed during the revolution of independence, reached its peak at the end of the 19th century as a part of the crisis of the liberal-conservative consensus. By contrast, Brazil's peaceful transition to independence took place impacted by the dangerous example of the victorious slave revolt in Haiti. That induced the white elite to moderate strong regionalisms and various conflicts of interests (Silva Dias 1975: 100).

As already mentioned, general ideas of the by then fully shaped European liberalism–individualism, property rights, limited role of the state and free trade–implied a clear distinction between and autonomy of political and economic activities. From the perspective of the principles firmly established by the mid-19th century, in Western Europe the long transition to the liberal political and economic order and to the formation of appropriate institutions was already 'ancient history'. Thus, also the lack of autonomy of the political and economic spheres, characteristic of the transition period, was a thing of the past.

But for Latin America and Central Europe that 'ancient history' was the present-in-the-making or only a plan for the future. Still, such a liberal plan was established in the ideological and political environment in which an autonomy of politics and economy was treated as the founding principle. Thus, the transition to the liberal order and its consolidation were overlapping and this had significant consequences. The differences in historical time, whose rhythm was set by social and economic changes in Western Europe on the one hand, and, until the mid-19th century, the relative isolation of Spanish America and concentration on other tasks on the other hand, make us ask about the reinterpretation of classical standards. In the process of assimilation of liberal ideas in Latin America, the process that defined consolidated liberalism appeared not as an autonomy of the two spheres, but as a hostile symbiosis between the elitist state and society. In Central Europe, in Poland in particular, the estrangement of the *real state* was until a certain moment the dominant factor, whereas modern nation-building revolved around the idea of a *future independent state*. In Spanish America on the other hand, one can speak of civil society's fundamental opposition to its own state. Tocqueville's grass-roots "habit" of cooperation appeared not as autonomy, but resistance to state institutions, law and the ruling elite (Forment 2003: 426ff, 440).

The liberalism of continental Europe, molded in the fight against the *ancien régime* was–whatever one can say about its "spiritual aristocratism" (Jedlicki 1993: 35, 38)–an ideology of liberation. In Latin America the replacement of strategic political elites and, partly, of commercial ones (the substitution of *peninsulares* with *criolles*) brought modest results in basic social structures and economic institutions. Emancipation abolished the symbols of colonial subordination, but not the system based on the matrix of real property relations and social relationships that mould people's concept of their interests. A succinct observation by a historian of Chile that in the first decades of independence, "a radical shift in society did not occur, was never intended, and would have been wholly unwelcome to the creoles" (Collier 1967: 361, 367f) applies to the whole continent. It looked different in the sphere of economic ideas put forward by critical authors in Peru in the latter half of the 19th century. Gootenberg (1993: 205), however, correctly points out that "[t]hese thinkers were producing a Peru that never was." The political break with the Colonial Pact (Halperin-Donghi 1975) did not dramatically increase the circle of social groups included in the political nation. Outside the city limits stretching out still was—and impoverished by destructive wars but with its basic structures intact—the world defined by this Pact: "the landed estate, rather than the nation-state, constituted the 'political universe'" (Lewis 2005: 4). As a result, Latin American liberalism did not revolutionize, but selectively modernized societies and economies.

Nevertheless, the very fact of the political break with the Colonial Pact required, as another step, a basic reorganization of political power and an adjustment of the colonial institutions to new economic challenges. In that sphere liberal leaders went beyond the pattern of limited transformation. Classical liberalism—concentrated on the problems of a republican form of government, individual freedom and constitutional order, hostile to corporate forms of property (the economic empire of the Church and the property of Indian communities) and the ideological dominance of the Church—played a very active role, although not dominant everywhere. The example of Juan Manuel Rosas' dictatorship in Argentina, was a symbol of the failure of the liberal project. His dreadful *La Mazorca* spread terror instead of liberalism. Whether Rosas' dictatorship was also a failure of the state- and nation-building project remains an open question. Benito Juárez and Mexican liberal *La Reforma* and also post-1860s Argentina were the opposite examples. The Creole nationalism of the period of the struggle for independence, which had been far from liberalism, transformed into a unique amalgamation of liberal and conservative values and progressive ideas. I shall return to this question shortly.

For obvious reasons liberalism in Central Europe looked different. In this region liberal projects appeared not only as elements of wider processes taking place in multinational monarchies ("non-nation states" in Breuilly's terminology), but also as national projects emerging in opposition to oppressive nation-states (such as the unified Germany). Liberalism in this region thus remained under constant pressure from the nationalist agenda. And that agenda included, beside *separation* (demand for independence), also *unification* (an identity between state borders and the area of national settlement) and *reform* (modern nation building) (Breuilly 1985: 11ff). In clash with the nationalist agenda, liberalism was marginalized.

From this point of view, the classical-liberal era on the Latin American continent, which lasted roughly until the 1850s, was clearly restricted as to its goals. Nation-building was a process dominated by state-building tasks. Therefore to maintain the unity of the state, that had for half a century been undermined by territorial disputes and by strong regional interests and loyalties (local *caudillos*), was a priority. The new state had to stand up to regional ambitions brought out in the revolutionary period. The distinction between the "private homeland" and the "ideological homeland" (Ossowski 1967) was expressed in the long-standing conflict between the regional homelands and the idea of state-based community.

For several decades the nation-building impact of the creation of sovereign states was quite limited. Latin American liberalism neither modernized the (non-existent) national community, nor managed to ensure liberal nationalism's victory. That concerned racially and culturally mixed states in particular. Needless to say, sparking national feelings (among other things through criticism of the colonial past and invocation of heroes of the revolution), just like the establishment of national educational and cultural institutions, was a permanent element of the new bureaucracy's activities. In Argentina and Uruguay *criollo-ismo*, argued Peruvian Marxist José Carlos Mariátegui (1971: 270f), already at the beginning of the 20th century became a clearly accentuated symbol of the nascent national consciousness in those racially and culturally homogenous countries. In Peru, on the other hand, "we have not even begun to fuse the racial elements that make up our population," and as a result the Peruvian criollo, who marginalized the Indian, "[had] not yet liberated himself spiritually from Spain." At this point however, Mariátegui is overgeneralizing. The Peruvian criollo did not take over the whole of Spain's spiritual heritage, but he did willingly take over its attitude, which was damaging to the Indian elite. It became fully manifest upon the suppression of Túpac Amaru II's rebellion in 1781. It is significant however that in the majority of countries national issues had not been under major debate until the turn of the 19th and 20th centuries. In the longer perspective it created a barrier, and one that was difficult to overcome, between state-centered identifications and those having other points of reference.

At that time, the amorphous *pueblo* under local *caudillos* remained by no means passive. Basadre's scathing opinion that the local "*el caudillaje* is ... a tropical adaptation of democracy," should not be taken literally. Nation-as-people often rebelled against the territorial state. More often than not, however, that was a defensive reaction when the matter concerned Indian communities and/or politically active urban artisans or when it was an expression of discord within the elite. Put in a nutshell, there is no reason to unreservedly accept the thesis that "outside the middle and upper sectors of the population, most Latin Americans were simply indifferent to the political struggle taking place–if they were even aware that they were happening" (Bushnell and Macaulay 1998: 35).

One can only observe here that the struggle for a state is not the only form of political activity. As a rule, resistance from below was also ineffective, or weak. Nevertheless, there was resistance. Meanwhile, the provincial segment of the Latin American elite–with the consent of the state and, at the same time, above it–exercised control not only over the land, but also over the life and labor of the rural population (different forms of non-market contracts and a complex set of patron–client relations). With due caution, in the analysis of certain cases of *el caudillaje*, one could refer to the role landed elites played under the second serfdom: "the institutionalization of servile relations served in many ways as a functional substitute for the state" (Badie and Birnbaum 1983: 68). All things considered, the formation of formally liberal Latin American states–embroiled in a clash with the 'culture of rebellion' against the national center–was taking place as the realization of the elite project of limited mobilization potential. As a result, "Latin Americans invested their sense of sovereignty horizontally in each other rather than vertically in government institutions" (Forment 2003: 430).

Nevertheless, bearing all these limitations in mind one cannot underestimate the breakthrough that the political emancipation of the continent was. After it the post-colonial elites acted in a new political context. Irrespective of the quality of the institutions established, and of the elites' capability of exercising political leadership, these states became both an object of rivalry as well as, in certain situations, autonomous actors. Also, placed onto the agenda was the problem of how to use this new instrument in relations with the outside world. Without a state, including the oligarchic state that had prevailed until the 1920s, the formation of Latin American nations would have been simply impossible.

Changes that occurred in the latter half of the 19th century, during the consolidation of the oligarchic state, were extremely interesting. Positivism ruled. In 1889 the Brazilian republic proclaimed the ideological domination of positivism, inscribing the words *Ordem e Progresso* on its flag. The conflict between liberalism and conservatism, characteristic of the mid-19th century, became less intense. The victory of the republican idea in Mexico (1867) and Brazil (1889) can be symbolically regarded as quickening the evolution toward 'scientific politics'. Consequently, post-independence liberalism underwent a double transformation: first, it became "universal heritage" and a "unifying myth," and second, as positivism, it metamorphosized into the ideological justification of the liberal-conservative consensus and modernization (Hale 1996: 134f, 152). Writing about Chile at the end of the 19th century, Pike (1963: 18) points out correctly that the erasure of differences between liberalism and conservatism was particularly evident with regard to the lower classes, and this in combination with a disparaging attitude. Consequently, "the social and political contact between the middle and upper groups led to a mingling of their philosophical principles." The case of Peru, and as a matter of fact of the majority of Latin American countries, was similar (Pike 1977: 158).

Having accomplished its task, elitist Latin American liberalism, concentrated almost exclusively on the state, encountered a more critical–although not new–problem, that of the synchronization of the ideal of political liberalism and the ideas of economic liberalism. The solution to this problem was a transformation of hitherto liberalism into positivist engineering and selective modernization. "One of the anomalies of the liberal legacy," writes Hale (1996: 145ff), "was the juxtaposition of political centralism and socio-economic individualism." In Latin America, the consequence of the latter was the failure of half-hearted projects to create foundations for greater development of medium-size rural property, and more generally to create the social and economic foundations for a fundamental 'reform' of the nation. Fernandes (1975: 50) well captures the historical uniqueness of Latin American liberalism when he points out that "the ideological motivations of liberalism were primarily of an economic and only then of a political character." A brief comment seems necessary here.

The anomaly mentioned by Hale implied a rather banal truth that property rights, especially those of powerful elites, are as a rule difficult to negotiate. The situation is different in the case of economically important, but politically weakened, traditional corporate groups (the Church, Indian communities, artisan guilds). Here, the victory of liberal ideals, although qualified, was nevertheless indisputable. It concerned especially the process of taking the corporate land property over by the state. However, the distribution of such property (similarly as of the lands of the former Spanish Crown) was, from the perspective of the liberal worldview (*Seamos Estados Unidos*–"Let us be [like the] United States," appealed Sarmiento), a complete fiasco (Hale 1996: 147, Bulmer-Thomas 2003: 91–95). As the example of Mexico under liberals and subsequently Porfirio Díaz clearly indicated, the distribution of such property revealed the collapse of projects designed to create a class of independent peasants. Although the *Ley Lerdo* of 1856 "is generally regarded as a sincere effort to transfer modern property rights to the peasant," in fact the pressures on part of the *hacendados*, railroad owners and survey companies meant that "the reform laws were corrupted ... and used ... to invalidate peasants' claims. The legal act was not reversed, but its intended effect was" (Dye 2006: 198, 200). Liberal reform led to a phenomenon described as a possibility of "the obvious persistence of inefficient property rights" (North 1990: 52). Thus Jaguaribe (1973: 437) was mistaken in his claims that it was the absence of state-owned lands and of the equivalent of the Homestead Act(s) that in the 19th century prevented the development of modern agriculture in Brazil. Economic historians' opinions on this issue are unequivocal: such a development, a clear case of path-dependency, was blocked by the political and economic power of agrarian elites, who in the process of distribution of state-owned lands consolidated the hitherto pattern of property rights and social stratification (Cárdenas, Ocampo and Thorp 2000, Abreu and Bevilaqua 2000).[6]

With the appearance in the 1870s of strong international market incentives and thus a chance of selective modernization, the liberal-conservative consensus became possible. It appeared as positivism with strong admixtures of biological taxonomy and social Darwinism, which, in turn, did not facilitate integration of multicultural/multiracial societies. In such societies deviations from the liberal standard were stressed even more strongly. The 'creole nation' was emerging next to Indian culture and communities, and in point of fact–against them.[7] A constitutive element of creole nationalism in Peru, i.e. a racist interpretation of the Indian and, at the same time, a selective appropriation of the Inca tradition, occurred earlier, when the North Peruvian and Lima creole elites confronted the Peruvian-Bolivian Confederation (1836–1839) arms in hand. In the fight against the Confederation and its leader Santa Cruz, the argument put forward was

---

[6] The Homestead Act(s) referred to the first-come, first-served rule, according to which public lands were distributed at a zero money price. It is another matter that homesteaders were by no means the main beneficiaries of that policy (Breton and Breton 1995: 109). On the other hand, distribution of public lands in Brazil and Mexico took place through sale and/or usurpation, alienating the landless poor, sharecroppers and immigrants. It was a peculiar application of E. G. Wakefield's scheme as an answer to the problems which appeared during the colonization of Australia. His concept providing for a sale of land (at a price "sufficient for the purpose"), not for its free distribution, in Latin America became an instrument for land concentration. See Kowarick (1987: chapters 3 and 4), Schwartz (1994: 123ff). Lewis (2005: 8n) interprets it in a rather cryptic way: "either states were too weak to implement 'development projects' or massive transfers of resources were narrowly [sic] conceived as mechanisms to consolidate regimes for example the *paz rocista* in the Argentine or the *porfiriato* in Mexico." For Argentina in the 1870s and 1880s see Díaz-Alejandro (1970: 38f).

[7] Under colonial rule, the Indian nobility (*curacas*) could move upward in the social hierarchy, which meant a change of their race and caste status. In the 19th century, the rate of caste-change was much lower. See Kubler (1952: 64f).

not only that Santa Cruz was Bolivian but, above all, that he had traces of Indian blood:

> The definition of what was 'national' would henceforth be determined not so much in accordance with a xenophobic rejection of foreign elements ... as by contempt towards, and segregation of, Indian elements (Méndez G. 1996: 206, 216).

It was on this basis that the liberal-conservative consensus in Peru was built. In Chile, where Indians did not play any significant role, an admixture of Indian blood (usually among lower classes) did not make life easier, either. Therefore, at the beginning of the 20th century Nicolás Palacios argued that *la raza chilena* meant in point of fact Basque or Gothic blood (Pike 1963: 29ff). In Brazil, the nation of whites was built, among other things, on utter contempt for black slaves. Following the 1888 abolition, added to contempt was an indifference toward socially marginalized Blacks. The world of the humiliating yet perversely rational slave plantation (Stein 1985) was over. The so-called native workers and European immigrants had deprived the former slaves of their economic bargaining power:

> Upon losing his privileged position as the only source of labor, the ex-slave also lost all that had made him an object of interest to the ruling classes. ... The former slave was left to whatever fate he could work out by and for himself (Fernandes 1969: 4).

All the more so that in spite of fear widespread in 1865 that, as in Haiti and the USA, "the slave will sign his letter of liberty with the blood of his oppressor," the abolition was preceded by decades of effective prevention that fragmented the slave community (Toplin 1972: 32f).

The modernizing community, if one describes this way the coalition of political forces and economic interests, and also the nation being formed at that time, maintained its elitist character, despite the rapid development of the urban economy.[8] The gulf between this kind of nation and 'the people' was sharply defined and felt. In Chile, which was a rather typical example, the emerging urban middle class aspired at the status of "hybrid aristocracy," an amalgamation of landed aristocracy and the nouveaux

---

[8] The term modernizing community reflects properly, I believe, the fundamental feature of the stage of development of nationalism in Latin America which was marking the end of the formation of states and the opening to the international market. Hobsbawm (1995: 317) writes; "Only those committed to progress or who at least accepted it, could be seen as the true members of the nation."

riches from the booming mining and commercial sectors (Pike 1963). At the same time, that elitism facilitated the opening up to the world. In the countries receiving great waves of immigration (Argentina, Uruguay and Brazil), the 'national socialization' of newcomers took place partly as subjugation, and partly in a limited distributional conflict with the modernizing community's ideals. That concerned towns and certain rural areas experimenting with modern farmer-type agriculture (Gallo 1977: 336ff).

However, the opening up of Latin American economies had wider implications. Thus, Francisco Weffort argued that it was a mistake to treat the modernizing community as an anti-national elite in 20th-century populist discourse. The opening-up it preferred was "not sufficient reason for us to think that there has come about a contradiction between nation and market in the country that is integrated into the international economic system" (quoted in Wallerstein 2000: 323). Nils Jacobsen (2005: 135) argued similarly when he wrote about economic liberalism in Latin America:

> the liberal reforms represented nation-building programs, that is the attempt to develop the nation through a feedback mechanism between building modern institutions and economic growth through exports. The interests of the nation and of those elites forming part of the liberal political accommodation were seen as identical.

Nation-building understood as the emergence of a modernizing community was nothing but an aspect of the policy of opening-up, while social Darwinism coupled with sectoral labor shortages justified also the open-door policy toward immigrants.

Should this phenomenon be described as an example of liberal economic policy carried out for nationalist reasons (Helleiner 2002: 319ff)? To some extent and selectively, yes, it should be. The strengthening of the economic foundations of the state and the consolidation of the nation-as-the-modernizing community made possible a combination of selective economic liberalism and a nationalist political project, as shown, for example, by Peru during the Guano Era (Gootenberg 1993: 19, 27ff). This liberal model of nationalism however encountered growing resistance, as did the related project of the nation. At the turn of the century it took the form of cultural resistance but also that of protectionist ad hoc reactions to the deteriorating terms of trade, next to appear as a symbiosis between populism and economic policy more ambitiously defined.

While trying to expand the space of freedom, Latin American liberalism could not at the same time undermine and demolish the social and economic matrix of backwardness. Theoretically, had the liberal elites really intended to concentrate on fundamental economic change, they would have, at least temporarily, had to question the limits of the hitherto political bargaining (Zeitlin 1984: 210ff). Up in the air would also have been the economic preferences of the dominant groups. To date, historians' search for instances of such fundamental change prior to the mid-19th century have not produced any major results.

By modifying or rejecting the classical doctrine, Latin American liberalism was thus creating a specific kind of nation and economy. The positivist political project included not only 'racial engineering' (as a response to backwardness), but authoritarian temptations as well (Hale 1996: 153f). On the other hand, the liberal *Weltanschauung*, seen against the background of the network of real property and social relations, justified in practice certain consequences that diverged far from the spirit of the classical doctrine. The continent's elites acted like a good filter: they accepted only some of the ideas and only a certain type of liberalism, and at the same time gave them a new meaning. In fact it was neither a fundamental economic transformation, nor perfect freedom. The following assessment of Central Europe applies, without major changes, to Latin America as well: "all of the newly created laws and institutions were controversial, often formally granted but strongly limited" (Berend 2003: 132).

Thus, positivist *científicos*, a circle of Mexican intellectuals and technocrats who supported the modernizing dictatorship, who legitimized authoritarain rule and, at the same time, selective modernization, became a major symbol of liberalism. In Alan Knight's (1990: 22f) bold interpretation of their economic ideas, those authoritarian modernizers

> saw foreign investment as a crucial factor in [Mexico's] development ... and they anticipated the day when ... domestic capital, already dominant in some sectors, would assume a greater, determining role within the economy. By the 1900s, indeed, a new economic nationalism emerged in Porfirian-Cientifico circles.

Arnaldo Córdova's (2003) and Paolo Riguzzi's (2009) arguments ran along similar lines; the first saw also elements of continuity in the economic policy of *científicos* and revolutionary Mexico.

At this point, a comparison with Witte's top-down industrialization comes to mind. Although their economic projects were radical, *científicos*, like Witte, were also enemies of political reform. However, this analogy should not be pushed too far. Witte's economic project was much more ambitious. Unlike *científicos*, Witte created a strong, diversified industrial base for modern growth, capital goods industries included. The Mexican economy under Porfirio Diaz evolved pursuing the classical, though radical, variant of 'easy' import substitution. Fundidora Monterrey, the first Latin American modern iron and steel plant–which started its operations in 1903–was an isolated example of going beyond the traditional pattern. Yet, as a productive and financial endeavor it was for many years a failure (Bulmer-Thomas 2003: 136). In Brazil the total production of iron and steel as early as 1929 equaled the output of Fundidora Monterrey (Baer 1969: 57, 61). And unlike in Russia, in Mexico the sectoral distribution of foreign investments followed a traditional pattern, observed in other Latin Amercian countries: heavy concentration on non-industrial export sectors (mining included), on transport infrastructure and on public utilities. In this sense, the economic nationalism of *científicos* was one of the forms of creating the modernizing community, characteristic of Latin America. In this endeavor they were indeed quite successful. In a nutshell, Porfirio Diaz was a drastic example of the transformation of the liberal of the *La Reforma* period into a modernizing autocratic leader (Łepkowski 1986: 289–307). Paradoxically his figure was immortalized by the Mexican revolution, not by Leo Tolstoy's raptures about Porfirio Díaz as the "modern Cromwell."

The liberal-conservative consensus hit rural areas particularly hard. Liberal practices affected Latin American peasants in a way that inevitably triggered resistance, although the patterns and intensity of that resistance varied dramatically throughout the continent: compared with Mexico, Bolivia and Peru, Chilean and Uruguayan rural areas were examples of comparative peace and tranquility. The Mexican revolution, on the other hand, did not arise from a mere rebellion caused by the growing feeling of political oppression and the waning legitimacy of the Diaz regime among the middle classes and sectors of the elite that had been alienated by the regime. The crucial element of the rebellion syndrome, which gave very strong force to the already started revolution, was the negation of the practice of liberalism in rural Mexico. A decade earlier, in 1899, during the Indian peasant revolt led by Pablo Zárate "Willka," Bolivia came across a similar phenomenon, though to a limited extent. The Indian struggle was both for communal lands (*tierras de origen*), seized in the course of liberal reforms, as well as for their place under the sun, i.e. citizen status (Irurozqui 2000, Pearse 1975: 137ff). Thus, Knight (1990: 167ff) argues passionately that it was precisely the combination of the peasant struggle for land and moral outrage against mounting injustice that were the source of strength of the Mexican revolution. State-enforced 'real liberalism' was the midwife of that explosive combination.

After all, lower classes were not the only ones to rebel against liberalism. The secular and positivist authoritarian state had many opponents. Among them was the Catholic Church, still an important economic factor as well as a spiritual force to be reckoned with and well-established in popular consciousness. The 1891 *Rerum novarum* encyclical, an answer to the "great labor question" in Europe–connected with the increasingly forceful questioning of the "condition of the working classes" by socialists–one can assume gave great succor to the evolution of Mexican Catholicism. This concerned particularly the provincial part of this institution, which remained in close contact with local dissatisfied middle classes and peasants. Thus there appeared a contradiction between the "Neo-Colonial Catholicism" of the ruling elites and the higher Church hierarchy on the one hand, and grassroots "Civic Catholicism" on the other. This would appear with full force in the first years of the revolution (Forment 2003: 437, Knight 1990: 39f). The small groups of socially and politically active Mexican protestants were from the very beginning of *porfiriato* staunch opponents of dictatorship. They saw in it a blatant betrayal of the liberal and democratic message of *La Reforma* (which also included strong measures aimed against the Catholic Church, but which were substituted by Porfirio Díaz with a far-reaching compromise with the Church hierarchy) (Bastian 1988). In Poland, the activities of the Catholic Church, although concerned with the "condition of the working classes," was nevertheless dominated by the national question (Skarbek 1986).

Brazil stood at the opposite pole. In this country, a similar set of social and economic relations allowed the bloodless introduction of liberals–protected by military Positivists–onto the political scene, connected with the abolition of slavery as well as the empire. Contrary to the expectations of some and the fears of others, the establishment of the republic did "not usher in any sharp break in economic policy or new departures in the social realm." By having established a republic and given power to liberals, "[t]he military ... emerged to assume an arbiter role in the nation's political life" (Schneider 1991: 65, 67; see also Kula 1987: 131). In fact, the military would decisively assume such a role only in the 1930s, as a result of the *compromisso* between Getúlio Vargas and the senior military command (McCann 2006: 132–136). The crippled constitutionalism, enforced at the birth of the Old Republic by men in uniforms with the consent of the traditional and new elites, would therefore be only a first attempt and harbinger of the moderator role of the armed forces–a basic parameter of Brazilian politics until 1980s.

Populist Response

The socially limited Latin American liberalism, additionally distorted at the time with a fascination with positivism, was reborn in some of the countries in the decade preceding WWI. It was not a lasting phenomenon, though. A powerful response to the conservative-liberal consensus and the problems engendered by rapid modernization came from another side in the subsequent decades. Its countrywide peasant mobilization made the Mexican Revolution of 1910 a unique phenomenon. Otherwise however–in view of it going beyond the elitist modernizing community–it was an indication of a wider process: the birth of an integral nationalism, which appeared as populism. Under its banner the elitist, creole *conciencia de sí* transformed itself into the idea of a modern nation, into a nationalism of the masses. "The Mexican Revolution was a great *national revolution*," argued Łepkowski (1992: 136), and "[p]erhaps this trend should be recognized as most significant ... most pioneering."

Liberalism was unable to fullfil this task. Under conditions prevailing in Latin America it could be nothing but a particularist ideology. It was a political negation of conservatism, but at the same time it was a complement to it. The societal actors who made up the liberal-conservative spectrum were able, each in his own way, to give an impetus only to particular fragments of social and economic life, such as state-building, education and the popularization of elements of social semantics, unified monetary and fiscal systems and the creation of export-trade infrastructure. After the epoch of the *caudillos*, the dynamics of the liberal program resuming in the latter half of the 19th century were largely confined to the duplication of Sarmiento's antinomy: *Civilizacíon y barbarie*, Europeanized regional centers versus the backward interior. The implementers of this catchword understood it in various ways: sometimes literally as, for example, the extermination of Indians in Argentina (Conquest of the Desert in 1870s) and Chile, sometimes as *mestizaje* and thus the solution of the problem of the 'biological inferiority' of the Indians, and finally as selective modernization. At the same time it was obvious that the diffusion of national ideology in rural areas was extremely limited. But even in towns liberalism was not able to carry out a wide range of integration tasks. Disarticulation not articulation of the new social groups' interests was on the agenda. The formal rules of the Chilean constitution of 1833, which continued until the mid-1920s, "limited political competition and preserved oligarchic control. ... it was also one of the most aristocratic of Latin American constitutions" (Dye 2006: 186). In Argentina, where, as in Uruguay, the process of the opening up of the political system to new societal actors was relatively advanced at the beginning of the 20th century, the landmark 1912 Sáenz Peña Law of 1912 and the questioning of *acuerdo* 'controlled democracy' did not cover the new immigrants (Munck 1987: 57f, Smith 1969: 21–26). What is more, the immigrant-unfriendly system of their naturalization created additional barriers preventing their transformation into 'Argentinians' (Solberg 1987: 30f). However, Uruguay and Argentina with their reforms were exceptions to the rule. In Brazil, the system for presidential elections, known as *café com leite*, i.e. an agreeent between the coffee elites of São Paulo and the dairy- and coffee-producing elites of Minas Gerais on the winning candidate, was questioned only in 1930.

Hence the populist answer.[9] It took extremely diverse forms, always however pacifying threats connected with conflicts generated by changes in stratification and class structures. Their escalation followed the period of export boom, after which came the double crisis caused by WWI, the postwar reconstruction of the world economy, and finally the 1929 crash. The first crisis was, in a way, a consequence of certain effects of the export boom, of the emergence–along with the urban economy–of new social groups: middle classes, workers and the urban poor. The oligarchic state had no answer to the fact of their presence, and especially to the questions about how they should be represented. The second crisis was a direct result of the problems the slowed down export dynamics were causing in the growing urban sectors.

Populism was an attempt to answer the double crisis. However, its gist was expressed not just in political prevention and controlled co-optation. In the most general sense, populism appeared as a form of political modernization and national integration, as a reform of the social order that made it possible to move to "a certain idea of modernity in Latin America:

---

[9] The literature on Latin American populism is enormous. Let me thus point only to Di Tella's (1965) classical analysis stressing the significance of social mobilization, to Ianni's (1975) interpretation linking the emergence of populism with import substitution industrialization, and to the new approaches delinking populism and specific economic policies, and placing in the forefront the concept of "political style" (Knight 1998, Weyland 2001). For a preliminary criticism of such approach see Szlajfer (2009), and for a useful presentation of recent contributions to the study of Latin American populism see Conniff (1999).

the inclusion of the excluded" (Castañeda 1993: 40). Populism was also a 'reform' of the nation: through granting the (selective) possibility to articulate social and political interests of new urban groups, there came to the questioning of its hitherto elitist model. If today the populist epoch is described as "a golden age of national self-assertion" (Castañeda 1993: 44), it is above all so in view of the rapid extension of the hitherto modernizing community.

At the same time, populism was a political instrument that demobilized and repressed certain protest movements and co-opted new urban classes. At work was the mechanism of "artificial corporatism by means of preemptive co-optation" (Schmitter 1971: 112). Politically and institutionally the populist state of the 1930s was antiliberal and paternalistic-administrative: integration through co-option manifested itself as corporatism and clientelism (Ericsson 1977: 52, Stein 1980). Last but not least, Latin American populism, initiated in the first three decades of the 20th century, was next, especially in bigger countries, closely connected with industrialization and economic nationalism. However, in view of the experience of agrarian populism in North America and the Balkans it is obvious that such a connection was not the necessary condition for the emergence of the populist movement and state.

Nevertheless, the ideas, which to a certain extent defined the populist variants of Latin American integral nationalism, reappeared in Europe, in the same way as socialism, anarchism, syndicalism and communism were European imports. It was in the Old World where new variants of political and economic nationalisms were formed after WWI. Mexican revolutionary nationalism and *La Reforma Universitaria* of 1918 that shattered positivist dogmas were significant exceptions. Let me add here the ideas of the Argentine Manuel Ugarte in the early 20th century. His concept of combining "democratic nationalism" with socialism can be treated as the prologue to Peronism (Miller 1999: 184ff).

Similar imports were encountered in East and Central Europe, although with significant exceptions. I mean here the mass political activation in certain countries (e.g. in Bulgaria, Romania and Poland) of peasants and the rural intelligentsia. The goals and political ideology (agrarianism) of peasant movements, however, diverged far from their counterparts in Scandinavia and other Western European countries, even though, like them, they strengthened populist tendencies and the peculiar grassroots "societal corporatism" (Schmitter quoted in Rockman 1989: 176; see also Harre 2006: 260). At the same time, nevertheless, they posed a serious threat to nationalist parties and movements springing up in towns.

In Poland it pertained mainly to the urban-based National Democracy (*endecja*). In Latin America, except for Mexico and, already after WWII, Bolivia, populism was overwhelmingly an urban phenomenon (in which new migrants from rural areas took part).

New incarnations of nationalism in Europe did not arise in an ideological void. Witte's shadow was discerned in Soviet debates at the end of the 1920s. The same could probably be said about Stolypin. The way the two authoritarian reformers treated 'human material' constituted an important experience which impressed on the mentality of the communist elites. Nonetheless, one should not extend these analogies too far, as does von Laue (1971: 36), according to whom Witte, "[i]mpatient to make Russia strong ... was a forerunner of Stalin rather than a contemporary of Nicholas II." Imperial reformers' projects never anticipated total social mobilization and a questioning of property rights. While it is true that Witte's concept of 'new autocracy' assumed a combination of the government and the people in "one common, almost superhuman effort," Witte would certainly not accept the exclusion of "spontaneity" from the economy (Laue 1969: 306). The analogy between collectivization-based Soviet modernization and the serf-based modernization initiated by Peter the Great sounds more convincing (Gerschenkron 1965: 147ff).

Aside from that unique phenomenon initiated in 1917, there also appeared the political and economic nationalisms of Italian fascism and German nazism, European authoritarianism and corporatism. Each of them was in its own way an answer to the post-war crisis of the liberal *Weltanschauung* and, at the same time, a perverted adaptation of democracy and mass politics to dictatorship and the anti-liberal backlash. In the cases of Italy and Germany we are dealing with an equally perverted combination between nationalism, syndicalism and socialism. These answers did not arise from nothing, either. They were a *possibility* contained in the history of Germany and Italy. After all, the *Sonderweg* was not a purely theoretical construct invented to make Germans unhappy (see Wehler 2001: 309f, 312f). On balance, fascism or nazism was not the pre-determined fate of these two countries. Thus it seems that Greenfeld (1993: chapter 4) went too far both in interpretation and her choice of words when describing the history of German nationalism as "the final solution of infinite longing."

Therefore, if integral nationalism in Latin America and Central Europe was to rule out capitulation to these ideological powers, it had to define itself in its own way. Imbibing new ideas required, once again, their re-interpretation. In Latin America, a part of the response was not, in keeping with Breuilly's terminology, separation or unification, but reform. Integral nationalism as a project of the new nation was at the same time merged with the problem of backwardness. In view of the only recently regained independence, in Central Europe matters stood somewhat differently. Here, the new tasks connected with reform appeared primarily as aspirations for unification, as a fight against the 'foreigner', defined as an internal threat and as the ever-present geopolitical uncertainty. The question of separation appeared chiefly in the demands made by the territorially concentrated minorities (German in Czechoslovakia, Hungarian in Romania and the Slovak part of Czechoslovakia, etc.).

But in both regions, an answer to the challenges posited by the metropolis was economic nationalism. Thus, it was one more ideological import, coupled with the authoritarian–corporatist and/or populist–corporatist variant of integral nationalism. However, because of the underdevelopment of the two areas, the tasks involved were basically different.

PART TWO

ECONOMIC NATIONALISM AT WORK

CHAPTER SIX

A PROTO-NATIONALIST INTERLUDE[1]

THE KINGDOM OF POLAND AND LATIN AMERICA:
SIMILARITIES AND DISSIMILARITIES

In the attempts at industrial development made in the first half of the 19th century one can discern both the germs of economic nationalism as well as practical problems associated with the policy aimed at overcoming backwardness. This lesson, though largely forgotten, lets us see 20th century economic nationalism in its proper historical perspective (see Batou 1990b, David 2001). The points of reference for such comparative analysis are the history of the state-led industrialization in the Kingdom of Poland[2] in the years 1815–1850, and parallel attempts to initiate industrial growth in certain Latin American countries.

In both regions these attempts were important fragments of wider state-building processes. In Latin America this concern played the main role throughout almost the entire 19th century. The collapse of this process in post-slavery Haiti was a dramatic instance of the difficulties encountered in carrying out this task. On the other hand, in the Kingdom of Poland one should recognize the (unsuccessful) attempt to strengthen the autonomy of the semi-sovereign state as the key focus. Also, in both cases, attempts at industrial development were made at the time of the "long wait" (Chavarria 1978: 48), i.e. at a time when contacts with the international market were–when seen from the perspective of the export boom in the second half of the 19th century–relatively underdeveloped.

---

[1] A preliminary version of this chapter was published in Batou (1990a).
[2] Following the decision of the Congress of Vienna, the Kingdom of Poland (127,300 sq. km with a 4.15 million population) was established as an autonomous state within the Russian empire on a part of the territory of the former Polish Commonwealth carved out by Russia at the end of the 18th century (Jezierski 1994: 68, 70). After the 1830–1831 anti-Russian uprising, the Kingdom of Poland was in practice deprived of its autonomy. The Polish army was disbanded and in 1841–1849 the Russian authorities installed the imperial monetary system and imperial weight and measurement standards. The last traits of formal autonomy of the Kingdom of Poland were liquidated after the second anti-Russian uprising in 1863–1864.

Let me start with a thesis formulated by Bairoch (1991: 33f; see also 1993: 102–106): "Around 1800, the future Third World had an income and an industrial product per inhabitant comparable to those of the presently developed countries." His calculations showed that the ratio between the GDP per capita of the (future) developed countries and the (future) Third World countries was 1:1 in 1750, 1.3:1 in 1830 and 1.9:1 in 1860. Angus Maddison (2003: 249) roughly confirms the Bairoch-implied trend. It seems plausible that the level of economic development in Asia, in China in particular, counted in per capita income, was around the 16th century similar to that in Western Europe. From the 16th century onward changes were gradual, although up until the mid-18th century Europe's advantage was not that clear. However, in 1820 Maddison noted an already 2:1 difference in per capita income to the advantage of Europe. This was a huge qualitative jump.

Until the early 19th century, both in Europe and Asia economies operated under Malthusian constraints. Kenneth Pomeranz (2000: 67f, 206) maintains that within these constraints by around 1750 China had achieved a development level at least equal to that in Western Europe. Considering the stronger demographic pressure in China in the three centuries preceding the Industrial Revolution in England, China's use of resources must have been more effective and labor productivity higher. Pomeranz concludes that "Western Europe was not uniquely productive or economically efficient." Thus, the English Industrial Revolution appeared as the breaking out of the Malthusian cycle, which was made possible owing to the substitution of organic fuels (wood) with coal. No such substitution took place in China. In a word, the uniqueness of the English Industrial Revolution seems to have been a random event; the transition to modern growth was a matter of chance and favorable location of new energy resources and centers for non-agricultural production.

This innovative hypothesis, however, requires further research (Stokes 2001). All the more so that, as Maddison observed, the Pomeranz-implied higher productivity in China around 1750 is debatable, although labor intensity in the rice economy was higher (a continued preference for labor-intensive technologies). Nevertheless, the question mark is quite appropriate here as in the grain areas population density in China around 1750 was much greater than in England. But, on the other hand, in the centuries between 1500–1700 the GDP per capita in England increased by 75 percent, whereas in China it stagnated at the 1500 level (Maddison 2003: 48, 249). Because of these and other contradictory statistical estimates, the questions raised by Pomeranz, and earlier by Frank (1998), will probably be a subject of intensive debate over the next years.

It can be implied, however, that the contrasting cases of China and Western Europe indicate that appropriate institutions and structure of incentives play quite an important role in explaining the transition to non-Malthusian cycles and growth; their absence blocks such transition. Frank's reference to the concept of path-dependent development and the role played by random events (Frank–Landes 1998) does not sound convincing: one cannot really recognize Great Britain's transition from organic to mineral fuels as a classical random event. Furthermore, the others copied this transition with considerable delay.[3] Neither can one treat as a random event the way the British economy dealt in successive decades with the negative impact on growth of the monopoly on the production and distribution of coal:

> Expansion of markets, technological changes, political action, all conspired to bring about [competition]. ... the railroad, the greatest single technical innovation in history, assured it a glorious and vigorous life of about a half a century (Sweezy 1938: 146f).

Thus, the blocking of the transformational potential of technical progress in the Middle Kingdom still remains an intriguing riddle. This applied also to the coke-based technology of iron production, which had been known for centuries. Hence, Needham (1984: 120) observed that Chinese culture, like the proverbial ostrich, had been able to digest iron with no consequences, whereas indigestion brought about the European transformation. Again, institutions, surely, played a key role in this undertaking. The Chinese homeostatic (although not inimical to innovation) system was, according to Arrow's interpretation of path-dependency, an example of "irreversibility" even in favorable conditions of constant and even diminishing returns.

Let me, however, return to Bairoch. The thesis he formulated begs the following questions: Is it really the case that around 1800 one can speak only about a *future* Third World? Are the indicators he mentioned sufficient for presenting the hierarchy of development potentials of particular countries and regions around 1800?

It seems that it was just around 1800 when the processes initiated 300–400 years earlier culminated, leading to the establishment, first within the Baltic and then within the Atlantic economy, of the first areas of modern backwardness. At the close of the 18th century, the economies of Latin America and Central Europe were examples of non-dynamic

---

[3] Around 1840 the coal output per one inhabitant of Great Britain reached 2.1 tons, in Belgium 0.9 tons, in France 0.09 tons, while in Poland 0.03 tons (David 2001: 78 table 7).

systems (although capable of short-lived prosperity, as in mid-18th century Mexico). Certainly those systems were evolving, and attempts were made at reform (such as in Poland in the latter half of the 18th century), nevertheless such evolution was neither quick and radical, nor was the outside world standing still.

These systems were export economies, primarily in Latin America, where exports, of silver and gold among other things, reached their peak at the end of the colonial period. But already at the beginning of the 19th century mine production dropped rapidly due, among other things, to the use of obsolete, labor-intensive technologies. (In Mexico, the 1796–1806 level of gold and silver production was achieved only in the years 1850–1870.) The mining boom of the mid-18th century was followed by a general economic slowdown which lasted until the Mexican Wars for Independence (Cardenas 1997: 71, 75, Salvucci 1997: 216). In Peru the drastic decline in silver mining after 1821 was stopped around 1825 but the 1800 level of production was achieved only in the early 1840s (Gootenberg 1989: 162).

These systems were also post-export economies. An example of such an economy was Poland, politically and economically paralyzed by the nobility and landed gentry (*szlachta*), which had earlier become rich trading in grain. Beginning from the mid-18th century, Polish grain was being driven out of the European market by countries where a more exploitative serfdom-based economy was backed by an absolutist state (e.g. Russia). The symptoms were clear: in the latter half of the 18th century, in the best year, Polish grain exports amounted to nearly 111,000 tons; during the 16th–17th century boom annual grain exports reached about 290,000 tons (Topolski 1971: 201).

There were no social groups capable of questioning the prevailing pattern of resource distribution or–the Polish 'specificity'–which would be capable of at least effectively supporting the state's greater share of revenues: "in Poland ... the state had become merely an institution stripped of all substance" (Braudel 1992b: 54). The eastern variant of the absolutist state, which combined refeudalization with the formation of centralized monarchies, capable of increasing the state's taxing potential (Anderson 1974), did not occur in Poland. Why it did not are to be found in insightful analyses by Antoni Mączak (1986: 134–140) and Jacek Kochanowicz (1989: 114–120), and regarding the wider context of Eastern Europe, also by Jenö Szücs (1988: 322–330). Next, the opening up of new possibilities of profitable exports of grain and other agricultural products required a technological revolution, which, in turn, was conditioned by institutional changes in agriculture, such that would drive surplus labor to towns.

This did not happen: the yield of grain per hectare grew relatively slowly in the first half of the 19th century. The food balance of the Kingdom of Poland was saved by the potato: in the years 1810–1848 per capita potato consumption increased six-fold (Jezierski and Leszczyńska 2001: 123, Kochanowicz 1981: 129).

In both cases we were dealing with economies characterized by low rates of growth in agricultural productivity. That was due, above all, to the persistence of traditional institutions: large grain-producing and cattle-breeding estates, serfdom and various forms of informal labor services. The Western European agrarian revolution which preceded, as well as made, the industrial revolution possible (Bairoch 1973) did not spread to the European periphery: "in the 15th–17th centuries the ratio of the acreage necessary to keep one consumer in Eastern Europe and Western Europe was 3:1" (Mączak 1967: 28). According to other estimates, in 1810 agricultural productivity in France amounted to 51 percent of the British level, whereas in Poland it was 19 percent (David 2001: 79 table 9). Put in a nutshell, "[p]re-partition Poland never attained the level of economic development of the turn of the 16th century" (Kula 1983b: 179; see also Topolski 2000: 95).

It cannot be ruled out that the results achieved by colonial Latin America were somewhat better (particularly from the mid-17th century). But they were not that much better so as to allow a questioning of the continent's stagnating agricultural productivity. In both cases, the extremely uneven distribution of resources and incomes led to the fragmentation of domestic markets and hampered their growth, limited the diffusion of technical innovation and favored the ossification of other phenomena characteristic of the Third World.

This way Latin America and Poland entered the 19th century as underdeveloped regions because of their basic economic structures and institutions, not because their per capita income and/or industrial output were so much lower that in Western Europe. That, of course, was not the case. The living standards of the Polish and Canadian peasants did differ, but it was a difference of degree rather than of quality. The Polish 19th-century countryside was described as "backward but rich" (Kaczyńska 1976: 265). Likewise, about the Canadian countryside it was said that the farmer lived in a "sane and wholesome kind of squalor" (Adelman and Morris 1977: 326). Already in 1800 the economic systems and social structures of Poland and Latin America were warped. Their chances of joining the countries contributing to the Industrial Revolution in the first half of the 19th century was highly debatable.

It was already mentioned in Chapter 3 that one of the traits of the Industrial Revolution of the turn of the 18th and 19th centuries was the absence of industrial methods of producing capital goods: machines to produce machines were lacking. The capital/labor ratio in industry was lower than in agriculture; therefore there were strong incentives for intersectoral capital transfers. From the point of view of the periphery that meant not only a (potential) possibility of mobilizing resources needed for industrialization, but also a chance to copy the existing technologies relatively cheaply (Bairoch 1975, Hobsbawm 1969: 58–61). Worth remembering is the pace at which technology was transferred and modern textile centers were established in Mexico and in the Kingdom of Poland. Change in this area began in the late 1830s, when in the British and subsequently in other countries' economies the so-called new industries were becoming increasingly important (Bairoch 1991: 5).

Another factor to be considered was the declining impact of the world economy. Until the early 1840s the British economy, although increasingly engaged in international trade, 'consumed' primarily internally the possibilities thrown up by the Industrial Revolution. Exactly at that time Latin American countries found themselves in a situation of enforced quasi-isolation (Platt 1985: 30, 32). The problem was made worse by debt defaults by new states. Thus, circumstances became favorable to the move away from the traditional agricultural and raw material orientation. This was even truer with regard to the Kingdom of Poland. Great Britain resumed its outward expansion with full force only in the 1840s.[4]

One should, however, give attention to certain striking differences between the two regions.

Compared to Latin America, the Kingdom of Poland's economic relations with Western Europe (primarily with Prussia and Austria) in the years 1817–1830 were relatively limited. Trade reached a ceiling in 1820 (£1.33 million), and in successive years (except in 1823) it did not drop below £893,000. In the years 1820–1834, the average annual trade with Prussia amounted to about £1 million, and in the years 1841–1850 it rose to £1.68 million. As regards imports from Prussia from 1820 through 1834, one can speak of downright stagnation: in the years 1820–1834, the average

---

[4] It was connected, among other things, with the growing scale of production and the drastic reduction of the cotton yard cost of production in the years 1786–1832. See Checkland (1964: 25), Mendelson (1959: 261, 263). The effects were spectacular: in the years 1830–1860 British per capita exports tripled, from $7.6 to $22.4. At that time per capita exports of the Brazilian model export economy grew from $3.3 to $7.3 (Bairoch 1991: 21, 23).

annual imports amounted to £603,000, and in 1841–1850 to £693,000 (Jezierski 1967).

The situation in Latin America was different. As a result of the Continental System, in the years 1805–1811, the still colonial Latin America became the second largest (after the USA) importer of British goods (worth about £12 million in the peak year). That was, however, a short-lived phenomenon, nevertheless it showed the enormous competitive power of British industry. Already in 1815 British exports to Latin America, compared to 1811, had fallen more than fourfold, and such a situation continued up until the 1820s. Peace brought only a short-term boom: in the years 1822–1825 British exports increased to £6.4 million, but in the successive years they fell sharply. This decline was, needless to say, connected closely with the 1825 crisis in England. Excessive exports to Latin America (well above the region's effective demand as well as payment potential) and £20 million debt accumulated by Latin American countries in 1820–1825 contributed to the crisis. But, contrary to popular wisdom, it was not in the new states defaulting on their debts that the causes of the 1825–1826 crisis should be looked for (Marichal 1989: 28, 46f). The 1825 trade level was achieved again only in 1840, and did not change much until 1850. In the years 1831–1850 British exports to Latin America grew 83 percent, but at the same time exports to Brazil grew more than 108 percent. As a result, Brazil's share in Great Britain's exports to Latin America fluctuated in the years 1831–1850 around 33–42 percent (Platt 1972, Mendelson 1959).

Therefore it seems obvious that, compared to Latin America, economic development of the Kingdom of Poland was much less dependent on foreign trade. All the more so that limited trade with Western Europe was accompanied by modest trade with Russia. The Russian market began to matter only after 1850 (Jezierski 1984: 130ff). This relative isolation of the Kingdom of Poland, combined with an attempt at an industrial spurt, induces one to think on the hypothesis of the crucial role protectionism played in initiating industrial development. I will return to this topic later in this chapter.

One more factor additionally deepened initial differences between the two areas.

The Kingdom of Poland entered upon the path of peaceful development in 1815. The extent of war damages was difficult to estimate. The decline of major cities, the weakening of the position of the landed gentry as well as the loss of traditional export markets were undeniable. The persisting serious budget deficit made things even more difficult. In 1821 the

Minister of the Treasury, Prince Xawery Drucki-Lubecki, took on deficit elimination, declaring, "I shall prove that the country shall not perish for finance" (Smolka 1984: 182). Most important, however, was the fact that the Kingdom of Poland was not a sovereign state, and following the defeat of the November Insurrection of 1830–1831, Polish economic decision-makers were deprived of any margin of flexibility whatsoever. On the other hand, at the time of the Napoleonic Wars the first substantial merchant and financial fortunes (Neumark, the Jakubowiczs, Steinkeller and Fraenkel) were made. The armament industry was thriving, and the abolition of serfdom in 1807 by Napoleon accelerated capitalization of land and a gradual transformation of agriculture. Under the tutelage of the state initial steps were made to foster the emergence of the new social class– the bourgeoisie (Kaczyńska 1979, Kołodziejczyk 1979).

Spanish America in 1815, however, was a region gripped by devastating revolution. According to fragmentary estimates, at the threshold of final victory, a decade after the Kingdom of Poland started its peaceful development, the economically most important regions of Spanish America were in ruin. The British Consul in Lima reported that war and low wages had dispersed skilled Indian miners. The value of silver and gold mined in Peru declined from US$6.1 million in 1805 to $3 million in 1826. In the years 1780–1800, liquid capital available in Lima was estimated at about US$15 million; in 1826 the value of that capital did not exceed $1 million. Consul Charles Rickett emphasized that such profound changes as well as the decline of handicrafts were a result of the Creole-forced emigration of Spanish artisans and merchants (Bonilla 1977a: 4f, 21f).

The economic decline of Mexico, of its silver mining in particular, was even more serious: "In 1821, the year Mexico won its independence from Spain, the output of the Mexico City mint was less than six million pesos. In the year before the war for independence began, it had been more than twenty-six million pesos" (Bushnell and Macaulay 1988: 55).[5] As in Peru, *gachupinos* (i.e. Spaniards) either emigrated or were slaughtered. As a consequence, it was only in the early Porfiriato that GDP per capita levels from the late colonial times were reached (Coatsworth 2005: 128n). It seems, however, that the Mexican economic crisis resulted first and foremost from general disorganization and damage in non-mining sectors. Although in 1800, at the threshold of independence, silver made up about

---

[5] Because of transfers of gold and silver in the years 1807–1820, the loss of capital was much greater (Cardenas 1997: 68).

75 percent of exports, at the same time it made up no more than 8 percent of Mexico's total production (Salvucci 1997: 230). Non-export handicrafts and manufactures did play a certain role in industrialization attempts made after gaining independence. The losses suffered by Venezuela and Banda Oriental were the most substantial. In the Caribbean, an economic gem of France, Saint-Domingue, was from the end of the 18th century being ravaged by internal wars and the fight against Napoleon's army. Only a few areas avoided major damage (Paraguay, Chile and Argentina and Brazil). Also, only a few countries avoided serious economic losses due to post-independence internal conflicts.

Compared to the Kingdom of Poland, Latin America was at least 10–15 years behind. That mattered a great deal.

After *Discontinuité Structurelle*

In the Polish discussion on Marx's concept of original accumulation (*ursprüngliche Akkumulation*) and the origin of capitalism, years ago there appeared two rival approaches.

The author of the first one, Jerzy Topolski, argued that provided the basic attribute of original accumulation was changes in the resource distribution and concentration, the second serfdom could be recognized as a period of such accumulation. Although second serfdom meant refeudalization, it was also the landed gentry's answer to declining incomes and a way of adjusting to the signals from the emergent modern European economy. That double answer expressed the specificity of the Polish economy and society. The change of the resource ownership structure, brought about at the time of the second serfdom, "after about three centuries, began to yield capitalist accumulation (from the mid-19th century)" (Topolski 1965: 82f, 134). In what way? Topolski did not take up this problem.

In turn, the author of the alternative approach, Witold Kula, maintained that the period of original accumulation had been "amazingly short" in Poland. In the period between 1815–1830, original and capitalist accumulations overlapped, even though the latter was "still weak" (Kula 1955: 95; see also Kołodziejczyk 1979: 78). In Jedlicki's opinion (1999: 52, 54), "the first, unmistakable signs of change" appeared somewhat earlier, around 1785. However, the loss of independence meant that "the first attempts at modernizing the economy were frustrated." Therefore it is clear that, unlike Topolski, Kula and Jedlicki, and also Małowist (2010: 242) were not inclined to treat the second serfdom as a prelude to the early 19th century capitalist development. Without strong external incentives, the economic dynamics of the second serfdom did not lead to the self-destruction which would have opened the road to the new economic system.

Yet, differences between Topolski's and Kula's approaches did not come down to mere chronology and length of the process. According to Kula, continuity of the process of original and capitalist accumulations concerned only the system shaped in the first half of the 19th century, which had *already* worked as a modern growth-oriented one. However, between the second serfdom, in the deep crisis in the 18th century, and the first half of the 19th century there occurred a "great *discontinuité structurelle*" (Kula 1983a: 204). The implications of that fact were significant:

> It is necessary to pose a question whether, regarding the economic development of Poland, it is possible to deduce capitalism from feudalism? ... it seems that the answer to this question must be negative. If so, the modern economic history of the whole world can be reduced to one question concerning the origins of capitalism in England (Kula 1996: 160).

Thus the emergence of the industrial economy in England was treated as the main factor shaping a new historical context of the Polish (and not only the Polish) economy. Kula discussed the case of Poland. Earlier, Weber (1966: 276) wrote the following about China's chance of modern development: "In the long run, no religious-ethical conviction is capable of barring the way to the entry of capitalism, *when it stands in full armor before the gate.*" Also, at that moment there arose the question of the phrasing of innovative responses in a situation where a repetition of classical development was impossible. "England is ... the exception rather than the model," wrote Bendix (1984: 102; see also Landes 1998: 235ff, O'Brien 1986: 293f). There had to emerge new strategies, new actors and new variables: the state, foreign capital, limited domestic resources promoting entrepreneurship, international competition.

Topolski's hypothesis, in turn, stressed the question of continuity of certain economic institutions having been established since the 16th century. Many elements of the second serfdom found their place in the Kingdom of Poland's nascent capitalism: the landed estate and the related pattern of unequal distribution of income and labor services (up until the 1860s). Kula would probably agree with such a suggestion, considering that he was the author (about which below) of the concept of the "coexistence of asynchronisms."

Similar phenomena and similar interpretation problems are encountered also in Latin America. According to some, "transition to capitalism" began in the 16th century, according to the others, only with liberal reforms in the latter half of the 19th century. What is more, interpretations that at first glance seemed surprising were proposed. For example, Guy Martinière (1978: 190) wrote that after 1825 "colonial feudalism" was replaced by "dependent capitalism," and "without modification of the 'structural' foundations" of Latin American economies at that. Such a statement made in reference to the systemic change in core economies would have been shocking.

In Central Europe, there was a gap between the period of consolidation of the second serfdom, started in the 16th century, and the period when that system, already in crisis, began to play an important role in shaping the initial conditions of the development of capitalism. A consequence of that discontinuity was, it seems, the need to repeat, in new conditions, the redistribution of resources. It appeared in combination with a new role of the state, unknown to Poland's second serfdom, that of "Treasury transfer" (Jedlicki 1976: 235). The industrialization that started in the Kingdom of Poland in the first half of the 19th century can thus be interpreted as not only a failed spurt to modernity, but also as a part of the renewed, successful original accumulation (Jedlicki 1964, Ihnatowicz 1982). Unlike the original accumulation of the period of the second serfdom, restricted primarily to reallocation of resources in agriculture, accumulation in the Kingdom of Poland also embraced intersectoral transfers.

In Latin America intersectoral transfers took place to a limited extent only. In a similar way as in the colonial economy, the main 'front' of the accumulation was raw materials and agriculture. Attempts at industrialization were limited to the protection of handicrafts and obsolete manufactures. In view of the scale of investments, Mexico, a *cause célèbre* of Latin American protectionists (Bulmer-Thomas 2003: 33), and, for different reasons, Paraguay were the exceptions.

Considering that the development of capitalism in Poland in the first half of the 19th century also took the form of original accumulation, this prompts a number of questions: What capitalism? Was the close overlapping of original and capitalist accumulations of a transitory or relatively enduring character? To what extent can the attempts at industrialization in the Kingdom of Poland and Latin America be placed within the framework of the variant of the theory of spurts Kula presented in his polemic with Gerschenkron?

So, what kind of capitalism? Well, it seems that from the moment of creation–by an industrializing Great Britain–of the new external environment, the development of capitalism in peripheral regions could no longer be described as determined: "the industrial revolution presented two alternative challenges–an opportunity to industrialize by example and an opportunity to trade" (Lewis 1978a: 12). It was not yet forejudged that the new economy and modernity would make their appearance as industrial society. The new context offered a new opportunity: capitalism without industry, primary-economy capitalism.

In Latin America enthusiasts of the new capitalist era were well aware of this opportunity. They had no trouble equating primary economy and lack of industry with modernity. Toward the end of the 1850s, Bolivian President Linares emphasized in his criticism of protectionism: "no one seems to have realized that the intelligent development of primary material exports could be a source of great wealth for us." A decade earlier, Colombian Treasury Minister thought the same (quoted in Lora 1977: 17; see also Reinhardt 1986: 84, Guerra Vilaboy 1980: 20ff). In the Kingdom of Poland, things looked somewhat more complicated because, among other things, of the prior industrial spurt. But in Poland, too, modernization that emphasized the primary role of industry was until the 1860s a preoccupation of state bureaucrats and the state-controlled bank and at the same time a goal "beyond the range of any greater interest of the 'enlightened strata'" (Kizwalter 1991: 179).

Thus the development of industry became a matter of choice of one of many possible ways leading to modernity. Lewis (1978b: 223) argued that one cannot forejudge which of them would be chosen simply by referring to the general theory of economic development. Bearing in mind the skewed structures with which the two areas were entering the 19th century, one may posit that industrial growth could not be initiated in any other way than through decisions from above.

We can pass over here a discussion on the relationships between original and capitalist accumulations in the peripheral economies. I would only like to mention that despite the predominance of dualistic approaches in Polish historiography, some attempts have been made at a more nuanced look at the role 'vestiges of feudalism' played in capitalist accumulation. For example, Elżbieta Kaczyńska (1975) suggested interpreting the underdeveloped regions of the Kingdom of Poland not as areas under feudalism, but as areas under "marginal capitalism." She made that suggestion in connection with the novel concept, which Kula presented in the late 1950s, of the "coexistence of asynchronisms:"

> On the one hand ... we are dealing with a harmonic symbiosis of mechanized industries and production stages with industries which were technologically obsolete. At the same time we are dealing ... with a harmonic

symbiosis of large-scale industry with petty-commodity production. These phenomena cannot be explained by the mere 'lagging behind' approach. They turn out to be permanent (Kula 1983b: 75).

Such coexistence was widespread in the two regions' agriculture as well.

Needless to say, in the first half of the 19th century, subordination of peasants and artisans to modern accumulation had not as yet occurred as symbiosis. Outside the main centers of commodity production, one can speak only about penetration by merchant capital. It frequently was just a resumption of relations, once established and subsequently severed (e.g. in Latin America's mining regions), and also continuation of the landed gentry-imposed commercialization of a part of peasant production (the gentry's monopoly on the production and sale of alcohol). However, the direction of the evolution leading to the "coexistence of asynchronisms" had already become apparent. The state-induced industrial growth in the Kingdom of Poland helped consolidate this. Coexistence of asynchronisms appeared in Latin America, too, although with a lesser intensity. This was a result of a slower pace of changes in the first half of the 19th century. Nevertheless, the direction was similar.

The above remarks imply that the molding of peripheral capitalism was taking place in conditions unfavorable to spontaneous transformation that would help industrial investments. Land estates, a limited domestic market, the weakness of private non-agricultural accumulation, underdeveloped infrastructure, limited labor mobility (primarily in Latin America), a shortage of skilled workers and international competition were just some of the factors hindering the development of industrial capitalism. Under such conditions, industry transformed this environment only gradually and at the same time was shaped by it. The fact that the results of the process did not exactly correspond to the 'classic' models was nothing but peripheral peculiarity.

Such was the hypothesis Kula (1983b: 82ff) presented with regard to the 19th century history of the Kingdom of Poland. It concerned not so much the existence of peculiarities of the industrial development of backward countries, as their shape and interpretation.

Generalizing the history of Poland's industrial development from the latter half of the 18th century through the 19th century, Kula argued that that history was characterized by several spurts: toward the end of the 18th century, in the 1820s and the 1830s, and in the 1880s. The analysis of those spurts indicated three "general statements:"

> not one of them represented a continuation of the previous one ... not one of them was a 'spurt' comparable to similar 'spurts' in more developed

countries ... [t]he process of capitalist industrialization in Poland showed a clear dominance of light industry (Kula 1983b: 85f).

I believe that the very concept of spurts, of non-linear development, does not raise serious doubts today, although its statistical verification remains a critical problem. The same applies to other moments of the economic breakthrough (Landes 1998: 195–198, Siegenthaler 1973). But Kula's first "generalization," namely that the lack of continuity in the location of industry was the basic indication of non-linear development in the 19th century, does not sound convincing.

Changes of location were caused, first and foremost, by technological changes related, among other things, to the switch from charcoal to hard coal. The lack of continuity between particular spurts was expressed, above all, in the technological regression of the old manufacturing centers, tied to organic energy sources. Where dependence on the location of such energy sources was limited, such continuity was preserved. The textile industry in Łódź, initiated during the second spurt and developed during the third one, and the metal industry in Warsaw, can serve as examples. A rapidly growing population in both cities in 1810–1910 can serve as a proxy of their rising economic importance (Jezierski 1994: 89). As concerns technological regression, it is worth remembering that in 1844 as much as 21 percent of iron production was coal-based. The development of the coal-based Dąbrowa Basin metallurgical center had already started at the time of the second spurt. All the same, in the subsequent decades, up until the 1870s, the share of these modern technologies in total iron output fell dramatically (Zientara, Mączak, Ihnatowicz and Landau 1965: 394). The same concerned coal mining: it was on the rise from 1820 to 1840, later to decline up until the late 1850s (Jezierski and Wyczański 2006: 234). Incidentally, this makes an interesting contribution to the discussion on Pomeranz's and Frank's theses.

However, successive "general statements" raise much greater doubts. These "statements" seem to have appeared as a one-sided generalization of the third spurt from the end of the 19th century, which blurred the distinctive features of the second spurt.

Was the spurt in the 1820s and 1830s, from a comparative perspective, too weak? Yes and no. If measured against the growth indices of iron production–maybe. Progress in other parts of Central Europe seems to have been faster. If measured against long-term effects, it was certainly too small. Poland did not enter the second half of the 19th century as a country remodeled by an industrial revolution. But if we were to measure it against the point of departure, taking into account the narrow rural market, then the spurt would certainly be too big. The high indices of underutilization of the productive capacities that were created showed this clearly. Last but not least, did that spurt indicate the primacy of light industry? Certainly not. The pillars of that spurt were the textile industry *as well as* the mining and metallurgical industries (the latter two were funded primarily by the state).⁶ What is more, it was precisely the "one-sided concentration of state investments in heavy industry" that contributed largely to the failure of that spurt (Jedlicki 1964: 365).

It seems impossible to apply the concept of spurts, as presented above, to the analysis of Latin America without prior significant modifications.

Save for Mexico and Paraguay, in no other country did there appear even an outline of an industrial development policy, let alone of a heavy industry development policy. The latter was taken into consideration only when attempts were made to recreate the technically obsolete iron production that dated back to colonial times or isolated private endeavors. In Brazil, in 1864, iron-smelting production, based on a modified old African *cadinho* technique (and also obsolete Italian and Catalan methods), amounted to a mere 1,550 tons (Baer 1969: 55). The late colonial Zona Metalúrgica in Minas Gerais was in crisis (the first modern iron and steel industry would emerge in Minas Gerais only in the late 1950s). In 1864, Poland produced 25,100 tons of pig iron and in Hungary pig iron production increased from 22,000 tons to 116,000 tons in 1840–1864. Production increased even faster in the more developed regions of Austria and the Czech lands (Jedlicki 1964: 316, Gross 1983, Slokar 1914).

In Brazil serious individual industrial endeavors were rare. Investments in the metal industry Irineu Evangelista de Sousa, Viscount de Mauá, made following the 1844 introduction of a protectionist tariff, were the example quoted most often. As was the fact that the first, 14 km, railroad was constructed by his firm. The conglomerate the British began to organize in 1834 at Nova Lima in Minas Gerais, around the Morro Velho gold mine (Eakin 1986), was another, smaller, endeavor. An international conglomerate that Mauá formed, next developed production activities and financial operations in Brazil, Argentina and Uruguay. At the peak of its

---

⁶ In another place Kula (1983b: 68) stressed that "inasmuch as in Western Europe ... only the needs of light industry induced the development of heavy industry," in Eastern Europe "the heavy and light industries frequently developed concurrently." Such a description fitted perfectly the situation in the Kingdom of Poland in the first half of the 19th century.

development, the shipyard and ironworks in Niterói employed circa 1,000 workers. The combined value of that investment amounted to US$600,000. For comparison: the capital of Banco de Comercio amounted at the time to US$1.25 million (Marchant 1965: 53f, Bushnell and Macaulay 1988: 248ff). Declining cotton exports, besides the 1844 tariff, were another factor conducive at that time to a certain reorientation of the agrarian elites toward the domestic market and small investments in the textile industry. In a word, Latin American states were interventionist, yet this as a rule did not concern modern industry. Thus, at the beginning of the 1870s, the disappointed and bankrupt Mauá wrote that "the action of capital is blocked as soon as it is gathered up for any purpose of public or private utility" (quoted in Marchant 1965: 61; see also Topik 1985). Toward the end of the 19th century, however, there appeared worthy successors to Mauá, above all Francisco de Paula Mayrink and the powerful industrialist Francisco Matarazzo. The first created a conglomerate embracing banks, industry and city transport, the other became an icon of Brazilian industrialism (Ridings 1994: 38).

At the time, the development of industry in Latin America was for the most part a continuation of colonial trends. However, the social composition of investors (new *empresarios*) changed to some extent. Because of the needs of the Treasury and the chronic foreign trade deficit, the state, of necessity, bolstered this tendency (first and foremost in silver mining) (Deustua 1986). Nothing rendered the orientation toward a colonial profile of industry better than Peru's fascination with silver in the first years of independence. Hipolito Unanué, Minister of the Treasury, in his 1825 Congress report stressed that Peru was "a mining country." When during the debates a proposal was made to set up a Sociedad Económica de Agricultura, the proposition was received with *"el silencio despectivo de la Camara"* (Romero 1949: 261, 264f). Such a mood infected the British. In connection with the visions of Latin American 'treasuries' at least 25 companies, with a combined capital of £3.5 million were set up in 1824 and 1825, and 'prince' Gregor McGregor, a former brigadier general in Bolivar's army, secured in London a loan for his fictitious Central American state 'Poyais' (Rippy 1959: 23f).

Variants of Industrialization

Attempts at industrialization in both regions in the first half of the 19th century came in three basic variants.

The first variant, exemplified by the Kingdom of Poland, appeared as the state-initiated and controlled spurt that embraced textiles and other consumer goods, and also iron and iron products (though production of capital goods was hardly perceptible). Therefore, in the case of the Kingdom of Poland one can speak "of the formation, in reference to the 18th century ideas, of a global economic ideology which presumed modernization of the entire country's economy" (Topolski 1982: 379). Stanisław Staszic and after him Drucki-Lubecki undoubtedly were representatives of such an idea, described in this book as holistic nationalism. Despite its limited scale and scope, this "global ideology" differed widely from the plans for natural development, which played down the significance of state-induced changes. In Latin America, the concept of natural development had strong support, among others, from the first constitutional president of Mexico. In the opinion of Guadalupe Victoria, the role of the government was to "remove the great obstacles, leaving the rest to the action and interest of private individuals" (quoted in Potash 1983: 21).

The industrial policy instruments used by the government of the Kingdom of Poland included tariff protection, etatism, and credit and tax policies which together made the choice of an appropriate investment mix possible. This was top-down industrialization in the full sense of the term; at the same time it was a conservative one with respect to the state's position on agrarian relations. It was also an attempt at holistic proto-nationalism, clearly aimed against inherited backwardness. Thus, Drucki-Lubecki wrote:

> Political independence must be complemented with economic independence. In the meantime foreign countries' industry abuses its advantage and keeps our [industry] underdeveloped and subordinated. It is therefore necessary to throw off this yoke, let the country participate in the benefits of industrial development based on domestic consumption and trade (quoted in Górski 1963: 218).

Under such circumstances the state acquires a new role:

> The position, alas, of the government in an underdeveloped country like ours is such that it has to take initiative in everything and on every field, because the level of education, distrust and deeply ingrained habits discourage the citizens from embracing all innovations, which elsewhere can be left to the endeavors of private persons acting in their own interests (quoted in Smolka 1984: 231).

Drucki-Lubecki's economic radicalism was just as striking. Not fearing a sudden rise in peasants' rebelliousness, he did not seek to create the illusion of economic security for each and every landowner. On the contrary, his tax policy, staked on the strong, destroyed the weak. He compelled them to modernize their manors for their own interest. The consequences were paradoxical:

> [Drucki-Lubecki] conducted ... policy in the interest of landowners. But they hated him. ... he conducted policy which was in the interest of land estates in particular, which were becoming capitalist, while the backbone of the opposition to him was Kalisz County,

i.e. a region that was modernizing fast (Kula 1979: 13f).

It is not easy to explain this contradiction. Perhaps, besides Drucki-Lubecki's authoritarian personality, the fact that it was quite some time before capitalization of land started to pay dividends also played a certain role. Additionally, the effective, and sometimes even brutal, tax collection and painful measures to eliminate the budget deficit increased the number of his opponents. His political meanderings, the vagueness of the goals he wanted to achieve (independence? autonomy?), also played into the hands of his opponents. A historian and admirer of Drucki-Lubecki attached special importance to his statement that Poland needed three things: schools, industry and trade, and arms factories (Smolka 1984: passim).[7]

The second variant, characteristic of the majority of Latin American countries, appeared as the policy of continuation, concentrated on the traditional branches of the processing and mining industries, and on handicrafts. Hardly perceptible were attempts to support the development of new kinds of production, except for those connected directly with the existing profile of internal and external demands. In this case the policy of industrialization was identical with the policy of tariff protectionism, and largely subordinated to the needs of the Treasury. Accumulation in agriculture followed the colonial pattern, and was in greater part re-invested back into the primary sector and trade. Additionally, it consolidated the agrarian structures adopted from the colonial period. Put in a nutshell, with regard to the majority of countries one

---

[7] Drucki-Lubecki explained the reasons why he wanted to sell off state-owned land (*dobra narodowe*) to Poles, not Russians, in a similar way. The capital thus obtained, he argued, "would be used to the benefit of the country," so as "to come to the industry's and trade's aid." What is more, state enterprises would be strengthened, and at the end of the day "[we] will be allowed to manufacture weapons, and the nation will have everything it needs to exist" (Smolka 1909: 198).

could hardly speak of any beginnings of industrialization at all. Representative in this respect was Argentina in the mid-19th century:

> With the disappearance of local crafts under the impact of competition by the sellers of machine-made products from abroad the comparative advantages of industrial activity were non-existent at this stage. The shortage of labour, the absence of organizing, administrative, and commercial experience in the industrial field, and the smallness of the market all militated against industrial growth. Only one industry of any consequence flourished in Argentina at this time: meat packing for export (Ferns 1960: 363).

Let me throw in other arguments here.

In Latin America common was the model of investments which enhanced an export drive (despite its weakening in the period discussed). Chile, for example, could from the 1830s through the 1870s mobilize considerable private and state resources for railroad construction and for development of coal and copper mining and smelting. But nearly all those investments were geared toward copper exports. The same applied to coal consumed by first and foremost the copper sector (Ortega 1982, Valenzuela 1992, Collier and Sater 1996: 76–80). A perfect example of such development was in the 1840s and 1850s the export-oriented mining empire of Matías Cousiño, combining coal and copper mining with modern copper smelting (Zeitlin 1984: 21ff). In sum, according to some estimates, in the early 1850s Chile:

> export oriented companies numbered 185 with capital assets about 100,000,000 pesos. Banks, which invested in domestic and export activities, accounted for 86,500,000 pesos, and domestically oriented companies (55) represented an investment of only 13,000,000 pesos (Oppenheimer 1982: 61).

Moreover, investment efforts in Latin America were probably relatively smaller than in the Kingdom of Poland. Assuming that industrialization potential is, to some extent, determined by the level of foreign trade, it is telling that in 1840 the absolute levels of the foreign trade of the Kingdom of Poland and, for example, Peru were similar; however the same could not be said about their respective levels of industrial development.[8] In Peru a few modern textile factories went into operation only in the late 1840s (Gootenberg 1989: 59). Last but not least, the high share of textile imports

---

[8] In 1840, the Kingdom of Poland's foreign trade amounted to £3.1 million, and that of Peru to £2.7 million (Jezierski 1967: 159, Platt 1972:). In that same year Brazilian imports from Great Britain were almost twice as large as the Kingdom of Poland's total imports (Jezierski 1967: 34, Platt 1972: 30).

in their total consumption was a consequence of Latin America's weaker industrial growth. In the Kingdom of Poland, in the years 1825–1850, imports' share in the consumption of textiles dropped from 51.5 percent to 5.5 percent. This reflected the dramatic rise in cotton textile production: from 489,000 meters in 1826 to 11.6 million meters in 1850 (Jezierski 1967: 52, Jezierski and Wyczański 2006: 242). In Colombia, which introduced a protectionist policy in the 1840s, in 1855 that share amounted to 28 percent (McGreevey 1971: 171). The differences were considerable. What is more, unlike in the Kingdom of Poland, in Colombia after 1855 imports grew quickly, while local, market-oriented textile production almost disappeared.

The industrialization policy carried out by Mexican conservatives does not fit the thus sketched picture. In the projects and activities of Lucas Alamán, in 1830–1832 the influential minister under President Anastasio Bustamente, one can see traces of the "global ideology." However, its practical implementation was different from the standard adopted in the Kingdom of Poland. It was thus a model giving exclusive preference to the textile industry, initiated by a strong state intervention, which only partially carried on the activities of the colonial industry. However, in the Mexican model conservative characteristics were more noticeable than in the Polish one. Although both Drucki-Lubecki and Alamán were in practice following Burke's advice to concentrate on "cautious experiment" and "at once to preserve and to reform" (Bluhm 1965: 403f), there is no doubt that the latter had more reasons for fearing peasant claims and Indian rebellions and for never testing the loyalty of the *hacendados*. The industrialization he had planned stopped at the border of the landed estates (owned by private individuals as well as the Church) (Randall 1977, Hale 1968). Incidentally, the Chilean state and its powerful landowning elite of Central Valley repeated that socially conservative model with even more efficiency. And the economic power of this elite and its export orientation were strengthened from the 1840s until the early 1870s by, successively, the California and Australia Gold Rushes and access to the British grain market. As a result, "[t]he patriarchal rural world (for so many, the real Chile), the world of *patrón* and inquilinos, was strengthened rather than undermined by the export economy" (Collier and Sater 1996: 83). The political and armed conflicts in 1851 and 1859, described by Maurice Zeitlin (1984: 69f) as an attempt at the first 'bourgeois revolution' in Chilean history, ended in the defeat of radical liberals and "suppression of an alternative and independent path of capitalist development." It seems, however, that such an alternative was rather illusory: the pro-industry appeals and emphasis laid down after the rebellion by the liberal journal *el Mercurio* on the need for "a peaceful revolution in landed property" did not reflect mainstream liberal ideas and the programs carried on from the late 1850s by Fusión Liberal-Conservadora. And as far as revolutionaries were concerned, there are serious doubts as to whether agrarian reform and industrial protectionism were really on their agenda (Ortega 1985, Valenzuela 1989: 295f).

Both in the Kingdom of Poland and Mexico, the main instruments enabling the initiation of industrial development were state banks. In the Kingdom of Poland it was the Bank Polski, established in 1828, in Mexico– the Banco de Avío para Fomento de la Industria Nacional, established in 1830.[9] Unlike the Banco de Avío, the Bank Polski was not only a readily available source of credit and the bank of issue, but also an investor. None of the Polish financiers or industrialists was able (or willing) to make risky and capital-intensive investments in the modern mining and iron industry. As concerns Alamán's 1831 attempt to extend the operations of the Banco de Avío, it was effectively blocked primarily by local interests (Potash 1983: 57). Then, unlike the capital of the Banco de Avío, the Bank Polski's capital, earmarked for investments in mining and metallurgy, came mainly from domestic sources, supplemented by foreign loans. Almost all of Banco de Avío's capital depended on customs duties.

These differences show that, unlike the Mexican government–which "was torn between the need to protect industry from foreign competition and the need to obtain revenue from taxes on foreign goods" (Randall 1977: 149)–the government of the Kingdom of Poland had much more room to maneuver. Etatism supported by domestic resources enhanced the effectiveness of this policy, while orders placed with private entrepreneurs increased their interest in industrialization. They also provided an opportunity to make a great profit and to privatize state accumulation (Jedlicki 1964). Moreover, in the Kingdom of Poland, with the help of the state steps conducive to the development of both the textile *and* the iron and machine-building industries, to investments in infrastructure and to the inflow of foreign experts were taken. Even before the Bank Polski was established, in one of the commissions subordinate to Drucki-Lubecki

---

[9] The Bank Polski was modeled after the Prussian Seehandlung-Companie which de facto was also an investment bank (Grodek 1963: 287). Before the Bank Polski was established, the investment program had been coordinated by a government commission subordinate to Drucki-Lubecki as the Treasury minister.

divisions whose names spoke for themselves–mining, metallurgy, machines and constructions–were set up (Szczepański 2008: 164).

On the other hand, in Mexico, the "global ideology" and also the activities of the government and the Banco de Avío reflected the compromise between the divergent interests of the groups of private entrepreneurs which were dominated by agrarian-commercial and speculative interests (*agiotistas*), and additionally by the interests of the Church as a major participant in financial transactions. The attitudes of these actors had a negative impact on state finances. As a result, it was difficult to accumulate adequate initial capital and the government never succeeded in ensuring a steady flow of capital allotted for industrial development. Consequently, the just created textile industry did not initiate industrial development, whereas Mexico "experience[d] only cosmetic adjustment (however impressive technologically and organizationally) to its traditional manufacturing structure" (Thomson 1990: 257f, 1985). Cost inflation was a rule, too. Therefore it was pointed out that "in Mexico the concept of essential expenses was not quite the same as that held in Manchester or Lowell" (Potash 1983: 154). All in all, in the case of the Kingdom of Poland one can speak of an obviously overheated economy, whereas in Mexico, the Banco de Avío had enormous difficulty raising the planned capital. Nevertheless, the results of the endeavors of the latter should not be treated with disdain: "the fact remains that as of 1846, a mechanized textile industry had been created ... The creation of this industry, moreover, was not a transitory achievement" (Potash 1983: 164f).

One can therefore posit that although both regions carried out, with various intensity, the policy of import-substitution, in the former region it was confined to textiles, while in the latter it embraced both textiles as well as certain investment goods. At the same time, unlike in the Kingdom of Poland, in Latin America the policy of import-substitution did not usually involve a technological breakthrough. Drucki-Lubecki was fascinated not only with Prussian industry, but, above all, with the English one, and it was with England, not Prussia, that he wanted to establish as close relations as possible. Particularly in machine-building (Szczepański 2008; Smolka 1984). However, in both regions in the mid-19th century industrial growth suffered a setback and the next spurt took place on an already new basis.

And finally, the third variant, very difficult to interpret, exemplified by Paraguay. Considering the role of the state, it resembled, especially from the mid-19th century, the Kingdom of Poland case. This variant differed, however, in the adopted solutions to the problem of institutions and accumulation in agriculture. Etatism, much stressed in the Kingdom's industrial policy, in Paraguay under the dictatorship of Dr. J. G. Rodrigues de Francia, "El Supremo" (1814–1840) also embraced large parts of agriculture and foreign trade. At the same time, this etatism was not all-embracing, it went hand in hand with the development of peasant holdings and with a relatively equal income distribution (compared to other Latin American countries) (Alperowicz 1981, Burns 1980, White 1978, Williams 1979). Thus Dr. Francia undoubtedly was a dictator, which was nothing unique in the Latin America of the time. At the same time he was the founder of a state whose social and economic structures toward the end of his life unquestionably differed from Latin American standards.[10]

On the other hand, attempts to develop industry made by Presidents Lópezes in the 1850s until 1864 were closely related to the country's security and independence. And not without reason, taking into account the growing strength of Paraguay's two–not necessarily friendly–neighbors (Brazil and Argentina). At the same time both presidents attempted a cautious and selective opening up of the economy to their neighbors and to Great Britain. Also, the opening up was accompanied by the formation of a new social group who gradually privatized the etatized economy:

> In the Paraguayan economy, this stratum represented private capital and at the same time, because of their membership of the ruling elite, they supported measures aiming at the consolidation of the role of the state in the economic life (Alperowicz 1981: 193).

Paraguay's investment effort made in the mid-1850s was presumably relatively greater than in Mexico or Peru. On the verge of independence, this land-locked part of the former Viceroyalty of the Rio de la Plata was just a poor cousin. Also, the small demographic potential of the country speaks volumes. According to certain new estimates, in 1864 the population of Paraguay should be estimated at 285,000–318,000, not a million, as reported

---

[10] Pastore (1994b: 577, 593) takes the opposite view. He derives Dr. Francia's etatism from the colonial model of agrarian relations, although he admits that the intensity of the measures taken by *El Supremo* was much greater. One of the consequences was the structure of the budget revenue, decidedly different from the one in the late colonial period. Therefore, having in mind the differences between colonial and post-colonial property relations in agriculture, to reduce the two variants to colonial mentality of "giving preference to the interests of the state over individual interests" seems to be an oversimplification.

earlier (Reber 1988: 307). Yet, this new estimate seems to be considerably understated. The 420,000 figure or more (with the maximum ceiling of 700,000) seems much more reliable. In 1850 the population of Mexico was 7.66 million, that of Peru 2 million (Madison 2003: 121). Let us add here that in 1870, i.e. right after the end of the destructive war of the Triple Alliance, the population of Paraguay was probably 110,000–210,000 (Whigham and Potthast 2002: 144ff). Still, the surpluses accumulated by the government allowed it after the mid-1850s to build, with the help of British experts (Plá 1976), ironworks, an arsenal and a railroad (as long as the one in Brazil at that time), and to diversify and increase agricultural production (particularly of yerba mate and tobacco) and cattle breeding. Paraguay started to build its own navy and tried to build ironclad steamships.

One should, however, take note here of the opinion of Mario Pastore (1994a: 307), who maintains that, first, "no estimates exist of the real value of state investments or of the product of state enterprises" and therefore "only a qualitative description [can] be made," and that, second, "the evidence does not justify the contention that anything even remotely akin to industrialization took place." In a nutshell, one should decidedly reject the hypothesis of state-led industrialization (see also Schneider 1984).

This is an extreme view. Moreover, the author makes criticism of his opponents easier by assuming implicitly that in the case of Paraguay, the discourse is not so much about the first steps toward the initiation of industrialization, as about an already advanced industrialization spurt. By definition, to treat such first steps as industrialization-in-the-making must lead to negative assessments. Open to doubt is also the author's thesis that within another "institutional structure" (read: less fiscality and state interventionism), Paraguay would have developed faster (Pastore 1994a: 323f). The trouble is that at the time of the Paraguayan experiment, the alternative structures existing in Latin America did not show any clear advantage, especially with regard to the development of industry. The author's conclusion that not only under Dr. Francia's dictatorship, but also in the 1850s and the early 1860s, and also from the late 1930s to the 1980s "Paraguay's ... experiment was nothing but the extension of colonial mercantilism, absolutism, and militarism" (Pastore 1994a: 322, 1994b: 594f) is an evident parachronism. In the same way, and for equally doubtful benefit, one might describe, for example, the economic policy pursued under Stalin in Russia in the 1930s. Which, after all is said and done, the author does, claiming that "[t]he numerous analogous features between [Dr. Francia's] economy and socialist economies suggest that all these economies may be of the same genus" (Pastore 1994b: 594f). On paper one can posit anything: both 'mercantilism' which blocks industrialization as well as 'mercantilism' which creates military-industrial power.

And the most difficult matter: unlike in the case of the first two variants, in the case of Paraguay we know a little about the beginnings of its industrialization, but we do not know its final results. The war of the Triple Alliance (Argentina, Brazil and Uruguay) in the years 1864–1870, which ended in the devastation of the country and in demographic catastrophe, interrupted the experiment in the selective opening up of the economy and in the initiation of industrialization. One can only presume that in view of the more favorable–from the point of view of industrial growth–agrarian structure and the experience in the controlled opening up to the outside world, potentially, Paraguay had a good chance to demonstrate the merits of an alternative capitalist model of development (Szlajfer 1986). But the tendencies that appeared in the Lopezes' time could just as well have led to the formation of an anti-development predatory state. Still, both these hypotheses are mere intellectual speculations.

As indicated above, the variants of industrialization and protonationalism outlined were an important element of the wider processes of the formation of new states. Despite social limitations as well as limited economic success, Latin American states became fact. The same applied to Paraguay where *El Supremo* carried out, using dictatorial methods, *The Social Contract* author's ideals of equality. Furthermore, the absence of large-scale mobilization of the rural population favored consolidation of the new states. The fate of the model slave colony, Saint Domingue (Haiti), was more dramatic.

In Haiti's case independence was a result of not only a political revolution, but of social and economic revolutions as well. Slave plantation and independence were irreconcilable. At the same time, an independent Haiti, without the economic foundations that inevitably could be provided, above all, by former black slaves, was a pipe dream. In a word, the prospects were tragic.

For decades after the Toussaint-L'Ouverture rebellion this basic issue was the subject of disputes and armed clashes that involved black and mulatto military elites, mulatto nouveaux riches, former slaves, and mulatto and black peasants. The conflicts also had their regional dimension: the division into the Black North (where sugar plantations prevailed) and the Mulatto South and West (which represented a more diversified production profile, combining landed estates and peasant holdings). All in all, inasmuch as the revolution expressed a distinctive "racial pride" which united the blacks and mulattos, the formation of a new order that implied new stratifications was entangled with destructive "colour prejudice" (David Nicholls quoted in Maginot 1992: 230).

The short rule of Toussaint-L'Ouverture's successor, Jean-Jacques Dessalines, was decisive for Haiti's future (Łepkowski 1964). Continuing his predecessor's policy focused on plantations as the main source of revenue, in 1805 Dessalines carried out a veritable economic revolution: he nationalized the plantations in the North. The British consul wrote that "nearly the whole of the North fell into the hands of this man," and once he had nationalized land estates, "he attached the labourers to the soil" (Mackenzie 1830: 145; see also Franklin 1971: 321). In the South, strong resistance from the mulatto elite prevented a solution of this kind. But mulatto landowners, like the black military elite, were without doubt interested in maintaining "work discipline" among black laborers. Successive governments recurrently duplicated the model of forced labor mobilization. Such attempts reached their peak when, in 1826, the Rural Code – which affirmed drastic limitations of individual freedom of plantation workers and established military commanders' supervision over agriculture– was promulgated. The importance of the plantation was reconfirmed, although laborers were no longer formal slaves and were called *cultivateurs, travaillant au quart*. The Rural Code stipulated: "The labourers attached to any plantation, labouring for one-quarter of the produce, shall have assigned to them for their personal use, a garden for provisions, which they shall cultivate during their hours and days of rest" (Rural Code 1970: 18f).

The attempts to draw the already free black Haitians into the regime of the export-oriented plantation economy and of forced labor mobilization ended in a fiasco. The victorious black peasant revolt (*picquete* rebellion) in the 1840s combined with mulatto resistance to the political-military dominance of the black elite, sealed it. Its consequence was the dramatic weakening of the state and, simultaneously, turning it into a predatory state. Masses of independent mulatto and black peasants stood for almost the entire 19th century in opposition to it. For them "comfortable self-sufficiency" was the alternative to plantation and great estate (Moya Pons 1978: 64f, Mintz 1974). The history of the first and in fact unique victorious anti-slavery revolution, and of the state which generously rendered a helping hand to Bolivar and his revolutionaries, came to a bitter end.

Selected Problems

This section discusses selected problems concerning the variants of industrialization outlined above.

Accumulation

Agriculture was the main source of accumulation both in the Kingdom of Poland and in Latin America. There were, however, significant differences in the methods of resource mobilization.

Although in 1807 Napoleon abolished serfdom on the territory of the future Kingdom of Poland, the new regulations did not settle the question of land ownership. As a result, a system of labor services (corvée) without serfdom appeared: "in order not to become a free pauper, the peasant had to provide labor services to the landlord" (Łepkowski 1967: 32f). The system was gradually eliminated through peasant buyouts of their obligations and land evictions, and on state-owned lands through enfranchisement. The number of landless peasants consequently rose. This way, parallel to the gradual development of peasant holdings, there was a transfer of some of the peasant land and money into the hands of the landed gentry (7.5 percent of the total population in 1827) (Jezierski 1994: 101). The result was the 'Prussian Road' to capitalist agriculture (Łukasiewicz 1982). The Land Credit Society (*Towarzystwo Kredytowe Ziemskie*), established in 1825 on the initiative of Drucki-Lubecki as a state-supported mortgage association, did not confine itself to saving debt-laden landowners (for the most part in Prussia): a mere 6 percent of landed estates were debt-free (Szczepański 2008: 155). The Society also aimed to help capitalization of land and modernization of agriculture. At the same time, the close financial relationship between the Society and the Bank Polski made it easier to involve landowners–voluntarily or involuntarily–in the government investment program. As a result, the program was partly financed by the landed gentry (Rutkowski 1953: 428, Jedlicki 1964: 44).

The indicated source of accumulation was of a private nature. But freedom of allocation was restricted by state control over a substantial part of resources: "No accumulation ... took place at that time without the state's participation. The state appropriated a large share in the national income ... A large part of that income lined the pockets of 'capitalists'" (Kula 1979: 15). Nevertheless, income redistribution related to state accumulation had, theoretically speaking, its good side, too, which was the lowering of private entrepreneurs' risk and transaction costs. The rise in investments in mining and metallurgy was evidence of the scale of state-controlled accumulation. In the years 1817–1827 those investments amounted to 2.7 million Polish złotys. The ambitious investment plan Drucki-Lubecki approved in 1827 provided, among other things, for the construction of 15 blast furnaces, 76 forges and eight rolling mills. Thus, in 1828–1833 the Bank Polski invested as much as 5.5 million Polish złotys (equal to £131,000) (Szczepański 2008: 165ff, Jezierski and Leszczyńska 2001: 121). The sums rose in the succeeding years.

The mechanism of state accumulation included a direct tax system which also applied to the landed gentry, and, first and foremost, indirect taxes (various kinds of state monopolies or monopolies leased from the state). To these one should add a £1 million foreign loan from Prussian and Dutch banks to finance, above all, investments in mining and metallurgy, and in infrastructure, and also sums obtained from the sale of state-owned lands. Meanwhile, the share of customs duties in the state budget was relatively small: in the years 1821–1850 it fluctuated between 7.7 and 10.3 percent (Jezierski and Wyczański 2006: 319, 322, Jedlicki 1964: 40, 51, Rutkowski 1953: 453f).

As concerns foreign capital, Drucki-Lubecki presented an ambiguous attitude. He unquestionably was a firm opponent of the influx of speculative "big capital from foreign money markets." He would "rather find capital at home, even if one had to wait longer." On the other hand, he was an enthusiastic supporter of immigrant skilled workers and technical experts (in 1824, 150,000 Germans settled in the Kingdom of Poland) (Smolka 1984: 239f). He also assumed that with the help of English experts and imported capital it would be possible to build local machine-building industry (Szczepański 2008: 168). A foreign loan secured by the state fit his vision of the Kingdom of Poland's growing economic independence.

As a managerial exercise, the system combining private and state accumulation, was, despite its complicated construction, effective. Regarding the peasantry, fiscal pressure initiated basic changes: direct and indirect taxation forced at least partial participation of the peasant household in market operations. In this way, alongside freeholders, peasants tied to the landed estate also found themselves, to a degree, within the orbit of the money economy. However, this kind of state activity did not facilitate modernization of agriculture or a rise in productivity or standard of living, while it definitely furthered income redistribution (Kochanowicz 1981: 185).

In Latin America, conversely, private accumulation took precedence. Except for some indirect taxes, as a rule, peasant surpluses did not go to the state budget. In Peru and Bolivia budgets were saved thanks, among other things, to the reintroduction of the old colonial tax on Indians, the *contribución de indigenas* (Kubler 1952, Bonilla 1980, Piel 1975). It was not a mere drainage of Indian resources as Indians treated this tax as the obligation for the state to curtail the privatization of communal lands (Irurozqui 2000). In turn, the lease of state monopolies often resulted in losses to the state budget. Such cases were noted in the Kingdom of Poland as well.[11]

Unlike the Kingdom of Poland, Latin American countries, as a rule, did not levy tax on *hacendados's* land. In certain countries possibilities to mortgage and capitalize landed property were limited. The principle of *mayorazgo* was holy gospel in Chile up until the mid-19th century (Bauer 1975). In this situation import duties and proceeds from certain monopolies (mainly on salt and tobacco) were the main sources of potential investments. At that time substantial foreign loans were out of the question. The majority of Latin American states did not pay debts that had been incurred before 1825. Moreover, the investment potential of the state was limited by the legacy of internal debts. In Bolivia they were paid back by handing over state-owned lands and confiscated Church property to *hacendados* (Bonilla 1980: chapter 4). Last but not least one should stress the inefficiency of the Latin American tax collection system (Deas 1982).

The picture of Paraguay was different. In that country considerable agricultural resources (particularly cattle breeding) were from 1814 under direct state control. This seems to have lessened the state fiscal pressure on peasants. In combination with effective control over foreign trade, in the 1850s it permitted, at least potentially, a concentration of resources siphoned off from agriculture on projects related with defense and development of the army in particular.

Labor

Inasmuch as in the Kingdom of Poland recruitment of labor for the nascent industry was no great trouble, in many parts of Latin America there were chronic labor shortages. This would partly explain the differences in the two areas' speed of industrial development. This thesis requires, however, a brief comment.

In the Kingdom of Poland changes in agriculture pushed surplus labor to the towns, although not at a pace permitting an all-out modernization of the rural economy as well as development of industry. This was one of the defining characteristics of "progress under conditions of growing

---

[11] See Walker (1984) on the tobacco monopoly in Mexico. In the Kingdom of Poland such a monopoly was in the 1830s in the hands of Maurycy Koniar. In both countries the leased monopoly was an instrument facilitating private accumulation at the expense of state revenues and tobacco growers.

backwardness" (Kula 1979: 23). Besides, productive use of the existing surplus labor required various non-market incentives and pressures (e.g. the formation in 1817 of the Mining Corps where miners and iron industry workers were employed for life). In many non-agricultural endeavors use was also made of unpaid labor of peasants tied to the landed estates. Freeholders too, pressed by tax collectors, searched for additional employment, for example in government-financed investment projects (Jedlicki 1964, Zientara, Mączak, Ihnatowicz and Landau 1965, Kochanowicz 1981). It was only in more or less the middle of the 19th century that one could speak of the formation of a modern labor market. Essentially, the problem of transformation of "hands *in potentia*" into actual employment persisted (Assorodobraj 1966: 270). But unlike in the 18th century, competition for labor between agriculture and manufacturing receded into the background.

In Latin America competition for labor was very strong, and this not only between agriculture and the town. In agriculture those competing for labor were export-oriented plantation/landed estates, domestic-market-oriented agriculture, and in the Indian regions–*hacendados* and Indian communities. Growing land concentration and extensive agricultural production restricted the mobility of labor, while labor services were widespread. The thesis of Polish historians that "labor services (corvée) without serfdom" was a unique Polish experience (Kula 1955, Łepkowski 1967) is thus unsustainable. *Inquilinos* in Chile and debt peonage, rife in the whole of Latin America, were sometimes complemented with more draconian methods, such as state-enforced *mandamientos* in Guatemala (Bauer 1975, McCreery 1986). In Bolivia and Peru, Indian communities immobilized the potential labor force (Bonilla 1980). On the other hand in towns, the formation of the modern labor market was blocked by politically powerful artisan guilds. It is not certain, however, whether their role was as negative as maintained with regard, for example, to Bolivia (Lora 1977).

Information on the beginnings of industrial protectionism in Colombia and Peru mentions the presence of *la plebe* in main towns and surroundings, just like in Poland in the second half of the 18th century (Flores Galindo 2001: 75f, Stafford 1965, Gootenberg 1982, 1989). Productive employment of that potential labor presented problems. Certain countries, such as Paraguay, resorted to administrative methods of labor mobilization: the ironworks of Ybycui were built by British experts and Indians working under the lash (Williams 1979: 181). Peru introduced economic mechanisms characteristic of the relatively modern labor market, though not on cotton and sugar plantations or in guano extraction. In the latter two, following the unsuccessful attempts to recruit Indians, labor shortage was solved by migration. Guano extraction and cotton and sugar plantations were sustained by the 90,000 Chinese who were in fact indentured and overexploited labor on eight-year contracts to have reached Peru in 1849–1874 (Levin 1960: 85–90, Gootenberg 1982: 346).

Handicraft
Unlike in the Kingdom of Poland, in Latin America in the first half of the 19th century artisans raised an outcry over the disastrous effects of British imports. Consul Rickett wrote in Lima in 1826 that in the years 1825 and 1826 the influx of British goods was so large that they were sold below cost (Bonilla 1977a: 23, 28). Historians sympathizing with hard pressed artisans write that British textiles "simply crushed local industry" (Stein 1970: 134; see also Gootenberg 1982, 1989). This thesis requires a commentary that will take into consideration the diversity of local artisan production.

When talk is about local handicraft, as a rule reference is made to statistics for marketable urban production. Statistics concerning the value of non-market production, primarily rural handicraft, are extremely rare. With regard to the Kingdom of Poland, such an estimate of the woven material production in the first half of the 19th century showed the following proportions: total production circa 6.16 million meters, of which 82.2 percent was for self-consumption, and 17.8 percent for sale (Rutkowski 1953: 362). In Minas Gerais, the center of Brazil's cottage industry, 5.8 million meters of cloth were produced in the late 1820s for home consumption and 2.34 million for sale outside the state (Libby 1991: 27). There are no such estimates with regard to Latin America as a whole. It is mentioned, however, that in the way of the development of a modern textile industry stood not only British imports, but also numerous rural weaving centers (Stafford 1965, Florescano 1977: 443, Bulmer-Thomas 2003). Thus, for lack of data researchers use first of all a division into domestic (primarily urban) market production and competing imports (McGreevey 1971: 169ff); their total value is treated as a rough estimate of total demand.

In a situation like this, to accept the hypothesis about a general decline of handicrafts in Latin America in the period discussed is rather a matter of intuition. Unquestionably such decline took place in urban handicrafts which faced direct British competition. Nine times out of ten those handicrafts were geared toward the production of luxury items, while such items were at the same time imported from Great Britain. Put briefly, this segment of Latin American handicrafts became a victim of global competition and nascent price convergence. Up until the end of the 1840s the situation in Lima was not unique:

> After the flurry of competing imports in the 1820s, demand shifted to ... less costly goods such as textiles, which dominated the import bill. As luxury needs dropped, those guilds closely associated with ornate colonial production suffered most acutely. ... If artisans 'erred,' it was their hesitancy to abandon an elite market that nearly ceased to exist. No attempts were made to reorient production to match needs of poorer consumers (Gootenberg 1982: 341f).

The majority of the most articulate protests made by artisans in Bolivia, Colombia and Peru came from manufacturers of precisely such luxury goods (Lora 1977, McGreevey 1971, Gootenberg 1982, 1989, Guerra Vilaboy 1980). In the La Plata region, too, this kind of handicraft was hit very badly. The same region also registered a significant foreign penetration of the cheap textiles market in the first half of the 19th century. According to the first diplomatic representative of the British Crown to Argentina,

> [t]he low prices of British goods, especially those suited to the consumption of the masses of the population of these countries, ensured a demand for them from the first opening of the trade. They are now become articles of the first necessity to the lower orders in South America (quoted in Ferns 1960: 79).

However, to Peru this triumphal report did not apply: "[rural artisans] proved flexible enough to survive Peru's first wave of industrial imports in the 1820s" (Gootenberg 1989: 48). Platt's view (1972: 12) of Latin America as a whole is unambiguous: handicrafts satisfying popular needs were not particularly threatened.[12]

It is nevertheless a fact that the fate of handicrafts in the Kingdom of Poland and in Latin America differed. According to some estimates, the number of independent artisans in the former rose in the years 1843–1861 from 66,000 to 95,000. At the same time the structure of craft production and the social composition of this social group changed due to the decline in the production of cotton and linen goods. Similar tendencies were observed in Hungary (Encyklopedia : 244, Ranki 1979: 142f). Also, a number of rural handicrafts established ties with modern textile production through the putting-out system. This led to a co-existence of asynchronisms, lowered productions costs but, at the same time, slowed down the mechanization of industry. That is why the development of crafts in the period discussed should be treated with mixed feelings (Kula 1979).

---

[12] Neither Consul Rickett nor the author of one of the first economic histories of Peru (Ugarte 1977) appreciated the significance of the provincial and rural industries.

The fate of handicrafts in the Polish territory seized by Prussia was much more dramatic. The Great Poland region, which in the latter half of the 18th century produced 70 percent of fabrics in Poland, in the 19th century, faced with competition from modern Prussian industry, was reduced to the role of rural hinterland (Topolski 1982: 380, Encyklopedia 1981: 244).

In Latin America handicrafts had absolutely no chance of transformation the way it happened in the Kingdom of Poland. Centers of modern textile production were in Great Britain, not in Lima or Bogota. As a result, urban handicrafts were largely destroyed by British competition, while technically obsolete rural industries, which profited from the isolation of local markets and from high transport costs, stagnated. Their transformation into an element of national structure was not possible, as illustrated by the example of southern Peru. Inasmuch as the elite-oriented urban and provincial textile mills collapsed, "textile production for lower strata" survived. And this concerned mainly the Indian and *mestizo* population. The existence of "a kind of double circulation of commodities and consumption made the survival of *chorrillos* and *obrajillos*" possible (Hünefeldt 1986: 38).

Also in Mexico, where a serious attempt was made to build a modern textile industry, its limited spread effects resulted, among other things, from strongly entrenched local interests. At the same time, local, technically obsolete *talleres* and *obrajes* became increasingly isolated. The transfer of the right to collect sales taxes from the central to state governments in 1828 meant that

> [tax] exemptions were given only to textiles produced in the state itself ... Since the [modern] textile industry would have had to have access to the entire national market to compete at all successfully with foreign textiles, state taxation policy went a long way toward inhibiting the growth of the domestic textile industry (Randall 1977: 136).

Alamán's attempt to enhance the market power of the Banco de Avío was his response to local restrictions. And his industrialization project provided for the development of the textile industry that would satisfy first of all popular needs.[13] Unlike President Guerrero (1828–1829), who wanted to

---

[13] What is needed are first of all "factories which produce articles of wider consumption, and which are also the easiest to establish. ... Inexpensive cotton, linen, and wool textiles ... are the things which should be promoted by encouraging Mexican and foreign capitalists to establish factories with the necessary machinery so that the goods will be available at a moderate price, a thing which will never be obtained without this assistance. ... Factories to produce articles of greater luxury should wait for the time being; we should not now seek to rival nations which have the industrial means we lack" (quoted in Potash 1983: 42f).

protect traditional manufacturers, Alamán favored tariffs which supported modern industry. Shortly before the establishment of the Banco de Avío he claimed: "The purely prohibitive system cannot by itself make factories flourish; other elements are needed such as an abundant population, capital, and adequate machinery" (quoted in Potash 1983: 42).

And finally, one could ask whether the fate of rural industries in Latin America and the Kingdom of Poland could contribute to the discussion on proto-industrialization (Mendels 1982, Clarkson 1985). The answer would be negative, especially with regard to Latin America (Gerst 1988, Libby 1991, Bulmer-Thomas 2003: 41, 129).

Tariffs, trade and industrialization

According to Stanley J. Stein (1967: 546), "the long-smouldering conflict between incipient industrializing sectors and mercantile interests flared up in the early decades of independence in the controversy over free trade versus protection" (see also Stein and Cortés Conde 1977: 13–16). This thesis posited by the outstanding economic historian was enthusiastically received by the followers of dependency theory (Frank, 1969: 21f, 1972: chapter 4). But other historians of Latin America are skeptical (Platt 1985, Ortega 1985). Gootenberg in his excellent monograph (1989) voiced his doubts with reference to Peru in the most articulate manner.

To perceive in Latin American protectionism of the first half of the 19th century the beginnings of the autonomous industrialization and a resemblance to the conflict between the North and South in the USA is a misinterpretation (Szlajfer 1986: 51 ff). In Argentina, the conflict between Rosas and his followers (*federales*) and Buenos Aires (*unitarios*), interpreted as a struggle for "economic independence" (Frank 1972: 53ff), actually concerned state building and the choice of the direction the development of agrarian and commercial capitalism should follow: "Excessive regard for the interests of the *estancieros* and the *saladeristas* forced government to exercise extreme caution when it came to extending a helping hand to the farmer and the industrialists" (Burgin 1946: 94). The protectionism Peruvian merchant and agrarian elites insisted on up until the 1840s, and the anti-foreign attitudes they demonstrated–aimed at both British and US merchants–did not result in the emergence of strong pro-industry groups and projects (Gootenberg 1989). Therefore, the peculiarly Janus face of protectionism should be mentioned here.

In the 19th century, the majority of Latin American countries experimented with protectionism. Depending on the country, the level of protectionism varied markedly. Inasmuch as the 1826 Reglamento de Comercio in Peru imposed an 80 percent tax on substitutes for local products, and the Brazilian tariff of 1844–a 60 percent one, Bolivian and Colombian taxes did not exceed the 20–40 percent level (Piel 1975: 260, Lora 1977: 16, McGreevey 1971: 35, Marchant 1965: 43). More often than not changes in tariffs were sharp, as, for example, in Peru where in 1836 the average tariff was reduced to 36 percent. And that was by no means the last change. By the end of the 1840s, Peruvian radical protectionism had given way to free trade (Ugarte 1977: 83, Gootenberg 1989).

It is debatable whether the customs tariff to the tune of 20 percent or 50 percent was sufficiently strong to protect local investments and production. If such was the real purpose of the tariff imposition. With the exception of Mexico, "the qualitative evidence suggests that domestic industry protection becomes a motivation for Latin American tariffs only in the late nineteenth century" (Bértola and Williamson 2006: 40f). Fiscal aims probably prevailed. At any rate, if one takes into account the scattered and incomplete statistics, one can conjecture that in the mid-19th century Latin American nominal tariffs were–when compared to those in Europe –very high:

> The tariff structure was inherited by independent Latin America from its colonial masters, and no great changes were observed in the first few decades after independence. ... [In 1840s] the average level of tariffs in Latin America was around 25 percent to 30 percent, with relatively few items admitted duty free (Bulmer-Thomas 2003: 137f; see also Coatsworth and Williamson 2004: 207ff).

The Kingdom of Poland imposed a strongly protectionist tariff in 1823 in response to the Prussian tariff that discriminated against Polish grain. With regard to textiles, finished iron products, woolen yarn, luxury goods and grain, the new tariff was prohibitive (the only exception being imports from Russia). On the other hand, import tax on industrial raw materials and capital goods was of a merely fiscal nature. It gave more effective protection to locally produced final goods. This tariff, with some minor changes, held until the end of the 1840s. At the same time, until 1831, Polish goods exported to Russia were tax exempt. By way of a reprisal for the 1830 uprising, Russians revoked the privilege for ten years (Jezierski 1967: 18–21, 24).

A comparison between the nominal protection ensured by the 1826 Peruvian tariff and the Polish one would probably reveal few differences. Hence, the degree of the tariff prohibitiveness does not explain why a country experienced or did not experience an industrial spurt. Attention must be paid to other factors, to terms of trade in particular.

As concerns Latin American countries, we have at our disposal detailed estimates of net barter terms of trade between France and Latin America in the first half of the 19th century (Schneider 1981). They were advantageous with regard to the majority of those commodities on which Latin America had a monopoly (or quasi-monopoly). With reference to these commodities, adequate supply was the problem. Net barter terms of trade with Great Britain were no different. For Latin America, at least until the 1870s, the 19th century was not an epoch of steadily deteriorating terms of trade (Bértola and Williamson 2006:, Williamson 2006). Needless to say, this did not rule out price fluctuations with respect to particular goods.

Therefore it does not seem that in the majority of Latin American countries unfavorable, supply-determined, income terms of trade were due to unfavorable barter terms of trade. The latter, however, contributed to the absence of strong incentives to change the production profile and initiate spontaneous structural changes. Moreover, investments in the hitherto structure of economic activities, reflected in the composition of the dominant social groups and the distribution of economic assets, were not flexible. A temporary immobilization of capital invested in agriculture, was a frequent strategy in times of crisis. Additionally, the need to liquidate the trade deficit through the sale of precious metals compelled–wherever possible–the maintenance of the colonial structure of non-agricultural investments. In such a situation, tariff protectionism was first and foremost an attempt at the defense of the balance-of-payments and resulted in fiscal squeeze.

The situation in the Kingdom of Poland was similar to the extent that supply determined export revenues. This is, however, where the similarities between Latin America and the Kingdom of Poland end.

The Kingdom of Poland exported to Western Europe primarily grain, the prices for which were clearly falling in the first half of the 19th century, because of, among other things, the Corn Laws. The fall in prices was particularly steep in the years 1817–1822. Because of the related negative trade balance, "the small bullion reserve was in danger of shrinking" (Jezierski 1967: 18). The decision to impose prohibitive tariffs was a response to that crisis and to the 1823 Prussian tariff. However, the consequence of these developments was a tariff war with Prussia. The Prussian blockade was the reason why prices for grain from the Kingdom of Poland continued to fall despite price increases in London in 1823–1825. At the beginning of the 1820s grain exports fell dramatically, accounting for a mere 6 percent of total production (Jezierski and Leszczyńska 2001: 123). In 1821–1830, the time of rapid deterioration of both net barter and income terms of trade,

Drucki-Lubecki initiated his investment program. In 1836–1840 terms of trade deteriorated again. This time the Bank Polski extended the program. Therefore one can assume that the changed terms of trade were a strong impetus for rethinking a policy that had been focused exclusively on grain trade and agriculture.[14]

Thus, in the Kingdom of Poland protectionism led to attempts at industrialization and became an element of the policy of industrialization. Where did protectionism lead in Latin America?

In the opinion of the 19th century opponents of protectionism, it was first of all exploitation of the consumer, an incentive to smuggle, a cause for the fall of finance, and also the surrender of the state to officials in charge of monopolies and to the corporate interests of artisans. Modern historians point to yet another aspect of Latin American protectionism. Lora (1977: 9) writes with regard to Bolivia that President Belzu's protectionist policy, protecting primarily urban handicrafts, was "an attempt to defend the country from [capitalist] development."[15] Regarding the Brazilian tariff of 1844, Richard Graham (1968: 107, 106) argues that protectionism in a backward country was nothing but an attempt "to shield a waning craft industry." It was only "after … the wealth produced by growing exports had pumped new life into the Brazilian economy … that industrialization became a serious possibility and free trade a drag rather than a boost." Lewis (1978b: 223) thought the same way, claiming that protectionism could be effective only in those countries which already had "a modernizing cadre, fired by economic nationalism to promote and protect industrial enterprise."

The old as well as the contemporary arguments are both convincing and doubtful. They are convincing as in the first half of the 19th century Latin American attempts to switch to modern production failed. They are doubtful because the example of the Kingdom of Poland belies them. So does the fact that irrespective of the relative stagnation in foreign trade, many Latin American countries had enough capital to initiate an industrial spurt. The problem was that capital was not in hands which

---

[14] Drucki-Lubecki wrote: "we would fare badly … if we applied the most elegant axioms of political economy, should they leave us at the mercy of this stagnation in which we have long been growing moldy" (quoted in Smolka 1984: 135, 1909: 82).

[15] However, it would be difficult to accept the hypothesis that e.g. President of Mexico Vincente Guerrero, when supporting in 1829 "wisely calculated prohibitions," had actually in mind, following Lora's reasoning, a struggle against the modern economy and not against "the bastard application of liberal economic principles" (quoted in Potash 1983: 30).

could use it to benefit industry. As a result, Latin American protectionism became what its old and present critics accused it of.

Finally, it is worth noting that the tariff policies of the Kingdom of Poland and of Latin America revealed also certain negative characteristics of import substitution policies development economists rediscovered more than a hundred years later. Underdevelopment of capital- and intermediary-goods industries was evident. Drucki-Lubecki was probably aware of this when he was planning investments in the machine-building industry. The neglect of non-export agriculture was equally evident.

Failure and Some Long-Term Consequences

The defeat of the industrial spurt in the Kingdom of Poland was devastating. At the end of the 1840s the etatized mining and iron industries were in deep crisis combined with technological decline. The climax of these processes was the privatization of the majority of mines and mills in the 1860s and bankruptcies. Further industrial development in the last quarter of the 19th century was dominated by the modern textile industry, and in the selectively reconstructed iron industry–by foreign capital. Such an end was a caricature of Drucki-Lubecki's long-range plans. He hoped that

> [w]ith God's help, the government will be able to relinquish [its] role as soon as possible, and its power of impulse, having put everything in motion, will commit themselves once more to the bounds of prudent rest (*dans une tranquillité réflechie*) (quoted in Smolka 1984 : 231f),

Historians debating the causes of that defeat listed, among other things, a limited domestic market, high production costs, an underdeveloped credit system and, after 1831, inefficient state bureaucracy and rising corruption. The parliament (*Sejm*) took note of these factors still in Drucki-Lubecki's day (Sejm Królestwa 1995: 360). Moreover, it is pointed out that in the peak years the newly-created iron industry used just 30–40 percent of its productive capacity, and from the mid-1840s–circa 10–20 percent. At the same time, an interesting hypothesis appeared that at the end of the 1850s privatization of this sector did not correspond to new domestic market trends and had perhaps been premature: "The idea of de-etatization was conceived just at the time when additional investments could probably have made the entire state-owned industry profitable" (Jedlicki 1964: 132, 166). Yet, the increase in domestic demand, conditioning such a solution, took place later, already after the protectionist tariffs had been lifted.

The problems besetting industry in the Kingdom of Poland were, although on a considerably larger scale, similar to those that also appeared in Latin America. The negative impact of obsolete textile mills on modern production found its reflection in the Kingdom of Poland in competition for a limited market between the government-owned industry and obsolete private mines and iron mills. However, money outlays in the latter were smaller than in the state-owned enterprises: unpaid peasant labor and free wood from landlord-entrepreneur's own forests made a difference. Insufficient domestic demand was equally painful in both regions. This shortcoming resulted in part from the blocked agrarian reforms as well as from modern industry's inability to compete with imports and with obsolete, but cheap, local manufacturers of simple iron tools and other products.

In the Kingdom of Poland, on the other hand, industrial boom, limited demand notwithstanding, was the effect of the unique characteristics of investments in heavy industry, which Tugan Baranovski described at the beginning of the 20th century as "production for the sake of production." Moreover, investments were propelled by corruption and cost inflation. Anyhow, in both regions, in the long run, the opportunity for industrial development was determined by institutions which were hindering the development of rural markets and ossifying sharply unequal income distribution. The urban market grew slowly, too. In the years 1827–1858, the share of urban inhabitants in the Kingdom of Poland's total population rose slowly, from 21.5 to 24.2 percent (Jezierski 1994: 88). The level of urbanization in Latin America at that time was decidedly lower.

Let me mention one more long-term difference that looms out of the comparative analysis presented.

In many Latin American countries, in the latter half of the 19th century, merchants, mine owners and *hacendados* formed a powerful alliance in support of the primary export economy. Researchers analyzing the case of Chile described this alliance as a tripod, *la mesa des tres patas* (Claudio Véliz quoted in Frank 1972: 60f). In Chile and other countries, however, *la mesa des tres patas* did not check the development of the textile and other non-durable consumer good industries at the time of booming primary exports at the turn of the 19th and 20th centuries. Quite to the contrary. As we will see, the growth of such industry was, within some bounds, a part of the export-economy's rationale. The attitudes and behaviors of the Peruvian merchant elite in the pre-guano period indicated that the alliance, which until the 1840s supported protectionist demands, was not inimical to liberalized trade and pro-export prospects:

> [I]n one form or another, the protectionist groups were also free traders. The merchant-industrialists could return to importing, artisans could try to rely

on increased effective protection and cheaper food imports, and agriculturalists could compensate with imported machinery. To some degree, all of Lima's protectionists were 'co-optable' by liberalism, since their economic interests did not bind them desperately to a protectionist regime (Gootenberg 1982: 357).

The Peruvian government's sudden movement away from protectionism to a liberal policy as soon as guano revenues poured in was a good illustration of that happening (Bonilla 1974, Gootenberg 1989).

No equally strong alliance was formed in the Kingdom of Poland, and the 'bourgeois-landowner alliance' could not be equated with the Latin American *mesa des tres patas*. Objectively speaking, the increasing demand for Polish grain in the 1850s and 1870s and the decline of the mining and iron industry built in the 1830s and 1840s were factors conducive to 'Latin Americanization' of the Polish economy and strategic elites. Nonetheless during the wheat crisis in the 1880s and 1890s, agriculture did not gain the support of the Russian state, which was understandable as Russia itself was a grain exporter. In the Kingdom of Poland it was no longer possible to form an export bloc based on the traditional primary sector. In the last quarter of the 19th century the Kingdom was already at a stage of relatively developed import substitution industrialization. Latin America reached that stage only at the beginning of the 20th century.

To some extent, such a result was a consequence of the industrial spurt in the first half of the 19th century, and also of the fragmentary inclusion of the peasantry in the market. In the Kingdom of Poland, state accumulation ensured the transfer of profits and resources to the private sector. Such were the beginnings of modern commercial and industrial capital, even if the quality of the latter was debatable: "The forced accumulation at the expense of the peasantry was spent on ailing industry" (Kula 1979: 17). From the 1850s onward, the significance of the Russian market, and along with it the chances for Polish industrial development, was growing. The share of exports to this market in Polish industrial production increased from 9 percent in 1850 to 20 percent in 1870, and to 66 percent in 1890 (Jezierski 1984: 238). In the end, the Tsarist land reform of 1864 was a nail in the coffin for the Polish variant of *la mesa de tres patas*: the enfranchisement of peasants weakened the landed gentry severely. The domestic market deepened, although with a lag. In Latin America, the 'land question' was still waiting to be settled.

In this way the Kingdom of Poland became an "intermediary zone between industrial and agricultural Europe" (Ihnatowicz 1982: 88).

CHAPTER SEVEN

ISSUES IN PRIMARY-SECTOR NATIONALISM: LATIN AMERICA

THE HERITAGE: A NOTE

The commercialized sectors of preindustrial peripheral economies were marked by a dual tension/specialization: between domestic primary production and the external market, and between domestic demand and external industrial supplies (Szlajfer 1985: chapter 2, Cardoso and Perez Brignoli 1979). According to Braudel, it was specifically those commercialized sectors that took part in the Atlantic economy, organized by capitalism understood as the internationalized top floor of commerce and finance, and next, of production as well.

That dual tension/specialization manifested itself most distinctly in the slave economies, which were a special variant of settler colonies. Export economies of this kind were extreme examples of the non-autonomous sub-systems created by the European center of the Atlantic economy. Adam Smith (2005: 469, 474) noted that in the English controlled sub-systems enforced specialization was very far advanced: colonies were "discouraged ... from refining their own sugar" and exports were limited to products "either in their rude state, or in ... the very first stage of manufacture." Raw material processing manufactories developed primarily in English harbor towns. In the sub-systems created by the French, Spanish and Portuguese, the metropolis' monopoly on processed products was not imposed so rigorously (Egerton 1903: 119, Davis 1973: 205).

But in other, less typical, instances, too, dual tension/specialization was a defining factor and determined a given country's participation in the emerging world economy. Such a dual tension/specialization was not questioned by the existence of local handicrafts and peasant-owned lands, which satisfied a substantial part of domestic demand, for elementary goods in particular. The history of Central Europe from the 15th century, especially of Poland, testifies to this. The export bias of the Polish economy neither eliminated the peasant holding as a (skewed) economic unit nor transformed every *szlachta* manor into an export-oriented business endeavor (Kula 1983a: 150, Topolski 2000). The Mexican, Argentine and Peruvian economies, which were not dominated by slave plantations, approximated this model. However, in part as a response to the development of dynamic production centers (such as silver mining in Peru and Mexico), in part as a response to demographic growth, both in urban centers and in agriculture, there emerged a dense network of local production. After all is said and done, even in the most typical slave economies, subsistence plots cultivated by slaves, and also other sideline activities, created a substitute for local production and market. In times of crisis they were the shock absorbers that enabled people to survive. In times of export boom, local supplies of food were substituted, for example in the British Caribbean, by deliveries from North American colonies. The peasant economy in Poland, distorted during the second serfdom and functionally integrated with the manor, played a similar role (Furtado 1967: chapter 6, Libby 1991: 21ff, Mintz 1978, Kula 1983a). In Brazil, in turn, once the 'sugar cycle' came to an end in the 17th century, first cattle-raising and other subsistence activities, and next migrations to the South led to the emergence of a relatively well integrated local economy in Minas Gerais in the 18th century (Caio Prado Jr. 1969). Its partial re-integration into the dual tension/specialization model took place after the country gained independence, during successive coffee and wild rubber cycles. In a nutshell, in both cases of the export-oriented economy, international specialization contributed to the weakening and disintegration of the urban economy and manufacturing, and blocked the development of the domestic economy.[1] From the historical point of view, it was not only the commodities actually produced by the periphery that were important, but equally important were the commodities not produced there.

As mentioned, this dual tension/specialization concerned the leading, commercialized sectors that directly participated in international trade. The degree of internationalization of the pre-industrial economies was considerable, although one should bear the proportions in mind (see the Mexican example quoted in chapter 6). In Brazil and Mexico, also at the turn of the 19th and 20th centuries, "70 to 80 per cent of economic activity was outside of international trade" (Marichal and Topik 2003: 362).[2] The situation in the Polish territories was likewise.

---

[1] Discussing the long-term impact of Western Europe's expansion into the Baltic region, Mączak (1972: 156) emphasized that, on the one hand, improvements in agriculture lessened Western Europe's dependence on food supplies from Central Europe, and on the other, Western industry's competitive advantage over Central Europe remained intact. See also Małowist (1973, 2010). For a good critical review of debates on this topic among Polish historians see Sosnowska (2004).

[2] For problems with research into the 19th century non-export and largely self-sufficient sectors see Bulmer-Thomas (2003: 38ff), Leff (1997: 40ff), Rutkowski (1953).

Despite the continuation of some colonial restrictions and monopolies, on winning independence the societal actors involved in domestic markets found an ally in a part of the nascent state apparatus. This concerned mainly artisans and a minuscule part associated with manufacturing production. The period of the post-revolutionary crisis and partial isolation from the international market were conducive to their economic strengthening. They were also favorable to the political and social upward mobility of the provincial elites. At the same time such mobility was made very difficult not only by overall backwardness, but also by transport barriers and the resulting isolation of particular regions. One element that is particularly appealing to the imagination is cabotage shipping in such countries as Brazil or Chile where particular regional economic centers were scattered along the coast or in its vicinity. In Brazil, as late as in the middle of the 19th century "a mere 7 percent of shipping commerce ... took place between Brazilian ports." The main destination ports were in Europe and the USA. Gradual changes were initiated in the 1880s, and in the 1930s interprovincial shipping reached one-third of all shipping (Topik 1985: 223f). In Brazil, as in the majority of other Latin American countries, rail transport was also slow to develop:

> the largest absolute rise in railways track occurred only in the twenty years before 1914. ... in 1914 the country had only 26,060 kilometers of track. This was a figure that the United States had surpassed by the 1850s (Leff 1997: 45).[3]

In the whole of Latin America the total length of rail tracks by 1913 had reached more than 83,000 kilometers (Bulmer-Thomas 2003: 105). In around 1842 the average freight cost per ton of merchandise from England to Mexico amounted to £2.5, but from the Mexican harbor to the capital £15.4. In the case of Bolivia, the respective rates were £4.5 and £21.6 (Prados de la Escosura 2005: 16). These factors ensured well into the second half of the 19th century, a kind of natural protection to the interior but at the same time constituting one of the most insurmountable barriers to the development of supraregional markets.

With such a legacy the newly-established Latin American countries and the Central European territories deprived of sovereignty entered the

---

[3] Other historians evaluate this delayed growth in a more positive way: "By 1888 Brazil had the largest rail system in Latin America. ... After 1889 railways grew rapidly so that in 1910 the national total was 21,325 kilometers" (Marichal and Topik 2003: 363). Well, in the small underdeveloped Kingdom of Poland (one half of the territory of the São Paulo state) there were 3,596 kilometers of railroad track in 1912 (Jezierski and Wyczański 2006: 252).

epoch of the Industrial Revolution–already in full swing in Western Europe and the USA. Until the 1870s the model thus sketched had been the dominant one:

> Before the mid nineteenth century it makes little sense to talk of national economies and thus of a *national* political economy, common to and integrating all regions and sectors, for most Latin American states (Jacobson 2005: 125).

The rapid rise in vertical trade during the globalization, until 1914, seemed to assert the traditional model. However, in certain countries that trade was the beginning of a gradual economic diversification and, at the same time, consolidation of the economic space. A complicated conversion of "archipelagic society into national society" (Jaguaribe 1969: 394) began. With a time lag institutions favoring opening up to new fields of economic activity and to new societal actors developed. But there is no doubt that at that time the Ricardian theory of comparative costs was liberal economists' and politicians' credo. Nevertheless, as Jonathan V. Levin (1960: 5f) rightly observed, at that time export expansion was not a result of natural factor endowments, but of the location of the least mobile factors (i.e. land and raw materials).[4]

The *raison d'être* of export economies was expressed in their growing participation in international trade. Thus, the outward orientation implied economic internationalism. To a small, as well as a large *fazendeiro* in Brazil the opinion expressed in 1902 that "coffee pays for everything" was obvious (Stein 1985: 38). At the same time, in this kind of economy, primary-sector nationalism was not merely a theoretical concept–it was a fact. Therefore questions arise as to its sources and the actors referring to it. Equally important is the question about the limits of the transformative potential of this type of nationalism.

The classical staple theory of growth was an approach that indicated the probability of a successful transition of primary export-oriented economies to a modern industrial economy. Western offshoots (but also e.g. Denmark) were prime examples. The role economic nationalism played in such transformation was positive, although all too often underestimated. The crucial 1929 Australian protectionism debate–which in fact

---

[4] This implied that in point of fact export economies functioned following Smith's vent for surplus model (Myint 1958, Cortés Conde 1974: 5f). For an analysis of models of export-led growth, which survived more or less until the 1920s, see Cardoso and Perez Brignoli (1979), and more recent, excellent contributions by Thorp (1998: chapter 3), Haber (1997), Cárdenas, Ocampo and Thorp (2000), Bulmer-Thomas (2003).

recapitulated the consequences of the economic processes and social and economic struggles of past decades–reinforced the plea for more equal income distribution *and* further action along the protectionist (i.e. pro-industry) line. However, the socio-economic background of that debate, a successful attempt to strengthen the labor-capital pressure on landed interests, which stood as a backbone of industrialization efforts, somehow disappeared in further discussions (see, however, Rogowski 1989: 43–47). Distribution of income was debated as if separate from the choice of a growth path and the early 20th century Liberal–Labor compromise on protectionism to which, after WWI, export-oriented agricultural interests (the Country Party) subscribed willy-nilly (Lloyd 2003: 412–416). Anyhow, "[t]he Australian debate, which indirectly led to the Stolper-Samuelson theorem," a seminal presentation of the income distributional consequences of protectionism (Irwin 1996: 175–181), provided a strong argument for seeing efficiency, coalition building and economic policy choices as intertwined.

Yet, Western offshoots were rather an exception to the rule. In the majority of cases, nationalism in export-oriented economies reflected not staple growth but accompanied a staple trap (Hirschman 1977a), later also called Dutch disease. Bearing this in mind, its transformative potential should be defined as undetermined.

In any case, the fact that in export economies particularistic nationalism frequently articulated also primary sector interests should induce us to carefully and more critically examine theses that laid emphasis on the causal nexus between nationalism, protectionism and industrialization. Protectionism linked with the scarce factor, i.e. more or less discriminated against in the free trade policy, was not the only one possible. At the time of an economic depression and other shocks a coalition so far favorable to free trade could also easily transform into one opting for protectionism (Rogowski 1989: 10). The same applied to such an abundant factor as 'land', i.e. agrarian interests. The example of the transformation of the Prussian Junkers, who until the 1870s had been "fanatical free traders," into staunch protectionists was classic (Gerschenkron 1989: 42ff, Kindleberger 1951). The support of agrarian interests for protectionist measures also had another source, such as a kind of trade-off concerning the state's tax policy in general (about which later). Moreover, according to Gellner (1994: 11), as important as industrialization itself was "the shadow cast by its coming." Berlin (2004: 171) thought likewise: in the world defined from the 19th century by industrialization, nationalism fed on industrialism but did not need it to develop.

Therefore, in the discussion on primary-sector nationalism and its transformative potential it seems useful to concentrate on the following selected issues. First, the problem of the state; second, varieties of export sectors and the differentiated form of the presence of foreign capital in export activities; third, the regional dimension of economic nationalism; and finally, the limits of the transformative potential of primary-sector economic nationalism.

An Internationalist Protectionist State

On more than one occasion the combination of the export economy model and the concept of the state-as-arena led to oversimplifications in the way the state was discussed. Above all, it was an oversimplification to confine oneself to a point of view that stressed that the particularistic economic nationalism that grew from the end of the 19th century involved the state only to a small degree. In fact, capital-market and transport-infrastructure development, but also the emergence of a modern consumer-goods industry and its structure, were "not completely endogenous to the process of economic growth; government regulation exerted powerful independent effects" (Haber 1997b: 170). A relative autonomy of the state was thinkable also in the liberal concept of the state-as-arena as a delicate act of balancing among contradictory internal pressures stemming from the modernizing community. Additionally, the very process of state-building and state-consolidation implied a relative distance from the dominant interest groups, fostered by the growing state bureaucracy. Thus, certain historians of the Brazilian economy assert that during the empire (until 1889) "a semi-autonomous 'mandarin' caste ... ruled as well as governed," whereas during the Old Republic (until 1930) "the export oligarchy had to share power" (quoted in Topik 1985: 204). Steven Topik, after presenting a detailed analysis of the monetary, fiscal and spending policies of Brazilian governments, points in the same direction: "the distribution of public economic policy benefits demonstrates that the Brazilian state between 1850 and 1930 was not simply the tool of the export oligarchy," although he does not suggest either a divorce between the main directions of the state's policy and the interests of the export-oriented landed elites or the predominance of "a self-seeking, independent patrimonial bureaucracy" (1985: 228, 1980: 615). The recent assessment by Marcelo de Paiva Abreu and Alfonso S. Bevilaqua (2000: 41) is an attempt to restore some balance when judging the limits of state autonomy under the empire and the Old Republic: "even with important qualifications, it is still true that to a large extent economic policy tended to reflect the interests of the rising coffee oligarchy and the long-established tradition of rent appropriation." Thus, it seems necessary to give attention to certain elements of the peculiar liberal interventionism that emerged before 1914 as a response to the "[d]emands of the international economy and of diverse domestic actors" (Marichal and Topik 2003: 349), the latter representing different forms of particularistic nationalism. Elaborating on Brazil's case, Topik (1980: 611) would suggest that "[t]he state came to participate extensively in the economy precisely because of its efforts to promote private enterprise." And in his reading of the *científicos*' programs and activities Knight (2000: 144) detected a proto-neoliberal approach to state intervention and market: strong state as competition-maker.

But this was only the beginning. Ultimately, something new appeared as a companion to the interventionist liberal-cum-internationalist protectionist state both in Mexico, Brazil, Argentina and Chile: industrialization.

"The impetus for industrial development came from the expansion of foreign trade" (Haber 2006: 560). No doubt about this. First, on the margins of the export economy, and next as an important part of it, there emerged strong incentives to develop *some kinds* of industrial production. No doubt about this, either. The lack of industry in the booming export-oriented economies before 1914 and also in the 1920s was a myth demolished decades ago by economic historians. Thus, Haber's (2006: 537) insistence that "there was substantial industry in Latin America well before 1930" and that such an argument "departs from the standard view" seems exaggerated. One could rather claim that his argument is a forceful reinstatement of the fact already well established in the literature (Gómez-Galvarriato and Williamson 2009: 667f).[5] Hence, the questions posed in the debate on the development of industry in the pre-1930 epoch, were not 'if', but 'how', to what extent, in which direction and at what speed. The same concerned the underdeveloped countries of Central Europe.

Let me move, however, to state budgets and customs tariffs.

Until more or less the end of the 1920s, Latin American states' budget receipts in the main consisted of revenues from import and export duties, excise duties and foreign loans. For instance, in Peru in the years

---

[5] Nevertheless, one should appreciate the sophistication of new approaches to studies of industrialization, Haber's own important contributions included. For a guide to recent literature see Bulmer-Thomas, Coatsworth and Cortés Conde (2006: 717–722).

1900–1920, import and export duties made up 57–60.5 percent of budget revenues; in Venezuela, in 1929, duties and royalties on crude oil made up 75.7 percent of state revenues (Mitchell 1983: 822). Thus it seems that the state's tax base in the 1920s did not differ much from the one in the last quarter of the 19th century, and definitely not from the one in 1913 (Bulmer-Thomas 2003: 178f). Until 1890 the average share of revenues from import duties in the budgets of Latin America's 11 most important countries approximated 58 percent (Clemens and Williamson 2002: 17). However, data from seven biggest Latin American countries (Argentina, Brazil, Chile, Colombia, Mexico, Peru and Venezuela) showed that in 1900–1930 customs as a percentage of total state receipts declined from 52.2 percent to 39.9 percent (with a sharp rise from 1900 to 1910). On the other hand, the rise of the share of income taxes in state budgets of this group was rather modest, from 2.5 percent in 1900 to 6.2 percent in 1920 and 9.1 percent in 1930 (Thorp 1998: 346). Thus the restructuring of the tax base started as early as in the last years of the *belle époque* of the export-drive, even though this was just a modest beginning. In Central Europe, foreign trade-linked revenues played a lesser role. Poland's budget receipts in the year 1927–1928 came mainly from internally-generated revenues, i.e. from excise and sales taxes (23 percent), industrial taxes (19 percent) and income taxes (19 percent). The share of customs duties was 25 percent. Likewise in Hungary. In industrially developed Czechoslovakia the share of customs duties was relatively small, slightly above 11 percent (Landau and Tomaszewski 1982: 269, Spigler 1986: 154ff).

The dependence of a large part of budget revenues on the global economy meant that protectionism, if understood as preference first of all for industry, was not so much unwelcome as entangled in a conflict-of-interest context which distorted its pro-industry impact. The vulnerability of primary exports, domestic effective demand, state budgets and industrial growth to external market volatility were of primary importance. Sudden changes also prompted investments with shortened pay-back periods, and speculative endeavors. The result was obvious: "The accretion of ad hoc policies means that the overall package of regulations, laws, and tax codes ... may work at cross-purposes to one another" (Haber 2006: 539; see also Luz 1978: 134f). Moreover, in a majority of cases, the levying of import and export taxes, apart from mutually excluding demands from particular interest groups, "was an art, not a science" (Bulmer-Thomas 2003: 33). The dominant liberal ideology deepened the inevitable dilemmas. The result was a reversed tariff-growth paradox: high import taxes went hand in hand with restricted industrialization (Bulmer-Thomas 2003: 33, Williamson 2002: 32, Bértola and Williamson 2006: 39f)).

That the nominal tariffs in major Latin American countries were exceptionally high is already a well documented fact. In Brazil in 1881 the share of customs revenue in total foreign trade was 20.82 percent, and in the heavily protected US economy "only" 13.1 percent (Mulhall 1884: 123). And that was not a transient phenomenon. Import tax in Brazil increased steadily to reach, by 1913, nearly 40 percent and in Venezuela nearly 46 percent (Bulmer-Thomas 2003: 139). From the mid-19th century until WWI, "Latin America was the most protectionist region in the world (except for the United States in the immediate post-Civil War era)" (Coatsworth and Williamson 2004: 206, 208f, 216–219, Bértola and Williamson 2006: 37).

However, a focus on nominal tariffs may lead to unwarranted conclusions regarding the level of protection that was assured to the already existing and also to incipient industries. Bulmer-Thomas presented elaborate arguments which force us to take a second look at the issue. The major argument concerns the effective rate of protection, the result of the structure of tariffs for both the final product and inputs. If Bulmer-Thomas is right, and we believe he is, then the evaluation of Latin American tariff levels suggests a less dramatic conclusion: "the true rate of industrial protection in the Latin American republics was not far below the rate in many other parts of the world" (Bulmer-Thomas 2003: 141). Let us bear this opinion in mind. Let us also remember that a positive effective rate of protection means also that the substitution of imported inputs will be difficult or even impossible. On the other hand, the types of pro-industry policy preferences are revealed in the tariff structure; the effective rates of protection are a strong signal indicating the relative weight attached to specific branches. In a word, the effective rate of protection is a double-edged sword.

The adoption by many Latin American countries of the gold standard in the 1890s and early 1900s additionally strengthened the upward trend in nominal tariffs. First of all, the adherence to the system eliminated such non-tariff instruments as manipulation of real exchange rates (Bértola and Williamson 2006: 39). Monetary stability linked with the gold standard was not however received as an unquestionable blessing. Neither did increased credibility in the eyes of foreign investors always counterbalance the risks linked with macroeconomic instability caused by international market fluctuations. Without going into detail one can say that the system was criticized first of all by those societal actors to whom an appreciated local currency meant losses, i.e. mainly agro-exporters and export-oriented mining entrepreneurs, and other groups closely dependent on exports. But other groups also joined in the dislike toward the gold standard and its stiff rules. In Brazil bankers and industrialists, but also planters-industrialists, were keenly interested in increasing money supply and in devaluation (Topik 1985: 206). For them the recourse to floating exchange rates was a bonus not a liability. And the never resolved dilemma and interplay between macroeconomic stability and private interests meant that "Latin America under the gold standard might be fairly termed Latin America 'on and off' the gold standard" (Salvucci 2006: 260).

Latin American states' adherence to the gold standard was frequently suspended. Incomplete information on 15 countries suggests that between 1870 and 1930, only Venezuela uninterruptedly remained in the system. Argentina and Brazil did not take part in it in the years 1924–1927, Chile in 1898–1926 and Peru in 1914–1930 (Salvucci 2006: 258f). All the same, the fact that Argentina and Brazil remained outside the system only after 1914 strengthens the hypothesis that the high level of tariffs after the 1890s was to some extent built into the operation of the gold standard in the region: "countries that went on the gold standard raised tariffs" (Bértola and Williamson 2006: 45). This however does not explain everything, and especially the fact that, for example, the tariff level in Argentina was considerably lower than in Uruguay, not to mention Brazil and Colombia.

The strong links between tariffs and budget receipts seems to be a convincing explanation of the high level of Latin American tariffs, with the state itself being the leading actor in this play. Pressure from societal actors would create a context in which the basic goals of the state bureaucracy–above all monetary policy, defense of the balance-of-payments and macroeconomic stability–would be carried out. Support for incipient industrialization would be a consequence of the choices made by the state in those strategically important fields. It would be a sort of side effect.

Today, however, this argument raises doubts. Thus in the case of Mexico a different interpretation was proposed, one grounded in an analysis of the effective rate of protection, implied by the tariff reforms carried out in the 1890s and early 1900s. The new structure of tariffs, it is argued, reflected a genuine autonomy of the state and an effort to support early industrialization. Revenue maximization was no longer of primary importance, and "tariff policy was ... increasingly freed from the fiscal concerns of the state" (Beatty 2002: 207). Other, less conspicuous and more debatable, examples are quoted: Brazil, Peru and Chile. Of course, there is no reason to question the factual basis of this interesting interpretation. But as already indicated 'the Mexican case' was merely a radical variant of the traditional pattern of early industrial development in Latin America. The demonstrated correlation between the cascading tariff structure and implied effective rates of protection and production reflects at least the skills of Porfirio Diaz's economic policy-makers. However, there is no proof that revenue maximization and other factors pushing toward higher tariffs were declining in importance. Thus, it would be hasty to discern 'developmentalism' in Mexican tariff and commercial policies. If by 'developmentalism' we are to understand List's classic argument, then "there is absolutely no pre-World I evidence from the periphery that would have supported infant industry argument" (Williamson 2006: 120).

The rise in protectionism since the 1880s was also strongly associated with pressure from budding industrial groups. The interpretation of this link, too, raises a number of questions.

In their important contribution to the debate, Bértola and Williamson (2006: 44f) presented two theses. First, that during the *belle époque* of the export drive, urban capitalists "managed to dominate oligarchic regimes" and "free-trade landowners formed the second dominant part of the governing oligarchy." Their unique position was translated into economic policy: "urban capitalists secured explicitly protectionist tariffs for existing and new industries beginning in the 1890s." Other economic historians would also argue that Latin American "national industrial elites were able to persuade their governments to erect high tariff barriers against foreign manufactures" (Haber 1997a: 12). On the second thesis see below.

The first remark that comes to mind concerns the relative strength of the urban capitalist. The evidence gathered by historians suggests the opposite. Until 1930, in the oligarchic system of government industrialists were the junior partner, both politically and economically. Needless to say, the degree of their relative vulnerability differed from country to country. Unquestionably in Argentina they were more vulnerable than in Brazil. It cannot be ruled out that Argentine tariffs and the relative lack of state support reflected this relative weakness. One can thus read that "[l]ike many neglected orphans, industry in Argentina had grown up in adversity and had emerged tough and independent" (Lewis 1990: 97). The tariff debates carried out in Brazil from the end of the 19th century, concerning support for industry, indicated that the bargaining power of industrialists was in point of fact limited. An attempt made in 1903 to radically strengthen, under the slogan "economic emancipation is the foundation of political emancipation," the famous *lei de similares* failed (Luz 1978: 132ff).

This does not mean, however, that industrialists had little bearing on tariffs and spending policies. On the contrary, they achieved a number of victories, but suffered setbacks as well. The "Aid to Industry" campaign mounted in 1892 by industrialists who pressed for financial assistance and subsequently also for higher tariffs was successful (Stein 1957: 93–96). Still, it is an exaggeration to suggest that it was mainly the industrial party that was behind the rising tariffs. The rise in protectionism "was not due to the rise of powerful industrial associations. ... their influence could not compare with that of the landowners and agro-exporters" (Bulmer-Thomas 2003: 144). The overall picture is further complicated by the large presence of planters, landowners and agro-exporters among the emerging class of industrialists. One can find among them also importers (Dean 1969: 26). Thus, in the relationships between industry and rural interests tariffs did not come as a zero-sum game. Lastly, surely the activistic state-as-arena would not undertake protectionist measures that would directly and obviously aim against the prevailing interests of the rural oligarchy. There is a subtle difference between a lack of direct preferences and/or weak preferences, on the one hand, and discriminatory measures on the other. Therefore, even though spending policy was relatively discriminating against powerful export-oriented sectors, this "does not necessarily reflect[ed] substantial power on the part of industrialists and farmers" (Topik 1985: 226). The coffee valorization scheme, about which see below, was a case which demonstrated the real strength of coffee elites when their vital interests were threatened. Against the strong initial opposition of the São Paulo state government the oligarchy-dominated sector prevailed, winning support the other societal actors were unable to think about:

> [valorization] absorbed about US $133,000,000 of federal funds (mostly borrowed from abroad) while São Paulo spent US $136,000,000 to protect crops. Between the two, they spent approximately the equivalent of the entire federal budget of 1929 (Topik 1980: 604).

Having said this, an important factor raised by Williamson (2006), which seems to have played a momentous role in increasing taxes, is worth mentioning: the impressive cuts in internal transport costs. As a result, the domestic economy became better integrated, but also natural protection of local non-agricultural production was eliminated and foreign competitors acquired easier access to previously closed markets.

The second, as yet unmentioned thesis, that of Bértola and Williamson, is in fact the conclusion they draw: "Tariffs in Latin America were viewed mainly as a revenue source, as a strategic policy response to trading partners' tariffs, as a redistributive device for special interests, and as a consequence of other political economy struggles. However, revenue needs were the central motivation behind those exceptionally high tariffs"

(Bértola and Williamson 2006: 46). Still, as Williamson (2006: 142) argues, such a conclusion would apply only to the period prior to the 1870s. For the four decades before WWI his empirical analysis "fails to find significant evidence that revenue needs still determined tariff rates in any ubiquitous and systematic way."[6] Unconvinced by Bértola and Williamson's arguments, I would thus follow the conclusion of Bulmer-Thomas (2003: 137): "Throughout the first century after independence the function of the tariff was primarily to raise revenue." No doubt, tariff duties served also state-building and subsequently state-consolidation. It is precisely at this point that state interventionism, the primary export economy and economic internationalism met, making up a cohesive *and* flexible system (see also Helleiner 2002). This system embraced also new societal actors such as industrialists, who along with the old, but restructured, rural interests made demands characteristic of particularistic nationalism.

The second issue, even more important, concerns the structure of industry, which emerged under the export economy and which was also aided by the state and tariffs. As mentioned above, effective rates of protection reflected the revealed preferences of both policy-makers and industrialists. But even pure revenue tariffs "will always give some protection" (Bulmer-Thomas 2003: 137). In other words, it shoul be of interest what kind of industrial nationalism emerged as a result of the workings of the export economy as well as state interventionism. In the present chapter I will merely touch on this question.

"Latin America," asserted Bértola and Williamson, "had to deal with the second industrial revolution before it had undergone the first." This eye-catching statement captured the structural problem of the emerging Latin American industry well. In all countries that recorded substantial industrial growth before 1914 the main emphasis was laid on the so-called natural industries. Food-processing and production of beverages, followed by the flagship textile and clothing industry, were the prime movers of such an industrial drive.

In 1937, the structure of the Argentine industry, molded during the primary export boom before 1914 and also under the impact of the two external shocks of WWI and the Great Depression, was telling: the share of the food and textile industries in total industrial production reached 34 percent, whereas that of the metal industry was 6.6 percent. In Canada,

---

[6] However, note should be taken of the change in Williamson's opinion on the matter. Elsewhere the caveat he made for the long period preceding WWI was absent (Williamson 2002: 32).

a country with natural endowments similar to those in Argentina, the share of these two industries was below 26 percent, and the share of the metal industry held at 16 percent. With a similar number of workforce employed in industry, in aggregate terms the value of Canada's industrial output was 3.5 times bigger than in Argentina (Solberg 1987: 44). A quarter of a century earlier, the share of the food and textile industries in Argentina's total industrial production reached almost 63 percent, in Brazil–74 percent, and in Peru–82 percent (Bulmer-Thomas 2003: 135). The second industrial revolution, which had for nearly four decades been in full speed in the USA and the developed parts of Europe, was indeed another, largely strange world.

Industry in some of the Central European countries was definitely more diversified. In Hungary, where in 1928 the share of the food processing and textile and clothing industries in total industrial production approached 28 percent, the engineering and metallurgical industries contributed 21 percent of total industrial output. But it was the textile industry which was the fastest growing one in the interwar period. Romania, with its oil and related industries enclave, was a kind of dual economy, surrounded by backward agriculture, handicrafts and small-scale industry. Poland, with its quite large modern industry, was, together with Hungary, an intermediary case between developed Czechoslovakia and the rest of East and Central Europe. In Bulgaria, as late as in 1938, the share of the food processing and textile industries in total industrial production was nearing 76 percent (Teichova 1986: 245, 248, 250, 255).

So, in the profile of industry that emerged from the export economy in Latin America, natural industries, sometimes called *indústrias nacionais* in Brazil, played a crucial role. Industries symbolic of the second industrial revolution were non-existent and/or at the very early stage of development. The category of natural industries was crucial here, both economically and sociologically. It reflected the unique process where a new social group emerged not as a breakup with the dominant agrarian and merchant elites, but as their outgrowth, as a group never attempting rebellion, preferring accommodation and evolutionary growth instead.

The already mentioned question of the social and national composition of the budding industrial class played an important role in affecting such attitudes. This is particularly true of the almost symbiotic relationship between industrialists and the dominant agricultural and exporting interests. I will touch upon this topic later, suffice here to refer to the example of Francisco Matarazzo, the most powerful Brazilian industrialist at the time of the export economy, and "the model of the immigrant-entrepreneur" (Dean 1969: 60).

In less than twenty years from his arrival in Brazil in 1881, this Italian middle-class immigrant first founded a commercial firm that sold agricultural products in the São Paulo state, then engaging in food processing, first of all in producing lard. His next step was to create a firm importing cotton and grain. At the beginning of the 1900s Matarazzo started building a commercial-industrial-financial conglomerate. His factories were chiefly flour mills and plants producing bean sacks. In about 1910 textile production became his main endeavor. Sugar and vegetable oil factories and also a phosphorus factory extend the conglomerate's activities. The consolidation of the vertically organized conglomerate, the Industrias Reundias Francisco Matarazzo (IRFM), and the entry into the financial sector were a qualitative breakthrough in terms of capital accumulation. Numerous branches of the conglomerate sprang up in Brazil, but also in Buenos Aires. In subsequent years Matarazzo extended his import and export activities as well as developed his commercial network in Brazil. By 1930 Matarazzo had formed Brazil's most powerful commercial-industrial-financial group (Dean 1969: 60–66, Reiss 1983: 71–76).

Although an immigrant, Matarazzo built his empire not on the fringes of the export economy, but in its center. If non-immigrant Brazilian entrepreneurs, descended from the landed elite, invested at all they tended to primarily in industries catering to mass consumers and in the processing of local, readily available materials such as cotton, sugar, cereals and vegetable oils. And the latter were usually provided by planters themselves who thus utilized land unsuitable for coffee trees (Dean 1969: 70). Similarly, in Argentina the role of landowner-industrialists was predominant, embracing also control over the Unión Industrial Argentina, set up in 1887 (Lewis 1990: 81). In this way the derivation of the category of natural industry was neither mysterious nor very complicated. Natural industry exploited a relatively narrow market, and its demand profile was a direct result of the low level of GDP per capita and of a relatively slow capital market development. The necessary capital was largely coming from the primary export sector. However, on the fringes of the export economy, but by no means in structural conflict with it, more diversified urban industry was springing up. It was composed of small, often artisan-type, shops. But not only. In Argentina in this sea of small-scale industry large private enterprises concentrated on such traditional sectors as textile, beer and cigarette production operated (Haber 2006: 546f).

These powerful financial groups (*grupos*) with their informal system of mobilizing financial resources reflected not only the underdevelopment of credit and the financial structure of the country (Pineda 2006) but also the skewed development of industry. The same can be said about the Mexican textile industry (Haber 1997).

No wonder that discussions on tariff protection in Brazil from the 1890s until WWI were largely about the protection of natural industries. Even the most radical, and failed, project for the protection of Brazilian industry, put forward in 1903 by a *mineiro* representative, emphasized the role of these industries (Luz 1978: 132f). In such a situation, any substantial development of 'artificial industries' was a priori doomed to failure. It was, after all, a general phenomenon, appearing in nearly all Latin American countries where agrarian and commercial elites possessed liquid capital surpluses, while investments in the main sector of their activity were, for various reasons, unprofitable. Periods of crisis were particularly favorable to diversification: when losses were obvious and export markets saturated, ad hoc measures were taken, including support for alternative crops and selective industrial protectionism (see Furtado 1964: 133–136). Supporters of the free market and economic internationalism become advocates of particularistic economic nationalism. This was illustrated clearly by the example of the elite La Sociedad Rural in Argentina, representing the largest cattle-breeders. During and right after WWI, when European demand for meat and hides slumped, La Sociedad vigorously supported demands for the protection of natural industries. In this particular case, the footwear industry (Solberg 1973). In Brazil, the *Encilhamento* speculative fever of the 1890s, followed by the financial crash and coupled with negative terms of trade shocks and devaluations are seen by certain historians as the beginning of cotton industry boom (Fishlow 1972: 318, Baer and Villela 1972).

The transition from natural to artificial industries could not take place in any way other than through an institutional revolution, although the experience with limited particularistic nationalism reflected in tariff policies should not be underestimated: "Colombia and Brazil were protectionist from the 19th century, and this was significant for the degree of diversification–perhaps the most significant factor of all" (Thorp 1998: 92). The same argument can be applied when comparing the industrial performance of Brazil and Mexico before 1913 (Gómez-Galvarriato and Williamson 2009). But this protectionism was not enough. What is more, a break with path-dependent development could not result from an evolutionary process. A combination of an external shock and a profound institutional change was necessary. That change involved, first and foremost, the state, the questioning of its internationalist protectionist-cum-liberal interventionist character. At the same time, one should bear in mind that the regulatory potential of the state, its capacity to allocate resources and make a strategic choice (Hirschman 1977a), was a function of both increased managerial skills as well as resources available and put under state control. Such regulatory potential in the export economy began to grow only at the end of the 19th century. The relatively slow growth of exports before the 1890s seriously curtailed the state's involvement in the economy. The narrow tax base of the Brazilian state, actually limited to import duties, was the main constraint, relaxed only after 1890 (Leff 1997: 50–54).

The limited growth of industry in export economies was also due to the fact that tariff protectionism still had its fierce opponents. First and foremost, the theory-predicted likelihood of an urban coalition (Rogowski 1989: 33, 35) did not materialize before the 1930s: "Capitalists did not ... look to labor for help" (Bértola and Williamson 2006: 44). However, there was something more to such an attitude than wrongly calculated private interests. "The social abyss ... separated the industrialist from his workers," wrote Dean (1969: 175) on Brazil. With regard to Argentine landowners and industrialists, Lewis (1990: 98) emphasized that "the liberalism they professed was the social Darwinian variety." Thus we saw urban workers and the middle class protest vigorously against protectionism.

Even if in 1896 the socialist leader Juan B. Justo raised—in connection with the financial crisis caused by Baring bank's insolvency—dependence on Great Britain, at the same time he claimed: "It is to delude oneself to say that the country's progress depends on establishing artificial industries" and that this can be attained and maintained only "at the expense of the basic sources of the country's wealth," i.e. agriculture and cattle-raising (quoted in Godio 1985: 151). Incidentally, in his stance on protectionism the Argentine socialist did not basically differ from, for instance, German or British Social Democrats. In both cases, defense of the worker as an urban consumer came to the fore (Gerschenkron 1989: 33, 35). Among the many factors which contributed to such a stance one should consider the possibility of producing an artificial labor surplus in towns, which in a period of economic slowdown would push wages down and facilitate the consolidation of pro-free-market sentiment among the urban classes. Not only in Argentina, but also in Brazil, Uruguay, Mexico and other countries, real wages lagged behind GDP per capita during the height of the export-economies' expansion (Bértola and Williamson 2006: 55); the distribution of national income discriminated against 'labor'. Similar were the consequences of overcoming labor shortages by international migrations:

> Overall, between 1885 and 1909 some 2.8 million European immigrants entered Brazil. Almost all of these people went to the southeast [coffee region]. ... the demand for workers also rose in manufacturing as well as in other activities in the booming southeast. *Despite these pressures on the demand side of the labor market, however, real wages apparently did not increase* (Leff 1997: 38f).

Other important, probably the most important, factors which should not be overlooked were the political weakness of labor and its limited bargaining strength. The overall negative pressure exerted by rural wages on the level of urban wages should be added to this list.

In such a situation it was quite unlikely that the urban classes would accept protectionism and the related rise in the cost of living. The policy of tariff protectionism, coupled with devaluation, was not an alternative in the eyes of consumers accustomed to cheaper imports. Members of these classes in Brazil "wanted the gold standard, balanced budgets, and low duties, not state intervention" (Topik 1984: 471). In Argentina such attitudes were even more distinct: "the pampa landed elite agreed with farmers as well as urban consumers that protectionism in an export-oriented economy would raise the cost of rural production and reduce aggregate real incomes" (Solberg 1987: 109). Thus there emerged factors which created favorable conditions for the socialist movement to enhance the export bias and to play–until WWI–the paradoxical role of the socially radical advocate of agricultural export interests (Veliz 1980: 183–188, Gallo 1970: 57f, Díaz-Alejandro 1970: 305f, Solberg 1973, Godio 1985: 167f). However, it is a matter of course that in times of crisis and/or growing foreign competition, threatening job losses, workers did not turn their backs on protectionist measures. Hence, in 1903, unemployed Chilean miners demanded a 25 percent tax on coal imported from Australia (Ortiz Letelier 1985: 168). In this they were not different from their worker-competitors in Australia. But it was clear that the Australian workers were much better organized and in the longer-run more successful (Lloyd 2003: 410f).

Unlike the non-export sectors, which remained under the control of the agrarian elites capable of enforcing protectionist tariffs, conflicts related to the competition of foreign goods in local markets for handicraft and a few small-enterprise products met with the state's disinterest in the latter half of the 19th century and the early 20th century (Lewis 1990: 31, 46).

As a result, economic nationalism connected with the development of the local market was in a structurally adverse situation. The already mentioned natural protectionism and international relative prices allowed economic nationalism to live on into the 20th century. Dean (1969: 10) wrote with regard to Brazil: "It is impossible to conceive of an export product so lucrative that it would pay for the importation of bricks." McGreevey (1971: 105) deployed the same argument with regard to Colombia. A matter of imagination, indeed. In fact, in the 19th century Brazil imported bricks from Germany, and salt from Portugal (Ridings 1994: 202). But at the end of the 19th century, with the development of the internal transportation network, significant changes in this respect took place. On the one hand, it played an integrating role in the centers of export production; on the other, it eliminated natural protectionism. Groups affected could be found among ardent supporters of raising customs duty rates, and thus the general level of customs protectionism (Bértola and Williamson 2006: 27f).

The function of the state as mediator, primarily in contacts with foreign commercial firms and financial institutions, should be interpreted somewhat differently. Those relations, although in the long run creating a peculiar community of interests between local and foreign capital and the state, contained the germs of conflict. They involved both the distribution of gains from foreign trade, different reactions to demand fluctuations and to crises in the international economy as well as the relatively privileged (due to their market power) position of foreign firms. Sometimes, as in Argentina during the financial crisis caused by the collapse of Barings Bank, the prevailing free market mentality was supplemented by violent nationalistic campaigns (Ferns 1960). In Brazil in the 1880s and late 1890s the clash between mainly foreign exporters of wild rubber and coffee and predominantly Brazilian intermediaries (factors) brought similar results: "factors, much less alien in nationality, appealed to the public as defenders of Brazilian economic sovereignty" (Ridings 1994: 123). On the railroads the Brazilian government imposed a new freight structure.

> that favored freight bound for the domestic market over freight bound for foreign markets, which meant that most of the gains from the railroads were captured by Brazilian agriculturalists and industrialists producing for the domestic market (Haber 1997: 26).

The example of Brazil was not widespread, though.

However, it is the already well researched history of the coffee sector in Brazil that can serve as the perfect example of rising particularistic primary-sector nationalism under the patronage of the state. Conflict-ridden relations with foreign merchants and intermediaries and the crisis in coffee trade were important factors shaping such nationalism. Monopsony secured by foreign trade houses in contacts between Brazilian coffee planters and foreign consumers automatically, as it were, gave rise to charges of exploitation and unfair pricing (Greenhill 1977b: 200f, 229). The introduction during the 1906 crisis of the coffee valorization scheme and supply control was the peak of this kind of nationalism and the ensuing forced mediation by the state. The São Paulo coffee elite, which controlled the greater part of Brazilian coffee production, played a leading role in initiating this innovative endeavor. In passing, the idea of such a scheme was first proposed in 1903 by Alexandre Sicíliano, an industrialist-merchant with strong financial and family links to coffee planters (Dean 1969: 75). Despite the initially negative attitude of the state and federal governments, after a period of dithering, foreign firms and banks, too, backed the Taubaté Agreement, signed in 1906 by representatives of São Paulo, Minas Gerais and Rio de Janeiro. On a certain condition, however: that in the 'coffee OPEC' of the time, the participation of the São Paulo state would be warranted. The condition was understandable: the valorization scheme was largely financed from a $73 million foreign loan (Thorp 1998: 93).

The novelty of the scheme, confirming the possibility of transforming free-market coalitions into protectionist ones, "lay in official adoption of the same business techniques to control foodstuffs, which had long characterized private manufacturing and mining" (Greenhill 1977b: 229f). It was possible due to the interplay of two factors: first, from the mid-19th century, the increase in world coffee consumption, particularly in the USA, was exponential, and second, Brazil's share of the world market of the time grew from 40 percent in the 1850s to more then 80 percent in 1911 (to stay at more than 50 percent until 1929). The Brazilian elite took the role of price-maker on the world coffee market (Abreu and Bevilaqua 2000: 36, 43). Both factors worked against the prospect of 'immiserizing growth' which could result from declining net barter terms of trade (Bhagwati 1958). A special tax in gold currency levied on exported coffee did not threaten the interests of the coffee elite: in the face of the diktat of the price-maker, the foreign consumer would pay for the losses incurred. The same applied to taxes on inputs to the coffee sector. However, in subsequent years the policy of supply control and of keeping prices for Brazilian coffee high weakened Brazil's quasi-monopolistic position and opened the door to competitors who had been marginalized until then (Abreu and Bevilaqua 2000). In the longer run, the low income elasticity of demand for coffee in the US and Europe favored more productive and/or aggressive suppliers. The failed–at roughly the same time–attempt to control prices and supply of Brazilian wild rubber was caused by the forceful entry of Asian competitors.

With hindsight, the valorization scheme can be seen to have set a precedent for direct, long-lasting government control over the key sector of the Brazilian economy. The conflict between planters and foreign trade houses was moved up to a new level. Valorization, next repeated in the years 1914–1918, in 1924 transformed into a 'permanent defense' under the supervision of the then just established Instituto do Café in São Paulo. Also, valorization provided a justification for operationalization of the concept of "national interest" as opposed to "cosmopolitan capitalism." This is how A. A. Leal da Cunha perceived the meaning of valorization in his book *Pela independencia econômica e emancipação commercial do Brasil*, published in 1912 (see Cortés Conde and Stein 1977: 238f). What is more, this instrument had proved effective, and the $73 million debt had been repaid by 1913. All the same, the short- and medium-term consequences of the scheme, its impact on primary export diversification and on industrial development in particular were probably negative (Furtado 1964: 136n). Colombia, the second largest coffee producer in Latin America, resorted to forceful intervention in the coffee market with a considerable delay. The Federación Nacional de Cafeteros Colombianos was founded only in 1927 and "endowed with quasi-state capacities" (Thorp 1998: 58ff). Those differences resulted, among other things, from different structures of the coffee sector in the two countries: a strong elite with access to the state bureaucracy in Brazil, and poorly organized coffee growers in Colombia.

In Brazil, however, what had been started via state patronage and backing, forced by the elite, in successive years transformed into a conflict. In the leading coffee-growing state, São Paulo, the increasingly autonomous bureaucracy was on course to cease playing a subsidiary role to the class of powerful coffee growers and exporters. Thus, already in 1926, the reform of the Instituto do Café "ended the representation of class interests within the institution." São Paulo state officials "argued that coffee policy, given its importance for the entire economy and for the State [of São Paulo] itself, could not remain subject to the guidance of private interests. 'Unity in direction' was the watchword" (Perissinotto 2003: 7). In the 1920s, there also appeared new threats: growing new urban classes, crop diversification and the rise of smaller farmers, the state government-aided breakup of inefficient plantations, split among the coffee oligarchy and its supporters and the emergence of "dissident oligarchies" (Welch 1999: 41, Schneider 1991: 109). At the outbreak of the 1929 crisis, followed by the Revolution of

1930, these creeping conflicts led to a fundamental split between the state and the São Paulo coffee elite. As a result of the progressing breakdown of the hitherto intimate relationship between the coffee elite and the state, and later the federal bureaucracy, there emerged a stronger, autonomous and centralized national state. In 1930 the Instituto do Café was put under the federal control of a Vargas-appointed intervenor, and in 1931–1933 coffee policy became the federal government's domain. The nationalism of the coffee planters transformed into *an element* of the wider policy of the economic nationalism of the Brazilian state. But the coffee elite, divided and weakened even before 1930, in the Revolution of 1930 mainly saw a threat to its values and interests. Confronted with Vargas's centralism and *tenentes'* radicalism, the coffee oligarchs and their industrial allies, the *classes cultas*, joined forces, and revolted in 1932 in the name of liberalism, regional autonomy and the status quo (Woodard 2006). However, their revolt, although widely supported, was not a demonstration of strength, but rather a sign of desperation and of their vanishing dominant economic and political role (Schneider 1991: 121–125).

The activities of foreign-controlled banking, public utilities, railroads and the merchant navy, provided a similar source of conflicts. Still, when tracing the origins of particularistic economic nationalism, it does not make a great difference to what extent the charges leveled by local economic elites corresponded with the facts and reflected the real behavior of foreign firms. Even if we assume that British capital in Latin America did not in the long run achieve extraordinarily high profits (Rippy 1959, Greenhill 1977a: 176), the subjective sense of inequality and discrimination was far more important, anyway. And that sense prevailed among the local elites. Let me once again repeat after Landes: "injustice perceived is injustice felt."

Varieties of the Export Sector and Economic Nationalism

The shaping of primary sector economic nationalism was to some extent dependent on the structure of the nascent modern export sector and on the role foreign capital played in its creation and functioning.

Singer (1950: 475) defined the sector as foreign-controlled export-oriented plantations and/or mining enclaves of limited spread effects which "should in fact be considered as domestic investment on the part of the industrialized countries" (see also Baran 1976, Kennwood and Lougheed 1971: 151). Cardoso and Faletto's (1979: 66–73) approach was more nuanced.

'Dependent development' marked not only the foreign-controlled enclave, but also the export sector where crucial assets and immediate production were under local elites' control.

The activities of the foreign-controlled export enclaves led to many frictions (also in contacts with a periphery state) and to an increase in the nationalistic mood among local economic elites. On a par with the issue of shares of profits, arose problems associated with competition for manpower, access to infrastructure and other supplementary resources. Conflicts were particularly strong in those areas where foreign companies were rapidly pushing out local capital and other forms of domestic economic activities (Lebergott 1980: 246–249). However, it is worth noting here that in Levin's (1960) seminal analysis the export enclave was defined as an essentially closed world, regulated by foreign factors of production, bringing in "luxury importers" that supplied foreign consumers and having weak links with the local economy. Describing Peru at the initial stage of the guano boom in the 1840s, he pointed out that "[l]abor came from China, capital from Great Britain, and entrepreneurship and management from both Peru and Europe" (Levin 1960: 14). A century later, in 1937, when the struggle for nationalization of the majority of foreign-owned oil companies in Mexico entered a decisive stage, the document prepared by a Mexican commission read:

> The principal oil companies operating in Mexico have never been fully integrated to the country ... [They] left in the Republic only wages and taxes, without in reality having cooperated in the social progress of Mexico (quoted in Wilkins 1974: 226).

And several years later Singer (1950: 4785) wrote that foreign-controlled enclaves "never became a part of the internal economic structure of ... underdeveloped countries themselves, except in the purely geographical and physical sense." A kind of *déjà vu*.

However, serious doubts began to emerge as to whether such totally isolated enclaves and export economies were really a rule, especially in larger Latin American countries (not to mention Central Europe). More recent approaches no longer refer to a so narrowly defined concept of the enclave-type of export economy (for Peru see Bonilla 1974, Thorp and Bertram 1978, Gootenberg 1993), although they do not rule out the appearance of narrowly understood enclaves, for instance, in the oil industry.

Thus, the activities of the foreign firms which controlled the enclaves did not always inevitably lead to the literal elimination of local capital. Under threat was a certain type of local entrepreneurship, but at the same time other local actors were included in the production cycle: directly in the enclave or indirectly via linkages. Nevertheless, there certainly occurred asymmetric market relations–a result of foreign firms' disproportionate bargaining power. In the case of the North American Cerro de Pasco Copper Corporation, which by 1915 had taken control of Peruvian copper, all these tendencies were visible (Mallon 1983: 181). Needless to say, in those enclaves exhibiting a tendency to create a closed world, isolated from the local economy, effects of this kind were limited. In such extreme cases, in relations with foreign companies, the fiscal interests of the state came to the fore.

Therefore can one posit the view that in enclave economies conflicts were sharper and created more favorable conditions for particularistic economic nationalism to arise than the conflicts arising in the variant of national control over the export sector? It would be very risky to generalize. In the two countries where national control over export-destined production was unquestionable, i.e. in Brazil and Argentina, their respective histories of the development of political and economic nationalisms in the 1930–1939 period, which was in many respects decisive, were decidely different. Above all the differences were manifested in the degrees of escalation of conflicts with foreign capital.

The challenge Argentine nationalists mounted in relation to Great Britain and, to a lesser extent, the USA, was serious, but primarily in the sphere of political ideas. It should be kept in mind that until 1943 it was not radical nationalists who dictated the economic policy of the government. Up until the early 1940s, the Concordancia had been perceived as an oligarchic answer to the UCR radical party, ousted from power. FORJA, the Radical Movement of the Young Argentina, a radical splinter group from the UCR, thus provided in the 1930s important political and ideological grounds for modern nationalism, although as a marginalized opposition. It should be added, however, that unlike the conservative and authoritarian nationalism of Leopoldo Lugones and the others, FORJA took a decidedly anti-imperialist stand, first of all anti-British, but without sympathies with German or Italian fascism. At the same time, the distinction between 'the people' and 'oligarchy' was an important element of FORJA's political message. In mid-1930 also other nationalist groups, like the Alianza de la Juventud Nacional, started to denounce both Marxism and "political, capitalist and latifundist" oligarchies. In successive years, the new nationalist current of Argentine historiography gave some support to the ideas advocated by FORJA and other dynamic (as opposed to nostalgic) nationalistic currents (Stemplowski 1975: 139–147, 183, 308–310,

Spektorowski 1994: 169ff, 179f). Thus, one can speak of a radical nationalism that was outside Concordancia and the conservative coalition of societal actors supporting it. The nationalism of FORJA and other groups gained practical significance only after 1943, when it became a part of the populism and economic nationalism associated with Juan Perón.

In the economic sphere, nationalist criticism of the 1930s concentrated, first and foremost, on the Roca-Runciman Treaty, signed in 1933. The treaty, meant to guarantee Argentine meat access to the British market, was actually asymmetric, decidedly favoring British interests. In the case of meat (about which more below), stipulations of the treaty fueled nationalist feelings. Also preferential opening up of the Argentine market to British industrial exports, guarantees for British investments in Argentina and a number of concessions, including a special railroad exchange rate and preferential exchange rate to service foreign debt, stirred up particularly strong emotions. One particular quote provides a vivid description of the attitudes of those who, on the one hand, expected and supported state intervention under crisis conditions, and on the other, were disappointed with the shape it took because of the treaty. Thus, in the state's actions critics detected

> a definite bias in favour of the interests of the 'establishment' and more specifically of British interests in Argentina. In their view economic reform during the 1930s, instead of transforming those aspects making the country vulnerable to instability and a victim of an unfair system of foreign relations, if anything reinforced them. For instance, it is argued that commercial policy consecrated the orientation of the Argentine economy towards one market–that of Great Britain ... The wide and nationally sensitive powers conferred on the newly created central bank were hardly compatible ... with the fact that representatives of foreign banks were seated on its board of directors.

To this one should add that many financial scandals at the time were linked "not so much to corruption as to leniency vis-à-vis some vested interest" (O'Connell 1984: 203). This largely traditional narrative of nationalist opponents of the treaty, amid attempts at revision, "still seems to hold water in the light of the available evidence" (Abreu 1984: 155). The practical implementation of Roca-Runciman Treaty was, however, less strict, especially as support for wheat and maize agriculture, local industry and infrastructural projects was concerned (Lewis 1990: 91f). Such an argument one can find, for example, in Peter Alhadeff's (1985) anti-*dependentista* analysis of the Roca Funding Loan which followed the Treaty. It is unclear, however, to what extent this was the result of a considerate policy as far as industry was concerned. It seems that pro-industry actions resulted not so much from the government's conversion to economic nationalism as from the growing difficulties with balance-of-payments.

The Argentine agricultural, wheat and maize sectors, also began forcefully to make nationalist demands. In a way this was natural and understandable. This was the sector after all that had been the first in contributing to Argentine's exports, hit hardest by the crisis. What was not natural was the fact that "no government between 1880 and 1930 enacted any significant policy reform or concession to aid wheat agriculture" (Solberg 1987: 28). The success of the relief operation–started in the early 1930s with the establishment of the Junta Reguladora de Granos (National Grain Board) and the introduction of minimum prices for wheat, linseed and maize–was qualified. The internal terms of trade continuously discriminated against the rural sector (O'Connell 1984: 206, Thorp 1984: 337). And finally industrialists also saw in the nationalist sentiment that was developing in the 1930s a chance to force through their demands for protectionism and state support (Lewis 1990: 97). Minuscule inflows of fresh foreign direct investments and balance-of-payments problems worked to the advantage of some of them, more successful in their relations with the state and state-controlled institutions.

Meanwhile, in Getúlio Vargas's Brazil, criticism of foreign capital and other elements epitomizing external dependence assumed the form of a rather mild conflict which was quickly obviated. In the dispute concerning the construction of a modern integrated iron and steel plant, Vargas's maneuvers between the USA and Nazi Germany never led to such tensions as in Argentina. And this despite strong dependence of Brazilian exports on the US market. Also Brazilian-German trade developed without dramatic protests. Although the share of Germany in Brazilian imports increased between 1934 and 1938 from 11–12 percent to 19–20 percent, "the increase of imports from Germany dislocated not American but British exports" (Abreu 1985: 383). However, one should add mainly British; the share of US imports also declined. Among the many factors which contributed to such an outcome one should mention the differences in exercising economic power by the US and Britain, respectively:

> in spite of American leverage in Brazil being at least as powerful as Britain's in Argentina, Brazil was never under real pressure to adapt her foreign economic policy to the advantage of the USA. ... During the 1930s ... the USA, in contrast with Britain, consistently adopted policies based on the most-favored-nation clause (Abreu 1984: 147f).

Incidentally, in their trade relations with Argentina in the 1930s, the US presented a rather strong British-like posture (Bértola and Porcile 2006: 9). On the other hand, the skilful use of the instruments of state intervention in the coffee sector essentially neutralized planters' nationalism. Alternative projects of nationalism and *brasilidade* were marginalized, too. After the unsuccessful revolt, the threat from the communist-backed ALN, led by famous Luís Carlos Prestes, and from the variant of anti-imperialism they propagated, was eliminated in 1935. Neither did Brazilian fascists (*Integralista* movement) find a reliable ally in Vargas or in the majority of the military, and their attempted putsch in 1938 ended in a fiasco.

In point of fact, in 1930 and thereafter Brazilian anti-imperialism, understood as defensive nationalism, was etatized and its intensity and direction subjected to top-down management-cum-manipulation. The establishment in 1937 of the authoritarian Estado Nôvo–a joint effort of the president and armed forces–gave Vargas considerably greater freedom of action. As a preemptive action it eliminated the threat posed by the renewed *paulista* opposition (Woodard 2006: 86f). Also, it enhanced earlier than in Argentina the etatist dimension of economic nationalism. Although the share of the Argentine state in total investments in the years 1930–1939 was on the rise (from 16.8 to 25.3 percent), until the very end of the 1930s this was not translated into well-orchestrated support for industry. "Concordancia's proagrarian bias" was visible (Lewis 1990: 90). New ideas concerning a more ambitiously understood role of the state arose later, in 1940, and next after 1943.

Initially, the sources of the Brazilian etatist bias in the 1930s were chiefly political. The tradition of regional loyalties and policy-making, strongly entrenched during the Old Republic, was a fact. To overcome the legacy of the 'politics of the governors' needed a much stronger cure than the creation of the *national* party. Attempts in 1930–1931 to build such a nationwide political structure, the Legion of October (*Legião de Outubro*), came to nothing (Flynn 1970, Schneider 1991: 142). Neither did subsequent attempts. Put briefly, until 1945 Vargas's nationalist party was simply the state, and more precisely: the federal state's bureaucratic structures and the army. Last but not least, in both Argentina and Brazil, although with different intensity, economic nationalism emerged as the policy of industrialization. Toward the end of the 1930s the nationalist and pro-industry character of Vargas's economic policy was much clearer than was the case in Argentina (Abreu 1985).

Comparing the reactions of the economic elites, for example, in Brazil and Peru, causes even more difficulties. Important sectors in the latter country, despite the differentiation of exports, can be described as enclaves *sensu largo*. After the outbreak of the 1929 crisis, local capital's attitude toward foreign investors was, however, considerably milder than in Brazil. What is more, irregularities in the behavior of Peruvian local capital were striking.

In two instances of the formation of export enclaves, i.e. in the guano era in the mid-19th century and in the copper era (from the beginning of the 20th century), reactions to the dominance of foreign companies were decidedly different. In the first case, from a certain moment the dispute over the lease of the state guano monopoly among groups of Peruvian entrepreneurs and foreign (chiefly British) investors was carried on in a rather grandiose atmosphere. The endorsement in 1849 by the Peruvian parliament of a contract with Antony Gibbs & Sons Co. was accompanied by patriotic declarations that in "all future guano contracts preference should be given to 'the sons of the country'" (Levin 1960: 77, Bonilla 1974). In this situation the curtailment of the role of foreign investors was not difficult to predict. All the more so given that local *consignatarios* had gained strong support from both the government and parliament. The arrangement finally established was quite an interesting one and unduplicated anywhere else in Latin America at that time:

> one striking feature of Peru's nineteenth-century export experience [was] the unique national-statist and entrepreneurial control which meant that an astonishing share of the final returns–some estimate more than 70 percent–remained at home. This record would not be approached again by other export nations until the mid-twentieth century (Gootenberg 1989: 84).

Well, around the late 1860s, also in neighboring Chile the share of local entrepreneurs in the returns from the locally-controlled copper and coal sectors were very high (Valenzuela 1992: 508, 544). In this sense Peru was not unique. All the same, the money involved in the guano business did excite the imagination.

Anyway, the support the government and public opinion gave to Peruvian entrepreneurs as well as the emergence of local sources of capital meant that toward the end of the guano boom, in 1868, "when a large share of the guano-export business was in Peruvian hands, a class of capitalist entrepreneurs had developed in Peru" (Levin 1960: 85). The quality of this class was another matter. If we leave aside here the consolidation of the state and its institutions, investments in guano were a classic case of a rent-creating activity (Bulmer-Thomas 2003: 36). Thus, local control and the struggle with foreign investors were important in defining the level of rent, but from the point of view of the country's development prospects, they were of no great consequence. As in the later case of the foreign-controlled copper mining sector, "the terms of [Peru's] integration into the international system" remained untouched (Thorp and Bertram 1978: 94; see also Platt 1977).

The expansion, begun in 1902, of the US Cerro de Pasco Copper Corporation met with a totally different reaction. In this case, two issues were involved: first, the attitudes and responses of the Peruvian mining elite to foreign capital entry, and second, the long-term benefits to (or losses for) the economy as a whole resulting from such an entry.

Regarding the first point, economic historians' conclusions are straightforward: local capital resigned itself to *La Compañía's* forceful entry with hardly any protest, although, as in the case of the guano boom, there were Peruvian entrepreneurs who could make profitable investments in copper mining: "[t]he capable and effective local mining capitalists of the 1880s and 1890s, with very few exceptions, welcomed and cooperated with foreign penetration" (Thorp and Bertram 1978: 80, 82ff, Bonilla 1974: 89ff). Hence, a question arises as to whether the appearance of the Cerro de Pasco Copper Corporation in actual fact took place "at the expense of local capitalists' development opportunities" (Flores Galindo 1974: 32).

Taking into account the attitudes of Peruvian mine-owners, such an opinion seems risky as examples of resistance to the take-over of the mines by *La Compañía* were rare, at best. Next, Peruvian historians point to the absence of any state protectionism that would support the national mining sector. This, however, assumed that local entrepreneurs, faced by a powerful corporation, really expected such support and pressed for it, whereas its absence forced them to capitulate. It was the Peruvian state, which "*se enfeudó al capital extranjero*" (Burga and Flores Galindo 1979: 77) and thus let them down. Yet, this argument does not sound convincing, either. Other historians have suggested instead that "the decision to sell was purely and simply a matter of price: the foreign firms, for some reason, valued Peruvian mineral deposits more highly than did the Peruvians" (Thorp and Bertram 1978: 85). However, looking at with a longer perspective, whatever the reasons behind local capitalists' decisions, one can plausibly argue that the entry of Cerro de Pasco "excluded local entrepreneurship and management ... contributing thereby to the erosion of local technological competence and the undermobilization of the society's creative potential" (Thorp and Bertram 1978: 95). And at the regional level, the company's activities, especially in the 1920s, meant that *La Compañía* "broke the delicate balance established with the regional economy": the delinking of mining and its immediate regional environment was a result (Drinot 2000: 176f). In other words, the spillover effects, social returns and also forward linkages one would expect from FDI like Cerro de Pasco–the things stressed by Haber (1997a: 10f) when taking account of crude variants of *dependentistas* arguments–were probably rather weak. In the case of oil in Peru, such effects were for all practical purposes nonexistent.

Regarding the second point, the conclusions one can draw are more complicated. The immediate effect of the entry of *La Compañía* and of its take-over of the mining sector was an increase of liquid capital in the hands of the Peruvian elite. Yet, Peruvian capitalists used the then huge sums obtained from *La Compañía*–about $8.5 million (against $15–20 million of total annual exports in the years 1900–1916)–in a largely unproductive way; additionally, under given domestic market conditions marked by limited demand, "only a rather small part of the liquid funds generated by Cerro's entry found profitable investment opportunities" (Thorp and Bertram 1978: 93ff; see also Mallon 1983). It seems therefore that the restrictions imposed on the long-term development of entrepreneurship were, to a large extent, a result of joint decisions taken by foreign and local capital. However, when looking at the returned value Cerro de Pasco left in the country, i.e. the proportion of the total value of exports 'returned' locally (locally purchased inputs, wages, taxes, locally accumulated profits, etc.) (Thorp and Bertram 1978: 19, 355), the balance sheet speaks against *La Compañía's* presence. Let me add, however, that the returned value the foreign-controlled copper industry left in Chile was much lower. If in Peru the returned value was 50–60 percent, in 1920 in Chile mining companies left a mere 11 percent of their earnings, and after income tax was for the first time imposed on them, an average in 1925–1931 of 39 percent. In other sectors of Chilean mining returned value in 1920 was decisively higher, reaching in the case of coal 91 percent and of nitrates 56 percent (Cortés Conde 1974: 73, 75). Foreign control over the Peruvian mining sector

> made only a small difference to the total amount of investment actually realized in the economy during the 1900s [and] caused foreign-exchange receipts from the First World War onwards to fall below the level which they would otherwise have attained (Thorp and Bertram 1978: 95).

This important incident, however, had a wider context and consequences. The concept of the collaborating elite, proposed by Ronald Robinson (1977: 138f) as an explanation of the limited conflict with foreign capital in underdeveloped countries, seems appropriate here (see also Platt 1977: 12). It implies that the interest groups dominant in a given country

> accepted the role of foreign capital either from motives of ideological belief of from personal economic interest. This was certainly the case in Peru at the turn of the century. ... Only one government between 1885 and 1930 systematically attacked foreign interests: that of José Pardo (1915–19) in the exceptional situation created by the First World War (Miller 1977: 374f).

Latin American anti-imperialist-cum-nationalist political vocabulary described the collaborating elites of the interwar period plainly and crudely as *vendepatrias* (nation-selling elites). Toward the end of the 1920s such attitudes were challenged from outside by radicalized middle-class leaders who were not part of the political and economic elites of the time. However, Haya de la Torre and APRA's bid for power at the 1932 elections and later during the 1934 revolt failed. The response was the appearance not of an authoritarian developmental regime but a relatively passive authoritarian one. Its policy toward foreign companies, especially in the oil sector, was far from assertive. The prediction that "countries that were enclaves have greater state capacity than non-enclaves" (Conning and Robinson 2009: 367) was not confirmed. Chile under the short-lived 1932 Socialist Republic was probably a different case (Stemplowski 1996). What was new was the partial recuperation of local entrepreneurship in Peruvian copper mining. The terms of the revival were quite interesting:

> Because the deposits brought into production by the new local companies were those which had remained out of the hands of the large foreign companies, there was no basis for a clash of interests between local and foreign capital; on the contrary, the two groups existed amicably side by side ... The largest and richest mineral deposits in Peru, however, typically remained in the hands of large foreign firms (Thorp and Bertram 1978: 161).

It seems that the examples quoted should warn against over-hasty generalizations which refer to a single-variable analysis, in this case to local versus foreign control over the export sector. However, I do not imply that the differentiation proposed by Cardoso and Faletto was of no value to the debates on issues of economic nationalism. It actually was of great importance to the formation of strategic economic elites, to the type of coalitions formed and to the directions of the state intervention. It seems, for example, that particularistic nationalism, if it manifested itself at all in enclave economies, found support above all among those economic elites who remained outside the dominant export sector, and also, in certain situations, among groups making up that amorphous category of 'the people'. In the variant of national control over the export sector, this nationalism found–particularly at the time of crisis–public support also among the agrarian export elite. In their protectionist behavior active representatives of this elite hardly differed from their French and German counterparts.

Yet, a deeper analyses necessitates one to take into account still other dimensions of the peripheral economy and society. Next to such issues as the degree of concentration/diversification of exports and imports, the share in the global production of a given commodity, the degree of integration in the international economy or the world market price for and income elasticities regarding particular products, one should also give attention to the potential for the autonomization of the state structures in different variants of the export economy.

One could argue that, theoretically, in specific situations, especially in medium-size and big countries, the enclave type of economy was favorable to different models of the autonomization of the state apparatus. Considering the main sources of state revenues (e.g. import taxes, licenses and foreign loans) and the vulnerability and low level of self-organization of societal actors, in this type of economy the bureaucratic apparatus seemed to remain under the much looser political and economic control of the local elites. Leguia's Peru in the 1920s was such a case. However, that does not imply that in the enclave economy, the autonomy of the state inevitably led–via increased state capacity–to holistic economic nationalism. On the contrary, in the period under consideration it usually manifested itself either in non-productive rent appropriation[7] or in a wasteful spending spree and rampant corruption. Leguia's Peru once more comes to mind. Increased rent-extraction capacity does not automatically translate into increased capacity in defining and executing developmental policy. Thus conflict between the state and foreign entrepreneurs usually expressed itself in the form of hard bargaining, less often as patronage over the particularistic nationalism of social groups uninvolved directly in the enclave economy. Venezuela under the long dictatorship of Juan Vicente Gómez (1908–1935) and the associated oil monoculture was an example of a largely predatory autonomy. One of the most important traits

---

[7] The example of the distribution of the extraordinary resources the Peruvian state obtained in the years 1840–1880 from the sale of guano is illustrative. From the $500–600 million obtained, about 80 percent was spent on the military and civilian bureaucracy, profits of foreign contractors and transfers to agrarian elites. 20 percent of the revenues was allocated to the construction of the railroads (Bonilla 1974: 146f, quoting Shane J. Hunt's estimates).

of this dictatorship was a skillful playing of British oil companies against US ones, with a preference for the latter and without undertaking any experiments with nationalism that went beyond the unscrupulous rent appropriation. In the opinion of American politicians and entrepreneurs, in the 1920s Venezuela was the 'healthy' opposite of unruly Mexico (Krenn 1990: chapter 6, Thorp 1998: 76f). The situation was different in those economies where national control prevailed over the export sector. In this case, far reaching state autonomy not only did not repeat the model of the predatory state, but in certain countries opened prospects for the transformation of the hitherto modernization community. Uruguay prior to 1929 can serve as an example. More about it below.

At the time of external shocks and/or rapid changes in the external demand profile, national control over the export sector favored export diversification and domestic market growth. This concerned, first of all, the more developed peripheral economies. However, to transform such a possibility into reality required support from a relatively autonomous state. All the same it was not the only requirement, as illustrated by the example of Argentina in the 1930s. Until the beginning of the 1940s, the Concordancia's rule and the related autonomization of the state meant a policy of muddling-through rather than a breakthrough. On the other hand, in the enclave economy, changes oriented toward export diversification and, above all, domestic market growth, were impeded because fundamental decisions on profit allocation were taken externally. Investment decisions by foreign firms were of primary importance: a kind of negative value added to changes in the world economy, to the limited domestic market and to the weakness of local entrepreneurship. This restricted intersectoral capital mobility, while constraints on the state's economic maneuvering were lifted only during violent political upheavals. At this point the example of Bolivia in the 1930s comes to mind.

The Regional Dimension

The regional dimension was an important aspect of particularistic economic nationalism. Nationalism of this type represented either the interests of entire sectors of production or their territorially concentrated parts ('sectoral nationalism') or those of different national (ethnic) groups in a given country ('national regionalism').

An example of the first type of regional nationalism was the conflict within the Argentine cattle-breeding sector between *criadores* (i.e. breeders supplying 8–10 month-old calves) from the interior (from La Pampa to Corrientes and Entre Ríos) on the one hand, and *invernadores* (i.e. fatteners supplying 2–3 year-old animals), mainly from Buenos Aires Province, on the other hand. That conflict intensified at the end of WWI, to be further exacerbated during the Great Depression.

The relationship between the upper-class *invernadores* and freezing plants (*frigoríficos*), crucial for the beef export business, was relatively close: "Reliable fatteners, who were usually large *estancieros*, were reasonably treated and benefited from consistent loyalty to one factory" (Crossley and Greenhill 1977: 312). The position of breeders was much weaker. The problem was aggravated by the actual monopoly on *frigoríficos* held by British investors and US firms ('Chicago companies') struggling with the British for a piece of the market. Before the 1929 crisis, for at least two decades, that fact had been a fertile ground for nationalist protests and campaigns: "Argentina's meat packing industry, epitomizing foreign capitalist exploitation of the republic's national resources and linked to the notorious Chicago companies, could hardly have expected popularity" (Crossley and Greenhill: 318). Even if accusations of permanent price overexploitation of Argentina's cattle-breeding sector as a whole were rather exaggerated, the very fact of monopolistic control (and monopolistic collusions) was sufficient to raise nationalistic reactions. The post-WWI cattle crisis and the rather uncompromising position taken by packinghouses vis-à-vis *estancieros* clearly demonstrated that such control and collusions were a reality. The same can be said about the grain trade, even more important for Argentina: "The Big Four [foreign] grain exporters, who handled 75 per cent of Argentina's grain trade, maintained the appearance but not the substance of competition" (Greenhill 1977a: 171).

The crisis of 1929 created conditions under which sectoral nationalism erupted. Because of the particular terms of the Argentine-British Roca-Runciman Treaty of 1933, which, among other things, provided for preferential treatment of the exports of the most profitable chilled, not frozen, beef, which discriminated against *criadores*, breeders from the interior invoked nationalistic slogans. They were directed against *invernadores* from Buenos Aires Province, large *estancieros* as well as British- and US-controlled packinghouses connected with them (Stemplowski 1975: 45, Murmis and Portaniero 1971: 27, Smith 1969:). In this way there appeared a sort of replica of the historical conflict from the first half of the 19th century: the 'barbarian' and at the same time 'truly national' interior epitomized by Rosas versus the 'civilization' of cosmopolitan and Europeanized Buenos Aires. Against *invernadores* (in 1937 their number was estimated at more than 6,400), who were usually absent, travelling intensively to Buenos Aires and Europe, were the *criadores*, "men of the country" (more than 18,200) (Smith 1969: 44f).

However, unlike Rosas and his ideological followers, the *criadores'* demands were not excessively ambitious: they demanded a greater share of the export quota and higher prices. The slogan *comprar a quien nos compra*,[8] popular among the Argentine elites, and launched as early as 1927 by a leader of influential elite La Sociedad Rural, which represented *invernadores* and the largest landowners, in the dispute between the two groups of breeders reflected a relatively mild radicalism. On the other hand, the newly established La Confederación de Asociaciones Rurales de Buenos Aires y La Pampa (CARBAP), representing the disadvantaged small ranchers and farmers, looked primarily after the economic interests of its members. What is more, while representing those interests, it was adamantly opposed to industrialization. Therefore it is argued by some historians that although the slogan proposed in the name of La Sociedad Rural contained "a grain of nationalism," the actual goal of La Sociedad and Argentine elites was to maintain close relations with Great Britain: "Dependence was thus promoted in the name of independence" (Smith 1969: 126). At the end of the day, *invernadores* got access to the British market with their chilled beef, and *criadores* and CARBAP got support from the Junta National de Carnes (National Meat Board), established in the 1930s.

However, one should interpret differently the inward-oriented anti-imperialism-cum-nationalism of Senator Lisandro de la Torre in the mid-1930s. By promoting the interests of *criadores* and small ranchers, and also by appealing to the middle and lower classes, at the same time he epitomized the "nonrevolutionary opposition to the aristocracy and foreign investments" (Smith 1969: 193ff). De la Torre's anti-imperialism was radical in the sense that for him his chief enemy was the oligarchy embodied by the Concordancia: "Though other politicians had resorted to anti-imperialism in the politics of beef, none had employed it as part of a broadside attack on the aristocracy and the government in general" (Smith 1969: 192f). As concerned people "in unquestioning service to [Anglo-American] refrigerating monopolies," de la Torre regarded, for instance,

---

[8] An identical phrase can be found in List's *System* (1922: 342). Writing about German trade with tropical colonies, he underscored that "we should give a preference to those ... which purchase manufactured goods from us; or, in short, *that we should buy from those who buy from us*."

Raúl Prebisch, president of the Central Bank of Argentina, as one of them (Puiggrós 1977: 321). In passing, one should bear in mind that the 1929 crisis facilitated the military coup in 1930, forced the radical party from power and restored the political role of the traditional elites. The fraud that accompanied the 1932 election of the new president, general Agustín Pedro Justo (the so-called *fraude patriótico*), the notorious Roca-Runciman Treaty, corruption and repressive measures marked the period of Concordancia's rule–*La Década Infame*–that lasted until 1943. However, in economic policy the Concordancia was not a simple and crude articulation of the interests of traditional elites: "the Concordancia was politically retrograde, but it managed nonetheless to be compatible with industrial progress. ... industrial interests gained ground steadily during the 1930s" (Lewis 1990: 85, 90). Yet, the pace of industrialization and structural change was distinctly slower than in Brazil. In Brazil, the crisis and internal conflicts within the coffee elite led in the 1930s to permanent political marginalization of the traditional oligarchy.

On the other hand, in Central Europe, nationalism connected with the economic role of national minorities ('national regionalism') was endemic. It included such precarious variants in which this nationalism was advanced by social groups belonging to the national majority who felt that minorities were undercutting its economic position. This kind of nationalism was exemplified by competition between Polish, Hungarian or Romanian and Jewish capital or between Polish capital and that of the German minority. According to Kofman (1997: 72–77), this was an outright copy-book example of–usually xenophobic–inward-oriented nationalism. It is worth adding here that its supporters often defined it as defensive nationalism. The terminology proposed in Poland by Rybarski (1997: 254) is evidence of the perceived intensity of this competition. On the analogy of protectionism directed against foreign companies, with reference to the economic activities of the Jewish minority, he wrote about the need to introduce "internal protectionism." Meanwhile, the authors of the Polish foreign ministry's 1935 program concerning the 'Jewish question' defined Polish-Jewish relations as "a state of war, without a formal declaration of one. The war waged by Jews is both defensive as well as offensive" (quoted in Chojnowski 1979: 222). The language used says something about the mentality of the program's authors and the degree of tension in Polish-Jewish relations. Such similarly strong emotions were felt only in Polish-German economic relations in Upper Silesia, but in this case the notion of defensive nationalism was largely justified.

In Latin America, particularly in the countries receiving large-scale immigration, such as Brazil and Argentina, such conflicts arose, too. The xenophobic attitude of conservative nationalists in Argentina toward immigrants was conspicuous (Stemplowski 1975). Also Peru and Mexico witnessed a division into traditional elites deriving their lineage from the colonial era and 'internal foreigners' (immigrants). Some researchers point to its negative impact on the formation of pro-industrial interests and the corresponding ideological and program consensus (Cornblit 1967). For instance in Brazil, the growing participation of immigrants in the industrialization of São Paulo gave rise at the beginning of the 20th century to strong xenophobic attacks against industry, especially the artificial one (Luz 1978: 151). It seems that the same can be said about difficulties in the formation of a pro-industry consensus in East and Central Europe, because of the strong economic role of Jewish and German minorities there (and of other minorities, depending on the country). However, in the case of Latin America, in view of the specific nature of nation-building processes in the region, it would not be appropriate to describe these immigrant economic groups as minorities.

Neither should we lose sight of regional nationalisms closely connected with a given territory and national and/or ethnic identities. It was often difficult to distinguish them from national separatisms and irredentist movements. In Czechoslovakia such nationalism inflamed relations between Czechs and Slovaks, between Czechs and Germans and between Slovaks and Hungarians, in Romania between Romanians and Hungarians (and to a lesser extent Germans), in Poland, among others, between Ukrainians and Lithuanians and Poles, and in Peru between the Creole-Mestizo coastal regions and Indian-Mestizo South and Sierra.

The case of developed and democratic Czechoslovakia was quite interesting and depressing. The clash of nationalisms in this country involved both urban-rural cleavages and conflicts among nationalities relatively similar in terms of occupational structure. In the first case, the predominantly urban Czech population confronted predominantly rural Slovak, Hungarian, Ukrainian and Ruthenian populations; in the second one, national conflicts involved highly urbanized (and 'industrialized') Czechs, Germans and Poles. Additionally, in the rural areas of Slovakia strong conflict between Slovaks and Hungarians continued. The situation of the German minority was precarious in the sense that in strictly economic terms "it managed to maintain its economic positions, which were more than proportionate to its share of the population of the republic"

(Průcha 2003: 182). To be more precise, they were overrepresented both among the industrial workers and the industrial technical and managerial elite. The policy of 'Czechization' of the economy, seen by the Germans as an aggressive undermining of their position, was interpreted by the Czechs as a legitimate attempt to reverse the pre-1918 Habsburg policy of 'Germanization'. However, until the ascent of Nazism in Germany a kind of a pragmatic compromise was achieved, first of all among Czech and German industrial elites: "in the economy there was relatively far-reaching goodwill regarding living together profitably" (Boyer 2000: 264, 271, 274). The Great Depression, which hit especially hard the export-oriented textile and metal industries in which the presence of German capital and workers was strongly accentuated, and the growing influence of Nazism among the German minority changed everything. Translated into political demands, in 1938 support for the secessionist movement among the Czech Germans reached 90 percent (Průcha 2003: 187). The democratic idea that underpinned the emergence of the Czechoslovak state was unable to withstand the pressure exerted by a combined strength of integral and economic nationalisms.

These nationalisms, although initially inward-oriented, overlapped with conflicts resembling in the popular perception conflicts with foreign companies. To some extent, such a conflict set the tone of regional relations in Poland, from underdeveloped, mainly rural Eastern Little Poland, with large segments of a Ukrainian population, to industrialized Upper Silesia. In the first case relations between Poles and Ukrainians were rationalized by Ukrainian nationalist movements as an example of an internal colony and/or colonization, with 'Polish landlords' (*polskie pany*) at the top. In the second case, the quite strong local separatism was entangled in a conflict with both the official policy of 'Polonization' and with German companies (Buła 1989: 75).

In the first three decades of the 20th century such occurrences took place also in Peru: both in the borderland between Peru and Bolivia as well as in the copper mining enclaves which employed Indian peasant workers.

In the first case we are dealing with Indian communities and llama breeders entangled in complex trade relationships, embracing foreign trading houses, local middlemen and *hacendados*, and foreign railroads. These groups, threatened by competition from cheaper products from the coast and abroad, invoked–something strongly encouraged by non-Indian middlemen–'national' arguments. The rise in railroad tariffs by the foreigners stimulated similar national campaigns (Thorp and Bertram 1978:

65f, Burga and Reategui 1981). And needless to say, the Indians never failed to raise the issue of the common lands they had lost to the *mistis*. This Quechua word denoted both a white person and at the same time the larger socio-economic category which included *hacendados*, merchants, state officials, in a word those on the top of social and economic hierarchy. The situation in Bolivia was similar. Here, however, from the end of the 19th century the Indians acted much more violently (Irurozqui 2000, Pearse 1975). However, with the Indian uprising in 1915–1917 in Puno, led by Rumi Maqui, in the 1920s there began a series of localized revolts in Sierra and the southern part of Peru. Indian economic demands were intimately linked with the more general protest against the (mis)rule of the *mistis*. There appeared slogans combining Indian nationalism and grievances with references to the Inca past and Tawantinsuyu. It is not clear though to what extent these utopian ideas influenced and motivated Indian peasants going into battle (Burga 1986, Kapsoli 1984, Flores Galindo 2001).

In the other case we are dealing with the reaction to the policy of *La Compañía*. In view of the increasing competition in the international copper market and the substantial modernization of the company-owned smelters (the modern La Oroya facilities were completed in 1922), Cerro de Pasco began to depart from the system of seasonal contract labor of Indian peasant-workers (*enganche*). The transition to a less numerous but more stable workforce inevitably hit local contractors and, first and foremost, Indian communities. Parenthetically, the *enganche* system first developed as a byproduct of commercial relations between coast sugar plantations and the northern Indian Sierra. The rising population pressure in Indian regions and land evictions resulted in an increased mobility of labor: *enganche* and permanent migrations to the coast (Drinot 2000: 165f).

As on the coast, also in the case of mining money earned by Indian peasant-workers counted in family budgets. Violent strikes by Indian miners in 1929–1930 (no longer peasant-worker *enganchados*, but already a modern workforce) for better work conditions reflected the decline of the *enganche* system. What is more, to the surprise of communists involved in the strikes, they turned out to be as much 'proletarian' as 'nationalistic'. Such a phenomenon of linking class and national perspectives was common in practically all foreign-owned firms, from copper mining and oil drilling to sugar plantations (Flores Galindo 1974: 89, Burga and Flores Galindo 1979: 168). A young radical Peruvian leader Victor Raul Haya de la Torre understood that duality well: he defined anti-imperialism as a populist national project.

In the mid-1920s *La Compañía* directly hit the interests of Indian communities and local Indian and non-Indian merchants when it attempted to cut back on purchases of meat from local markets. A direct impetus for such a policy was the environmental disaster caused by the La Oroya smelter (*cuestión de los humos*). Cerro de Pasco's more or less legal takeover of the contaminated land, cutbacks in purchases, followed by the establishment of its own Ranching Division (*División Ganadera*) and the gradual decontamination of the seized land gave an impetus to another national (Indian) campaign (Flores Galindo 1974: 46–50, 89, Mallon 1983: chapter 5). The growing neglect of the Indian and regional economy by *La Compañía* as well as the appropriation of Indian lands were powerful reasons stimulating anti-foreign feelings.

Transformational Potential of Primary-Sector Nationalism

Historical experience and theoretical interpretations not only affirm the possibility of the emergence and consolidation of particularistic primary-sector nationalism, but also indicate the variable–due to economic fluctuations–composition of the social coalitions championing such nationalism. Although conflicts taking place in primary-sector economies led to various forms of particularistic nationalism, this nationalism had a decidedly limited transformational potential (Szlajfer 1990, Becker and Komlosy 2004: 47ff). Above all, it did not question the logic of the export economy but hindered the evolutionary transition to holistic nationalism.

This was apparent in the economies highly integrated into the world market. In their case, the economic and political costs of an exit from the system or even of a greater curbing of its influence would have been extremely high indeed. The already mentioned relative delinkage of tariffs and industrial growth (a reversed tariff-growth paradox) speaks volumes about this matter. Bulmer-Thomas's assertion (2003: 141, 396) that the level of protection of industry in Latin America "was almost certainly less than what was required to achieve an industrial performance consistent with the level of real income per head and population size," seems very much to the point here. In a word, "Latin America was underindustrialized before the First World War." Incidentally, this is what the Polish economist Ludwik Landau (1939: 128f) drew attention to toward the end of the 1930s, when he compared the high per capita income and the relatively low level of Argentina's industrialization. The figures quoted by Maddison (2003: 60,

143) are telling: in 1914, the per capita income, calculated in 1990 international dollars, amounted to $3,302 in Argentina, and to $3,059 in Germany.

In order to enter the path of industrialization and initiate a transition toward holistic nationalism above all required breaking with particularistic nationalism. As a rule, it happened at the time of strong negative shocks (to a limited extent–during the WWI, and on a larger scale–during the Great Depression). Customs tariffs were an important instrument of such transformation, but were nowhere near enough. It should be kept in mind that in 1905 nominal tariffs in Uruguay were 2.5 times higher than in Canada (Clemens and Williamson 2002: 9). The explanatory potential of the commodity lottery should not be exaggerated, either. Grain production in Argentina and Canada led to distinctly different results: "by 1925–29 automobiles were Canada's sixth-largest export at a time when Argentina still imported all its motor vehicles" (Solberg 1987: 43; see also Weaver 1980: 88ff). For the critically important variables one should look rather into the institutional framework of agriculture, respectively in Argentina and Canada, and the emergence in both countries, already in the second half of the 19th century, of a different kind of economic elites (Engerman and Sokoloff 1997: 281, Solberg 1987: 46f). In a word, if "there is not necessarily a one-to-one correspondence between a staple and 'its' sociopolitical environment" and if "the same staple ... may unexpectedly lend strength to two totally different social arrangements and political regimes" (Hirschman 1977a: 97, 98), then the choice between staple growth and staple trap cannot be determined within the framework of the endogenous evolution of particularistic nationalism. External shocks were required.

Within the limits set by the logic of the export economy and bargaining, particularistic economic nationalism in Latin America appeared in an extremely radical and modern form in Uruguay in José Batlle y Ordóñez's era (1903–1907, 1911–1915). That Colorado Party leader, unique in his time, "pushed for both social democracy and economic nationalism with a great deal of success" (Krenn 1990: 27). Still, this quite commonly shared opinion does not fully convey the fact that *batllismo* constituted a radical proposal not only because of the pioneering character of the solutions which redefined the hitherto modernizing community and nation (and showed the possibilities inherent in populism). This radicalism can be described as the achievement within the export economy–with the help of selective economic nationalism–of the maximum limit of its transformational potential. And this without questioning the economy's foundations: land ownership and social relations in agriculture.

At the turn of the centuries, the traditionalist nationalism of rural Uruguay–close to the ideological message of Argentine *federales* from a half century earlier–nearly led to the country's disintegration. José Batlle y Ordóñez's era, begun in 1903, put an end to the crisis. At the same, the country's capital gained importance. Montevideo, where at a certain moment 40 percent of the country's population lived, metamorphosed into a real political center, a point of reference for agrarian elites and rapidly developing new urban societal actors. The new model radically extended the scope of activities of both the modernizing agrarian and export elites as well as new urban groups interested in the development of the domestic market (Sierra 1977: 434f, Cardoso and Faletto 1979: 95f). Meanwhile, state autonomy made it possible to reconcile free-market preferences of agrarian elites and their demand for the status quo and stable property rights with a protectionism that would favor industrialists and with a degree of protection ensured to workers. Such distancing of Uruguayan politics from the immediate pressure of dominant rural interests was sometimes interpreted in a very radical way: "the Uruguayan political system was its own representative" (J. P. Barran and B. Nahum quoted in Rial and Klaczko 1982: 235). However, such an interpretation does not seem fully convincing. The fact that the increased autonomy of the Uruguayan state became possible probably resulted from both political conditions for a solution to the crisis as well as the sociological characteristics of the leading societal actors. The split in agrarian elites and a considerable share of newly arrived immigrants in urban elites meant–among many other factors–that "the interests of the property-owning class as a whole ... were under-represented in the political system" (Finch 1985: 264).

But what really set the Uruguay of the *batllismo* period apart from other countries of the continent was its novel solution to the problem of social democracy, of the 'labor question' in particular. That question defined the unique role of "an economic organization" and tasks of "state socialism," as Batlle put it (Krenn 1990: 28). Recognition of several economic and social rights of urban workers (8-hour working day, the right to organize labor unions and to strike, factory inspection, indemnity for accidents, etc.) was a real achievement and a political innovation. As was the right to divorce granted to women. With one distinctive exception, though: agriculture (mainly cattle- and sheep-rising) and rural laborers remained outside that pioneering–in Latin America–welfare state. In its relations with politically weakened but economically powerful rural elites *batllismo* represented caution and a decidedly conservative attitude. A kind of trade-off was arranged: taxes for stability. The status quo in agriculture was exchanged for a tax levied on land property, which in turn created new revenues for the state budget and facilitated experiments in urban economy. In a cautiously worded assessment of Batlle's policy one can read:

> Although no evidence exists that agricultural exports were crippled by Batllismo, the rate of taxation was significantly higher than in other countries that pursued export-led growth, and the ideology of Batllismo certainly encouraged nonexport urban activities (Bulmer-Thomas 2003: 170).

Nevertheless, progress was enormous. In São Paulo, the economic center of Brazil, as late as in the 1920s the social question and "worker agitation" were treated, according to Washington Luis Pereira de Sousa, the last President of the Old Republic, as "a question that concerns public order more than the political order" (quoted in Kula 1987: 142). However, in a comparative perspective the degree of self-organization of labor and capital in Uruguay was not high enough to substantially strengthen the developmental impact of protectionism. The economic preeminence of agrarian and commercial elites was not undermined substantially. Meanwhile, the exclusion of rural workers from innovative efforts decidedly weakened the protectionist coalition's appeal.

It seems that it is against this basic background that problems related to *batllismo's* position with regard to foreign companies and nationalization should be interpreted.

There is no reason to question the opinion that the basic goals in this sphere were to curtail the thus far overwhelming presence and power of foreign investors in infrastructure and urban economy, to increase domestic investments and to limit the need for new loans, which Batlle defined as a "considerable sacrifice" (Krenn 1990: 28). No doubt, *batllismo* was marked by a firm bargaining posture in relations with foreign, mainly British, companies. Such bargaining dynamics led, in turn, to state intervention, nationalization of many foreign firms (some of them inefficient), and also to the establishment of state-run enterprises competing with foreign investors in banking, insurance, public utilities, transport and harbor services, and in the end, also in the key *frigoríficos* business (Finch 1985). These moves were aided by tariff protectionism that favored local production of industrial consumer goods. In a word, according to a British consular report, this was a prime example of a "nationalising fanatic" (Finch 1985: 258; see also Di Tella 2007: 38).

However, as in the case of social democracy, nor should *battlismo's* conflicts with foreign capital be interpreted anachronistically. All the steps taken by Batlle stayed within the logic of bargaining, not that of elimination of foreign companies.[9] It is noteworthy that although the British investors in Uruguay lavished such epithets on Batlle as "a damned socialist," "a public nuisance" or "anti-foreign," neither the volume nor the profitability of British investments changed much during his second term in 1911–1915 (Finch 1985: 266, Rippy 1959: chapter 12). Within the logic of bargaining, but also of populist discourse, Batlle supported streetcar drivers striking for higher wages: "Without that strike the wage surplus would emigrate to London and Berlin along with a major part of the immense profits. ... Now it will stay here, distributed among our people" (quoted in Wittman 1980: 368). Stimulating controlled popular nationalism by a charismatic leader was a part of the same distributional conflict. In passing, precisely this aspect of *batllismo* has been criticized by some radical researchers who have argued that the mechanisms of co-optation used by Batlle "disorganized the working class" and weakened the transformational potential of industrial conflicts (Sierra 1977: 436). A historian and sociologist of Latin American political parties agrees: "Batllismo ... had an important leftist component, and probably this fact delayed the growth of a Socialist movement with enough support in the ballot box" (Di Tella 2007: 38).

All in all, the example of Uruguay in the days of Batlle shows all the basic forms of particularistic nationalism. Its radicalism resulted from both the combination of these forms and from their combination with solutions to 'the labor question' that were novel in Latin America at that time. Both in the policy of nationalization and in the way new social groups were co-opted and integrated, Uruguayan nationalism was an exception in the then Latin America. At the same time, it showed that economic and political nationalism could develop without traumatic upheaval: at the cost, however, of resignation from social and economic radicalism in rural areas. The Mexican revolution that started at the same time represented an alternative model of social and political change. Thus, *batllismo* was an example of populism, but one that appealed not to an authoritarian, but to a democratic, agenda which embraced not only social democracy, but political democracy as well. Still, Batlle-imposed presidential power reform (*colegiado*)–an anomaly under the prevailing constitutional arrangements in Latin America–barely survived its originator.

---

[9] Thus the assessment of Batlle's program of nationalization as "intended to substitute state control for foreign" (Jorrín and Martz 1970: 232) seem to be an overstatement.

All the same, Uruguayan economic nationalism remained particularistic. As concerns the economy, its obvious untouchable reference points were the traditional, although undergoing modernization, rural and export-oriented interest groups, this time embedded in the political autonomy of the state and 'reform' of the nation. Increasing the share of the state and local elites in income and opening up to new urban actors did not threaten the export economy and the foundations of economic internationalism. On the contrary, all statistics demonstrate that it was in full bloom. Until WWI, Uruguay, like Argentina, was a successful case of integration with the world market, of convergence in GDP per capita with developed industrial countries and of export performance (Bértola and Porcile 2006). However, in a comparative perspective, when looking at countries such as Uruguay and New Zealand, which were strikingly similar in terms of size, population and natural endowments, such an enthusiastic opinion should be qualified. From the very beginning, say from 1870–1890, both countries diverged and this

> can be explained by the existence of different institutions governing the agricultural sectors of the two countries, which in turn generated different distributions of both land property rights and product shares in the agricultural sector. ... such institutional differences crucially affected industrial development ... through their impact on income distribution (Àlvarez, Bilancini, D'Alessandro and Porcile 2010: 27).

Was Uruguay therefore different in terms of a substantial rearrangement of relations between urban and rural classes in favor of the former? Can one see in Batlle's industrial and protectionist policies a "significant exception" (Rogowski 1989: 47n) to the prevailing pattern of the export economy? The answers have to be negative. There was, however, a substantial diversification and enhancement of the social environment of such an economy and the emergence of a strong public sector. Batlle's nationalism and social democracy created a unique hybrid: the lack of a basic transformation of economic structures was combined with an urban-based populist politics and elements of the modern welfare state.

The experiment was put to the test in the 1930s. The result was unfavorable.

CHAPTER EIGHT

PIECES OF A PUZZLE: TOWARD HOLISTIC NATIONALISM

The Restrained Nationalism of Industrialists

In advanced peripheral economies, the end of the 19th century marked the beginnings of the local consumer goods industry. Its development during WWI (chiefly in Latin America, but also in Bulgaria) and in the years following the post-war recession did not basically change the situation of those economies in the short run. However, the long-term effects were significant, due, among other things, to the rising importance of the social groups that industry had brought into existence. But was it really an industrialization? For Bértola and Williamson (2006: 47f), who challenge the commonly accepted terminology, it was not:

> If by industrialization we mean a process by which manufacturing output grows faster than that of other sectors for a long enough time to significantly alter output mix, then it appears that industrialization was never achieved in Latin America prior to the 1930s.

Other historians had earlier made a similar claim (Baer and Villela 1972). In all countries the rate of export growth in the years 1900–1929 was higher than the GDP rate. And exports were exclusively agricultural products and raw materials. Only in Brazil and Chile, and for different reasons, did GDP grow faster than exports (Thorp 1998: 52). The situation changed dramatically only in the 1930s with the fall in export/GDP ratios in the major countries of both regions.

In East and Central Europe, in the countries which in the majority had until 1918 been deprived of sovereignty, industrial development was initiated or resumed under much more complicated circumstances. After 1918, the Latvian, Estonian, Hungarian and Czechoslovak economies emerged as structures separated from the larger economic space which had thus far defined the directions of their respective development. The process was of a particularly complex nature in Poland, where economic *unification* was the order of the day. Internal polarization and a lack of economic cohesion of the newly established state were very much apparent. Post-1918 Poland comprised, on the one hand, underdeveloped regions of the peasant economy, previously parts of the former Austria-Hungary and Russia, and on the other, the modern mining and iron and steel industries of Upper Silesia taken from Germany. Assuming that in 1913 the per capita income in the Prussian partition sector was 100 percent, then in the Kingdom of Poland it stood at 56 percent and in Galicia at 34 percent (Jezierski and Leszczyńska 2001: 214, Kwiatkowski 1989: 173–176). Let me add to this picture the legacy of three different legal, educational, measurement, taxation and railroad systems, etc. and we see a kind of a patchwork economy. To an outside observer, the situation immediately after WWI looked desperate indeed: "Poland is an economic impossibility with no industry but Jew-baiting" (Keynes 1920: 291). His first judgment was wrong. There was industrial potential, especially that the formerly Russian partition sector (Kingdom of Poland) had been one of the leading industrial areas of the Russian empire. To put this potential into operation was, however, a more complicated thing. What had up to 1914 been the most important Russian market for the Kingdom's textile and other industrial products after 1918 simply disappeared: "In 1929 the share of the USSR in the total exports of Poland was only 6.8 per cent, and 1.8 per cent in the case of imports" (Drabek 1985: 421). Thus, the 1913 level of industrial production was achieved as late as in 1938, although after 1932 Polish industry finally entered a growth path, interrupted only by the outbreak of WWII (Teichova 1986: 230f). As to his other observation, Keynes exaggerated, but his irony was not without foundation. And it applied not only to Poland. Post-1918 East and Central Europe was a region composed of small and medium-sized multinational states where minority-baiting was a rather common occurrence (Berend 1998: Rothschild 1974: passim). Meanwhile, in the successor states formed in the place of the Austro-Hungarian empire, such as Hungary and Czechoslovakia, overcoming the crisis caused by their *separation* from the Austro-Hungarian economic area, was the problem. Baltic countries, previously integrated into the Russian empire, encountered similar difficulties (Lewis 1949: 21, Matis 1983, Köll 2000).

As already indicated, until the Great Depression, in peripheral economies industry developed as a fairly uncomplicated substitution of imports of selected consumer goods. One of the methods for illustrating the change can be–along with general information on the number of workers and enterprises and capital invested–a look at the imports of those countries: basic changes in the directions of their development were immediately reflected in a shift from imports of industrial consumer goods to imports of capital goods and intermediate products (Díaz-Alejandro 1988: 92). This concerns, first and foremost, the more advanced import-substituting economies, where an increased share of capital goods and semi-finished products in total imports was already apparent. For instance, in the years 1901/1907–1928 the share of capital goods in Brazilian imports increased from 7.1 percent to 26.7 percent. In 1929, that share in Argentine imports was 31.8 percent, in Polish imports 30 percent, and in Romanian imports 44.4 percent. In less developed economies, the share of capital goods in imports was visibly smaller: in Bolivia–16.6 percent, and in Bulgaria–barely 5.6 percent (Villela and Suzigan 1973: 72, Díaz-Alejandro 1970: 15, Drabek 1985: 471ff, Chalkley 1931: 95, Hobson 1931: 21, 23f). Therefore it can be said that development of import substitution in peripheral economies resulted in both the modernization of their economic structures and their links with the international economy. The dual tension/specialization characteristic of pre-industrial export economies, mentioned in the previous chapter, no longer applies in its entirety. The problem of the balance-of-payments, and especially of import capacity, in this modernization process was related not only with the question of imports of consumer goods and machinery indispensable to the primary export sector. To an ever greater extent it was under the pressure of imports necessary for the smooth functioning of the domestic import-intensive substituting industries which produced mass consumption industrial non-durables.

In the circumstances of the time this meant that in the peripheral economy, the development of industry found support primarily in relatively strong forward linkages connected with final consumer demand. Backward linkages were definitely weaker. In the 1920s the share of consumer goods in total industrial production stood at at least 56.1 percent in Argentina, 81.4 percent in Chile, 58.4 percent in Romania, and 62.9 percent in Hungary (Weaver 1980: 102, Teichova 1985: 248). But differences in the degree of industrial development in the two regions were enormous. Certain countries (e.g. Poland and, above all, Czechoslovakia) had had well developed elements of heavy industry before 1929; only after 1929 did others begin to develop traditional light industries on a large scale (e.g. Bolivia, Venezuela, Bulgaria and the Baltic states).

Tariff policies reflected those trends. In the majority of East and Central European economies, in 1927 the level of tariffs for imported capital goods, chemicals and vehicles did not exceed 40 percent ad valorem. In Argentina, in that same year, an import duty on investment goods was much lower than the average tariff level (Drabek 1985: 411, Díaz-Alejandro 1970: 283, 290). A positive effective rate of protection for local industry was the result. Thus a mechanism typical of industrialization through import substitution had entered the scene:

> the greater the difference between the level of protection accorded to the import-substituting industry and that applying to its imported inputs, the more will the profit margin of the industry depend on preventing domestic production of inputs (Hirschman 1968: 18).

In a word, the trap built into import substitution was expressed in negative incentives for the development of industries unrelated to final consumer demand. Lack of capital goods, transport equipment and metallurgical industries, to name just a few, and also the stagnation of local technological capabilities, were the result.

But even this limited industrialization, complementing the primary export economy, led to the enhancement and differentiation of a social environment that supported particularistic nationalism; it also introduced new forms of it. Along with local industry other societal actors also appeared who sought state support and expected protection against foreign competition. For obvious reasons, groups related to natural industries were most vociferous in their demands. As shown by the already quoted example of La Sociedad Rural in Argentina, agreement between the agrarian export sector and industrialists was reached relatively easily, especially at times of crisis. Sometimes, those were not separate groups but the same entrepreneurs who were active in different sectors. Industrial protectionism which sprang up against such a background, enhanced by regional nationalisms, was a common occurrence. The history of the textile and food processing industries in the majority of peripheral economies is testimony of this (Stein 1957, Lewis 1978b: 164ff).

What is more, even before 1929 industrial groups found an ally in the state bureaucracy. Its support was the result of a mix of factors, including personal contacts and the need to solve balance-of-payments problems rather than of doctrinal premises. The experience of WWI also mattered. The excess industrial capacity created earlier turned out to be a blessing when links with Europe were severed and imports from Europe dwindled. Additionally, it was noticed that the decline in import duties was partially compensated by taxes on consumption of locally produced industrial goods (Luz 1978: 152f). The attitude toward the demands of industrialists began to change; despite overlapping and often contradictory pressures exerted by particular interest groups, even before 1929. Increasingly often industrial actors' demands were considered to be justified and in accordance with 'the national interest'. Also before 1929, the state bureaucracy and the army showed a certain interest in artificial industries. In Poland, under the influence of the tasks involved in the unification process, the pro-industry and strongly interventionist First Economic Brigade–with strong links to the powerful military-bureaucratic elite–was particularly active in the period before the Great Depression. For more about this, see below in this chapter.

An accelerated process of domestic market formation was one of the most significant consequences of import substitution industrialization. Protection of this market through tariffs and other instruments also provided strong investment incentives to encourage foreign firms. This time, however, the point was not supply-oriented investments alone, but also market-oriented ones. Nevertheless, the former did not lose significance. Far from it: they were on the rise. The share of agriculture and oil in total US FDI increased between 1914 and 1929 from 28.9 percent to 44.2 percent (Bulmer-Thomas 2003: 158), fueling on the way Latin American political and economic nationalism. At the same time, market-oriented subsidiaries and/or assembly plants of foreign companies quickly found their place among advocates of protectionism, just as had been the case in Witte's Russia. Such occurrences, engaging British investors, were reported, for example, in Brazil:

> [in 1903] the British flour mill ... contributed fully to efforts to erect a tariff barrier against the imported article. Other Britishers had joined Brazilian industrialists in 1882 to demand protective tariffs against foreign imports generally (Graham 1968: 140).

But in the age of the first globalization one could observe the mere beginnings of the change, primarily in the bigger Latin American countries. In 1929, industrial investments made up only 9.9 percent of the US's direct investments in South America; however in Argentina their share amounted to 24.7 percent, in Brazil to 23.6 percent, but in Colombia to less than 3 percent (Wilkins 1974: 55, 57).[1] On the other hand, in Poland, 40 percent of total capital of all joint-stock companies was foreign owned, and in industrial firms over 90 percent (Teichova 1985: 304, Landau and Tomaszewski 1981: 30).

The limited development of modern sectors of the economy in the two regions meant that foreign capital actually exercised disproportionally extensive control over dynamic economic centers. This was particularly apparent in new industries, such as car manufacturing, oil refineries, chemical, iron and steel and machine-building. Until the end of the 1930s, in the Brazilian iron and steel industry, the Companhia Siderúrgica

---

[1] Bulmer-Thomas (2003: 158) quotes a lower share of manufacturing in the total of US direct investment: 6.3 percent in 1929 compared with 2.9 percent in 1914.

Belgo-Mineira, established in 1921 by the Belgian-Luxembourg group Aciéries Reunies de Burbach-Elch-Dudelange (ARBED), held the dominant position. In the next years it substantially developed its charcoal-based integrated steelworks. Nevertheless, until the end of the 1930s the iron and steel industry was clearly underdeveloped. While in the years 1920–1940 imports of pig iron and steel ingots declined from 33.2 percent of total domestic demand to nil and from 100 percent to 4.5 percent, respectively, in the case of technically advanced rolled-steel products, the share of imports remained extremely high: 99.9 percent in 1925 and 69.4 percent in 1940 (Baer 1969: 60–64). In Poland, in 1931 foreign capital was predominant in the oil, mining, metallurgical and electric machine-building industries (the degree of control fluctuated between 58 and 87 percent). In subsequent years foreign control extended also to the chemical industry (Landau and Tomaszewski 1982: 96). The presence of foreign firms in traditional industries was much less apparent. However, according to information on Central Europe, Brazil, Peru and Chile, in this sector foreign companies were also as a rule in the group of the largest enterprises (Teichova 1985, Evans 1979: 135, 140ff, Thorp and Bertram 1978: 123, Stemplowski 1985/1986).

These developments were of great importance from the point of view of the emerging particularistic nationalism of industrialists. The evolution of foreign companies' market strategies inevitably widened the potential for conflicts with national entrepreneurs and triggered nationalistic feelings. These were inevitable when foreign-owned businesses entered local capital's sphere of interests and/or tried to seize control over important natural resources. From the turn of the century this type of clash of interests was increasingly rationalized as, for instance, in Brazil through anti-foreign attitudes. In 1912, the Centro Industrial do Brasil started attacking foreign investors, charging them with a "financial *conquista* of Brazil" and attempts to seize control over natural resources (Luz 1978: 148; see also Wirth 1970: 82). Also at that time the famous book by Alberto Tôrres *O problema nacional brasileiro*, was published, two decades later becoming a kind of Bible of Brazilian nationalism. In oil-rich Romania such anti-foreign attitudes appeared in 1900, but that could not prevent–after initial refusal–the granting in 1904 of a concession to the US's Standard Oil (Wilkins 1974: 221, Murgescu 2006: 236). In modern industries, on the other hand, because of the absence of local entrepreneurship, conflicts were quite rare. If they occurred they usually were focused on the threat of *desnacionalização* and involved foreign capital and the state and/or local politicians (Luz 1977: 176). In no-man's-land, where modern technologies and products were at stake, the particularistic nationalism of local industrialists was markedly subdued in tone, and their attitudes were ambivalent. This concerned electrical and chemical industries, petroleum products, car manufacturing, metal products and machine-building. The launching of a car assembly plant in Brazil by General Motors and, on a large scale, by Ford (25,000 cars in the mid-1920s) (Garcia 2000: 11) did not provoke protests. All in all, "from scattered evidence one can estimate that foreigners controlled roughly one-half of all industry in 1930" (Topik 1989: 90).

Needless to say, as in the case of primary sector nationalism and that concerning foreign-controlled urban infrastructure, transportation, banks and mining, so, too, in the case of industry nationalists frequently employed such slogans as 'plunder' and 'exploitation'. High profits–and sometimes, as in Argentina in the 1920s, they were fantastically high–were not the only cause of resentment: "US companies were resented for their size, their power (or potential power), their profits ... and for their just being alien enterprise[s]" (Wilkins 1974: 61f, 158). To this one should also add the growth of company towns with their tightly structured hierarchies and social distances in the rapidly developing foreign-controlled mining and oil enclaves. The extent to which higher wages and medical care provided to the local workforce could offset feelings of national deprivation was uncertain, to say the least.[2] In situations like this state support and intervention were expected. And in the disputes with individual foreign firms and banks, bigger Latin American states were usually not on the losing side. Either in the 19th century or in the first decades of the 20th century (Platt 1985: 32, Ferns 1960: 487ff). This was particularly the case if the intentions of potential investors were not clear. The prolonged negotiations, carried out after WWI, of foreign capital's access to iron ore deposits in Minas Gerais, originally connected with a project to develop a modern iron and steel industry, ended in failure: access was denied. A mixture of local *mineiro* politicians' nationalism and more profound negative attitudes among potential foreign investors was at work in this case:

> foreign financial interests connected with steel [were] concerned mainly with obtaining Brazilian iron ore and manganese for European and American steel plants. There was little interest in constructing new steel works in an underdeveloped region (Baer 1969: 67, Wirth 1970: 78).

---

[2] In her meticulously researched history of American multinationals, Wilkins (1974: 123–127) prefers to emphasize benefits.

This example was instructive for yet another reason: in the case of iron and steel it appeared that the development of this type of artificial capital-intensive industry was beyond the reach of Brazilian private investors. Also the flagship of the Brazilian interventionist state, the valorization scheme, was successfully defended in the mid-1920s: in this case against the US administration which, before approving the loan Brazil had asked for, wanted Brazilians to dismantle the scheme (Garcia 2000: 38–41).

The size of the domestic market also mattered. There is no doubt that in labor-intensive economies effective demand depended, among other things, on the absolute number of the population:

> Size was ... important, and in more ways and more deeply than might be thought at first. In the extreme case of Brazil, size provided ... an internal market that made local reinvestment of the export sector surplus profitable, as was the case as well in Colombia. ... In Uruguay, size limited the interest of foreign investors in solving the problems affecting the livestock and manufacturing industries (Thorp 1998: 88).

However, the population argument should not be overstated. When elaborating on the impact of population size on the development of industry, Bértola and Williams (2006: 49f) were right to point out that population mattered only in concert with other factors, such as level of general poverty, low per capita income, unequal income distribution (made even more unequal at the peak of primary export-led growth). In our approach, however, analytically the absolute size of the population does not seem to have been of crucial importance in the early 1900s. Also, the proposal to compare the population in Latin American countries with that of the major, more populous, developed European countries–although interesting–does not seem persuasive. The case of the Western offshoots, except for the USA, is more telling. In around 1900 the population of Canada approached 5.4 million and that of Australia 3.7 million. At the same time, Argentina was populated by 4.7 million, Brazil by 18 million and Mexico by 13.5 million. In Europe, Romania's population was 11 million and Bulgaria's 4 million, compared to Belgium's 6.7 million and Denmark's 2.5 million (Maddison 2003: 36, 81, 121). Such a comparison seen against the data on income per capita and on literacy levels prompts the following conclusion: "[w]hat is important ... is the increase, not in population, but in purchasing power. The increase in the number of paupers does not broaden the market" (Kalecki 1980: 355). In Canada, Australia and New Zealand, population constraints–no doubt serious–were neutralized by pro-growth patterns of institutional development of agriculture and industry. In their case, the size of the population was a problem, but not an insurmountable obstacle to more diversified and robust development of the modern domestic market.

Also the already mentioned origins of the group of industrialists played an important, albeit complementary, role. In many countries they largely came from traditional agrarian and commercial sectors and in their market behavior represented a mix of various types of particularistic nationalisms except the one related with artificial industries. In Brazil, next to agrarian- and merchant-industrialists, immigrants also contributed greatly to the foundation and development of urban industry, particularly in São Paulo (Bresser Pereira 1964, Dean 1969: passim). In Peru, in the 1890s, alongside sugar planters and planter-exporters, merchants, financiers and relatively recent immigrants also played a role in the development of industry. But in the years 1900–1930, the old elite-controlled industry gave way above all to immigrants, small-scale entrepreneurs and foreign firms (Thorp and Bertram 1978: 32, 121). In Argentina, as in Brazil, the genealogy of this group differed depending on the type of industry. However, the contribution made before WWI by immigrants was enormous. Immigrants predominated among 'foreigners' who in 1914 made up 65 percent of the group of industrial entrepreneurs. Only in textiles did Argentines prevail. In the next 20 years their share in the group of owners of industrial establishments increased slightly from 32 percent to 39 percent (Díaz-Alejandro 1970: 215). Yet, the elite of the business community was formed by powerful *grupos*, merchant-industrial-banking conglomerates, resembling the Matarazzo empire in Brazil. The degree of diversification of their operations was well illustrated by the composition of the business profile of the Tornquist group: insurance, wool textiles, hotels, mining, glass, tobacco, porcelain fixtures, biscuits, motors, farming, metallurgy, real estate, beer, commercial fishing and bottled mineral water. It can be said that empire building and economic security clearly prevailed over specialization, productivity growth and technological excellence. The group of new industrialists that emerged after 1930 and was involved mostly in artificial industries was to a large extent dependent on the government's direct and indirect support (Lewis 1990: 40, 57, 62).

At first glance, relations in Poland both in the 19th century and in the interwar period resembled those in Latin America. This concerned first of all a considerable segment of non-Polish groups within the urban entrepreneurial class (Kaczyńska 1979: 311). One should, however, bear in mind the distinction between the immigrant entrepreneur in Latin America and the national minority one in Central Europe. The social and political position of the latter was decidedly weaker, and bargaining power substantially curtailed. Thus in the Łódź textile center ('the Polish Manchester'), in 1890, out of the nearly 5,000 strong group of modern entrepreneurs and merchants, 25 percent were German, 33 percent Jewish and 25 percent Polish. In terms of economic power, Germans clearly dominated. Estimates for interwar Poland suggest that Germans made up 3–4 percent, Jews circa 43 percent and Poles 51 percent of the 260,000 strong group of bourgeoisie. Yet, these percentages hardly reflect the distribution of real economic power and influence, especially in industry, banking, transportation and public utilities. The role of foreign investors and of the state in those sectors was not only very noticeable, but also on the rise (Kołodziejczyk 1979: 123, 152f). Hence, the powerful private Polish entrepreneur was the exception rather than the rule. In such a situation, inward-oriented economic nationalism aimed, first of all, against national minority capitalists, was inevitably concomitant with the growing impact of integral political nationalism. The place occupied by the immigrant entrepreneur in Latin America was different; certainly not comfortable, as illustrated by the public reactions to the Brazilian cotton textile industry campaign in 1928–1929 to limit imports of cheaper textiles and machinery:

> Nationalism was on the rise in Brazil during the 1920s and the 'foreigner' came in for more than his share of criticism. The task of isolating foreign- from Brazilian-born industrial figures was relatively simple ... the leading figures among textile entrepreneurs long resident in Brazil were called Portuguese, Italian, Syrian, or English, not Brazilians (Stein 1957: 128).

But the main target of particularistic nationalism was increasingly different: foreign capital. In the 1920s and 1930s varieties of anti-imperialism substituted for immigrant-bashing.

It has already been mentioned that the emergent particularistic nationalism of industrialists found—at the peak of export-economy development—only limited support among the urban middle class and workers. As entrepreneurs and workers in the national industry, these groups should, potentially, support protectionism. The same could be expected of that part of the middle-class whose incomes depended directly on government spending. As consumers, however, the urban classes were against protectionism, and the fight against inflation and the rising cost of living was to a large extent concomitant with criticism of local industry. The attitude that prevailed depended on specific circumstances, including the evolution of the consumer habits of the new immigrants, as was the case in Argentina (Díaz-Alejandro 1970: 305f). The labor market situation and the relative strength of the urban classes were certainly an important, if not the most important, variables. From this point of view, the Great Depression meant a qualitative change. It is from this moment on that one can speak of a relatively enduring relationship–under government tutelage–between the drastically transformed particularistic nationalism of industrialists and popular nationalism.

Moreover, let us pay attention to a certain additional factor that emerged in the 1920s and which additionally limited the bargaining power of the particularistic nationalism of industrialists of the time.

It is a fact that in the 1920s in Latin America and to a lesser degree in East and Central Europe it became much easier to finance government deficits and expenditures with foreign loans (Winkler 1933, Stallings 1987, Eichengreen 1988). US capital played a crucial role both in this international lending expansion and in the surge of direct investments. FDI increased between 1914 and 1929 by a factor of 2.85, from $1.27 billion to $3.64 billion. Portfolio investments increased even more spectacularly, by a factor of 4.7, from $0.36 billion to $1.72 billion. Loans to Latin American governments between 1926 and 1928 approached $1 billion (net). And "this inflow of resources ... was beyond the absorptive capacity of the recipient country, and stories of graft and corruption were legion" (Bulmer-Thomas 2003: 158, 179, Stallings 1987: 72ff). However, the assessment of the situation in East and Central Europe should be different. The allocated loans and FDI were of no match to those in Latin America. Between 1924 and 1928 the net imports of long- and short-term capital of the four major countries (Poland, Hungary, Romania and Yugoslavia) were in the range, depending on the method of calculation, of $610–730 million (Nötel 1986: 189). And the purpose of the loans was defined in much stricter terms; they were–taking Poland as an example–focused primarily on achieving monetary stabilization after the years of post-WWI devastating inflation and debt servicing. The gross inflow of FDI was not impressive: $77 million to Poland in 1924–31 and $67 million to Hungary (Nötel 1986: 270).

This 'dance of the millions' in Latin America, as the loan bonanza was described in Colombia and other countries in the 1920s, was both a blessing for industrial growth as well as a disaster. First and foremost, from the point of view of the state bureaucracy, less restricted access to international financing made the policy of raising tariffs less attractive, postponed basic decisions on structural changes until a future date, and, at the same time, ensured a relatively conflict-free deficit-based growth of the autonomy of the state apparatus. And the causal relation was different from the one usually expected: namely that it was deficits that followed loans and not vice versa (Stallings 1987: 211, 273). With reference to Colombia at that time, Thorp (1998: 92) writes about the misfortune the borrowing possibilities caused from the point of view of the pro-industry protectionist policy. An analysis of Peru in the 1920s also shows a strong relationship between the inflow of foreign capital and loans, the state budget's decreasing dependence on customs revenue, and the decline of industry (Thorp and Bertram 1978:). Assessment of the situation in Central Europe is similar: foreign loans were of no great help in raising productivity in the region's economies and their debt-service capacities (Berend 1998: 233). On the other hand, however, the 1920s are also perceived differently: as a period of relatively fast although unstable and sector-specific industrial growth in some Latin American countries. I shall return to this question.

The arguments put forward so far, touching upon the industrial development of Brazil, Colombia and Argentina until the Great Depression, can be presented as a triad: an interplay between the absolute size of the existing domestic market, surpluses of capital at the disposal of agrarian and commercial elites, and pro-industrial protectionism (Thorp 1998: 88–93). This protectionism was consolidated by the revenue-maximizing tariff and fiscal linkages resulting from the disbursement of state revenues. The significant presence of immigrants in the urban economy was–regardless of all limitations on their bargaining power–an additional factor. In Brazil, sizeable foreign currency reserves accumulated during WWI also played an important role, favorable to industrial development in the 1920s (Fishlow 1972: 321, Lewis 1986). And finally, one cannot pass over the seemingly eccentric attitudes and behavior of the primary export elites who were "as unwilling as the industrialists to reduce the rates of the tariff schedule." In this way, all other things being equal, they contributed to pro-industry protectionism. In many interpretations of such behavior the following argument is put forward:

> Their acquiescence was, in fact, *faute de mieux*. ... [In republican Brazil] the tariff continued to be ... the only significant source of revenue that the planters would grant. The available alternatives would obviously be more painful to them: a tax on land or a tax on incomes or profits (Dean 1969: 70f; see also Bulmer-Thomas 2003: 144, Marichal and Topik 2003: 355).

However, such a solution to the problem of government revenues inhibited modernization of the revenue-raising apparatus and meant that in the 1930s there occurred a "contrast between an antiquated revenue system and an advanced expenditure program containing provisions for liberal social services and other needs" (Wallich 1944: 127; see also Bulmer-Thomas 2003: 179).

The limitations of the pro-industry triad mentioned by Thorp were however obvious. They were also reflected in the composition of pro-industry coalitions formed before 1929: local and foreign producers of manufactured agricultural products and industrial goods, a few nationalist and pro-industry writers, and treasury officials (Díaz-Alejandro 1970: 306ff). However, the context in which these actors operated was more complex. Instead of open conflict pushing industrialists and agrarian-export elites into a deadly zero sum game, it favored a strengthened synergy of attitudes and interests: "The industrialists realized that in the broadest sense their prosperity was dependent on the agricultural sector" (Dean 1969: 130). Hence, one can see industrialists' particularistic nationalism as a part of the efficient functioning of the export-oriented primary economy. The country's domestic market for manufactured necessities depended on this sector, and the powerful textile entrepreneurs were well aware of this important linkage. In such a system balance-of-payments and primary sector-dependent import capacities were critically important variables. Dependency of this kind was reflected also in the demands regarding state support. Thus, inasmuch as competition between planters and industrialists for governmental support was real and at the same time timid, this was not the case regarding the antagonism between the industrialists and the importers. For example, in the late 1920s, both Brazilian planters and industrialists, capitalizing on the inflationary policy, and worried because of over-production of textiles, moved against importers. The victims of such an alliance were, however, not only merchant houses, because urban classes also paid a price (Dean 1969: 136, Stein 1957: 126–131).

The basic context within which the nationalism of industrial groups and other related societal actors developed also set a discreet but effective upper limit to the radicalism of industrialists. Such a limit was also reflected in the structure of the industry that had been developing since the 1880s. At least until the Great Depression the particularistic nationalism of industrialists had been mostly confined to natural industries, a lowest common denominator of a kind:

> One is struck by the absence, in all the polemical literature of the industrialists between the wars, of any exhortations in behalf of new industries. ...

their concern for the protection of industry embraced only existing lines of production. During this period it was not the 'entrepreneurs' but engineers, journalists, and bureaucrats who spoke in favor of the immediate creation of steel, petroleum, and chemical industries (Dean 1969: 148).

Economic nationalism of industrialists thus appeared restrained by their own history, a hostage to the primary export economy and the constraints it imposed, and also its beneficiary.

Did the outbreak of the Great Depression undermine the tacit, yet structurally conditioned, alliance from the past? In the situation of economic crisis, open conflict between the two types of particularistic nationalism for government support seemed inevitable. The hot disputes about the directions of state policy in Brazil and Poland after 1929 seemed to confirm this. Would therefore the ultimate success of the industrial party be the outcome of the way in which the conflict between the societal actors representing different variants of particularistic nationalism was resolved? In other words, were the decline of the agricultural-export elite and the victory of the industrialists a result of an endogenous process, the clash between societal actors shaped under the export economy? And more specifically, can we allow the possibility suggested by Hirschman (1968: 19) that the resistance to backward linkage could be overcome without a recourse to state action?

It has already been mentioned that a clash between societal actors could lead to substantial shifts in trade policy. When analyzing the different reactions of European governments to the massive imports of grain from the Western offshoots after 1870, Kindleberger (1951: 45) suggested that to explain this fact required "an adequate theory of large groups and their components ... as an adjunct to the analytical tools of the market." This interesting suggestion was subsequently made use of in the pathbreaking study by Gourevitch (1986) in his analysis of societal actors' different reactions to crisis situations in the 19th and 20th centuries.

However, there arises a question as to how the concept of "large groups" should be defined. Narrowing it to those societal actors struggling for influence in the state ('state-as-arena') was probably justified in the case of the crisis Kindleberger analyzed. Similar reactions in Germany and France indicated that despite basic differences between the strong protectionist German state and the weak French republic, in both cases the "influence of societal actors [on the state] in this period appears to have been relatively naked and raw. ... It seems likely that even a republican Germany with a weak state, or an authoritarian France with stronger leadership, would have adopted the same policy" (Gourevitch 1986: 23). Especially so given that toward the end of the 19th century the government's main instrument of action was tariff protectionism, not modern 'mercantilism', which would have required more robust and efficient institutional mechanisms, making possible a choice across a wide spectrum of economic variables, and thus a precise allocation of "rewards and constraints" (Gourevitch 1986: 53). Such 'mercantilist' mechanisms appeared for the first time at the end of the 19th century, primarily as cascading tariffs, i.e. effective rates of protection. On a larger scale, more developed and refined institutional mechanisms appeared in the 1930s. The experience of the European war economy and the immediate post-WWI non-market adjustments played a role here.

The approach proposed in this book points in a similar direction. To explain the origins and logic of the new type of economic nationalism that emerged in many peripheral economies after 1929 requires that we pay attention to the formation of the state of holistic nationalism which would attempt to subsume all earlier forms of particularistic nationalism. To question and reject the interventionist liberal-cum-internationalist protectionist state–a variety of the state-as-arena model–becomes inevitable, whereas the "large group" concept requires a redefinition. It should also embrace the state as an autonomous actor and arbiter able to set new rules for resolving the distributional conflicts and competition among societal actors. What is more, if it is societal actors who create demand for protectionism, then "suppliers of protectionism are state ... institutions" (Borchardt 1991: 2, 12). The state, which until then had mediated conflicts among particularistic nationalisms, came forward as an active protagonist of a new form of economic nationalism. At that moment it symbolized self-emancipation of a kind and the breakup with the prevailing economic ideology and mentalities. The state's embeddedness in social relations constitutes, no doubt about it, the necessary context of its activities. Yet, fundamental choices are made not by following the societal actors' revealed preferences alone: "Knowing preferences and coalitions is not the same as knowing power" (Gourevitch 1986: 58). The fiscal linkage is a case in point: assuming the state's "will and ability to stake a claim ... on the resources" as given, in the structure of linkage "the importance of the political context is immediately manifest" (Hirschman 1977a: 91). Moreover, those in power should not only deliver results, they should look for and ensure the legitimacy of their action as well. That was granted by political nationalism, and to be more precise–by its integral variant.

Holistic Nationalism as an Enforced Process

The questioning of primary-sector nationalism and the development in the regions under study of elements of holistic economic nationalism constituted a pragmatic and, with a lag, also an ideological response to emergencies such as wars and/or crises. With regard to the majority of East and Central European countries, the focus should be shifted somewhat. Here, territorial and administrative integration and/or reconstruction, i.e. the state-building, were strong incentives to forming the ideology and practice of economic nationalism: "warlike import restrictions" were a result (Berend 1998: 235). In Poland, war damages, disruptions accompanying territorial changes and the disappearance of the Russian market meant that "Poland's trade, which must have been one of the highest at the beginning of the century, suddenly turned out to be much lower than that of most trading nations after the War" (Drabek 1985: 385). Quite influential in Poland, protagonists of etatism and new nationalism strongly emphasized also the need to link the economic unification with planning studies and development of infrastructure and artificial industries. And this still before the 1929 crash (Kofman 1986: chapter 4, Gołębiowski 1985: chapter 3, Janus 2009: 237). One can treat these circumstances unique to East and Central Europe as a substitute for crisis.

Nevertheless, the hypothesis that the Great Depression was conducive to the development of industry in peripheral states and certain colonies and that it speeded up evolution toward holistic nationalism requires substantiation here. Despite appearances, it is by no means obvious.

When writing about colonial India, Chandra (1979: 13) did not doubt that "if the First World War marked the firm foundation of Indian capitalism, the Depression can be said to be the period of its coming of age." The same was said about Latin America: "Wars and depressions have historically no doubt been most important in bringing industries to countries of the 'periphery'" (Hirschman 1968: 4). For Frieden (2006: 221) the time of the Great Depression was probably one of the most significant moments in the economic history of the underdeveloped part of the world:

> In Latin America and other advanced developing nations the Depression and subsequent years played a role analogous to that of the Civil War in the United States: It brought down internationalist economic interests and brought nationalist to the fore.

Still, this is not a universally held opinion. According to Thorp (1998: 125),

> there is a great difference between industrialization that reflects export sector interests and industrialization that leads the economy, backed by a state

taking on new functions. The first is what principally occurred in the 1930s. The second is a reasonable description of the larger Latin American economies by the 1950s.

Lewis (2005: 14) argues likewise: in the 1930s "economic policy was piecemeal and directed towards export (sic) substitution–'economic internalisation'–rather than industrialization *per se*." And finally, let us bring in Haber's (2006: 538f) firm assertion that

> it is clear that there is no neat divide between the pre- and post-1930 periods in terms of government policies, the adaptation of mechanized technologies, the scale of enterprise, or the inward-looking nature of industry. ... The notion that governments are 'autonomous' entities that frame development 'strategies' is social-science fiction.

Indeed, compared with the developments in the 1950s, the industrial growth and structural transformations of the Brazilian economy in the 1930s may seem very limited and attained as a result of primarily emergency policies. Moreover, the role played by the primary sector was, after domestic final demand, second in importance for recovery and resumption of growth after 1932 (Bulmer-Thomas 2003: 208f). However, it has not been settled the extent to which this sector "flourished alongside rapid expansion of the industrial sector" and to what extent it was a prime-mover of industrial expansion in the late 1930s (Thorp 1998: 116, 125). Nevertheless, the results of the 1930s and the way they were achieved, especially in the second half of the decade, should not be underestimated. There was a difference between policies preceding the Great Depression and initial reactions to the 1929 crash, and the pro-industry policies pursued thereafter (Dean 1969, Wirth 1970), although one can find another opinion, according to which the "[c]ontinuity of federal economic thought and policies," as far as pro-industry and developmental goals were concerned, "was a dominant characteristic of the entire Vargas period" (Hilton 1975: 756). And specifically, such a difference between pre- and post-1929 developments was reflected in the industrial product mix at the end of the 1930s and in the increased autonomy of state structures. In a word, a transition to holistic nationalism began.

Let me, however, first mention briefly the WWI impact on industrial development in Brazil, the clear case of shock and/or war-induced growth. The classic hypothesis, put forward in the 1930s, held that the breakdown of economic relations in this period resulted in the spontaneous and unintended acceleration of industrial growth of the country, first initiated under *Encilhamento* in the 1890s. In his pathbreaking historical analysis of Brazilian cotton manufacturing, Stein (1957: 107), too, asserted that "[w]hat high tariffs had done for the Brazilian cotton manufacture between 1900 and 1913, the disruption of international trade during the First World War continued." Such a claim can also be made concerning Chile, Bulgaria in East and Central Europe but not Argentina. Compared to Brazil, Argentina's industrial sector came out as unable to flexibly respond to domestic demand: "the shaky data for this period show a drop in manufacturing output during 1914–17. The common opinion that the war boosted industrialization appears to be at best a very partial view" (Díaz-Alejandro 1970: 218; see also Bulmer-Thomas 2003: 183). In Brazil, however, at the time of WWI, the industrial workforce, the number of industrial establishments and the value of capital invested were on the rise. As a result, in 1917–1918 the average annual growth of aggregate industrial output reached 6.8 percent, a quite impressive achievement when compared with 5.5 percent in 1901–1910 and 4.4 percent in 1921–1930 (Versiani 1984: 166, Singer 2009: 64).

The sources and quality of such a growth were, however, the most interesting part of that WWI experience. In an interpretation of this hotly debated issue, historians pointed to two seemingly contradictory developments: on the one hand, a relatively fast growth of the production of textiles and other industrial consumer goods from 1914 to 1918, and on the other, a dramatic fall in the consumption and imports of indispensable industrial inputs. Curtailment of investments, reflected in falling consumption of steel and cement and of machinery imports, suggests that the impressive growth rate of industry was a sign of the increased "utilization of food and textile producing capacity that had been created prior to the war" (Baer 2008: 29, 33f; see also Haber 2006: 554f). The strength of this prewar expansion was illustrated by the fact that "[a]pproximately half of Brazil's cotton textile equipment as of 1945 was installed and in operation by 1915" (Stein 1957: 103). But it was also a testimony to the long-term technological decline of the Brazilian cotton industry. Moreover, the new firms created during the war in response to the demand previously satisfied by imports were technically less advanced and smaller than those established before 1914 (Baer 2008: 31f). Thus the rapid growth of textile output was impressive, indeed; nevertheless it was a mere adjustment of the Brazilian economy to war-imposed conditions. Such an adjustment also embraced an innovative although momentary attempt to develop an ersatz capital goods production. Majority of the firms established in São Paulo during the war as substitutes for missing capital goods imports were in fact immigrant-run small underfunded firms and repair shops. Their role as a kind of emergency assistance was significant but their contribution to the overall long-term development of industry very limited. After 1918 only a few survived (Dean 1969: 97ff, 104, Marson 2010).

Developments in the 1920s were equally interesting although of a different kind. Although the growth of total industrial output slowed, new important developments characterized this growth. First, regarding the textile industry, the crowding in effect emerged. From 1919 through 1925, the demand 'bonanza' of the WWI period was translated into substantial new investment in this sector. At the same time, however, a growing part of the demand was reclaimed by imports. The result was over-production, a slowdown in growth of textile production and excess capacities (an important factor when explaining the growth of industry before the mid-1930s). The ban on imports of textile machinery industrialists extorted in 1928 from the state–renewed in the 1930s–was the result; as was the shift toward more labor-intensive technologies. The ties linking, until mid-1930s, this industrial "business oligarchy" with the state were of enormous importance for pursuing their particularistic nationalism, however at the cost of growing economic and technological obsolescence (Stein 1957: chapter 10, 186f, Haber 1992). Second, it was in the 1920s that erratic and volatile but at the same time relatively substantial investments in new sectors were noted. Chemicals and metallurgy were growing well ahead the average for total industrial output. In 1925, at the height of the cotton industry investment drive the share of this sector in total machinery imports reached 34 percent; in 1929 it declined to 12 percent. Together with the–as yet limited–inflow of foreign market-oriented direct investments, these new developments "helped to establish the foundations for an expansion and diversification of industrial output in the following decade" (Versiani 1984: 169, 179).

How can one interpret the period of the 1930s against this background? Once again, changes in the interwar tariff policy, intensified in the 1930s, seem to provide a good starting point for a discussion.

Referring to the fiscal nature of Latin American countries' tariff policies at the time of the export boom, Bulmer-Thomas (2003: 143) observed that

> a tax imposed primarily for revenue reasons would never give the same rate of protection as a tax imposed primarily for protectionist purposes. Thus the rate of tariff protection in the United States may have appeared to be the same as in Argentina, but in practice US protection was much higher because the duties were concentrated on those products deemed to need protection from foreign competition (see also Irwin 2006: 152, 157, Bértola and Williamson 2006: 40).

It seems however that irrespective of the earlier nature of Latin American tariffs, the substantial redefinition of their economic role was undertaken only after WWI. They gradually turned from an instrument of fiscal policy into an instrument of protection and promotion of industry (Coatsworth and Williamson 2004). The process speeded up in the following decade. Links between the new trade policy and the gradual widening of the domestic tax base and employment of new financial instruments evolved and were strengthened, while the policies toward foreign capital and role of foreign trade were gradually modified. It was under the influence of the crisis that the Concordancia introduced income tax in Argentina, which was a move rejected first in 1915 and which the UCR radicals in power from 1916 had not dared to make. In Chile such a tax and the taxation of capital investments and property had been introduced twenty years earlier, in response to dwindling nitrate prices and exports at the beginning of WWI (Bulmer-Thomas 2003: 177, Díaz-Alejandro 1970, Collier and Sater 1996: 169). With regard to Central Europe on the other hand, it was pointed out that it was the Great Depression that put an end to the largely "spontaneous protectionism" that had prevailed up until 1929 (Kofman 1997: 109–112). It was in 1932 that a new customs tariff was introduced in Poland and "this was the first postwar customs tariff adapted to the needs of Poland" (Spigler 1986: 164, Landau and Tomaszewski 1982:). However, its role in strengthening the pro-industry policy fell short of expectations; the recourse to non-tariff measures was probably of greater importance (Kofman 1997: 133). Another distinctive feature of the late 1930s in Poland, Bulgaria and Romania was the increasing tendency to tie (not without the influence of the relevant Soviet and German experience) "new protectionism" not only with political, but also developmental, goals (Kofman 1997: 148, 156f, 181). And increasingly the new tariff schedules introduced after 1929 were seen and employed in both regions and in fact, around the world, as an internationally traded commodity, a bargaining chip in the hands of governments when dealing with trade partners/competitors. The Polish 1932 tariff played such a role, and so did the Brazilian tariffs introduced in 1931 and 1934. In a word, "[the] tariff policy ... ceased to be a gentlemanly game of small favors arranged clandestinely. ... the tariff schedule had to be mobilized for national purposes" (Dean 1969: 196).

At this point it should be emphasized once again that the level of nominal tariffs alone does not explain much. In Latin America in the 1930s they remained very high. The novelty was that after 1929 the core countries, too, raised tariffs: "The emergence of a protectionist and nationalistic Centre was the greatest shock to Latin American economies during the 1930s, going beyond its direct negative impact on the region's terms of trade" (Díaz-Alejandro 1984: 21). This time the effect of Latin American tariffs was strengthened by the combination of monetary policy and manipulation of exchange rates, quantitative import restrictions (QR), foreign exchange controls, direct and indirect subsidies and compensatory trade. Similar policies emerged in East and Central Europe, although the timing of intervention varied depending on the country. The difference lay in the fact that non-tariff instruments were used in the region (with different degrees of intensity and in different packages) practically from the end of WWI. In this sense, in both regions protection of the domestic market and industry was much more intensive than indicated by the levels of nominal rates alone. Because of poor coordination and complicated web of interests pressing for specific tariffs and other instruments of protection, these defensive measures often were duplicated (Kofman 1997: 120–123, Berend 1998: 234–239).

In the 1930s, all Latin American and Central European countries had to find a way out of the protracted crisis on their own. Hence, their growing criticism of the existing economic structures and attempts to adjust them to a situation where growth—if it were to recur—had to be backed by incentives (and resources) other than those the international market had provided so far. The crisis of the 1930s enforced and made stronger the link between distributional conflicts that engaged both new and traditional societal actors and the critical assessment of the hitherto development model and the level of industrialization achieved. However, the outlines of a new policy and the accompanying institutional change leading to 'independent industrialization' resulted not from theoretical reflection but from immediate defensive policy measures. The theory came later (Love 1996: 209). Burgin (1944: 228) stressed that with reference to Argentina:

> [industrialization] was not so much the result of a conscious and deliberate government policy as it was a consequence of a series of fortuitous circumstances over which the government had little or no control, but which at times forced the government to re-examine its commercial and economic policies.

Villela and Suzigan (1973: 79) wrote about Brazil in a similar vein: "it was monetary policy ... that was mostly responsible for the limited industrial growth in Brazil before 1945, even more so until the end of the 1920s." And the same pattern prevailed in East and Central Europe:

> It would be anachronistic to see the trend towards deficit financing as the result of clearly defined policies, for governments' measures to help

industry, agriculture, and trade ... were uncoordinated, even impressionistic (Spigler 1986: 1341).

Notwithstanding the initial reasons, such circumstance-enforced adjustments could be interpreted in some of the peripheral economies as the take-off in the transition to holistic nationalism. Thus the largely spontaneous industrialization that continued roughly up until the end of 1920s, faced with the shock of the Great Depression, gradually became, through trial and error, a policy of industrial development (Furtado 1967).

In both regions transition to holistic nationalism meant first of all widening the scope of direct as well as indirect government intervention. The traditional preoccupation with the state budget, balance-of-payments and tariff policy had not disappeared; it became a part of a greater whole. Interventionism became more intrusive, collectivism and new forms of interest articulation and representation were on the rise and the growing share of state expenditures in national incomes became a common occurrence. Needless to say, in Poland, irrespective of the etatism, strongly emphasized already in the 1920s, the nascent holistic nationalism was initially far from embracing macroeconomic planning. Thus in the mid-1930s–having the example of large-scale government interventions in the USA and other countries in mind–Eugeniusz Kwiatkowski (since 1935 Deputy Primer Minister in charge of the economy) wrote that Poland needed not planned, but strongly interventionist, government and an "organic" economy. In such an economy the role of the state was to "establish certain basic principles and guidelines," so that one could choose "among numerous possibilities for economic development ... those that would benefit society most" (quoted in Drozdowski 1989: 80, 84). In the following years, upon taking over economic policy-making in Poland, Kwiatkowski fundamentally changed his attitude toward planning in practice. The experience of preparing and subsequently carrying out in the late 1930s the ambitious Central Industrial Region (COP) project was of enormous importance: "in fact, Poland advanced farther down the path of government planning than its neighbors did" (Berend 1998: 271). In Brazil the transformation from strongly interventionist state to sectoral and/or indicative planning was in the 1930s much less advanced: the Volta Redonda iron and steel project "did not result from a clearly defined master solution. Instead, it followed from a long series of decisions that were influenced by circumstances, political and social groups, and personalities" (Wirth 1970: 217).

In a word, the first steps in the transition to holistic nationalism and the policy of industrialization were for the most part very loosely coordinated.

What is more, having the inherited pre-1929 industrial structure at hand, in the short run the crucial question was how to increase the rate of utilization of the existing capacities without substantially changing the prevailing demand profile. Thus, Kaufman (1979: 203, 1990: 115) asserted that such a process "did not require the hegemony of any particular class coalition, or any specific set of political-institutional arrangements" and the policy-making in the 1930s "[was] made possible by earlier growth of state decision-making structures with some capacity to resist external economic pressures and to regulate trade and finance." That was certainly the case at the start of the processes sparked by the Great Depression. The first years of the Vargas government did not as yet indicate a chance and/or will to introduce fundamental institutional and policy changes. However, already in the mid-1930s the need to introduce new institutional solutions became pressing, particularly when the growth of artificial capital goods industries became the priority. Also the financial institutions created in many countries in the 1920s with the aim of streamlining–under the gold standard rule–monetary, fiscal and credit policies were gradually changing their original character. This concerned, for example, central banks established in the Andean countries on the advice of the Princeton professor and 'money doctor' Edwin W. Kemmerer:

> Although these institutions were constructed entirely around restoration of the gold standard ... his innovations produced financial institutions that would nevertheless serve for the long run, laying the foundation for an increased role for government (Thorp 1998: 121).

The circumstance-enforced transition to holistic nationalism was characteristic of those economies which at a certain time switched from passive to non-orthodox reactive economic policy. This useful distinction proposed by Díaz-Alejandro (1984) allows us to see not only similarities in the policies of Brazil and Poland, but basic differences as well, especially in the years 1930–1935. Deflation psychosis reigned in Poland, the terrible experience of the post-war hyperinflation downright paralyzing decision-makers. Thus it was only in 1936 when the Polish government decided to introduce foreign exchange controls and import restrictions. These psychological-cum-policy limiting factors were largely absent in Brazil. Despite those differences, in the mid-1930s the above-mentioned tendencies appeared in both countries. At the same time, to resume and sustain growth meant entering upon the path of accelerated industrialization and holistic nationalism. Differences between particular reactive countries concerned not the main direction, but the timing, sequence and effectiveness of the measures undertaken. Hence, in some countries a move toward 'independent industrialization' meant steps toward deepened import substitution in the capital goods sector (e.g. in Poland and Brazil), and in some others, an acceleration of the historically earlier stage of substitution for industrial non-durables (e.g. in Bulgaria).

Prior to the Great Depression, industry in some of the Latin American countries developed slightly faster than the main sectors of the export economy. In the 1930s the rate of industrial growth was in all major countries already far ahead of the growth of national income (Thorp 1998: 318, 322). However, without going into detail, with regard to Latin American countries which were pursuing reactive policies, the rate of growth of national income and/or aggregate industrial output alone could not be a measure of the structural changes initiated. In absolute terms, Argentine industry was in the late 1920s much bigger than that in Brazil, but its share in GDP was, if we follow data quoted by Abreu (1993: 10), far below the relevant figure for Brazil. In the late 1920s the difference amounted to 5 percentage points.[3] Thus, industrial progress in pre-Great Depression Brazil was probably more advanced, taking also into account the enormous gap in incomes per capita in favor of Argentina.

However, even if data quoted by Abreu overestimate the progress made by Brazil until the late 1920s, the *relative* weakness of an industrial party in Argentina was apparent: all industries, from textile to capital goods, "were ... less advanced than could legitimately be expected in a country of Argentina's wealth" (Bulmer-Thomas 2003: 288). In explaining such differences, before 1929 and thereafter, the crucial variable seems to be the effects of political economy in both countries. Although before 1930 both Brazilian and Argentine industrialists were part of the export-economy dynamic, the former were definitely more successful in arguing their case. And there is no easy answer to the question of how to measure the results of an interplay between government short-term policies aimed at adjustment and survival, and policies fostering structural change, including the development of new industries. We can only assume that the acceleration of the industrialization of Brazil from the early 1950s, which included high rate of growth of the capital goods industry (Serra 1979: 121), was rooted in the results of policies of the late 1930s. Between 1920 and 1940 the share of the so-called modern industries (metal products and metallurgy, machinery, chemicals, transport equipment) in the

---

[3] According to Bulmer-Thomas (2003: 221), the reverse was true: in the 1930s the respective shares of industry in GDP of Argentina and Brazil were 22.7 percent and 14.5 percent.

industrial output increased from 12.3 percent to 23.9 percent; the next spurt took place in the 1950s when the 40.2 percent level was reached (Evans 1979: 72).

Díaz-Alejandro concluded his extensive and sophisticated evaluation of Argentina's progress in the 1930s favorably, although not without some doubts. The main one concerned the glaring discrepancy between the relatively high rate of GDP and industrial growth and the very low level of capital formation, a shift in the structure of demand from fixed investments to consumption. However, the reason he gave for such an unfavorable development did not sound convincing:

> The decrease in the capacity to transform domestic savings into machinery and equipment, can be blamed almost wholly on world conditions, which suddenly turned against an economy built on the premise that world trade would in the long run continue to expand (Díaz-Alejandro 1970: 102).

No doubt about it as far as the early 1930s were concerned. But afterwards? The Brazilian government, which until the mid-1930s had pursued a similar policy, at the end of the decade decided to move in the different direction, with the Volta Redonda project a sign of the change. One can also note not only the growing, after 1932, consumption of cement (the same took place in Argentina) but also the resumption of massive capital goods imports and rising consumption of steel; employment in the iron and steel industry in the 1930s more than doubled (Baer 2008: 31, 169: 65, Bulmer-Thomas 2003: 210n). The rate of growth of the transport equipment and electrical industries in São Paulo was in this period far above the growth rate of industry as a whole; the share of capital goods industries in the industrial output doubled (Marson 2008). An even more ambitious industrialization project was initiated in the late 1930s in Poland, under much greater hardship imposed by "world conditions." At the very early stage of the COP project development, the industries which between 1928 and 1938 reported rise in employment were metallurgy, chemicals and electric power, and this growth should be seen against the decline in total industrial employment between 1928 and 1938 (Teichova 1985: 245).

Thus, both countries took the first, although delayed, steps toward a more advanced stage in import-substitution; they clearly began to deviate from the growth path of industry reflecting primarily export sector interests and neglect of backward linkage. It was in these countries that one can claim with hindsight that "structural changes were more impressive than overall growth" (Díaz-Alejandro 1984: 37) and where industrialization, as understood by Bértola and Williamson, started. And in both cases one can find at least a partial answer to the important questions raised by Díaz-Alejandro (1970: 78) in his analysis of Argentine example:

> What would have happened if the strategy of import substitution had been different? In particular, what would have happened if activities such as steel, oil-extraction, and petrochemicals had received priority over the expansion of light consumer goods industries?

And as already mentioned, to all intents and purposes the awareness that the *belle époque* of the primary export economy was over was growing and around 1932–1933 it was already widespread and firmly established in both regions. The attempts at adjustment policy in 1930–1932, which brought limited positive results in some countries and disappointment in others, were accompanied by the deepening world crisis. The hoped-for change for the better in the international economy was not coming. Thus in 1935 Kwiatkowski (1988: 98) wrote that "the fundamentals of economic *Weltanschauung* were lost through the destruction of the rules of the old system and inability to formulate a new one." In Argentina such a mood was well reflected in the statement Luís Duhau, the Minister of Agriculture, made in 1933:

> The historical stage of our prodigious growth under the direct stimulus of the European economy has finished. ... the country should look in itself, with its own resources, for the relief for its present difficulties. [El Plan de Acción Económica Nacional] proposes to stimulate efficiently industrial output (quoted in Díaz-Alejandro 1970: 104).

It is noteworthy that that was an opinion voiced by a former leader of the La Sociedad Rural.

However, the immediate effects of Duhau's declaration were limited, notwithstanding strong interventions in agriculture, rapid development of public works (mainly road building) and growing state expenditures. Although the economic situation in Argentina after 1933 was not as bad as depicted by contemporary critics of Concordancia and some economic historians thereafter, the improvements fell short of expectations. Thus, in 1940, Concordancia's Minister of the Treasury and former independent socialist Federico Pinedo introduced his radical plan for a coordinated transition to the policy of industrialization including provisions for long-term loans, development of infrastructure, a housing program and stronger government intervention in agriculture. Although the plan was spiked by the UCR opposition, nevertheless "it showed how far the dominant thinking, even of the old elites, had moved away from classical liberalism toward the ideas of economic nationalism and state regulation" (Lewis 1990: 93).

Three years later that plan turned out to be politically dead. The military, representing 'the national interest', stepped in with a different, even more radical project for economic nationalism. And on the way, they pushed aside not only Concordancia but also demands for democracy. In the years to come Juan D. Perón moved the policy of holistic nationalism to the frontier of radical economic populism.

Against Foreign Domination: Yes, But...

Although the economic policies of the 1930s were enforced by circumstances and only through trials and errors found answers to the situation of imposed quasi-isolation, they did not emerge in an intellectual vacuum. Studies on the evolution of economic and social thought indicate a gradual formation, already from the latter half of the 19th century, of concepts emphasizing the need to embrace a different, industry-based, idea of modernity. The ideas of Peruvians Juan Copello and Luis Petriconi from the 1870s, presented in *Estudio sobre la independencia económica del Perú*, and rediscovered in the 1970s, were a prime example of the critical analysis of the guano era impact on the long-term development of the country. The answer to the crisis, proposed by both the authors, was a policy of industry-centered tariff protectionism, understood also as "the only means to ... resolve the problem of economic independence, and with it, all of the problems of our political existence." This, however, should be the first step. "Well-organized protectionism" should be strengthened by "direct protectionism" (*protección directa*), i.e. a package of measures in support of certain enterprises, imports of experts, industrial exports, etc. (Gootenberg 1993: 172, 176ff; see also Bonilla 1974: 169ff).

In the annotated bibliography by Cortés and Stein (1977), indispensable to studies of the economic history of Latin America, one can find information on other attempts to approach this problem. However, while giving credit to forerunners, we should, however, bear in mind the late birth of theoretical-historical reflection concerning underdevelopment and industrialization. Until the 1940s its place in mainstream historiography had been marginal; such a subordinate position was well reflected by the following observation concerning research into the economic history of Latin America:

> the first major bibliography of publications on the economy of Latin America ... prepared by Harvard University's Bureau for Economic Research in Latin America (1935), has no section entitled 'economic history' nor one which today would be designated 'economic development' (Stein and Hunt 1971: 233).

Latin America was not an isolated example in this respect. In Central Europe academic studies on economic development were initiated–under the strong influence of the German Historical School–as late as the beginning of the 20th century. That a unique and largely precursory debate on certain issues of structurally determined underdevelopment took place in Romania in the 1920s was brought to the attention of historians outside Romania pretty late (Love 1996a, Kofman 1997: passim).

Also, during the Great Depression the role of the state was not discovered but reformulated and reemphasized. In 19th century Peru, the intellectual state-centered "counter-liberal tradition" of debating "elaborate alternatives," which pointed out to an "imagined development," was a critical (and not exclusively utopian) response to real issues. But it was not a uniquely Peruvian tradition:

> Many historians now identify ongoing statist and nationalist traditions that never quite dried up under the liberal pause and that simply assumed greater weight with the loss of world markets and finance in the Great Depression (Gootenberg 1993: 205f, 209).

In the case of Brazil, historians argued along the same lines, stressing the rather weak commitment of economic elites to free trade (Topik 1980, Abreu 1993).

No doubt, historically established patterns of political behavior and conflict resolution, and also the impact of inherited and/or borrowed ideologies on the processes affecting state action did matter. It seems, however, that there was sufficient diversity in the policies of Latin American states and the behavior of their elites and popular societal actors before and also during the interwar crisis to warn against overemphasizing the one-model-fits-all approach. I mean here the model of the "organic-statist" tradition proposed by Alfred Stepan as an historical-theoretical explanation of the phenomenon of the Latin American strong state: "Organic-statist concepts of the political community and of the state's responsibility for the common good imply strong constraints on laissez-faire market individualism." Such a state, a kind of middle ground between liberal and communist visions of state–society relations, and at the same time a juxtaposition of liberal "associational patterns" and non-liberal "government chartered interest groups" ends as an autonomous, "clearly interventionist and strong" actor (Stepan 2001: 40, 42, 59, 62, 68). It seems, however, that it would be difficult to subsume the state in Argentina and in Brazil and the political economies of both countries under the one-size-fits-all organic-statist variant. Examples are abundant. The solutions to the 1890s financial crises found by the two countries were poles apart. In the case of Argentina a weakening of the state's role in the economy was a result, in Brazil the speculative boom was probably the most important step leading to the strengthening of the position of industrialists and at the same time it "brought recognition in government circles that the state might play an important role in fostering industry" (Stein 1957: 90, 96f). What is more, the structurally and historically determined divorce between the state and civil society in many Latin American countries in the 19th century–a case strongly argued by Forment (2003)– should not be discarded here.

Let me stop here, however. What is clear is the fact that in the interwar period a strong, interventionist state played a major role in both regions, although the degree of intrusiveness and the main direction of its actions were different before and after 1929: "if the twenties could be regarded as the epilogue of the old, the thirties might be regarded as the prologue of the new period" (Ránki and Tomaszewski 1986: 5f).

The earliest to appear in Latin American debates, along with the problem of the state, was that element of economic nationalism which expressed suspicion of and/or hostility toward foreign capital and 'foreigners'. Without going into history too deeply, certain contemporary and modern interpreters have reduced the causes of the 1891 dramatic end of President Balmaceda's rule in Chile to a conspiracy of British firms in control of a considerable part of nitrate deposits. It is an undeniable fact that these firms supported conspirators financially and that British navy officers backed the rebels. However, a considerable part of the Chilean elite, already well established in the nitrate business and threatened by economic moves planned by Balmaceda, also went against him. Balmaceda's plans such as the opening of this monopolistically structured sector to new Chilean entrepreneurs did not arouse their enthusiasm (Zeitlin 1984: chapter 3). On the other hand, the constitutional dispute unified almost the whole of the political class against Balmaceda (Collier and Sater: 152). Let me add here that a similar explanation was given, especially in Peru, to the war between Chile, Bolivia and Peru (The Pacific War 1879–1883). The Peruvian nationalist narrative associated the loss of guano and nitrate deposits with the expansion of Great Britain and British entrepreneurs and intra-imperialist rivalries. The Pacific War, as Luis Esteves wrote in the 1880s, had been a "war of foreign interests against the guano and other riches of Peru" (quoted in Gootenberg 1993: 191). Historians have already convincingly demonstrated the limitations of such a "phantasmagoric interpretation of the national history" (Bonilla 1980: 184, 153–175).

From the turn of the century, in these rationalizations the place of British capital and interests was becoming increasingly often taken by North American capital. Not without reason.

The United States' activities in the Caribbean and Central America demonstrated to Latin Americans not only the civilizational might of the northern power, but also the threat it posed. But at that time Latin American nationalism found, for the most part, a literary answer to those new developments. For an economic answer it was still too early. Its first outlines began to appear during the 1910s, although one work worth mentioning is the "forgotten in many ways" precursor economic history of Peru by Luis Esteves, published in 1882. His *Apuntes para la historia económica del Perú* included an extensive discussion on the negative impact of British imperialism on Peru's economic development, "a theme broached openly for the first time in Peru's economic literature" (Gootenberg 1993: 187, 190). *Ariel,* by the Uruguayan José Enrique Rodó (1900), was probably the best example of this literary type of nationalism, today described as *arielista* anti-imperialism (Miller 1999: 174ff). The Cuban José Martí was its critical continuator. Rubén Darío's ode to Theodore Roosevelt (1901), widely circulated in Central and South America, and *El diario de Gabriel Quiroga: Opiniones sobre la vida argentina* (1910) by the Argentine Manuel Gálvez were classic examples of nationalism calling for a defense of the cultural identity of Latin America against the 'materialist civilization' and its values and against the external expansionism of the great neighbor. *La evolución política y social de Hispano-América* by the Venezuelan Rufino Blanco-Fombona, *La creación de un continente* (1912) by the Peruvian Francisco García Calderón, and finally *El destino de un continente* (1923) by the Argentine erstwhile socialist and later 'democratic nationalist' Manuel Ugarte fall into the same tradition. At this point there occurs an analogy with the Polish fear of materialist civilization and dilemmas in the 19th century, described by Jedlicki (1999). By the way, this important heterogeneous tradition of *arielista* anti-imperialism-cum-nationalism is clearly detested by certain modern US scholars who describe it as "a largely irrational" and full of "vitriol and indignation" body of writings, documenting rising "Yankeephobia" (Jorrín and Martz 1970: 204).

The book by Ugarte–preceded by his commentaries focused on the economic background of the United States political and military expansion ("El peligro yanqui" from 1901)–represented an in-between position in that current. The author's obvious pro-industry sympathies and his strong emphasis on US economic expansionism distinguished *El destino de un continente* from classic *arielista* anti-imperialism. From the latter half of the 1920s, populist currents, among others, in Peru but first of all in Argentina, referred to the theses laid out by Ugarte. The fact that Victor Raúl Haya de la Torre, the future leader of the populist and (initially) anti-American APRA, did not even suspect the existence of economic imperialism when he was a student in the late 1910s shows what a revelation Ugarte's book was. In his 1923 comments on the book, Haya de la Torre wrote, "I must say that the awareness of the threat posed by North American imperialism is news to me." It was only the appearance in Peru of a 'technical commission' from the USA, which as part of the agreement concerning a foreign loan for Peru took over control of customs revenues, brought home to him the extent of Peru's and other countries' "subordination to *al capitalismo de Yanquilandia*" (Haya de la Torre 1976: 16).

From the point of view of the formation process of Latin American self-identity and nationalism, it is not terribly important whether, because of its elitism and reference to the mythologized past, we call *arielista* anti-imperialism-cum-nationalism 'oligarchic' and 'reactionary' or whether we recognize it as a stage in the process of the cultural and social emancipation of Latin America. Surely, an emblematic figure of traditionalist attitudes at the turn of the 19th and 20th centuries was Aparicio Saravia in Uruguay, an opponent of the modernizer Batlle (the one who, as his opponents claimed, being a mason, removed crosses from hospitals). Saravia and his death from wounds sustained in battle "incarnated the gaucho legacy" (Burns 1980: 80). In the opinion of Manuel Gálvez, an outstanding representative of traditional nationalism and *hispanidad*, Saravia was *el gaucho de la libertad*. Ultimately, this legendary leader became a part not only of the elite, but also national history, a reflection of its paradoxical ambiguity (Rodríguez Monegal 2003). His was not an isolated case.

In the subsequent decades of the 20th century elite nationalism was transformed in a symptomatic way. One way or another it was incorporated into the cultural and political credo of considerable sections of modern urban groups, thus shaping the mentality and attitudes of the modernizing community. After all, it was not a unidirectional movement. As relations with the modern economy and foreigners developed, in parallel to elite nationalism there also developed the nationalism of the lower classes, popular nationalism (Burns 1980), which became an important premise of the future populist movements. In this sense, the forms of nationalism referred to here can be treated as the psychological and cultural foundations of holistic economic nationalism. They were not, however, the prime movers of this type of nationalism.

In Central Europe, up to 1918, outward-oriented nationalism developed and occurred in different forms. Attitudes toward foreign capital were formed primarily in the context of nation-building and unstable intra-national relations; after 1918 added to this was a certain angst over the stability of the newly-emerged states. That is why it is so difficult to distinguish between defensive nationalism and aggressive nationalism. One can try to define them; however, this requires reference to the wider, historical context of the state- and nation-building processes in the region. Without such a point of reference any discussion becomes impossible. Needless to say, such elucidation may not be confined to the adoption of a one-size-fits-all interpretation, and meant to apply to Romanians and Hungarians, Ukrainians and Poles or Slovaks and Czechs. That would be a utopian and politically explosive endeavor. Morgenthau's "A-B-C paradox" occurred with full force in the interwar period. What is meant is rather a sketch of a map illustrating the areas and spread of conflicts (economic conflicts included), connected with the formation of national and multi-national states after 1918. Interpretation of the character of these conflicts (defensive? aggressive?) remains a matter resolved one way or another but depending on the national viewpoint.[4]

However, even if we confine our deliberations to relations between the Central European economies and foreign capital the problem does not become less complicated. At first glance, the outburst in the 1930s of anti-French feelings in Poland and the nationalization of a French-owned textile enterprise (the so-called Żyrardów affair) (Landau and Tomaszewski 1964: 117–126) or general hostility to foreigners in Romania (the Liberal Party's "On our own" slogan which was raised as early as 1904) would suggest an analogy with the situation in Latin America. So would the fear of foreign capital domination over a weak domestic economy, widespread in Poland. Stefan Starzyński, the founder of the First Economic Brigade connected with the military-bureaucratic elite that seized power

---

[4] For the situation on the eve of independence of Poland and other countries in the region in 1917–1918 see, above all, Chlebowczyk (1988), and also a succinct discussion in Rothschild (1974: 3–14).

following Józef Piłsudski's 1926 coup, insisted not just upon strong government interventionism. During the 1925–1926 discussions on a possible foreign loan and imposed external control over it, he charged those advocating accepting such a loan with lack of patriotism, and thundered that they wanted "to eliminate Poland from the world scene." He argued that the financial stability of the state must be secured by internal resources, without the entry of foreign capital into the Bank Polski (Janus 2009: 178, 183). Socialists and radical nationalists argued similarly (Landau and Tomaszewski 1984: 191f). In fact, in 1927 former US Assistant Secretary of Treasury Charles S. Dewey was appointed member of the Bank Polski Board and advisor to the Polish government. And foreign controllers as well as lien on taxes and property mortgages–a collateral of the loans– were a common occurrence in many Latin American and Central European states at the time (Łapa 2002: 114, Winkler 1933: passim, Stallings 1987: 132f, Landau and Tomaszewski 1984: 181ff, 187ff). The 'match loan' and 'tobacco loan' in Poland were names of collaterals involving mortgages of state excise from the sales of matches and tobacco.

However, such direct analogies would be deceptive.

In Latin America, the presence of foreign capital was seen as a reflection of the *monocentric* domination of Great Britain, above all. The same concerned foreign trade. Until the outbreak of WWI such a perception did not clash with real tendencies, although the situation in Central America and the Caribbean, where US preeminence and 'dollar diplomacy' were already a well-established fact, should be tackled differently. With regard to South America in the period between 1914 and 1929, this picture of British monocentric dominance became more complicated. The British position in trade weakened markedly. In the years 1914–1929, the share of imports from the USA in the total import trade of Latin America increased from 24.5 percent to 38.8 percent. In 1929 the United States was the largest supplier of imports to the bigger countries, Argentina included. On the other hand, Great Britain still mattered as an export market, even though in 1929 it was the USA which was the main export market for Brazil, Chile and Peru. In the 1930s Great Britain as an export market was still of primary importance to Argentina and Chile, and second in importance to Peru, but marginal to Brazil. The overall importance of the US to Latin America's imports in the 1930s remained the primary one, although those imports declined somewhat compared with 1929 (to 35.8 percent). The share of British imports was reduced to 12.2 percent, having been overtaken by German imports (17.1 percent). And in the 1930s, Nazi Germany and Japan joined the countries trading intensively with Latin America.

In Brazil, Chile and Peru German imports ranked second after those from the US.

As a trading partner the USA was thus after 1914 on the road to replacing Great Britain, and in 1920, its role was already preponderant. However, the predominance of Great Britain and the USA taken together in Latin American foreign trade was unquestionable and overwhelming. The combined share of these two powers in Latin American exports rose from 52.5 percent in 1910 to 56.5 percent in 1930; the respective figures for imports were 54 and 57 percent (Thorp 1998: 349). Analysis of these trends in Hirschman's (1980: 102, 105) study shows that the level of Latin American trade concentration in the interwar period was close to those in the British Empire and the countries of South Eastern Europe (including Hungary) and Turkey.

As far as the presence of foreign capital is concerned, the USA relatively quickly replaced Great Britain. US net capital exports to Latin America after WWI far outpaced British investments (Taylor 2006: 71). However, British presence in certain Latin American countries had been well entrenched and it took American firms and banks a bit longer to dislodge their competitors. In Argentina, until 1914 a privileged area of British investments, the share of US investments in total foreign investments amounted to 1.2 percent in 1913, and to 14 percent in 1927 (Solberg 1987: 38). In Brazil, the share of US firms and banks in total foreign investments increased from 4 percent in 1914, to 21 percent in 1930 (Evans 1979: 82). As far as disbursed loans were concerned, between 1918 and 1931 US financial institutions outstripped British banks by a factor of 8 ($2 billion gross against $0.25 billion); the acceleration of this process took place only after the international commercial crisis of 1920–1921 (Taylor 2006: 69, Marichal 1989). However, although most of the loans were now coming from the USA, the role of the British and other European banks was not marginal. Thus, in the interwar period, the previously monocentric dominance of the British was replaced by a duopoly of a sort with US firms and finances rapidly substituting such Old World preeminence. Except for Argentina, in the late 1930s the term 'foreigner' began to stand for 'American' (or, abusively, *gringo* and/or Yankee).

Meanwhile, East and Central Europe from the end of WWI to the late 1930s was confronted with the *polycentric*, highly dispersed dominance of foreign capital and the considerably lower geographic concentration of foreign trade. That concerned, first of all, Poland and Czechoslovakia. The levels of foreign trade concentration in both countries were far lower than in Latin America, and falling in the years 1925–1937 (Hirschman 1980: 102).

First of all, Germany's initially high share in Polish imports in 1929 (27.3 percent) fell in 1935 to 14.4 percent. Although in 1938 this share reached 23 percent, it, however, represented already combined imports from Germany and Austria. In 1929, imports from other countries were dispersed, from 12.3 percent in the case of the United States, to 6.9 percent in the case of France, with Great Britain and Czechoslovakia in between. In that year the leading export markets were Germany (31.1 percent), Austria (10.4 percent), Czechoslovakia (10.5 percent) and Great Britain (10.2 percent) (Landau and Tomaszewski 1982: 390). In 1938, the share of Great Britain increased to 18.1 percent, and of the markets in the Western Hemisphere to 8.6 percent (Rocznik 1939: 167). Germany's relatively limited share in the foreign trade of Poland, Czechoslovakia and to some extent Romania contrasted, however, with the experience of Bulgaria and Yugoslavia, especially after 1934. In the latter case, the growth of their foreign trade was strongly dependent on the compensatory trade expansion of Nazi Germany (Drabek 1985: 436).

As far as foreign capital is concerned, in the immediate postwar years, the traditional position of French and British firms and banks, established before 1914, seemed unchallenged. However, in this region, too, US investments and finances began to appear. But unlike investments and loans provided by France and Great Britain they were not strongly intertwined with the political priorities of the USA. Central Europe was, first of all, a place for limited private investments, relief operations (after 1918) and some state-supported loans, not for international politics. As in Latin America in the 1920s, the US government played in the region a "rather passive, supervisory role over private lending" (Stallings 1987: 141).

As in the case of foreign trade, foreign investments in Poland were dispersed too. In the years 1929–1938 the share of French capital in overall foreign investments fluctuated between 30.4 and 26.2 percent, of US capital between 12.1 and 18.6 percent, of Belgian capital between 14.8 and 13.3 percent, and of German capital between 24.1 and 13.3 percent (Landau and Tomaszewski 1981: 31).[5] Such a pattern of dispersed foreign investments was also characteristic of other countries of the region (Teichova 1985; 293, Landau and Tomaszewski 1981). However, if we look at the six major countries of the region as a whole, a kind of French-British preeminence can be detected. In 1935 investors from both countries controlled 42 percent of the capital assets of East and Central European enterprises, against

---

[5] Landau and Tomaszewski (1984: 201) assert that the share of German capital was underestimated.

10 percent controlled by the Germans, primarily in Poland. The share of US investors amounted to 18 percent (Nötel 1986: 275). The important difference between the patterns of foreign investments in Latin America and East and Central Europe was also reflected in their sectoral distribution. Of the $550 million FDI in East and Central Europe in 1937, $450 million was in industry, mining and oil, and $50 million in banking. And they were relatively highly concentrated: in 1937, the FDI in the integrated metallurgical and mining sectors in Czechoslovakia and Poland amounted to about $144 million, and in the Romanian oil sector to about $60 million, i.e. to 45 percent of total FDI in the East and Central European industry, mining and oil (Nötel 1986: 281).

Thus, Latin American nationalism developed as, first of all, outward-oriented, anti-British and increasingly anti-Yankee and therefore directed at the centers of the world economy. Looking with hindsight at the 1930s, the Brazilian historian Werneck Sodre's (1960: 30, 31) answer to the question "Why nationalism?" was simple: "the external economic forces today are the biggest obstacle to our development. ... Hence nationalism emerges as liberation." In this respect, nationalism in East and Central Europe was in the 1920s ambivalent; with two exceptions, however. First, strong peasant movements in Bulgaria, Czechoslovakia, Poland, Romania, Estonia and Latvia–with their ideology of 'agrarianism' and rather weak international coordination (the Green International based in Prague and controlled by Czechoslovak Agrarians)–were essentially anti-foreign and anti-liberal but not necessarily anti-development and/or anti-urban (Rothschild 1974: 16ff). However, one should keep in mind that ideological and program cohesion was not the strong point of these movements either in underdeveloped Bulgaria or in industrialized Czechoslovakia. The most glaring case was Bulgaria in the early 1920s, with the anti-foreign, authoritarian and also anti-urban Agrarian Union in power (Bell 1977). The Czechoslovak farmer movement adopted a completely different attitude regarding development and parliamentary democracy. In Romania, the anti-urban and largely anti-etatist mentality of peasant party leaders led them in the 1920s to opposing nationalization of land (with subsoil oil reserves) and to fostering an 'open door' policy toward foreign investments (Murgescu 2006: 239). Second, strong anti-foreign sentiment against Germans and German capital permeated politics and economic policies primarily in Poland and Czechoslovakia, but also in Estonia and Latvia. In the latter two countries, independence–but also the earlier national revolutionary movements–led to the elimination of stratifications based on a juxtaposition of the mainly German landowners and Estonian and Latvian peasantry. German landlords were forced out and their relatively well developed lands (*Rittergut*) were redistributed as a result of the post-WWI land reforms. And what is more, the egalitarian medium-size farm-based agrarian structure which emerged as a result of these reforms in both countries was unique in East and Central Europe (Köll 2006: 151f, 2000).

To some extent, the ambivalence of East Central European outward-oriented economic nationalism and its chief preoccupation with the 'German agenda' and/or 'Austrian agenda' were paradoxical but at the same time–in the case of Poland and Czechoslovakia–understandable. The economic power of the German neighbor and the memory of Austro-Hungarian dominance created a political and economic syndrome difficult to dislodge. On the other hand, considering the degree of control over the East and Central European economies by British and French capital, German control over modern industrial branches in the region as a whole was not overwhelming. The country where a preoccupation with foreign control was both before WWI and in the 1920s most intensively articulated, and at the same time not reduced to the 'German agenda', was Romania. Attacks against 'foreign capital and Jews' were common as was a striving to enlarge national control over the critically important oil industry. The results were impressive but not decisive: the degree of foreign control decreased between 1914 and 1922 from 94 percent to 88–85 percent and in 1936 it declined to 74 percent, although "[t]he Romanian state was more successful in obtaining the nomination of Romanian officials in top management positions" (Murgescu 2006: 238, 241, Ránki and Tomaszewski 1986: 8f, Nötel 1986: 281, 282). The leading role in the oil industry played by Royal Dutch-Shell (Astra Română) and Standard Oil of New Jersey (Româno-Americana) was preserved amid a strong nationalistic campaign in 1920s. With regard to inward-oriented economic nationalism, about which in a moment, the situation looked different.

It is also unclear why modern nationalism took the form of anti-imperialism in Latin America, whereas in East and Central Europe this kind of terminology did not take root. It would be pointless to maintain that the diverse impact of communist parties and the Komintern explains this difference. Both in Latin American as well as in East and Central Europe (save for Chile and Czechoslovakia) that impact was very weak. Somewhat different should be the appraisal of the influence of the Komintern as a 'propaganda machine' which introduced a new language and new topics into Latin American discussions at the time (Caballero 1986, Szlajfer 1989). Anti-imperialism-cum-nationalism became an important element in the political rhetoric of also Latin American governments and populist leaders. From the 1930s it selectively drew its slogans and arguments also from the Italian fascist propaganda. Concepts developed by Robert Michels and Dino Grandi, highlighting the fate of "proletarian nations" and the significance of "the class struggle between nations," reached a much wider audience than Komintern manifestoes did (Gregor 1979, Kula 1987: 237ff).

At any rate, in keeping with the hypothesis presented above, one can claim, referring to the example of Poland and Czechoslovakia, that the potential risk related to the presence and economic predominance of foreign capital, although rising in public perception and reflected in government policies in the 1930s, was placed in a wider context, going beyond the limits delineated by economic analysis alone. Unlike in the larger Latin American countries, the presence of foreign capital was understood and evaluated as primarily a political issue, as threat to state sovereignty (or as a factor strengthening independence), and to a lesser extent as economic exploitation. Czechoslovakia (to a lesser extent Poland) was a perfect example of such a highly politicized approach:

> with the active support of Czech bankers and industrialists, the government tried to achieve political and economic consolidation with the help of Allied capital investments ... in order to dislodge German and Austrian economic influence from key positions (Teichova 1985: 295).

Meanwhile, the strong presence of US firms in the Polish oil industry raised no great interest and/or passions. Prior to the Great Depression, Kwiatkowski (1988: 82) wrote that the inflow of foreign capital, French, British, American and Czech in particular, "should be considered beneficial." In passing, the strong anti-Russian and anti-Soviet feelings in Poland and Romania had little in common with the economy.

Taking into account such a wider context, it is not surprising that the attitude toward US firms in the region was not particularly negative, except in Romania. The rhetoric used by the leader of the Liberal Party and the Prime Minister in 1904, at the final stage of the (lost) battle for national control over oil was quite unique:

> Taking as a model the motto of the Americans, 'America for Americans,' I have as my motto 'Europe for Europeans' and especially 'Romania for Romanians.' ... Guard yourselves against the Standard Oil Trust and all who are in league with it (quoted in Murgescu 2006: 235; see also Harre 2006: 257).

Poles did not change their feelings even after 1931, when the presence of US capital became more visible than that of German capital. The exception was the William A. Harriman group. From 1928 it had been operating in the Upper Silesian mining and the iron and steel industry as a minority partner in the "Wspólnota Interesów" [Community of Interests] Friedrich Flick group, which together controlled about 50 percent of metallurgical production in Poland. Following the slump in Flick's large-scale exports of rolled steel products to the Soviet Union (the so-called *Russengeschäfte*) toward the end of 1931, the Harriman group presumably lost interest in further investments in Poland (Jezierski and Leszczyńska 2001: 293). The reasons for its continued presence in Polish heavy industry began to arouse suspicions. Not without reason. The evidence suggests that a strong case can be made that from as early as 1928 Harriman had been acting as a front for German capital. The nationalization of Flick's "Wspólnota Interesów" in 1936 was justified by *raison d'état* and financial mismanagement, and delivered by the Polish government to the public as the need to limit German economic influence (Landau and Tomaszewski 1964: 317–332). Parenthetically speaking, the consequences of the highly politicized economic relations in Upper Silesia were far-reaching. It was striking that until 1939 this industrial center had been unable to act as the growth pole of the Polish economy. German capital's hostile attitude toward the newly-emerged state must have been a reason. This in turn aroused distrust among the Poles. Thus, starting from 1937, COP had been built not as an extension of the Upper Silesian industrial center, but apart from it.

Let me now consider briefly inward-oriented nationalism, directed primarily against the Jewish minority. In Poland, but also in other countries (except for Czechoslovakia), this nationalism exerted a strong impact on the ideology of economic nationalism. Romania, in the first days of WWII, detained the powerful Jewish industrialist and manager Max Auschnitt. All his property was confiscated (Nötel 1986: 345). That was a signal to weaken substantially 'Jewish capital'. In Hungary, which after the 1920 Trianon treaty re-emerged as a territorially reduced state with a 90 percent Hungarian majority, anti-Semitism was elevated to a level of importance not known in the pre-WWI Austria-Hungary empire: "Economic nationalism re-appeared in the form of economic anti-Semitism" (Pogány 2006: 228). In interwar Poland, despite the rhetoric of radical nationalists and the post-1936 increasing government support for "economic struggle" with Jewish trade and handicraft, tensions in Polish-Jewish relations were, when seen from a comparative perspective, weaker. Until the early 1939 the tendency had been, however, similar.

It is important that anti-Jewish, inward-oriented, nationalism was an autonomous phenomenon, bearing no relation to the preeminence of the core countries' capital. Nevertheless, in the eyes of the nationalists the

Jewish minority was also an active participant in the anti-Polish, anti-Romanian or anti-Hungarian 'conspiracy'. For radical Polish nationalists like Doboszyński (1936), the external threat posed by German capital and the internal one posed by Jews were the two sides of the same coin. The already quoted call by Rybarski to introduce anti-Semitic "internal protectionism" or attempts at defining self-sufficiency as liberation from Jewish economic influence (Mendelsohn 1983: 71) showed that this kind of nationalism was felt intensely. All the more so that in the 1930s Polish-Jewish economic competition grew harsher. Needless to say, one should bear in mind that economic conflict was neither the only one, nor the most important. Such conflict, in concert with expansive authoritarian integral nationalism, exacerbated the political and cultural clash between Polish and Jewish national identities (Tomaszewski 1999: 144, 2006: 137, Mendelsohn 1983: 76–83). But it was the prolonged crisis and the ongoing modernization of trade, where Jewish presence was very much visible, that formed an explosive mixture and enhanced popular nationalist appeals. The tendency to 'Polonize' this sector was apparent: in 1921, about 77 percent of those employed in mainly small- and medium-sized commerce businesses were Jews, against 48 percent in 1938 (Jezierski and Leszczyńska 2001: 317). Put in a nutshell, inward-oriented nationalism aroused much greater passion, particularly among the urban middle class and peasants, than the foreign investments. German capital being the only exception. The government's position on this issue, expressed in the often quoted 1936 speech by the Polish Prime Minister ("An honest host does not allow anybody to be harmed in his house. Economic struggle [with the Jews]–yes! But no harm"), in fact, reflected a surrender to widespread anti-Jewish sentiment, not an urgent economic need. In the opinion of a Jewish scholar, "the government and its followers, in contrast with the Endeks [National Democrats] and other fascists, were more concerned over foreign capital than Jewish ownership." He adds, all the same, "the nationalization of Jewish-owned factories was undoubtedly projected in the long-run" (Marcus 1983: 366, 106). Well, until early 1939, there had been a lot of talk about this subject in the press and in parliament, but in fact nothing was decided.[6]

---

[6] The shift in Polish foreign policy, which led to the military guarantees by Great Britain and France (illusory as it turned out in September 1939) in fact barred the development of any plan for a large-scale assault against Jews and Jewish property. Marcus's approach to this issue seems excessively speculative and biased.

Meanwhile in Latin America, in the countries where inward-oriented nationalism occurred on a larger scale it was closely related to the growing fear of and dependence on Europe and the United States. This did not rule out an attack against local competitors in a situation of crisis. Writing about the "repugnant and noble" faces of "spontaneous nationalism" during the Mexican revolution, Łepkowski (1986: 137) pointed out that it was "Chinese and Arabs in particular that had been attacked, Jews more seldom, besides, needless to say, the Yankees." This applied above all to northern states. But it was not "spontaneous nationalism" alone and it was not aimed against the Yankees in the first place. Prior to 1924, in Sonora, which until Cardenas's time had brought to power the strongest group of "intelligent and amoral" leaders, persecution of the Chinese manifested in both massacres as well as, for instance, the ban on interracial marriage. In Sonora, the rallying call of the revolution *México para los mexicanos* found also a sinister expression (Carr 1973: 320, 336f). As concerns 'the Yankees', in one pogrom in Torreón at the beginning of the revolution over 250 Chinese died–"more than all the American civilians to be killed in ten years of revolutionary violence" (Knight 1990: 208).

In other countries, the struggle against the internal threat in the interwar period, although in less dramatic forms, was nevertheless continued. The 1938 administratively enforced assimilation of immigrants in Getúlio Vargas's Brazil was an effect of the desire to curtail alleged foreign control and influence. This concerned primarily immigrants from Italy, Germany and Japan. Although authoritarian Brazil traded intensively with Nazi Germany, still Vargas, despite Berlin's protests, prohibited NSDAP activities in Brazil (Wirth 1970: 238). The selective nationalization of foreign capital, intensive indigenization of foreign companies' personnel (e.g. in Chile in 1939) and the policy of national incorporation were perceived as a part of a single whole. It was not a completely new practice. Already in the 1920s half or more jobs in foreign-owned banks, telegraph offices and on ships involved in coastal trade were reserved for Brazilians (Topik 1980: 602).

Even if we take into consideration all the differences between Latin America and Central Europe, it remains true that the Great Depression speeded up the crystallization of behaviors increasingly hostile toward foreigners. Inasmuch as prior to 1929 foreign capital had been denounced mainly by radical students and intellectuals and, less frequently, the industrial or military elite, after that year the situation changed radically. Apprehension in the face of growth in nationalist mood, voiced in the 1920s by a representative of one of the US firms, proved right: "the woods are full of [nationalistic] lions" (quoted in Krenn 1990: 37). Thus, for instance, a British consul in Peru reported in 1931, after the overthrow of President Leguía, that "revolution brought in its train a very strong wave of antiforeign feeling. This feeling had its genesis in the knowledge that the richest natural resources were in the hands of foreigners" (Gurney 1931: 9).

However, much more revealing is the example of Brazil where until the 1930s economic nationalism, although practiced, was nevertheless a marginal intellectual current. As in other Latin American countries, cultural nationalism, which had been developing since the early 20th century, did not refer to economic arguments (Schmitter 1971: 61, Luz 1977: 176). Hence, although Tôrres's book was read, it would play an important ideology-shaping role only after 1929. Neither did relations with the United States present problems. According to contemporary American observers, in the 1920s "[e]conomic nationalism appeared to be a dead letter in Brazil." In 1926, the US Ambassador maintained also that there were "probably few countries where the Communist or Socialist Parties [found] less terrain in which to operate successfully than in Brazil" (Krenn 1990: 124, 126). Both changed completely after the start of the Great Depression. This is vividly illustrated by the fortunes of the activists earlier committed to cultural nationalism:

> Plínio Salgado became the leader of the fascist Integralist party, Oswaldo de Andrade flirted with Communism, Cassiano Ricardo and Menotti del Picchia favored the labor parties, Sérgio Millet, Sérgio Buarque de Holanda and Mário de Andrade, the democratic left (Burns 1968: 67).

At the same time, since 1929 economic nationalism became Brazil's quasi-official policy.

In the 1930s, nationalism directed against the 'selfishness' of foreign investors and financiers became an integral part of common perception. In both regions, governments generally complained about the outflow of profits and capital. Disputes with foreign firms escalated. Describing the situation in Poland, one of the main participants in the interwar economic discussions pointed out that

> [t]he extent and character of foreign control of Polish industry was a source of many difficulties and anomalies. ... The problem of profits and dividends had not only an internal domestic aspect but had also to be regarded from the standpoint of transfer. The control of prices had to be viewed in the same way (quoted in Nötel 1986: 286n).

Sometimes such disputes ended in nationalization. In Latin America, they usually and above all concerned raw materials, as, for instance, in Bolivia which nationalized Standard Oil in 1937. It is worthwhile devoting some attention to this particular case.

Following the 1936 defeat in the war with Paraguay (*La Guerra del Chaco*) and the young colonels' (David Toro, German Busch) coming to power, conceptions of political and economic modernization, which simultaneously referred to socialism, corporatism and fascism (Kula 1999: 29ff) were propagated. That was an enormous change. As late as in the 1920s, the call for nationalization of Bolivia's natural resources–*tierras al pueblo y minas al estado*–by Tristán Marof (1926: 27, 32)[7] had been perceived as dangerous radicalism. After all is said and done it was not without reason that the slogan coined by Tristán Marof became extremely popular. At the same time, extraordinary guarantees and privileges granted by the Bolivian government in the 1920s as collateral to the North American bank loan were treated as nothing out of the ordinary (Haring 1928: 227). Until the 1930s, the three Bolivian tin tycoons' (Simón Patiño, Félix Avelino Aramayo and Mauricio Hochschild) close cooperation with foreign firms, detrimental to Bolivia's interests, had been treated as something equally normal. As Bolivia did not have indigenous tin smelters, its major export commodity was tin ore, with profits taken above all from refined tin produced abroad. In such a situation the "primary objective was to obtain ore at the cheapest possible price. The lower the value of the ore they shipped abroad the less they paid their national government in export taxes" (Pike 1977: 155). The young colonels' junta with its ideological mixtum compositum was a desperate response to the blatant exploitation of the country's resources. Here one should add that the radical project of the Socialist Republic of Chile in 1932, although definitely a more elaborate one, belonged to the same category of nationalist responses to the crisis: "Chilean economic nationalism was related to Chilean state socialism" (Stemplowski 1996: 389). In political terms, however, the difference between these two cases was enormous: the development of a strong socialist party and party-based politics in Chile contrasted with the development of revolutionary-national populism in Bolivia.

Many countries in the two regions either brought up to date or hurriedly passed acts constraining foreign control over natural resources and the banking system as well as indigenizing many areas of social and economic life. In Brazil, "Vargas nationalized the job market by limiting the number of foreigners who could be employed and by restricting many

---

[7] This was the pseudonym of Gustavo A. Navarro, at that time a young diplomat and a future cofounder of the Bolivian Left.

public offices to native-born Brazilians" (Burns 1968: 85). Nostrification (indigenization) campaigns in East and Central Europe were even more radical (Kofman 1997: passim). And from the perspective of foreign firms, all those changes meant also the emergence of a new business culture. Unrestricted access to markets and foreign capital-friendly governments were replaced by centralization and a 'negotiated environment'. The change was well captured by an executive of a US oil company operating in Czechoslovakia, who when faced with the government's offer to join a national cartel agreement said:

> While these combinations were theoretically voluntary, no company–certainly no foreign company–could invite the consequences of acting counter to the wishes of the locally owned companies and the urge of the government (Wilkins 1974: 205, 235).

All the same, when highlighting the range of this and other practices included in the arsenal of nationalist economic policy ('enlightened autarky' as they put it in Poland), we must not lose sight of the fact that the foreign capital attacked was at the same time a scarce commodity and very much sought after. The same could be said of the access to foreign markets. Grumbling about foreign firms' egoism concerned both the high profits they made (and took out) and their reluctance to make new investments. Poland's deflationary policy as a proof of good economic conduct and creditworthiness was not enough to secure new loans. Hence Polish disappointment with the foreign banks' unfavorable attitude toward the COP investment program. The only loan obtained was from France. At the initial stage of the program implementation, i.e. in 1936/37, its share in total investment outlays reached 12.5 percent, declining to 2 percent in the following year (Drozdowski 1963: 137). After the lack of financial aid at the beginning of the 1930s, that was another signal that the country should rely, first of all, on domestic resources. Thus, in 1936 Kwiatkowski (1988: 107) wrote: "Let us cooperate with foreign capital whenever possible ... but let us not count on a foreign volunteer army" (see also Landau and Tomaszewski 1989: 282f, Landau and Roszkowski 1995: 46, 194f). Vargas was more successful. He skillfully overcame the US government's and business circles' negative attitude toward the program for development of a modern steel industry in his country: first, he approached a German competitor, and then made the most of new external circumstances, i.e. growing international tensions preceding the outbreak of WWII (Baer 1969: 68–76, Wirth 1970: part 2). Thus, nationalist moods in the two regions were stirred up by both the actual losses due to the crisis and the reluctant position taken by foreign banks and investors. This was already thinking in categories of holistic nationalism. The development of new artificial industries and re-orientation toward the development of the domestic market were elements of that change.

'THOSE WHO DON'T OBEY THE RULES WIN': BEYOND ORTHODOXY

After 1929 all countries in the two regions experienced deflationary policies, as recommended by mainstream economics. All of them also registered little if no success with it. But in the majority of countries (although not in Poland) this episode did not last very long. Governments tried to find ways out of crisis beyond liberal economic theory and, actually, in defiance of it. Non-orthodoxy was the product of disappointment. At the same time, the larger Latin American countries parted with passive economic policies much faster than Poland. In point of fact, it was this practice, even during the period of deflationary policy, that was the decisive factor in the birth of holistic nationalism. The defense of the balance-of-payments, and even a minimum level of domestic effective demand in backward countries, gradually initiated a mechanism favorable for 'internal market orientation'. The pace of change was different in particular countries: relatively quick, for instance, in Brazil and Romania, slow in Poland, with Argentina in the middle. This does not change the general picture in the 1930s of giving a definite national character to economic processes in the peripheries, and of increasingly relating them to internal priorities and incentives.

The term 'internal marker orientation' oversimplifies, to some extent, the specific character of these changes. In practice, they involved measures close to later Keynesianism, which in view of the use of the unorthodox methods combined to push state interventionism to a new level and new direction: deficit-financed public works and support for agriculture, devaluation, quantitative restrictions (QR) on imports and other aggressive methods of foreign trade promotion. Although still framed in the orthodox deflationary policy, in Poland, already in 1930 the share of direct and indirect subsidies to exports reached 30 percent (Nötel 1986: 232). And this was only the beginning.

This was, however, a particular kind of Keynesianism: intuitive or "inadvertent," which only in the early 1950s was "rationalized, legitimized, theorized, and institutionalized by ECLA" (Drake 2005: 75).

The concept of intuitive Keynesianism has a triple meaning.

Firstly, it indicates the appearance of specific methods for supporting domestic effective demand, first of all in agriculture. For understandable reasons. In 1935 Kwiatkowski (1988: 101) wrote in desperation that Poland "need[ed] neither tariffs nor protectionism ... but she need[ed] the domestic consumer, which [was] not there." Agrarian interventionism was designed to save such a consumer. Parenthetically, the importance of such particular demand was also strongly emphasized on the global scale. The hypothesis that the persistence of the Great Depression resulted from the combination of economic nationalism of the core countries, the global overproduction of food and the appearance of the 'price scissors problem' sounds plausible (see Lewis 1949: 57, 155, 197, Latham 1981: passim).

Needless to say, the policy of protecting rural income and attempts to control prices for and supply of agricultural products was launched on a large scale in developed countries as well. Suffice to mention the robust programs of the F. D. Roosevelt administration (Garraty 1986). In underdeveloped countries, however, such policy had a different significance as it concerned not only the majority of the population, but also the strategically important export sector. Therefore historians relate the effectiveness of the anti-crisis policy to the effectiveness (and scale) of the agricultural support programs. In the opinion of Landau (1972), the insufficient scale of such policy in Poland contributed to the aggravation of crisis, whereas its effectiveness (and grand scale) in Brazil, argued Furtado (1967), enabled the resumption of growth of both GDP and industry. Although in the early 1970's Furtado was criticized for his bold hypothesis that deficit-financed intervention in the coffee sector played the major role in extricating the Brazilian economy out of crisis in the early 1930s, in the end, however, leading historians have proved his hypothesis to have been right (see Baer 2008: 39f, Fishlow 1972: 327ff).

What is more important, programs to protect the purchasing power of the rural population and, above all of the coffee sector, were favorable to that part of the economic elite that until 1929 had exerted a decisive influence on the peripheral state and its economy. Thus, together with the maintenance of the social status quo in the countryside, the conditions were created for including traditional societal actors in new, already pro-industry, coalitions. In Brazil, following the defeat of the *paulista* revolt in 1932, the agrarian elites found their place in the new state, although they lost their dominant political influence (Schmitter 1971: 371ff). In Chile, the foundation in 1935 of the Corporación de Fomento a la Producción (CORFO)–the leading institution implementing elements of the holistic nationalism program–was in point of fact possible owing to the compromise struck in the 1930s with agrarian elites regarding labor (and property) relations in agriculture (Collier and Sater 1996: 265ff, 269, Thorp 1998: 121). This compromise exerted a strong influence on both the industrialization process itself and the social development of the periphery in the decades that followed.

Secondly, the concept of intuitive Keynesianism went beyond a short-term intervention in agriculture. It embraced the idea that in backward countries 'internal market orientation' had to lead to reallocation of resources, and thus to the policy of industrialization or at least attempts to initiate one. Under the continuing disintegration of the world economy, the resumption and maintenance of growth could not just be a result of short-term measures aimed at protecting the balance-of-payments and supporting, via budget deficits and devaluations, the hitherto demand profile. Increasing the level of capacity utilization was linked with the creation of new productive capacities in new lines of production. The economists of the time saw and stressed the difference between Keynes' theory and intuitive Keynesianism (Studentowicz 1939), something that is obvious today. In passing, already before WWI, the preoccupation with the structure of national income and criticism of abstract "distribution" and financial flows was the guiding motif of the nationalist conceptions of the Italian Alfredo Rocco (De Rosa 2000: 180f). Thus, a proper product-mix, the essence of economic independence, made up the basic element of nascent holistic economic nationalism. "For entire centuries," Kwiatkowski (1989: 301) wrote, "we have been a nation of peasants; today, we must become a multifunctional nation, a community of merchants, industrialists, farmers, blue- and white-collar workers."

Such nationalism was developing partly as a spontaneous and partly as a top-down process of 'creeping into' industrialization. Passing over all other factors, all the same the combination of economic policy, spontaneity and unpredictability, and also the composition of the coalition of societal actors who supported industrialization after 1929, meant that initiating and continuing it was by no means a linear process. That applied to Brazil after 1945 when the country temporarily returned to the export economy model (Love 1996b: 214f, 1996: 148; Ianni 1971: chapter 3). In Peru, attempts to return to the old model were made already in the 1930s: "instant default, gaining of room for manoeuvre, and move back into pattern of following exports. This route ... reflected in the relatively slow growth of industry and the few signs of progress in import-substitution" (Thorp and Londoño 1984: 102; see also Cheesman Rajkovic 1986). And finally, the attempts at industrialization made by and large did not prove

Gerschenkron's hypothesis that late industrialization led to the transfer of the latest technologies (Teichova 1985: 253). With regard to Brazil, Fishlow (1972: 311) argued that the impulse of the Great Depression "represented technologically inferior [import] substitution." Hence, the examples of the earlier industrial spurts were not followed. To what extent, however, such a conclusion is applicable to investment projects in Brazil and Poland in the late 1930s (and in Brazil after WWII) remains a subject of controversy. In the assessment of holistic nationalism, this issue is of key importance.

Thirdly, in certain underdeveloped countries state interventionism manifested itself as etatism which, admittedly, Keynes did not rule out, but was not very enthusiastic about. The growth of the public sector, which made progress alongside the growth of private protection markets of cartelized sectors (Yeager 1980), was reflected in the redistribution of power in the economy and society. The state not only supported and assisted, but gradually took over the leading role, including the already existing private capital groups in industrialization projects. Consequently, holistic economic nationalism as an ideological construct appears to be, above all, in praise of the state and an embodiment of the *raison d'état*, and in the majority of cases as ideological justification of authoritarian rule.

The theoretical implications of the emerging holistic nationalism were something more than criticism–via actual practice–of the agrarian-export orientation. One should always bear in mind that the mainstream economics of the time either ignored the phenomenon of industrialization in backward countries or treated it as an anomaly. The descriptions and empirical analyses published usually abided by a similar convention. "It will not be the privilege of the present generation," insisted one US observer in the 1920s, "to witness anything like an industrialization of South America" (Haring 1928: 30). The recommendations of the 1931 Sir Otto Niemeyer mission to Brazil stressed only the need to diversify agriculture, while disregarding industry (Burns 1970: 308, Baer 2008: 44). Such an intellectual atmosphere made it hard to formulate an answer to the question about appropriate industrial development directions after 1929. On the other hand, in the peripheries theories justifying the abandonment of the dominant economic orthodoxy were relatively rare. Manoilescu's theory of protectionism was an exception (Kofman 1997: 13ff). "The national-economic ideal of nationalism" (Michels 1931: 585), expressed in the criticism of the primary export orientation, and the suggestions pointing to the need to adjust the supply profile to the domestic demand profile did not belong to the mainstream economics of the time. The nascent holistic nationalism was therefore inevitably a rebellion; it assumed that "[t]hose who don't obey the rules win" (Bairoch 1993: 168; see also Chang 2005: passim).

Non-orthodoxy as a response to the exogenously determined collapse of trade and terms of trade, international finance and investments and to the general decline in trust and creditworthiness became the norm. Along with dumping, clearing agreements and other forms of control over trade, exchange controls were imposed, foreign loan defaults declared and negotiations for debt conversion initiated. The first to default in Latin America, in January 1931, was Bolivia. In that same year, Chile, Ecuador, Peru and Brazil suspended debt payments (Marichal 1989: 212f). In East and Central Europe, Hungary was the first to introduce, in July 1931, exchange controls, soon to be followed by others, with the exception of Poland. The next step was to declare, between 1932 and 1933, moratoriums on transfers. In Latin America as of the end of 1935, the default index (the ratio of defaulted loans to all loans) reached 71.8 percent, in East and Central Europe 88.4 percent against the world average of 35.3 percent (Stallings 1987: 77). With their backs to the wall because of the balance-of-payments crisis the governments of particular countries desperately made debt payments conditional—as the Chilean government put it in 1931—on "the restoration of trade and of conditions that [would] promote it" (quoted in Winkler 1933: 249).

And such non-orthodoxy paid off: "the data for the 1930s suggest a positive relationship between default and subsequent economic performance" (Eichengreen and Portes 1989: 26). The reasoning behind the non-orthodox behavior of Brazil was well reflected in the memo prepared by a Rothschild and Sons representative:

> the Brazilians knew that they had no credit and ... they thought therefore that they might as well cease payments on their External Debt. There were many people who wished to devote sums now used to pay interest to the internal needs of the Country and that were exerting strong pressure on the President and the Finance Minister to cease payments (quoted in Eichengreen and Portes 1992: 18).

Poland suspended debt payments only in 1936, having added in the preceding years to the exogenously determined shocks the costs of "unsparing domestic deflation" (Nötel 1986: 228); this resulted in depressed domestic demand, in an overvalued złoty and in net transfers of capital. As a consequence, between 1929 and 1935, the outflow of capital amounted to $340 million, equal to 75 percent of investment outlays between 1936 and 1939 (Drozdowski 1963: 135, Landau and Tomaszewski 1982: 396). Paradoxically, what helped reduce East and Central European debt most was the devaluation, in the 1930s, of the creditor countries' currencies. On this account alone, the total debt of the region, which in 1931 stood at $3.8 billion, was by 1937 cut down to $2.2 billion (Nötel 1986: 261; for Poland see Drozdowski 1963: 243).

At this point, one should take note of the controversial and often misinterpreted problem of autarky.

In the relatively advanced peripheral countries, such as Poland, Mexico and Brazil, behaviors directed against foreigners and rejection of 'obeying the rules' were never expressed in a preference for a literally understood self-sufficiency or autarky. Autarky would be tantamount to a total economic collapse. That is why "the tendency to fence oneself off," observed by Kurt Baumann[8] (1933) when he wrote about East and Central Europe, or Latin America's aspirations for "economic independence" (Behrendt 1941) should not be understood as intentional cutting off of the economies from the outside world. The external shocks forced the emergence of such tendencies: the world crisis brought into question not just the economic rationality of the hitherto policy and economic structures. Along with the declining trade and foreign capital inflows, pressure on the state from particular societal actors increased and as a result ever new economic spheres came within the orbit of the state bureaucracy's interest and intervention. General and particularistic interest were intertwined in this process. In this way, the Brazilian ban on imports of textile machines in the 1930s resulted not from an autarkic policy but from the demands of the industrialists, who warned of a danger of overproduction. The terms of trade shocks and drastic restrictions in access to external financial assets demanded that internal resources of financing and growth be sought and mobilized.

As a policy choice (and ideological option), however, autarky was actually a marginal current (Heilperin 1960: 27). After all is said and done, Baumann assessed the situation wrongly. His claim, that one of the main sources of autarkic tendencies was the policies of the Central European authoritarian governments, and speaking more broadly–of the countries aiming to create "national industrial capitalism," was wrong on two counts. First, at that time industrialization was in core countries misleadingly

---

[8] That was the pseudonym of the future co-founder of development economics Kurt Mandelbaum, who until his emigration to Great Britain had been linked with the Frankfurt Institute for Social Research.

considered equivalent to autarky, particularly in Germany. The "Sombart paradox" was in the ascendency. At the same time many peripheral countries were desperately trying to combine attempts at import substitution with an increased volume of primary exports necessary to finance essential capital goods imports. A contemporary observer rightly noted that during the crisis, Latin American countries "[went] in for some industrialization but they [did] not want to sacrifice their foreign markets" (Bonn 1938: 189). The same could be said about Central Europe (for Poland see Drozdowski 1963: 174). The results in the major Latin American countries, except for Argentina, were positive: "[they] found ... delicate balance whereby they could diversify without killing the goose that laid the golden eggs–the export sector" (Thorp 1998: 116). In East and Central Europe in the years 1929–1933, the decline in foreign trade in value terms was much deeper than the world average. As in Latin America, East and Central Europe's immediate response to the balance-of-payments and domestic market collapse was a dramatic increase in the volume of exports and curtailment of imports (Drabek 1985: 433, 456). The ever higher degree of self-sufficiency was, however, the result, not the cause. Second, peripheral Europe's economic significance to the European economy as a whole was negligible: in 1938 the region's contribution to the overall European industrial output was 8 percent (Rothschild 1974: 15). It was simply impossible for underdeveloped East and Central Europe to fulfill the role of one of the "autarky centers."

Of course, on a graph showing the continuum of attitudes toward foreign capital and self-sufficiency, it would not be difficult to identify the political currents opting for isolation from the international market and for autarky. In Germany, in the period preceding Hitler's rise to power, such an option was represented by *Die Tat,* the influential conservative revolutionary (*konservativen Revolutionäre*) and elitist monthly and its circle. It was precisely *Die Tat* circle which rediscovered for the German public the concept of autarky, understanding it, after all is said and done, not selectively, but totally (Hoffmann 1932: 500). Werner Sombart, venerated by nationalist circles, enhanced this tendency. Among the nine variants of autarky analyzed by Hoffmann one can find, alongside *Die Tat* circle, also the concepts of the NSDAP economic ideologues, "national Bolsheviks" and anti-capitalist Nazis from the Otto Strasser group. For other reasons, communists, too, were in favor of autarky (Hoffmann 1932, Mommsen 1996: 348–350, Leibovitz 1969: chapter 6).

Differences apart, all contemporary concepts of autarky referred in one way or another to the practice of protectionism and economic ideas developed in previous decades. In the 1930s they took the form, among other things, of the conception of an economic bloc that would include Germany and Central and South Eastern Europe and that would compete with the West (*Die Tat* circle project). The Nazis presented this idea as a concept of the Economy of the Great Area (*Grossraumwirtschaft*) and of "living space" (*Lebensraum*) (Hossbach 1949, Overy 2003: 176f). In Mussolini's Italy strong autarkic tendencies appeared as early as in 1926, primarily in response to outside shocks. These tendencies manifested themselves in the Battle for Grain (that followed a crop failure) and the Battle for the Lira (that followed the Italian currency slump) (Gregor 1979: 140–152, De Rosa 2000). And, needless to say, one should not pass over the USSR, where the program of forced industrialization had–with some important exceptions such as imports of modern technologies–a quasi-autarkic nature. After all, Evgeny Preobrazhensky, a Bolshevik leader and theoretician, wrote about "socialist protectionism" several years ahead of the Stalinist industrial spurt. Such protectionism would be an integral part of accelerated industrialization, which implied the operation of "the law of primitive socialist accumulation" and "non-equivalent exchange with the countryside" (Preobrazhensky 1965: 121f; see also Berend 1998: 214–217).[9]

In a word, in underdeveloped countries the autarkic option never became a major political-economic and/or ideological current. The frequently raised problem of greater control over foreign capital, of restricting its political influence and of subordinating it to the 'national interest' did not mean the choice of forming an iron curtain that would isolate the nation from the international market. Let me add here that in his famous article Keynes did not at all raise this ambivalence inherent in the nationalism of the periphery. For him it was obvious that industrialization understood as self-sufficiency was possible. Underdevelopment and industrialization were not his field of interest. Political and economic nationalism as the "future" of the world and as a "new dynamic force" was praised also by such moderate advocates of etatism and economic nationalism as Kwiatkowski in Poland; however, it was not understood as an appeal for total isolation. After all, it was characteristic that a socialist critic of Kwiatkowski interpreted his words as praise of reactionary

---

[9] Yet, the self-sufficiency about which Preobrazhensky wrote did not mean total isolation. Communist economic nationalism never led–because of mimetic industrialization–to breaking off the relationship with the international market (Szlajfer 1997: 51f, Díaz Alejandro 1978, Senghass 1985). A Polish contemporary observer of the first two years of the Soviet industrialization spurt rightly pointed out the role of foreign trade in that project (Kwiatkowski 1989: 242–247).

inward-oriented nationalism (Żuławski 1939: 221ff). Autarky as a nonoption was also obvious for Polish radical integral nationalists who insisted on the creation of a national economy based on small property ("the socialization of property") as an alternative to capitalist and Marxist materialism. Pointing out that "a nation taking its first steps along the road to industrialization will be content with partial tariff protection of its industry," would also need a flow of "honest foreign capital" (Doboszyński 1939: 111). The National Democratic party (*endecja*), the very incarnation of Polish integral nationalism, accepted these theses without qualification.

At the opposite end of the political spectrum, when in 1931 Victor Raúl Haya de la Torre was beginning his struggle for power in Peru, representing the revolutionary-populist APRA, both in propaganda and in confidential talks with the US ambassador and business people, he dissociated himself from the conception of discriminating against foreign capital in general (Davies, Jr.: 1978: 138f). On the contrary, his conception of imperialism as "*la primera etapa del capitalismo*" in peripheral countries and the revolutionary-national and corporatist "Aprista state" implied industrialization without breaking ties with the world economy and in cooperation with foreign investors (Haya de la Torre: 1931, 1972, 1977, Hirschman 1961: 10f).

One can suppose that the position of Haya de la Torre was to some extent influenced by the experience of Mexico. Despite his violent dispute with oil companies and the government of the United States, President Calles, while attacking the "conquistador capital," thought it was obvious that Mexico needed foreign capital, which was "conscious of its mission in the modern world" (quoted in Dobrzycki 1986: 194f). It was, so to speak, natural. In relations with foreign capital, the policy of post-revolutionary governments did not differ much form the policy toward Mexican entrepreneurs. The concept of the "revolutionary capitalist" presented in *Decalogo del Capitalista Revolucionario* by Alberto J. Pani (otherwise the effective minister of finance under President Calles) served as propaganda of the idea that the creation of a strong class of Mexican entrepreneurs was a key element of the Mexican national revolution (Córdova 2003: 367f, Dobrzycki 1986: 194f).[10] This concept was evidence of the revolutionary leaders' conviction that the "socialism of the Mexican revolution" brought workers and peasants as well as local entrepreneurs under a protective umbrella. That was also the approach taken in the 1930s by President

---

[10] The first paragraph of that "Decalogue" read: *No mantendras ocioso tu capital y lo invertiras de modo reproductivo en tu pais* (Thou shalt not use your capital inactively, but thou shalt invest it in a productive way in your country) (quoted in Córdova 2003: 367f).

Lazaro Cárdenas, wrongly accused of bolshevism. Although strongly supportive of labor unions and peasants, he nevertheless decidedly dissociated himself from Soviet "state communism" as from an "exotic system" (Dobrzycki 1986: 244f).

Thus, the conception of the closed economic system, tested during WWII–with horrifying results–in the German *Grossraumwirtschaft* and the Japanese Greater East Asia Co-Prosperity Sphere, could not materialize in peripheral economies, because such attempts were never made. By definition, bringing the projects of holistic nationalism into effect assumed maintaining, not severing, the tightly controlled relations with the world economy.

Nevertheless, in conditions when autarky was a non-option and the export economy was a variant of the market economy that "refused to function" (Polanyi 1957: 239), it was extremely difficult to determine where particularistic nationalism ended and the outlines of holistic economic nationalism appeared. On the other hand, however, a holistic nationalism that was out of touch with the interests of societal actors was unthinkable. Despite the shock caused by the Great Depression nowhere did the economic autonomy of the state express itself in the marginalization of economic elites and complete disregard of their opinion and influence. Not even in Hitler's Germany or Mussolini's Italy, even though initially fascists' anti-class economic slogans worried and bewildered "also the classes that helped Fascism into power" (Röpke 1935: 89). After all, political marginalization did not mean social and/or economic annihilation (Turner 1985: 338, Gregor 1979: passim).

Those complicated relationships found their reflection both in historians' debates as well as in real economic processes. In Brazil, these issues emerged as arguments about *intencionalidade* and the continuity of Vargas's industrial policy in the 1930s. For certain historians, contrary to Furtado, Dean and Wirth, Vargas's 'developmentalism' had appeared as a well-thought out project already in the early 1930s. Thus the transition to the authoritarian regime only accelerated industrialization and accompanying institution-building (Hilton 1975, Fonseca 2003). Polish discussions concentrated, in turn, on the questions as to why only as late as 1936 did economic decision-makers resort to strong interventionism, this time clearly aimed at industrialization, and why until 1936 had state interventionism been reflecting, instead of development goals, "the principle of the golden mean" (Kofman 1986: 122).

Among the many factors blocking such a transition, Kofman points out in particular the effects of the political economy: until 1936, the economic policy of the Polish governments had practically been a hostage to the unresolved conflict between industrial and agrarian-commercial groups. The lack of "a modern, clear conception of the country's development," underpinned by a deflationary psychosis and the principle of a 'sound budget', was its consequence. Wojciech Roszkowski shares this view: "The controversy over the choice of either the industrial or agricultural development path of the Polish economy was not decided in a definitive way." He adds, however, that "it resulted primarily from concern for the social and political stability of the state, which had good reasons to worry about its existence anyway" (Landau and Roszkowski 1995: 216). It is difficult to regard such justification of the "golden mean" policy as convincing. At this point, however, I will pass over this issue.

But it is important that these two leading Polish historians have shown how until 1936 state policy had been hindered by a deadlock imposed by the conflicting interests of societal actors. The post-1926 authoritarian regime was a part of, not a solution to, this problem also in the first years of the Great Depression. And the risk-avoiding industrialists who– like the agrarian sector– focused their attention and efforts on control of labor costs, tax concessions and state subsidies, were of limited help in pushing toward a more resolute countercyclical policy. The government's indecision in the early years of the crisis was, according to Roszkowski, proof that "it is hard to say that the policy of the Polish governments was unequivocally 'class-based'" (Landau and Roszkowski 1995: 218). He is probably right. Still, the passiveness this kind of state autonomy-in-reverse implied resulted in prolonged crisis. Unlike the Polish government, whose activity had been until 1936 paralyzed by political-economic deadlock, the Vargas government demonstrated, in 1930–1935, a greater degree of flexibility and determination in dealing with the crisis and societal actors' demands. The exchange controls imposed in 1931 outraged both planters and industrialists, the massive coffee purchases rescued the former but at the same time the newly-introduced land tax "appeared to them to be a kind of confiscation" (Dean 1969: 192). In hindsight, the 1932 armed conflict with *paulistas* turned out to be an important development, leading to a redefinition and weakening of the role of traditional elites.

The Polish government moved beyond autonomy-as-passivity only in the final years preceding WWII. The political stability and *raison d'état* arguments, quoted by Roszkowski as justification for passivity, were used in the new increasingly volatile context of European politics as arguments for rapid change. The "principle of the golden mean" was replaced by a policy of accelerated industrialization and questioning the primacy of particularistic societal actors' interests, including those of private industrial groups. In May 1936, Kwiatkowski submitted a four-year investment plan, to be financed primarily through domestic savings and credits. The plan provided for investment spending to the tune of $310–340 million. In fact, from 1936 until mid-1939 circa $450 million was invested (in the years 1936/1937–1938/1939 total budget receipts amounted to $1.44 billion). A part of this plan was the ambitious COP project (Drozdowski 1963: 27, 68, 137, 234). At the same time, foreign debt payments were suspended, negotiations on loan conversion initiated, foreign exchange and trade control tightened and certain key foreign-owned companies nationalized. In this way the autonomy of the state was redefined. However, the cost of passivity that preceded this breakthrough was enormous.

One can speak of a similar rupture in the case of Brazil, once the Estado Nôvo was established. Immediately after the 1937 *autogolpe*, three measures were introduced by the Vargas government: suspension of all payments on external debt, monopoly in the sale of foreign exchange and a tax on all exchange transactions. What is more, although "Vargas continued to search for ways of stimulating exports, the conception of priorities had dramatically altered." The new situation the transition to authoritarian regime created "evoked no opposition from the industrialists. It can be imagined that many ... found much in the new order with which to console themselves" (Dean 1969: 212, 209). New corporatist-cum-technocratic style channels of interest articulation and of influencing policy-making were created.

As already mentioned, intellectual attempts to break with the traditional export orientation had been made earlier, in the latter half of the 19th century. Yet, at that time projects for state-initiated and coordinated robust industrialization represented a keen intuition rather than a practical program. The ideas promoted by Alejandro E. Bunge in Argentina, in the years 1918–1927, should be assessed differently. His point of departure was Argentina's already advanced industrial development and the problems connected with its continuation. When writing about *la independencia económica de que hasta hoy carecemos* (Bunge 1918: 253), he referred above all to the experience of WWI. The sudden fall in imports from Britain, which caused economic chaos and inflation, was a signal for him that a far-reaching diversification of the country's economic structure was necessary. He also maintained that the lessening of external dependence required much greater protectionism than the one ensured by the current tariffs. Moreover, import substitution should not be limited to natural industries alone. In Bunge's opinion, the adjustment process forced by the war showed that, despite the high cost, it was feasible. What is more, also the loss of the comparative advantage in Argentina's grain and meat exports justified greater industrial protectionism, import of capital goods and diversification of the economy. The relevant measures should be supplemented with Argentina's participation in the establishment of a Unión Aduanera del Sud (Solberg 1973, Haring 1928, Lewis 1990). Yet, contrary to the hopes Bunge had pinned on the Unión Industrial Argentina, the activities of that organization in the 1920s fell short of his expectations. And this despite the strong leadership of Luís Colombo, the "wunderkind" of Argentine politics and industry. Like Bunge, Colombo, too, "brushed aside any distinction between natural and artificial industry. ... He also denied that industrial and agrarian interests were opposed" (Lewis 1990: 89).

However, among the precursors of holistic nationalism in Latin America, Roberto C. Simonsen, from the late 1920s "Brazil's most influential spokesman for industry" (Love 1996a: 11) and the "creator of a persuasive ideology of national independence through industrialization" (Schmitter 1971: 147) ranks highest. Although under the Estado Nôvo the political influence of Simonsen, strongly involved with the *paulista* elite, was limited, nevertheless he played an important leadership role in public debates, both toward the end of the Old Republic, and during Vargas's rule.

Not only Simonsen, but other members of the 1928 established Centro das Indústrias do Estado de São Paulo (CIESP), also knew Manoilescu's *Theory of Protectionism*, and it was CIESP that led to its publication in 1931. According to Eugênio Gudin, a liberal critic of Simonsen and Manoilescu, the book was "distributed as a kind of bible of protectionism" (Love 1996a: 145). However, unless the *Theory* was confined to the technical problem of protectionist tariffs alone, translating the theory of the Romanian economist into practical recommendations was not easy. The difficulties were reflected glaringly in Simonsen's conceptions formulated prior to 1930, especially in their guarded low-voice polemical tone concerning agricultural interests. This ambiguity first and foremost testified to the resistance of the agrarian elite to plans for more intensive industrialization, which implied a re-allocation of resources, particularly of labor, to industry. This applies in particular to Simonsen's 1928 program statement he made as the first vice-president of CIESP, in which he presented industrialists' broad view of Brazil's future.

Powerful Francisco Matarazzo, CIESP president, set the tone of Simonsen's address, saying: "It is obvious that there is an absolute correlation between the ends that industrialists have in view and the true interests of the nation" (quoted in Dean 1969: 141). Simonsen (1973: 53–65) took up this idea:

> Brazilians who combat the implementation and diffusion of industries in the country are consciously or unconsciously acting on behalf of foreign nations interested in the conquest of our markets, working to return us to the position of a colony of foreign producers.

Engaging in polemics with opponents of the development of industry (of artificial industries in particular), he put forward a number of historical and statistical arguments to the effect that "[e]conomic independence, and thus perfect political independence [could] exist ... in the countries where agriculture and industry [were] harmoniously united." He defended the development of artificial industries, referring to the example of Great Britain, which imported most raw materials for its industries, to the opinion of the Argentine Manuel Ugarte, and to the threat to Brazilian interests posed by the industrial expansion of the Argentine rival. Next, he rejected one of the agrarian elite's main objections that industrial development had thus far disorganized the rural labor market by drawing labor away from the coffee sector. In subtle and toned-down criticism of the elite he highlighted that industry could not be held responsible for such a state of affairs: 3.8 percent of the economically active population employed in industry (1 percent in the modern industry) could not bring such negative results. He added that industrial development would become a necessity also in view of agricultural countries' unfavorable terms of trade. He refuted the charge that protectionism contributed to rising costs of living, arguing that the current high tariffs were primarily of a fiscal, not pro-ndustry, nature; thus, while contributing to rising costs of living anyway they could not be used to provide support for industrial development. To posit modern customs tariffs and a change in tariff policy preferences was therefore logical.

Simonsen's address was a precisely constructed argument aimed at convincing economic elites of the need to accelerate industrialization. Still Simonsen evaded defining the area of conflicting interests of industrial groups on the one hand, and agrarian and commercial groups on the other. As Dean (1969: 145) observes, his criticism of the latter was indirect and unsatisfactory:

> it is obvious that industry does indeed increase the wages of labor, and an aggressive and fervent promoter of industrialization would almost certainly claim this effect as his principal goal. But Simonsen could not. It would derail the alliance he sought to achieve: *Paulista* industrialization would have to be contained within the existing structure.

Well, Simonsen's timid and unsatisfactory answer misled neither the representatives of the powerful Associação Comercial of Rio de Janeiro, acting for the merchant elite, and the influential Sociedade Rural Brasileira (Schmitter 1971: 148, 431, Luz 1978: 162). They sensed, correctly, that there was something new and threatening in his presentation, and that Simonsen's plea for a modern tariff schedule went beyond the traditional bargaining position of industrialists.

Nonetheless, those oblique utterances meant that the dispute on how to interpret Simonsen's address lasted for several decades. Put in a nutshell, was Simonsen striving to extend the industrial groups' political and economic role within the coalition controlled by the agrarian and export elite or was he rather trying to outline Brazil's new prospects for economic development, and in effect, for a coalition of a new type?

Juxtaposing Simonsen's views with the radical protectionism of Alexandre Siciliano Jr., Dean is inclined to accept the former interpretation. However, one should bear in mind that this influential industrialist expressed his views in 1931, that is in a completely different political and economic situation. At any rate, in Dean's (1969:144) opinion, Simonsen "remained ... thoroughly the product of the plantation society in his understanding, or lack of understanding, concerning the power of industry to transform society." On the other hand, Schmitter (1971: 148) tends to accept the latter interpretation. In his opinion, Simonsen's address was "a virtuoso performance." Although it revealed a tendency to maintain "natural harmony among the specialized components of the 'productive classes'," essentially it

> marked the beginning of a new ideology of industrialization. ... this ideology gradually became the orthodox nationalist position. In Simonsen, the Brazilian industrial class found its most articulate spokesman and its most active interest-group entrepreneur.

I think Schmitter's opinion is more convincing, even though he confines himself to analyzing Simonsen's pre-1930 position (see also Luz 1978: 163). In point of fact, the case of Simonsen showed vividly the situation in which representatives of industrialists and other economic interest groups found themselves at the threshold of changes initiated by the Great Depression shock. They were ready to accept the blessing of industrialization and nationalism, but only within a clearly defined institutional framework that would elevate their role. The evolution of Simonsen's views in the 1930s suggested a flexible adjustment of his initial position to new developments taking place under Vargas authoritarian rule. In the late 1930s he was no longer speaking *sotto voce*, but was on Vargas's side. The famous Simonsen-Gudin debate of 1944–1945 marked a symbolic end to any doubts concerning his understanding of the epoch-making role of industry.

Economic Independence as State Business: *Étatisme*

In 1928 and the early 1930s, Simonsen and the CIESP were exponents of the industrial groups already present in the political and economic life of Brazil, aspiring for greater autonomy. Their ongoing emancipation from the tutelage of traditional commercial associations was a fact (Diniz 1989, Schmitter 1971, Luz 1978). Nevertheless, it would be wrong to equate the idea and practical experience of the Brazilian industrialization of the 1930s with these particular groups and their ambitions. Another group of decision-makers and other societal actors and institutions acted as protagonists of holistic nationalism. This became very visible in the latter half of the 1930s, after the Estado Nôvo had been established. The transition to authoritarian rule meant a rapid autonomization of the state and accelerating growth of a "state technostructure" (*tecnoestructura estatal*), a process which had already started in the early 1930s. This new structure, unifying political and economic decision-making and subordinated to executive power, remained beyond the control of traditional interest groups and, until 1937, of parliament (Ianni 1971: 4, 8, 25). At the same time new channels for private sector (subordinate) participation in the drafting of economic policies were created. A strengthened federal state also meant a rapid rise in the bureaucracy. Between 1920 and 1940, employment in federal institutions more than doubled, having increased sharply after 1937 (Schmitter 1971: 33).

Simonsen and the CIESP's reference group, primarily the industrial elite of São Paulo, represented an initially rival model of industrialization. This elite not only tried to find a place for itself in the ideology of economic nationalism, but also wanted to become a subject and the main point of reference of the industrialization project. Therefore it was apparent that at least until the mid-1930s Simonsen had neither foreseen nor, subsequently, supported economic nationalism in the etatized form. On the contrary, although he saw the need for state intervention, he nevertheless opposed the concept of the state-as-producer to the concept of the strong regulatory state. Industrialization was a task for private investors. When, however, after 1937 the development of the capital-intensive, modern iron and steel industry had been put on the agenda, Simonsen changed his viewpoint substantially. It was obvious for him that private investors were unable to bear the burden of this type of investment. What is more, he began to equate the concept of government intervention not only with tariffs, devaluations and other protectionist measures, but also with planning and direct involvement in production. In 1939, still before Vargas had made a final decision on the Volta Redonda project, his worries concerned precisely the lack of a clearly devised state economic policy and of coordination (Simonsen 1973: 43). But even before 1937, when discussing a trade treaty with the USA, he proposed the creation of a national export institute with quite an impressive mandate: from export promotion and quotas negotiations to rationalization of "industrial and agricultural production, and consumption in the domestic market. ... However vaguely worded, it was a proposal to associate interest groups directly in the planning process" (Wirth 1970: 48f). At the same time Simonsen did not become an unswerving etatist. The concept of state-private mixed enterprises was a way to defend the interests of his reference group. Mergers with foreign capital and other forms of private investors' participation in government projects were one of the variants of involving Brazilian entrepreneurs in the industrialization projects he was considering (Wirth 1970: 83, 126f).

Before Simonsen turned to planning and the concept of mixed enterprises, his views on the role of the private sector in industrialization had largely coincided with the position taken by the influential entrepreneurs' organizations in Poland. This concerned in particular the ideas developed and policies pressed for by Lewiatan, the powerful Central Union of Polish Industry, Mining, Trade, and Finance, led until 1939 by Andrzej Wierzbicki. However, unlike Simonsen, in the 1920s and 1930s Wierzbicki and Lewiatan members remained extremely orthodox opponents of the growing role of the state-as-producer and thus of the etatist variant of industrialization and economic nationalism. And planning, going beyond the protectionism and cartel policies in support of big industry, definitely was not on their agenda (Dziewulski 1981, Kofman 1986). At the same time, until 1929 they had simply overestimated the strength of the Polish private sector. That was clearly demonstrated in 1926, when during a meeting with the Prime Minister, Wierzbicki declared on behalf of Lewiatan: "We do not come to you, Mr. Prime Minister, as supplicants ... we come here in order to ... reach an agreement with Mr. Prime Minister on how to join forces to pursue State policy" (quoted in Janus 2009: 218). Still in the 1920s Wierzbicki and Lewiatan also counted in their anti-etatist crusade on support from foreign capital. This turned out to be a pipe dream: the balance of gros long term capital movement between 1926 and 1929 showed only a modest surplus of $136 million. Lewiatan's program appeared an outdated one (Łapa 2002: 134, Kofman 1986: 113–118). Also the little interest that foreign investors showed in the 1930s in the government's investment program meant that Lewiatan remained a passive actor regarding the development of the COP project and the rising economic role of the state-owned enterprises. The reluctant support Lewiatan gave to Deputy Prime Minister Kwiatkowski in the late 1930s–criticism of the "overgrowth of etatism" notwithstanding–was a second-best choice, an expression of the failure of its concepts so far, as well as the lack of an alternative (Kofman 1986: 181–188). At the same time, the Lewiatan circle began to treat the government's post-1936 policy of curbing the role of foreign, mainly German, capital "as the elimination of a foreign competitor to Lewiatan's advantage" (Jezierski and Leszczyńska 2001: 311f). This was, however, a small consolation to Lewiatan members, falling short of their previously demonstrated ambitions.

The two leaders of the national industrial groups suffered a defeat in the latter half of the 1930s, when the concept of the regulatory state was replaced, in the transition to holistic nationalism, by the state-as-producer policy. The state was really becoming Oakeshott's "enterprise association." At the same time, the breakthrough leading to the new, state-centered policy of industrial development was in some respects not so much a blessing as a risk to the traditional industrial elites. On the agenda was not so much the question of their leadership in the industrialization process as their relative marginalization and participation in government projects. This was the case particularly in Poland where etatism was more strongly accentuated (Kofman 1986: 125f, 189, Gołębiowski 1985: passim).

Simonsen and Wierzbicki's defeat cannot be interpreted as accidental. The main constraint on the influence of private interest groups in Brazil "was their own inability to command sufficient resources independently of the government. Thus they approached the State not as powerful initiators but as suppliants with hat in hand" (Wirth 1970: 220). Such a conclusion was fully applicable also to Poland, although Wierzbicki believed that Lewiatan's economic potential was big enough to avoid the suppliant's position. However, policy-makers harbored no illusions. In 1936 Kwiatkowski, a benign etatist, said with frankness: "No doubt overgrowth of etatism is occuring in Poland. Yet, this etatism developed not as a result of the etatist doctrine, but of insufficient private initiative" (quoted in Drozdowski 1989: 108f). Relatively weak institutional representation of industrial interest groups was an additional factor, especially in Brazil. Thus, when it came to the shock of 1929 and the state stepped in, economic elites, industrialists included, "found themselves insufficiently organized to resist" (Topik 1989: 100). In such a situation, following the understanding of the concept of holistic nationalism proposed in Chapter 1, the transition to new economic nationalism was a sort of a dual operation. First, it meant a redefinition of the main lines of economic policy and their points of reference; second, it defined the methods of carrying them out under conditions of crisis, and considering the relative strength of particular societal actors. The merger of the two notions, of state and economic independence, was the result of that dual operation.

Before discussing these questions, a comment on the wider context and implications of that emerging symbiosis is necessary.

The etatist variant of economic nationalism was not merely an economic project. It was also an attempt at etatizing integral political nationalism. Authoritarian regimes once installed were the main instrument enabling the fulfillment of such ambitions. The state appeared not only as a major economic actor, but also as a point of reference and a political structure which strived to redefine and monopolize the 'national idea'. In the Europe of the time, Italian fascism was the model case of such a variant of nationalism, trying to subordinate to the state the main ideas of integral nationalism that preceded fascism. In Poland and Brazil of the 1930s such a process was much less advanced, nevertheless the tendency was clear. It may be described as follows:

> the national state ... proceeds to find for 'the nation' a place in the global order of capital, while striving to keep the contradictions between capital and the people in perpetual suspension. All politics is now sought to be subsumed under the overwhelming requirements of the state-representing-the-nation (Chatterjee 1986: 168; see also Gramsci 1961).

The consequences of the symbiosis between the state and economic independence posed perhaps the most serious challenge to the hitherto integral nationalism. Integral nationalism, while extolling the state, tried nevertheless to retain some space for autonomous action by the broadly defined middle class. For this type of nationalism, in Poland exemplified by the *endecja*, the primacy of the well-organized and monopolistic 'national idea' did not mean, however, the "total solution" that would blur the boundaries between the state and the economy, and eliminate, as Rybarski (2002: 275, 283, 285) put it, the difference between "economic freedom and coercion." Dispersed property rights and entrepreneurship ("socialization of property"), not the economy subordinated to the state, was the ideal (see Dziewulski 1981: 63–72). In the 1930s this anti-etatist integral nationalism clashed with a different, never precisely defined, new variant of integral nationalism. Etatism, different from traditional interventionism, defined by Rybarski as state capitalism, signified a close relationship between the ascendance of the redefined 'national idea' and the vanishing 'economic freedom'. In Poland, the direction of the political evolution of the authoritarian pro-government Camp of National Unity (OZON) was obvious: *étatisme* in economic matters and "a desire to capture the clientele of the national camp," i.e. "to carry out the *endecja* policy without *endecja*" (Majchrowski 1985: 194, see also Chojnowski 1979: 239). The increase in anti-Jewish inward-oriented political and economic nationalism and growing tensions with the Ukrainian minority in southeastern Poland were part of this struggle for ideological and political primacy.

In Brazil, similar tendencies appeared after the suppression of the *paulista* revolt, and reached their zenith with the establishment of the authoritarian regime in 1937. With one basic difference, though. Integral nationalism, poorly developed before 1929, was not Vargas's chief political rival. His rival was regional nationalism: of São Paulo, Minas Gerais but also of his native state of Rio Grande do Sul. The *Queima das Bandeiras* holiday, which Vargas decreed a month after the *autogolpe*, was intended as a confirmation of the primacy not only of the federal state, but of state-based political and economic nationalism. The burning of the flags of particular Brazilian states, combined with celebrations of the second anniversary of the suppression of the communist-backed revolt (*Intentona Comunista*), were meant to validate "an agenda of statist, anti-regionalist, antiliberal, eugenicist politics of national modernization. ... in symbolism, the *Queima* was the essence of the authoritarian state" (Williams 2006: 66).

Such consequential political and economic change, a sort of paradigm shift, took place in a wider international and political-ideological context. Even if the crisis depressed trade and investments, at the same time it accelerated the circulation of and 'trade' in political and economic ideas. Latin America was a quite heavy, although careful, borrower.

As far as economic ideas were concerned, close to the hearts of representatives of radical, etatist economic nationalism were those threads of Italian fascist ideology which conceived visions of economic self-reliance, of the primacy of the domestic sources of savings and investments, of development of infrastructure and heavy industry, and of the growing role of the state in these processes. Apart from the fascist ideological sources of holistic nationalism and borrowed institutional patterns (corporatism, anti-parliamentarism, etc.), similarities between the ideology of holistic nationalism and the concepts of the Italian economic nationalist Alfredo Rocco were striking. The ideas he had developed before WWI, were in the 1920s subsumed under the basic canons of fascist economic policy. Thanks to a perverted symbiosis of the totalitarian state and the 'national idea' fascism was thus nationalized (Gregor 1979: 133–140, De Rosa 2000).

An analogy with Italian fascism seems in a way natural and understandable. Francisco Matarazzo, the future leader of the influential CIESP, returned from his trips to Italy in 1923 and 1925 delighted (Dean 1969: 171f). This, no doubt, strengthened his pro-industry position. Italian economic nationalism was made additionally attractive by the emphasis Rocco and supporters of industrialization laid on the issue of economic backwardness and interregional disparities, the formation of capital and the development of new branches of production. Against this background the need to make the state the main focus of economic decisions acquires a proper historical dimension. The example of economically developed Nazi Germany–although used in pro-industry propaganda, especially during the debate over the Volta Redonda project–was too abstract; it diverged too far from specific problems of peripheral economies.

And last but not least, one should not ignore the influence exerted at that time by Soviet planning and industrialization. The reaction to that experience, like that of fascism, was very selective. In certain countries, representatives of diametrically different political and social groups used the Soviet experience as an argument in discussions on the future direction of development. In Poland, before the 1929 crash, Stefan Starzyński, the founder of the First Economic Brigade, referred to the merits of planning and quoted the achievements of the German ministry of economy and the Soviet GOSPLAN. Representatives of Lewiatan immediately accused him of disseminating bolshevik ideas (Dziewulski 1981: 78, 80, 145, Janus 2009: 192). After 1929, those achievements were praised by the populist-revolutionary APRA in Peru, while government economists in Chile referred to the Soviet example. In the latter country, during the short-lived Socialist Republic, economic nationalism found its theoretical validation mainly in the late 19th-century German tradition of "state socialism" (Stemplowski 1996). And in Brazil it was

> remarkable how frequently the conservative ... elite referred to the Soviets. ... The revolution itself had frightened them briefly, but the image that endured was that of a central government directing an orderly and rapid economic development (Dean 1969: 146).

In passing, in the United States at that time the president of the National Industrial Conference Board claimed that the Soviet Union was "the most capitalistic country in the world because it [spent] a larger part of its working energy in creating the means of production" and that "subjecting [the Soviet population] to arbitrary and tyrannical discipline" was justified. Other entrepreneurs and financiers spoke about the USSR as of a "gigantic corporation" and the "most extreme type" of capitalism (Wilson 1974: 11f). Meanwhile, according to a former vice-governor of the National Bank of Belgium, "[the] pathetic and already conclusive experiment" carried out in the Soviet Union should be seen as a warning to those who experiment with *étatisme*: it was "not a matter of communism, but rather, indeed, of state capitalism pushed to its furthest extremes" (Zeeland: 92f). It is worth adding here that in the case of US industrial corporations, their enthusiasm was by no means fortuitous. Between 1927 and 1932, and especially after the first Five-Year Plan was launched, the Soviet Union became a valuable partner of European and American firms.[11]

Of course, the focus of such a selective perception of the Soviet experiment was determined by growing specific internal demand for new ideas when economic orthodoxy was rejected. Thus, it was not by chance that debaters referred to the Soviet Five-Year Plan as, above all, an example of economic patriotism, proof that a top-down, well-coordinated and planned struggle against backwardness and for economic independence was feasible. In his 1944 polemics with Gudin, Simonsen (2011: 7) strongly linked his project to quadruple Brazilian national income within 15 years with planning, "as in Russia and Turkey." The Peruvian Haya de la Torre and the Indian Nehru were unanimous in such a selective reading of Soviet industrialization, too (Chatterjee 1986: 143ff, 164). What is more, such a reading of the Soviet experiment allowed a free combination of the demand for planned state-led industrialization with elements of fascist ideology and native tradition. The Soviet experiment was also perceived– as in the cases of China and Japan–as an example of a more general phenomenon of economic nationalism. Preaching the idea of "revolutionary internationalism" notwithstanding, wrote Lorwin (1933: 363), Soviet Russia had "in its economics pursued a distinctly nationalistic policy based upon the exclusive reservation of the domestic market for its own industries."

---

[11] Thus, US exports to the Soviet Union increased from $65 million in 1927 to $114 million in 1930, only slightly to decline in 1931 to $104 million (4.3 percent of total US exports): in those years "Russia [became] the largest foreign customer for American industrial machinery" (Siegel 1996: 133).

Moreover, there is no doubt that, while searching for new directions of national development, the state began to question liberal orthodoxy also with regard to the role of foreign trade. The already mentioned radical project concerning state-controlled trade presented by Simonsen in 1935, although rejected both by the government and agricultural groups ("they wanted fewer government control, not more"), was a clear sign of such a change coming (Wirth 1970: 49). Uncertain was, first and foremost, the concept of foreign trade as an engine of growth. Gradually the benefits of foreign trade began to be seen not in categories of comparative advantages and factor endowments, but as a vent for surplus model and the imports subordinated to the new domestic demand profile. Thus, in the document submitted to the Colombian parliament in 1937, Gabriel Sanín Villa posited that, concerning the initiation of industrialization, what counted was the absolute level of imports and not comparative costs and/or economies of scale in foreign trade (see Cortes Conde and Stein 1977: 425f). Rybarski (2002: 273–276) in Poland continuously emphasized the "antagonism between [the 'national idea'] and the principle of the advanced international division of labor." The building of an economic bloc by Nazi Germany in the succession states and in the Balkans also questioned the traditional model of trade. Disregarding the political and military goals of Nazi Germany, an important side- and unplanned effect of compensatory trade was support for the fragmentary industrialization of backward succession states.[12]

In passing, such an approach had been since the late 1920s characteristic also of the Soviet, and next of the Soviet-type, industrialization policy. After WWII, the guidelines of Poland's long-term plan, prepared in 1947 by the Central Planning Office (CUP), which was at that time still controlled by socialists, stuck to similar principles:

> The entire economy shall be oriented primarily toward supplying the home market and increasing the per capita income consumed. The volume of exports shall depend on import requirements. Emphasis shall be laid on increasing agricultural exports (CUP 1983: 438).

---

[12] "Contrary to frequent allegations at the time and since," wrote Rothschild (1974: 22), "Germany did not flood East Central Europe with cuckoo clocks, aspirin, and thermometers in exchange for grains, minerals, and timber; rather, it supplied capital goods for industry, encouraged the diversification of vulnerable one-crop agricultures, and supplied a steady market at reasonable prices." Hirschman (1980: 36) claimed the opposite: "one of the great principles of German foreign economic policy [was] to prevent the industrialization of her agricultural trading partners." Rothschild's opinion was supported by earlier analyses by Basch (1943: 178–181).

Whichever way one looks at it, in these guidelines one finds all the basic assumptions of ideal economic nationalism: an adjustment of resources to the domestic demand profile, the subordination of foreign trade to internal developments, a relative isolation from the influence of the international market, planning. The guidelines were soon revised substantially: per capita income consumed was replaced by accelerated growth in the heavy and defense industries.

Seen against such a wider context the dual operation implied by the emergence of holistic nationalism resulted in basic changes in the way the national interest was understood and operationalized. At the height of the export economy the coffee valorization scheme was a model example of how the national interest was defined (particularistic nationalism writ large) and transformed into policy. In the 1930s the determination of national interest and its operationalization became the domain of the emerging state technostructure.

In Brazil after 1937 the asymmetric relation between state structures and private societal actors was well established. Wirth (1970: 222) implies that during the Vargas authoritarian rule, "economic nationalism was broadened in scope from protecting natural resources to supporting policies that called for the utilization of these resources." Ianni (1971: 25–28) represents a similar view; in his opinion, in 1934, with the appointment of the Conselho Federal de Comércio Exterior (the Federal Council of Foreign Trade) Brazil went over from a "defensive" to an "offensive" economic policy. The former "consisted first of all in the protection ... of the existing sectors," while the latter in creating "conditions for the expansion and diversification of the economy." As early as 1933–1934 the Nazi government became aware that such a shift in resource allocation was being considered: "More quickly than Americans, the Germans realized ... that Brazilian nationalism was maturing into an ideology of industrial expansion" (Wirth 1970: 43). The detailed draft plan prepared in Berlin in early 1935, entitled "Fundamentals for the Industrial Development of Brazil with German Help" (the translation in Wirth 1967) can be read both ways: as a description of Germany's general plan for investments in and compensatory trade with Brazil, and, what seems more interesting, as a good understanding and summary of Brazil's new economic priorities. Berlin knew that the development of iron ore deposits and of the iron and steel industry, and an improvement in domestic military supply chain had been intensely debated since the early 1930s, well before the Volta Redonda project was launched. Thus, the transition to an authoritarian regime in 1937 resulted in the next stage of the decision-making process (Hilton 1975, Fonseca 2003).

The Polish decision to build COP should be analyzed in a similar manner. The fact that in the end the state took the initiative actually meant a fiasco for the Lewiatan-proposed division of roles between private industry and the state. Not just transport infrastructure construction, but also modern industrial production became a quasi-monopoly of the state (Kofman 1986: 189). Industrial development was focused on new industrial branches, with particular emphasis on the modern steel and iron, machine-building and chemical industries. At the same time, Kwiatkowski's four-year plan was merged with the six-year plan for the development of the country's defense potential as prepared by the military. Both plans provided for a qualitative jump in the development of indigenous modern technologies, and in this way they deviated from the classic import-substitution pattern. The path to attaining such goal was cleared in the 1930s by the state-controlled and technologically advanced defense industry (Gołębiowski 1985: 124–141, Hauner 1986: 110–116).

Thus, the transition to holistic nationalism and to new directions in economic development was combined with the rejection of the radicalized particularistic nationalism of industrial groups writ large. However, this was not a clear-cut choice made at the beginning of the process. Both in Brazil and Poland, pressure from the military for etatism notwithstanding, the state was considered to be a mere temporary substitute of private interests. This is not sheer speculation. In Poland, it was assumed by government that as a result of the 1936 nationalization of Flick's powerful "Wspólnota Interesów" group, shares in this new state holding would quite soon change hands, passing from the state to the private sector and local governments (Landau and Tomaszewski 1964: 317–323). Until 1939 such plans remained on paper: there was no private capital that could take over the integrated iron and steel industry, which at the time of nationalization employed more than 27,000 workers, technicians and engineers (Gołębiowski 1985: 182, 184). In Brazil, the decision that Volta Redonda would be a government project, backed with a foreign loan, was taken relatively late, after other schemes had failed and/or been rejected under pressure from the military (Wirth 1970: 103–113).

These examples indicate that Brazilian, Polish and Hungarian etatism (the latter epitomized by the 1938-announced Győr five-year economic plan) was not a matter of choice. In fact, it was a historical turning point distinguishing two models of economic development. In the case of Poland, this trend seemed to be much more persistent and noticeable. Despite Lewiatan's criticism and government attempts to reduce the role of the state, etatism was very strong as early as in the 1920s. The historical circumstances mentioned earlier played a role in strengthening the trend.

In 1929, explaining the fiasco of the earlier-declared anti-etatist policy, Prime Minister Kazimierz Bartel said: "the government has been driven to take action of an 'etatist' nature, because no group of capitalists felt like taking proper measures" (quoted in Gołębiowski 1985: 86). It was not without reason that Stefan Starzyński claimed in 1928 that in point of fact "the biggest capitalist and entrepreneur in ... Poland was the state itself" (quoted in Janus 2009: 254). There was no exaggeration in his claim. According to estimates by Michał Kalecki and Ludwik Landau, the Polish capital share in total accumulation amounted to 14 percent, foreign capital to 19 percent, and that of the state to 66.7 percent (Gołębiowski 1985: 231). In the 1930's, the etatization of the Polish economy gained momentum. According to Kazimierz Secomski's estimates, between 1936–1939, the government's share in total investment outlays reached 76.8 percent. In other words, the strategic change of economic priorities and the transition to holistic nationalism, expressed in the COP project, took place with the marginal involvement of private capital. In such a situation, Lewiatan's complaints about the "overgrowth" of etatism were hardly justified. In spite of tax reliefs and other incentives, private investors were reluctant. Not without reason, a newspaper close to the government wrote about the "laziness and tardiness of the private sector" (Gołębiowski 1985: 231, 229). Needless to say, in accordance with the ideology of inward-oriented nationalism and the policy of 'Polonization', Jewish entrepreneurs were kept well away from the COP (Marcus 1983: 267, Drozdowski 1963: 147). In this respect the Hungarian Győr investment plan was more radical: its financing was founded in part on "[t]he hidden program of Aryanisation" (Pogány 2006: 225).

Yet, a look at the actors involved in such a redirection of economic policy priorities in Brazil and in Poland indicates that there were significant differences. The Volta Redonda project was a relatively isolated case of building modern large-scale heavy industry. The development of other sectors of the capital-goods industry was less capital-intensive and thus definitely within the reach of Brazilian industrialists. In the 1930s the profile of São Paulo industry changed but relative discrimination against the machine building industry was noticeable (Marson 2008). The Brazilian state-as-producer appeared to be less expansive, leaving a large part of small-scale, technologically inferior capital-goods industry in the hands of the private sector. In a word, one can treat developments in the 1930s as a sign of major changes to come, a promise. In Poland, government investment projects focused on capital-intensive branches of industry and on industrial infrastructure were planned as a radical reorganization and remodeling of industry as a whole. The inicial direct and indirect effects of the COP project were to affect circa 107,000 people (Drozdowski 1963: 148). Thus, the etatism of the Brazilian state was selective, whereas in Poland it was overwhelming. However, differences apart, in both cases the growing etatist trend indicated that the transition from countercyclical policy to holistic nationalism implied a change of policy instruments. The assertion that until the outbreak of WWII, devaluations, deficit spending and tariffs had been strong enough macroeconomic policy parameters, and within them the state left "extensive scope ... for private market decisions" (Kaufman 1990: 116), was no longer convincing.

In the 1930s, economic independence was described relatively simply, particularly in propaganda. Vargas maintained in 1939 that "iron, coal and oil are the foundation of the economic emancipation of every country" (Ianni 1971: 62). There was a grain of truth in that catchword inasmuch as at the stage of industrial development of the time, steel and iron and the related industries, and also the chemical industry, energy resources and development of public and private transportation were still the distinguishing marks of technological and economic progress. They also were an important reference point for military planners and technocrats. But it was precisely in these areas, because of initially large capital expenditures and the relatively long pay-back period, that the state had the natural advantage over the private sector (Baer, Kerstenetsky and Villela 1973, Fishlow 1972).

The operationalization of the concept of economic independence constituted a much more complicated problem. The translation of this concept into decisions concerning the growth rates of specific industries and other sectors was only touched upon toward the end of the decade. If such operationalization was to take the form of planning, in the 1930s in most cases it appeared only in its most rudimentary form.

As in the case of etatism, the transition to planning was also much faster and more resolute in Poland than in Brazil, even though the authoritarian Brazilian constitution of 1937 authorized "direct and indirect [government] intervention" and "direct [economic] management (*gestão directa*)" (Ianni 1971: 46). Still, it should be noted that authoritarianism in both countries, although facilitating transition to *étatisme* and planning, was not a factor which could explain the speed and intensity of such a move. Compared with the Estado Nôvo, the regime in Poland was not yet a fully developed authoritarian system. Although weakened, the traditional channels of political and economic interest articulation were nevertheless still in place.

Kwiatkowski's Four-Year Investment Plan (1936–1940) was completed ahead of schedule. However, its coordination with a more ambitious plan for the years 1936–1942, prepared by the military, was a problem. For this plan presupposed not only bigger investments, but also implied strong criticism of the taboo of the "sound budget" as well as a demand for "planned inflation" (Gołębiowski 1985: 203–214, Drozdowski 1989: 152f, Kofman 1986). This did not occur, although the pressure of defense priorities speeded up investments in the machine-building, iron and steel and related industries, and slowed down investments in infrastructure in COP (Drozdowski 1963: 138, 144, 271f, Kostrowicka 1989: 333ff).

However, the four-year plan was only the first step toward national planning and accelerated industrial drive. The initial success of the COP project allowed Kwiatkowski to present–at the end of 1938–the guidelines for the more ambitious Fifteen-Year Plan (1939–1954). Divided into five stages (three-year plans), it encompassed the entire economy. It anticipated, successively, development of the defense industry (the first stage), social infrastructure and the automotive and aviation industries (the second stage), accelerated large-scale industrialization and urbanization (the fourth stage), and, finally, a considerable reduction of interregional disparities (Kostrowicka 1989: 336). The outbreak of the war meant that the plan remained on paper only.

In Brazil the transition to planning in the 1930s and in the subsequent years was much slower. The main quasi-planning role was played by the numerous advisory and regulatory bodies (*conselhos, comissãos, institutos*), above all the Conselho Federal de Comércio Exterior (CFCE) and the Conselho de Economia Nacional that had been created ad hoc since the early 1930s and also, to some extent, autarchic institutions focused on specific sectors and products (coffee, sugar, cocoa, etc.) (Ianni 1971: chapter 2, Schmitter 1971: 126, Diniz 1989: 106ff). The importance of *conselhos* and technical commissions, particularly in the case of iron and steel, and petroleum, grew after 1937. The National Petroleum Council founded in 1938 by General Horta Barbosa and the Executive Commission for the National Steel Plan appointed in 1940 and presided over by Guilherme Guinle (with the participation of top military experts) emphasized the importance of the new priorities. In addition, the former epitomized the problem of national control over mineral resources (Wirth 1970: 155, 159). At the same time new state-owned companies were created. The Fabrica Nacional de Motores and Companhia Nacional de Álcalis had been set up during the war (Evans 1979: 89). Upon completing negotiations with the US over the Volta Redonda project, the Companhia Siderúrgica (CSN) was established in 1941, and in 1942 the Coordenação de Mobilização Econômica, a superministry of a kind, was created (Ianni 1971: 48).

The creation of an institutional and social environment favorable to planned industrialization was, nevertheless, particularly until 1937, a largely spontaneous process. After all is said and done, the case of Brazil was not a unique one. The establishment of CORFO in Chile was above all a response to the havoc caused by an earthquake. Furthermore, the national holding Instituto per la Riconstruzione Industriale, an Italian public holding, initially was an ad hoc institution established in 1933 by the fascist regime for the time of crisis. In Brazil, a broader discussion on national planning started as late as during the war. The 1942–1943 report of the US Cooke Mission (supportive of planning but not etatism) (Baer 2008: 45), discussion between Simonsen and Gudin in 1944–1945, the experience of the management of the 'war economy' were elements enhancing the legitimacy of planning (or the *mística do plano* according to Gudin). The *Carta Econômica de Teresópolis*, the result of the conference of *das Classes Produtoras do Brasil*, published in May 1945, was the main accent at this stage of the debate. The *Carta* stressed the need for economic planning which would enable "greater productivity and develop natural richness" (quoted in Ianni 1971: 57). However, the transition to effective national planning did not occur until the early 1950s.

In both countries the transition from countercyclical policies to policies defining new priorities and structural change implied the emergence of new channels of interest articulation and new societal actors. Brazil, particularly after the imposition of authoritarian rule, was to some extent a model case for authoritarian policy-making. It is worthwhile quoting here at length Schneider's (1991: 146) excellent, succinct summary of the system created by Vargas:

> With parties ruled out, the answer [to state-society relations] was a network tying together the Vargas-appointed interventors, the growing array of governmental agencies, and the sectoral organizations fostered by the basically corporativist design of the Estado Novo. This ... would provide a means for accommodating emerging interests while at the same time easing the decline of traditional elites ... Centralization was made more palatable by furnishing a widening variety of groups with new avenues of quite direct access to policy making and implementation just above the working level. The resulting system of co-optative clientelism enhanced the viability of the Vargas-designed state by channeling the concerns and energies of politically relevant elements into relatively narrow struggles over policy in particular areas–hence away from broader questions of the regime's basic orientation and underlying priorities.

In such a system the merger between the state and economic independence was relatively easy. It was not, though, a case of unconcealed political and social engineering and/or manipulation. The system created by Vargas was not a transitory phenomenon: "observers have failed to notice the very profound changes that took place in the nature of intermediary political associations, the scope of government policy, and the interpenetration of the two" (Schmitter 1971: 127). The new priorities embodied in state policy found strong and direct support among new societal actors: new industrialists, the armed forces and state bureaucracy.

The initially passive São Paulo industrialists, hostile to Vargas's political leadership, were not the only actors. The structure of Brazil's industrialist group underwent a basic transformation in the 1930s. Among the industrial enterprises registered in 1940, 70 percent were firms established in the 1930s (Diniz 1989: 106). Unlike traditional elites, "the emerging industrial elite's view of the desirability of state intervention in the economy came to coincide with that held by key regime figures–as well as that of some important elements in the armed forces" (Schneider 1991: 147).

The change of economic priorities reflected, above all, the increasing role of the army and federal bureaucracy. It was by no means an accident that in Brazil and Poland the military played the primary role among the supporters of industrialization. In the *conselhos* responsible for development of the iron and steel industry the voice of the military was the important one. One can suggest that, in practice, the *compromisso* stricken by Vargas and the military command in 1937 provided not only for an arbiter role for the army, but also transformed the army and its experts into (co)managers of structural change. However, Vargas leadership was not questioned.[13] At the same time, the belief–widespread among the top military command in the 1930s that "national security demanded greater military-industrial autonomy"–in subsequent years was transformed into a coherent ideology, combining national security and industrialization under the armed forces' protective umbrella (Hilton 1982: 652, 666). The role of the state bureaucracy grew in parallel with that. The Brazilian

---

[13] It should be noted that some historians questioned the leadership role of the military in forcing the iron and steel program–a thesis propounded by Wirth in his pioneering study. According to Hilton (1973, 1982), the large-scale iron and steel program was from the very beginning Vargas's idea which after 1937 was carried out with the reluctant support of Brazilian top command. The armed forces' chief immediate interest in the 1930s was focused on rapid improvements in supply of war material. However, the evidence Hilton quotes refers primarily to the pre-1937 period and he does not mention the 'oil problem'.

Departamento Administrativo do Serviço Público (DASP) created in 1938 not only controlled federal state structures but also had a major task of improving their efficiency. *Técnicos*, managers in the state-owned enterprises and other public institutions, who emerged under the Estado Nôvo, were an important part of that group (Ianni 1971: 66). Their hour came a quarter century later, under the military dictatorship.

In Poland, where the industrialization project was in the hands of Deputy Prime Minister Kwiatkowski and the state bureaucracy, the army played both the role of the strongest, radical pressure group and the powerful participant in the decision-making process. Even though the growing disintegration of the ruling camp following Marshall Piłusdski's death (1935) created space for relatively autonomous action for politicians like Kwiatkowski, the veto power was firmly in the hands of the top military command.

What is more, the military and the emerging modern bureaucracy were among the supporters of the radical, etatist variant of holistic nationalism. This was particularly the case of Poland. In the 1930s the army quite determinedly insisted on decreasing the role of private capital in modern, strategically important investments (Gołębiowski 1985: 138–141). Thus, already in the 1920s the defense industry was organized as a military-industrial complex of a kind. This trend became decidedly stronger in the 1930s. According to tentative estimates, at the end of 1938 the state-owned defense industry employed 34–35 thousand people, mainly in modern large-scale enterprises. Total employment in state-owned and state-controlled industry reached 142 thousand, i.e. 19 percent of the industrial workforce in Poland (Gołębiowski 1985: 135, 294). At the same time, in the 1930s the army quite determinedly insisted on decreasing the role of private capital in modern, strategically important investments. The military's attitude toward private capital was characterized by both disdain (because of its weakness) as well as a large measure of suspicion (because of their doubtful patriotism). With such tendencies in mind, Landau (1975: 19) suggested that "a military-economic complex ... replaced the traditional financial oligarchy." The situation in Brazil was different. According to Hilton (1982: 656f), emphasis there was laid on "nationalization" of defense and industrial potential, i.e. on national control, not on etatization. Hence, the Brazilian army was more than willing to cooperate with the private sector to the extent that the latter were able to satisfy the armed forces' demands.

However, the army did not always have the upper hand, as illustrated by the example of Argentina in the 1930s:

> [the] relatively late development of the basic iron and steel industry in Argentina, in spite of the strong interest shown in it by the powerful armed forces, suggests that either 1) this activity can only be carried out at very high costs or 2) that the power of industrial users if imported iron and steel was a good match to that of the armed forces (Díaz-Alejandro 1970: 247n).

A change was initiated with a certain delay, in the 1940s. But at that time the plans of the Argentine military were much more ambitious:

> Economic nationalism meant something different for the army than it did for businessman ... Not only was industry to be fostered and protected from competition, but it also had to produce in accordance with a national plan. Prices, wages, credit, and the allocation of fuels and raw materials were all to be regulated by the state. ... Certain areas of the economy considered vital for national defense, such as fuels, transportation, and energy, would be managed directly by the state. Businessmen soon found that, under military rule, there was less opportunity then ever for organized interests to influence policy-making (Lewis 1990: 93f).

Also in Poland the draft program prepared at the end of 1938 by the pro-government OZON clearly demonstrated a willingness to take outright totalitarian political and economic measures. Influential groups of the state bureaucracy and the army demanded that "rigorous and radical methods should be used, together with the realization of the new economic system and planned economy" (quoted in Drozdowski 1989: 132; see also Kofman 1986: 169). Not only the economy, but also education and civic organizations, were to be subordinated to the State Economic Plan. Traditional integral nationalists were not the only ones to act against such 'total' projects. Lewiatan, too, came forward to harshly criticize them, at the same time seeing Kwiatkowski's etatism as a lesser evil (Drozdowski 1963: 280, Majchrowski 1985: 101ff, 116). Life itself verified the Argentine military's plans. However, those extreme variants, approximating 'war economy' conditions and displaying a radical authoritarian mentality, well reflected the feelings and sense of an extraordinary situation.

Lastly, a situation where the increase in government investments was considerably greater than the increase in private investments in the long run threatened the marginalization of local private capital. In the modern, capital-intensive sectors in particular. In Brazil and Poland, the early symptoms of such a process were already clearly visible, although, again more so in Poland than in Brazil. That is why, for instance in Brazil, Simonsen and Guilhermo Guinle, the latter the first president of the CSN, were fighting a desperate struggle to prevent–in spite of the United States Steel Corporation's last minute withdrawal from the Volta Redonda project–the nascent iron and steel industry from becoming fully dominated by the state, and to have it operate as a mixed company. Simonsen insisted on a similar solution for oil. But despite the strenuous efforts of the two private capital did not become involved in the newly-created CSN (Wirth 1970: 159, 124f). The CSN was created as a state-owned company, co-financed by the US Export-Import bank loan. For radical nationalists among the army and bureaucracy that was an ideal solution. In 1945, Simonsen's opponent Gudin returned to the conception of transforming the CSN into a mixed company, proposing to reserve 30–40 percent of shares for foreign investors (Ianni 1971: 56), that is to the conception discussed with the United States Steel Corporation years earlier. The Brazilian military also opted for mixed enterprises, but in which Brazilian capital would have a stake.

The case of Volta Redonda showed clearly that at that time it was impossible to solve the problem of etatism with the help of private, local as well as foreign, capital. Consequently, in those countries where the progress of industrialization (including the capital-goods industries) was considerable, the etatist variant of holistic nationalism became inescapable. In Brazil, the relatively weak local capital could not counter this trend either in the 1930s or in the succeeding years. One should note that among the largest national economic groups that existed at the end of the 1950s a mere 5 percent was formed between 1930 and 1945 (Evans 1979: 105). Lewiatan could not play such role in Poland, either. As a matter of fact, at the end of the 1930s it was not even indicating it would play such a role. Hence, from the very start COP was a state-initiated and state-run investment project. In the last months preceding WWII, Polish industrialists began to change their attitude toward the COP project. Nevertheless, the rules of the game remained unchanged: the modus vivendi with the government placed private investors in a subordinate role.

In the 1930s these problems were merely hinted at. In Brazil, they emerged with full force in the 1950s and in the two following decades. In East and Central Europe, on the other hand, this problem became a non-issue. In Brazil, the emergent informal coalition of the state, foreign capital and local entrepreneurs, the famous *tri-pé*, or tripod (Evans 1979: 228–273) matured under military dictatorship. This kind of development was however in contrast with the conceptions of the 1950s, staked as it was on the leadership role of 'national capitalists'. Half a century earlier Witte had tried to deal with such a problem in Russia. The stormy debate in the mid-1970s on anti-*estatização* (anti-statism), followed by a *democratização* debate, did not bring any fundamental solution, although it contributed to the decline of the military dictatorship (Evans 1979: 268f, Diniz 1989: 111–116).

This is, however, another chapter in the history of economic nationalism.

CONCLUSIONS

In the analysis presented many important questions were either only alluded to or not touched upon at all. The final part of the book is not the proper place to fill in these gaps. Nevertheless, it seems worthwhile to stress the point mentioned at the very beginning of my analysis, concerning the wider context in which Latin America's and Central Europe's encounter with economic nationalism should be placed. Some tentative conclusions will follow.

Economic nationalism was neither a time-restricted nor region-specific episode in the history of capitalism. At the most general level, combined with a history-sensitive approach, economic nationalism reflected and still reflects the great challenge of "making state and market congruous" (Hont 2005: 155), of accommodating the state and global dynamic of capital and of placing the development-underdevelopment dilemma within the framework of such political economy. Convergence of "national community" and "national economy"–as Polish economists of the beginning of the 20th century put it (Głąbiński 2002: 373; Rybarski 2002: 368)– was an important part of this history. The former was treated as incomplete or imperfect if it did not find support in the "unified economic space" (Braudel 1977: 99), the latter as unfeasible without a national state.

The explosive development of protectionist practices at the end of the 19th century and subsequently in the interwar period overshadowed and pushed to the background the centuries-long maturation of economic nationalism. Therefore, Kohn's thesis that "[t]he close political and cultural identification of the individual with his nationality ... extended to the economic field only during the latter part of the nineteenth century," just like Pollard's contention that only in the 1870s did "frontiers [begin to] gel ... into economically meaningful barriers," seem untenable. Developments preceding the relatively rapid shift to economic nationalism at the time of first globalization mattered. And this does not apply only to the instances of early 19th century economic proto-nationalism discussed in this book. The analytically superb presentation of the 17th–18th century "Jealousy of trade debate" by Hont is a major contribution to the understanding of economic nationalism as *longue durée*.

Economic nationalism was also a worldwide phenomenon. Thus Ronald Findlay (1995: 148) rightly pointed out in his remarks concerning Gellner's approach to nationalism and industrialization that his model "fails to predict any 'nationalist' outcome for the 'old continuous nations' of England and France and, for that matter, Japan. ... in his view there could not be such a thing as 'old industrial country' nationalism. Nationalism therefore becomes exclusively an 'ideology of delayed industrialization.'" A similar, self-imposed restrictive reasoning is also to be found among economic nationalists for whom the 'national idea' and economic nationalism were a particular nation-specific opposite pole of universalism of any kind (Rybarski 2002: 274). However, the claimed uniqueness of economic nationalism was in point of fact a universal historical experience. Different countries in different continents gave similar nationalistic responses to the problem of economic development and/or underdevelopment. Notwithstanding certain limitations of Greenfeld's important contribution to the debate, her historical-sociological analysis of core countries' economic nationalism was a persuasive rebuttal of economic nationalism-as-region specific and anti-universalistic hypothesis. Such an approach opens up a possibility for both a typology of and comparative study into economic nationalism.

The critical test of economic nationalism in both regions were the 1930s. In certain underdeveloped countries, which faced unparalleled exogenous shocks, nationalist ideology evolved in the direction described by the concept of holistic nationalism. The structural crisis of the first globalization was a good time for the self-consciousness of backwardness to grow and of the realization that the hitherto pattern of modernity was breaking. Thus it was not accidental that such perception of the crisis was transformed into a nationalistic agenda, with the state structures and apparatuses taking the role of substitute economic nationalists. A new balance between the private sector interests and the machinery of the state was set. The ideal of the national economy as a unique structure driven by the endogenous mechanisms of industrial transformation found its reflection in state technostructure. For some researchers, however, such a 'usurpation' on the part of the state was not articulated strongly enough. For Kohli (2004: 160) "neither Vargas's developmental mission nor his commitment to economic nationalism was well developed." This is a debatable assessment, although in comparative perspective the limits of the Brazilian "cohesive-capitalist state" were strongly accentuated. There is no doubt, however, that in both regions spirit of capitalism-as-economic nationalism appeared first as modern underdevelopment, and later as industrial modernity fostered by the nationalist state.

Inasmuch as holistic nationalism pushed the state to the foreground as the *spiritus movens* of industrialization, traditional particularistic nationalism(s) was (were) preserved and reemphasized under its protective umbrella. This reflected a complicated processes of coalition-forming which merged political innovation with social and economic conservatism so dear to the rural elites. Such a limiting factor was present, with a different degree of intensity, both in Brazil and Poland. However, with all shortcomings and barriers making the transition to the new model of modernity difficult, it appeared clear that the escape from the trap of underdevelopment was not crudely predetermined by the 'iron laws' of the hitherto peripheral integration into the world economy. Such an escape was possible, and the 'hidden secret' of success stories should be looked for in the structure of winning coalitions. Peter Evans (1995), Alice H. Amsden (2001) and Atul Kohli (2004) have in recent years contributed the most to the debate on this subject. In further studies on political economy and history of economic nationalism this issue should be given a more prominent place than I have been able to do it in this book.

However, in the period under study these structural and institutional changes were largely eclipsed by authoritarianism. What is more, it seemed that precisely authoritarianism was the essence of economic nationalism. It was expected therefore that the restoration of the normal conditions of international trade would bring about, along with democratization, also the end of nationalist experiments. This concerned the state backed industrialization in particular.

The first post-WWII decades did not confirm these expectations. A return to the epoch preceding the Great Depression became impossible. A historian thus wrote that "[t]he post-war economy had to start anew. The former priority for balance-of-payments equilibrium had to make way for the domestic interests of the national economy" (Wee 1987: 33). The road to the second globalization led through a complex interdependence between tasks related to the growth of national economies and economic internationalism. Moreover, the establishment, within that process, of the European economic communities, also reflected that dualism (Milward and Sørensen 1994).

Did thus holistic nationalism measure up to the expectations placed on it?

With regard to Poland in the 1930s, Łepkowski (1984: 84) wrote that attempts then made "to etatize the economy did not (could not? did not have time to?) achieve the goal of building a unique model of a strong state of 'national capitalism'." With regard to the entire East and Central European region we have the rather pessimistic assessment of Rothschild (1974: 15): "Despite strenuous, if often misapplied efforts ... to increase the area's wealth through industrialization, in 1938 ... the fate of the several states' economies was annually determined by the single, hazardous, factor of weather." Hofbauer and Komlosy (2000: 481) see no positive aspects of the experiments of the 1930s: "it became evident that both national independence and colonial status were compatible." Berend (1998: 244f) adds more specific arguments to those negative assessments:

> Despite important short-term economic successes, the region failed to adjust in the long term to the transforming world economy, modern technology, and related industrial structures. The short term achievements of import-substitution promoted relatively rapid growth in the textile and other light industries. But this road to industrialization produced systems that failed to incorporate the structural changes occurring in the already industrialized world. ... The developing industries in Central and Eastern Europe represented nineteenth-century economic sectors not suitable for twentieth-century competition.

Such a bird's eye view implies, however, an excessive homogeneity of the highly diversified region. Instead, I would suggest, taking into account interstate differences that grew in the region particularly in the 1930s, and thus the fact that in certain countries there appeared at that time conditions for accelerating structural change as well as rate of growth (see Kofman 1997). And it was precisely the tendency to move beyond the 'easy' import-substitution industrialization in the late 1930s that was the main defining element of economic policy in Poland (and to some extent also in Brazil). In passing, stressing the role of the textile industry is justified in the case of Hungary or Bulgaria, but certainly not in Poland. Changes in the occupational structure of industry between 1929 and 1938 show that, unlike in the former countries, in Poland employment in light industry declined, rising, in turn, in metallurgy and engineering, chemicals and electric power (Teichova 1985: 245, Landau and Tomaszewski 1971: 564f).

The war and subsequently the decades of communist rule disrupted this experiment. Therefore it is impossible to answer the question of whether the changes initiated in Poland in the 1930s could, among other things, have narrowed the technological gap and improve industrial competitiveness. It is worthy of note, however, that, surprisingly, the transition to the communist planned economy and the industrial spurt that followed showed that internal resources in Poland or Hungary were much greater than had been presumed in the interwar period. Within another political and institutional framework, and assuming that WWII never happened, these resources could have been mobilized and allocated in a more efficient and less wasteful way. The fifteen-year plan outlined by Kwiatkowski was not simply wishful thinking. In other words, Czechoslovakia, which was an industrialized country already before WWII, would not have had, following this counterfactual scenario, to become a 'museum of technology' in the 1970s and 1980s, while Poland, at its disposal the potential of Upper Silesia and COP, would have been able to go on with modern industrial development, speeded up in the 1930s.

Assessment of the situation in Latin America, where the historical continuity of political and economic development was maintained, is much more complicated. The industrialization of Brazil and other countries, which accelerated in the 1930s, transformed the region over the subsequent decades. Latin American economies in 1930 and thirty years later were two different worlds (Thorp 1998: 159). At the same time, the post-WWII history of Latin America shows that the 1930s were not a short-lived anomaly caused by the final breakdown of the first globalization, but a period of experimenting in some countries with holistic economic nationalism. Leaving all other cases aside for now, Brazil's post-1945 experience demonstrated that this nationalism had turned out to be a long-term trend, the sine qua non for successful late industrialization. Accelerated industrialization became a fact both under the democratic-populist system (until 1964) and the authoritarian-bureaucratic regime, and in both cases state-owned enterprises played the leadership role in the capital goods industry, social infrastructure, etc. (Evans 1979: passim, Serra 1979). In hindsight, the fact that today Brazil is on a good track is, to some extent, a result of its "total history."

However, the import substitution industrialization as carried out in Brazil and other countries of the region was, according to critical historians, in the long term a comparatively suboptimal solution. Berend's opinion regarding the technological lag in Central Europe's import substituting economies also roughly applies to post-WWII Latin America until the early 1950s. Under the umbrella of high nominal and effective tariffs, "higher than Latin America had applied in earlier periods" (Bulmer-Thomas 2003: 271), the manufacturing boom created a relatively outdated and non-competitive industry. The transition from demand-supported industrialization, as in the 1930s and early 1950s, to the supply-sensitive one proved to be very costly. Hence, Bulmer-Thomas's (2003: 279) negative assessment of post-WWII developments: the ISI model "cannot be defended." One should also add that foreign capital did not offer much help to this transition. Foreign direct investments, which played a negligible role in the industrial drive in the 1930s, in the 1950s and 1960s were focused on the production of durable consumer goods. Foreign capital was reluctant to invest in the intermediate and capital-goods industries "that governments were hoping to see established" (Bulmer-Thomas 2003: 273). However, the recent estimates of the long-term productivity growth in Brazilian industries do not confirm the harsh criticism of the ISI, in fact they rather "lend support to a qualified view of the efficiency performance of import-substitution industrialization in postwar Brazil" (Colistete 2009: 14; see also Thorp 1998: 163–167).

Thus, one is left with a picture of 'lights and shadows' mixing. This impression is enhanced by the successful performance of economic nationalism and of the "cohesive-capitalist states" in East Asia since the 1960s. In such a comparative perspective the cost of political and economic compromises reached in Latin America in the interwar period and over the subsequent decades has proved quite high. Also the quality of the state techno-structure, its ability to prioritize economic policy seems to be suboptimal. There are limits to such direct comparisons, though. The political and social context of the impressive East Asian growth was disparate. For instance, Korea's and Taiwan's solution to their respective land question was, politically, simply not available to Brazil, Argentina or Chile. The muddling through approach taken in the latter was the obvious result of their political economy. This fact substantially held back Latin America's growth potential. The elite-formation processes in the former countries were completely different, too. In a word, with hindsight, the industrial sector that emerged in Latin America due to the developments in the 1930s and after was, contrary to the *leyenda negra* of ISI, a qualified success (Thorp 1998: 197, Serra 1979). Holistic nationalism did work. Yet, it failed miserably as far as income distribution and the social dimension of this process were concerned. The dedication with which Bulmer-Thomas provided his economic history of Latin America well renders this problem: "For the 30 percent who receive 5 percent–a ray of hope; for the 5 percent who receive 30 percent–a warning."

Inasmuch as economic nationalism in Latin America and Central Europe toward the end of the 1930s was, despite all reservations, future oriented, the communist variant of economic nationalism ended up as devolution. According to some estimates, compared to Italy and Spain, economic position of Poland and Hungary had been improving until 1960, and rapidly declined thereafter (Eva Ehrlich quoted in Marer 1989: 49). In strictly technical terms,

> [a]s long as the economic world was ruled by the industrial and technological structures typical of the thirties or forties, the European socialist

countries were capable of reducing to some extent the huge ... headstart of Western Europe and North America (Průcha 1991: 267).

Interpreting this defeat, Hobsbawm (1994: 497), not without irony, referred to Marx: "Rarely has there been a clearer example of Marx's forces of production coming into conflict with the social, institutional and ideological superstructure ... up to the point where they turn from forces into fetters of production." The defeat of communist economic nationalism was a practical reply to the paradox inherent in Michał Kalecki's sarcastic remark on Soviet-type 'socialism': "Yes, the overthrowing of capitalism has gone well, now the only problem left is to get out of feudalism" (quoted in Małecki-Tepicht 2003: 123).

Yet, the way the implosion of "actually existing socialism" in the USSR and East and Central Europe occurred was not the only model of bypassing communist economic nationalism and "getting out" of "feudalism." The inconclusive experience of China's modernization strategy remains an alternative, authoritarian variant of breaking with such nationalism. Outdated and inefficient communist economic nationalism has been replaced by expansive, internationally competitive nationalistic state capitalism, fueled by extraordinarily high investment and infrastructure outlays, FDIs, an undervalued currency and export expansion.

Economic nationalism as a global phenomenon has found a very strong ally in a China that has been pursuing export-led industrialization. Even before China and other third-tier NICs began their impetuous export expansion, Bairoch (1993: 168) had pointed out that "if the entire Third World now had to export per capita the same amount of manufactures as the 'Four Dragons', this would be the equivalent of almost all of the consumption of manufactures of all the Western developed countries." Samuelson (1985: 511), when analyzing the first effects of the second globalization on the core countries in the 1970s, did not sound terribly optimistic: "The political pressures [in those countries] for protectionism, I suspect, are about to intensify." In the 1980s he suggested a way out:

> No matter how vibrant remains Japan's entrepreneurship, the capacity of the rest of the world to absorb and tolerate the expansion of Japanese exports needed to pay for the raw materials she would consume after attaining the American level of affluence will be limited. ... Put your best minds to work to *reduce your dependence on export-led growth* (Samuelson (1985: 508).

China's entry into the international market, followed by India, Brazil and other new regional economic powers, increased the already high tensions and gross disequilibria in the world economy enormously. The financial crisis and dramatic fall in world trade in 2008–2010 contributed to growing nationalism as well. The signs are abundant; therefore one example will suffice here: in December 2011, members of the South America's Mercosur trading bloc decided to increase by 35 percent tariffs on 100 commodities, from capital goods to textiles. Latin American countries "have voiced fears that Asian exporters might seek to offset soft demand in the U.S. and Europe by flooding Latin America with cheap manufactured goods" (Romig 2011).

However, China as a final production platform and a link in the intra-industry trade should also be seen as a part of the larger worldwide 'export engine' combining East Asian economies and the US, European and Japanese firms and their markets (Foster and McChesney 2012). The fact that the export drive was laid down as the backbone of the policy of internal restructuring and modernization makes China's position increasingly vulnerable. Its export expansion has been until now well ahead of its internal market-oriented industrialization: China's export mix "does not reveal the stage of [its] industrial sophistication" (Kasahara 2004: 17). Thus, the recently announced policy aimed at strengthening the nationally-controlled domestic potential adds a new dimension to economic nationalism already manifest in export expansion. The growing friction with foreign firms is but the first sign of such a change. In short, the state-supported political and economic nationalism, combined with unorganized and cheap labor and substantial foreign currency reserves, is a country-specific national response that permits both export-led industrialization as well as gradual reshaping of the hitherto dependence on FDI.

And finally, let me pose some questions: Can the endurance of economic nationalism as the economic policy option cause misfortunes such as those in the interwar period? Is nationalism, today manifested in unlimited export expansion, a model for all backward countries to copy, or an option for the few? Will new mercantilism and increasing competition for natural resources determine the future of second globalization?

The pessimistic scenario does not necessarily have to come true:

- if the crucial reform of capitalism, initiated in the 1930s (Kalecki's "full employment capitalism") is not totally rejected under the growing pressure from both the MNCs and low-labor-cost economies,
- if adjustment processes in the present-day core countries do not result in a dramatic social backlash internally, and increased protectionism internationally,

– if the new 'dragons' economies rebalance their respective investment and consumption levels, and adjust their priorities accordingly,
– if at a certain moment the new 'dragons' open up their domestic markets, in this way greatly increasing global demand.

There are many such ifs.

It is a matter of speculation, not knowledge, if the answers to these and other questions confirm the permanent break from the political passions and madness that have so far accompanied the (few) successes and (many) defeats of economic nationalism. Following the path charted by David Hume in his anti-mercantilist crusade, one can, of course, believe that rejection of the jealousy of trade, of "this narrow and malignant opinion" implying a zero-sum game, can be combined with a definite kind of economic nationalism. In a word, one can also imagine the reappearance of economic nationalism as *le doux commerce* and "calm passion" (Hirschman 1977).

However, such a belief would make sense only if the current economic strategies underpinning the globalization change. The blend of political and economic nationalism and an unconstrained export-drive founded on cheap labor is a prescription for trouble.

REFERENCES

Abdelal, Rawi. 2001. *National Purpose in the World Economy: Post-Soviet States in Comparative Perspective*. Ithaca and London: Cornell University Press.

Abraham, Gary A. 1991. "Max Weber: Modernist Anti-Pluralism and the Polish Question." *New German Critique* 53: 33–66.

Abreu, Marcelo de Paiva. 1984. "Argentina and Brazil during the 1930s: The Impact of British and American International Economic Policies", in Rosemary Thorp, ed., *Latin America in the 1930. The Role of the Periphery in World Crisis*. London: Macmillan in association with St. Antony's College, Oxford.

———. 1985. "Anglo-Brazilian Economic Relations and the Consolidation of American Preeminence in Brazil, 1930–1945", in Christopher Abel and Colin M. Lewis, eds., *Latin America, Economic Imperialism and the State: The Political Economy of the External Connection from Independence to the Present*. London: Athlone.

———. 1993. *The Political Economy of Protectionism in Argentina and Brazil, 1880–1930*. Rio de Janeiro: PUC-Rio Departamento de Económia Texto para Discussão No. 306, Agosto.

——— and Afonso S. Bevilaqua. 2000. "Brazil as an Export Economy, 1880–1930", in Enrique Cárdenas, José Antonio Ocampo and Rosemary Thorp, eds., *An Economic History of Twentieth-Century Latin America. Vol. 1: The Export Age: The Latin American Economies in the Late Nineteenth and Early Twentieth Centuries*. Basingstoke: Palgrave in association with St. Antony's College, Oxford.

Acemoglu, Daron. 2003. "Why Not a Political Coase Theorem? Social Conflict, Commitment, and Politics." *Journal of Comparative Economics* 31: 620–652.

———, Simon Johnson and James Robinson. 2004. *Institutions as the Fundamental Cause of Long-run Growth*, Cambridge, MA: NBER Working Paper No. 10481, May.

———, Simon Johnson and James Robinson. 2005. "The Rise of Europe: Atlantic Trade, Institutional Change and Economic Growth." *The American Economic Review* 95 No. 3: 546–579.

Acton-Dalberg, John E. E. 1907. "Nationality", in John E. E. Dalberg-Acton, *The History of Freedom and Other Essays*. London: Macmillan and Co. First published in 1862.

Adelman, Irma and C. Taft Morris. 1977. "A Typology of Poverty in 1850." *Economic Development and Cultural Change* 25 (Supplement): 314–343.

Adler, John H. with the assistance of Paul W. Kuznets, ed. 1967. *Capital Movements and Economic Development*, London and New York: Macmillan and St Martin's Press.

Albertone, Manuela and Alberto Masoero, eds. 1994. *Political Economy and National Realities*. Torino: Fondazione Luigi Einaudi.

Albrecht, Catherine. 2001. "The Rhetoric of Economic Nationalism in the Bohemian Boycott Campaigns of the Late Habsburg Monarchy." *Austrian History Yearbook* 32: 47–67.

Alhadeff, Peter. 1985. "Dependency, Historiography and Objections to the Roca Pact", in Christopher Abel and Colin M. Lewis, eds., *Latin America, Economic Imperialism and the State: The Political Economy of the External Connection from Independence to the Present*. London: Athlone.

Allen, G. C. 1972. *A Short Economic History of Modern Japan 1867–1937*. London: George Allen & Unwin (3rd edition).

Alperowicz, Moisiej S. 1981. *Dyktatura doktora Francii w Paragwaju (1814–1840)*. Wrocław: Ossolineum.

Àlvarez, Jeorge, Ennio Bilancini, Simone D'Alessandro and Gabriel Porcile. 2010. *Agricultural Institutions, Industrialization and Growth: The Case of New Zealand and Uruguay in 1870–1940*. Center for Economic Research Working Paper 53, Modena, November.

Amsden, Alice H. 2001. *The Rise of "The Rest:" Challenges to the West from Late-Industrializing Economies*. New York: Oxford University Press.
Anderson, Benedict. 1983. *Imagined Communities: Reflections on the Origin and Spread of Nationalism*. London: Verso Editions and NLB.
Anderson, Perry. 1974. *Lineages of the Absolutist State*. London: NLB.
Andersson, Jan Otto. 1976. *Studies in the Theory of Unequal Exchange between Nations*. Åbo: Akademi Press.
Arieli, Yehoshua. 1966. *Individualism and Nationalism in American Ideology*. Baltimore: Penguin Books.
Arrow, Kenneth J. 2004. "Path Dependence and Competitive Equilibrium", in Timothy Guinnance, William W. Sundgtrom and Warren Whatley, eds., *History Matters. Essays on Economic Growth, Technology, and Demographic Change*. Stanford: Stanford University Press.
Arthur, W. B. 1989. "Competing Technologies, Increasing Returns, and Lock-In by Historical Events." *Economic Journal* 99 No. 394: 116–131.
Ascher, Abraham. 2001. *P. A. Stolypin: The Search for Stability in Late Imperial Russia*. Stanford: Stanford University Press.
Assorodobraj, Nina. 1966. *Początki klasy robotniczej. Problem rąk roboczych w przemyśle polskim epoki stanisławowskiej*. Warszawa: PWN.
Ayal, Eliezer B. 1966. "Nationalist Ideology and Economic Development." *Human Organization* 25 No. 3: 230–239.
Baack, Bennet D. and Edward J. Kay. 1974. "Tariff Policy and Comparative Advantage in the Iron and Steel Industry: 1870–1929." *Explorations in Economic History* 11 No. 1: 3–23.
Babb, Sarah. 2001. *Managing Mexico: Economists from Nationalism to Neoliberalism*. Princeton and Oxford: Princeton University Press.
Badie, Bertrand and Pierre Birnbaum. 1983. *The Sociology of the State*. Chicago and London: The University of Chicago Press.
Baer, Werner. 1969. *The Development of the Brazilian Steel Industry*. Nashville: Vanderbilt University Press.
——. 2008. *The Brazilian Economy: Growth and Development*. Boulder: Lynne Rienner Publishers (6th edition).
—— and Anibal Villanova Villela. 1972. "Crescimento industrial e industrialização: revisões nos estagios do desenvolvimento econômico do Brasil." *Dados* 9: 114–131.
——, Isaac Kerstenetsky and Anibal Villanova Villela. 1973. "The Changing Role of the State in the Brazilian Economy." *World Development* l No. 11: 23–34.
Bagchi, Amiya Kumar. 2000. "The Past and the Future of the Developmental State." *Journal of World-Systems Research* VI No. 2: 398–442.
Bairoch, Paul. 1973. "Agriculture and the Industrial Revolution 1700–1914", in Carlo Cipolla, ed., *The Fontana Economic History of Europe*. Vol. 3: *The Industrial Revolution*. Glasgow: Fontana/Collins.
——. 1975. *The Economic Development of the Third World since 1900*. London: Methuen.
——. 1991. "How and Not Why? Economic Inequalities between 1800 and 1913: Some Background Figures", in Jean Batou, ed., *Between Development and Underdevelopment 1800–1870. The Precocious Attempts at Industrialization of the Periphery*. Geneva: Centre of International Economic History/ Librairie Droz.
——. 1993. *Economics and World History. Myths and Paradoxes*. London: Harvester Wheatsheaf.
—— and Richard Kozul-Wright. 1996. *Globalization Myths: Some Historical Reflections on Integration, Industrialization and Growth in the World Economy*. Geneva, UNCTAD Discussion Paper No. 113.
Baran, Paul. 1976. *The Political Economy of Growth*. Harmondsworth: Penguin Books. First published in 1957.
Barkey, Karen and Sunita Parikh. 1991. "Comparative Perspectives on the State." *Annual Review of Sociology* 17: 523–549.

Basadre, Jorge. 1965. "Conciencia de sí", in R. A. Humphreys and John Lynch, eds., *The Origins of the Latin American Revolutions, 1808–1826*. New York: Alfred A. Knopf.
Basch, Antonín. 1943. *The Danube Basin and the German Economic Sphere*. New York: Columbia University Press.
Bastian, Jean Pierre. 1988. "Las sociedades protestantes y la oposición a Porfirio Díaz, 1877–1911." *Historia Mexicana* 37 No. 3: 469–512.
Batou, Jean, ed. 1990a. *Between Development and Underdevelopment 1800–1870. The Precocious Attempts at Industrialization of the Periphery*. Geneva: Centre of International Economic History/Librairie Droz.
———. 1990b. *Cent ans de resistance au sous-developpement. L'industrialisation de l'Amérique latine et du Moyen-Orient face au defi européen*. Genève: Centre of International Economic History/ Librairie Droz.
———. 1993. "Nineteenth-Century Attempted Escapes from the Periphery: The Cases of Egypt and Paraguay." *Review* 16 No. 3: 279–318.
——— and Thomas David. 1996. "Nationalisme économique et industrialisation de la périphérie européenne: de la révolution industrielle à la deuxieme guerre mondiale", in Paul Bairoch and Eric J. Hobsbawm, eds., *Storia d'Europa*, Vol. V: *L'Eta contemporanea. Secoli XIX–XX*. Torino.
Bauer, Arnold J. 1975. *Chilean Rural Society from the Spanish Conquest to 1930*. Cambridge: Cambridge University Press.
Bauer, Peter T. 1972. *Dissent on Development. Studies and Debates in Development Economics*. Cambridge, MA: Harvard University Press.
Bauer, Ralph and José Antonio Mazzotti. 2009. "Introduction: Creole Subjects in the Colonial Americas", in Ralph Bauer and José Antonio Mazzotti, eds., *Creole Subjects in the Colonial Americas: Empires, Texts, Identities*. Chapel Hill: University of North Carolina Press for the Omohundro Institute of Early American History and Culture, Williamsburg, Virginia.
Baumann, Kurt. 1933. "Autarkie und Planwirtschaft."*Zeitschrift für Sozialforschung* 2 No. 1: 79–103.
Bazylow, Ludwik. 1966. *Polityka wewnątrzna caratu i ruchy społeczne w Rosji na początku XX wieku*. Warszawa: Książka i Wiedza.
Beatty, Edward. 2002. "Commercial Policy in Porfirian Mexico: The Structure of Protection", in Jeffrey L. Bortz and Stephen Haber, eds., *The Mexican Economy, 1870–1930. Essays on the Economic History of Institutions, Revolution, and Growth*. Stanford: Stanford University Press.
Becker, Joachim and Andrea Komlosy. 2004."Grenzen und Räume – Formen und Wandel. Grenztypen von der Stadtmauer bis zum 'Eisernen Vorhang', in Joachim Becker and Andrea Komlosy, eds., *Grenzen Weltweit. Zonen, Linien, Mauern im historischen Vergleich*. Wien: Promedia Verlag & Südwind.
Behrendt, Richard F. 1941. *Economic Nationalism in Latin America*. Albuquerque: The School of Inter-American Affairs, University of New Mexico Short Papers No. 1.
Belaunde, Víctor Andrés. 1965. "The Origins of Spanish American Nationalism", in R. A. Humphreys and John Lynch, eds., *The Origins of the Latin American Revolutions, 1808–1826*. New York: Alfred A. Knopf. First published in 1938.
Bell, John D. 1977. *Peasants in Power. Alexander Stamboliski and the Bulgarian Agrarian National Union, 1899–1923*. Princeton: Princeton University Press.
Bendix, Reinhard. 1984. *Force, Fate and Freedom: On Historical Sociology*. Berkeley and Los Angeles: University of California Press.
Berend, Ivan T. 1998. *Decades of Crisis. Central and Eastern Europe before World War II*. Berkeley: University of California Press.
———. 2003. *History Derailed. Central and Eastern Europe in the Long Nineteenth Century*. Berkeley: University of California Press.
Berger, Mark T. 2000. "Specters of Colonialism: Building Postcolonial States and Making Modern Nations in the Americas." *Latin American Research Review* 35 No. 1: 151–171.

Berlin, Isaiah. 2003. *Rosyjscy myśliciele*. Warszawa: Prószyński i S-ka.
——. 2004. *Pokrzywione drzewo człowieczeństwa*. Warszawa: Prószyński i S-ka.
Bértola, Luis and Jeffrey G. Williamson. 2006. "Globalization in Latin America before 1940", in Victor Bulmer-Thomas, John H. Coatsworth and Roberto Cortés Conde, eds., *The Cambridge Economic History of Latin America*, Vol. II: *The Long Twentieth Century*. Cambridge: Cambridge University Press.
—— and Gabriel Porcile. 2006. Convergence, Trade and Institutional Policy: Argentina, Brazil and Uruguay in the International Economy, 1900–1980. Paper presented at the XIV International Economic History Association Congress, Helsinki.
Bhagwati, Jagdish. 1958. "Immiserizing Growth: A Geometrical Note." *Review of Economic Studies* 25 No.3: 201–205.
——. 1989. *Protectionism*. Cambridge, MA: The MIT Press.
Bibó, István. 1991. "The Distress of the East European Small States", in István Bibó, *Democracy, Revolution, Self-Determination. Selected Writings*. Highland Lakes: Atlantic Research and Publications. First published in 1946.
Bielecki, Jan Krzysztof. 2011. "Myślę, jak to państwo wzmocnić." *Gazeta Wyborcza* April 7: 17–18.
Bils, Mark. 1984. "Tariff Protection and Production in the Early U. S. Cotton Textile Industry." *The Journal of Economic History* XLIV No. 4: 1033–1045.
Blaug, Mark. 1996. *Economic Theory in Retrospect*. Cambridge: Cambridge University Press.
Bluhm, William T. 1965. *Theories of the Political System. Classics of Political Thought and Modern Political Analysis*. Englewood Cliffs, N.J.: Prentice-Hall.
Blum, Jerome. 1978. *The End of the Old Order in Rural Europe*. Princeton: Princeton University Press.
Bobbio, Norberto. 1998. *Liberalizm i demokracja*. Kraków: Wydawnictwo Znak.
Bonilla, Heraclio. 1974. *Guano y burguesía en el Perú*. Lima: Instituto de Estudios Peruanos.
—— (ed.). 1977a. *Gran Bretaña y el Perú 1826–1919: informes de los consules britanicos*, Vol. I. Lima: Instituto de Estudios Peruanos–Fondo del Libro del Banco Industrial del Perú.
——. 1977b. *Gran Bretaña y el Perú: los mecanismos de una control económico*. Lima: Instituto de Estudios Peruanos–Fondo del Libro del Banco Industrial del Perú.
——. 1980. *Un siglo a la deriva. Ensayos sobre el Perú, Bolivia y la Guerra*. Lima: Instituto de Estudios Peruanos.
Bonn, Moritz J. 1938. *The Crumbling of Empire: The Disintegration of World Economy*. London: Allen & Unwin.
Bonnell, Victoria E. 1980. "The Uses of Theory, Concepts and Comparison in Historical Sociology." *Comparative Studies in Society and History* Vol. 22 No. 2: 156–174.
Borak, Neven. 2000. "Economic Background to National Conflicts in Yugoslavia", in Alice Teichova, Herbert Matis and Jaroslav Pátek, eds., *Economic Change and the National Question in Twentieth-century Europe*. Cambridge: Cambridge University Press.
Borchardt, Knut. 1991. *Perspectives on Modern German Economic History and Policy*. Cambridge: Cambridge University Press.
Borejsza, Jerzy W. 1981. *Rzym a wspólnota faszystowska. O penetracji faszyzmu włoskiego w Europie Środkowej, Południowej i Wschodniej*. Warszawa: Książka i Wiedza.
Boulanger, Éric. 2002. *Le nationalisme économique dans la pensée et les politiques publiques du Japon: particularisme, pragmatisme et puissance*. Montréal : Cahiers de recherche – CEIM, Université du Québec, Février.
Boyer, Christoph. 2000. "Nationality and Competition: Czech and Germans in the Economy of the First Czechoslovak Republic (1918–1938)", in Alice Teichova, Herbert Matis and Jaroslav Pátek, eds., *Economic Change and the National Question in Twentieth-century Europe*. Cambridge: Cambridge University Press.
Bradford, Jr., Colin I. 1990. "Policy Interventions and Markets: Development Strategy Typologies and Policy Options", in Gary Gereffi and Donald L. Wyman, eds., *Manufacturing Miracles. Paths of Industrialization in Latin America and East Asia*. Princeton: Princeton University Press.

Braudel, Fernand. 1977. *Afterthoughts on Material Civilization and Capitalism.* Baltimore and London: The Johns Hopkins University Press.
——. 1990. *The Identity of France*, Vol. II: *People and Production.* New York: HarperCollins Publishers.
——. 1992a. *Civilization and Capitalism, 15th–18th Century.* Vol. 2: *The Wheels of Commerce.* Berkeley and Los Angeles: University of California Press.
——. 1992b. *Civilization and Capitalism, 15th–18th Century.* Vol. 3: *The Perspective of the World.* Berkeley and Los Angeles: University of California Press.
Bresser Pereira, Luiz Carlos. 1964. "Origens étnicas e sociais do empresário paulista." *Revista de Administração de Empresas* 11 No. 4: 83–103.
——. 1993. "Economic Reforms and Cycles of State Intervention." *World Development* 21 No. 8: 1337–1353.
——. 2009a. "From the Patrimonial State to the Managerial State", in Ignacy Sachs, Jorge Wilheim and Paulo Sérgio Pinheiro, eds., *Brazil: A Century of Change.* Chapel Hill: The University of North Carolina Press.
——. 2009b. *From the National-Bourgeois to the Associated Dependency Interpretation of Latin America.* São Paulo: Escola de Economia de São Paulo da Fundação Getulio Vargas Textos para Discussão 185, Abril.
Breton, Albert. 1964. "The Economics of Nationalism." *The Journal of Political Economy"* Vol. LXXII No. 4: 376–386.
—— and Margot Breton. 1995. "Nationalism Revisited", in Albert Breton, Gianluigi Galeotti, Pierre Salmon and Ronald Wintrobe, eds., *Nationalism and Rationality.* Cambridge: Cambridge University Press.
Breuilly, John. 1985. *Nationalism and the State.* Chicago: The University of Chicago Press.
Bujak, Franciszek. 1976. *Wybór pism. Nauka, społeczeństwo, historia* Vol. 1. Warszawa: PWN. First published in 1906–1925.
Bukharin, Nikolai. 1973. *Imperialism and World Economy.* New York: Monthly Review Press. First published in 1915.
Bulmer-Thomas, Victor. 2003. *The Economic History of Latin America since Independence.* Cambridge: Cambridge University Press (2nd edition).
——, John H. Coatsworth and Roberto Cortés Conde, eds. 2006. *The Cambridge Economic History of Latin America,* Vol. II: *The Long Twentieth Century.* Cambridge: Cambridge University Press.
Bunge, Alejandro 1918. "La económia positiva y la política económica argentina." *Revista de Economía Argentina* 1 No. 3: 241–258.
Buła, Alojzy. 1989."Obrona Ślązaków." *Kwartalnik Polityczny KRYTYKA* 31: 70–81 (samizdat publication).
Burga, Manuel. 1980. "Los profetas de la rebelión, 1920–1923 (Imaginación y realidad en una sublevacion andina)", in J. P. Deler and Y. Saint-Geours, eds., *Estados y naciones en los Andes. Hacia una historia comparativa: Bolivia – Colombia – Ecuador – Perú,* Lima: Instituto de Estudios Peruanos y Instituto Frances de Estudios Andinos.
—— and Alberto Flores Galindo. 1979. *Apogeo y crisis de la Republica Aristocratica. Oligarquia, aprismo y comunismo en el Perú 1895–1932.* Lima: Ediciones "Rikchay Peru".
—— and Wilson Reategui. 1981. *Lanas y capital mercantil en el Sur. La Casa Ricketts, 1895–1935.* Lima: Instituto de Estudios Peruanos.
Burgin, Miron. 1944. "Argentina", in Seymour E. Harris, ed., *Economic Problems of Latin America.* New York and London: McGraw-Hill Book Company.
——. 1946. *The Economic Aspects of Argentine Federalism, 1820–1852.* Cambridge, MA: Harvard University Press.
Burnell, Peter J. 1986. *Economic Nationalism in the Third World.* Brighton: Wheatsheaf.
Burns, E. Bradford. 1964. "The Role of Azeredo Coutinho in the Enlightenment of Brazil." *The Hispanic American Historical Review* 44 No. 2: 145–160.
——. 1968. *Nationalism in Brazil: A Historical Survey.* New York: Frederick A. Praeger.
——. 1970. *A History of Brazil.* New York: Columbia University Press.

———. 1980. *The Poverty of Progress. Latin America in the Nineteenth Century.* Berkeley and Los Angeles: University of California Press.
Bushnell, David and Neill Macaulay. 1988. *The Emergence of Latin America in the Nineteenth Century.* New York: Oxford University Press.
Caballero, Manuel. 1986. *Latin America and the Comintern 1919–1943.* Cambridge: Cambridge University Press.
Calleo, David P. 2001. *Rethinking Europe's Future.* Princeton: Princeton University Press.
Cameron, Rondo. 1996. *Historia gospodarcza świata. Od paleolitu do czasów najnowszych.* Warszawa: Książka i Wiedza.
Cárdenas, Enrique. 1997. "A Macroeonomic Interpretation of Nineteenth-Century Mexico", in Stephen Haber, ed., *How Latin America Fell Behind: Essays on the Economic Histories of Brazil and Mexico, 1800–1914.* Stanford: Stanford University Press.
———, José Antonio Ocampo and Rosemary Thorp, eds. 2000. *An Economic History of Twentieth-Century Latin America.* Vol. 1: *The Export Age: The Latin American Economies in the Late Nineteenth and Early Twentieth Centuries.* Basingstoke: Palgrave in association with St. Antony's College, Oxford.
Cardoso, Ciro F. S. and Hector Perez Brignoli. 1979. *Historia económica de América Latina.* T. 1: *Sistemas agrarios e historia colonial* T. 2: *Economias de exportación y desarrollo capitalista.* Barcelona: Editorial Crítica.
Cardoso, Fernando H. 1979a. "On the Characterization of Authoritarian Regimes in Latin America", in David Collier, ed., *The New Authoritarianism in Latin America*, Princeton: Princeton University Press.
———. 1979b. "The Originality of the Copy: The Economic Commission for Latin America and the Idea of Development", in *Toward a New Strategy for Development. A Rothko Chapel Colloquium.* New York: Pergamon Press.
——— and Enzo Faletto. 1979. *Dependency and Development in Latin America.* Berkeley and Los Angeles: University of California Press.
Carmagnani, Marcello. 1990. "Some Comments on Economic Nationalism," in Henryk Szlajfer, ed., *Economic Nationalism in East-Central Europe and South America, 1918–1939.* Geneva: Centre of International Economic History/ Librairie Droz.
Carr, Barry. 1973. "Las peculiaridades del norte mexicano, 1880–1927: ensayo de interpretación." *Historia Mexicana* XXII No. 3: 320–346.
Carr, Edward H. 1985. "States and Nationalism: The Nation in European History", in David Held *et al.*, eds., *States and Societies.* Oxford : Basil Blackwell in association with The Open University. First published in 1945.
Castañeda, Jorge G. 1993. *Utopia Unarmed. The Latin American Left after the Cold War.* New York: Alfred. A. Knopf.
Chalkley, H.O. 1931. *Economic Conditions in the Argentine Republic. Report by...* London: Department of the Overseas Trade.
Chandra, Bipan. 1979. *Nationalism and Colonialism in Modern India.* New Delhi: Orient Longman.
Chang, Ha-Joon. 2005. *Kicking Away the Ladder. Development Strategy in Historical Perspective.* London: Anthem Press.
Chapple, Simon. 1993. "Kalecki's Theory of the Business Cycle and the General Theory." *History of Economics Review* 20: 120–139.
Chapple, Simon. 1995. "The Kaleckian Origins of the Keynesian Model." *Oxford Economic Papers* 47: 525–538.
Chatterjee, Partha. 1986. *Nationalist Thought and the Colonial World. A Derivative Discourse?* London: Zed Books.
Chavarría, José. 1978. "The Colonial Heritage of National Peru: An Overview". *Boletin de Estudios Latinoamericanos* 25: 37–49.
Checkland, S.G. 1964. *The Rise of Industrial Society in England, 1815–1885.* New York: St. Martin's Press.

Cheesman Rajkovic, Roxanne. 1986. "Politicas de reactivación económica en la crisis de 1929", in Heraclio Bonilla, ed., *Las crisis económicas en la historia del Perú*. Lima: Centro Latinoamericano de Historia Economica y Social-Fundación Friedrich Ebert.
Chehali, H. E. and Juan J. Linz. 1998. "A Theory of Sultanism 1: A Type of Nondemocratic Rule", in H. E. Chehali and Juan J. Linz, eds., *Sultanistic Regimes*. Baltimore: The Johns Hopkins University Press.
Child, Josiah. 1751. *A New Discourse of Trade*. Glasgow: Robert and Andrew Foulis. First published in 1670.
Chlebowczyk, Józef. 1983. *O prawie do bytu małych i młodych narodów. Kwestia narodowa i procesy narodotwórcze we wschodniej Europie Środkowej w dobie kapitalizmu (od schyłku XVIII do początków XX w.)*. Warszawa–Kraków: Śląski Instytut Naukowy/ PWN.
——. 1988. *Między dyktatem, realiami a prawem do samookreślenia. Prawo do samookreślenia i problem granic we wschodniej Europie Środkowej w pierwszej wojnie światowej oraz po jej zakończeniu*. Warszawa: PWN.
Chojnowski, Andrzej. 1979. *Koncepcja polityki narodowościowej rządów polskich w latach 1921–1939*. Wrocł Ossolineum.
Clark, Ian. 1991. *The Hierarchy of States. Reform and Resistance in the International Order*. Cambridge: Cambridge University Press (revised edition).
Clarkson, L. A. 1985. *Proto-Industrialization: The First Phase of Industrialization?* London: Macmillan.
Clay, Henry. 1958. "Speech on the Tariff, March 31, 1824," in Richard Hofstadter, ed., *Great Issues in American History. From the Revolution to the Civil War, 1765–1865*. New York: Vintage Books. First published in 1824.
Clemens, Michael A. and Jeffrey G. Williamson. 2001. *A Tariff-Growth Paradox? Protection's Impact the World around 1875–1997*. Cambridge, Mass: NBER Working Paper No. 8459, September.
Clemens, Michael A. and Jeffrey G. Williamson. 2002. Closed Jaguar, Open Dragon: Comparing Tariffs in Latin America and Asia before World War II. Cambridge, MA: NBER Working Paper No. 9401, December.Coatsworth, John H. 2005. "Structures, Endowments, and Institutions in the Economic History of Latin America." *Latin American Research Review* 40 No. 3: 126–144.
Coatsworth, John H. and Jeffrey G. Williamson. 2004. "Always Protectionist? Latin American Tariffs from Independence to Great Depression." *Journal of Latin American Studies* 36 No. 2: 205–232.
Coleman, D. C. 1969. "Eli Heckscher and the Idea of Mercantilism", in D. C. Coleman, ed., *Revisions in Mercantilism*. London: Methuen.
Colistete, Renato P. 2009. Revisiting Import-Substitution Industrialization in Brazil: Productivity Growth and Technological Learning in the Post-War Years. Paper presented at the International Conference on Latin American Economies: History and Globalization, UCLA, Los Angeles, April 24–25.
Collier, Simon. 1967. *Ideas and Politics of Chilean Independence 1808–1833*. Cambridge: Cambridge University Press.
—— and William F. Sater. 1996. *A History of Chile 1808–1994*. Cambridge: Cambridge University Press.
Conniff, Michael L., ed. 1999. *Populism in Latin America*. Tuscaloosa and London: The University of Alabama Press.
Conning, Jonathan H. and James A. Robinson. 2009. "Enclaves and Development: An Empirical Assessment." *Studies in Comparative International Development* 44: 359–385.
Córdova, Arnaldo. 2003. *La ideología de la revolución mexicana: la formación del nuevo régimen*. México: Editorial Era (2nd edition).
Cornblit, Oscar. 1967. "European Immigrants in Argentine Industry and Politics" in Claudio Veliz, ed., *The Politics of Conformity in Latin America*. London: Oxford University Press.
Cortés Conde, Roberto. 1974. *The First Stages of Modernization in Spanish America*. New York: Harper & Row, Publishers.

———. 2000. "The Vicissitudes of an Exporting Economy: Argentina, 1875–1930", in Enrique Cárdenas, José Antonio Ocampo and Rosemary Thorp, eds., *An Economic History of Twentieth-Century Latin America*. Vol. 1: *The Export Age: The Latin American Economies in the Late Nineteenth and Early Twentieth Centuries*. Basingstoke: Palgrave in association with St. Antony's College, Oxford.

——— and Stanley J. Stein. 1977. "Editors' Introduction", in Roberto Cortés Conde and Stanley J. Stein, eds., *Latin America: A Guide to Economic History, 1830–1930*. Berkeley: University of California Press.

Crisp, Olga. 1991. "Russia", in Richard Sylla and Gianni Toniolo, eds., *Patterns of European Industrialization. The Nineteenth Century*. London and New York: Routledge.

Croce, Benedetto. 1933. *History of Europe in the Nineteenth Century*. New York: Harcourt, Brace and Company.

Crossley, Colin and Robert Greenhill. 1977. "The River Plate Beef Trade", in Desmond C. M. Platt, ed., *Business Imperialism 1840–1930. An Inquiry Based on British Experience in Latin America*. Oxford: Oxford University Press.

Cunningham, William. 1891. "Nationalism and Cosmopolitanism in Economics." *Journal of the Royal Statistical Society* 54 No. 4: 644–662.

[CUP] 1983. "Wytyczne planu długoterminowego na lata 1950–1973", in Hanna Jędruszczak, ed., *Wizje gospodarki socjalistycznej w Polsce 1945–1949: początki planowania. Materiały źródłowe*. Warszawa: PWN. Prepared in 1947.

Czarnowski, Stefan. 2002. "Nacjonalizm", in Wojciech Józef Burszta, Joanna Nowak and Krzysztof Wawrucha, eds., *Polska refleksja nad narodem. Wybór tekstów*. Poznań: Wydawnictwo Poznańskie. First published in 1912.

Dangerfield, George. 1965. *The Awakening of American Nationalism, 1815–1828*. New York: Harper & Row, Publishers.

David, Paul A. 1985. "Clio and the Economics of QWERTY." *American Economic Review* 75, No. 2 (Papers and Proceedings): 332–337.

David, Thomas and Elisabeth Spilman. 2006. "Proto-Economic-Nationalism in the Early Nineteenth Century", in Helga Schultz and Eduard Kubů, eds., *History and Culture of Economic Nationalism in East Central Europe*. Berlin: Berliner Wissenschafts-Verlag.

———. 2009. *Nationalisme économique et industrialisation: L'experience des pays d'Europe de l'Est (1789–1939)*. Genève: Librairie Droz.

Davies Jr., Thomas M. 1978. "The Indigenismo of the Peruvian Aprista Party: A Reinterpretation", in Francisco Miró Quesada, Franklin Pease and David Sobrevilla, eds., *Historia, problema y promesa. Homenaje a Jorge Basadre*. Lima: Pontificia Universidad Católica del Perú.

Davis, Ralph. 1969. "English Foreign Trade, 1700–1774", in W. E. Minchinton, ed., *The Growth of English Overseas Trade in the Seventeenth and Eighteenth Centuries*. London: Methuen.

———. 1973. *The Rise of the Atlantic Economies*. London: Weidenfeld and Nicolson.

Deák, István. 1990. "The Revolution and the War of Independence", in Peter F. Sugar, ed., *A History of Hungary*. Bloomington and Indianapolis: Indiana University Press.

Dean, Warren. 1969. *The Industrialization of São Paulo 1880–1945*. Austin: The University of Texas Press.

Deas, Malcolm. 1982. "The Fiscal Problems of Nineteenth-Century Colombia." *Journal of Latin American Studies* 14 Part 2: 287–328.

De Rosa, Luigi. 2000. "Economic Change and Nationalism in Italy in the Twentieth Century", in Alice Teichova, Herbert Matis and Jaroslav Pátek, eds., *Economic Change and the National Question in Twentieth-century Europe*. Cambridge: Cambridge University Press.

Deutsch, Karl W. and A. Eckstein. 1961. "National Industrialization and the Declining Share of the International Economic Sector, 1890–1959." *World Politics* 13, No. 2: 267–299.

Deustua, Jose. 1986. *La minera peruana y la iniciación de la republica, 1820–1840*. Lima: Instituto de Estudios Peruanos.

Díaz-Alejandro, Carlos F. 1970. *Essays on the Economic History of the Argentine Republic*. New Haven and London: Yale University Press.

―――. 1978. "Delinking North and South: Unshackled or Unhinged?", in Andres Velasco, ed., *Trade, Development and the World Economy. Selected Essays of Carlos F. Díaz-Alejandro.* Oxford: Basil Blackwell.

―――. 1984. "Latin America in the 1930s", in Rosemary Throp, ed., *Latin America in the 1930s. The Role of the Periphery in World Crisis.* Oxford: Oxford University Press.

Diniz, Eli. 1989. "The Post-1930 Industrial Elite", in Michael L. Conniff and Frank D. McCann, eds., *Modern Brazil: Elites and Masses in Historical Perspective.* Lincoln and London: University of Nebraska Press.

Di Tella, Torcuato S. 1965. "Populism and Reform in Latin America", in Claudio Veliz, ed., *Obstacles to Change in Latin America.* New York: Oxford University Press.

―――. 2007. *History of Political Parties in Twentieth-Century Latin America.* New Brunswick: Transaction Publishers.

Doboszyński, Adam. 1936. *Gospodarka narodowa.* Warszawa (no publisher) (2nd edition).

Dobrzycki, Wiesław. 1986. *Myśl polityczna rewolucji meksykańskiej.* Warszawa: PWN.

Donham, Wallace B. 1933. "National Ideals and Internationalist Idols", in James G. Hodgson, ed., *Economic Nationalism.* New York: The H. W. Wilson Company.

Dowrick, Steve and J. Bradford DeLong. 2003. "Globalization and Convergence", in Michael D. Bordo, Alan M. Taylor and Jeffrey G. Williamson, eds., *Globalization in Historical Perspective.* Chicago: University of Chicago Press.

Drabek, Zdenek. 1985. "Foreign Trade Performance and Policy", in Michael C. Kaser and E. A. Radice, eds., *The Economic History of Eastern Europe 1919–1945,* Vol. I: *Economic Structure and Performance between the Two Wars.* Oxford: Oxford University Press.

Drake, Paul W. 2005. "The Hegemony of US Economic Doctrines in Latin America", in Valpy FitzGerald and Rosemary Thorp, eds., *Economic Doctrines in Latin America. Origins, Embedding and Evolution.* Basingstoke: Palgrave Macmillan in association with St. Antony's College, Oxford.

Drinot, Paulo. 2000. "Peru, 1884–1930: A Beggar Sitting on a Bench of Gold", in Enrique Cárdenas, José Antonio Ocampo and Rosemary Thorp, eds., *An Economic History of Twentieth-Century Latin America.* Vol. 1: *The Export Age: The Latin American Economies in the Late Nineteenth and Early Twentieth Centuries.* Basingstoke: Palgrave Macmillan in association with St. Antony's College, Oxford.

Drozdowski, Marian Marek. 1963. *Polityka gospodarcza rządu polskiego 1936–1939.* Warszawa: PWN.

―――. 1989. *Eugeniusz Kwiatkowski. Człowiek i dzieło.* Kraków: Wydawnictwo Literackie.

Dye, Alan. 2006. "The Institutional Framework", in Victor Bulmer-Thomas, John H. Coatsworth and Roberto Cortés Conde, eds., *The Cambridge Economic History of Latin America,* Vol. II: *The Long Twentieth Century.* Cambridge: Cambridge University Press.

Dziewulski, Kazimierz. 1981. *Spór o etatyzm. Dyskusja wokół sektora państwowego w Polsce międzywojennej 1919–1939.* Warszawa: PWN.

Eakin, Marshall C. 1986. "Business Imperialism and British Enterprise in Brazil: The St. John d'el Rey Mining Company, Limited, 1830–1960." *The Hispanic American Historical Review* 66 No. 4: 697–741.

Egerton, Hugh E. 1903. *The Origin and Growth of Greater Britain.* Oxford: Oxford University Press.

Eichengreen, Barry. 1992. "The Origins and Nature of the Great Slump Revisited." *The Economic History Review.* New Series 45 No. 2: 213–239.

―――. 2008. *Globalizing Capital: A History of the International Monetary System.* Princeton and Oxford: Princeton University Press (2nd edition).

――― and Richard Portes. 1989. *Dealing with Debt. The 1930s and the 1980s.* Washington, D.C.: The World Bank Policy, Planning, and Research Working Papers No. 259, August.

――― and Richard Portes. 1992. "After the Deluge: Default, Negotiation, and Readjustment during the Interwar Years", in Barry Eichengreen and Peter H. Lindert, eds., *The International Debt Crisis in Historical Perspective.* Cambridge, MA: The MIT Press.

[Encyklopedia] 1981. *Encyklopedia historii gospodarczej Polski do 1945 roku.* Warszawa: Wiedza Powszechna.

Engerman, Stanley L. and Kenneth L. Sokoloff. 1997. "Factor Endowments, Institutions, and Differential Paths of Growth Among New World Economies: A View from Economic Historians of the United States", in Stephen Haber, ed., *How Latin America Fell Behind: Essays on the Economic Histories of Brazil and Mexico, 1800–1914.* Stanford: Stanford University Press.

Ericsson, Kenneth P. 1977. *The Brazilian Corporative State and Working-Class Politics.* Berkeley: University of California Press.

Evans, Peter. 1979. *Dependent Development. The Alliance of Multinational, State, and Local Capital in Brazil.* Princeton: Princeton University Press.

——. 1992. "The State as Problem and Solution: Predation, Embedded Autonomy, and Structural Change", in Stephan Haggard and Robert R. Kaufman, eds., *The Politics of Economic Adjustment.* Princeton: Princeton University Press.

——. 1995. *Embedded Autonomy: States and Industrial Transformation.* Princeton: Princeton University Press.

——. 2005. "The Challenge of the 'Institutional Turn': New Interdisciplinary Opportunities in Development Theory", in Victor Nee and Richard Swedberg. eds., *The Economic Sociology of Capitalist Institutions.* Princeton: Princeton University Press.

Fernandes, Florestan. 1969. *Negro in Brazilian Society.* New York: Columbia University Press.

——. 1975. *A revolução burguesa no Brasil. Ensaio de interpretação sociológica.* Rio de Janeiro: Zahar Editores.

Ferns, Henry S. 1960. *Britain and Argentina in the Nineteenth Century.* Oxford: Oxford University Press.

Ferrero, Mario. 1995. "The Economics of Socialist Nationalism: Evidence and Theory", in Breton, Albert, Gianluigi Galeotti, Pierre Salmon and Ronald Wintrobe, eds., *Nationalism and Rationality.* Cambridge: Cambridge University Press.

Finch, M. H. J. 1985. "British Imperialism in Uruguay: the Public Utility Companies and the battlista State, 1990–1930", in Christopher Abel and Colin M. Lewis, eds., *Latin America, Economic Imperialism and the State: The Political Economy of the External Connection from Independence to the Present.* London: Athlone.

Findlay, Ronald. 1995. "Notes on the Political Economy of Nationalism", in Albert Breton, Gianluigi Galeotti, Pierre Salmon and Ronald Wintrobe, eds., *Nationalism and Rationality,* Cambridge: Cambridge University Press.

—— and Kevin H. O'Rourke. 2001. Commodity Market Integration, 1500–2000. Paper presented at NBER Conference on Globalization in Historical Perspective, Santa Monica, California, May 3–6.

Fishlow, Albert. 1972. "Origins and Consequences of Import Substitution in Brazil", in Luis Eugenio di Marco, ed., *International Economics and Development. Essays in Honor of Raúl Prebisch.* New York: Academic Press.

FitzGerald, E. V. K. 1994. "ECLA and the Formation of Latin American Economic Doctrine," in David Rock, ed., *Latin America in the 1940s: War and Postwar Transitions.* Berkeley: University of California Press.

Flandreu, Marc and Juan Flores. 2010. *Hamlet without the Prince of Denmark: Relationship Banking and Conditionality Lending in the London Market for Foreign Government Debt, 1815–1913,* Geneva: Graduate Institute of International and Development Studies Working Paper No. 08.

Flores Galindo, Alberto. 1974. *Los mineros de la Cerro de Pasco 1900–1930. Un intento de caracterización social.* Lima: Pontificia Universidad Católica del Perú.

——. 2001. *Los rostros de la plebe.* Barcelona: Crítica.

Florescano, Enrique. 1977. "México: ensayo de interpretación", in Roberto Cortés Conde and Stanley J. Stein, eds., *Latin America: A Guide to Economic History, 1830–1930.* Berkeley: University of California Press.

Flynn, Peter. 1970. "The Revolutionary Legion and the Brazilian Revolution of 1930", in Raymond Carr, ed., *Latin American Affairs, St. Antony's Paper* No. 22. Oxford: Oxford University Press.

Fonseca, Pedro Cezar Dutra. 2003. "Sobre a intencionalidade da política industrializante do Brasil na década de 1930." *Revista de Económia Política* 23 No. 1: 133–148.

Forbes, Ian L. D. 1978. "German Informal Imperialism in South America before 1914." *The Economic History Review*. New Series 31 No. 3: 384–398.

Forment, Carlos A. 2003. *Democracy in Latin America 1760–1900* Vol. 1: *Civic Selfhood and Public Life in Mexico and Peru*. Chicago and London: The University of Chicago Press.

Foster, John Bellamy and Robert W. McChesney. 2012. "The Global Stagnation in China." *Monthly Review* 63 No. 9.

Fox Przeworski, Joanne. 1978. "Mines and Smelters: the Role of the Coal Oligopoly in the Decline of the Chilean Copper Industry." *Nova Americana* 1: 169–213.

Frank, Andre Gunder. 1969. *Capitalism and Underdevelopment in Latin America. Historical Studies of Chile and Brazil*. Harmondsworth: Penguin Books (revised edition).

———. 1972. *Lumpenbourgeoisie and Lumpendevelopment. Dependency, Class, and Politics in Latin America*. New York: Monthly Review Press.

———. 1998. *ReOrient: Global Economy in the Asian Age*. New Dehli: Vistaar Publications.

[Frank-Landes] 1998. *Frank-Landes Debate. 'ReOrient' vs. 'The Wealth and Poverty of Nations'*. World History Center at Northeastern University, December 2 (stenographic report).

Franklin, James. 1971. *The Present State of Hayti, (Saint Domingo) with Remarks on Its Agriculture, Commerce, Laws, Religion, Finances and Population, etc. etc*. London: Frank Cass. First published in 1825.

Frieden, Jeffrey A. 2006. *Global Capitalism: Its Fall and Rise in the Twentieth Century*. New York And London: W. W. Norton & Company.

Friedman, Milton. 1997. "John Maynard Keynes." *Federal Reserve Bank of Richmond Economic Quarterly* 83 No. 2: 1–23.

Furtado, Celso. 1964. *Development and Underdevelopment. A Structural View of the Problems of Developed and Underdeveloped Countries*. Berkeley: University of California Press.

———. 1967. *Rozwój gospodarczy Brazylii*. Warszawa: PWN.

Gallo, Ezequiel. 1970. "Agrarian Expansion and Industrial Development in Argentina, 1880–1930", in Raymond Carr, ed., *Latin American Affairs, St. Antony's Paper* No. 22. Oxford: Oxford University Press.

———. 1977. "The Cereal Boom and Changes in the Social and Political Structure of Santa Fe, Argentina, 1870–95", in Kenneth Duncan and Ian Rutledge, eds., *Land and Labour in Latin America. Essays on the Development of Agrarian Capitalism in the Nineteenth and Twentieth Centuries*. Cambridge: Cambridge University Press.

Garcia, Eugênio Vargas. 2000. *Anglo-American Rivalry in Brazil: the Case of the 1920s*. Oxford: University of Oxford Centre for Brazilian Studies Working Paper CBS-14-00 (P).

Garraty, John A. 1979. *Unemployment in History. Economic Thought and Public Policy*. New York: Harper & Row, Publishers.

———. 1986. "Agriculture in the Great Depression and in the 1970s", in Ivan T. Berend and Kurt Borchardt, eds., *The Impact of the Depression of the 1930s and Its Relevance for the Contemporary World: Comparative Studies*. Berne: 9th International Economic History Congress.

Garvy, George. 1975. "Keynes and the Economic Activists of Pre-Hitler Germany." *The Journal of Political Economy* 83 No. 2: 391–405.

Gatrell, Peter and Boris Anan'ich. 2003. "National and Non-national Dimensions of Economic Development in Nineteenth- and Twentieth-Century Russia", in Alice Teichova and Herbert Matis, eds., *Nation, State and the Economy in History*. Cambridge: Cambridge University Press.

Gellner, Ernest. 1981. "Nationalism." *Theory and Society* No. 10: 753–776.

———. 1994a. *Encounters with Nationalism*. Oxford: Basil Blackwell Publishers.
———. 1994b. *Conditions of Liberty. Civil Society and Its Rivals*. New York: Allen Lane/The Penguin Press.
———. 2006. *Nations and Nationalism*. Oxford: Basil Blackwell Publishers (2nd edition). First published in 1983.
Gerschenkron, Alexander. 1965. *Economic Backwardness in Historical Perspective. A Book of Essays*. New York: Frederick A. Praeger.
———. 1968. *Continuity in History and Other Essays*. Cambridge, MA: Harvard University Press.
———. 1989. *Bread and Democracy in Germany*. Ithaca and London: Cornell University Press. First published in 1943.
Gerst, Thomas. 1988. *Die wirtschaftliche Entwicklung Mexikos und das Problem der Proto-Industrialisierung am Ausgang der Kolonialzeit*. München: Wilhelm Fink Verlag.
Gide, Charles and Charles Rist. 1916. *A History of Economic Doctrines from the Time of the Physiocrats to the Present*. Boston and London: D. C. Heath and Company.
Giffen, Robert. 1904. *Economic Inquiries and Studies*, Vol. II. London: George Bell and Sons.
Gilpin, Robert. 2001. *Global Political Economy. Understanding the International Economic Order*. Princeton: Princeton University Press.
Głąbiński, Stanisław. 2002. "Teorja ekonomiki narodowej", in Wojciech Józef Burszta, Joanna Nowak and Krzysztof Wawrucha, eds., *Polska refleksja nad narodem. Wybór tekstów*. Poznań: Wydawnictwo Poznańskie. First published in 1927.
Godio, Julio. 1985. *Historia del movimiento obrero latinoamericano*, Vol. II: *Anarquistas y Socialistas, 1850–1918*. San José: Editorial Nueva Sociedad.
Golay, Frank H., Ralph Anspach, M. Ruth Pfanner and Eliezer Ayal. 1969. *Underdevelopment and Economic Nationalism in Southeast Asia*. Ithaca and London: Cornell University Press.
Gołębiowski, Jerzy. 1985. *Sektor państwowy w gospodarce Polski międzywojennej*. Warszawa: PWN.
Gómez-Galvarriato, Aurora and Jeffrey G. Williamson. 2009. "What It Prices, Productivity or Policy? Latin American Industrialisation after 1870." *Journal of Latin American Studies* 41: 663–694.
Gonzales, Michael J. 1994. "United States Copper Companies, the State and Labour Conflict in Mexico, 1900–1910." *Journal of Latin American Studies* 26 Part 3: 631–681.
Good, David F. 2003. "The State and Economic Development in Central and Eastern Europe", in Alice Teichova and Herbert Matis, eds., *Nation, State, and the Economy in History*. Cambridge: Cambridge University Press.
Gootenberg, Paul. 1982. "The Social Origins of Protectionism and Free Trade in Nineteenth-Century Lima." *Journal of Latin American Studies* 14 Part 2: 329–358.
———. 1989. *Between Silver and Guano. Commercial Policy and the State in Postindependence Peru*. Princeton: Princeton University Press.
———. 1993. *Imagining Development: Economic Ideas in Peru's 'Fictitious Prosperity' of Guano, 1840–1880*. Berkeley and Los Angeles: University of California Press.
———. 2004. "Review: Between a Rock and a Softer Place: Reflections on Some Recent Economic History of Latin America." *Latin American Research Review* 39 No. 2: 239–257.
Gould, John D. 1973. *Economic Growth in History. Survey and Analysis*. London: Methuen.
Gourevitch, Peter. 1986. *Politics in Hard Times: Comparative Responses to International Economic Crisis*. Ithaca and London: Cornell University Press.
Górski, Janusz. 1963. *Polska myśl ekonomiczna a rozwój gospodarczy 1807–1830. Studia nad początkami teorii zacofania gospodarczego*. Warszawa: PWN.
Grady, Robert C. 2002. Studies of the State and Fragmentation Politics: The Demise and Restoration of Pluralism in Early Political Science. Paper prepared for the Southern Political Science Association Annual Meetings, Savannah, Georgia, November 6–9.
Graham, Richard. 1968. *Britain and the Onset of Modernization of Brazil 1850–1914*. Cambridge: Cambridge University Press.

Gramsci, Antonio. 1961. "Filozofia Benedetta Croce", in *Pisma Wybrane*, Vol. 1. Warszawa: Książka i Wiedza. First published in the early 1930s.
Grantham, George. 2003. Guiding Concepts in Economic History. A Sketch of a History of Ideas. Paper prepared for the Canadian Conference on the Future of Economic History, University of Guelph, Ontario, October 17–19.
Greenfeld, Liah. 1993. *Nationalism. Five Roads to Modernity.* Cambridge, MA: Harvard University Press.
———. 1995. "The Worth of Nations: Some Economic Implications of Nationalism." *Critical Review* 9, No. 4: 555–584.
———. 2003. *The Spirit of Capitalism. Nationalism and Economic Growth.* Cambridge, MA: Harvard University Press.
Greenhill, Robert. 1977a. "Merchants and the Latin American Trades: An Introduction", in Desmond C. M. Platt, ed., *Business Imperialism 1840–1930. An Inquiry Based on British Experience in Latin America.* Oxford: Oxford University Press.
———. 1977b. "The Brazilian Coffee Trade", in Desmond C. M. Platt, ed., *Business Imperialism 1840–1930. An Inquiry Based on British Experience in Latin America.* Oxford: Oxford University Press.
Gregor, A. James. 1979. *Italian Fascism and Development Dictatorship.* Princeton: Princeton University Press.
Gregory, Paul R. 1991. "The Role of the State in Promoting Economic Development: the Russian Case and Its General Implications", in Richard Sylla and Gianni Toniolo, eds., *Patterns of European Industrialization. The Nineteenth Century.* London and New York: Routledge.
Gregory, Theodore E. 1933. "Economic Nationalism in the Modern World", in James G. Hodgson, ed., *Economic Nationalism.* New York: The H. W. Wilson Company.
Grodek, Adam. 1963. *Wybór Pism.* Vol. 1: *Studia z historii myśli ekonomicznej.* Warszawa: PWN.
Gross, Nachum. 1983. "Austria-Hungary in the World Economy", in John Komlos, ed., *Economic Development in the Habsburg Monarchy in the Nineteenth Century.* New York: Columbia University Press.
Guerra Vilaboy, Sergio. 1980. *La' Republica artesana' en Colombia.* La Habana: Editorial de Ciencias Sociales.
Gurney, W. M. 1931. *Report on the Economic Conditions in Peru.* London: Department of the Overseas Trade.
Haber, Stephen. 1992. "Business Enterprise and the Great Depression in Brazil: A Study of Profits and Losses in Textile Manufacturing." *The Business History Review* 66 No. 2: 335–363.
———. 1997a. "Introduction: Economic Growth and Latin American Economic Historiography", in Stephen Haber, ed., *How Latin America Fell Behind: Essays on the Economic Histories of Brazil and Mexico, 1800–1914.* Stanford: Stanford University Press.
———. 1997b. "Financial Markets and Industrial Development: A Comparative Study of Governmental Regulation, Financial Innovation, and Industrial Structure in Brazil and Mexico, 1840–1930", in Stephen Haber, ed., *How Latin America Fell Behind: Essays on the Economic Histories of Brazil and Mexico, 1800–1914.* Stanford: Stanford University Press.
———. 2006. "The Political Economy of Industrialization", in Victor Bulmer-Thomas, John H. Coatsworth and Roberto Cortés Conde, eds., *The Cambridge Economic History of Latin America,* Vol. II: *The Long Twentieth Century.* Cambridge: Cambridge University Press.
Habermas, Jürgen. 1992. "Citizenship and National Identity: Some Reflections on the Future of Europe." *Praxis International* 12 No. 1: 1–19.
Haggard, Stephan. 1990. *Pathways from the Periphery. The Politics of Growth in the Newly Industrializing Countries.* Ithaca and London: Cornell University Press.
Hale, Charles A. 1968. *Mexican Liberalism in the Age of Mora 1821–1853.* New Haven and London: Yale University Press.

———. 1996. "Political Ideas and Ideologies in Latin America, 1870–1930", in Leslie Bethell, ed., *Ideas and Ideologies in Twentieth Century Latin America*. Cambridge: Cambridge University Press.

Hall, John A. 2003. "Introduction: Nation-States in History", in T. V. Paul, G. John Ikenberry, John A. Hall, eds., *The Nation-State in Question*. Princeton: Princeton University Press.

Halperin-Donghi, Tulio. 1975. *Politics, Economics and Society in Argentina in the Revolutionary Period*. Cambridge: Cambridge University Press.

Hamilton, Alexander. 1958. "Opinion on the Constitutionality of the Bank, February 23, 1791", in Richard Hofstadter, ed., *Great Issues in American History. From the Revolution to the Civil War, 1765–1865*. New York: Vintage Books. First published in 1791.

Handelsman, Marceli. 1973. *Rozwój narodowości nowoczesnej*. Warszawa: Państwowy Instytut Wydawniczy. First published in 1923.

Hansen, Alvin H. 1947. "Keynes on Economic Policy", in Seymour E. Harris, ed., *The New Economics. Keynes' Influence on Theory and Public Policy*. London: Dennis Dobson.

Harcave, Sidney. 2004. *Count Sergei Witte and the Twilight of Imperial Russia: A Biography*. Armonk, NT: M. E. Sharpe.

Hardt, Michael and Antonio Negri. 2001. *Empire*. Cambridge, MA: Harvard University Press.

Haring, Clarence H. 1928. *South America Looks at the United States*. 1928. New York: The Macmillan Company.

Harlen, Christine Margerum. 1999. "A Reappraisal of Classical Economic Nationalism and Economic Liberalism." *International Studies Quarterly* 43: 733–744.

Harre, Angela. 2006. "Economic Nationalism in Romania", in Helga Schultz and Eduard Kubů, eds., *History and Culture of Economic Nationalism in East Central Europe*. Berlin: Berliner Wissenschafts-Verlag.

Hatton, Timothy J. 2010. *The Cliometrics of International Migration: A Survey*. Institute for the Study of Labor (IZA) Discussion Paper No. 4900, April.

Hauner, Milan. 1986. "Military Budgets and the Armaments Industry", in Michael C. Kaser and E. A. Radice, eds., *The Economic History of Eastern Europe 1919–1945*, Vol. II: *Interwar Policy, the War and Reconstruction*. Oxford: Oxford University Press.

[Haya de la Torre Victor Raúl]. 1931. "El APRA no esta contra el capital extranjero." *APRA: Organo del Frente Unico de Trabajadores Manuales e Intelectuales* 4.

Haya de la Torre, Victor Raúl. 1972. *El antimperialismo y el APRA*. Lima: Editorial–Imprenta Amauta S.A. First published in 1936.

———. 1976. *Obras completas* Vol. I. Lima: Editorial Juan Mejia Baca.

Hechter, Michael. 2000. "Nationalism and Rationality." *Studies in Comparative International Development* 35 No. 1: 3–19.

Heckscher, Eli F. 1969. "Mercantilism", in D. C. Coleman, ed., *Revisions in Mercantilism*. London: Methuen.

Heilbroner, Robert and William Milberg. 1995. *The Crisis of Vision in Modern Economic Thought*. Cambridge: Cambridge University Press.

Heilperin, Michael A. 1960. *Studies in Economic Nationalism*. Geneva and Paris: Librairie E. Droz/ Librairie Minard.

Helander, Sven 1955. *Das Autarkieproblem in der Weltwirtschaft*. Berlin: Duncker & Humblot.

Helleiner, Eric. 2002. "Economic Nationalism as a Challenge to Economic Liberalism? Lessons from the 19th Century." *International Studies Quarterly* 46 No. 3: 307–329.

———. 2005. "The Meaning and Contemporary Significance of Economic Nationalism", in Eric Helleiner and Andreas Pickel, eds., *Economic Nationalism in a Globalizing World*, Ithaca and London: Cornell University Press.

Hellmuth, Eckhardt. 2002. "The British State", in H. T. Dickinson, ed., *A Companion to Eighteenth-Century Britain*. Oxford: Basil Blackwell Publishers.

Henderson, William O. 1983. *Friedrich List: Economist and Visionary, 1789–1846*. London: Cass.

Hilferding, Rudolf. 1958. *Kapitał finansowy. Studium o najnowszym rozwoju kapitalizmu*. Warszawa: PWN. First published in 1910.

Hill, Christopher. 1969. *Reformation to Industrial Revolution 1530–1780*. Harmondsworth: Penguin.
Hilton, Stanley E. 1973. "Military Influence on Brazilian Economic Policy, 1930–1945: A Different View." *The Hispanic American Historical Review* 53 No. 1: 71–94.
———. 1975. "Vargas and Brazilian Economic Development, 1930–1945: A Reappraisal of His Attitude Toward Industrialization and Planning." *The Journal of Economic History* 35 No. 2: 754–778.
———. 1982. "The Armed Forces and Industrialists in Modern Brazil: The Drive for Military Autonomy (1889–1954)." *The Hispanic American Historical Review* 62 No. 4: 629–673.
Hingley, Ronald. 1970. *The Russian Secret Police. Muscovite, Imperial Russian and Soviet Political Security Operations 1565–1970*. London: Hutchinson & Co.
Hinshaw, Randall. 1947. "Keynes Commercial Policy", in Seymour E. Harris, ed., *The New Economics. Keynes' Influence on Theory and Public Policy*. London: Dennis Dobson.
Hirschman, Albert O. 1961. *Latin American Issues: Essays and Comments*. New York: The Twentieth Century Fund.
———. 1968. "The Political Economy of Import-Substituting Industrialization in Latin America." *The Quarterly Journal of Economics* 82 No. 1: 1–32.
———. 1977a. "A Generalized Linkage Approach to Development, with Special Reference to Staples." *Economic Development and Cultural Change* 22: 67–98 (Supplement).
———. 1977b. *The Passions and the Interests: Political Arguments for Capitalism before Its Triumph*. Princeton: Princeton University Press.
———. 1980. *National Power and the Structure of Foreign Trade*. Berkeley: University of California Press. First published in 1945.
Hobsbawm, Eric J. 1969. *Industry and Empire*. Harmondsworth: Penguin.
———. 1990. *Nations and Nationalism since 1780. Programme, Myth, Reality*. Cambridge: Cambridge University Press.
———.1994. *The Age of Extremes. A History of the World, 1914–1991*. New York: Pantheon Books.
———. 1995. "Nationalism and Nationality in Latin America", in Etemad Bouda, Jean Batou and David Thomas, eds., *Pour une histoire économique et sociale internationale. Mélanges offerets à Paul Bairoch*. Geneva: Editions Passé Présent.
Hobson, H. A. 1931. *Economic Conditions in Bolivia. Report by...* London: Department of the Overseas Trade.
Hobson, John M. 2002. "The Two Waves of Weberian Historical Sociology in International Relations", in Stephen Hobden and John M. Hobson, eds., *Historical Sociology of International Relations*. Cambridge: Cambridge University Press.
———. 2004. *The Eastern Origins of Western Civilisation*. Cambridge: Cambridge University Press.
Hodgson, James G. 1933. "What Is Economic Nationalism?", in James G. Hodgson, ed., *Economic Nationalism*. New York: The H. W. Wilson Company.
Hodgson, Geoffrey M. 2001. *How Economics Forgot History. The Problem of Historical Specificity in Social Science*. London and New York: Routledge.
Hofbauer, Hannes and Andrea Komlosy. 2000. "Capital Accumulation and Catching-Up Development in Eastern Europe." *Review* 23 No. 4: 459–501.
Hoffmann, F. 1932. "Der Ruf nach Autarkie in der deutschen politischen Gegenwartsideologie."*Weltwirtschaftliches Archiv* 36, No.4: 496–511.
Hont, István. 2005. *Jealousy of Trade: International Competition and the Nation-State in Historical Perspective*. Cambridge, MA and London: The Belknap Press of Harvard University Press.
[Hossbach] 1949. "Hossbach Memorandum (Nov. 10, 1937)", in *Documents on German Foreign Policy 1918–1945. Series D Vol. 1: From Neurath to Ribbentrop (September 1937 – September 1938)*. Washington, D.C.: U.S. Government Printing Office. Prepared in 1937.
Hoston, Germaine A. 1994. *The State, Identity, and the National Question in China and Japan*. Princeton: Princeton University Press.

Hroch, Miroslav. 2000. *Social Preconditions of National Revival in Europe. A Comparative Analysis of the Social Composition of Patriotic Groups among the Smaller European Nations.* New York: Columbia University Press.
Hünefeldt, Christine. 1986. "Viejos y nuevos temas de la historia económica del Siglo XIX", in Heraclio Bonilla, ed., *Las crisis economicas en la historia del Perú.* Lima: Centro Latinoamericano de Historia Economica y Social–Fundación Friedrich Ebert.
Hymer, Stephen H. and Stephen A. Resnick. 1971. "International Trade and Uneven Development", in Jagdish N. Bhagwati et al., eds., *Trade, Balance of Payments and Growth. Papers on International Economics in Honor of Charles P. Kindleberger.* Amsterdam and London: The North Holland Publishing.
Ianni, Octavio. 1971. *Estado e planejamento econômico no Brasil 1930–1970.* Rio de Janeiro: Civilização Brasileira.
———. 1975. *A formação do estado populista na América Latina.* Rio de Janeiro: Civilização Brasileira.
Ihnatowicz, Ireneusz. 1982."Przemysł, handel, finanse", in Stefan Kieniewicz, ed., *Polska XIX wieku. Państwo, społeczeństwo, kultura.* Warszawa: Wiedza Powszechna.
Irurozqui, Marta. 2000. "The Sound of the Pututes. Politicisation and Indigenous Rebellions in Bolivia, 1826–1921." *Journal of Latin American Studies* 32 No. 1: 85–114.
Irwin, Douglas A. 1996. *Against the Tide: An Intellectual History of Free Trade.* Princeton: Princeton University Press.
———. 2006. "Interpreting Tariff-Growth Correlation", in Jean-Pierre Dormois and Pedro Lains, eds., *Classical Trade Protectionism, 1815–1914.* London and New York: Routledge.
——— and Peter Temin. 2001. "The Antebellum Tariff on Cotton Textiles." *The Journal of Economic History* 61, No. 3: 777–798.
Islamov, Tofik M. 1992. "From *Natio Hungarica* to Hungarian Nation", in Richard L. Rudolph and David F. Good, eds., *Nationalism and Empire. The Habsburg Empire and the Soviet Union.* New York: St. Martin's Press.
Jacobsen, Nils. 2005. "*Liberalismo Tropical*: The Career of a European Economic Doctrine in Nineteenth-Century Latin America", in Valpy FitzGerald and Rosemary Thorp, eds., *Economic Doctrines in Latin America. Origins, Embedding and Evolution.* Basingstoke: Palgrave Macmillan in association with St. Antony's College, Oxford.
Jaguaribe, Hélio. 1969. "Political Strategies of National Development in Brazil", in Irving Louis Horowitz, Josué de Castro and John Gerassi, eds., *Latin American Radicalism. A Documentary Report on Left and Nationalist Movements.* New York: Vintage Books.
———.1973. *Political Development: A General Theory and a Latin American Case Study.* New York: Harper & Row.
James, Harold. 2001. *The End of Globalization: Lessons from the Great Depression.* Cambridge, MA: Harvard University Press.
Janowski, Maciej. 1996/1997. "Kozy i jesiotry. Uwagi o specyfice liberalizmu w Europie Środkowo-Wschodniej między rewolucją francuską a I wojną światową." *Roczniki Dziejów Społecznych i Gospodarczych* LVI-LVII: 69–92.
———. 1998. *Polska myśl liberalna do 1918 roku.* Kraków: Społeczny Instytut Wydawnicza Znak/Fundacja im. Stefana Batorego.
Janus, Piotr. 2009. *W nurcie polskiego etatyzmu. Stefan Starzyński i Pierwsza Brygada Gospodarcza 1926–1932.* Kraków: Avalon.
Jaszczuk, Andrzej. 1986. *Spór pozytywistów z konserwatystami o przyszłość Polski 1870–1903.* Warszawa: PWN.
Jaśkiewicz, Leszek. 1982. *Absolutyzm rosyjski w dobie rewolucji 1905–1907. Reformy ustrojowe.* Warszawa: PWN.
Jedlicki, Jerzy. 1964. *Nieudana próba kapitalistycznej industrializacji. Analiza państwowego gospodarstwa przemysłowego w Królestwie Polskim XIX w.* Warszawa: Książka i Wiedza.
———. 1976. "W sprawie automatycznego krachu feudalizmu", in *Między feudalizmem a kapitalizmem. Studia z dziejów gospodarczych i społecznych. Prace ofiarowane Witoldowi Kuli.* Wrocław: Ossolineum.

——. 1993. *Źle urodzeni czyli o doświadczeniu historycznym. Scripta i postscripta.* Londyn – Warszawa: Aneks–Polityka.
——. 1999. *A Suburb of Europe. Nineteenth-Century Polish Approaches to Western Civilization.* Budapest: Central European University Press.
Jefferson, Thomas. 1958a. "The Importance of Agriculture, 1784", in Richard Hofstadter, ed., *Great Issues in American History. From the Revolution to the Civil War, 1765–1865.* New York: Vintage Books. First published in 1784.
——. 1958b. "Recollections of the Hamiltonian System, 1818", in Richard Hofstadter, ed., *Great Issues in American History. From the Revolution to the Civil War, 1765–1865.* New York: Vintage Books. Prepared in 1818.
Jessop, Bob. 1990. *State Theory. Putting the Capitalist State in Its Place.* Cambridge: Polity Press.
——. 2001. *The Political Scene and the Politics of Representation: Periodizing Class Struggle and the State in 'The Eighteenth Brumaire'.* Lancaster: Department of Sociology, Lancaster University.
Jezierski, Andrzej. 1967. *Handel zagraniczny Królestwa Polskiego 1815–1914.* Warszawa: PWN.
——. 1984. *Problemy rozwoju gospodarczego ziem polskich w XIX i XX wieku.* Warszawa: Książka i Wiedza.
——, ed. 1994. *Historia Polski w liczbach* Vol. I: *Ludność, terytorium.* Warszawa: Zakład Wydawnictw Statystycznych GUS.
—— and Cecylia Leszczyńska. 2001. *Historia gospodarcza Polski.* Warszawa: Wydawnictwo Key Text.
—— and Andrzej Wyczański, eds. 2006. *Historia Polski w liczbach* Vol. II: *Gospodarka.* Warszawa: Zakład Wydawnictw Statystycznych GUS.
Joelsohn, Walter. 1952. *Die Theorie der säkularen Stagnation. Eine Darstellung und kritische Würdigung.* Wien: Springer-Verlag.
Johnson, Harry G. 1968a. "The Ideology of Economic Policy in the New States", in Harry G. Johnson, ed., *Economic Nationalism in Old and New States.* Chicago and London: The University of Chicago Press.
——. 1968b. "A Theoretical Model of Economic Nationalism in New and Developing States", in Harry G. Johnson, ed., *Economic Nationalism in Old and New States.* Chicago and London: The University of Chicago Press.
Jones, Charles. 1977. "Commercial Banks and Mortgage Companies", in Desmond C.M. Platt, ed., *Business Imperialism 1840–1930. An Inquiry Based on British Experience in Latin America.* Oxford: Oxford University Press.
Jorrín, Miguel and John D. Martz. 1970. *Latin-American Political Thought and Ideology.* Chapel Hill: The University of North Carolina Press.
Kaczyńska, Elżbieta. 1976. "Tak zwane przeżytki feudalne i kapitalizm marginalny w Królestwie Polskim w drugiej połowie XIX wieku", in *Między feudalizmem a kapitalizmem. Studia z dziejów gospodarczych i społecznych. Prace ofiarowane Witoldowi Kuli.* Wrocław: Ossolineum.
——. 1979. "Burżuazja", in Witold Kula and Janina Leskiewiczowa, eds., *Przemiany społeczne w Królestwie Polskim 1815–1864.* Wrocław: Ossolineum.
Kahan, Arcadius. 1968. "Nineteenth-Century European Experience with Policies of Economic Nationalism", in Harry G. Johnson, ed., *Economic Nationalism in Old and New States.* Chicago and London: The University of Chicago Press.
Kaldor, Nicolas. 1970. "The Case for Regional Policies." *Scottish Journal of Political Economy* XVII, No. 3: 337–348.
Kalecki, Michał. 1938. Review of the book by M. Manoilescu. *Economic Journal* 48, No. 4: 192.
——. 1972. "Political Aspects of Full Employment", in Emery H. Hunt and Jesse G. Schwartz, eds., *A Critique of Economic Theory: Selected Readings.* Harmondsworth: Penguin. First published in 1943.

———. 1980. *Teoria dynamiki gospodarczej. Rozprawa o cyklicznych i długofalowych zmianach gospodarki kapitalistycznej*. Warszawa: Państwowe Wydawnictwo Ekonomiczne. First published in 1954.

———. 1984. "The Mechanism of the Business Upswing", in John Bellamy Foster and Henryk Szlajfer, eds., *The Faltering Economy. The Problem of Accumulation Under Monopoly Capitalism*. New York: Monthly Review Press. First published in 1935.

Kamiński, Antoni Z. 1994. "Reformowalność i potencjał rozwojowy ustrojów polityczno-ekonomicznych. Przypadek komunizmu", in Witold Morawski, ed., *Zmierzch socjalizmu państwowego. Szkice z socjologii ekonomicznej*. Warszawa: PWN.

Kamiński, Bartłomiej and Antoni Z. Kamiński. 2004. *Korupcja rządów. Państwa postkomunistyczne wobec globalizacji*. Warszawa: Wydawnictwo TRIO/ ISP PAN.

Kapsoli, Wilfredo. 1984. *Ayllus del Sol. Anarquismo y utopia andina*. Lima: TAREA.

Kasahara, Shigehisa. 2004. *The Flying Geese Paradigm: A Critical Study of Its Application to East Asian Regional Development*. Geneva, UNCTAD Discussion Paper No. 169.

Kaufman, Robert R. 1979. "Industrial Change and Authoritarian Rule in Latin America: A Concrete Review of the Bureaucratic-Authoritarian Model", in David Collier, ed., *The New Authoritarianism in Latin America*. Princeton: Princeton University Press.

———. 1990. "How Societies Change Developmental Models or Keep Them: Reflections on the Latin American Experience in the 1930s and the Postwar World", in Gary Gereffi and Donald L. Wyman, eds., *Manufacturing Miracles. Paths of Industrialization in Latin America and East Asia*. Princeton: Princeton University Press.

Kawalec, Stefan. 2011. "Udomowić banki." *Gazeta Wyborcza*, November 7: 22–23.

Kenwood, A. G. and A. L. Lougheed. 1971. *The Growth of the International Economy 1820–1960. An Introductory Text*. London: George Allen & Unwin.

Keynes, John M. 1920. *The Economic Consequences of the Peace*. New York: Harcourt, Brace, and Howe.

———. 2003. "The End of laissez-faire", in Steven G. Medema and Warren J. Samuels, eds., *The History of Economic Thought: A Reader*. London and New York: Routledge. First published in 1926.

———. 1933a. "National Self-Sufficiency." *The Yale Review* 22, No. 4: 755–769.

———. 1933b. "An Open Letter to President Roosevelt." *New York Times*, December 31.

———. 1936. *Abstract of Conversation with Mr. John Maynard Keynes. Recorded by A. P. Chew*. Washington, D. C.: Department of Agriculture, May 4 (mimeo).

———. 1964. *The General Theory of Employment, Interest and Money*. New York: Harcourt, Brace & World. First published in 1936.

———. 1947a. "The General Theory", in Seymour E. Harris, ed., *The New Economics. Keynes' Influence on Theory and Public Policy*. London: Dennis Dobson. First published in 1937.

———. 1947b. "The Anglo-American Financial Arrangements. Speech delivered before the House of Lords, December 18, 1945", in Seymour E. Harris, ed., *The New Economics. Keynes' Influence on Theory and Public Policy*. London: Dennis Dobson.

Kindleberger, Charles P. 1951. "Group Behavior and International Trade." *The Journal of Political Economy* 59 No. 1: 30–46.

———. 1962. *Foreign Trade and the National Economy*. New Haven and London: Yale University Press.

———. 1974. "Size of Firm and Size of Nation", in John H. Dunning, ed., *Economic Analysis and the Multinational Enterprise*. London: Allen & Unwin.

———. 1987. *The World in Depression 1929–1939*. Harmondsworth: Penguin (revised edition).

———. 1996. *World Economic Primacy: 1500–1990*. New York and Oxford: Oxford University Press.

Kirchner, Walther. 1981. "Russian Tariffs and Foreign Industries before 1914: the German Entrepreneur's Perspective." *The Journal of Economic History* 41 No. 2: 361–379.

Kizwalter, Tomasz. 1991. *'Nowatorstwo i rutyny'. Społeczeństwo Królestwa Polskiego wobec procesów modernizacji (1840–1863)*. Warszawa: PWN.

Kleer, Jerzy. 1975. *Gospodarka światowa. Prawidłowości rozwoju*. Warszawa: PWE.

Knight, Alan. 1985. "The Political Economy of Revolutionary Mexico, 1900–1940", in Christopher Abel and Colin M. Lewis, eds., *Latin America, Economic Imperialism and the State: The Political Economy of the External Connection from Independence to the Present*. London: Athlone.
———. 1990. *The Mexican Revolution*, Vol. 1: *Porfirians, Liberals and Peasants*. Lincoln and London: University of Nebraska Press.
———. 1998. "Populism and Neo-populism in Latin America, Especially Mexico." *Journal of Latin American Studies* 30 No. 2: 223–248.
———. 2000. "Export-led Growth in Mexico, c.1900–30", in Enrique Cárdenas, José Antonio Ocampo and Rosemary Thorp, eds., *An Economic History of Twentieth-Century Latin America*. Vol. 1: *The Export Age: The Latin American Economies in the Late Nineteenth and Early Twentieth Centuries*. Basingstoke: Palgrave Macmillan in association with St. Antony's College, Oxford.
Knothe, Tomasz. 1985. "Kapitał zagraniczny w rozwoju rosyjskiego kapitalizmu monopolistycznego. Dyskusje w historiografii radzieckiej." *Studia z Dziejów ZSRR i Europy Środkowe* XXI: 33–62.
Kochanowicz, Jacek. 1981. *Pańszczyźniane gospodarstwo chłopskie w Królestwie Polskim w I połowie XIX w.*. Warszawa: Wydawnictwo Uniwersytetu Warszawskiego.
———. 1983. "*Teoria ekonomii...* w oczach krytyków", in Witold Kula, *Teoria ekonomiczna ustroju feudalnego*. Warszawa: PWN (2nd expanded edition).
———. 1989. "The Polish Economy and the Evolution of Dependency", in Daniel Chirot, ed., *The Origins of Backwardness in Eastern Europe: Economics and Politics from the Middle Ages until the Early Twentieth Century*. Berkeley and Los Angeles: University of California Press.
Kofman, Jan. 1986. *Lewiatan a podstawowe zagadnienia ekonomiczno-polityczne Drugiej Rzeczypospolitej. Z ideologii kół wielkoprzemysłowych*. Warszawa: PWN.
———. 1997. *Economic Nationalism and Development. Central and Eastern Europe between the Two World Wars*. Boulder, Colorado: Westview Press.
Kohli, Atul. 2004. *State-directed Development. Political Power and Industrialization in the Global Periphery*. Cambridge: Cambridge University Press.
———. 2009. "Nationalist Versus Dependent Capitalist Development: Alternative Pathways of Asia and Latin America in a Globalized World." *Studies in Comparative International Development* 44: 386–410.
Kohn, Hans. 1955. "Nationalism", in Hans Kohn, ed., *Nationalism: Its Meaning and History*. Princeton: D. Van Nostrand Company.
———. 1967. *The Idea of Nationalism. A Study in Its Origins and Background*. New York: Collier Books. First published in 1944.
Köll, Anu Mai. 2000. "Economy and Ethnicity in the Hands of the State: Economic Change and the National Question in Twentieth-Century Estonia", in Alice Teichova, Herbert Matis and Jaroslav Pátek, eds., *Economic Change and the National Question in Twentieth-century Europe*. Cambridge: Cambridge University Press.
———. 2006. "Agrarianism and Ethnicity – an East Central European Survey", in Helga Schultz and Eduard Kubů, eds., *History and Culture of Economic Nationalism in East Central Europe*. Berlin: Berliner Wissenschafts-Verlag.
Kołodziejczyk, Ryszard. 1979. *Burżuazja polska w XIX i XX wieku. Szkice historyczne*. Warszawa: Państwowy Instytut Wydawniczy.
Kostrowicka, Irena. 1989. "Koncepcje i polityka planowania", in *Problemy gospodarcze Drugiej Rzeczypospolitej*. Warszawa: PWE.
Kowalik, Tadeusz. 1992. *Historia ekonomii w Polsce 1864–1950*. Wrocław: Ossolineum.
Kowarick, Lucio. 1987. *The Subjugation of Labour: The Constitution of Capitalism in Brazil*. Amsterdam: CEDLA.
Krasner, Stephen D. 1989. "Sovereignty: An Institutional Perspective", in James A. Caporaso, ed., *The Elusive State. International and Comparative Perspectives*, Newbury Park, Calif.: Sage Publications.

Krenn, Michael L. 1990. *U.S. Policy Toward Economic Nationalism in Latin America, 1917–1929*. Wilmington, DE: Scholarly Resources Inc.
Krieger, Leonard. 1975. *An Essay on the Theory of Enlightened Despotism*. Chicago and London: The University of Chicago Press.
Kubler, George. 1952. *The Indian Caste of Peru, 1795–1940. A Population Study based upon Tax Records and Census Reports*. Washington, D.C.: Smithsonian Institution.
Kudliński, Romuald and W. Siwiński. 1985. *Szkice o gospodarce światowej*. Warszawa: PWN.
Kula, Marcin. 1987. *Historia Brazylii*. Wrocław: Ossolineum.
———. 1991. *Narodowe i rewolucyjne*. Londyn–Warszawa: Aneks/ Więź.
———. 1999. *Anatomia rewolucji narodowej (Boliwia w XX wieku)*. Wrocław: Wydawnictwo Leopoldinum/Fundacja na Rzecz Nauki Polskiej.
Kula, Witold. 1955. *Kształtowanie się kapitalizmu w Polsce*. Warszawa: PWN.
———. 1963. *Problemy i metody historii gospodarczej*. Warszawa: PWN.
———. 1979. "Wprowadzenie: rozwój gospodarczy w warunkach rosnącego zacofania", in Witold Kula and Janina Leskiewiczowa, eds., *Przemiany społeczne w Królestwie Polskim 1815–1864*. Wrocław: Ossolineum.
———. 1983a. *Teoria ekonomiczna ustroju feudalnego*. Warszawa: PWN (2nd expanded edition).
———. 1983b. *Historia, zacofanie, rozwój*. Warszawa: Czytelnik.
———. 1996. *Rozdziałki*. Warszawa: Wydawnictwo TRIO.
Kurczewska, Joanna. 1979. *Naród w socjologii i ideologii polskiej. Analiza porównawcza wybranych koncepcji z przełomu XIX i XX wieku*. Warszawa: PWN.
Kuznets, Simon. 1951. "The State as a Unit in Study of Economic Growth." *The Journal of Economic History* 11 No. 1: 25–41.
———. 1963. "Economic Growth of Small Nations", in E. A. G. Robinson, ed., *Economic Consequences of the Size of Nations*. London: Macmillan.
———. 1966. *Modern Economic Growth. Rate, Structure and Spread*. New Haven and London: Yale University Press.
[Kwiatkowski, Eugeniusz] 1988. Marian M. Drozdowski, ed., *Eugeniusz Kwiatkowski 'Rzecz najważniejsza Polska'. Wybór myśli politycznych i społecznych*, Kraków: Wydawnictwo Literackie. First published in 1929–1936.
Kwiatkowski, Eugeniusz. 1989. *Dysproporcje. Rzecz o Polsce przeszłej i obecnej*. Warszawa: Czytelnik. First published in 1932.
Kymlicka, William. 1996. *Multicultural Citizenship. A Liberal Theory of Minority Rights*. Oxford: Oxford University Press.
Lademacher, Horst. 1988. "Kosmopolitismus, Solidarität und Nation. Einige Bemerkungen zum Wandel von Begriff und Wirklichkeit im internationalen Sozialismus", in Frits van Holthoon and Marcel van der Linden, eds., *Internationalism in the Labour Movement, 1830–1940*, Leiden: International Institute of Social History.
Lal, Deepak. 1998. *Unintended Consequences: The Impact of Factor Endowments, Culture and Politics on Long-Run Economic Performance*. Cambridge, MA: The MIT Press.
Landau, Ludwik. 1939. *Gospodarka światowa. Produkcja i dochód społeczny w liczbach*. Warszawa: Instytut Gospodarstwa Społecznego.
Landau, Zbigniew. 1972."Dwusektorowy układ gospodarki Polski międzywojennej i jego konsekwencje." *Przegląd Historyczny* 3: 452–467.
———. 1975. "Gospodarcze aspekty Wielkiego Kryzysu gospodarczego. Wybrane zagadnienia." *Dzieje Najnowsze* VII No.2: 16–19.
——— and Jerzy Tomaszewski. 1964. *Kapitały obce w Polsce 1918–1939. Materiały i dokumenty*. Warszawa: Książka i Wiedza.
——— and Jerzy Tomaszewski. 1971. *Robotnicy przemysłowi w Polsce 1918–1939. Materialne warunki bytu*. Warszawa: Książka i Wiedza.
——— and Jerzy Tomaszewski. 1981. "The International Movement of Capital in Central and South-Eastern Europe before the Second World War", in Nina Assorodobraj-Kula, Czesław Bobrowski, Henryk Hagemejer, Witold Kula and Jan Łoś, eds., *Studies in*

Economic Theory and Practice. Essays in Honor of Edward Lipiński. Amsterdam and New York: North-Holland Publishing Company.
—— and Jerzy Tomaszewski. 1982. *Gospodarka Polski międzywojennej,* Vol. 3: *Wielki Kryzys 1930–1935.* Warszawa: Książka i Wiedza.
—— and Jerzy Tomaszewski. 1984. *Polska w Europie i świecie 1918–1939.* Warszawa: Wiedza Powszechna (2nd enlarged edition).
—— and Jerzy Tomaszewski. 1986. "Foreign Policy and International Business in Poland: 1918–39", in Alice Teichova, Maurice Lévy-Leboyer and Helga Nussbaum, eds., *Multinational Enterprise in Historical Perspective.* Cambridge: Cambridge University Press.
—— and Wojciech Roszkowski. 1995. *Polityka gospodarcza II RP i PRL.* Warszawa: PWN.
Landes, David. 1990. "Does It Pay to Be Late?", in Jean Batou, ed., *Between Development and Underdevelopment 1800–1870. The Precocious Attempts at Industrialization of the Periphery.* Geneva: Centre of International Economic History/Librairie Droz.
——. 1998. *The Wealth and Poverty of Nations: Why Some Are So Rich and Some So Poor.* London: Abacus.
Lange, Oskar. 1973. "Rola państwa w kapitalizmie monopolistycznym", in *Dzieła,* Vol. l. Warszawa: PWN. First published in 1931.
Latham, A. J. H. 1981. *The Depression and the Developing World, 1914–1939.* London and New Jersey: Croom Helm.
Laue, Theodor H. von. 1954. "A Secret Memorandum of Sergei Witte on the Industrialization of Imperial Russia." *The Journal of Modern History* XXVI No. 2: 60–74.
——. 1969. *Sergei Witte and the Industrialization of Russia.* New York: Atheneum.
——. 1971. *Why Lenin? Why Stalin? A Reappraisal of the Russian Revolution 1900–1930.* New York: HarperCollins Publishers (2nd edition).
[League of Nations] 1942. *Commercial Policy in the Interwar Period: International Proposals and National Policies.* Geneva: League of Nations.
Lebergott, Stanley 1980. "The Returns to U. S. Imperialism. 1890–1929." *The Journal of Economic History* XL No. 2: 229–252.
Leff, Nathaniel H. 1997. "Economic Development in Brazil, 1822–1923", in Stephen Haber, ed., *How Latin America Fell Behind: Essays on the Economic Histories of Brazil and Mexico, 1800–1914.* Stanford: Stanford University Press.
Levi-Faur, David. 1997. "Economic Nationalism: from Friedrich List to Robert Reich." *Review of International Studies* 23: 359–370.
——. 1998. "The Competition State as a Neomercantilist State: Understanding the Restructuring of National and Global Telecommunications." *Journal of Socio-Economics* 27 No. 6: 665–686.
Levin, Jonathan V. 1960. *The Export Economies. Their Pattern of Development in Historical Perspective.* Cambridge, MA: Harvard University Press.
Lewin, Moshe. 1985. *The Making of the Soviet System. Essays in the Social History of Interwar Russia.* New York: Pantheon Books.
——. 1995. *Russia/USSR/Russia: The Drive and Drift of a Superstate.* New York: The New Press.
Lewis, Cleona. 1948. *The United States and Foreign Investment Problems.* Washington, D.C.: The Brookings Institution.
Lewis, Colin M. 1986. "Industry in Latin America before 1930", in Leslie Bethell, ed., *The Cambridge History of Latin America,* Vol. IV: *c. 1870 to 1930.* Cambridge University Press.
——. 2005. *States and Markets in Latin America: The Political Economy of Economic Interventionism.* London: LSE Department of Economic History Working Paper No. 9.
Lewis, Paul H. 1990. *The Crisis of Argentine Capitalism.* Chapel Hill and London: The University of North Carolina Press.
Lewis, W. Arthur. 1949. *Economic Survey 1919–1939.* London: George Allen & Unwin.
——. 1978a. *The Evolution of the International Economic Order.* Princeton: Princeton University Press.

———. 1978b. *Growth and Fluctuations 1870–1913*. London: George Allen & Unwin.
Libby, Douglas C. 1991. "Proto-industrialisation in a Slave Society: The Case of Minas Gerais." *Journal of Latin American Studies* 23 Part 1: 1–35.
Lindert, Peter H. and Jeffrey G. Williamson. 2002. *Does Globalization Make the World More Unequal?* NBER Working Paper 8228, Cambridge, MA, April.
Linz, Juan J. 1975. "Totalitarian and Authoritarian Regimes", in Fred J. Greenstein and Nelson W. Polsby, eds., *Handbook of Political Science* Vol. 3: *Macropolitical Theory*. Reading, MA: Addison and Wesley.
Lippmann, Walter. 1933. "A New Social Philosophy", in James G. Hodgson, ed., *Economic Nationalism*. New York: The H. W. Wilson Company.
Lipsey Robert. E. 1963. *Price and Quantity Trends in Foreign Trade of the United States*. Princeton: Princeton University Press.
List, Friedrich. 1922. *The National System of Political Economy*. London: Longmans, Green and Co. First published in 1841.
Lloyd, Christopher. 2003. "Economic Policy and Australian State Building: From Labourist-Protectionism to Globalization", in Alice Teichova and Herbert Matis, eds., *Nation, State and the Economy in History*. Cambridge: Cambridge University Press.
Lora, Guillermo. 1977. *A History of the Bolivian Labour Movement*. Cambridge: Cambridge University Press.
Lorwin, Lewis L. 1933. "Economic Nationalism and World Coöperation." *Pacific Affairs* 6 No. 7: 361–372.
Love, Joseph L. 1996a. *Crafting the Third World. Theorizing Underdevelopment in Rumania and Brazil*. Stanford: Stanford University Press.
———. 1996b. "Economic Ideas and Ideologies in Latin America since 1930", in Leslie Bethell, ed., *Ideas and Ideologies in Twentieth Century Latin America*. Cambridge: Cambridge University Press.
Luz Vilela, Nícia. 1977. "Ensaio de interpretação", in Roberto Cortés Conde and Stanley J. Stein, eds., *Latin America: A Guide to Economic History, 1830–1930*. Berkeley: University of California Press.
———. 1978. *A luta pela industrialização do Brasil*. São Paulo: Editora Alfa–Omega. First published in 1961.
Łapa, Małgorzata. 2002. *Modernizacja państwa. Polska polityka gospodarcza 1926–1929*. Łódź: Ibidem.
Łepkowski, Tadeusz. 1964. *Haiti. Początki państwa i narodu*. Warszawa: PWN.
———. 1967. *Polska: narodziny nowoczesnego narodu 1764–1870*. Warszawa: PWN.
———. 1984. "Myśli o historii Polski i Polaków." *Zeszyty Historyczne* 68: 66–154.
———. 1986. *Historia Meksyku*. Wrocław: Ossolineum.
———. 1988. "Sobre la historia y los historiadores habla ..." *Estudios Latinoamericanos* 11: 11–45.
———. 1992. "Rewolucja Meksykańska i rewolucje antyzależnościowe XX wieku", in *Historia i wyobraźnia. Studia ofiarowane Bronisławowi Baczce*. Warszawa: PWN.
Łuczak, Czesław. 1988. *Od Bismarcka do Hitlera. Polsko-niemieckie stosunki gospodarcze*. Poznań: Wydawnictwo Poznańskie.
Łukasiewicz, Juliusz. 1982. "Drogi rozwoju rolnictwa na ziemiach polskich", in Stefan Kieniewicz, ed., *Polska XIX wieku. Państwo, społeczeństwo, kultura*. Warszawa: Wiedza Powszechna.
Machlup, Fritz. 1986. *Integracja gospodarcza: narodziny i rozwój idei*. Warszawa: PWN.
Mackenzie, Charles. 1830. *Notes on Haiti Made During a Residence in That Republic*, Vol. 2. London: Henry Colburn and Richard Bentley.
Maddison, Angus. 1985. *Two Crises: Latin America and Asia 1929–38 and 1973–83*. Paris: OECD.
———. 2003. *The World Economy: Historical Statistics*. Paris: OECD.
Magdoff, Harry. 1978. *Imperialism: From the Colonial Age to the Present*. New York and London: Monthly Review Press.

Mahoney, James. 2001. "Path-Dependent Explanations of Regime Change: Central America in Comparative Perspective." *Studies in Comparative International Development* 36 No. 1: 111–141.
Maier, Charles S. 1993. "Democracy since the French Revolution", in John Dunn, ed., *Democracy. The Unfinished Journey, 508 BC to AD 1993*. Oxford: Oxford University Press.
Maingot, Anthony P. 1992. "Race, Color, and Class in the Caribbean", in Alfred Stepan, ed., *Americas: New Interpretative Essays*. New York and Oxford: Oxford University Press.
Majchrowski, Jacek. 1985. *Silni – zwarci – gotowi. Myśl polityczna Obozu Zjednoczenia Narodowego*. Warszawa: PWN.
Mallon, Florencia E. 1983. *The Defence of Community in Peru's Central Highlands. Peasant Struggle and Capitalist Transition, 1860–1940*. Princeton: Princeton University Press.
Małecki-Tepicht, Stefan. 2003. *Ekonomiczne źródła wzrostu i upadku gospodarki socjalistycznej*. Warszawa: PWN.
Małowist, Marian. 1973. *Wschód a Zachód Europy w XIII–XVI w. Konfrontacja struktur społeczno-gospodarczych*. Warszawa: PWN.
———. 2010. "Economic and Political Divisions in Medieval and Early Modern Europe", in Jean Batou and Henryk Szlajfer, eds., *Western Europe, Eastern Europe and World Development 13th–18th Centuries. Collection of Essays of Marian Małowist*. Leiden and Boston: BRILL. First published in 1991.
Manchester, Alan K. 1933. *British Preeminence in Brazil: Its Rise and Decline. A Study in European Expansion*. Chapel Hill: The University of North Carolina Press.
Mandel, Ernest. 1971. *The Formation of the Economic Thought of Karl Marx: 1843 to 'Capital'*. New York and London: Monthly Review Press.
Marchant, Anyda. 1965. *Viscount Mauá and the Empire of Brazil. A Biography of Irineu Evangelista de Sousa (1813–1889)*. Berkeley and Los Angeles: University of California Press.
Marcus, Joseph. 1983. *Social and Political History of the Jews in Poland 1919–1939*. Berlin-New York-Amsterdam: Mouton.
Marer, Paul. 1989. "The Economies and Trade of Eastern Europe", in William E. Griffith, ed., *Central and Eastern Europe: The Opening Curtain?* Boulder: Westview Press.
Mariátegui, José Carlos. 1971. *Seven Interpretative Essays on Peruvian Reality*. Austin and London: University of Texas Press. First published in 1928.
Marichal, Carlos. 1989. *A Century of Debt Crises in Latin America: From Independence to the Great Depression, 1820–1930*. Princeton: Princeton University Press.
——— and Steven Topik. 2003. "The State and Economic Growth in Latin America: Brazil and Mexico, Nineteenth and Early Twentieth Centuries", in Alice Teichova and Herbert Matis, eds., *Nation, State and the Economy in History*. Cambridge: Cambridge University Press.
Marof, Tristán [Gustavo A. Navarro]. 1926. *La justicia del Inca*. Bruselas: La Edición Latino Americana/ Libreria Falk Fils.
Marson, Michel Deliberali. 2008. "A indústria de bens de capital no processo de industrialização na décad de 1930: crescimento e diversificação no estado de São Paulo." *Revista Economia* 9 No.3: 577–597.
———. 2010. *Origens dos empresários e evolução do setor de bens de capital no estado de São Paulo, 1901–1922*. São Pulo, Novembre (mimeo).
Martinière, Guy. 1978. *Les Amériques latines. Une histoire économique*. Grenoble: Presses Universitaire de Grenoble.
Marx, Karl. 1975. "Draft of an Article on Friedrich List's Book 'Das Nationale System der Politischen Ökonomie'", in Karl Marx and Friedrich Engels, *Collected Works* Vol. 4: 1844–45. Moscow: Progress Publishers. Prepared in 1845.
———. 1973. *Grundrisse. Foundations of the Critique of Political Economy (Rough Draft)*. Harmondsworth: Penguin Books in association with New Left Review. Prepared in 1857–1858.
———. 1922. *The Gotha Program*. New York: Socialist Labor Party. First published in 1875.

—— and Friedrich Engels. 2004. *German Ideology*. New York: International Publishers. First published in 1846.
—— and Friedrich Engels. 1998. *Communist Manifesto*. London: Verso. First published in 1848.
Matis, Herbert. 1983. "Disintegration and Multinational Enterprise in Central Europe during the Post-war Years (1918–23)", in Alice Teichova and P. L. Cottrell, eds., *International Business and Central Europe, 1918–1939*. New York: St. Martin's Press.
Mayall, James. 1990. *Nationalism and International Society*. Cambridge: Cambridge University Press.
Mączak, Antoni. 1967. *U źródeł nowoczesnej gospodarki europejskiej*. Warszawa: PWN.
——. 1972. *Między Gdańskiem a Sundem. Studia nad handlem bałtyckim od połowy XVI do połowy XVII w.* Warszawa: PWN.
——. 1986. *Rządzący i rządzeni. Władza i społeczeństwo w Europie wczesnonowożytnej*. Warszawa: Państwowy Instytut Wydawniczy.
McCann, Frank D. 2006. "The Military and the Dictatorship: Getúlio, Góes, and Dutra", in Jens R. Hentschke, ed., *Vargas and Brazil. New Perspectives*. New York: Palgrave Macmillan.
McCraw, Thomas K. 1994. "The Strategic Vision of Alexander Hamilton." *The American Scholar* 63, No. 1: 31–57.
McCreery, David. 1986. "'An Odious Feudalism': Mandamiento Labor and Commercial Agriculture in Guatemala, 1858–1920." *Latin American Perspectives* 13 No. 1: 99–117.
McGreevey, William Paul. 1971. *An Economic History of Colombia 1845–1930*. London: Cambridge University Press.
Mendels, Franklin F. 1982. "Proto-industrialisation: Theory and Reality. General Report. 'A' Themes". Budapest: Eight International Economic History Congress.
Mendelsohn, Ezra. 1983. *The Jews of East Central Europe between the World Wars*. Bloomington: Indiana University Press.
Mendelson, L. 1961. *Teoria i historia kryzysów i cykli ekonomicznych* Vol. 1. Warszawa: PWN.
Méndez G., Cecilia. 1996. "Incas Sí, Indios No: Notes on Peruvian Creole Nationalism and its Contemporary Crisis." *Journal of Latin American Studies* 28 Part 1: 197–225.
Michels, Robert. 1931. "Das Problem der Strukturänderung in einigen südamerikanischen Staaten insbesondere Argentinien und Brasilien, zumal im Hinblick auf den italienischen Einfluss." *Weltwirtschaftliches Archiv* 34: 565–597.
Mill, John Stuart. 1992. *On Liberty and Utilitarianism*. New York: Alfred A. Knopf. First published in 1859–1863.
Miller, Nicola. 1999. *In the Shadow of the State. Intellectuals and the Quest for National Identity in Twentieth-Century Spanish America*. London and New York: Verso.
Miller, Rory. 1977. "British Firms and the Peruvian Government, 1885–1930", in Desmond C. M. Platt, ed., *Business Imperialism 1840–1930. An Inquiry based on British Experience in Latin America*. Oxford: Oxford University Press.
Milward, Alan S. and Vibeke Sørensen. 1994. "Interdependence or Integration? A National Choice", in Alan S. Milward and Vibeke Sørensen, eds., *The Frontier of National Sovereignty. History and Theory 1945–1992*. London and New York: Routledge.
Minchinton, Walter E. 1969. "Editor's Introduction", in Walter E. Minchinton, ed., *The Growth of English Overseas Trade in the Seventeenth and Eighteenth Centuries*. London: Methuen.
Mintz, Sidney W. 1978. "Caribbean Marketplaces and Caribbean History." *Nova Americana* 1: 333–344.
Mises, Ludwig von. 2004. "Economic Nationalism and Peaceful Economic Cooperation", in *Ludwig von Mises Institute*, Auburn, Alabama, June 3. First published in 1943.
Mitchell, Broadus. 1967. *Postscripts to Economic History*. Totowa, NJ.: Littlefield, Adams & Company.
Mitchell, R. B. 1983. *International Historical Statistics: The Americas and Australasia*. London: Macmillan.
Mintz, Sidney W. 1974. *Caribbean Transformation*. Chicago: Aldine Publishing.

Moffat, James E. 1928. "Nationalism and Economic Theory." *The Journal of Political Economy* 36 No. 4: 417–446.
Molyneaux, Peter. 1933. *Economic Nationalism and Problems of the South*, Dallas, Texas: Arnold Foundation Studies in Public Affairs Vol. II No. 2.
Mommsen, Hans. 1996. *The Rise and Fall of Weimar Democracy*. Chapel Hill and London: The University of North Carolina Press.
Mommsen, Wolfgang J. 1984. *Max Weber and German Politics 1890–1920*. Chicago and London: The University of Chicago Press.
———. 1990. "The Varieties of the Nation State in Modern History: Liberal, Imperialist, Fascist and Contemporary Notions of Nation and Nationality", in Michael Mann, ed., *The Rise and Decline of the Nation State*. Oxford: Basil Blackwell.
Moore, Jr., Barrington. 1969. *Social Origins of Dictatorship and Democracy. Lord and Peasant in the Making of the Modern World*. Harmondsworth: Penguin.
Moya Pons, Frank. 1978. *La dominación haitiana, 1822–1844*. Santiago: Universidad Católica Madre y Maestra.
Mulhall, Michael G. 1884. *Dictionary of Statistics*. London: George Routledge and Sons.
Mun, Thomas. 1895. *Englands's Treasure by Forraign Trade or, The Balance of our Forraign Trade is The Rule of our Treasure*. New York and London: Macmillan and Co. First published in 1664.
Munck, Ronaldo, with Ricardo Falcon and Bernardo Galitelli. 1987. *Argentina: From Anarchism to Peronism. Workers, Unions and Politics, 1855–1985*. London: Zed Press.
Munck, Thomas. 1990. *Seventeenth-Century Europe: State, Conflict and the Social Order in Europe, 1598–1700*. London: PalgraveMacmillan.
Murgescu, Bogdan. 2006. "Anything but Simple: the Case of the Romanian Oil Industry", in Helga Schultz and Eduard Kubů, eds., *History and Culture of Economic Nationalism in East Central Europe*. Berlin: Berliner Wissenschafts-Verlag.
Murmis, Miguel and Juan Carlos Portantiero. 1971. *Estudios sobre los orígines del peronismo*. Buenos Aires: Siglo XXI Argentina Editores.
Myint, Hla. 1954–1955. "The Gains from International Trade and the Backward Countries." *The Review of Economic Studies* 22 No. 2: 129–142.
———. 1958. The 'Classical Theory' of International Trade and the Underdeveloped Countries." *The Economic Journal* 68 No. 270: 317–337.
Nairn, Tom. 1977. "The Twilight of the British State." *New Left Review* 101/102.
Nakano, Takeshi. 2007. "Alfred Marshall's Economic Nationalism." *Nations and Nationalism* 13 No. 1: 57–76.
Nash, Manning. 1968. "Economic Nationalism in Mexico", in Harry G. Johnson, ed., *Economic Nationalism in Old and New States*. Chicago and London: The University of Chicago Press.
Needham, Joseph. 1969. *The Grand Titration: Science and Society in East and West*. London: George Allen & Unwin.
Nicholson, J. Shield. 1922. "Introductory Essay", in Friedrich List, *The National System of Political Economy*. London: Longmans, Green and Co.
Nötel, Rudolf. 1986. "International Capital and Finance", in Michael C. Kaser and E. A. Radice, eds., *The Economic History of Eastern Europe 1919–1945*, Vol. II: *Interwar Policy, the War and Reconstruction*. Oxford: Oxford University Press.
North, Douglass C. and Robert P. Thomas. 1973. *The Rise of the Western World. A New Economic History*. Cambridge: Cambridge University Press.
———. 1990. *Institutions, Institutional Change and Economic Performance*. Cambridge: Cambridge University Press.
O'Brien, Patrick K. 1982. "European Economic Development: The Contribution of the Periphery." *The Economic History Review*. New Series 35 No. 1: 1–18.
———. 1986. "Do We Have a Typology for the Study of European Industrialization in the XIXth Century?" *The Journal of European Economic History* 15 No. 2: 291–333.

———. 2003. "Political Structures and Grand Strategies for the Growth of the British Economy, 1688–1815", in Alice Teichova and Herbert Matis, eds., *Nation, State and the Economy in History*. Cambridge: Cambridge University Press.

Ocampo, José Antonio and María Mercedes Botero. 2000. "Coffee and the Origins of Modern Economic Development in Colombia", in Enrique Cárdenas, José Antonio Ocampo and Rosemary Thorp, eds. 2000. *An Economic History of Twentieth-Century Latin America*. Vol. 1: *The Export Age: The Latin American Economies in the Late Nineteenth and Early Twentieth Centuries*. Basingstoke: Palgrave in association with St. Antony's College, Oxford.

O'Connell, Arturo. 1984. "Argentina into the Depression: Problems of an Open Economy", in Rosemary Thorp, ed., *Latin America in the 1930. The Role of the Periphery in World Crisis*. London: Macmillan in association with St. Antony's College, Oxford.

O'Donnell, Guillermo A. 1979a. *Modernization and Bureaucratic-Authoritarianism. Studies in South American Politics*. Berkeley: Institute of International Studies University of California (2nd edition).

———. 1979b. "Tensions in the Bureaucratic-Authoritarian State and the Question of Democracy", in David Collier, ed., *The New Authoritarianism in Latin America*, Princeton: Princeton University Press.

Okita, Saburo and Takeo Miki. 1967. "Treatment of Foreign Capital: A Case Study for Japan", in John H. Adler with the assistance of Paul W. Kuznets, ed., *Capital Movements and Economic Development,* London and New York: Macmillan and St Martin's Press.

Oliveira Filho, Virgilio Roma de. 2007. "A revolução nacional isebiana – H. Jaguaribe e N. W. Sodré." *Estudos de Sociologia* 5 No. 9: 1–45.

Olson, Jr., Mancur. 1982. *The Rise and Decline of Nations: Economic Growth, Stagflation, and Social Rigidities.* New Haven and London: Yale University Press.

———. 1990. "Is Britain the Wave of the Future? How Ideas Affect Societies", in Michael Mann, ed., *The Rise and Decline of the Nation State.* Oxford: Basil Blackwell.

———. 1996. "Big Bills Left on the Sidewalk: Why Some Nations are Rich, and Others Poor." *Journal of Economic Perspectives* 10 No. 2: 3–24.

———. 2000. *Power and Prosperity: Outgrowing Communist and Capitalist Dictatorships.* New York: Basic Books.

[Olson, Jr., Mancur] 1999. *Capitalism, Socialism and Dictatorship: Outgrowing Communist and Capitalist Dictatorships. Conference Proceedings.* Luxembourg: Luxembourg Institute for European and International Studies.

Oppenheimer, Robert. 1982. "National Capital and National Development: Financing Chile's Central Valley Railroads." *Business History Review* 56 No. 1: 54–75.

O'Rourke, Kevin H. and Jeffrey G. Williamson. 2000. *When Did Globalization Begin?* Cambridge, MA: NBER Working Paper No. 7632, April.

Ortega, Luis. 1982. "The First Four Decades of the Chilean Coal Mining Industry, 1840–1879." *Journal of Latin American Studies* 14 Part 1: 1–32.

———. 1985. "Economic Policy and Growth in Chile: From Independence to the War of the Pacific", in Christopher Abel and Colin M. Lewis, eds., *Latin America, Economic Imperialism and the State: The Political Economy of the External Connection from Independence to the Present.* London: Athlone.

Ortiz Letelier, Fernando. 1985. *El movimiento obrero en Chile 1891–1919.* Madrid: Ediciones Michay.

Ossowski, Stanisław. 1967. "Analiza socjologiczna pojęcia ojczyzny", in Stanisław Ossowski, *Dzieła* Vol. III: *Z zagadnień psychologii społecznej.* Warszawa: PWN.

Overy, Richard J. 2003. "German Business and the Nazi New Order", in Terry Gourvish, ed., *Business and Politics in Europe, 1900–1970. Essays in Honour of Alice Teichova.* Cambridge: Cambridge University Press.

Pagano, Ugo. 1995. "Can Economics Explain Nationalism?", in Albert Breton, Gianluigi Galeotti, Pierre Salmon and Ronald Wintrobe, eds., *Nationalism and Rationality.* Cambridge: Cambridge University Press.

Parrington, Vernon L. 1987. *Main Currents in American Thought* Vol. 1: *The Colonial Mind, 1620–1800*. Norman: University of Oklahoma Press. First published in 1927.
Pastore, Mario. 1994a. "State-led Industrialisation: The Evidence on Paraguay, 1852–1870." *Journal of Latin American Studies* 26 Part 2: 296–324.
———. 1994b. "Trade Contraction and Economic Decline: The Paraguayan Economy under Francia, 1810–1840." *Journal of Latin American Studies* 26 Part 3: 539–595.
Pelaez, Carlos Manuel. 1976. "The Theory and Reality of Imperialism in the Coffee Economy of Nineteenth-Century Brazil." *The Economic History Review* 2nd Series 29 No. 2: 276–290.
Perez, Joseph. 1977. *Los movimientos precursores de la emancipacion en Hispanoamérica*. Madrid: Editorial Alhambra.
Perissinotto, Renato Monseff. 2003. "State and Coffee Capital in São Paulo's Export Economy (Brazil 1989–1930)." *Journal of Latin American Studies* 35 No. 1: 1–23.
Pickel, Andreas. 2005. "False Oppositions: Recontextualizing Economic Nationalism in a Globalizing World", in Eric Helleiner and Andreas Pickel, eds., *Economic Nationalism in a Globalizing World*. Ithaca and London: Cornell University Press.
Piel, Jean. 1975. *Capitalisme agraire au Pérou. Vol. I: Originalité de la société agraire péruvienne au XIXe siècle*. Paris: Éditions Anthropos.
Pierson, Paul. 2000. "Increasing Returns, Path-dependence, and the Study of Politics." *American Political Science Review* 94 No. 2: 251–267.
Pike, Frederick B. 1963. "Aspects of Class Relations in Chile, 1850–1969." *The Hispanic American Historical Review* 43 No. 1: 14–33.
———. 1977. *The United States and the Andean Republics: Peru, Bolivia, and Ecuador*. Cambridge, MA and London: Harvard University Press.
Pineda, Yovanna. 2006. "Sources of Finance and Reputation: Merchant Finance Groups in Argentine Industrialization 1890–1930." *Latin American Research Review* 41 No. 2: 3–30.
Pipes, Richard. 1990. *Rosja carów*. Warszawa: Wydawnictwo Magnum.
———. 2000. *Własność a wolność*. Warszawa: MUZA SA.
Pietschmann, Horst. 2009. "On the Origins of the Latin American States", in Ryszard Stemplowski, ed., *On the State of Latin American States: Approaching the Bicentenary*. Kraków: Andrzej Frycz Modrzewski Krakow University.
Plamenatz, John. 1976. "Two Types of Nationalism", in Eugene Kamenka, ed., *Nationalism: The Nature and Evolution of an Idea*. London: Edward Arnold.
Plá, Josefine. 1976. *The British in Paraguay, 1850–1870*. Richmond: The Richmond Publishing in association with St. Antony's College, Oxford.
Platt, Desmond C. M. 1972. *Latin America and British Trade, 1806–1914*. London: Adam and Charles Black.
———. 1977. "Introduction", in Desmond C. M. Platt, ed., *Business Imperialism 1840–1930. An Inquiry Based on British Experience in Latin America*. Oxford: Oxford University Press.
———. 1985. "Dependency and the Historian: Further Objections", in Christopher Abel and Colin M. Lewis, eds., *Latin America, Economic Imperialism and the State: The Political Economy of the External Connection from Independence to the Present*. London: Athlone.
Pogány, Ágnes. 2006. "Economic Anti-Semitism in Hungary after Trianon", in Helga Schultz and Eduard Kubů, eds., *History and Culture of Economic Nationalism in East Central Europe*. Berlin: Berliner Wissenschafts-Verlag.
Pogge von Strandmann, Hartmut. 2001. "Introduction: Walther Rathenau, a Biographical Sketch", in Hartmut Pogge von Strandmann, ed., *Walther Rathenau: Industrialist, Banker, Intellectual, and Politician. Notes and Diaries 1907–1922*. New York: Oxford University Press. First published in 1967.
Polanyi, Karl. 1957. *The Great Transformation. The Political and Economic Origins of Our Time*. Boston: Beacon Press. First published in 1944.
Pollard, Sidney. 1981. *Peaceful Conquest: The Industrialization of Europe, 1760–1970*. Oxford: Oxford University Press.

Pollock, Friedrich. 1933. "Bemerkungen zur Wirtschaftskrise." *Zeitschrift für Sozialforschung* 2 No. 3: 321–353.
Pomeranz, Kenneth. 2000. *The Great Divergence: China, Europe and the Making of the Modern World Economy*. Princeton: Princeton University Press.
Porter, Brian. 2000. *When Nationalism Began to Hate. Imagining Modern Politics in Nineteenth-Century Poland*. New York: Oxford University Press.
Portes, Alejandro and Lori D. Smith. 2008. "Institutions and Development in Latin America: A Comparative Analysis." *Studies in Comparative International Development* 43: 101–128.
Potash, Robert A. 1983. *Mexican Government and Industrial Development in the Early Republic: The Banco de Avío*. Amherst: The University of Massachusetts Press.
Prado, Caio, Jr. 1969. *The Colonial Background of Modern Brazil*. Berkeley and Los Angeles: University of California Press.
Prados de la Escosura, Leandro. 2005. *Colonial Independence and Economic Backwardness in Latin America*. London: LSE Department of Economic History Working Paper No. 10.
Preobrazhensky, Evgeny. 1965. *The New Economics*. London: Oxford University Press. First published in 1926.
Průcha, Vacláv. 1991. "Changes in the Structure of the Manufacturing Industry in the Countries of Central-East and South-East Europe after the Second World War", in *Sectoral Changes in Industry after World War II*. Prague: Institute of History of the CSAS.
——. 2000. "The Economy and the Rise and Fall of a Small Multinational State: Czechoslovakia, 1918–1992", in Alice Teichova and Herbert Matis, eds., *Nation, State and the Economy in History*. Cambridge: Cambridge University Press.
Puiggrós, Rodolfo. 1977. "La Argentina en la decada de los treinta", in Pablo Gonzales Casanova, ed., *América Latina en los años treinta*. México: Universidad Nacional Autónoma de México.
Randall, Laura. 1977. *A Comparative Economic History of Latin America 1500–1914: Vol. I (Mexico)*. Ann Arbor: University Microfilms International.
Ránki, Györgi. 1979. "The Role of Small Industry in Hungarian Capitalist Development", in Ivan T. Berend and Györgi Ranki, *Underdevelopment and Economic Growth. Studies in Hungarian Economic and Social History*. Budapest: Akademiai Kiado.
—— and Jerzy Tomaszewski. 1986. "The Role of the State in Industry, Banking and Trade", in Michael C. Kaser and E. A. Radice, eds., *The Economic History of Eastern Europe 1919–1945, Vol. II: Interwar Policy, the War and Reconstruction*. Oxford: Oxford University Press.
Rawls, John. 2002. *The Law of Peoples: with 'The Idea of Public Reason Revisited'*, Cambridge, MA: Harvard University Press.
Reber, Vera Blinn. 1988. "The Demographics of Paraguay: A Reinterpretation of the Great War, 1864–70." *The Hispanic American Historical Review* 68 No. 2: 289–319.
Reinhardt, Nola. 1986. "The Consolidation of the Import-Export Economy in Nineteenth-Century Colombia." *Latin American Perspectives* 13 No. 1: 75–98.
Reiss, Gerald Dinu. 1983. "O crecimento da empresa industrial na economia cafeeira." *Revista de Economica Politica* 3 No. 2: 67–101.
Renan, Ernest. 1996. "What is a Nation?", in Geoff Eley and Ronald Grigor Suny, eds., *Becoming National: A Reader*. New York and Oxford: Oxford University Press. First published in 1882.
Rial, Juan and Jaime Klaczko. 1982. "Review Essay: Historiography and Historical Studies in Uruguay." *Latin American Research Review* 17 No. 3: 229–250.
Ridings, Eugene W. 1994. *Business Interest Groups in Nineteenth-Century Brazil*. Cambridge: Cambridge University Press.
Riguzzi, Paolo. 2009. "From Globalisation to Revolution? The Porfirian Political Economy: An Essay on Issues and Interpretations." *Journal of Latin American Studies* 41 No. 2: 347–368.
Rippy, J. Fred. 1959. *British Investments in Latin America 1822–1949: A Case Study in the Operations of Private Enterprise in Retarded Regions*. Minneapolis: University of Minnesota Press.

Roberts, Luke S. 1998. *Mercantilism in a Japanese Domain. The Merchant Origins of Economic Nationalism in 18th-Century Tosa.* New York: Cambridge University Press.
Robinson, Joan. 1939. *Wstęp do teorii zatrudnienia,* Warszawa: Wydawca Polityka.
———. 1964. *Economic Philosophy.* Harmondsworth: Penguin.
———. 1972. "The Second Crisis of Economic Theory." *The American Economic Review* 62 No. 1-2: 1–10.
———. 1980. "Michal Kalecki", in *Collected Economic Papers,* Vol. V. Cambridge, MA: The MIT Press.
Robinson, Ronald. 1977. "Non-European Foundations of European Imperialism: Sketch for a Theory of Collaboration", in Roger Owen and Bob Sutcliffe, eds., *Studies in the Theory of Imperialism.* London: Longman.
Rockman, Bert A. 1989. "Minding the State – or a State of Mind? Issues in the Comparative Conceptualization of the State", in James A. Caporaso, ed., *The Elusive State. International and Comparative Perspectives.* Newbury Park, Calif.: Sage Publications.
[Rocznik] *Mały Rocznik Statystyczny 1939.* Warszawa: Główny Urząd Statystyczny.
Rodríguez Monegal, Emir. 2003. "La muerte y las vidas de Aparicio Saravia", in *Obra selecta.* Caracas: Biblioteca Ayacucho.
Roett, Riordan. 1978. *Brazil: Politics in a Patrimonial Society.* New York: Praeger Publishers (revised edition).
Röpke, Wilhelm. 1935. "Fascist Economics." *Economics.* New Series 2 No. 5: 85–100.
———. 1942. *International Economic Disintegration.* London: William Hodge & Co.
Rogowski, Ronald. 1989. *Commerce and Coalitions: How Trade Affects Domestic Political Alignments.* Princeton: Princeton University Press.
Romero, Emilio. 1949. *Historia económica del Perú.* Buenos Aires: Editorial Sudamericana.
Romig, Shane. 2011. "South American Trade Group Raises Import Tariffs." *The Wall Street Journal* December 21.
[Roosevelt, Theodore]. 1909. "Theodore Roosevelt: The Threat of Japan." Papers of Theodore Roosevelt, Manuscript Division, Library of Congress (the internet archive).
Root, Franklin R. 1978. *International Trade and Investment.* Cincinnati: South–West Pub.
Rose-Ackerman, Susan. 2003. "Was Mancur a Maoist? An Essay on Kleptocracy and Political Stability." *Economics and Politics* 15 No. 2: 163–180.
Rosenau, James N. 1989. "The State in an Era of Cascading Politics: Wavering Concepts, Widening Competence, Withering Colossus, or Weathering Change?", in James A. Caporaso, ed., *The Elusive State. International and Comparative Perspectives*, Newbury Park, Calif.: Sage Publications.
Rosenberg, Hans. 1943. "Political and Social Consequences of the Great Depression of 1873–1896." *The Economic History Review* 13 Nos. 1–2: 58–73.
Rosenberg, Nathan. 1976. *Perspectives on Technology.* Cambridge: Cambridge University Press.
Rosenbloom, Joshua L. 2002. *Path Dependence and the Origins of Cotton Textile Manufacturing in New England.* Cambridge, MA: NBER Working Paper No. 9182, September.
Rostow, W.W. 1990. *Theorists of Economic Growth from David Hume to the Present. With a Perspective on the Next Century.* New York: Oxford University Press.
Rothbard, Murray K. 2010. *Keynes, the Man.* Auburn, Alabama: Ludwig von Mises Institute.
Rothschild, Joseph. 1974. *East Central Europe between the Two World Wars.* Seattle and London: University of Washington Press.
Rousseau, Jean Jacques. 1923. *The Social Contract and Discourses.* London and Toronto: J. M. Dent and Sons. First published in 1762.
Rozman, Gilbert. 1990. "The Rise of the State in China and Japan", in Michael Mann, ed., *The Rise and Decline of the Nation State.* Oxford: Basil Blackwell.
[Rural Code] 1970. "The Rural Code of Haiti: in French and English, with a Prefatory Letter to the Right Hon. the Earl Bathurst, K.G., etc.", in *West Indian Slavery: Selected Pamphlets.* Westpoint, CT: Negro Universities Press. First published in 1827.

Rutkowski, Jan. 1953. *Historia gospodarcza Polski (do 1864 r.)*. Warszawa: PWN
Rybarski, Roman. 1932. *Przyszłość gospodarcza świata*. Warszawa (no publisher).
——. 1997. *O narodzie, ustroju i gospodarce*. Warszawa: First published in 1922–1939.
——. 2002. "Idea gospodarstwa narodowego", in Wojciech Józef Burszta, Joanna Nowak and Krzysztof Wawrucha, eds., *Polska refleksja nad narodem. Wybór tekstów*. Poznań: Wydawnictwo Poznańskie. First published in 1919.
Safford, Frank R. 1965. "Foreign and National Enterprise in Nineteenth Century Colombia." *Business History Review* 39 No. 4: 503–526.
Salter, Arthur. 1933. "Future of Economic Nationalism", in James G. Hodgson, ed., *Economic Nationalism*. New York: The H. W. Wilson Company.
Salvucci, Richard J. 1997. "Mexican National Income in the Era of Independence, 1800–40", in Stephen Haber, ed., *How Latin America Fell Behind: Essays on the Economic Histories of Brazil and Mexico, 1800–1914*. Stanford: Stanford University Press.
——. 2006. "Export-Led Industrialization", in Victor Bulmer-Thomas, John H. Coatsworth and Roberto Cortés Conde, eds., *The Cambridge Economic History of Latin America*, Vol. II: *The Long Twentieth Century*. Cambridge: Cambridge University Press.
Samuelson, Paul A. 1986. *The Collected Scientific Papers of Paul Samuelson*, Vol. 5. Edited by Kate Crowley. Cambridge, MA: The MIT Press.
Say, Jean-Baptiste. 1960. *Traktat o ekonomii politycznej czyli prosty wykład sposobu, w jaki się tworzą, rozdzielają i spożywają bogactwa*. Warszawa: PWN. First published in 1803–1810.
Saxonhouse, Gary R. 1993. "Economic Growth and Trade Relations: Japanese Performance in Long-Term Perspective", in Takatoshi Ito and Anne O. Krueger, eds., *Trade and Protectionism* Vol. II. Chicago: University of Chicago Press.
Schacht, Hjalmar. 1937. "Germany's Colonial Demands." *Foreign Affairs* 15, No. 2: 223–234.
Schmitter, Philippe C. 1971. *Interest Conflict and Political Change in Brazil*. Stanford: Stanford University Press.
Schneider, Jürgen. 1981. *Frankreich und die Unabhängigkeit Spanisch-Amerikas. Zum französischen Handel mit den entstehenden Nationalstaaten (1810–1850)*, Vol. 1. Stuttgart: Klett–Cotta.
——. 1984. "Wirtschaft und Aussenhandel Paraguays in den ersten fünfzig Jahren nach der Unabhängigkeit. Der Mythos von der Industrialisierung durch Isolation." *Lateinamerika Studien* 14: 131–146.
Schneider, Ronald M. 1991. *'Order and Progress'. A Political History of Brazil*, Boulder: Westview Press.
Schroeder, Paul W. 1994. *The Transformation of European Politics 1763–1848*. Oxford: Oxford University Press.
Schularick, Moritz. 2006. "A Tale of Two 'Globalizations': Capital Flows from Rich to Poor in Two Eras of Global Finance." *International Journal of Finance and Economics* 11: 339–354.
Schultz, Helga and Eduard Kubů, eds. 2006. *History and Culture of Economic Nationalism in East Central Europe*. Berlin: Berliner Wissenschafts-Verlag.
Schumpeter, Joseph A. 1974. *Imperialism. Social Classes. Two Essays*. New York: The New American Library. First published in 1919–1927.
——. 1975. *Capitalism, Socialism and Democracy*. New York: Harper Colophone Books. First published in 1942.
——. 1986. *History of Economic Analysis*. New York: Oxford University Press.
Schwartz, Herman M. 1994. *States versus Markets: History, Geography, and the Development of the International Political Economy*. New York: St. Martin's Press.
Seers, Dudley. 1983. *The Political Economy of Nationalism*, London: Oxford University Press.
[Sejm Królestwa]. 1995. Janina Leskiewiczowa and Franciszka Ramotowska, eds., *Sejm Królestwa Polskiego o działalności rządu i stanie kraju 1816–1830*. Warszawa: Wydawnictwo Sejmowe. First published in 1816–1830.
Senghaas, Dieter. 1977. "Friedrich List and the New International Economic Order." *Economics* 15: 78–93.

———. 1985. *The European Experience. A Historical Critique of Development Strategy.* Leamington Spa: Berg Publishers.

Serra, Antonio. 1958. "Krótki traktat o przyczynach, które mogą sprowadzić obfitość złota i srebra w krajach nie posiadających kopalni", in *Merkantylizm i początki szkoły klasycznej. Wybór pism ekonomicznych XVI i XVII wieku.* Warszawa: PWN. First published in 1613.

Serra, José. 1979. "Three Mistaken Theses Regarding the Connection between Industrialization and Authoritarian Regimes", in David Collier, ed., *The New Authoritarianism in Latin America*, Princeton: Princeton University Press.

Shafaeddin, Mehdi. 2000. *What Did Frederick List Actually Say? Some Clarifications on the Infant Industry Argument.* Geneva: UNCTAD Discussion Paper No. 149, July.

Siegel, Katherine A. S. 1996. *Loans and Legitimacy. The Evolution of Soviet-American Relations, 1919–1933.* Lexington: The University Press of Kentucky.

Siegenthaler, Jürg K. 1973. "A Scale Analysis of Nineteenth-Century Industrialization." *Explorations in Economic History* 10, No. 1: 75–107.

Sierra, Geronimo de. 1977. "Consolidación y crisis del 'capitalismo democratico' en Uruguay", in Pablo González Casanova, ed., *América Latina: historia de medio siglo.* Vol. 1: *América del Sur.* México: Siglo XXI Editores.

Silva Dias, Maria Odila. 1975. "The Establishment of the Royal Court in Brazil", in A. J. R. Russell-Wood, ed., *From Colony to Nation. Essays on the Independence of Brazil.* Baltimore and London: Johns Hopkins University Press.

Simon, Matthew. 1967. "The Pattern of New British Portfolio Foreign Investment, 1865–1914", in John H. Adler, ed., *Capital Movements and Economic Development.* London and New York: Macmillan and St. Martin's Press.

Simonds, Frank H. and Brooks Emeny. 1935. *The Great Powers in World Politics: International Relations and Economic Nationalism.* New York: American Book Company.

Simonsen, Roberto C. 1973. *Evolução industrial do Brasil e outros estudos.* São Paulo: Editora Nacional e Editora da Universidade de São Paulo. First published in 1928–1935.

———. 2011. "A indústria e o desenvolvimento do Brasil." *Jornal Hora do Povo.* Janury 26–27: 7. First published in 1944.

Singer, Hans. 1950. "The Distribution of Gains between Investing and Borrowing Countries." *The American Economic Review* 40 No. 2 (Papers and Proceedings): 473–485.

Singer, Paulo. 2009. "Economic Evolution and International Connection", in Ignacy Sachs, Jorge Wilheim and Paulo Sérgio Pinheiro, eds., *Brazil: A Century of Change.* Chapel Hill: The University of North Carolina Press.

Skarbek, Jan. 1986. "W dobie rozbiorów i braku państwowości (1772–1918)", in Jerzy Kłoczowski *et al.*, *Zarys dziejów Kościoła katolickiego w Polsce.* Kraków: Wydawnictwo Znak.

Skidelsky, Robert. 1992. *John Maynard Keynes*, Vol. II: *The Economist as Saviour, 1920–1937.* London: Macmillan.

———. 1995. *The World after Communism: A Polemic for Our Times.* London: Macmillan.

———. 2001. "The Mystery of Growth." *The New York Review of Books* 40, No. 4: 28–31.

Skocpol, Theda. 1979. *States and Social Revolutions. A Comparative Analysis of France, Russia, and China.* Cambridge and New York: Cambridge University Press.

———. 1984. "Emerging Agendas and Recurrent Strategies in Historical Sociology", in Theda Skocpol, ed., *Vision and Method in Historical Sociology.* Cambridge and New York: Cambridge University Press.

Slokar, J. 1914. *Geschichte der österreichischen Industrie und ihrer Forderung unter Kaiser Franz I. Mit besonderer Berücksichtigung der Grossindustrie und unter Benutzung archivalischer Quellen verfasst.* Wien: F. Tempsky.

Smith, Adam. 2005. *An Inquiry into the Nature and Causes of the Wealth of Nations.* Hazleton, PA: The Pennsylvania State University (Electronic Classics Series). First published in 1776.

Smith, Anthony D. 1972. *Theories of Nationalism.* New York: Harper & Row.

———. 1998. *Nationalism and Modernism: A Critical Survey of Recent Theories of Nations and Nationalism.* London and New York: Routledge.
Smith, Peter H. 1969. *Politics and Beef in Argentina. Patterns of Conflict and Change.* New York and London: Columbia University Press.
Smolka, Stanisław. 1909. *Korespondencya Lubeckiego z ministrami sekretarzami stanu Ignacym Sobolewskim i Stefanem Grabowskim, T. I: 1821–182.* T. III: *1827–1830.* Kraków: Akademia Umiejętności.
———. 1984. *Polityka Lubeckiego przed powstaniem listopadowym.* T. 1. Warszawa: Państwowy Instytut Wydawniczy. First published in 1907.
Snyder, Louis L. 1990. *Encyclopedia of Nationalism.* New York: Paragon House.
Sodré, Nelson Werneck. 1960. *Raízes históricas do nacionalismo brasileiro,* Rio de Janeiro: Instituto Superior de Estudos Brasileiros (2nd edition).
Solberg, Carl E.. 1973. "The Tariff and Politics in Argentina 1916–1930." *The Hispanic American Historical Review* 53 No.2: 260–284.
———. 1987. *The Prairies and the Pampas. Agrarian Policy in Canada and Argentina, 1880–1930.* Stanford: Stanford University Press.
Sombart, Werner. 1913a. *Luxus und Kapitalismus.* München und Leipzig: Verlag von Duncker & Humblot.
———. 1913b. *Krieg und Kapitalismus.* München und Leipzig: Verlag von Duncker & Humblot.
———. 1928. *Der moderne Kapitalismus. Historisch-systematische Darstellung des gesamteuropäischen Wirtschaftslebens von seinen Anfängen bis zur Gegenwart.* III Bd.: *Das Wirtschaftsleben im Zeitalter des Hochkapitalismus.* München und Leipzig: Verlag von Duncker & Humblot.
———. 1932. *Die Zukunft des Kapitalismus.* Berlin–Charlottenburg II: Buchholz & Weisswange.
———. 1954. *Die deutsche Volkswirtschaft im 19. Jahrhundert und im Anfang des 20. Jahrhunderts. Eine Einführung in die Nationalökonomie.* Darmstadt: Wissenschaftliche Buchgemeinschaft E. V. (reprint of the 7th edition from 1912).
Sosnowska, Anna. 2004. *Zrozumieć zacofanie. Spory historyków o Europę Wschodnią (1947–1994).* Warszawa: Wydawnictwo TRIO.
Spektorowski, Alberto.1994. "The Ideological Origins of Right and Left Nationalism in Argentina, 1930–43."*The Journal of Contemporary History* 29 No. 1: 155–184.
Spigler, Iancu. 1986. "Public Finance", in Michael C. Kaser and E. A. Radice, eds., *The Economic History of Eastern Europe 1919–1945,* Vol. II: *Interwar Policy, the War and Reconstruction.* Oxford: Oxford University Press.
Stallings, Barbara. 1987. *Banker to the Third World. U.S. Portfolio Investment in Latin America, 1900–1986.* Berkeley: University of California Press.
———. 1990."The Role of Foreign Capital in Economic Development", in Gary Gereffi and Donald L. Wyman, eds., *Manufacturing Miracles. Paths of Industrialization in Latin America and East Asia.* Princeton: Princeton University Press.
Staniland, Martin. 1985. *What Is Political Economy? A Study of Social Theory and Underdevelopment.* New Haven and London: Yale University Press.
Steensgaard, Niels. 1981. "Violence and the Rise of Capitalism: Frederic C. Lane's Theory of Protection and Tribute." *Review* V, No. 2: 247–273.
Stein, Stanley J. 1957. *The Brazilian Cotton Manufacture. Textile Enterprise in an Underdeveloped Area 1850–1950.* Cambridge, MA: Harvard University Press.
———. 1967. "The Tasks Ahead for Latin American Historians", in Howard F. Cline, ed., *Latin American History: Essays on Its Study and Teaching 1895–1965,* Vol. 2. Austin: University of Texas Press.
———. 1985. *Vassouras: A Brazilian Coffee County, 1850–1900.* Princeton: Princeton University Press. First published in 1958.
—— and Barbara Stein. 1970. *The Colonial Heritage of Latin America. Essays on Economic Dependence in Perspective.* New York: Oxford University Press.

—— and Shane J. Hunt. 1971. "Principal Currents in the Economic Historiography of Latin America." *The Journal of Economic History* 31, No. 1: 222–253.
Stein, Steve. 1980. *Populism in Peru. The Emergence of the Masses and the Politics of Social Control.* Madison, Wisconsin: The University of Wisconsin Press.
Stemplowski, Ryszard. 1975. *Zależność i wyzwanie. Argentyna wobec rywalizacji mocarstw anglosaskich i Trzeciej, Rzeszy.* Warszawa: Książka i Wiedza.
——. 1985/1986. "Empresas europeas y Chile en la epoca de la Gran Depresión, 1930–1933." *Estudios Latinoamericanos* 10: 135–145.
——. 1996. *Państwowy socjalizm w realnym kapitalizmie: Chile w 1932 roku.* Warszawa: Wydawnictwo TRIO.
Stepan, Alfred. 2001. *Arguing Comparative Politics.* Oxford: Oxford University Press.
Štiblar, Franjo. 1997. "The Rise and Fall of Yugoslavia: An Economic History View", in Alice Teichova, ed., *Central Europe in the Twentieth Century. An Economic History Perspective.* Aldershot: Ashgate Publications.
Stokes, Gale. 1989. "The Social Origins of East European Politics", in Daniel Chirot, ed., *The Origins of Backwardness in Eastern Europe: Economics and Politics from the Middle Ages until the Early Twentieth Century.* Berkeley and Los Angeles: University of California Press.
——. 2001. "The Fates of Human Societies: A Review of Recent Macrohistories." *The American Historical Review* 106, No. 2: 508–525.
Studentowicz, Kazimierz. 1939."Od tłumacza", in Joan Robinson, *Wstęp do teorii zatrudnienia.* Warszawa: Wydawca Polityka.
Summerhill, William R. 2006. "The Development of Infrastructure", in Victor Bulmer-Thomas, John H. Coatsworth and Roberto Cortés Conde, eds., *The Cambridge Economic History of Latin America,* Vol. II: *The Long Twentieth Century.* Cambridge: Cambridge University Press.
Supple, Barry. 1973. "The State and the Industrial Revolution 1700–1914", in Carlo M. Cipolla, ed., *The Fontana Economic History of Europe* Vol. 3: *The Industrial Revolution.* Glasgow: Fontana/Collins.
Sutcliffe, Robert. 1977. "Imperialism and Industrialization in the Third World", in Roger Owen and Robert Sutcliffe, eds., *Studies in the Theory of Imperialism.* London: Longmans.
Svennilson, Ingvar. 1963. "The Concept of the Nation and Its Relevance to Economic Analysis", in E. A. G. Robinson, ed., *Economic Consequences of the Size of Nations.* London: Macmillan.
Sweezy, Paul M. 1938. *Monopoly and Competition in the English Coal Trade 1550–1850.* Cambridge, MA: Harvard University Press.
—— and Harry Magdoff. 1972. *The Dynamics of U. S. Capitalism.* New York: Monthly Review Press.
Sylla, Richard and Gianni Toniolo. 1991. "Introduction: Patterns of European Industrialization during the Nineteenth Century", in Richard Sylla and Gianni Toniolo, eds., *Patterns of European Industrialization. The Nineteenth Century.* London and New York: Routledge.
Szacki, Jerzy. 1994. *Liberalizm po komunizmie.* Kraków: Społeczny Instytut Wydawniczy Znak/ Fundacja im. Stefana Batorego.
—— 1997."Wstęp. Powrót idei społeczeństwa obywatelskiego", in Jerzy Szacki, ed., *Ani książę, ani kupiec: obywatel. Idea społeczeństwa obywatelskiego w myśli współczesnej.* Kraków: Wydawnictwo Znak.
——. 2002. *Historia myśli socjologicznej.* Warszawa: PWN (new edition).
Szczepański, Jerzy. 2008. *Książę Ksawery Drucki-Lubecki (1778–1846).* Warszawa: DiG.
Szlajfer, Henryk. 1985. *Modernizacja zależności. Kapitalizm i rozwój w Ameryce Łacińskiej.* Wrocław: Ossolineum.
——. 1986. "Against Dependent Capitalist Development in Nineteenth-Century Latin America: the Case of Haiti and Paraguay". *Latin American Perspectives* 13, No. 1: 45–73.

——. 1989. "Latin America and the Comintern: An Interesting Book with Many Mistakes. Review Essay." *Boletín de Estudios Latinoamericanos y del Caribe* 46: 111–118.

——, ed. 1990. *Economic Nationalism in East-Central Europe and South America, 1914–1939*. Geneva: Centre for International Economic History/Librairie Droz.

——. 1997. "Promise, Failure and Prospects of Economic Nationalism in Poland: The Communist Experiment in Retrospect", in Alice Teichova, ed., *Central Europe in the Twentieth Century. An Economic History Perspective*. Aldershot: Ashgate Publishing.

——. 2005. *Droga na skróty. Nacjonalizm gospodarczy w Ameryce Łacińskiej i Europie Środkowo-Wschodniej w epoce pierwszej globalizacji*. Warszawa: Instytut Studiów Politycznych PAN.

——. 2009. "Latin American 'Classical' Populism and Economic Nationalism: Style and Content Revisited", in Andrzej Dembicz, ed., *América Latina: interpretaciones a inicios del siglo XXI*. Warszawa: CESLA/CEISAL.

Szporluk, Roman. 1991. *Communism and Nationalism. Karl Marx versus Friedrich List*. New York: Oxford University Press (2nd edition).

——. 2003. *Imperium, komunizm i narody. Wybór esejów*. Kraków: Wydawnictwo ARCANA.

Szücs, Jenö. 1988. "Three Historical Regions of Europe", in John Keane, ed., *Civil Society and the State*. London and New York: Verso.

Tagore, Rabindranath. 2002. *Nationalism*. New Delhi: Rupa & Co. First published in 1917.

Tamir, Yael. 1993. *Liberal Nationalism*. Princeton: Princeton University Press.

Taylor, Alan M. 2006. "Foreign Capital Flows", in Victor Bulmer-Thomas, John H. Coatsworth and Roberto Cortés Conde, eds., *The Cambridge Economic History of Latin America*, Vol. II: *The Long Twentieth Century*. Cambridge: Cambridge University Press.

Twomey, Michael J. 1998. "Patterns of Foreign Investment in Latin America in the Twentieth Century", in John H. Coatsworth and Alan M. Taylor, eds., *Latin America and the World Economy Since 1800*. Cambridge, MA: Harvard University and David Rockefeller Center for Latin American Studies.

Teichova, Alice. 1985. "Industry", in Michael C. Kaser and E. A. Radice, eds., *The Economic History of Eastern Europe 1919–1945*, Vol. I: *Economic Structure and Performance between the Two Wars*. Oxford: Oxford University Press.

Tennenbaum, Henryk. 1942. *Europa Środkowo-Wschodnia w gospodarstwie światowem*, London: M. I. Kolin (Publisher).

Thomas, Brinley. 1967. "The Historical Record of International Capital Movements to 1913", in John H. Adler with assistance of Paul W. Kuznets, ed., *Capital Movements and Economic Development*. London and New York: Macmillan and St. Martin's Press.

Thomson, Guy P. C. 1985. "Protectionism and Industrialization in Mexico, 1821–1854: the Case of Puebla", in Christopher Abel and Colin M. Lewis, eds., *Latin America, Economic Imperialism and the State: The Political Economy of the External Connection from Independence to the Present*. London: Athlone.

——. 1990. "Continuity and Change in Mexican Manufacturing, 1800–1870", in Jean Batou, ed., *Between Development and Underdevelopment 1800–1870. The Precocious Attempts at Industrialization of the Periphery*. Geneva: Centre of International Economic History/Librairie Droz.

Thorp, Rosemary. 1998. *Progress, Poverty and Exclusion: An Economic History of Latin America in the 20th Century*. Baltimore: Inter-American Development Bank.

—— and Geoffrey Bertram. 1978. *Peru 1890–1977. Growth and Policy in an Open Economy*, London: The Macmillan Press.

—— and C. Londoño. 1984. "The Effects of the Great Depression on the Economies of Peru and Columbia", in Rosemary Thorp, ed., *Latin America in the 1930s. The Role of Periphery in World Crisis*. London: Macmillan in association with St Antony's College, Oxford.

Tijn, Theo van. 1988. "Nationalism and the Socialist Workers' Movement", in Frits van Holthoon and Marcel van der Linden, eds., *Internationalism in the Labour Movement, 1830–1940*. Leiden: International Institute of Social History.

Timmer, Ashley S. and Jeffrey G. Williamson. 1998. "Immigration Policy Prior to the 1930s: Labor Markets, Policy Interactions, and Globalization Backlash." *Population and Development Review* 24 No. 4: 739–771.

Tipton, Frank B. Jr. 1981. "Government Policy and Economic Development in Germany and Japan: A Skeptical Reevaluation." *The Journal of Economic History* 41 No. 1: 139–150.

Toledo, Caio Navarro de. 1998. "ISEB Intellectuals, the Left, and Marxism." *Latin American Perspectives* 25 No. 1: 109–135.

Tomaszewski, Jerzy. 2000. "Economic Differentiation and the National Question in Poland in the Twentieth Century", in Alice Teichova, Herbert Matis and Jaroslav Pátek, eds., *Economic Change and the National Question in Twentieth-century Europe*. Cambridge: Cambridge University Press.

———. 2006. Review of the book by H. Szlajfer, *Droga na skróty*. *The Polish Quarterly of International Affairs* 15 No. 3: 134–138.

Topik, Steven. 1980. "State Interventionism in a Liberal Regime: Brazil, 1889–1930." *The Hispanic American Historical Review* 60 No. 4: 593–616.

———. 1984. "State Autonomy in Economic Policy: Brazil's Experience 1822–1930." *Journal of Interamerican Studies and World Affairs* 26 No. 4: 449–476.

———. 1985. "The State's Contribution to the Development of Brazil's Internal Economy, 1850–1930." *The Hispanic American Historical Review* 65, No. 2: 203–228.

———. 1989. "The Old Republic", in Michael L. Conniff and Frank D. McCann, eds., *Modern Brazil: Elites and Masses in Historical Perspective*. Lincoln and London: University of Nebraska Press.

Toplin, Robert B. 1972. *The Abolition of Slavery in Brazil*. New York: Atheneum Publishers.

Topolski, Jerzy. 1965. *Narodziny kapitalizmu w Europie XVI–XVII wieku*. Warszawa: PWN.

———.1971. "Gospodarka", in Bogusław Leśnodorski, ed., *Polska w epoce Oświecenia. Państwo, społeczeństwo, kultura*. Warszawa: Wiedza Powszechna.

———. 1982. *Prawda i model w historiografii*. Łódź: Wydawnictwo Łódzkie.

———. 2000. *Przełom gospodarczy w Polsce XVI wieku i jego następstwa*. Poznań: Wydawnictwo Poznańskie.

Triffin, Robert. 1963. "The Size of the Nation and Its Vulnerability to Economic Nationalism", in E. A. G. Robinson, ed., *Economic Consequences of the Size of Nations*. London: Macmillan.

Turnell, Sean. 2002. *Keynes, Economics and War: A Liberal Dose of Realism*. Sydney: Macquarie University, Department of Economics Research Papers No. 0207.

Turner, Henry A., Jr. 1985. *German Big Business and the Rise of Hitler*. New York and Oxford: Oxford University Press.

Ugarte, Cesar Antonio. 1977. *Bosquejo de la historia económica del Perú*. Lima: Delva Editores. First published in 1926.

[UNCTAD] 1996. *Trade and Development Report, 1996*. New York and Geneva: United Nations.

[U.S. Tariff Commission] 1934. *The Tariff and Its History*. Washington, D.C.: U.S. Tariff Commission.

Valenzuela, Luis. 1989. "Plebeians and Patricians in 19th Century Chile." *Journal of Historical Sociology* 2 No. 3: 287–301.

———. 1992. "The Chilean Copper Smelting Industry in the Mid-Nineteenth Century: Phases of Expansion and Stagnation, 1834–58." *Journal of Latin American Studies* 24 Part 3: 507–550.

Veblen, Thorstein B. 1920. Review of the book by J. M. Keynes *The Economic Consequences of Peace*. *Political Science Quarterly* 35.

Veliz, Claudio. 1980. *The Centralist Tradition of Latin America*. Princeton: Princeton University Press.

Versiani, Flavio Rabelo. 1984. "Before the Depression: Brazilian Industry in the 1920s", in Rosemary Thorp, ed., *Latin America in the 1930s. The Role of Periphery in World Crisis*. London: Macmillan in association with St. Antony's College, Oxford.

Villanova Villela, A. and Anibal W. Suzigan 1973. *Politica do governo e crescimento da economia brasileira 1899–1945.* Rio de Janeiro: IPES.
Viner, Jacob. 1969. "Power versus Plenty as Objectives of Foreign Policy in the Seventeenth and Eighteenth Centuries", in D. C. Coleman, ed., *Revisions in Mercantilism.* London: Methuen.
Wade, Robert. 1990. "Industrial Policy in East Asia: Does It Lead or Follow the Market?", in Gary Gereffi and Donald L. Wyman, eds., *Manufacturing Miracles. Paths of Industrialization in Latin America and East Asia.* Princeton: Princeton University Press.
Waldenberg, Marek. 1992. *Kwestie narodowe w Europie Środkowo-Wschodniej. Dzieje. Idee.* Warszawa: PWN.
Walicki, Andrzej. 1965. "Wstęp", in Andrzej Walicki, ed., *Filozofia społeczna narodnictwa rosyjskiego,* Vol. I. Warszawa: Książka i Wiedza.
———. 1983. *Polska, Rosja, marksizm. Studia z dziejów marksizmu i jego recepcji.* Warszawa: Książka i Wiedza.
Walker, D. W. 1984. "Business As Usual: The Empresa del Tabaco in Mexico, 1837–44." *The Hispanic American Historical Review* 64, No. 4: 675–705.
Wallerstein, Immanuel. 1974. *The Modern World-System: Capitalist Agriculture and the Origins of the European World-Economy in the Sixteenth Century.* New York: Academic Press.
———. 2000. *The Essential Wallerstein.* New York: The New Press.
———. 2004. *World-System Analysis. An Introduction.* Durham and London: Duke University Press.
Wallich, Henry C. 1944. "Fiscal Policy and the Budget", in Seymour E. Harris, ed., *Economic Problems of Latin America.* New York and London: McGraw-Hill Book Co.
Wapiński, Roman. 1980. *Narodowa Demokracja 1893–1939. Ze studiów nad dziejami myśli nacjonalistycznej.* Wrocław: Ossolineum.
———. 1988. *Roman Dmowski.* Lublin: Wydawnictwo Lubelskie.
Wasserman, Mark. 1973. "Oligarquía e intereses extranjeros en Chihuahua durante el porfiriato." *Historia Mexicana* XXII No. 3: 279–319.
Weaver, Fredrick Stirton. 1980. *Class, State, and Industrial Structure. The Historical Process of South American Industrial Growth.* Westport, Conn.: Greenwood Press.
Weber, Max. 1994. "The Nation State and Economic Policy (Inaugural lecture)", in Max Weber, *Political Writings.* Edited by Peter Lassman and Ronald Speirs. Cambridge: Cambridge University Press. First published in 1895.
———. 1966. *General Economic History.* New York: Collier Books. First published in 1920.
———. 1978. *Economy and Society. An Outline of Interpretative Sociology.* Berkeley and Los Angeles: University of California Press. First published in 1920.
Wee, Herman Van der. 1987. *Prosperity and Upheaval. The World Economy 1945–1980.* Harmondsworth: Penguin.
Wehler, Hans-Ulrich. 2001. *Modernizacja, nacjonalizm, społeczeństwo. Eseje i artykuły.* Warszawa: Wiedza Powszechna.
Weiss, R. W. 1968. "Economic Nationalism in Britain in the Nineteenth Century", in Harry G. Johnson, ed., *Economic Nationalism in Old and New States.* Chicago and London: The University of Chicago Press.
Welch, Cliff. 1999. *The Seed was Planted. The São Paulo Roots of Brazil's Rural Labor Movement, 1924–1964.* University Park, PA: The Pennsylvania State University Press.
Wereszycki, Henryk. 1975. *Pod berłem Habsburgów. Zagadnienia narodowościowe.* Kraków: Wydawnictwo Literackie.
Weyland, Kurt. 2001. "Clarifying a Contested Concept: Populism in the Study of Latin American Politics." *Comparative Politics* 34 No. 1: 1–22.
Whigham, Thomas Lyle. 1978. "The Iron Works of Ybycui: Paraguayan Industrial Development in the Mid-Nineteenth Century." *The Americas* 35 No. 2: 201–218.
——— and Barbara Potthast. 2002. "Refining the Numbers: A Response to Reber and Kleinpenning." *Latin American Research Review* 37 No. 3: 143–148.

White, Richard Allen. 1978. *Paraguay's Autonomous Revolution, 1810–1840*. Albuquerque: University of New Mexico Press.
Wilkins, Mira. 1974. *The Maturing of Multinational Enterprise: American Business Abroad from 1914 to 1970*. Cambridge, MA: Harvard University Press.
Williams, Daryle. 2006. "Civicscape and Memoryscape: The First Vargas Regime and Rio de Janeiro", in Jens R. Hentschke, ed., *Vargas and Brazil. New Perspectives*. New York: Palgrave Macmillan.
Williams, Gwyn. 1981. "Economic Development, Social Structure and Contemporary Nationalism in Wales." *Review* V, No. 2: 275–310.
Williams, John Hoyt. 1979. *The Rise and Fall of the Paraguayan Republic, 1800–1870*. Austin: University of Texas Press.
Williamson, Jeffrey. 2002. Is Protection Bad for Growth? Will Globalization Last? Looking for Answers in History. Paper presented at the XIII International Economic History Association Congress, Buenos Aires, July 21–26.
———. 2006. *Globalization and the Poor Periphery before 1950*. Cambridge, MA: The MIT Press.
Wilson, Charles. 1957. "Mercantilism: Some Vicissitudes of an Idea." *The Economic History Review*. New Series 10 No. 2: 181–188.
———. 1969. "The Other Face of Mercantilism", in D. C. Coleman, ed., *Revisions in Mercantilism*. London: Methuen.
Wilson, Joan Hoff. 1974. *Ideology and Economics. U.S. Relations with the Soviet Union, 1918–1933*. Columbia: University of Missouri Press.
Wimmer, Andreas and Nina Glick Schiller. 2003. "Methodological Nationalism, the Social Sciences, and the Study of Migration: An Essay in Historical Epistemology." *International Migration Review* 37 No. 3: 576–610.
Winkler, Heinrich August. 1976. "From Social Protectionism to National Socialism: The German Small-Business Movement in Comparative Perspective." *The Journal of Modern History* 48 No. 1: 1–18.
Winkler, Max. 1933. *Foreign Bonds. An Autopsy. A Study of Defaults and Repudiations of Government Obligations*. Philadelphia: Roland Swain Company.
Wirth, John D. 1967. "A German View of Brazilian Trade and Development, 1935." *The Hispanic American Historical Review* 47 No. 2: 225–235.
———. 1970. *The Politics of Brazilian Development*. Stanford: Stanford University Press.
Witte, Sergei Iu. 1921. *The Memoirs of Count Witte*. Garden City, N.J. and Toronto: Doubleday, Page & Company.
———. 1954. "Report of the Minister of Finance to His Majesty on the Necessity of Formulating and Thereafter Steadfastly Adhering to a Definite Program of a Commercial and Industrial Policy of the Empire", in Theodor H. von Laue. "A Secret Memorandum of Sergei Witte on the Industrialization of Imperial Russia." *The Journal of Modern History* XXVI, No. 2: 64–74. Prepared in 1899.
Wittman, Tibor. 1980. *Historia de América Latina*. Budapest: Akademiai Kiado.
Woodard, James P. "'All for São Paulo, All for Brazil': Vargas, the *Paulistas*, and the Historiography of Twentieth-Century Brazil", in Jens R. Hentschke, ed., *Vargas and Brazil. New Perspectives*. New York: Palgrave Macmillan.
Woroncow, W. 1965. "Losy kapitalizmu w Rosji", in Andrzej Walicki, ed., *Filozofia społeczna narodnictwa rosyjskiego*, Vol. 2. Warszawa: Książka i Wiedza. First published in 1882.
Woroniecki, Jan. 1990. *Obcy kapitał w gospodarce radzieckiej. Doświadczenia i współczesność*. Warszawa: PWN.
Wright, Gavin. 2003. "The Role of Nationhood in the Economic Development of the USA", in Alice Teichova and Herbert Matis, eds., *Nation, State and the Economy in History*. Cambridge: Cambridge University Press.
Yeager, Mary A. 1980. "Trade Protection as an International Commodity: the Case of Steel." *The Journal of Economic History* XL, No. 1: 33–42.

Zeitlin, Maurice. 1984. *The Civil Wars in Chile (or the bourgeois revolutions that never were)*. Princeton: Princeton University Press.

Zeeland, Paul van. 1933. *A View of Europe, 1932. An Interpretative Essay on Some Workings of Economic Nationalism*. Baltimore: The Johns Hopkins Press.

Zientara, Benedykt, Antoni Mączak, Ireneusz Ihnatowicz and Zbigniew Landau. 1965. *Dzieje gospodarcze Polski do 1939 r.* Warszawa: Wiedza Powszechna.

Zimmermann, Erich W. 1931. "The Resource Hierarchy of Modern World Economy." *Weltwirtschaftliches Archiv* 33: 431–463.

Żuławski, Zygmunt. 1939. *Refleksje*. Warszawa: Wydawnictwo Komisji Centralnej Związków Zawodowych.

INDEX[1]

Abdelal, Rawi 2, 39, 53
Accumulation, original 191–194
Acemoglu, Daron 41, 82, 104
Acton-Dalberg John E. E. 53, 148, 150, 152
Ação Integralista Brasileira *see also* Fascism 108, 249, 310
Adams, John Quincy 18, 50f
Africa 122, 125f, 197
Agrarian Union [Bulgaria] 304
Agrarianism 177, 304
Alamán, Lucas 202f, 215f
Alianza de la Juventud Nacional 246
ALN [Aliança Nacional Libertadora] *see also* Communism 108, 249
Amsden, Alice H. 349
Anderson, Benedict 11n, 13, 163
Andersson, Jan Otto 40, 128n
Andrade, Mario de 310
Andrade, Oswaldo de 310
APRA *see* Haya de la Torre
Arabs 309
Aramayo, Félix Avelino 311
ARBED group *also* Companhia Siderúrgica Belgo-Mineira 273f
Argentina 6, 19, 88, 106f, 115, 117, 119f, 125–129, 135, 165f, 169n, 171, 175f, 191, 197, 201, 205, 207, 214, 216, 229f, 232f, 236–241, 246–249, 255f, 258f, 262f, 267, 271–278, 280, 286–289, 292–294, 297, 299, 301f, 313, 319, 324f, 344, 352
Arrow, Kenneth J. 20, 185
Asia *also* East and South East Asia 6, 23, 32, 41f, 61, 112f, 122, 125f, 129f, 145, 184, 243, 322, 352, 354
Associação Comercial of Rio de Janeiro 327
Asynchronisms, coexistence of 192, 194f, 214
Atlantic economy 122, 185, 223
Auschnitt, Max *see also* Jews 307
Australia *see also* Western offshoots 12, 19, 123f, 126–129, 135, 160, 169n, 202, 240, 276
Australian protectionist debate 226f
Austria 34, 65, 188, 197, 303, 305f

Austro-Hungarian empire 118, 147, 270, 305
Autarky 68, 70, 312, 318f, 321f
Authoritarianism 7, 22, 73, 106–108, 139, 141, 147, 157f, 160f, 172, 174, 178f, 246, 249, 253, 282, 304, 308, 316, 318, 322–324, 328, 331f, 336, 339, 341, 344, 349, 351, 353
Autocracy 26n, 81, 143, 145, 155–160, 178
Ayal, Eliezer B. 23f, 112
Azeredo Coutinho, José Joaquim da Cunha de 62

Badie, Bertrand 43n, 100, 102n, 143, 167
Baer, Werner 173, 197, 238, 269, 274f, 286, 293, 312, 314, 316, 339, 341
Bairoch, Paul x, 4f, 7, 18, 43, 51, 70, 88f, 122, 125, 128, 131, 134, 184f, 187f, 317, 353
Balicki, Zygmunt 99
Balmaceda, Manuel José 119, 297
Baltic countries 270f
Baltic economy 185, 224n
Banco de Avío para Fomento de la Industria Nacional 203f, 215f
Banco de Comercio *see also* Mauá 198
Bank Polski (1) 203, 209f, 219
Bank Polski (2) 301
Baran, Paul 31, 98, 244
Baring Brothers Bank 115, 119, 239, 241
Barbosa Horta, Júlio Caetano 340
Bartel, Kazimierz 338
Batlle y Ordóñez, José *also* batllismo 263–267, 299
Batou, Jean 7, 26n, 183
Baumann, Kurt *see* Mandelbaum, Kurt
Belgium 185n, 276
Belzú, Manuel 219
Benavides, Oscar R. 107
Bendix, Reinhard 3, 192
Berend, Ivan T. 34n, 62, 89, 107, 151n, 172, 270, 280, 284, 289f, 320, 350f
Berlin, Isaiah 17, 227
Berlin 266, 309, 336
Bértola, Luis 6, 18, 217f, 230–235, 239, 241, 249, 267, 269, 276, 287, 293

---

[1] Central Europe, East and Central Europe, Western Europe, Latin America, Central America and South America are omitted from the index.

INDEX

Bertram, Geoffrey 245, 251–253, 260, 274, 277, 280
Bhagwati, Jagdish N. 6n, 103, 105, 190, 242
Bielecki, Krzysztof 78
Birnbaum, Pierre 43n, 100, 102n, 143, 167
Bismarck, Otto 12, 83, 91f, 147, 152, 154, 157
Blanco-Fombona, Rufino 298
Bogota 215
Bolivar, Simón 163, 198, 208
Bolivia 163, 173, 178, 194, 210–212, 214, 217, 219, 225, 255, 260, 267, 271, 297, 310f, 317
Bonilla, Heraclio 134, 190, 211–213, 222, 245, 250f, 254n, 295, 298
Borchardt, Knut 7, 283
Boyer, Christoph 260
Braudel, Fernand 15, 31n, 37, 43, 45, 48, 63, 80, 85, 90, 100, 186, 223, 347
Brazil 3, 6, 25, 31, 62, 78n, 93, 102, 105n, 106–108, 112f, 118, 120, 123f, 126–129, 133, 135, 163, 167, 169–171, 173–176, 188n, 189, 191, 197f, 201n, 205–207, 213, 217, 219, 224–226, 228–233, 236–244, 246, 248–250, 258f, 265, 269, 273–278, 280, 282, 285f, 288–293, 296f, 301f, 309–311, 313–318, 322, 324–333, 336–345, 348–353
Bresser Pereira, Luiz Carlos 102–104, 113, 277
Breton, Albert 23f, 32, 109, 114, 120, 130, 169n
Breuilly, John 11n, 17, 149, 162, 165f, 179
Buarque de Holanda, Sérgio 310
Bücher, Karl 78, 85
Buenos Aires 216, 237, 256f
Bukharin, Nikolai 84
Bulgaria 107, 177, 236, 269, 271, 276, 286, 288, 292, 303f, 350
Bulmer-Thomas, Victor 34n, 111, 128n, 133, 168, 173, 193, 213, 216f, 224n, 225, 226n, 229n, 230f, 234–236, 251, 262, 265, 273, 279–281, 285–288, 292f, 351f
Bunge, Alejandro 324f
Burke, Edmund 202
Busch, German 311
Bustamante, Anastasio 202

Cabotage *also* coastal shipping 225, 309
California 132, 202
Calles, Plutarco Elías 115, 116n, 321
Canada *see also* Western offshoots 19, 124, 128f, 135, 160, 235f, 263, 276
Capitalism, transition to 192–194
Capitalism, spirit of 3, 14, 16, 348
CARBAP [Confederación de Asociaciones Rurales de Buenos Aires y La Pampa] 257

Cárdenas, Lázaro 115, 116n, 309, 322
Cardoso, Fernando H. 106, 112, 244, 253, 264
Carey, Henry 55
Carmagnani, Marcello 15–17, 23
Carr, Edward H. 33, 125, 152
Carranza de la Garza, Venustiano 115
Caribbean Basin 123, 126, 191, 224, 298, 301
Carta Econômica de Teresópolis 341
Catalonia 17
Catholic Church 165, 168, 174, 202, 204, 211
Cavour, Camillo Benso di 147, 155
Conselho de Economia Nacional *see also* Planning 340
Central Industrial Region *see* COP
Centro Industrial do Brasil *see also* Protectionism 274
Cerro de Pasco Copper Corporation 246, 251f, 261f
CFCE [Conselho Federal de Comércio Exterior] *see also* Planning 336, 340
Chang, Ha-Joon 6, 35n, 99n, 317
Chatterjee, Partha 11n, 331, 334
Chenery, Hollis B. 87
Chihuahua 115
Child, Josiah 39f, 44
Chile 35, 105, 107, 114, 119, 133, 162–164, 170, 173, 175f, 191, 201f, 211f, 221, 225, 229f, 232, 250, 252f, 269, 271, 274, 286, 288, 297, 301f, 305, 309, 311, 314, 317, 333, 341, 352
China 126, 130f, 184f, 192, 245, 334, 353f
Chinese 213, 309
Científicos *see also* Mexico 172f, 229
CIESP [Centro das Indústrias do Estado de São Paulo] *see also* Industry 325, 328, 333
Cipolla, Carlo M. 1
Clay, Henry 18, 51f
Clark, Colin xi, 38
Coal *also* charcoal 119, 184f, 196, 201, 240, 250, 252, 274, 339
Coatsworth, John H. 2n, 34n, 130, 190, 217, 229n, 231, 288
Cobden, Richard 62
Cobden–Chevalier Treaty 19
Coffee, valorization scheme 102, 234, 241–243, 276, 336
Colbert, Jean Baptiste de 38, 44f
Collier, Simon 162–164, 201f, 288, 297, 315
Colombia 194, 202, 214, 217, 230, 232, 238, 241, 243, 273, 276, 279f, 335
Colombo, Luís 325
Colonial Pact 164f
Commodity lottery *see also* Disjunctive exchange 128n, 263

INDEX 397

Communism *also* Komintern 6, 22, 26, 28, 32, 70, 81, 85f, 106n, 108, 115, 158, 172, 178, 206, 249, 261, 296, 305f, 310, 319f, 322, 332, 334, 350, 352f
Comte, August 151
Concert of Powers 154
Concordancia *see also* Argentina 246f, 249, 255, 257f, 288, 294f
Cooke Mission *see* Planning
Coordenação de Mobilização Econômica *see also* Planning 341
Copper mining 35, 115n, 119, 201, 246, 250–253, 260f
Cooper, Thomas 51, 62, 99
COP [Centralny Okręg Przemysłowy] *see also* Planning 25, 290, 293, 307, 312, 324, 330, 337–340, 345, 351
Copello, Juan 295
CORFO [Corporación de Fomento a la Producción] 314, 341
Corn Laws 59, 218
Cortés Conde, Roberto 34n, 216, 226n, 229n, 243, 252, 335
Cousiño, Matías 201
Creole *also* criolles 162–166, 169, 175, 190, 259
Crimean War 139, 154
Croce, Benedetto 147, 151–153
Cromwell, Oliver 173
CSN *see* Volta Redonda project
Cuba 133n
Culture, personal and civic 81f
Cunningham, William x, 38, 45
CUP [Central Planning Office] 335
Czechoslovakia 34, 105, 107f, 161, 179, 230, 236, 259, 270f, 302–307, 312, 351

Darío, Rubén 298
DASP [Departamento Administrativo do Serviço Público] 343
Davenant, Charles 38, 41
David, Thomas 26n, 28f, 183, 185n, 187
Davis, Ralph 4, 48, 223
Dąbrowa Basin 196
Dean, Warren 78n, 234, 237, 239, 241f, 277, 280–282, 285, 287f, 322–324, 326f, 333
Debt, foreign 45, 50, 119, 123, 189, 243, 247, 279, 318
Defaults 188, 211, 315, 317, 324
Deflation 71, 291, 312f, 317, 323
Denmark 226, 276
Dependency theory 111n, 112, 216, 252
Dessalines, Jean-Jacques 208
Dewey, Charles S. 301

Díaz-Alejandro, Carlos F. 107, 128n, 169n, 240, 270f, 277f, 281, 286, 288f, 291, 293f, 344
Díaz Porfirio Mori, José de la Cruz 120, 168, 173f, 233
Disjunctive exchange *see also* Commodity lottery 40, 128
Doboszyński, Adam 308, 321
Drozdowski, Marian M. 290, 312, 318f, 326, 330, 338–340, 344
Drucki-Lubecki, Franciszek Xawery 63, 190, 199f, 200n, 202–204, 203n, 209f, 219f
Duhan, Luis 294
Dutch *also* Dutch disease 19, 45, 134, 210, 227

East India Company 41, 44
ECLA/CEPAL 111f
Ecuador 317
Encilhamento *see also* Industry 238, 285
Endecja 159, 178, 308, 321, 331f
Engels, Friedrich 7, 55n, 83
Engerman, Stanley L. 130, 263
England *see* Great Britain
Estado Nôvo *see* Brazil
Esteves, Luis 298
Estonia 107, 269, 304
Etatism *see also* State and Planning 57, 152, 199, 203, 205, 284, 290, 316, 320, 328, 330, 332, 334, 337–339, 341, 344f
Evans, Peter 26n, 82n, 86n, 100, 104f, 274, 293, 302, 340, 345f, 349, 351
Export economy 30, 186, 188n, 202, 221, 223f, 226, 228f, 235, 237, 239, 245, 262f, 267, 271, 282, 294, 315
Export–Import Bank *see also* Volta Redonda project 345

Faletto, Enzo 112, 244, 253, 264
Fascism 106n, 108, 139f, 154, 155n, 178, 246, 249, 260, 310f, 319f, 322
Fasenfest, David 8
Federación Nacional de Cafeteros Colombianos 243
Fernandes, Florestan 106f, 112, 168, 170
Ferns, Henry S. 201, 241, 275
Fichte, Johann G. 56, 72
Findlay, Ronald 17, 125, 347
First Economic Brigade *see* Starzyński Stefan
Fishlow, Albert 238, 280, 314, 316, 339
Flick, Friedrich 307, 337
Flores Galindo, Alberto 212, 251, 261f
Foreign capital and investments 4f, 28, 37, 84n, 101, 109–111, 113–120, 123f, 132–136,

141–144, 146, 155, 192, 210, 215n, 220, 228, 241, 244, 246, 248, 251–253, 256, 265, 273–275, 278–280, 288, 297, 300–306, 308f, 312, 319–321, 329f, 338, 345, 351, 353f
FORJA [Fuerza de Orientación Radical de la Joven Argentina] 246f
Forment, Carlos A. 164, 167, 174, 297
France 15, 19, 24, 27, 38, 43–45, 48n, 61, 80, 83n, 123f, 161, 185n, 187, 191, 218, 282, 303, 308n, 312, 348
Francia, José Gaspar Rodrigues de 205f
Fraenkel, Samuel Antoni 190
Frank, Andre Gunder 16on, 184f, 196, 216
Friedman, Milton 58, 66, 70, 103
Fundidora Monterrey 173
Furtado, Celso 224, 238, 243, 290, 314, 322

Gage, Thomas 162
Gálvez, Manuel 298f
García Calderón, Francisco 298
Gellner, Ernest 11n, 13, 16f, 23, 27, 33n, 53f, 80, 83f, 99, 149, 155n, 227, 347
German Historical School 30, 38, 47, 61, 63, 78, 85, 91, 296
Germans, minority 210, 259f, 278, 304
Germany 12, 19, 24, 27, 33, 38, 45, 52–57, 65, 70f, 73, 83n, 91, 93, 120, 123f, 131, 138f, 141, 144n, 145, 147, 150, 154, 156, 160f, 165, 178, 188, 203n, 204, 209f, 215, 217f, 227, 241, 248, 260, 263, 270, 282, 301, 303, 309, 319f, 322, 333, 335f
Gerschenkron, Alexander 17, 19n, 24, 26n, 27, 55n, 79, 137, 138n, 141, 143, 145, 155f, 158f, 178, 193, 227, 239, 316
Gilpin, Robert 1, 82n, 84n, 101
Globalization *also* world economy ixf, 1f, 4–6, 8, 16, 19, 24, 28, 30f, 35, 37, 43, 47, 65, 67f, 72f, 75, 78, 83–86, 88–90, 98f, 101, 104, 111, 121f, 129, 134–136, 145f, 148m 176, 188, 223, 226, 255, 273, 304, 315, 321f, 347–351, 353–355
Głąbiński, Stanisław 78, 347
Gold standard 19, 65–68, 71f, 135, 142, 231f, 240, 291
Gołębiowski, Jerzy 284, 330, 337f, 340, 343
Gómez, Juan Vicente 115, 254
Gootenberg, Paul 2n, 152, 164, 171, 186, 201, 212–214, 216f, 222, 245, 250, 295f, 298
Gould, John D. 19, 61, 86n, 88n, 122, 144
Gourevitch, Peter 5, 27, 37, 105, 134
Graham, Richard 219, 273
Grandi, Dino 306
Grantham, George 47f

Great Britain *also* England x, 1, 13, 15, 19, 24, 38–48, 53, 56, 58–62, 65, 71, 83n, 88n, 103, 113n, 120, 123, 126, 133, 160f, 184f, 188f, 192f, 201, 204f, 213, 215, 218, 225, 239, 245–247, 257, 298, 301–303, 308n, 318n, 326, 348
Great Depression 104, 235, 322 (as shock), 31, 263, 282–285, 288, 290f (and holistic economic nationalism)
Greenfeld, Liah 3, 11n, 13–17, 24, 35n, 41, 47, 48n, 49, 55n, 82n, 83n, 111, 114n, 145, 155n, 161f, 178, 348
Greenhill, Robert 242, 244, 256
Gregor, A. James 106, 306, 320, 322, 333
Gregory, Paul R. 142
Gregory, Theodore E. 114n
Growth, new theory of 82
Guano 171, 212f, 221f, 245, 250f, 254n, 295, 297f
Gudin, Eugênio 325, 328, 334, 341, 345
Guerrero, Vicente 215, 219n
Guinle, Guilhermo 340, 344
Györ Program 25, 337f

Haber, Stephen 111, 116, 124, 226n, 228–230, 229n, 230, 233, 237f, 241, 252, 285–287
Habermas, Jürgen 131, 148
Haiti 163, 170, 183, 207f
Hale, Charles A. 167f, 172, 202
Hamilton, Alexander 50f
Handicraft *also* artisans 154, 166, 168, 190f, 193, 195, 200, 212–215, 219, 221, 223, 225, 236f, 240, 307
Hansen, Alvin H. 64, 73f
Haring, Clarence H. 311, 316, 325
Harriman, William A. 306f
Hawaii 132
Haya de la Torre, Victor Raúl 253, 261, 294, 321, 334
Heckscher, Eli F. 38, 42–46, 64
Heilperin, Michael A. 21f, 34, 70, 74, 155, 318
Helleiner, Eric 28, 35n, 52, 124, 171, 235
Herder, Johann Gottfried 53
Hilferding, Rudolf 34, 84, 98
Hilton, Stanley E. 285, 322, 336, 342f, 342n
Hinze, Otto 56, 101
Hirschman, Albert O. 3, 47, 77, 128n, 227, 239, 263, 272, 282–284, 302, 321, 335n, 355
Hitler, Adolf 70, 154, 319, 322
Hobsbawm, Eric J. 11n, 14n, 15, 29, 48, 120f, 170n, 188, 353
Hobson, John A. 34
Hobson, John M. 43n, 47, 99, 103, 105, 160

INDEX 399

Hochschild, Mauricio 311
Hoffman, Walther G. 87
Homestead Act(s) 169
Hont, István 13, 42–45, 60. 161, 347
Hoston, Germaine A. 140, 145
Humboldt, Alexander von 162
Hume, David 44, 102, 355
Hungary 53, 107, 150, 151n, 197, 214, 230, 236, 270f, 279, 302, 307, 317, 350, 352
Hunt, Shane J. 254n, 296
Hymer, Stephen H. 37, 84n

Ianni, Octavio 112, 176n, 315, 328, 336, 339–341, 343, 345
Imperialism *also* anti-imperialism 22, 34, 56f, 83f, 118, 120, 131, 154, 249, 257, 261, 278, 298f, 305f, 321
India 1, 12, 31, 41, 77n, 122, 126f, 130f, 284, 353
Indians *also* Indian 163, 165f, 168–170, 173, 175, 190, 202, 210–213, 215, 259–262
Indigenization 23, 125, 309, 312
Indonesia 31
Industrial Bank of Japan 135, 141
Industry 35, 238f, 259, 272, 276f, 284, 291, 313, 325f (artificial), 235–238, 272, 28f, 325 (natural), 1, 119, 137, 145, 188, 196–199, 201–204, 213–215, 220f, 235–238, 260, 270, 272, 277f, 281, 286f, 300, 318, 350 (textile), 142, 173, 197, 221, 248, 270f, 273–276, 290, 293, 307, 332, 336–338, 340, 342, 344, 345 (iron and steel)
Industrialization 19n, 26f, 29, 31f, 46, 86–88, 111, 113, 129, 138, 140, 142f, 172f, 193, 198–207, 220, 229, 233f, 263, 269, 271f, 284f, 289–294, 315f, 324–329, 336f, 339–341, 349–352
Inflation 204, 221, 278f, 281, 291, 324, 340
Instituto do Café *see also* Coffee 243f
Ireland 126, 131, 133
ISEB [Instituto Superior de Estudos Brasileiros] 112
IRI [Instituto per la Riconstruzione Industriale] 341
Irwin, Douglas A. 6n, 42, 69, 94n, 113, 137, 227, 287n
Italy 19, 48n, 53, 73, 95, 106, 123, 131, 137, 138n, 153f, 178, 320, 322, 333, 352

Jackson, Andrew 18, 51, 60
Jaguaribe, Helio 102, 112, 169, 226
Jakubowiczs 190
James, Harold x, 65, 68n
Janowski, Maciej 63, 149–152, 151n

Japan 6, 19, 21, 24, 48n, 73, 89, 111, 123, 130, 135f, 138–140, 142, 144f, 156, 160f, 301, 322, 334, 348, 353f
Jedlicki, Jerzy 7, 61, 63, 110, 148, 150, 164, 191, 193, 197, 203, 209f, 212, 220, 298
Jefferson, Thomas 50f
Jessop, Bob 97, 102n, 103, 105
Jews *also* anti-Semitism 29, 63, 83n, 118, 131, 151, 258f, 270, 278, 305, 307–309, 332, 338
Jezierski, Andrzej 2n, 119, 183n, 187, 189, 196, 201n, 202, 209f, 217f, 221f, 225n, 270, 307f, 330
Johnson, Harry G. 14, 24, 32, 114, 120, 130
Juárez, Benito 123, 165
Junkers [Prussian landlords] 91f, 227
Junta Nacional de Carnes [National Meat Board] *see also* Argentina 257
Junta Reguladora de Granos [National Grain Board] *see also* Argentina 248
Justo, Agustín Pedro 258
Justo, Juan B. 114, 239

Kaczyńska, Elżbieta 187, 190, 194, 277
Kahan, Arcadius 17–20, 25f, 49, 136–138
Kaldor, Nicolas 78, 87n
Kalecki, Michał 71, 73, 104, 276, 338, 353f
Kamiński, Antoni Z. 4, 8, 90
Kaufman, Robert R. 107, 291, 339
Kawalec, Stefan 78
Kellogg, Frank B. 116n
Kemmerer, Edwin 291
Keynes, John M. 26, 43, 63–75, 78, 270, 315f, 320
Keynesianism 64, 70f, 313–315
Kindleberger, Charles P. 57, 65, 68, 79, 88, 128n, 227, 282
King, Gregory 38
Kingdom of Poland *see* Poland
Knight, Alan 115, 172–174, 176n, 229, 309
Knox, Philander C. 132
Kochanowicz, Jacek 8, 31n, 186f, 210, 212
Kofman, Jan ix, 3, 6n,7f, 16, 21, 23f, 27, 34n, 35, 107f, 113, 258, 284, 288f, 296, 312, 316, 322, 329f, 337, 340, 344, 350
Kohli, Atul 6, 31, 35n, 106, 112n, 113, 348f
Kohn, Hans 11, 33n, 147, 151n, 162, 347
Kokueki, concept of 48n
Kokutai, concept of 140
Koniar, Maurycy 211n
Korea, Republic of 138, 352
Kossuth, Lajos 56n, 148
Kozul-Wright, Richard x, 88f, 122, 125, 134
Krasner, Stephen D. 20n, 90, 105

Krenn, Michael L. 35, 116, 255, 263–265, 310
Kula, Marcin 11n, 174, 306, 311
Kula, Witold 30, 31n, 61, 89, 187, 191–196, 197n, 200, 212, 214, 222–224
Kurczewska, Joanna 99
Kuznets, Simon 25, 38, 79, 87f, 124, 135
Kwiatkowski, Eugeniusz 270, 290, 294, 306, 312, 314f, 320, 324, 330, 337, 340, 343f, 350
Kymlicka, William 149

Labor 110, 127f, 171, 195, 201, 211–213, 240, 326 (shortage), 32, 41, 126, 167, 187, 208f, 212, 261 (control and mobilization), 227, 239, 278 (and protectionism)
Labor unions 107, 125, 131, 240, 264, 322
Lal, Deepak 87, 102n, 113, 138, 140, 145
Land, property relations 165, 168f, 169n, 203, 205n, 211f, 265, 267
Land reform 112, 222, 305, 352
Landau, Ludwik 129, 262, 338
Landau, Zbigniew 196, 212, 230, 273f, 288, 300f, 303, 307, 312, 314, 318, 337, 343, 350
Landes, David 3, 16, 81, 88, 141, 145, 192, 196, 244
Lange, Oskar 98
Latvia 107, 269, 304
Laue, Theodor H. von 62, 157–159, 178
Lautenbach, Wilhelm 71
Leal da Cunha, Alfredo Alberto 243
Leff, Nathaniel H. 224n, 225, 239f
Leguía, Augusto 254, 310
Leszczyńska, Cecylia 187, 210, 218, 270, 307f, 330
Levi-Faur, David 8, 35n, 60
Levin, Jonathan V. 213, 226, 245, 250
Lewiatan [Centralny Związek Polskiego Przemysłu, Górnictwa, Handlu i Finansów] 329f, 333, 337f, 344f
Lewin, Moshe 145, 158
Lewis, Cleona 116
Lewis, Colin M. 165, 169n, 280, 285
Lewis, Paul H. 107, 117, 233, 237, 239f, 247–249, 258, 277, 295, 325, 344
Lewis, W. Arthur 62, 77, 88, 126–131, 194, 219, 270, 272, 314
Liberal-conservative consensus 161, 164, 167–175
Liberalism, economic 18f, 71, 152–154, 168, 171, 219n, 222, 226, 229, 294
Liberalism, Latin America and Central Europe 118, 147, 150–152, 159, 161, 163–166, 168f, 171f, 175f, 193, 202f, 239, 244, 296
Liberal Party see also Romania 300, 306

Lima 169, 190, 213, 215, 222
Linares, José María 194
Linz, Juan J. 102, 106n
Lippmann, Walter 95
Lipsey, Robert E. x, 74n
List, Friedrich 26, 33, 37, 47, 49, 51–63, 74, 78, 98, 110, 114, 120, 125, 132, 135, 141, 144, 147, 155, 158, 233, 267n
Loans, foreign 134, 203, 211, 254, 265, 279f, 301–303, 312, 317
London 65f, 198, 218, 266
Lópezes, Carlos Antonio and Francisco Solano 205, 207
Lorwin, Lewis L. 67, 72, 334
Louis XI 38
Louis XIV 38
Love, Joseph L. 31n, 111–113, 289, 296, 315, 325
Lugones, Leopoldo 246
Luxemburg, Rosa 34
Łepkowski, Tadeusz 31, 173, 175, 208f, 212, 309, 349
Łódź 119, 196, 278

Maddison, Angus 6, 38, 184, 262, 276
Magdoff, Harry 84n
Malthus, Thomas also Malthusian 87, 184
Małowist, Marian 30, 191, 224n
Mandelbaum, Kurt 32, 318
Manoilescu, Mihail 113, 316, 325
Mariátegui, José Carlos 166
Marichal, Carlos 119f, 133, 189, 224, 225n, 229, 280, 302, 317
Marof, Tristán 311
Martí, José 298
Martyn, Henry 41f
Marx, Karl 2, 7, 54f, 55n, 59, 82f, 83n, 93n, 193, 353
Marxists also Marxism 31, 34, 73, 82, 85, 102n, 140f, 166, 246, 321
Matarazzo, Francisco also IRFM 198, 236f, 277, 325, 333
Mauá [Irineu Evangelista de Souza] 197f
Mayall, James 12, 35n, 80
Mayrink, Francisco de Paula 198
Mazzini, Giuseppe 148, 155
Mączak, Antoni 186f, 196, 212, 224n
McGregor, Gregor 198
Meiji Restoration 25, 111, 139
Mercantilism 16, 37, 39f, 42–44, 46, 48f (general), 38f (dual interpretation), 41 (social)
Mercosur 354

INDEX

Mexico 6, 88, 92f, 116, 120, 123f, 134f, 163, 167f, 169n, 172f, 178, 186, 188, 190f, 193, 197, 199, 203–206, 211n, 215, 217, 219n, 224f, 229f, 232, 238f, 245, 255, 259, 276, 309, 318, 321
Michels, Robert 131, 306, 316
Migrations *also* migrants 8of, 91, 117f, 121, 125–127, 130–132, 155, 161, 169n, 170f, 176, 178, 210, 213, 237, 240, 259, 261, 264, 277f, 286, 309
Military, role of 174f, 208, 272f, 295, 300f, 337, 340, 342–345
Mill, John Stuart 47, 79, 148, 150–153
Miller, Nicola 162, 177, 298
Miller, Rory 253
Millet, Sergio 310
Minas Gerais 176, 197, 213, 224, 242, 275, 332
Mistis 261
Modernizing community 170f, 173, 175, 177, 228, 263, 299
Molier [Jean-Baptiste Poquelin] 48
Molyneaux, Peter 94
Mommsen, Hans 72, 319
Mommsen, Wolfgang J. 91, 93, 147, 154
Montevideo 264
Moore Jr., Barrington 1, 11n, 139, 145
More, Thomas 41
"Morgenthau Paradox" ix, 300
Moscow 119
Müller, Adam 47, 56
Munn, Thomas 39, 44
Mussolini, Benito 70, 320, 322
Myint, Hla 127, 130

Napoleon Bonaparte 191, 209
Napoleonic wars 46, 52, 147, 190
Narodniks 140
Nation-building 11, 13f, 20, 23, 28, 161, 164–166, 171, 259, 300
National Democrats *see* Endecja
National economy 5, 15–18, 20f, 26f, 30, 37–39, 46–49, 52–55, 63f, 73, 77–80, 82–86, 89–92, 94, 101, 321, 347–349
Nationalism, economic 1–4, 7, 14, 17f, 20f, 23–25, 31, 33–35, 49, 322, 347f (general), 29, 183–222 (proto-nationalism), 5, 21, 50, 56, 91–99, 104, 136f, 262f, 269, 283–285, 289–293, 312–317, 322, 328, 330f, 336f, 343, 351f (holistic and particularistic), ix, 60, 166, 249, 258, 300 (defensive), 28, 171 (liberal), 11–13, 16, 25, 43, 105–108 (and political nationalism), ix, 334 (as economic patriotism), 27f, 48n, 62, 94, 216, 226f, 241f, 244–257, 262, 267, 284, 336 (of primary sector groups), 94, 233f, 236, 238f, 272, 278f, 281f, 323f, 327f, 329f, 337 (of industrial groups), 6, 26, 32, 85f, 95, 319, 320n, 352f (communist)
Nationalism, political 109f, 146f, 149f, 160, 166 (liberal) 28f, 109f, 125, 146f, 151n, 155, 159–162, 175, 177–179, 308, 321, 331f (integral)
Nationalization 23, 28, 45, 115–117, 133, 245, 265f, 300, 304, 307–311, 337, 343
National Petroleum Council *see* Oil
National Steel Plan, Executive Commission for *see* Industry
Nazism *see* Fascism
Needham, Joseph 185
Nehru, Jawaharlal 324
Netherlands 15
Neumark, Ignacy 190
New York 32
New Zealand *see also* Western offshoots 124, 128, 267, 276
Niemeyer, Sir Otto 316
Niterói 198
Nitrates 119, 252, 288, 297f
North, Douglass C. 2, 20n, 82, 169
North–North axis *also* income convergence x, 124f, 134, 267
North–South axis 122, 125, 134
Norway 135
Nostrification *see* Indigenization
NSDAP *see* Fascism

Oakeshott, Michael 102n, 330
Obóz Zjednoczenia Narodowego *see* OZON
O'Brien, Patrick K 4, 19n, 33, 43f, 43n, 46, 99, 192
Obshchina 157
O'Donnell, Guillermo 106
Ohlin, Bert 113
Oil 35, 115–117, 142, 230, 236, 245, 252–255, 261, 273–275, 282, 294, 304–306, 311f, 321, 339f, 342n, 345
Old Republic *see* Brazil
Olson Jr., Mancur 3, 17, 26n, 81f, 97
O'Rourke, Kevin H. x, 15, 121, 125
Oroya, La 262
Ossowski, Stanisław 166
OZON 332, 344

Pacific War 297f
Pagano, Ugo 24, 80
Paiva Abreu, Marcelo de
Palacios, Nicolás 170

Palacký, František 150, 151n
Pani, Alberto J. 321
Paraguay 118, 163, 191, 193, 197, 204–207, 211f, 311
Pardo, José 253
Pastore, Mario 205n. 206f
Pasvolsky, Leo 34
Path-dependent development *see also* Dutch disease 2, 20, 22, 90, 169, 185, 238
Patiño, Simon 311
Paulistas *see* São Paulo
Pazos, Felipe 77
Peasants *see also* Agrarianism and Indians 91, 155–159, 168, 173–175, 187, 195, 189, 202, 205, 207–212, 221–224, 269, 308, 315, 321f
Pelaez, Carlos Manuel 128f
Peninsulares *also* gachupinos 162, 164, 190
Pepys, Samuel 45
Pereira de Sousa, Washington Luis 265
Perón, Juan D. *also* Peronism 107, 127, 247, 295
Peru *also* Tawantinsuyu 107, 134, 163f, 166, 168–171, 173, 186, 190, 198, 201, 205f, 210, 212–217, 221–224, 229, 230, 232, 236,245f, 250–254, 259, 260f, 274, 277, 280, 295–299, 301f, 310, 315, 317, 321, 333f
Peruvian-Bolivian Confederation 169
Petriconi, Luis 295
Picchia, Paulo Menotti del 310
Pickel, Andreas 2, 35n
Piłsudski, Józef 18on, 301
Pinedo, Federico 294
Pipes, Richard 145, 157
Pitt, William 61
Planning *see also* State 114, 153, 284, 290, 329, 333–337, 339–341
Plantation 30, 62, 129f, 132, 170, 207f, 212f, 223, 243f, 261, 327
Platt, Desmond C. M. 123, 188f, 201n, 214, 216, 251, 253, 275
Poland 3, 25f, 30, 53f, 56, 58, 61, 63, 77f, 88, 92, 95, 107, 110, 114, 117f, 134, 150, 151n, 159, 16on, 164, 174, 177, 183, 185n, 186–197, 199–204, 209–224, 225n, 230, 236, 258–260, 269–274, 277–279, 282, 284, 288, 290–293, 300–307, 310, 312–314, 316–320, 329–333, 335, 337–339, 342–345, 349–352
Polanyi, Karl 38, 97, 100, 153f, 322
Pollard, Sidney 34, 56, 80n, 88n, 133, 142, 347
Pomeranz, Kenneth 5, 184, 196

Population and market size 276f
Populism 162, 171, 175–178, 247, 263, 266, 295, 311
Positivism 151f, 167–169, 172, 174f, 177
Potash, Robert A. 203f
Prague 304
Prebisch, Raúl 31, 62, 111, 113n, 258
Preobrazhensky, Evgeny 320
Prestes, Luis Carlos 249
Protection, rate *also* nominal tariffs 231f, 271, 351 (effective), 217m 231, 257, 263, 287–289, 351 (nominal)
Protectionism 7f, 18f, 27, 33f, 49, 51f, 57, 59–61, 64f, 67, 72, 88f, 94–98, 113f, 152, 155, 160, 189, 193, 212, 221f, 226–228, 230, 233f, 238, 254, 264, 280, 288f, 319, 339, 347 (in general), 225, 234, 241 (natural), 18f, 51, 55n, 57, 65, 94–96, 98, 118f, 125,137f, 141–145, 197, 200, 202, 216–220, 229, 231f, 234f, 240, 263, 265, 271, 273, 280, 283, 287f, 295, 321, 324, 326f, 351 (tariff), 6, 19, 66, 101, 138n, 141, 231, 288f, 313, 323 (non-tariff), 136f, 316 (private, public), 152, 154 (social and national, solidarity), 320 (socialist)
Protestants 14, 174
Prussia *see* Germany
Prussia, tariff war with 218
Puno 261

Racism *also* xenophobia 130–132, 151, 16of, 169, 170, 258f
Radziszewski, Henryk 54
Railroads *also* transport and transport revolution 4, 15, 49, 56, 80, 87, 115, 119, 121, 124, 133–135, 144, 168, 173, 185, 197f, 201, 206, 215, 225, 228, 234, 241, 244, 247, 254n, 260, 265, 270, 272, 275, 278, 292f, 337, 339, 344
Ranki, Györgi 25, 214, 297, 305
Rawls, John 4, 150
Renan, Ernest 12
Ricardo Leite, Cassiano 310
Ricardo, David 1, 52, 54, 62, 69, 79
Rio de Janeiro 242
Rio Grande do Sul 332
Robinson, Joan ix, 58, 65, 71, 78
Robinson, Ronald 252
Roca–Runciman Treaty 247, 256, 258
Rocco, Alfredo 315, 333
Rockman, Bert A. 103f
Rodó, José Enrique 298
Röpke, Wilhelm 65, 95, 322

INDEX 403

Rogowski, Ronald x, 156, 227, 239, 267
Romania *also* Romanians 71n, 107, 150, 177, 179, 236, 258f, 271, 274, 276, 279, 288, 296, 300, 303–308, 313, 325
Roosevelt, Franklin Delano 65–67, 116n, 314
Roosevelt, Theodore 93, 132
Rosas, Juan Manuel 165, 216, 256f
Rosenberg, Hans 147, 152
Rosenberg, Nathan 88
Rosenstein-Rodan, Paul 32
Rostow, W. W. 19, 58
Roszkowski, Wojciech 312, 323
Rothschilds bank 123, 317
Rothschild, Joseph 108n, 270, 300n, 304, 319, 335n, 349
Rousseau, Jean Jacques 148
Rubber, wild 224, 241, 243
Rumi Maqui 261
Russia *also* Russians and Russian 19, 25, 27, 32, 62, 72, 88, 95, 111, 117–119, 133, 135, 137–145, 151n, 155–160, 173, 178, 183n, 186, 189, 200n, 217, 222, 269f, 273, 284, 306, 334, 345
Rutkowski, Jan 209f, 213, 224n
Rybarski, Roman 39, 78, 88, 90, 92, 258, 308, 331f, 335, 347f
Rykov, Aleksey I. 77n

Sáenz Peña Law *see also* Argentina 176
Salgado, Plinio 310
Salter, Arthur 95f
Samuelson, Paul A. 63, 78, 96, 353
Sanín Villa, Gabriel 335
Santa Cruz, Andrés de 169f
São Paulo 112, 176, 225n, 234, 237, 242–244, 249, 259, 265, 277, 286, 293, 314, 323, 325f, 328, 332, 338, 342
Saravia da Rosa, Aparicio 299
Sarmiento, Domingo Faustino 168, 175
Sater, William F. 162f, 201f, 288, 297, 315
Say, Jean-Baptiste 48
Schmitter, Philippe C. 177, 310, 314, 325, 327f, 340, 342
Schmoller, Gustav von 38, 46f, 56, 78, 137
Schneider, Jürgen 206, 218
Schneider, Ronald M. 174, 243f, 249, 341f
Schumpeter, Joseph A. 34, 40, 51f, 63, 98, 114, 130
Scotland 17
Secomski, Kazimierz 338
Seehandlung-Companie 203n
Self-sufficiency 21f, 51, 56f, 63, 67, 69, 72f, 208, 308, 318–320

Serfdom 31n, 63, 139, 167, 186f, 190–193, 209, 212, 224
Serra, Antonio 39f
Serra, José 292, 351f
Siciliano Jr., Alexandre 25, 242, 327
Sierra 259, 261
Silesia, Upper 258, 260, 270, 307, 351
Silver mining 39f, 133, 186, 190, 198, 224
Simonsen, Roberto C. 325–330, 334f, 341, 344f
Singer, Hans 128f, 244f
Singer, Paulo 133, 286
Skidelsky, Robert 7, 22, 69f, 71n, 82n
Skocpol, Theda 3, 101, 103, 105
Slavery *also* slaves 5, 51, 62f, 163, 170, 173, 183, 207f, 223f
Slovakia *also* Slovaks 259, 300
Smith, Adam 26, 45, 47, 54, 56–59, 61f, 78f, 82, 87, 96f, 102, 223, 226n
Smith, Anthony D. ix, 11n, 14n, 27, 29n, 33, 148
Smith, Peter H. 176, 256f
Socialism *also* socialists 35, 53, 83, 93n, 114, 154, 159, 160n, 174, 177f, 239, 240, 253, 264, 266, 294, 298, 301, 310f, 320f, 333, 335
Sociedad Rural *see also* Argentina 238, 257, 272, 294
Sociedade Rural Brasileira 327
Sodré, Nelson Werneck 112, 304
Sokoloff, Kenneth L. 130, 263
Sombart, Werner 14, 25, 46, 99, 113f, 319
"Sombart Paradox" x, 74, 88, 319
Sonora 309
Soviet Union 32, 73, 77n, 111, 178, 288, 306f, 322, 333f
Spain 123, 162f, 166, 190, 352
Spencer, Herbert 151
Spilman, Elisabeth 29
Stalin, Joseph *also* Stalinist 26n, 32, 70, 73, 111n, 159, 178, 206, 320
Stallings, Barbara 113, 279f, 301, 303, 317
Standard Oil of New Jersey 274, 305f, 311
Staple theory and growth 128, 226f, 263
Starzyński, Stefan 272, 300, 333, 338
Staszic, Stanisław 54, 199
State, autonomy of 2, 5f, 12, 16, 21f, 31f, 37, 40, 44f, 50, 53, 55, 57f, 70, 74, 92, 95, 97, 99–106, 112f, 140f, 143, 152f, 156f, 164, 172, 177, 199, 205f, 208, 228f, 243f, 249, 254f, 263f, 272f, 279f, 282f, 290–297, 316, 322–324, 328–331, 336, 348
Stein, Stanley J. 123, 170, 213, 216, 226, 234, 243, 272, 278, 281, 286f, 295–297, 335
Steinkeller, Piotr 190

Stemplowski, Ryszard 7f, 35, 114, 246, 253, 256, 259, 274, 311, 333
Stepan, Alfred 296f
Stolper-Samuelson theory 28, 227
Stolypin, Peter 158, 178
Strasser, Otto 319
Struve, Peter 140
Sucre, Antonio José de 163
Supiński, Józef 77, 117
Supple, Barry 19, 133
Surowiecki, Wawrzyniec 54, 117
Sutcliffe, Robert 87
Svennilson, Ingvar 79
Sweezy, Paul M. 73, 84n, 285
Szacki, Jerzy ix, 149, 153, 159
Szlachta [Polish landlords] 63, 86, 223
Szlajfer, Henryk 7f, 26n, 31f, 176n, 207, 216, 221, 262, 305, 320n
Szporluk, Roman 11n, 53, 55n, 62

Tagore Rabindranath 161
Taiwan 138, 352
Tamir, Yael 11n, 149
Tariff-growth paradox 19, 230, 262
Tarrifs see Protectionism and Protection, rate
Teichova, Alice 236, 270f, 273f, 293, 303, 306, 316, 350
Tennenbaum, Henryk 27, 95
Terms of trade 112, 124, 127–130, 171, 218f, 238, 242, 317f, 326
Thorp, Rosemary 34n, 116, 169, 226n, 230, 238, 242f, 245, 248, 251–253, 255, 260, 269, 274, 276f, 280f, 284f, 291f, 302, 315, 319, 351f
Tipton, Frank B. Jr. 138
Tocqueville, Alexis de 152, 164
Tolstoy, Lev 173
Tomaszewski, Jerzy 8, 25, 230, 273f, 288, 297, 300f, 303, 305, 307f, 312, 318, 337, 350
Topik, Steven 118, 123, 198, 224f, 228f, 232, 234, 240, 275, 280, 296, 309, 331
Topolski, Jerzy 186f, 191f, 199, 215, 223
Tornquist group 277
Toro, David 311
Torre, Lisandro de la 257
Torreón 309
Tôrres, Alberto 274, 310
Toussaint-L'Ouverture 207f
Towarzystwo Kredytowe Ziemskie [The Land Credit Society] 209
Trade see also Protectionism 302
(concentration), 122f, 124, 134, 226
(vertical), 27, 79 (domestic), 89, 129, 335

(as an engine of growth), 15, 60, 65, 282, 288 (policy)
Triple Alliance, war of the 118, 206f
Tugan Baranovski, Mikhail J. 140, 221
Túpac Amaru II 163, 166
Turkey 302, 334

UCR [Unión Civica Radical] see also Argentina 246, 288, 294
Ugarte, Cesar Antonio 214n, 217
Ugarte, Manuel 177, 298f, 326
Ukrainians 259f, 300, 332
Unanue, Hipolito 198
Unión Aduanera del Sud 325
Unión Industrial Argentina 237, 325
United States Steel Corporation 345
Uruguay 6, 125, 127f, 135, 166, 171, 173, 176, 197, 207, 232, 239, 255, 263–267, 276, 299
USA also North America 19, 21, 24, 27, 32, 47f, 48n, 55, 66, 71n, 78, 88n, 89, 114f, 120f, 123, 125–127, 131, 135, 141, 160–162, 170, 177, 189, 216, 224–226, 236, 242, 246, 248, 256, 276, 290, 298f, 301–303, 311, 329, 353

Vargas, Getúlio 25, 174, 244, 248f, 285, 291, 309, 311f, 322–325, 327–329, 332, 336, 339, 341f, 342n, 348
Veblen, Thorstein B. 57, 72
Venezuela 88, 115, 123, 163, 191, 230–232, 254f, 271
Versiani, Flavio Rabelo 286f
Victoria, Guadalupe 199
Vienna 62
Vienna, Congress of 183n
Villa, Francisco (Pancho) 115
Viner, Jacob 27, 44, 48f, 113
Volta Redonda project 25, 290, 293, 329, 333, 336–338, 340, 344f
Voltaire [François M. Arouet] 42

Wakefield, Edward K. 169n
Walicki, Andrzej 140f
Wallerstein, Immanuel 1n, 17, 31n, 38, 84f, 101, 103
War, economic consequences of 25, 34, 60, 190, 284–287
Warsaw 196
Washington, George 50
Weber, Max ix, 2f, 11–14, 38, 91–93, 99n, 100f, 105, 120, 133, 192
Wehler, Hans-Ulrich 11n, 12, 53, 178
Western offshoots 12, 105, 125, 226f, 276, 282
Wierzbicki, Andrzej 329f

Wilkins, Mira 115, 117, 134, 273–275, 312
Williamson, Jeffrey G. x, 4, 15, 18f, 28, 121, 125–129, 131f, 217f, 229–235, 238f, 241, 263, 269, 287f, 293
Wilson, Charles 38, 41
Wirth, John D. 31, 93, 274f, 285, 290, 309, 312, 322, 329f, 335–337, 340, 342n, 345
Witte, Sergey 14, 25, 62, 88, 111a, 137, 139–145, 147, 155–160, 172, 178, 273, 345
Woroncow, Wasyl P. *see* Narodniks

"Wspólnota Interesów" *see* Flick
Wuttenberg 51

Ybycui 212
Yeager, Mary A. 136f, 316
Yugoslavia 107, 279, 303

Zaibatsu groups 136
Zárate "Willka", Pablo 173
Zeeland, Paul Van 34, 64, 67, 96, 334
Zeitlin, Maurice 119, 172, 201f, 297